Southern Living®

2010 ANNUAL RECIPES

Oxmoor
House®

❧ *Best Recipes of 2010*

Not all recipes are created equal. At *Southern Living*, only those that have passed muster with our Test Kitchen staff and Food Editors—not an easy crowd to please—make it onto the pages of our magazine. Members of our Food staff gather almost every day to taste-test recipes to ensure not only that they're reliable, but also that they taste as good as they possibly can. Here we share this year's favorites.

Banana Bread Cobbler ▶
(page 43) If you're craving a little down-home comfort, don't miss this spectacular dessert that combines the flavors of two Southern favorites.

◀ Lemon Hard Sauce with Gingerbread *(page 33)* Drizzled over warm gingerbread, this melt-in-your -mouth sauce boasts a hint of lemon and vanilla.

Two-Step Pound Cake *(page 96)*, not pictured, Who would guess that with just six ingredients and two quick steps you could have a scrumptious Southern dessert?

Best-Ever Scones *(page 286)*, not pictured, Create eight sweet and savory variations from one basic recipe.

Pam-Cakes with Buttered Honey Syrup *(page 31)* Our staff affectionally named these fluffy flapjacks after Test Kitchen Pro Pam Lolley, who created them.

Easy Chicken Gumbo *(page 42)* A brown
roux that whisks up in just five minutes serves as
the base for this hearty one-dish meal.

◄ **Stir-and-Roll Biscuits** *(page 43)* Made from scratch in just 15 minutes, these light and fluffy favorites use vegetable oil instead of shortening.

Grilled Peaches with Blackberry-Basil Butter *(page 104)*, not pictured, Butter, basil, and blackberry preserves make a tasty topping for one of summer's sweetest fruits.

Carolina-Style Mignonette *(page 106)*, not pictured, We gave this classic French vinegar-based sauce that's traditionally served with oysters a Southern spin by adding a barbecue base and a hint of horseradish. It's delicious served alongside shrimp.

▼ **Buttermilk Fried Chicken** *(page 42)* An overnight soaking in buttermilk makes this Southern specialty extra tender and juicy.

Bacon-and-Leek Tart *(page 79)* A flaky pastry crust topped with a mixture of hickory-smoked bacon, leeks, Gruyère cheese, and fresh thyme makes a delicious main-dish meal.

▲ **Stuffed Mushrooms with Pecans** *(page 79)* Chopped pecans give this classic appetizer a Southern twist.

Chocolate Truffle Bites *(page 111)*, not pictured, Refrigertated piecrusts serve as the base for these delightful nibbles of chocolate made with chocolate bars and whipping cream.

Buttermilk Fried Okra *(page 115)*, not pictured, The secret ingredient in this regional side dish is a sprinkling of sugar in the corn-meal coating that caramelizes as the okra cooks.

◄ **Tex-Mex Shrimp Cocktail** *(page 73)* Fiery jalapeño pepper jelly combined with mango add a sweet and spicy kick to this sassy twist on a traditional hors d'oeuvre.

7

Strawberry-Orange Shortcake Tart and Vanilla-Stuffed Strawberry Cupcakes *(page 72)* One of the South's favorite brings a burst of flavor and color to these showstopping desserts.

Homemade Apple Pie (*page 157*), not pictured, The cornmeal crust dough is the unbelievable secret behind this cherished fall dessert.

Chocolate Truffle Cheesecake (*page 247*), not pictured, A rich chocolaty filling atop a crunchy cookie crust swimming in chocolate ganache ensures that you won't be able to stop at just one bite.

Tiny Caramel Tarts (*page 248*), not pictured, The cream-cheese pastry shells make these bite-size treats extra special.

Caramel Pecan Bars (*page 248*), not pictured, Save room to enjoy this irresistible bar cookie with a crunchy crust and a gooey caramel middle.

Caramel Crunch Ice-Cream Pie (*page 250*), not pictured, This frozen sensation gets its incredible texture and flavor from the Buttered Pecans.

▼ **Pavlova with Lemon Cream and Berries** (*page 95*) With a crispy outside and pillow-soft interior, this meringue-based dessert is crowned with a lemon-curd mixture and assorted fresh berries.

Caramel-Cream Cheese Flan *(page 251)*, not pictured, Perfect for holiday entertaining, caramelized sugar tops this rich custard dessert that can be made up to two days ahead.

Caramel Sauce *(page 251)*, not pictured, No one will believe that just four ingredients make up this rich buttery sauce.

Super-Moist Cornbread *(page 258)*, not pictured, A can of cream-style corn adds to the abounding flavor of this Southern specialty.

▼ **Lemon-Garlic Potato Salad** *(page 90)* Summer comfort food at its best, buttery Yukon gold potatoes and heart-friendly sweet potatoes serve as the base for this hearty side dish.

Spicy Cheddar "Long" Straws *(page 275)*, not pictured, Sharp cheddar cheese, butter, crushed red pepper, and half-and-half team team up to make these crispy Southern snacks.

Red Velvet Soufflés with Whipped Sour Cream *(page 282)*, not pictured, These showstoppers get a flavorful hint of chocolate from a bittersweet chocolate baking bar.

Sweet Potato Chips *(page 271)*, not pictured, The secret to these extra-crispy appetizers is to fry them in small batches.

◀ **Big Daddy's Grilled Blue Cheese-and Bacon Potato Salad** *(page 90)* A mayonnaise base mixed with Dijon mustard, red onion, blue cheese, and bacon tossed with grilled potatoes help make this recipe an enormous hit.

Red Velvet Brownies with Cream Cheese Frosting *(page 283)*, not pictured, All the key ingredients for red velvet cake are here inside these fun little nibbles.

▼ **Okra-and-Corn Maque Choux** *(page 115)* Smoked sausage mixes with a host of fresh-from-the-garden summer vegetables for an irresistible dish.

Mocha Latte Ice Cream *(page 119)*
Enjoy the smooth combination of coffee, chocolate, and vanilla in every bite of this cool dessert.

Profiteroles with Coffee Whipped Cream *(page 103)* These easy-to-make treats boast delicious Coffee Whipped Cream sandwiched between flaky cream puffs drizzled with hot fudge topping.

Angela's Spicy Buffalo Wings (*page 146*) Test-kitchen professional Angeal Sellers shares the secrets to making one of her best entertaining recipes.

Pam's Country Crust Bread (*page 150*) With a tender crumb and soft crust, this melt-in-your-mouth favorite is pure bliss.

Blackberry Wine Sorbet *(page 132)* The sweet flavors of blackberry wine, fresh blueberries, blackberries, and raspberries along with the brightness of lime juice combine for a refreshing make-ahead late summer dessert.

Meet the *Southern Living* Food Staff

For over 40 years, the *Southern Living* Food Staff has been the trusted source of Southern cuisine. On these pages, we invite you to match the names and faces of the people who plan, kitchen-test, and write about our favorites.

▲ Scott Jones, *Executive Editor;* Lyda Jones Burnette, *Test Kitchen Director;* Shannon Sliter Satterwhite, *Food Editor;* Pat York, *Editorial Assistant*

◀ (seated) Marian Cooper Cairns, *Test Kitchen Specialist/Styling;* Rebecca Kracke Gordon, *Assistant Test Kitchen Director;* Norman King, *Test Kitchen Professional;* (standing, from left,) Vanessa McNeil Rocchio, *Test Kitchen Specialist/Styling;* Pam Lolley *and* Angela Sellers, *Test Kitchen Professionals*

(from left)
Mary Allen Perry, *Senior Food Editor;*
Ashley Leath, *Senior Recipe Editor;*
Shirley Harrington, *Senior Food Editor;*
Ashley Arthur, *Assistant Recipe Editor;*
and Donna Florio, *Senior Writer* ▶

Our Year at Southern Living®

Dear Food Friends,

Each year the *Southern Living* Food staff creates the recipes, photographs, and stories in the magazine that embody the spirit of the South. The magazine pages reflect what Southerners are cooking in their kitchens today, while at the same time honoring the traditions that have been passed down through generations of cooks.

Columns such as "Mama's Way or Your Way?" illustrate this by presenting two takes on time-honored Southern recipes: more traditional and a speedier, just-as-delicious version. Another favorite, "Cooking Class," provides a little more step-by-step instruction to preparing some favorite Southern dishes. And readers get the answers to some of their most challenging cooking problems with our new column, "Ask the Test Kitchen." *Southern Living* readers are also conscious of living well, which is why we are always looking for ways to make our Southern favorites more nutritional and share the best information on good foods in our *Healthy Living* section.

> *"The magazine pages reflect what Southerners are cooking in their kitchens today ..."*

This year has been a busy one at *Southern Living,* as you'll see by the abundance of recipes we tested as you flip through the pages of this month-to-month scrapbook of food. Be sure not to miss the Test Kitchen Notebook tips scattered throughout the chapters that reveal our top secrets for cooking success. And the Test Kitchen Favorite recipes, a few of our extra favorites added to some stories this year. I'm also particularly fond of this year's "Make-Ahead" bonus section that begins on page 291. It's filled with recipes that will help you fit time in the kitchen into your busy lives.

This year, we'd like to save a place for you at our *Southern Living* table. We'd love for you to share your favorite recipes with us for possible publication. Thanks for inviting us into your homes, and I look forward to hearing from you and seeing more of your recipes soon.

Sincerely,

Scott Jones
Executive Editor
sl_foodedit@timeinc.com

ISBN-13: 978-0-8487-3345-2
ISBN-10: 0-8487-3345-2
ISSN: 0272-2003

Printed in the United States of America
First printing 2010

To order additional publications, call 1-800-765-6400.

For more books to enrich your life, visit **oxmoorhouse.com**

To search, savor, and share thousands of recipes, visit **myrecipes.com**

Cover: Spice Cake with Citrus Filling, page 264

Page 1: Sweet Potato Pie with Marshmallow Meringue, page 239

Southern Living

Executive Editor: Scott Jones
Food Editor: Shannon Sliter Satterwhite
Senior Writer: Donna Florio
Senior Food Editors: Shirley Harrington, Mary Allen Perry
Senior Recipe Editor: Ashley Leath
Assistant Recipe Editor: Ashley Arthur
Test Kitchens Director: Lyda Jones Burnette
Assistant Test Kitchens Director: Rebecca Kracke Gordon
Test Kitchens Specialists/Food Styling: Marian Cooper Cairns, Vanessa McNeil Rocchio
Test Kitchens Professionals: Norman King, Pam Lolley, Angela Sellers
Editorial Assistant: Pat York
Production Manager: Jamie Barnhart
Copy Chief: Susan Emack Alison
Assistant Copy Chief: Katie Bowlby
Copy Editor: JoAnn Weatherly
Assistant Copy Editors: Marilyn R. Smith, Ryan Wallace
Senior Food Photographer: Jennifer Davick
Photographers: Ralph Anderson, Beth Dreiling Hontzas
Senior Photo Stylist: Buffy Hargett
Assistant Photo Stylist: Amy Burke
Production Coordinators: Christy Coleman, Paula Dennis, Mary Elizabeth McGinn
Production Services Photo Coordinator: Ginny P. Allen

Oxmoor House, Inc.

VP, Publishing Director: Jim Childs
Editorial Director: Susan Payne Dobbs
Brand Manager: Daniel Fagan
Senior Editor: Rebecca Brennan
Managing Editor: Laurie S. Herr

Southern Living 2010 Annual Recipes

Editor: Susan Hernandez Ray
Photography Director: Jim Bathie
Senior Production Manager: Greg A. Amason

Contributors

Designer: Nancy Johnson
Copy Editor: Donna Baldone
Editorial Consultant: Jean Liles
Proofreader: Julie Gillis
Indexer: Mary Ann Laurens
Index Copy Editor: Jasmine Hodges
Editorial Interns: Christine T. Boatwright, Caitlin Watzke

Contents

✤ *Favorite Columns*

Each month, we focus on topics that are important to our readers—from delicious menus to healthy options to handy tips for almost anything.

Mama's Way or Your Way?

♥ Nothing is cozier on a cold winter evening than curling up in front of a fire with a bowl of steaming chicken and dumplings. In one version, we remain true to the stick-to-your-ribs classic recipe. In the other, we've created a recipe easy enough for a weeknight dinner, yet wholesomely satisfying (page 36).

♥ Even country music star Miranda Lambert misses her mama's homecooked meatloaf when she's on the road. We've devised a way to make Mama's recipe healthier, so her traveling daughter can take it on the road as a way of carrying a little piece of home with her. (page 47).

♥ Lemon squares hold all of the citrusy tanginess of summer. Try Luscious Lemon Bars for a taste of the good, ol' days in your mama's kitchen, or discover our new version, Lemon Drop Squares, to enjoy these tasty treats any night of the week (page 66).

♥ The rich smell of baking ham is as Southern as sweet tea. We've taken a mouthwatering classic and turned it into a quicker, easier dish that families are sure to love (page 78).

♥ Celebrate summer by making one of two delicious squash casseroles. The richer, traditional Two-Cheese Squash Casserole bakes in the oven, while the tasty Summer Squash Casserole occupies your microwave for only 10 minutes (page 97).

♥ Enjoy the summery goodness of fresh peaches in either a traditional, down-home cobbler, or our So-Easy Peach Cobbler that takes just 30 minutes to make (page 105).

♥ Nothing beats a lazy afternoon by a beautiful lake, except maybe the delicious catfish you can prepare as a result of your fishing success! We've provided a traditional fried catfish recipe, and we've created an oven-fried version that's low fat and tasty (page 123).

♥ Mama's way is a made-from-stratch masterpiece of rich flavor and lemony goodness. Your way is a no-bake lemonade pie with a cheesecake-like texture. Both ways are guaranteed to refresh and impress (page 144).

♥ Heaps of cheese, mounds of mushrooms, and piles of chicken and noodles form the perfect comfort food. Chicken tetrazzini provides the ideal way of warding off cool evenings, and we've worked to create a dish that enhances the traditional version (page 153).

♥ Just as the scrumptious cinnamon scent begins to float from the kitchen, you'll reminisce about melt-in-your-mouth cinnamon rolls your mom used to make. Now, you can either make that beloved classic, or try a new twist, Bite-Sized Cinnamon-Pecan Twirls (page 209).

♥ Try the traditional version of corn pudding with its rich, creamy texture. Our new version uses less dairy and eggs and has a speedy preparation time (page 289).

Healthy Living

♥ Delicious, calorie-laden desserts often come with a heaping side of guilt. But with recipes like these, you can indulge your sweet tooth without worrying about the scale. Chocolate Fudge Pie and Lemon-Cheesecake Bars offer yummy satisfaction and sweet alternatives to traditionally regretful indulgences (page 48).

♥ Enjoy a healthy punch of nutrition by introducing a rainbow of healthful, colorful fruits and vegetables to your diet. The richer the color, the more nutrients in the produce (page 60).

♥ If you love the crunch of fried foods but are looking for a healthy way to enjoy a crispy dish, look no further than our Coconut Shrimp recipe. Oven "frying" rather than deep frying lends a tasty crunch with less fat (page 93).

♥ Barbecue and banana pudding go together like a Southern twang and country music. Miraculously, this recipe brings all of that creamy banana flavor with less fat and calories (page 112).

♥ Be sure to use Key limes, rather than regular limes, when making this delicious, lightened pie. Bottled lime juice won't do the trick either. Invest in fresh Key limes for a memorable, tropical delight (page 122).

♥ Potato salad traditionally swims in gobs of mayonnaise. We decided to give the fat-saturated salad a makeover by using olive oil, seasonings, and lemon juice to create a lighter, healthier side dish (page 139).

♥ Avocados add a tasty buttery zing to guacamole, but they also offer 5 nutritional benefits in extraordinary ways. This vitamin-packed fruit can help lower cholesterol and help regulate blood pressure, all while being a great source of vitamin E (page 155).

♥ Keep your skillet cornbread moist and delicious while also making it lighter and healthier. Use kitchen staples to make the perfect side to any meal of the day (page 214).

♥ A Thanksgiving favorite finally gets the perfect makeover. With our new version of a sweet potato casserole, we keep all of the creamy, crunchy toppings without sacrificing any of the delicious richness (page 240).

♥ Try our new twist on an old favorite. Bread pudding already offers warm sweetness, but with our recipe makeover, the dish gives you warm fulfillment without heaping on extra calories (page 252).

♥ Pomegranates have more to offer than tangy flavor. From preventing arthritis to protecting your skin and teeth, this wonder fruit just keeps giving (page 253).

Cooking Class

♥ Create perfectly fluffy omelets for either breakfast or dinner. Our Test Kitchen shows you how to blend, tilt, and fold until your omelets equal perfection (page 84).

♥ With only six ingredients and two easy steps, our new twist on a classic pound cake recipe makes this delicious dessert practical for any night of the week (page 96).

♥ Baby back ribs are the perfect addition to any backyard barbecue, but learning how to cook these ribs can be tricky. Follow our Test Kitchen's advice to spice, stack, and baste a slab of ribs into melt-in-your-mouth perfection (page 136).

Half-Hour Hostess

♥ Host your own Super Bowl party with three easy-to-fix recipes. Super Quick Chili is deliciously filling, while Blue Cheese Ranch Dip offers guests a creamy, rich snack to munch on while they cheer for their favorite team (page 50).

♥ Pull out your wide-brimmed hat and julep cups to host an unforgettable Kentucky Derby party. Our Mint Julep recipe is a must for guests enjoying the race. Pair the famous beverage with our adorable Derby Cheese Hat appetizer, and you're all set for a day at the races (page 98).

Ask the Test Kitchen

♥ A plate of steamed asparagus is a refreshing dish, but the healthful vegetable has much more dinner-table excitement to offer. Adding pesto or pistachios to asparagus not only spices up a favorite side-dish standby, but also offers a nutritional punch (page 55).

♥ Cucumbers arrive in hearty amounts during the summer months. Try out the Test Kitchen's twist on familiar cucumber-laden dishes. Enjoy this versatile vegetable fried, enhancing a soup, or gracing a salad (page 138).

Cook's Chat

Our readers chat online about what they think of our recipes and how they use them. Here, they brag about some of their favorites.

Appetizers and Beverages

Pancetta Crisps with Goat Cheese and Pear, page 32—"Impressive, delicious, and easy to make. I gave the pears a swipe with a cut lemon to keep the color appetizing."

Kentucky Mimosa, page 65—"I made Kentucky mimosas for Sunday brunch, and there wasn't a drop left. My husband wanted more bourbon in it, but a guest added orange juice to mitigate the bourbon in hers. I think we'll be making these mimosas a lot this summer!"

Raspberry Beer Cocktail, page 71—"I just mixed up this cocktail, and it is fantastic! I added a can of Sprite to the mix, as the recipe as is was a little too tart for my taste. Now it is perfect! It will definitely be my summertime, by-the-pool drink."

Carolina Peach Sangria, page 104—"I made this for a girls' night party at my house for 12 friends. Good thing I made two pitchers full! It's not like the typical heavy, spiced sangria. Can't wait to make it again this weekend!"

Spicy Glazed Shrimp and Vegetable Kabobs, page 107—"We used this recipe for shrimp only, and it is delicious! It's both spicy and sweet at the same time. This is going to be a 'go-to' recipe for a quick and different way to grill shrimp."

Entrées

Pork Chops with Pepper Jelly Sauce, page 28—"I absolutely love this recipe! I was a little skeptical at first about red pepper jelly, but this is fantastic! It's definitely one of our new favorites! I made El Charro Beans and green salad for a perfect dinner! It's great for everday or special occasions, and it can easily be doubled for larger get-togethers!"

Pam-Cakes with Buttered Honey Syrup, page 31—"This was an amazing take on pancakes! My daughter, who is the pickiest eater ever, had four! The Buttered Honey Syrup was a bit runny, but it tasted so amazing that no one cared."

Sausage-and-Cheese Frittata, page 35—"This is excellent! I made one for my Bible study group, but made it a little healthier by using egg substitute for four of the eggs, and baking it in a glass dish coated with cooking spray, skipping the butter. My husband liked it so much that he made another one himself to cut up and have for breakfast for the next few days. Yum!"

Linguine with Sun-Dried Tomatoes, page 41—"This is a wonderful dish, fast to whip up, and it tastes as though you spent lots of time preparing. I will serve this dish often."

Sizzling Flounder, page 53—"I am not a 'fish' person, but even I loved this recipe, not only for its good taste but also for its ease! This is a very simple recipe that takes no time at all to make, and doesn't taste fishy. My local grocery store didn't have flounder, so I used tilapia instead, which worked great. This will be a recipe I use quite a few times a year."

Pasta with Zesty Pecan Sauce, page 58—"This was so easy! I love that the ingredients are things I have in my pantry. My husband, who does not like pecans or lemons, thought this was good."

Sweet Potato-and-Edamame Hash, page 74—"I made a meatless version by using two ham seasoning packets instead of the ham. We had it for Easter dinner, and it was wonderful! I loved how colorful it was. We had it with ham and broccoli salad—a wonderful combination."

Spinach-and-Cheese Omelet, page 84—"This is a refreshing change to a traditional omelet. It's a delightful combination of flavor—light, fresh, and fabulous."

Spicy Grilled Pork Tenderloin with Blackberry Sauce, page 86—"This is hands down one of the best recipes I've ever tried. It's so delicious, and I think the sauce would be excellent on chicken or shrimp."

Grilled Chicken-and-Veggie Tortellini, page 135—"This dish was a huge hit in my kitchen. Preparation is a breeze, and the final product delivers a beautiful, summery presentation. Overall, a delicious dinner that I'll be cooking again soon!"

King Ranch Chicken, page 218—"It was a rainy night in Virginia, and this wonderful slow-cooker casserole really hit the spot. This will be a new comfort food in our house. It also will be nice to serve to guests for a casual supper."

Soups and Sandwiches

Easy Chicken Gumbo, page 42—"I will surely make this recipe again. My husband loved it. It made quite a big amount, so we had leftovers several times, and he did not complain a bit."

Baby Carrot Soup, page 62—"I did it just like the recipe, and it came out outstanding. I love soup, and this is a great starter dish for any meal!"

Cheesy BBQ Sloppy Joes, page 82—"This is so quick and easy! Everyone liked it at our house. I'll make it again with my favorite BBQ Sauce."

Greek Turkey Burgers, page 121—"Delicious! I normally make some type of change, but I didn't change anything for this recipe. They turned out wonderfully! I'll definitely make these again."

Caribbean Crab Sandwich, page 134—"One word: awesome! The flavors in this recipe are to die for. It's super-easy to make with only a few ingredients. It tasted good as leftovers the next day too."

Creamy Cucumber Soup, page 138—"Loved this recipe! Quick, easy, refreshing. When I made it, I made it in the food processor, but forgot to save some of the chopped cucumber. As a result, the soup was smoother, but excellent."

Salads

Strawberry-Avocado Salad, page 57—"Excellent and easy. I added cubed seasoned chicken for a complete, refreshing meal."

Roasted Asparagus Salad, page 57—"Having never roasted a vegetable before, I was intrigued by the recipe. Very light. Really delicious! Can't wait to make it again this weekend! It was delicious, so much so that I have made it three times in the last week. I took some to work, and it was devoured!"

Chicken-and-Melon Chopped Salad, page 64—"Fantastic salad! The ingredients sounded like a strange combination, but they worked together delightfully. We decided to try it while on vacation at the beach, and it was perfect. We'll definitely make this again."

Grilled Shrimp-and-Green Bean Salad, page 87—"I tried this recipe and all I have to say about it is. . . wow! I didn't serve it on cornbread. Just mix it all up and serve it on a plate, and it looks really pretty! I cooked the green beans for 6 minutes instead of 4, as they were a little too crisp for me. This is an excellent recipe. Give it a try! It's awesome!"

Big Daddy's Grilled Blue Cheese-and-Bacon Potato Salad, page 90—"Delicious! This potato salad is so rich and creamy. I'm going to make it over and over. It's great with steak or hot dogs."

Creole Potato Salad, page 91—"My family liked this very much. It holds up well for the next day, if you want to make it ahead. I served this with brisket."

Simple Beet Salad, page 95—"This was my first time to prepare beets, and this recipe was easy and very good. It adds a little something extra to the table, and the color is beautiful."

Strawberry Fields Salad, page 141—"A definite summer salad keeper! My entire family loved this salad. A great combination of sweet and salty, fresh greens, fruits, terrific light dressing and easy to put together! Delicious! Salad and fruit lovers will not be disappointed."

Sides

Cauliflower Gratin with Almond Crust, page 46—"It was very good, and I'm not all that fond of cauliflower! I would serve this to company."

Grilled Rainbow Peppers, page 56—"For the ease of prep, this is a great recipe! So yummy and quick to make with very little cleanup."

Sweet Corn and Zucchini, page 56—"This is one of the best, fresh-tasting side dishes you can make in a hurry, and it is very attractive. Frozen corn works great!"

Oregano Green Beans, page 77—"I just had this dish last week and am already craving it again! I wasn't too sure about the combination of some of the ingredients, but wow, do they work together! It is a must-try! I am adding this recipe to my list of absolute favorites!"

Black Beans and Coconut-Lime Rice, page 94—"I fixed this recipe on Memorial Day for my family with shish kabobs. It was a huge hit! Everyone loved the layers of flavor. I have added this to my favorite recipes."

Heirloom Tomatoes with Fresh Peaches, Goat Cheese, and Pecans, page 116—"I saw this recipe and had to try it. It sounded so unusual. My husband and I loved the salad. I have leftover dressing that I am going to use tomorrow night with more tomatoes and lettuce. I can't wait to have it again, and I also can't wait to take it to an occasion."

Breads

Pam's Country Crust Bread, page 150—"I just made this bread, and it is awesome! It came out perfectly after following the directions. I made the whole-wheat version from wheat that I had ground myself. I would highly recommend this recipe!"

Jordan Rolls, page 208—"This recipe is very easy to follow, and you will not be disappointed with the results. Keep this recipe on hand for the holidays to come. Your guests will love them."

Desserts

Easy Berry Cobbler, page 33—"My first attempt at cobbler and it was amazing! The cobbler came out perfect! Just juicy enough and not too dry; the topping was sweet, but not overpowering for the berries. I will keep this one in my arsenal for a quick dessert anytime!"

Salted Caramel-Chocolate Cupcakes, page 39—"I made the salted caramel cupcakes today, and yum! Deliciousness! The frosting reminds me of the sweet/salty taste of kettle corn. I never would've thought of putting salt in the frosting, but it totally enhances the flavors. I will definitely be making these again."

Banana Bread Cobbler, page 43—"My new favorite comfort food! I had this at a friend's house where we all devoured it while it was still warm. She served it without the streusel, and it was still great. I might serve vanilla ice cream on the side when I make it."

Benne Brittle, page 54—"This was delicious and fun to make...and I learned a lot about melting sugar. When it clumps up and you think you have ruined it, keep on stirring and the sugar will melt beautifully."

Strawberry-Orange Shortcake Tart, page 72—"This is the best new spring recipe I've made this year! The flavors were fantastic together, and I had no problem at all preparing the tart. It came together in 5 minutes! A fantastic, stunning, delicious spring dessert. I even shared slices with a few neighbors, who also raved about it."

Pavlova with Lemon Cream and Berries, page 95—"This dessert was so light, refreshing, and delicious. I highly recommend this dessert recipe, perfect for spring and summer."

Pineapple Upside-Down Carrot Cake, page 151—"This cake is fantastic! It is very moist. I will make this again and again!"

January

Fall in Love With Cast Iron

Use your nonstick pan all the time? Don't forget about the versatile cast iron tucked away in your cabinet. Here's why you should use it tonight.

You might remember it as the heavy black skillet grandma fried chicken in (and later passed down to you). But versatile cast iron goes from stovetop to oven to grill with such ease that you can bake a gooey upside-down cake in it as well as fry unbelievably crisp catfish. And it's a regional icon that will boost your reputation as a savvy cook. So pull out your hand-me-down skillet, or buy a new preseasoned one—once you try these recipes, you'll be a cast-iron convert.

Pork Chops with Pepper Jelly Sauce

MAKES 6 SERVINGS
HANDS-ON TIME: 39 MIN.
TOTAL TIME: 39 MIN.

- 4 (¾-inch-thick) bone-in pork loin chops (about 2¼ lb.)
- 1 tsp. salt
- ¾ tsp. freshly ground pepper
- 3 Tbsp. butter, divided
- 3 Tbsp. olive oil
- 1 Tbsp. all-purpose flour
- 1 large jalapeño pepper, seeded and minced
- ⅓ cup dry white wine
- 1 cup chicken broth
- ½ cup red pepper jelly

1. Sprinkle pork with salt and pepper. Melt 1 Tbsp. butter with oil in a 12-inch cast-iron skillet over medium-high heat. Add pork chops, and cook 8 minutes; turn and cook 10 minutes or until a meat thermometer inserted into thickest portion registers 150°. Remove from skillet, and keep warm.
2. Add flour and jalapeño to skillet. Cook, stirring constantly, 1 to 2 minutes or until flour is golden brown. Add wine, stirring to loosen particles from bottom of skillet; cook 1 minute or until almost completely reduced.
3. Add chicken broth, and cook 2 to 3 minutes or until mixture begins to thicken. Whisk in pepper jelly until melted and smooth. Cook 3 to 4 minutes or until thickened. Remove from heat. Stir in remaining 2 Tbsp. butter. Season with salt and freshly ground pepper to taste. Return pork to skillet; turn to coat. Serve pork with sauce.

Note: We tested with Braswell's Red Pepper Jelly.

RUST ERASER
Rub this handy tool on rust stains, and then reseason pan. Find it at hardware stores, bike shops, or woodworking shops.

Caring for Cast Iron

When cared for properly, cast iron develops a shiny patina called "seasoning" that makes it nearly nonstick. Here are our secrets for perfectly preserved pans.

- Clean with a stiff brush or plastic scrubber under running water while the cast iron is still warm but cool enough to handle with ease. Kosher salt is also a good scrubbing agent for baked-on stains. The most important tip is to never use soap!
- Before cooking, apply vegetable oil to the cooking surface, and preheat the pan on low heat, increasing the temperature slowly.
- Never marinate in cast iron. Acidic mixtures will damage the seasoning.
- Reseason if food particles start to stick, rust appears, or you experience a metallic taste. A seasoned skillet is a happy skillet. Learn how to season yours with our step-by-step video: *southernliving.com/january2010*.

Parmesan-Pecan Fried Catfish with Pickled Okra Salsa

MAKES 6 SERVINGS

HANDS-ON TIME: 23 MIN.

TOTAL TIME: 1 HR., 33 MIN. (INCLUDING SALSA)

Create a sensational main dish with two Southern favorites in Parmesan-Pecan Fried Catfish With Pickled Okra Salsa. (pictured on page 163)

- 2 lb. catfish fillets, cut into 1-inch-wide strips
- 1 cup buttermilk
- 1 cup ground pecans
- ⅔ cup plain yellow cornmeal
- ⅔ cup grated Parmesan cheese
- 1 Tbsp. Cajun seasoning
- 1 Tbsp. paprika
- 2 large eggs, beaten
  Vegetable oil
  Pickled Okra Salsa

1. Place catfish and buttermilk in a large zip-top plastic freezer bag. Seal and chill 1 hour. Remove catfish from buttermilk, discarding buttermilk.
2. Combine pecans and next 4 ingredients in a shallow bowl. Dip fish in eggs; dredge in pecan mixture, shaking off excess. Arrange on a baking sheet. Pour oil to depth of 1½ inches into a cast-iron Dutch oven or 12-inch (2¼-inch-deep) cast-iron skillet; heat to 350°. Fry fish, in batches, 2 to 3 minutes or until golden brown and fish flakes with a fork. Drain on a wire rack over paper towels. Serve with Pickled Okra Salsa. **RECIPE FROM BARBARA JONES** CORDOVA, TENNESSEE

Note: We tested with Zatarain's Creole Seasoning.

TRY THIS TWIST!
Parmesan-Pecan Fried Chicken: Substitute 2 lb. chicken breast tenders for catfish. Fry 3 minutes or until done.

Pickled Okra Salsa:

good for you • make-ahead

MAKES ABOUT 1½ CUPS **HANDS-ON TIME:** 10 MIN. **TOTAL TIME:** 10 MIN.

- 5 whole pickled okra, sliced
- ½ cup chopped sweet onion
- 4 tsp. chopped fresh cilantro
- 1 tsp. fresh lime juice
- ¼ tsp. salt
- ⅛ tsp. freshly ground pepper
- 1 (14.5-oz.) can diced tomatoes with mild green chiles, drained

1. Pulse first 6 ingredients and half of tomatoes in a food processor 4 to 6 times or until thoroughly combined. Stir in remaining diced tomatoes. Serve immediately, or cover and chill. Store in refrigerator up to 7 days. If refrigerated, let stand at room temperature 15 minutes before serving.

Upside-Down Caramelized Apple Cake

MAKES 8 TO 10 SERVINGS

HANDS-ON TIME: 38 MIN.

TOTAL TIME: 1 HR., 38 MIN.

A buttery mixture of pecans, brown sugar, and tart Granny Smiths make this an irresistible treat. To get a true reading of doneness, insert the wooden pick only halfway through the cake when testing.

- ½ cup chopped pecans
- 2 large Granny Smith apples, peeled and cut into ½-inch-thick slices
- 1 Tbsp. lemon juice
- 2 tsp. vanilla extract, divided
- ¾ tsp. ground cinnamon, divided
- ½ cup butter, softened and divided
- 2 tsp. brandy
- 1 cup firmly packed light brown sugar
- ¾ cup granulated sugar, divided
- 2 large eggs, separated
- ¾ cup milk
- ½ cup sour cream
- 2 cups all-purpose baking mix
- ⅛ tsp. ground nutmeg

1. Preheat oven to 350°. Bake pecans in a single layer in a shallow pan 8 to 10 minutes or until toasted and fragrant, stirring after 5 minutes. Increase oven temperature to 375°.
2. Toss apple slices with lemon juice, 1 tsp. vanilla extract, and ½ tsp. cinnamon.
3. Melt ¼ cup butter in a 10-inch cast-iron skillet over low heat. Remove from heat; stir in brandy. Sprinkle with brown sugar.
4. Sprinkle pecans over brown sugar mixture. Arrange apples in 2 concentric circles over pecans.
5. Beat ½ cup granulated sugar and remaining ¼ cup butter at medium speed with an electric mixer until blended. Add egg yolks, 1 at a time, beating just until blended after each addition. Add milk, sour cream, and remaining 1 tsp. vanilla, beating just until blended.
6. Whisk together baking mix, nutmeg, and remaining ¼ tsp. cinnamon in a medium bowl. Add nutmeg mixture to butter mixture, beating just until blended.
7. Beat egg whites in a large bowl at high speed until soft peaks form. Gradually beat in remaining ¼ cup granulated sugar until stiff peaks form. Fold into batter. Spread batter over apples in skillet.
8. Bake at 375° for 50 to 54 minutes or until a wooden pick inserted halfway into center of cake comes out clean. Cool in skillet on a wire rack 10 minutes. Carefully run a knife around edge of cake to loosen. Invert cake onto a serving plate, replacing any topping that sticks to skillet on cake.
Note: We tested with Bisquick Original All-Purpose Baking Mix.

Roasted Sweet Potato Salad With Citrus Vinaigrette

good for you

MAKES 4 SERVINGS **HANDS-ON TIME:** 20 MIN.
TOTAL TIME: 1 HR., 10 MIN. (INCLUDING VINAIGRETTE)

- 1 lb. medium-size sweet potatoes, peeled and cut into wedges
- 1 medium-size sweet onion, cut into wedges
- 1 Tbsp. olive oil
- 1 garlic clove
- ¾ tsp. salt
- ½ tsp. freshly cracked pepper
- 1 (5-oz.) package fresh mâche, thoroughly washed
  Citrus Vinaigrette

1. Preheat oven to 400°. Heat a 17- x 10-inch cast-iron pan or 12-inch cast-iron skillet in oven 10 minutes. Toss together sweet potato wedges and next 5 ingredients in a large bowl. Place sweet potato mixture in hot pan.
2. Bake at 400° for 25 minutes. Stir once, and bake 15 more minutes or until potatoes are tender and begin to caramelize.
3. Spoon potato mixture over mâche; drizzle with Citrus Vinaigrette.

Citrus Vinaigrette:

make-ahead • quick-prep

MAKES ABOUT ½ CUP **HANDS-ON TIME:** 10 MIN. **TOTAL TIME:** 10 MIN.

- 1 (½-inch) piece fresh ginger, peeled
- 2 Tbsp. red wine vinegar
- 1 Tbsp. chopped sweet onion
- 1 Tbsp. honey
- 1 tsp. orange zest
- ¼ tsp. dry mustard
- ¼ tsp. salt
- ¼ cup olive oil

1. Pulse first 7 ingredients in a blender or food processor until blended. With blender running, add olive oil in a slow, steady stream, processing until smooth. Pour through a fine wire-mesh strainer into a bowl; discard solids.

Pamper Yourself With Pancakes

This weekend make Pam-Cakes! That's what we affectionately call our Food staff's favorite, fluffy, buttermilk flapjacks created by Test Kitchen pro Pam Lolley. Plan to drench them, hot off the griddle, with one of our easy syrups.

Dress Up Your Maple Syrup

We can't get enough of our Buttered Honey Syrup and fruit preserve toppings. We also love the flavor of good ol' maple syrup, which is why we're featuring these easy, jazzed-up versions. Get our results by using pure maple syrup, not pancake syrup. We know it's pricey, but it's worth the splurge.

Vanilla Maple Syrup: Pour 1 cup maple syrup into a saucepan. Split 1 (3-inch) vanilla bean in half lengthwise; scrape seeds into syrup. Place vanilla bean in syrup. Cook over medium-low heat 5 minutes. Remove from heat; discard vanilla bean. Makes 1 cup. Hands-on time: 10 min.; Total time: 10 min.

Apple-Pecan Pie Maple Topping

Apple-Pecan Pie Maple Topping: Prepare Vanilla Maple Syrup as directed. Stir in 1 (12-oz.) package frozen spiced apples, thawed. Bring to a boil, reduce heat, and simmer 5 minutes. Stir in ½ cup chopped toasted pecans. Makes about 2½ cups. Hands-on time: 10 min.; Total time: 23 min. (including Vanilla Maple Syrup)
Note: We tested with Stouffer's Harvest Apples.

Blueberry-Lemon Maple Syrup: Combine ½ cup maple syrup, 1 (12-oz.) package frozen blueberries*, 1 tsp. lemon zest, and 2 tsp. lemon juice in a large saucepan. Bring to a boil over medium-high heat; reduce heat to low, and simmer 5 minutes. Serve warm. Makes about 2 cups. Hands-on time: 10 min.; Total time: 15 min.
*1 (12-oz.) package frozen mixed berries may be substituted.

Pam-Cakes with Buttered Honey Syrup

Editor's Favorite

MAKES ABOUT 16 (4-INCH) PANCAKES **HANDS-ON TIME:** 34 MIN. **TOTAL TIME:** 34 MIN.

Use a light hand when stirring the batter; overmixing will cause a rubbery texture. When using a griddle to cook pancakes, set the temperature dial to 350°. (pictured on page 3)

- 1¾ cups all-purpose flour
- 2 tsp. sugar
- 1½ tsp. baking powder
- 1 tsp. baking soda
- 1 tsp. salt
- 2 cups buttermilk
- 2 large eggs
- ¼ cup butter, melted
  Buttered Honey Syrup

1. Combine flour and next 4 ingredients in a large bowl. Whisk together buttermilk and eggs. Gradually stir mixture into flour mixture. Gently stir in butter. (Batter will be lumpy.)
2. Pour about ¼ cup batter for each pancake onto a hot buttered griddle or large nonstick skillet. Cook pancakes 3 to 4 minutes or until tops are covered with bubbles and edges look dry and cooked. Turn and cook 3 to 4 minutes or until golden brown. Place pancakes in a single layer on a baking sheet, and keep warm in a 200° oven up to 30 minutes. Serve with Buttered Honey Syrup.

Buttered Honey Syrup:
quick-prep

MAKES ABOUT ¾ CUP
HANDS-ON TIME: 5 MIN.
TOTAL TIME: 5 MIN.

1. Melt ⅓ cup butter in a small saucepan over medium-low heat. Stir in ½ cup honey, and cook 1 minute or until warm.
Note: Buttered Honey Syrup cannot be made ahead. The heated honey will crystallize when cooled and will not melt if reheated.

Test Kitchen Notebook

PERMISSION SLIP: When it comes to buttering the griddle or skillet for cooking pancakes, peel paper away from one end of a stick of butter and rub on hot surface. Store in fridge for the next time you need to butter a clean pan.

3 Fruit Preserve Toppings

Once you drizzle Pam-Cakes with Buttered Honey Syrup, add more flavor with a delicious topping. Finish off with fresh blueberries, toasted almonds, or toasted pecans.

1 Cherry-Almond Topping: Microwave ½ cup cherry preserves at HIGH 1 minute, stirring at 20-second intervals. Stir in ⅛ tsp. ground nutmeg and ⅛ tsp. almond extract. Makes ½ cup. Hands-on time: 5 min.; Total time: 5 min.
Note: We tested with Smucker's Cherry Preserves.

2 Pear-Orange Fruit Topping: Microwave ½ cup pear preserves at HIGH 1 minute, stirring at 20-second intervals. Stir in 1 tsp. orange zest and ⅛ tsp. ground cinnamon. Makes ½ cup. Hands-on time: 5 min.; Total time: 5 min.

3 Apricot-Ginger Topping: Microwave ½ cup apricot or peach preserves and 1½ tsp. finely chopped crystallized ginger* at HIGH 1 minute and 20 seconds, stirring at 20-second intervals. Makes ½ cup. Hands-on time: 5 min.; Total time: 5 min.
* ¼ tsp. ground ginger may be substituted.
Note: Crystallized ginger adds texture and a subtle ginger flavor. Using ground ginger yields a thinner mixture, but a spicier flavor.

Coffee Craving

MAPLE COFFEE: Cook 2 cups half-and-half and ¾ cup maple syrup in a saucepan over medium heat until thoroughly heated. (Do not boil.) Stir in 3 cups strong brewed coffee. Top with frothed half-and-half, if desired. Makes 6 cups.

Try it with chocolate-dipped biscotti from the supermarket bakery.

This Year's Recipes To Know by Heart

From an elegant five-ingredient appetizer to a hearty chili to tempting desserts, these top-rated staff favorites are so easy you'll use them again and again.

Pancetta Crisps with Goat Cheese and Pear

quick-prep

MAKES 6 APPETIZER SERVINGS
HANDS-ON TIME: 15 MIN.
TOTAL TIME: 33 MIN.

"A short ingredient list with wow-factor results makes this my favorite appetizer," says Ashley Leath, Senior Recipe Editor. Readers say it's ideal for New Year's Eve.

Preheat oven to 450°. Arrange 12 thin pancetta slices (about ⅓ lb.) in a single layer on an aluminum foil-lined baking sheet. Bake 8 to 10 minutes or until golden. Transfer to a paper towel-lined wire rack. Let stand 10 minutes or until crisp. Core 1 red Bartlett pear, and cut crosswise into 12 thin rings. Arrange on a serving platter. Top with pancetta and ½ (4-oz.) package goat cheese, crumbled; sprinkle with freshly cracked pepper. Drizzle with honey just before serving.

Blackberry-Basil Vinaigrette

quick-prep • make ahead

MAKES 1 CUP
HANDS-ON TIME: 10 MIN.
TOTAL TIME: 10 MIN.

Mary Allen Perry, Senior Food Editor, touts this dressing as one to use throughout the year. Drizzle it over salad greens topped with grilled or sautéed chicken breasts; apple or peach slices; crumbled blue or feta cheese; and roasted, glazed pecan pieces. (Find the nuts on the produce aisle.)

½ (10-oz.) jar seedless blackberry preserves
¼ cup red wine vinegar
6 fresh basil leaves
1 garlic clove, sliced
½ tsp. salt
½ tsp. seasoned pepper
¾ cup vegetable oil

1. Pulse blackberry preserves, red wine vinegar, and next 4 ingredients in a blender 2 to 3 times or until blended. With blender running, add vegetable oil in a slow, steady stream, processing until smooth.

Turkey-Black Bean Chili

quick-prep • make ahead

MAKES 6 TO 8 SERVINGS
HANDS-ON TIME: 21 MIN.
TOTAL TIME: 36 MIN.

Black Bean Chili using meat crumbles or ground round received a "definitely a keeper" comment from readers when we first shared it. Here's our update using ground turkey.

3 (15-oz.) cans black beans
1 large sweet onion, chopped
1 lb. ground turkey
1 Tbsp. olive oil
4 tsp. chili powder
1 tsp. ground cumin
½ tsp. salt
½ tsp. pepper
1 (14-oz.) can low-sodium fat-free chicken broth
2 (14.5-oz.) cans petite diced tomatoes with jalapeño peppers
Toppings: sour cream, shredded Cheddar cheese, sliced jalapeño peppers, chopped fresh cilantro, chopped tomatoes, lime wedges, corn chips

1. Drain and rinse 2 cans black beans. (Do not drain or rinse third can.)
2. Sauté chopped onion and ground turkey in hot oil in a large Dutch oven over medium heat, stirring often, 8 to 10 minutes or until turkey crumbles and is no longer pink. Stir in chili powder and next 3 ingredients; sauté 1 minute. Stir in drained and undrained beans, chicken broth, and diced tomatoes.
3. Bring to a boil over medium-high heat; cover, reduce heat to low, and simmer 10 minutes. Serve chili with desired toppings.

Sausage-and-Ravioli Lasagna

quick-prep • make ahead

MAKES 6 TO 8 SERVINGS
HANDS-ON TIME: 25 MIN.
TOTAL TIME: 1 HR.

"Make this dish once, and you'll have it down," says Marion McGahey, Assistant Food Editor. "Keep the ingredients on hand, and you'll be ready to assemble when the craving for Italian hits."

- ½ lb. ground Italian sausage
- 1 (24-oz.) jar tomato-and-basil pasta sauce
- 1 (6-oz.) package fresh baby spinach, thoroughly washed
- ½ cup refrigerated pesto sauce
- 1 (25-oz.) package frozen cheese-filled ravioli (do not thaw)
- 1 cup (4 oz.) shredded Italian six-cheese blend

1. Preheat oven to 375°. Cook Italian sausage in a skillet over medium heat, stirring often, 10 minutes or until sausage crumbles and is no longer pink; drain well. Stir pasta sauce into sausage.
2. Chop spinach, and toss with pesto in a bowl.
3. Spoon one-third of sausage mixture (about ½ cup) into a lightly greased 11- x 7-inch baking dish. Top with half of spinach mixture. Arrange half of ravioli in a single layer over spinach mixture. Repeat layers once. Top with remaining sausage mixture.
4. Bake at 375° for 30 minutes. Sprinkle with shredded cheese, and bake 5 to 8 minutes or until hot and bubbly.
Note: We tested with Buitoni Pesto With Basil.

TRY THIS TWIST!

Shrimp-and-Ravioli Lasagna: Omit Italian sausage. Substitute 1 (15-oz.) jar Alfredo sauce for pasta sauce. Stir ¼ cup vegetable broth* into Alfredo sauce. Proceed with recipe as directed, sprinkling 1 lb. peeled, coarsely chopped cooked shrimp over first layer of ravioli. Sprinkle with ⅛ tsp. paprika before serving. Hands-on time: 20 min., Total time: 55 min.
*Chicken broth may be substituted.
Note: We tested with Bertolli Alfredo Sauce with Aged Parmesan Cheese.

 ## Lemon Hard Sauce with Gingerbread

quick prep • make-ahead

MAKES ABOUT 1 CUP HARD SAUCE
HANDS-ON TIME: 10 MIN.
TOTAL TIME: 10 MIN.

Reader Jean Smith of Brookhaven, Mississippi, inspired this delicious topping for gingerbread. Make your own favorite gingerbread recipe, or use a mix. (pictured on page 2)

- ½ cup butter, softened
- 1 tsp. lemon zest
- 1 Tbsp. lemon juice
- 1½ cups powdered sugar
- 1 Tbsp. vanilla extract
  Warm gingerbread

1. Beat softened butter, lemon zest, and lemon juice at medium speed with an electric mixer until creamy. Gradually add powdered sugar and vanilla, beating until light and fluffy. Serve immediately with warm gingerbread.

RECIPE INSPIRED BY JEAN SMITH, BROOKHAVEN, MISSISSIPPI
Note: Store sauce in refrigerator up to 1 week. Let stand 20 minutes before serving.

Easy Berry Cobbler

quick prep

MAKES 6 SERVINGS
HANDS-ON TIME: 10 MIN.
TOTAL TIME: 1 HR.

This dessert appeared on our cover in July 2008 and is a favorite of Pam Lolley, Test Kitchen Professional. It was originally made with fresh fruit, but Pam retested using frozen berries. She added a version that uses frozen sliced peaches flavored with peach schnapps for fun. Decrease bake times 5 to 10 minutes when using fresh fruit.

Preheat oven to 375°. Place 4 cups frozen blackberries* in a lightly greased 8-inch square baking dish; sprinkle with 1 Tbsp. lemon juice. Stir together 1 large egg, 1 cup sugar, and 1 cup all-purpose flour in a medium bowl until mixture resembles coarse meal. Sprinkle over fruit. Drizzle 6 Tbsp. melted butter over topping. Bake 40 to 45 minutes or until lightly browned and bubbly. Let stand 10 minutes. Serve warm with sweetened whipped cream, if desired.
*4 cups frozen mixed berries may be substituted.
Note: For individual cobblers, prepare recipe as directed, and bake at 375° for the same amount of time in 6 (8-oz.) ramekins on an aluminum foil-lined baking sheet.

TRY THIS TWIST!

Easy Peach Cobbler: Substitute 4 cups frozen sliced peaches for blackberries. Prepare recipe as directed, sprinkling 1 Tbsp. peach schnapps and ½ tsp. ground cinnamon over peaches with lemon juice, and baking cobbler 1 hour to 1 hour and 5 minutes or until lightly browned and bubbly. Hands-on time: 10 min.; Total time: 1 hr., 20 min.

A New Take on New Year's Favorites

Two Southern favorites—black-eyed peas and greens—get a flavor makeover.

Potluck Gathering

SERVES 4 TO 6

Hoppin' John Stew with White Cheddar Cheese Grits

Good-for-You Collards

Bakery brownies

Hoppin' John Stew with White Cheddar Cheese Grits

MAKES 4 TO 6 SERVINGS
HANDS-ON TIME: 33 MIN.
TOTAL TIME: 48 MIN. (INCLUDING GRITS)

A tasty alternative to chili, this hearty, updated twist is served with creamy, quick-cooking grits instead of rice.

- 1 Tbsp. butter
- 1 cup chopped smoked ham
- 1 medium onion, chopped
- 2 (15-oz.) cans black-eyed peas, drained and rinsed
- 2 (10-oz.) cans diced tomatoes with green chiles, undrained
- 1 cup frozen corn kernels
- 1 tsp. sugar
- ¼ cup chopped fresh cilantro
  White Cheddar Cheese Grits

1. Melt butter in a Dutch oven over medium heat; add ham and onion, and sauté 3 to 5 minutes or until onion is tender. Stir in black-eyed peas and next 3 ingredients. Cover, reduce heat to low, and cook, stirring occasionally, 15 minutes. Remove from heat, and stir in cilantro. Serve immediately over White Cheddar Cheese Grits.

White Cheddar Cheese Grits:

quick prep

MAKES 4 TO 6 SERVINGS
HANDS-ON TIME: 10 MIN.
TOTAL TIME: 15 MIN.

- 2 cups chicken broth
- 2 Tbsp. butter
- ½ cup uncooked quick-cooking grits
- 1 cup (4 oz.) shredded white Cheddar cheese

1. Bring chicken broth and butter to a boil in a medium saucepan over medium-high heat. Gradually whisk in grits, and return to a boil. Reduce heat to medium-low, and simmer, stirring occasionally, 5 minutes or until thickened. Stir in cheese until melted. Serve immediately.

RECIPE FROM LLOYD ROCZNIAK
ROCHESTER, MINNESOTA

Good-for-You Collards

freezable • good for you

MAKES 4 TO 6 SERVINGS
HANDS-ON TIME: 50 MIN.
TOTAL TIME: 55 MIN.

Smoky bits of lean Canadian bacon and light beer are the secrets to this dish's fabulous flavor. We also love the easy convenience of packaged collards.

- 6 Canadian bacon slices, chopped
- 1 medium-size sweet onion, chopped
- 1 Tbsp. canola oil
- 1 (16-oz.) package fresh collard greens, washed and trimmed
- 1 (12-oz.) can light beer
- 2 Tbsp. fresh lemon juice
- 2 Tbsp. balsamic vinegar
- 1 Tbsp. butter
- 1 tsp. salt
- ½ tsp. pepper

1. Sauté Canadian bacon and onion in hot oil in a large Dutch oven over medium-high heat 5 minutes or until onion is tender. Add collards, in batches, and cook, stirring occasionally, 5 minutes or until wilted. Stir in beer, and bring to a boil. Reduce heat to low, and cook, stirring occasionally, 25 minutes or to desired degree of tenderness. Stir in lemon juice and remaining ingredients.

RECIPE FROM SUSAN VAN DETTE
HIXSON, TENNESSEE

What's for Supper?

Streamline weeknight cooking with these three delicious main-dish ideas.

Chicken Dijon

quick prep

MAKES 6 SERVINGS HANDS-ON TIME: 25 MIN.
TOTAL TIME: 45 MIN.

Easy side: Prepare frozen mashed sweet potatoes according to package directions. Stir in chopped fresh sage, butter, and salt and pepper to taste.

- 6 skinned and boned chicken breasts (about 2 lb.)
- ½ tsp. salt
- ½ tsp. pepper
- 3 Tbsp. butter
- 1 medium-size red bell pepper, cut into thin strips
- 1 medium-size sweet onion, diced
- 1 (14½-oz.) can chicken broth
- 3 Tbsp. all-purpose flour
- 3 Tbsp. Dijon mustard

1. Sprinkle chicken with salt and pepper.
2. Melt butter in a large skillet over medium-high heat; add chicken, and cook 3 to 4 minutes on each side or until golden brown. Remove chicken from skillet; add bell pepper and onion, and cook, stirring often, 4 to 5 minutes or until vegetables are tender. Return chicken to skillet.
3. Whisk together broth and next 2 ingredients, and pour over chicken. Cover, reduce heat to low, and simmer 20 minutes or until chicken is done.

RECIPE FROM FRANCES MATTHEWS
BIRMINGHAM, ALABAMA

Smoked Turkey Monte Cristo Sandwiches

Quick & Easy

MAKES 4 SERVINGS
HANDS-ON TIME: 22 MIN.
TOTAL TIME: 22 MIN.

Easy side: Pulse 1 (28-oz.) can Italian-seasoned tomatoes in a food processor until finely diced. Stir together tomatoes, 1 (26-oz.) can tomato soup, 1 (32-oz.) container chicken broth, and ½ tsp. freshly ground pepper in a Dutch oven. Cook over medium heat, stirring occasionally, 10 minutes or until thoroughly heated.

- 4 Tbsp. whole grain mustard
- 8 honey-wheat bread slices
- ½ lb. thinly sliced smoked deli turkey
- 4 (1-oz.) Swiss or mozzarella cheese slices
- 2 large eggs
- ⅓ cup milk
- 2 Tbsp. butter
- 2 Tbsp. blackberry preserves
- 1 Tbsp. powdered sugar (optional)

1. Spread mustard over 1 side of each bread slice. Layer 4 bread slices, mustard sides up, with turkey and cheese slices. Top with remaining bread slices, mustard sides down.
2. Whisk together eggs and milk in a shallow dish. Dip both sides of each sandwich into egg mixture.
3. Melt 1 Tbsp. butter in a large non-stick skillet over medium heat; cook 2 sandwiches in skillet 3 to 4 minutes on each side or until lightly browned. Repeat procedure with remaining butter and sandwiches. Serve immediately with blackberry preserves. Dust with powdered sugar, if desired.

Sausage-and-Cheese Frittata

quick prep

MAKES 6 SERVINGS
HANDS-ON TIME: 25 MIN.
TOTAL TIME: 48 MIN.

Easy side: Toss together fresh spinach leaves, sliced red onions, and toasted almonds with your favorite bottled vinaigrette.

- 1 (12-oz.) package reduced-fat ground pork sausage
- 8 large eggs
- ⅓ cup milk
- ½ tsp. pepper
- ¼ tsp. salt
- 1 Tbsp. butter
- 1 cup (4 oz.) shredded 2% reduced-fat Cheddar cheese

1. Preheat oven to 350°. Brown sausage in a 10-inch ovenproof nonstick skillet over medium-high heat 10 minutes or until meat crumbles and is no longer pink; drain and transfer to a bowl. Wipe skillet clean.
2. Whisk together eggs and next 3 ingredients until well blended.
3. Melt butter in skillet over medium heat; remove from heat, and pour half of egg mixture into skillet. Sprinkle with cooked sausage and cheese. Top with remaining egg mixture.
4. Bake at 350° for 23 to 25 minutes or until set.

RECIPE FROM MARY PAPPAS
RICHMOND, VIRGINIA

Mama's Way or Your Way?
Chicken and Dumplings

One is a luscious, from-scratch favorite.
The other is cozy, easy, and delicious.

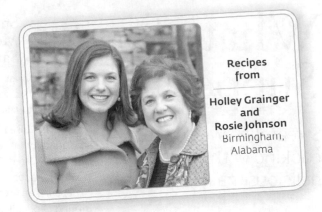

Recipes
from

**Holley Grainger
and
Rosie Johnson**
Birmingham,
Alabama

♣ WHY WE LOVE
Mama's Way

- Tender homemade dumplings
- One-dish family meal
- Makes enough to share

Classic Chicken and Dumplings

MAKES 8 SERVINGS
HANDS-ON TIME: 55 MIN.
TOTAL TIME: 2 HR., 25 MIN.

- 1 (3¾-lb.) whole chicken
- ½ tsp. garlic powder
- ½ tsp. dried thyme
- 2½ tsp. salt, divided
- ¾ tsp. pepper, divided
- 1 tsp. chicken bouillon granules
- 3 cups self-rising flour
- ½ tsp. poultry seasoning
- ⅓ cup shortening
- 2 tsp. bacon drippings*
- 1 cup milk
  Garnish: chopped fresh parsley

1. Bring chicken, water to cover, garlic powder, thyme, 1½ tsp. salt, and ½ tsp. pepper to a boil in a Dutch oven over medium heat. Cover, reduce heat to medium-low, and simmer 1 hour. Remove chicken; reserve broth.
2. Cool chicken 30 minutes; skin, bone, and shred chicken. Skim fat from broth. Add chicken, bouillon,

and remaining 1 tsp. salt and ¼ tsp. pepper to broth. Return to a simmer.
3. Combine flour and poultry seasoning in a bowl. Cut in shortening and bacon drippings with a pastry blender until crumbly. Stir in milk. Turn dough out onto a lightly floured surface. Roll to ⅛-inch thickness; cut into 1-inch pieces.
4. Drop dumplings, a few at a time, into simmering broth, stirring gently. Cover and simmer, stirring often, 25 minutes. Garnish, if desired.
*2 tsp. butter plus ¼ tsp. salt may be substituted.

♣ WHY WE LOVE
Your Way

- Only 7 ingredients
- Easy enough for weeknights
- Rich, flavorful broth

Easy Chicken and Dumplings
freezable

MAKES 4 TO 6 SERVINGS
HANDS-ON TIME: 30 MIN.
TOTAL TIME: 40 MIN.

Deli-roasted chicken, cream of chicken soup, and canned biscuits make a quick-and-tasty version of this favorite. One roasted chicken yields about 3 cups of meat. (pictured on page 162)

- 1 (32-oz.) container low-sodium chicken broth
- 3 cups shredded cooked chicken (about 1½ lb.)
- 1 (10¾-oz.) can reduced-fat cream of chicken soup
- ¼ tsp. poultry seasoning
- 1 (10.2-oz.) can refrigerated jumbo buttermilk biscuits
- 2 carrots, diced
- 3 celery ribs, diced

1. Bring first 4 ingredients to a boil in a Dutch oven over medium-high heat. Cover, reduce heat to low, and simmer, stirring occasionally, 5 minutes. Increase heat to medium-high; return to a low boil.
2. Place biscuits on a lightly floured surface. Roll or pat each biscuit to ⅛-inch thickness; cut into ½-inch-wide strips.
3. Drop strips, 1 at a time, into boiling broth mixture. Add carrots and celery. Cover, reduce heat to low, and simmer 15 to 20 minutes, stirring occasionally to prevent dumplings from sticking.

February

A Sweet and Sparkling Celebration

Get the girls together for bite-size cupcakes, sparkling wine, and fun. Everything you need is right here—delicious recipes and the bubblies to pair with them.

Basic Cupcake Batter:
Bite-Size Sour Cream-Pound Cake Cupcakes

freezable •make-ahead

MAKES 6 DOZEN MINIATURE CUPCAKES
HANDS-ON TIME: 45 MIN.
TOTAL TIME: 2 HR., 12 MIN.

- ½ cup butter, softened
- ½ (8-oz.) package cream cheese, softened
- 2 cups sugar
- 4 large eggs
- 1 tsp. vanilla extract
- 3 cups all-purpose flour
- 1 tsp. baking powder
- ½ tsp. baking soda
- ½ tsp. salt
- 1 (8-oz.) container sour cream
  Desired Buttercream or Glaze

1. Preheat oven to 350°. Beat butter and cream cheese at medium speed with an electric mixer until creamy. Beat in sugar until light and fluffy. Add eggs, 1 at a time, beating until blended after each addition. Stir in vanilla.
2. Combine flour and next 3 ingredients. Gradually add to butter mixture alternately with sour cream, beating until blended. Spoon batter by rounded tablespoonfuls into lightly greased miniature muffin pans.
3. Bake at 350° for 13 to 15 minutes or until a wooden pick inserted in centers comes out clean. Cool in pans on wire racks 5 minutes. Remove from pans to wire racks, and cool completely (about 30 minutes). Spread cupcakes with desired buttercream, or dip in glaze.

RECIPE FROM PAULA HUNT HUGHES
BIRMINGHAM, ALABAMA

Note: To prepare regular-size cupcakes, spoon batter into 2 lightly greased 12-cup muffin pans, filling two-thirds full. Bake at 350° for 22 to 24 minutes or until a wooden pick inserted in centers comes out clean. Cool and decorate as desired. Makes 2 dozen.

Basic Buttercream:
Vanilla Buttercream

MAKES ABOUT 3 CUPS
HANDS-ON TIME: 10 MIN.
TOTAL TIME: 10 MIN.

- ½ cup butter, softened
- 1 (3-oz.) package cream cheese, softened
- 2 tsp. vanilla extract
- 1 (16-oz.) package powdered sugar
- 3 to 4 Tbsp. milk

1. Beat first 3 ingredients at medium speed with an electric mixer until creamy.
2. Gradually add powdered sugar alternately with 3 Tbsp. milk, beating at low speed until blended and smooth after each addition.
3. If desired, beat in remaining 1 Tbsp. milk, 1 tsp. at a time, until desired consistency.

Dessert Party Sparklers for $15 or Less

"The secret is to pump up the fun quotient, not get too serious. To make this work you need slightly sweeter wines," says Food Executive Editor Scott Jones.

SCOTT'S TOP PICKS

- Domaine Ste. Michelle, Frizzante, Washington
- Freixenet, Spumante, Spain
- Ballatore, Gran Spumante, California
- Martini & Rossi, Asti, Italy

WORTH THE SPLURGE

- Pommery, POP Rosé, France

Fun, New Cupcake Flavors

Perk up the party with these updated variations on our basic batter and buttercream.

1 Fresh Citrus Cupcakes with Orange Buttercream

Prepare Cupcakes (facing page) as directed, omitting vanilla and adding 1 Tbsp. orange zest and 2 Tbsp. fresh orange juice to batter. Pipe or spread Orange Buttercream onto cupcakes.

Orange Buttercream: Substitute 1 Tbsp. orange zest for vanilla. Reduce milk to 2 Tbsp. Prepare Buttercream (facing page) as directed in Steps 1 and 2, beating in 2 Tbsp. fresh orange juice with 1 Tbsp. milk in Step 2. Beat in remaining 1 Tbsp. milk as directed in Step 3. Beat in 1 drop red food coloring and 1 drop yellow food coloring until blended, if desired.

2 Fresh Citrus Cupcakes with Ruby Red Grapefruit Glaze

Prepare Cupcakes (facing page) as directed, omitting vanilla and adding 1 Tbsp. orange zest and 2 Tbsp. fresh orange juice to batter. Drizzle tops of cupcakes with Ruby Red Grapefruit Glaze, and top with pink grapefruit-flavored jelly beans.

Ruby Red Grapefruit Glaze: Stir together 3 cups powdered sugar, 1 tsp. grapefruit zest, 5 to 6 Tbsp. fresh grapefruit juice, and 1 drop red food coloring until blended. Makes about 1½ cups.

3 Salted Caramel-Chocolate Cupcakes

(pictured on page 161)
Prepare Cupcakes (facing page) as directed, substituting 1¼ cups granulated sugar and ¾ cup firmly packed dark brown sugar for 2 cups granulated sugar. Microwave 8 oz. chopped semisweet chocolate and ¼ cup whipping cream in a microwave-safe bowl at HIGH 1 minute, stirring at 30-second intervals. Whisk in 2 Tbsp. whipping cream until smooth. Dip tops of cupcakes in chocolate mixture, and let stand until chocolate is set (about 30 minutes). Pipe or spread Salted Caramel Buttercream onto cupcakes. Garnish with sea salt flakes and caramels, cut into quarters. Note: We tested with Artisan Salt Company Cyprus Mediterranean Flake Salt.

Salted Caramel Buttercream: Prepare Buttercream (facing page) as directed in Step 1, using 3 Tbsp. milk and adding ¼ tsp. kosher salt with butter. Melt 15 caramels with 1 Tbsp. milk in a small microwave-safe bowl at HIGH 1 minute or until smooth, stirring at 30-second intervals. Fold caramel mixture into buttercream, creating swirls. (Do not completely blend.)

4 Cappuccino Cupcakes

(pictured on page 161)
Prepare Cupcakes (facing page) as directed. Pipe or spread Double Shot Latte Buttercream onto cupcakes. Garnish with instant espresso, ground cinnamon, and chocolate-covered coffee beans, if desired.

Double Shot Latte Buttercream: Prepare Buttercream (facing page) as directed, beating in 1½ Tbsp. instant espresso with butter.

5 Mocha Latte Cupcakes

(pictured on page 161)
Microwave 1 (12-oz.) package dark chocolate morsels at HIGH 1½ minutes or until melted and smooth, stirring at 30-second intervals. Prepare Cupcakes (facing page) as directed, stirring melted chocolate into batter. (Batter will be very thick.) Bake 11 to 13 minutes or until a wooden pick inserted in centers comes out clean. Cool as directed. Top with Double Shot Latte Buttercream. Garnish with chocolate shavings, if desired. Makes 6½ dozen.

Double Shot Latte Buttercream: Prepare Buttercream (facing page) as directed, beating in 1½ Tbsp. instant espresso with butter.

Freshly Baked Valentines

Share the love with
a batch of easy,
homemade cookies.

COOKIE CARDS Fold pretty paper, punch holes, and secure cookies with ribbon.

Lemon Butter Cookies

freezable • make-ahead

MAKES ABOUT 4 DOZEN (2¼-INCH) OR
2 DOZEN (3¼-INCH) COOKIES **HANDS-ON TIME:**
30 MIN. **TOTAL TIME:** 1 HR., 29 MIN.
(INCLUDING ICING AND GLAZE)

- 1 cup butter, softened
- 1 tsp. lemon zest
- 1 cup powdered sugar
- 2 cups all-purpose flour
- ¼ tsp. salt
    Parchment paper
    Royal Icing
    Colorful Glaze

1. Preheat oven to 325°. Beat butter and zest at medium speed with a heavy-duty electric stand mixer until creamy. Gradually add sugar, beating well.
2. Combine flour and salt; gradually add to butter mixture, beating until blended. Shape dough into a disc.

3. Roll dough to ⅛-inch thickness on a lightly floured surface. Cut with a 2¼- or 3¼-inch heart-shaped cutter; place ½ inch apart on parchment paper-lined baking sheets. If desired, cut 1 or 2 holes at top of each cookie (to hang or thread ribbon through after baking).
4. Bake at 325° for 12 to 14 minutes or until edges are lightly browned. Cool on baking sheets 5 minutes. Transfer to wire racks; cool completely (about 20 minutes). Decorate as desired with Royal Icing and Colorful Glaze.

Royal Icing:

MAKES ABOUT 1¾ CUPS **HANDS-ON TIME:**
5 MIN. **TOTAL TIME:** 5 MIN.

- 3 cups powdered sugar
- 2 Tbsp. meringue powder
- ¼ cup cold water
    Food coloring paste

1. Beat first 3 ingredients at high speed with a heavy-duty electric stand mixer, using whisk attachment, until glossy, stiff peaks form. Tint icing with desired amount of food coloring paste, and beat until blended. Place a damp cloth directly on surface of icing (to prevent a crust from forming) while icing cookies.

Colorful Glaze:

MAKES ABOUT 1 CUP
HANDS-ON TIME: 5 MIN.
TOTAL TIME: 5 MIN.

Use the glaze for dipping, and use Royal Icing for piping.

- 1 (16-oz.) package powdered sugar
    Food coloring paste

1. Stir together powdered sugar and 6 Tbsp. water. Tint glaze with desired amount of food coloring paste, and stir until blended.
Note: Purchase food coloring paste at cake-supply and crafts stores or supercenters.

For Your Valentine

SAY "BE MINE" WITH A SOUTHERN ACCENT: February makes us think red—roses, candy boxes, and these luscious strawberries. They're super easy. If your microwave has an "on" button, you can make them. Melt chocolate in your microwave, give strawberries a quick dip, and then add a Southern touch by rolling them in chopped pecans. Tell your sweetie you made them especially for him—with just a little help from Cupid.

Speedy Pasta Suppers

From Creamy Alfredo Pasta to classic Sesame Noodles, these recipes are satisfying, easy to make, and ready in 30 minutes or less.

Sesame Noodles

quick prep

MAKES 6 SERVINGS
HANDS-ON TIME: 23 MIN.
TOTAL TIME: 23 MIN.

1. Prepare 1 (14.5-oz.) package multi-grain spaghetti according to package directions. Toss with ½ cup Thai peanut sauce, 3 sliced green onions, ½ cup diced red bell pepper, 2 Tbsp. chopped fresh cilantro (optional), and 1 Tbsp. fresh lime juice. Sprinkle with 1 Tbsp. toasted sesame seeds.
Note: We tested with House of Tsang Thai Peanut Sauce.

TRY THESE TWISTS!

Shrimp Sesame Noodles: Prepare the recipe as directed. Stir in 1 lb. peeled anddeveined medium-size cooked shrimp (31/35 count), cut in half lengthwise.
Chicken Sesame Noodles: Prepare the recipe as directed. Stir in 2 (6-oz.) packages fully cooked grilled chicken strips.
Note: We tested with Oscar Mayer Grilled Chicken Breast Strips.

Linguine with Sun-Dried Tomatoes

quick prep

MAKES 6 SERVINGS
HANDS-ON TIME: 16 MIN.
TOTAL TIME: 26 MIN.

1 (16-oz.) package linguine
1 (7-oz.) jar sun-dried tomatoes in oil
¼ cup pine nuts
3 garlic cloves, minced
¼ cup extra virgin olive oil
1 (4-oz.) package crumbled feta cheese
2 Tbsp. thin fresh basil strips

1. Prepare linguine according to package directions.
2. Drain tomatoes, reserving 2 Tbsp. oil. Cut tomatoes into thin strips.
3. Heat pine nuts in a large nonstick skillet over medium-low heat, stirring often, 5 minutes or until toasted and fragrant. Remove nuts from skillet.
4. Increase heat to medium, and sauté garlic in 2 Tbsp. reserved oil and olive oil in skillet 1 minute or until garlic is fragrant. Stir in tomatoes, and remove from heat.
5. Toss together tomato mixture, hot cooked pasta, feta cheese, and basil in a large bowl. Sprinkle with toasted pine nuts.

RECIPE FROM SUSAN LEONARD
CAMERON PARK, CALIFORNIA

TRY THIS TWIST!

Linguine with Tuna and Sun-Dried Tomatoes: Prepare recipe as directed. Stir in 2 (6-oz.) aluminum foil pouches solid white tuna chunks, drained, and 1 (3-oz.) can sliced black olives, drained.

Creamy Alfredo Pasta

quick prep

MAKES 6 TO 8 SERVINGS
HANDS-ON TIME: 17 MIN.
TOTAL TIME: 17 MIN.

Finely grate fresh Parmesan for smooth sauce—pre-grated doesn't work as well.

½ (16-oz.) package cellentani (corkscrew-shaped) pasta
2 cups half-and-half
⅓ cup butter
2 garlic cloves, pressed
1½ oz. fresh Parmesan cheese, finely grated (1 cup)
1 Tbsp. chopped fresh parsley
¼ tsp. salt
Freshly ground pepper to taste

1. Prepare pasta according to package directions.
2. Meanwhile, cook half-and-half and next 2 ingredients in a large heavy non-aluminum saucepan over medium heat, whisking often, 12 minutes or until reduced by one-third (do not boil). Remove from heat.
3. Whisk in cheese, next 2 ingredients, and desired amount of pepper until sauce is smooth. Toss sauce with hot cooked pasta. Let stand 5 minutes before serving.

Southern Favorites Made Simple

Craving a little down-home comfort? Have we got the dish for you. Learn our secrets to weeknight easy gumbo, perfectly fried chicken, and a warm banana bread cobbler that's to die for.

I magine whisking up a rich brown roux in five minutes flat. Or coming home to slow-cooked pork chops simmered with pan-fried onions and field peas. How about a wickedly delicious Lowcountry pilau loaded with crumbled bacon or featherlight biscuits that stir together as easily as a mix? Well, pull up a chair and settle in at the kitchen table, because here's the scoop on how we do it.

READER RECIPE Easy Chicken Gumbo

quick prep • make-ahead

MAKES 6 SERVINGS
HANDS-ON TIME: 28 MIN.
TOTAL TIME: 48 MIN., INCLUDING PILAU

Adding flour to hot oil creates a fast and flavorful roux. (pictured on page 4)

- ½ cup peanut oil
- ½ cup all-purpose flour
- 1 cup chopped sweet onion
- 1 cup chopped green bell pepper
- 1 cup chopped celery
- 1½ to 3 tsp. Cajun seasoning
- 2 tsp. minced garlic
- 3 (14-oz.) cans chicken broth
- ½ lb. andouille sausage, cut in ¼-inch-thick slices
  Okra Pilau
- 4 cups chopped cooked chicken

1. Heat oil in a large Dutch oven over medium-high heat; gradually whisk in flour, and cook, whisking constantly, 5 minutes or until flour is chocolate colored. (Do not burn mixture.)
2. Reduce heat to medium. Stir in onion and next 4 ingredients, and cook, stirring constantly, 3 minutes. Gradually stir in chicken broth and sausage. Increase heat to medium-high, and bring to a boil. Reduce heat to low, and simmer, stirring occasionally, 20 minutes.
3. Meanwhile, prepare Okra Pilau. Stir chicken into gumbo; cook, stirring occasionally, 5 minutes. Serve with Okra Pilau.

RECIPE FROM CHARLES STEIN
DUBLIN, OHIO

Kitchen Express Note: We love the flavor of fresh onion, bell pepper, and celery, but to make it even quicker you can substitute 1 (10-oz.) package frozen diced onion, red and green bell peppers, and celery.

Okra Pilau:

MAKES 6 SERVINGS
HANDS-ON TIME: 20 MIN.
TOTAL TIME: 20 MIN.

- 3 bacon slices
- 1 large sweet onion, chopped (about 2 cups)
- 1 (16-oz.) package frozen sliced okra, thawed
- 2 (8.5-oz.) packages ready-to-serve Cajun-style rice

1. Cook bacon in a large skillet over medium-high heat 5 to 7 minutes or until crisp; remove bacon, and drain on paper towels, reserving 2 Tbsp. drippings in skillet. Crumble bacon.
2. Sauté onion and okra in hot drippings over medium-high heat 6 to 8 minutes or until tender.
3. Prepare rice according to package directions. Stir rice and crumbled bacon into okra mixture in skillet.

Buttermilk Fried Chicken

MAKES 4 SERVINGS
HANDS-ON TIME: 40 MIN.
TOTAL TIME: 9 HR. 10 MIN.

Soaking the chicken overnight in buttermilk keeps it extra tender and juicy. The pieces quickly brown in a skillet and then get a fuss-free finish in the oven. (pictured on page 5)

- 1 (3¾-lb.) cut up whole chicken
- 3 cups buttermilk
- 2 tsp. salt
- 2 tsp. pepper
- 2 cups all-purpose flour
  Vegetable oil

1. Combine chicken and buttermilk in a large nonmetal bowl; cover and chill 8 to 12 hours. Drain chicken, discarding buttermilk.
2. Preheat oven to 350°. Combine salt and pepper; sprinkle half of salt mixture over chicken. Combine remaining

salt mixture and flour in a large zip-top plastic freezer bag. Place 2 pieces of chicken in bag; seal bag, and shake to coat. Remove chicken. Repeat procedure with remaining chicken.

3. Pour oil to depth of ¼ inch in a large skillet. Fry chicken pieces, in 2 batches, in hot oil over medium-high heat 5 to 6 minutes on each side or until browned. Place chicken on a wire rack in a jelly-roll pan.

4. Bake at 350° for 30 minutes or until done.

Stir-and-Roll Biscuits

freezable • quick prep • make-ahead

MAKES 18 BISCUITS
HANDS-ON TIME: 15 MIN.
TOTAL TIME: 25 MIN.

Vegetable oil replaces solid shortening in these light, high-rising biscuits. (pictured on page 5)

2¼ cups all-purpose soft-wheat flour
1 Tbsp. baking powder
1 tsp. salt
⅔ cup milk
⅓ cup vegetable oil
 Wax paper

1. Preheat oven to 475°. Sift together first 3 ingredients. Stir in milk and oil, using a fork until dough leaves the sides of the bowl and forms a ball.

2. Turn dough out onto lightly floured wax paper; knead 8 to 10 times. Roll or pat dough into a ½ inch thick rectangle (about 8 x 6½ inches). Cut with a 2-inch round cutter, rerolling scraps as needed. Place ¾-inch apart on a lightly greased jelly-roll pan.

3. Bake at 475° for 10 to 12 minutes or until lightly browned.

Note: We tested with White Lily All-Purpose Soft Wheat Flour.

Slow-Cooker Pork Chops and Field Peas

MAKES 6 SERVINGS
HANDS-ON TIME: 30 MIN.
TOTAL TIME: 6 HR., 30 MIN.

Browning the pork chops and onions adds an extra layer of flavor to this dish. We love it served with hot cooked rice and chowchow.

1 (16-oz.) package frozen field peas with snaps, thawed
1½ tsp. dry mustard
1 tsp. salt
½ tsp. garlic powder
6 (1-inch-thick) bone-in pork chops (about 3½ lb.)
½ cup all-purpose flour
2 Tbsp. vegetable oil
1 large sweet onion, sliced
1 (10½-oz.) can condensed chicken broth

1. Place peas in a lightly greased 6-qt. slow cooker.

2. Combine mustard and next 2 ingredients; sprinkle over pork chops. Dredge pork in flour.

3. Cook pork, in batches, in hot oil in a large nonstick skillet over medium-high heat 3 to 4 minutes on each side or just until browned. Transfer pork to slow cooker. Reserve drippings in skillet.

4. Sauté onion in hot drippings over medium-high heat 6 to 7 minutes or until tender. Add chicken broth, and cook 2 minutes, stirring to loosen particles from bottom of skillet. Spoon onion mixture over pork in slow cooker. Cover and cook on LOW 6 hours.

 ## Banana Bread Cobbler

quick prep

MAKES 8 SERVINGS
HANDS-ON TIME: 15 MIN.
TOTAL TIME: 1 HR., 5 MIN., INCLUDING STREUSEL TOPPING

(pictured on page 2)

1 cup self-rising flour
1 cup sugar
1 cup milk
½ cup butter, melted
4 medium-size ripe bananas, sliced
 Streusel Topping
 Vanilla ice cream

1. Preheat oven to 375°. Whisk together flour and next 2 ingredients just until blended; whisk in melted butter. Pour batter into a lightly greased 11- x 7-inch baking dish. Top with banana slices, and sprinkle with Streusel Topping.

2. Bake at 375° for 40 to 45 minutes or until golden brown and bubbly. Serve with ice cream.

Streusel Topping:

MAKES 3¼ CUPS
HANDS-ON TIME: 10 MIN.
TOTAL TIME: 10 MIN.

¾ cup firmly packed light brown sugar
½ cup self-rising flour
½ cup butter, softened
1 cup uncooked regular oats
½ cup chopped pecans

1. Stir together brown sugar, flour, and butter until crumbly, using a fork. Stir in oats and pecans.

RECIPE FROM ANN WILSON
LEXINGTON, NORTH CAROLINA

What's for Supper?

Streamline weeknight cooking with these three delicious main dishes.

Mexican Beef 'n' Rice

MAKES 6 SERVINGS
HANDS-ON TIME: 24 MIN.
TOTAL TIME: 24 MIN.

Easy side: Prepare 1 (19-oz.) package white cornbread mix according to package directions, stirring 1 cup freshly grated Monterey Jack cheese and 1 jalapeño pepper, seeded and finely chopped, into batter.

- 1½ lb. lean ground beef
- ½ cup chopped onion
- 1 (15.5-oz.) can black beans, drained and rinsed
- 1 cup refrigerated salsa
- 2 Tbsp. chopped fresh cilantro
- 1 Tbsp. fresh lime juice
- 1 (8.5-oz.) pouch ready-to-serve whole-grain Santa Fe rice
  Toppings: chopped fresh cilantro, salsa, guacamole, shredded Cheddar cheese

1. Cook ground beef and onion in a large skillet over medium-high heat, stirring often, 6 to 8 minutes or until meat crumbles and is no longer pink; drain. Wipe skillet clean.
2. Combine ground beef mixture, beans, and next 3 ingredients in skillet, and cook 3 to 4 minutes or until thoroughly heated.
3. Prepare Santa Fe rice according to package directions. Stir into beef mixture. Serve with desired toppings.
Note: We tested with Uncle Ben's Ready Whole Grain Medley Santa Fe Rice.

Chicken Parmesan Pizza

MAKES 4 SERVINGS
HANDS-ON TIME: 15 MIN.
TOTAL TIME: 30 MIN.

Easy side: Toss together romaine lettuce, freshly cracked pepper, and grated Parmesan cheese; toss with your favorite bottled Caesar dressing. Sprinkle with croutons. (pictured on page 183)

- 1 (10-oz.) package frozen garlic bread loaf
- ½ cup canned pizza sauce
- 6 deli fried chicken strips
- 1 cup (4 oz.) shredded Italian three-cheese blend
- 2 Tbsp. chopped fresh basil

1. Preheat oven to 400°. Arrange garlic bread, buttered sides up, on a baking sheet.
2. Bake at 400° for 8 to 9 minutes or until bread is lightly browned. Spread pizza sauce over garlic bread.
3. Cut chicken strips into ½-inch pieces, and arrange over pizza sauce. Sprinkle with cheese and basil.
4. Bake at 400° for 8 to 10 minutes or until cheese melts. Serve immediately.

Shrimp and Grits

MAKES 6 SERVINGS **HANDS-ON TIME:** 30 MIN. **TOTAL TIME:** 35 MIN.

Easy side: Gently toss chopped fresh spinach leaves, toasted pecans, and thinly sliced onions with bottled balsamic vinaigrette.

- 1½ lb. unpeeled, large raw shrimp (31/40 count)
- 1 lb. fresh asparagus
- 3 cups chicken broth
- 1 cup uncooked quick-cooking grits
- ½ cup half-and-half
- 4 Tbsp. butter, divided
- 1 (8-oz.) package sliced fresh mushrooms
- 1 bunch green onions, cut into ½-inch pieces
- ½ tsp. dried thyme
- ½ tsp. salt

1. Peel shrimp; devein, if desired. Snap off and discard tough ends of asparagus. Cut asparagus into 1-inch pieces.
2. Bring chicken broth to a boil in a medium saucepan over medium-high heat; whisk in grits and half-and-half. Cook, whisking constantly, 7 minutes or until thickened. Remove from heat. Stir in 2 Tbsp. butter. Keep warm.
3. Melt remaining 2 Tbsp. butter in a large skillet over medium-high heat. Add asparagus, mushrooms, green onions, and thyme, and sauté 3 to 4 minutes. Add shrimp, and cook 2 to 3 minutes. Stir in salt; cook 3 minutes or just until shrimp turn pink. Serve immediately over warm grits.

Perfect for Brunch

SOUR CREAM SAUCE: Beat ⅓ cup butter, softened, and 1 cup powdered sugar at medium speed with an electric mixer until smooth. Add ½ cup sour cream, ½ tsp. lemon juice, and ¼ tsp. vanilla, beating until creamy. Cover and chill until ready to serve (up to 8 hours). Makes about 1¾ cups. Hands-on time: 10 min., Total time: 10 min.

Drizzle this rich, make-ahead sauce over fresh fruit in your favorite glassware.

Dress Up Winter Veggies

Showcase the season's freshest produce—whether serving a creamy gratin or a crisp salad.

Risotto with Fennel, Pear, and Prosciutto

MAKES 4 SERVINGS
HANDS-ON TIME: 45 MIN.
TOTAL TIME: 45 MIN.

- ½ cup finely chopped sweet onion
- 2 Tbsp. butter
- 1 garlic clove, minced
- 2 Tbsp. olive oil, divided
- 1 cup uncooked Arborio rice (short-grain)
- 3 to 3¼ cups low-sodium chicken broth, divided
- ¼ cup dry white wine
- ¼ cup freshly grated Parmesan cheese
- 2 firm Bosc pears, peeled and chopped
- ½ medium-size fennel bulb, thinly sliced
- ¼ lb. thinly sliced prosciutto, chopped
  Salt and pepper to taste

1. Stir together first 3 ingredients and 1 Tbsp. olive oil in a 2½-qt. microwave-safe glass bowl. Microwave at HIGH 3 minutes. Stir in rice, and microwave at HIGH 2 minutes.
2. Stir in 2¾ cups broth and ¼ cup wine. Cover tightly with plastic wrap. (Do not vent.) Microwave at HIGH 9 minutes. Carefully swirl mixture in bowl, without uncovering, to incorporate mixture. Microwave at HIGH 8 minutes. Carefully remove and discard plastic wrap. Stir in cheese and ¼ cup chicken broth, stirring 30 seconds to 1 minute or until creamy. Add remaining ¼ cup broth, 1 Tbsp. at a time, if necessary, for desired consistency.
3. Sauté pears and fennel in remaining 1 Tbsp. hot olive oil in a large nonstick skillet over medium-high heat 7 minutes or until tender and golden. Stir in prosciutto, and cook 1 minute or until slightly browned. Stir pear mixture into risotto. Season with salt and pepper to taste. Serve immediately.
Note: We tested with RiceSelect Arborio Italian-Style Rice and an 1,100-watt microwave oven. We found that self-sealing plastic wraps do not work in this application.

Ginger-Parsnip Soup with Bacon-Parmesan Crisps

quick prep

MAKES 4 SERVINGS (ABOUT 5 CUPS SOUP)
HANDS-ON TIME: 22 MIN.
TOTAL TIME: 1 HR., 10 MIN. (INCLUDING CRISPS)

- 1 small sweet onion, chopped
- 2 celery ribs, chopped
- 1 Tbsp. olive oil
- 1 Tbsp. grated fresh ginger
- 2 Tbsp. maple syrup
- 1 (32-oz.) container chicken broth
- 1 lb. parsnips, peeled and chopped
- ½ cup half-and-half
  Salt to taste
  Bacon-Parmesan Crisps

1. Sauté first 2 ingredients in hot oil in a Dutch oven over medium heat 5 to 6 minutes or until tender. Stir in ginger and maple syrup, and sauté 1 minute. Stir in broth and parsnips; cover and bring to a boil over medium-high heat. Reduce heat to medium-low, and simmer 18 to 20 minutes or until parsnips are tender. Remove from heat, and let cool 10 minutes.
2. Process parsnip mixture with a hand-held blender 1 minute or until smooth. Stir in half-and-half; cook over low heat 2 to 4 minutes or until thoroughly heated. Season with salt to taste. Serve with Bacon-Parmesan Crisps.

Bacon-Parmesan Crisps:

MAKES ABOUT 1 DOZEN
HANDS-ON TIME: 15 MIN.
TOTAL TIME: 25 MIN.

- ½ (8.5-oz.) French bread baguette, cut into ½-inch-thick slices
  Vegetable cooking spray
- ¼ cup (1 oz.) shredded Parmesan cheese
- 2 cooked bacon slices, crumbled
  Salt and pepper to taste

1. Preheat oven to 400°. Arrange bread slices on a baking sheet; lightly coat bread with cooking spray. Bake 5 minutes or until lightly browned.
2. Combine Parmesan cheese and crumbled bacon. Sprinkle cheese mixture on bread slices, and season with salt and pepper to taste.
3. Bake at 400° for 5 minutes.

Hearts of Palm-and-Jicama Salad

quick prep • good for you

MAKES 6 TO 8 SERVINGS
HANDS-ON TIME: 20 MIN.
TOTAL TIME: 1 HR., 20 MIN.

- 1 (14.4-oz.) can hearts of palm, drained and rinsed
- ¼ red onion, thinly sliced
- 1 yellow bell pepper, diced
- 1 jicama, peeled and cut into ⅛-inch strips
- 1 jalapeño pepper, seeded and minced
- ¼ cup chopped fresh cilantro
- ¼ cup fresh lime juice
- ¼ cup fresh orange juice
- 2 Tbsp. olive oil
- 1 tsp. salt
- ½ tsp. ground cumin
- 1 avocado, diced

1. Cut hearts of palm crosswise into ½-inch slices. Stir together hearts of palm and next 10 ingredients in a large bowl. Cover and chill 1 to 8 hours. Stir in avocado just before serving.

Shredded Celery Root-Apple Salad

quick prep • make-ahead

MAKES 5 TO 6 SERVINGS
HANDS-ON TIME: 15 MIN.
TOTAL TIME: 35 MIN.

Serve with grilled sausage.

- 1 lb. celery root, peeled and sliced
- 2 small Honeycrisp apples, sliced*
- ⅔ cup mayonnaise
- 2 Tbsp. lemon juice
- 2 Tbsp. coarse-grained mustard
- ½ tsp. salt
- ¼ tsp. pepper

1. Shred celery root and apples in a food processor using shredding disc; place in a large bowl.
2. Stir together mayonnaise and next 4 ingredients. Pour over celery root mixture; toss to coat. Cover and chill 20 minutes to 24 hours before serving.
*Pink Lady apples may be substituted.

Roasted Turnips with Honey Butter

quick prep

MAKES 4 SERVINGS
HANDS-ON TIME: 20 MIN.
TOTAL TIME: 50 MIN.

- 3 Tbsp. butter
- 3 Tbsp. honey
- 2 lb. turnips, peeled and cubed
- 1 tsp. salt
- ½ tsp. pepper
- ¼ cup chopped fresh parsley

1. Preheat oven to 400°. Place butter and honey in a glass measuring cup. Microwave at HIGH 40 to 45 seconds or until melted. Stir until blended.
2. Place turnips on an aluminum foil-lined baking sheet; sprinkle with salt and pepper. Drizzle with butter mixture, tossing to coat.
3. Bake at 400° for 30 to 35 minutes or until golden brown. Transfer turnips to a serving bowl; pour any accumulated liquid over turnips. Toss turnips with parsley.

Cauliflower Gratin With Almond Crust

quick prep

MAKES 6 SERVINGS
HANDS-ON TIME: 25 MIN.
TOTAL TIME: 43 MIN.

This tasty dish is perfect for a dinner party or a weeknight supper.

- ¼ cup butter
- 1 head cauliflower (about 2¼ lb.), separated into florets
- 1 small onion, chopped
- 2 garlic cloves, minced
- 2 Tbsp. all-purpose flour
- 2 tsp. chopped fresh thyme
- ½ tsp. salt
- ½ cup whipping cream
- 1 cup (4 oz.) shredded Gruyère cheese
- ⅔ cup Japanese breadcrumbs (panko)
- ¼ cup sliced almonds
- ¼ cup grated Parmesan cheese

1. Preheat oven to 400°. Melt butter in a large skillet over medium-high heat. Add cauliflower and next 2 ingredients; sauté 10 minutes or until golden and just tender. Sprinkle with flour and next 2 ingredients; stir well. Remove from heat.
2. Spoon cauliflower mixture into an 11- x 7-inch baking dish, and drizzle with cream. Sprinkle with Gruyère cheese and next 3 ingredients.
3. Bake at 400° for 18 to 20 minutes or until golden.

Mama's Way or Your Way?
Two Takes on Meatloaf

Country music star Miranda Lambert can't live without her mama's meatloaf. She asked us to make a healthier version for her to take on the road.

Recipes from

Miranda Lambert and Bev Lambert
Lindale, Texas

Bev's Famous Meatloaf
quick prep

MAKES 10 SERVINGS
HANDS-ON TIME: 15 MIN.
TOTAL TIME: 1 HR., 50 MIN.

- 2 lb. lean ground beef
- 1 lb. ground pork sausage
- 18 saltine crackers, crushed
- ½ green bell pepper, diced
- ½ onion, finely chopped
- 2 large eggs, lightly beaten
- 1 Tbsp. Worcestershire sauce
- 1 tsp. yellow mustard
- ½ cup firmly packed brown sugar, divided
- ½ cup ketchup

"My mom and I have cooked together as far back as she could bring a stool to the kitchen counter, and her meatloaf has always been my favorite recipe."

—*Miranda Lambert*

1. Preheat oven to 350°. Combine first 8 ingredients and ¼ cup brown sugar in a medium bowl just until blended. Place mixture in a lightly greased 11- x 7-inch baking dish, and shape mixture into a 10- x 5-inch loaf.
2. Bake at 350° for 1 hour. Remove from oven, and drain. Stir together ketchup and remaining ¼ cup brown sugar; pour over meatloaf. Bake 15 more minutes or until a meat thermometer inserted into thickest portion registers 160°. Remove from oven; let stand 20 minutes. Remove from baking dish before slicing.

Better-for You Turkey Meatloaf
quick prep • good for you

MAKES 10 SERVINGS
HANDS-ON TIME: 15 MIN.
TOTAL TIME: 2 HR., 10 MIN.

- ¾ cup uncooked quick-cooking oats
- ¾ cup diced green bell pepper
- ¾ cup finely chopped onion
- ¾ cup milk
- 1 large egg, lightly beaten
- 1 Tbsp. Worcestershire sauce
- 1 tsp. salt
- 1 tsp. yellow mustard
- 2 lb. lean ground turkey
- 1 (16-oz.) package reduced-fat ground turkey sausage
- 1 (15.5-oz.) can stewed tomatoes with green peppers and onions, drained
- 1½ Tbsp. brown sugar

1. Preheat oven to 350°. Combine first 8 ingredients in a medium bowl. Add ground turkey and sausage; combine mixture just until blended, using hands. Place mixture on a lightly greased rack in an aluminum foil-lined broiler pan; shape mixture into a 10- x 5-inch loaf. Top with stewed tomatoes, and sprinkle with brown sugar.
2. Bake at 350° for 1 hour and 35 minutes or until a meat thermometer inserted into thickest portion registers 165°. Remove from oven; let stand 20 minutes.

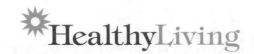
Guilt-Free Desserts

No need to deprive yourself. These yummy sweets are full of flavor without all the calories.

Chocolate Fudge Pie

MAKES 10 SERVINGS **HANDS-ON TIME:** 20 MIN. **TOTAL TIME:** 4 HR., 50 MIN. (pictured on page 164)

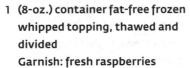

- ½ (14.1-oz.) package refrigerated piecrusts
- 6 oz. unsweetened chocolate baking squares, chopped
- 1 (14-oz.) can fat-free sweetened condensed milk
- 1 (8-oz.) container fat-free frozen whipped topping, thawed and divided
  Garnish: fresh raspberries

JUST FOUR INGREDIENTS

1. Preheat oven to 425°. Fit piecrust into a 9-inch pie plate according to package directions; fold edges under, and crimp. Line piecrust with aluminum foil, and fill with pie weights or dried beans.

2. Bake at 425° for 8 minutes. Remove weights and foil, and bake 5 to 7 more minutes or until golden brown. Cool completely on a wire rack (about 15 minutes).

3. Meanwhile, microwave chocolate in a large microwave-safe bowl at HIGH 1 to 1½ minutes or until melted and smooth, stirring at 30-second intervals. Whisk in milk until smooth; let stand 2 minutes. Fold half of whipped topping into chocolate mixture until combined; pour mixture into crust.

4. Cover and chill 4 to 8 hours. Spread remaining whipped topping over pie; garnish, if desired.

PER SERVING: CALORIES 329; **FAT** 14.4G (**SAT** 7.5G, **MONO** 2.7G, **POLY** 0.3G); **PROTEIN** 5.6G; **CARB** 47G; **FIBER** 2.8G; **CHOL** 7.5MG; **IRON** 2.9MG; **SODIUM** 144MG; **CALC** 119MG.

Lemon-Cheesecake Bars

MAKES 8 SERVINGS **HANDS-ON TIME:** 20 MIN. **TOTAL TIME:** 9 HR., 35 MIN.

Use fresh orange juice and zest instead of lemon for a different flavor profile. (pictured on page 165)

BEST WHEN SERVED CHILLED

BUTTER CRUST

- ⅓ cup butter, softened
- ¼ cup firmly packed dark brown sugar
- ¼ tsp. salt
- ¼ tsp. ground mace or nutmeg
- 1 cup all-purpose flour
  Vegetable cooking spray

LEMON FILLING

- 1 cup 1% low-fat cottage cheese
- 1 cup granulated sugar
- 2 Tbsp. all-purpose flour
- 1 Tbsp. lemon zest
- 3½ Tbsp. fresh lemon juice
- ¼ tsp. baking powder
- 1 large egg
- 1 egg white

GARNISH

Lemon rind curl

The Best Sugar Substitute

As a dietitian, I'm always looking for new products that are not only better for you, but also taste good—especially when it comes to sugar substitutes. The search is over. I found a sugar sweetener that tastes *exactly* like the real thing. It's called Whey Low, an all-natural blend of crystalline fructose (fruit sugar), lactose (milk sugar), and sucrose (table sugar). Here's the exciting part—it has about 75% fewer calories than regular sugar! I love it in my coffee (no aftertaste), and it substitutes perfectly in these desserts. Look for it at natural food markets, or order online at *wheylow.com*. It's a bit pricey but well worth the splurge. —BY SHANNON SLITER SATTERWHITE, M.S., R.D.

1. Preheat oven to 350°. Prepare Crust: Beat first 4 ingredients at medium speed with an electric mixer until smooth. Add 1 cup flour, beating at low speed until well blended. Press mixture on bottom of an 8-inch square pan coated with cooking spray.

2. Bake at 350° for 20 minutes.

3. Meanwhile, prepare Filling: Process cottage cheese in a food processor 1 minute or until smooth, stopping to scrape down sides as needed. Add granulated sugar and next 6 ingredients, and process 30 seconds or until well blended. Pour filling over prepared crust.

4. Bake at 350° for 25 minutes or until set. (Edges will be lightly browned.) Cool 30 minutes. Cover and chill 8 hours. Cut into bars. Garnish, if desired.

Note: For cleaner cuts, freeze 10 minutes before slicing.

PER BAR: CALORIES 289; FAT 8.9G (SAT 5.2G, MONO 2.2G, POLY 0.5G); PROTEIN 6.2G; CARB 47.5G; FIBER 0.5G; CHOL 45.1MG; IRON 1.1MG; SODIUM 262MG; CALC 76MG.

TRY THIS TWIST!

Reduced-Sugar Lemon-Cheesecake Bars: Substitute brown sugar sweetener for brown sugar and granular sweetener for granulated sugar.

Note: We tested with Whey Low 100% All Natural Gold Brown Sugar Sweetener and Granular Sweetener.

PER BAR: CALORIES 172; FAT 8.9G (SAT 5.2G, MONO 2.2G, POLY 0.5G); PROTEIN 6.2G; CARB 45.8G; FIBER 0.5G; CHOL 45.1MG; IRON 1MG; SODIUM 259MG; CALC 70MG

Oatmeal, Chocolate Chip, and Pecan Cookies

freezable • quick prep • good for you

MAKES 3 DOZEN

HANDS-ON TIME: 20 MIN.

TOTAL TIME: 1 HR., 26 MIN.

The mini-morsels disperse better in the batter, but you can use regular chocolate chips too.

¼	cup chopped pecans
1¼	cups all-purpose flour
1	cup uncooked regular oats
½	tsp. salt
½	tsp. baking powder
¼	tsp. baking soda
¾	cup granulated sugar
½	cup firmly packed brown sugar
⅓	cup butter, softened
1½	tsp. vanilla extract
1	large egg
⅓	cup semisweet chocolate mini-morsels
	Parchment paper

1. Preheat oven to 350°. Bake pecans in a single layer in a shallow pan 8 to 10 minutes or until toasted and fragrant.

2. Whisk together flour and next 4 ingredients. Beat sugars and butter at medium speed with an electric mixer until well blended. Add vanilla and egg, beating until blended. Gradually add flour mixture, beating at low speed just until combined. Stir in toasted pecans and mini-morsels.

3. Drop dough by tablespoonfuls 2 inches apart onto parchment paper-lined baking sheets.

4. Bake at 350° for 12 minutes or until edges of cookies are lightly browned. Cool on baking sheets 2 minutes. Transfer to wire racks, and cool completely (about 20 minutes).

PER COOKIE: CALORIES 83; FAT 3G (SAT 1.5G, MONO 1G, POLY 0.4G); PROTEIN 1.1G; CARB 13.2G; FIBER 0.5G; CHOL 9.5MG; IRON 0.5MG; SODIUM 62MG; CALC 12MG.

TRY THIS TWIST!

Reduced-Sugar Oatmeal, Chocolate Chip, and Pecan Cookies: Substitute granular sweetener for granulated sugar and brown sugar sweetener for brown sugar.

Note: We tested with Whey Low 100% All Natural Granular Sweetener and Gold Brown Sugar Sweetener. This variation is slightly more dense and has a chewier texture, but it's equally delicious.

PER COOKIE: CALORIES 58; FAT 3.1G (SAT 1.5G, MONO 1G, POLY 0.4G); PROTEIN 1.1G; CARB 12.7G; FIBER 0.5G; CHOL 9.5MG; IRON 0.4MG; SODIUM 60MG; CALC 9MG.

Half-Hour Hostess

Satisfy hungry fans at your **SUPER BOWL PARTY** in just 30 minutes with a speedy chili, a thick, flavorful dip, and an effortless snack mix.

Prepare Super Quick Chili as directed; keep it warm in a slow cooker during the game.

1 Super Quick Chili

MAKES 8 SERVINGS **HANDS-ON TIME:** 12 MIN. **TOTAL TIME:** 27 MIN.

Slice tops from 16 (1-oz.) hearty round dinner rolls, and then let guests hollow out centers and spoon chili into them.

- 2 lb. lean ground beef
- 2 Tbsp. chili powder
- 1 Tbsp. Creole seasoning
- 1 tsp. ground cumin
- 2 (16-oz.) cans diced tomatoes with green pepper and onion
- 2 (16-oz.) cans small red beans
- 2 (8-oz.) cans tomato sauce
  Toppings: shredded Cheddar cheese, sliced green onions, diced tomatoes

Recipe Note

Make the most of your time by prepping chili toppings while browning the beef. Prepare the dip and snack mix while the chili simmers.

1. Brown beef in a Dutch oven over medium-high heat, stirring often, 6 to 8 minutes or until beef crumbles and is no longer pink; drain well. Return beef to Dutch oven; sprinkle with chili powder, Creole seasoning, and cumin, and sauté 1 minute.
2. Stir in diced tomatoes and next 2 ingredients, and bring to a boil over medium-high heat, stirring occasionally. Cover, reduce heat to low, and simmer, stirring occasionally, 15 minutes. Serve with toppings.

Look for precut carrot and celery sticks in the produce department.

2 Blue Cheese Ranch Dip

Stir together 1 (16-oz.) container **sour cream**, 1 (1-oz.) package **Ranch dip mix**, 1 (4-oz.) package **blue cheese crumbles**, and 2 Tbsp. chopped fresh **chives**. Serve with **carrot and celery sticks**, sturdy **potato chips**, and **hot wings**. Makes 2½ cups. Hands-on time: 5 min., Total time: 5 min.

Stack cups in your team's colors next to Easy Snack Mix so guests can help themselves.

3 Easy Snack Mix

Toss together 5 cups **rice cereal squares**, 2 (19.2-oz.) bags **candy-coated chocolate pieces**, 1 (16-oz.) bag **pretzel twists**, 1 (16-oz.) container **honey-roasted peanuts**, and 1 (13.7-oz.) package bite-size **white Cheddar cheese crackers** in a large bowl. Store in an airtight container. Makes 30 cups. Hands-on time: 5 min., Total time: 5 min.

March

Try a Taste of Charleston

These time-tested classics and new favorites are perfect for any occasion. All showcase the city's unbeatable flavor.

South Carolina Supper

SERVES 6 TO 8

Spicy Pickled Shrimp

Lowcountry Punch

Sizzling Flounder (double recipe)

Bacon-Fried Okra (double recipe)

Hoppin' John Salad

Hot Slaw à la Greyhound Grill

Benne Brittle

Long before chefs made Lowcountry food famous, Charlestonians were eating high on the hog. We enjoyed rice at nearly every meal, fresh local shrimp, deviled crabs, okra soup, and benne wafers. We didn't realize this was local cuisine at its finest until much later.

When we wanted to learn to cook these foods, we turned to "the bible," *Charleston Receipts*. This must-have

cookbook has been guiding Lowcountry cooks for 60 years (and new cooks still consider it essential). It's full of timeless recipes and glimpses of the lifestyle that made the city famous. (To order, visit *jlcharleston.org,* or call 843-763-5284.) We adapted some of its recipes—and added a few of our own—to give you a delicious taste of Charleston's home cooking.

Spicy Pickled Shrimp

MAKES 12 SERVINGS

HANDS-ON TIME: 15 MIN.

TOTAL TIME: 23 MIN. PLUS 1 DAY FOR CHILLING (pictured on page 166)

2 lb. unpeeled, large raw shrimp (26/30 count)
3 small white onions, thinly sliced
½ cup olive oil
¼ cup tarragon vinegar
2 Tbsp. pickling spices
2 tsp. salt
1 tsp. sugar
1 tsp. Worcestershire sauce
½ tsp. dry mustard
¼ tsp. ground red pepper
¼ cup chopped fresh parsley

1. Peel shrimp; devein, if desired.
2. Cook shrimp in boiling water to cover 3 to 5 minutes or just until shrimp turn pink; drain. Rinse with cold water.
3. Layer shrimp and onions in a large bowl. Whisk together oil and next 7 ingredients; pour over shrimp and onions. Cover and chill 24 hours, stirring occasionally. Stir in parsley just before serving.

ADAPTED FROM *CHARLESTON RECEIPTS*

Lowcountry Punch

MAKES 11 CUPS

HANDS-ON TIME: 14 MIN.

TOTAL TIME: 1 HR., 14 MIN.

Charleston parties were once known for their vats of potent tea-based concoctions like this one. Use rye whiskey, Irish whiskey, or brandy for the whiskey in the ingredient list.

1½ cups boiling water
4 green tea bags
½ to 1 cup sugar
2½ cups whiskey
1½ cups rum
½ cup fresh lemon juice
½ cup orange liqueur
1 (32-oz.) bottle seltzer water, chilled

5 Traditional Ingredients

- **Rice** was one of the largest pre-Civil War cash crops. Cooks created many rice dishes, including "purlo" or pilau (a main dish that uses meat, seafood, or vegetables) and red rice.

- While most Hoppin' John recipes call for black-eyed peas, locals know that you use **field peas**, small brownish-red peas. You can find them canned in much of the South, but dried peas are elusive. In Charleston, Piggly Wiggly is the sure source (you'll also find the hog jowl to season them there).

- Slaves reportedly brought sesame or **benne seeds** to the Lowcountry. Their nutty flavor is best enjoyed in benne seed wafers and brittle.

- **Okra** is a favored vegetable, starring in okra soup and okra pilau.

- **Shrimp** show up in all manner of dishes, most notably shrimp and grits. Some locals use cast nets to harvest shrimp from tidal creeks.

---

1. Pour boiling water over tea bags; cover and steep 4 minutes. Remove and discard tea bags. Stir in ½ cup sugar until dissolved, adding additional sugar (up to ½ cup) if desired. Combine tea, whiskey, and next 3 ingredients in a pitcher. Cover and chill 1 to 4 hours. Stir in seltzer water. Serve over ice.

Note: We tested with Triple Sec orange liqueur.

ADAPTED FROM CHARLESTON RECEIPTS

Sizzling Flounder

MAKES 4 SERVINGS
HANDS-ON TIME: 10 MIN.
TOTAL TIME: 31 MIN.

While flounder is a Charleston favorite, use any firm-fleshed fish, such as tilapia, grouper, or catfish. Adjust the cooking time according to the thickness of the fish. (pictured on page 167)

- ¼ cup grated Parmesan cheese
- 1 tsp. paprika
- 4 (6-oz.) flounder fillets
- ¾ tsp. salt
- ¼ tsp. pepper
- ½ cup butter
- 2 Tbsp. fresh lemon juice

1. Place 1 oven rack 5 inches from heat; place a second rack in middle of oven. Combine Parmesan cheese and paprika. Season fish with salt and pepper.

2. Preheat oven to 450°. Heat butter in a broiler-safe 13- x 9-inch baking dish in oven 8 minutes or until butter is melted and beginning to brown. Place fish in hot butter, skin sides up.

3. Bake at 450° on middle oven rack 10 minutes. Carefully flip fish, and baste with pan juices. Sprinkle with lemon juice and Parmesan cheese mixture. Bake 5 more minutes or just until fish flakes with a fork. Remove from oven; increase oven temperature to broil.

4. Broil fish on oven rack 5 inches from heat 2 to 3 minutes or until bubbly and golden.

ADAPTED FROM CHARLESTON RECEIPTS

Bacon-Fried Okra

MAKES ABOUT 4 SERVINGS **HANDS-ON TIME:** 15 MIN. **TOTAL TIME:** 15 MIN.
(pictured on page 167)

1. Finely chop ½ lb. fresh okra. Sauté in 2 Tbsp. hot bacon drippings in a medium skillet over medium-high heat 10 to 12 minutes or until lightly browned. Sprinkle with salt to taste.

ADAPTED FROM CHARLESTON RECEIPTS

Hoppin' John Salad

MAKES 8 SERVINGS **HANDS-ON TIME:** 30 MIN. **TOTAL TIME:** 2 HR., 30 MIN.

- ½ cup uncooked long-grain rice
- ¼ cup fresh lemon juice
- ¼ cup olive oil
- 1 jalapeño pepper, seeded and minced
- 1 garlic clove, pressed
- 1 tsp. salt
- ¼ tsp. pepper
- 1 (15-oz.) can seasoned tiny field peas, drained and rinsed
- ½ cup chopped celery
- ⅓ cup loosely packed fresh parsley leaves, chopped
- ¼ cup chopped green onions

1. Prepare rice according to package directions.

2. Meanwhile, whisk together lemon juice, olive oil, jalapeño pepper, garlic, salt, and pepper in a large bowl. Stir in rice, peas, celery, and parsley until blended. Cover and chill 2 hours. Sprinkle with green onions just before serving.

Hot Slaw à la Greyhound Grill

MAKES 6 SERVINGS **HANDS-ON TIME:** 31 MIN.
TOTAL TIME: 36 MIN.

This tangy slaw is a favorite of native sons and award-winning cookbook authors Matt and Ted Lee. Pair it with broiled fish or pulled pork. (pictured on page 167)

- ½ **large red cabbage (about 1½ lb.), shredded**
- ½ **large green cabbage (about 1½ lb.), shredded**
- 4 **thick bacon slices, diced**
- ½ **cup cider vinegar**
- ½ **tsp. celery seeds**
- ¼ **tsp. dried crushed red pepper**
- 2 **tsp. salt**
- 1 **tsp. freshly ground black pepper**
  Pepper vinegar to taste (optional)

1. Bring 3½ qt. water to a boil in a large stockpot. Cook shredded cabbage in boiling water 4 minutes or just until it turns a dull gray purple. Remove from heat; drain well.
2. Cook bacon in a skillet over medium-low heat 8 minutes or just until crisp; remove bacon, and drain on paper towels, reserving drippings in skillet.
3. Stir cider vinegar, celery seeds, and red pepper into hot drippings, stirring to loosen particles from bottom of skillet. Stir in cabbage, salt, black pepper, and bacon; cook, stirring occasionally, 4 minutes or until cabbage is tender and red cabbage turns a bright magenta color. Place mixture in a serving dish, and, if desired, sprinkle with pepper vinegar to taste.

MATT AND TED LEE
THE LEE BROS. SOUTHERN COOKBOOK

Benne Brittle

MAKES ABOUT 1 LB. **HANDS-ON TIME:** 23 MIN.
TOTAL TIME: 43 MIN.
(pictured on page 167)

- 1¼ **cups benne (sesame) seeds**
- 2 **cups sugar**
- 1 **tsp. vanilla extract**

1. Cook benne seeds in a large heavy skillet over medium heat, stirring often, 8 minutes or until seeds begin to turn brown. Remove from skillet.
2. Cook sugar and 2 Tbsp. water in skillet over low heat, stirring constantly, 10 minutes or until sugar is melted. Quickly stir in benne seeds and vanilla. Pour onto a well-buttered baking sheet. Quickly spread to ⅛-inch thickness, using a metal spatula. Cool completely (20 minutes). Break into pieces. Store in an airtight container.

ADAPTED FROM *CHARLESTON RECEIPTS*

A Little Southern Know-How
Crawfish 101

Think of them as Louisiana lobster. Here's how to make quick work of the shell and get to those tasty morsels.

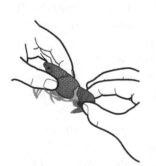  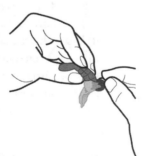 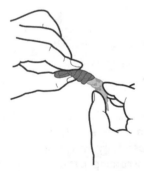

GRASP
Hold crawfish on both sides of the tail joint, your thumb on one side of the shell and your index finger on the other.

TWIST AND SNAP
With a twisting motion, snap the head away from the tail. (Optional step for diehards: Suck the juice from the crawfish head.

PEEL
Use your thumbs to peel away the shell from the widest part of the tail, pulling back from the center, just as you would peel a shrimp.

TUG
Hold the tip of the tail and gently tug out the tender meat. Enjoy! (Don't live on the bayou? Order online at **lacrawfish.com**.)

I'm Tired of Steamed Asparagus

Can you suggest recipes to make it more exciting?

Asparagus Pesto

MAKES ABOUT 2½ CUPS
HANDS-ON TIME: 18 MIN.
TOTAL TIME: 18 MIN.

Toss with cooked pasta, or spread on crostini and top with chopped tomatoes and bacon.

- 1 lb. fresh asparagus
- ½ cup freshly grated Parmesan cheese
- ½ cup pine nuts
- ½ cup olive oil
- 1 garlic clove
- 1 Tbsp. lemon juice
- ¾ tsp. salt

1. Snap off and discard tough ends of asparagus. Cook asparagus in boiling water to cover 3 to 4 minutes or until crisp-tender; drain.
2. Plunge asparagus into ice water to stop the cooking process; drain. Coarsely chop asparagus.
3. Process asparagus, cheese, and remaining ingredients in a food processor 30 seconds to 1 minute or until smooth, stopping to scrape down sides as needed.

Roasted Orange-Ginger Asparagus

MAKES 6 TO 8 SERVINGS
HANDS-ON TIME: 15 MIN.
TOTAL TIME: 30 MIN.

Southern Favorite

- 2 lb. fresh asparagus
- ¼ cup orange juice
- 2 Tbsp. olive oil
- 1 Tbsp. grated fresh ginger
- 1 Tbsp. Dijon mustard
- ½ tsp. salt
- ¼ tsp. pepper
  Garnishes: orange zest, chopped fresh basil

1. Preheat oven to 400°. Snap off and discard tough ends of asparagus; place asparagus on a lightly greased baking sheet. Whisk together orange juice, olive oil, and next 4 ingredients; drizzle mixture over asparagus, tossing to coat.
2. Bake at 400° for 15 minutes or to desired degree of tenderness, turning once after 8 minutes. Garnish, if desired.

Fresh Pistachio Vinaigrette

MAKES 1 CUP
HANDS-ON TIME: 10 MIN.
TOTAL TIME: 10 MIN.

1. Process ⅓ cup fresh **lemon juice**; 1 **shallot**, chopped; 2 Tbsp. chopped fresh **tarragon**; 1 Tbsp. **red wine vinegar**; 1 tsp. **sugar**; 2 tsp. **Dijon mustard**; ¾ tsp. **salt**; and ½ tsp. **pepper** in a blender until smooth. With blender running, add ¾ cup **olive oil** in a slow, steady stream, processing until smooth. Turn off blender; add ¼ cup **pistachios**, and pulse until pistachios are finely chopped.

Serving Suggestions: Drizzle 1 lb grilled **asparagus** with 3 to 4 Tbsp. vinaigrette, or try it over **grilled salmon** or other meat. Store any remaining vinaigrette in an airtight container in refrigerator 3 to 5 days.

Delicious, Easy Sides

Simple prep, plus a clever shortcut or two, bring garden-fresh flavor to your table.

1 | Grilled Rainbow Peppers

Crumbled goat cheese and basil add the finishing touches.

Preheat grill to 350° to 400° (medium-high) heat. Quarter 3 **bell peppers**; lightly coat with **vegetable cooking spray**. Grill peppers, covered with grill lid, 5 minutes on each side or until tender; arrange, cut sides up, on a serving platter. Whisk together 3 Tbsp. **olive oil**, 2 Tbsp. **balsamic vinegar**, and 1 Tbsp. **brown sugar**; drizzle over peppers. Sprinkle with ½ cup crumbled **goat cheese**, ½ cup loosely packed torn fresh **basil** leaves, and **salt** and freshly ground **pepper** to taste. Makes 4 to 6 servings. Hands-on time: 20 min.; Total time: 20 min.

2 | Roasted Fennel and Summer Squash

Preheat oven to 450°. Trim stalks from 2 small **fennel** bulbs. Cut bulbs lengthwise into ½-inch-thick wedges; chop 2 Tbsp. fronds. Toss wedges with 3 cups coarsely chopped **yellow squash**, 1 cup coarsely chopped **sweet onion**, 2 Tbsp. **olive oil**, 1 tsp. freshly ground **pepper**, and ½ tsp. **salt**. Place in a lightly greased large roasting pan. Bake 25 minutes. Stir once, and bake 15 minutes or until fennel is tender and begins to caramelize. Sprinkle with chopped fronds. Makes 4 to 6 servings. Hands-on time: 15 min.; Total time: 55 min.

3 | Sweet Corn and Zucchini

Sauté 2 cups coarsely chopped **zucchini** and ½ cup diced **sweet onion** in 3 Tbsp. **butter** in a large skillet over medium-high heat 5 minutes. Add 2 cups fresh **corn kernels**, ¼ cup chopped fresh **chives**, and 2 tsp. **taco seasoning mix**; sauté 5 minutes or until tender. Makes 4 to 6 servings. Hands-on time: 20 min.; Total time: 20 min.

4 | Gorgonzola-Walnut Potatoes

Quarter 2 lb. small **Yukon gold potatoes**; boil in salted water to cover 20 minutes or until tender. Drain potatoes, and coarsely mash with ⅔ cup crumbled **Gorgonzola cheese**, ½ cup **half-and-half**, ¼ cup **butter**, ¼ cup chopped fresh **parsley**, ¾ tsp. freshly ground **pepper**, and ¼ tsp. **salt**. Sprinkle with ½ cup chopped toasted **walnuts**. Makes 6 servings. Hands-on time: 10 min.; Total time: 30 min.

5 | Roasted Green Beans and Cashews

Preheat oven to 450°. Toss 1 (16-oz.) package frozen whole **green beans**, thawed, with ⅓ cup **sliced shallots**; 2 Tbsp. each minced fresh **ginger**, **sesame oil**, and **soy sauce**; and ½ tsp. dried crushed **red pepper**. Spread in a 13- x 9-inch baking dish, and bake, stirring occasionally, 20 minutes or until crisp-tender. Remove from oven, and sprinkle with ½ cup chopped roasted, lightly salted **cashews**. Makes 4 to 6 servings. Hands-on time: 10 min.; Total time: 30 min.

6 | Rice Pilaf

This sweet-and-tangy dish is hearty enough for lunch or a light supper.

Sauté 1 cup diced **red onion** in 3 Tbsp. melted **butter** in a large skillet over medium-high heat until tender; stir in 1½ cups halved seedless **red grapes**, ½ cup sweetened **dried cranberries**, and 2 Tbsp. white or regular **balsamic vinegar**. Stir in 2 (8.5-oz.) pouches ready-to-serve **basmati rice***, ¾ cup chopped toasted **pecans**, ½ cup chopped fresh **parsley**, and ½ tsp. **salt**; cook, stirring often, until thoroughly heated. Makes 6 servings. Hands-on time: 20 min.; Total time: 20 min.
*2 (8.8-oz.) pouches ready-to-serve whole grain brown-and-wild rice may be substituted; omit salt.

First Taste of Spring

SPRING POTATO TOSS: Gently toss together cooked quartered small red potatoes with cooked fresh sweet peas, refrigerated pesto, and lemon juice. Sprinkle with cooked, crumbled bacon.

♣

Store-bought refrigerated pesto livens up this seasonal side dish.

7 | Ravioli with Watercress Pesto

Pulse 2 cups loosely packed **watercress** leaves, ½ cup chopped toasted **pecans**, ½ cup freshly grated **Parmesan cheese**, ½ cup **olive oil**, 2 **garlic** cloves, and ¼ tsp. **salt** in a food processor until coarsely chopped. Prepare 2 (9-oz.) packages refrigerated cheese-filled tiny **ravioli** according to package directions; toss with watercress mixture. Makes 6 servings. Hands-on time: 15 min.; Total time: 25 min.
Note: We tested with Buitoni Three Cheese Ravioletti.

8 | Strawberry-Avocado Salad

Whisk together ¼ cup fresh **lime juice**, 2 Tbsp. **olive oil**, 2 Tbsp. **honey**, ¾ tsp. freshly ground **pepper**, and ¼ tsp. **salt** in a large bowl. Add 2 cups sliced fresh **strawberries**; 1 large **avocado**, diced; ¼ cup sliced **green onions**; and ¼ cup chopped fresh **cilantro**. Toss to coat, and serve over 4 cups fresh **arugula**. Makes 4 to 6 servings. Hands-on time: 15 min.; Total time: 15 min.

9 | Asiago Cheese Grits

Bring 3 cups water, 3 cups **milk**, and 1 tsp. **salt** to a boil in a large saucepan; gradually whisk in 1½ cups uncooked **quick-cooking grits**. Cook, stirring often, 6 to 7 minutes or until thickened. Remove from heat. Stir in 2 cups (8 oz.) shredded **Asiago cheese**; ⅓ cup each chopped fresh **basil**, **chives**, and **parsley**; 3 Tbsp. **butter**; and **salt** to taste, stirring until blended. Makes 6 servings. Hands-on time: 16 min.; Total time: 21 min.

10 | Fresh Spring Couscous

Prepare 1 (10-oz.) package plain **couscous** according to package directions. Stir in 1½ cups frozen sweet **green peas**, thawed; ¾ cup crumbled **feta cheese**; ⅓ cup sliced **green onions**; ¼ cup chopped fresh **mint**; 2 tsp. **lemon zest**; ¾ tsp. freshly ground **pepper**; and **salt** to taste. Makes 6 to 8 servings. Hands-on time: 10 min.; Total time: 15 min.

What's for Supper?

Streamline weeknight cooking with these delicious main-dish ideas.

Jamaican Chicken Burgers

family favorite

MAKES 4 SERVINGS
HANDS-ON TIME: 24 MIN.
TOTAL TIME: 54 MIN.

Easy side: Coat frozen sweet potato fries with olive oil and Jamaican jerk seasoning; bake according to package directions.

- 1 lb. ground chicken*
- ¼ cup mayonnaise
- 1 Tbsp. grated onion
- 1½ tsp. Jamaican jerk seasoning
- ½ tsp. salt
- 1 Tbsp. vegetable oil
- 4 hamburger buns
  Toppings: fresh mango slices, lettuce leaves, sweet-hot pickles

1. Combine first 5 ingredients in a large bowl. Shape into 4 (3-inch) patties. Cover and chill 30 minutes.
2. Cook patties in hot oil in a large nonstick skillet over medium-high heat 7 to 8 minutes on each side or until done. Serve on buns with desired toppings.
*Ground pork may be substituted.

Pasta with Zesty Pecan Sauce

MAKES 4 SERVINGS
HANDS-ON TIME: 20 MIN.
TOTAL TIME: 35 MIN.

Easy sides: Split 1 (12-oz.) French bread loaf lengthwise, and brush cut sides with ½ cup melted butter. Top with 6 garlic cloves, pressed; 1 tsp. dried oregano; and ½ tsp. dried parsley flakes. Bake until lightly browned and crisp. Serve with a tossed salad or green vegetable.

- ½ cup finely chopped pecans
- ¼ cup chopped fresh parsley
- 1 tsp. lemon zest
- 1 (12-oz.) package linguine
- 1 (14-oz.) can quartered artichoke hearts, drained
- ½ cup freshly grated Parmesan cheese
- 1 (3-oz.) package cream cheese, softened
- 3 Tbsp. olive oil
- 2 garlic cloves
- ½ tsp. freshly ground pepper
  Salt to taste

1. Heat pecans in a medium-size nonstick skillet over medium-low heat, stirring often, 5 to 7 minutes or until lightly toasted and fragrant. Remove from skillet. Let cool 5 minutes. Stir together pecans, parsley, and zest.
2. Cook pasta according to package directions; drain pasta, reserving ¼ cup cooking liquid.
3. Process artichoke hearts and next 5 ingredients in a food processor or blender until smooth, stopping to scrape down sides as needed. Add ¼ cup reserved cooking liquid. Pulse 3 to 4 times or until smooth. Toss with hot cooked pasta; season with salt to taste. Top each serving with pecan mixture.

RECIPE INSPIRED BY JANICE ELDER
CHARLOTTE, NORTH CAROLINA

Sesame-Ginger Shrimp

MAKES 4 SERVINGS
HANDS-ON TIME: 20 MIN.
TOTAL TIME: 30 MIN.

Quick dessert: Serve peach or vanilla frozen yogurt with ginger snaps.

- 4 oz. fresh snow peas
- 1 lb. large, peeled raw shrimp (26/30 count)
- 1 (11-oz.) package Asian-style noodles with soy-ginger sauce
- ⅛ tsp. salt
- 1 Tbsp. vegetable oil
- 2 Tbsp. lime juice
  Toppings: chopped fresh peanuts, chopped fresh cilantro

1. Trim ends and remove strings from snow peas; discard ends and strings. Devein shrimp, if desired.
2. Cook noodles according to package directions, reserving sauce and topping packets. Drain and keep warm.
3. Sprinkle shrimp with salt. Sauté shrimp in hot oil in a large nonstick skillet over high heat 2 minutes or just until shrimp turn pink. Remove shrimp from skillet, and keep warm.
4. Sauté snow peas in skillet over high heat, stirring often, 2 to 3 minutes or until tender. Return shrimp to skillet; stir in reserved sauce packet and lime juice, and cook 30 seconds. Stir in hot cooked noodles. Serve with desired toppings. Sprinkle with reserved sesame seed topping packet.
Note: We tested with Simply Asia Soy Ginger Noodles.

Test Kitchen Notebook

Oven Chicken Risotto

MAKES 6 SERVINGS

HANDS-ON TIME: 20 MIN.

TOTAL TIME: 1 HR.

Easy sides: Cook 1 lb. tiny green beans (haricots verts) in boiling salted water until crisp-tender; drain and sprinkle with freshly cracked pepper. Add hot buttered rolls, and dinner is served.

- 2 Tbsp. butter
- 2½ cups chicken broth
- 1 cup uncooked Arborio rice (short-grain)
- ½ small onion, diced
- ½ tsp. salt
- 2 cups chopped deli-roasted chicken
- 1 (8 oz.) package fresh mozzarella cheese, cut into ½-inch cubes
- 1 cup cherry or grape tomatoes, halved
- ¼ cup shredded fresh basil

1. Preheat oven to 400°. Place butter in a 13- x 9-inch baking dish; bake 5 minutes or until melted. Stir in broth and next 3 ingredients.
2. Bake, covered, at 400° for 35 minutes. Remove from oven. Fluff rice with a fork. Stir in chicken, mozzarella, and tomatoes; sprinkle with shredded basil. Serve immediately.

RECIPE INSPIRED BY LORI MEGDALL
MUNDELEIN, ILLINOIS

Cajun Steaks with Louisiana Slaw

MAKES 4 SERVINGS

HANDS-ON TIME: 37 MIN.

TOTAL TIME: 37 MIN.

Easy side: Serve with roasted potato wedges from the frozen food aisle.

- ½ cup mayonnaise
- 1 Tbsp. apple cider vinegar
- 2 Tbsp. Creole mustard, divided
- 1½ tsp. Cajun seasoning, divided
- 1 (16-oz.) package shredded coleslaw mix
- 4 (6-oz.) chuck-eye steaks
- ½ tsp. salt
- 1 medium-size red onion, cut into ½-inch-thick slices

1. Stir together mayonnaise, vinegar, 1 Tbsp. Creole mustard, and 1 tsp. Cajun seasoning in a medium bowl until blended. Stir in coleslaw. Cover and chill.
2. Meanwhile, brush steaks with remaining 1 Tbsp. mustard, and sprinkle with salt and remaining ½ tsp. Cajun seasoning. Heat a grill pan over medium-high heat. Cook steaks in pan 6 minutes on each side or to desired degree of doneness. Cook onion 5 minutes on each side. Serve steak and onions immediately with coleslaw.
Note: We tested with McCormick Cajun Seasoning.

Hamburger Steak with Sweet Onion-Mushroom Gravy

test kitchen favorite

MAKES 4 SERVINGS

HANDS-ON TIME: 23 MIN.

TOTAL TIME: 31 MIN.

Easy side: Serve with crusty French bread and colorful steamed veggies.

- 2 honey-wheat bread slices
- 1 lb. ground round
- 1 large egg, lightly beaten
- 2 garlic cloves, minced
- ½ tsp. salt
- ½ tsp. freshly ground pepper
- 1 (1.2-oz.) envelope brown gravy mix
- 1 Tbsp. vegetable oil
- 1 (8-oz.) package sliced fresh mushrooms
- 1 medium-size sweet onion, halved and thinly sliced

1. Process bread slices in a food processor 10 seconds or until finely chopped. Place breadcrumbs in a mixing bowl; add ground round and next 4 ingredients. Gently combine until blended, using your hands. Shape into 4 (4-inch) patties.
2. Whisk together gravy and 1½ cups water.
3. Cook patties in hot oil in a large skillet over medium-high heat 2 minutes on each side or just until browned. Remove patties from skillet. Add mushrooms and onion to skillet, and sauté 6 minutes or until tender. Stir in prepared gravy, and bring to a light boil. Return patties to skillet, and spoon gravy over each patty. Cover, reduce heat to low, and simmer 8 to 10 minutes.
Note: To make ahead, proceed with Step 1 as directed. Wrap each patty individually in plastic wrap, and place in a large zip-top plastic freezer bag. Freeze up to 3 months. Thaw frozen patties in refrigerator 8 hours; proceed with Steps 2 and 3.

Boost Nutrition With Color

Take advantage of the healthful benefits offered in bright, fresh produce.

Color is a key indicator that antioxidants and other powerful nutrients are present in fruits and vegetables (nature's way of helping us pick foods that are good for us). Start with a plateful of cancer-fighting goodness in Roasted Asparagus Salad. Or power up your immune system with bright orange Baby Carrot Soup (on page 62). We've even included a creamy, heart-healthy dessert. Whichever you choose, these delicious, good-for-you recipes offer a rainbow of colors and are your pot of gold for good health.

Roasted Asparagus Salad

MAKES 8 SERVINGS
HANDS-ON TIME: 20 MIN.
TOTAL TIME: 43 MIN.

Add even more color by roasting squash, zucchini, carrots, or other favorite veggies with the asparagus.

- 1½ lb. fresh asparagus
- ½ cup olive oil, divided
- 1½ Tbsp. chopped fresh basil, divided
- ½ tsp. lemon pepper
- ½ tsp. salt, divided
- ¼ cup balsamic vinegar
- 1 garlic clove, minced
- 1 cup halved cherry tomatoes (about ½ pt.)
- ½ cup chopped red bell pepper
- ¼ cup finely chopped red onion
- 1 head Bibb lettuce, torn into bite-size pieces
- 1 avocado, sliced

1. Preheat oven to 425°. Snap off and discard tough ends of asparagus; remove scales with a vegetable peeler, if desired.
2. Stir together 1 Tbsp. olive oil, 1½ tsp. chopped basil, ½ tsp. lemon pepper, and ¼ tsp. salt in a large bowl.
3. Add asparagus to olive oil mixture, and toss gently to coat. Place asparagus on a lightly greased baking sheet.
4. Bake asparagus at 425° for 13 to 15 minutes or to desired degree of tenderness. Cool 10 minutes.

5. Whisk together balsamic vinegar, garlic, and remaining 7 Tbsp. olive oil, 1 Tbsp. basil, and ¼ tsp. salt.
6. Toss together tomatoes, bell pepper, onion, and 1 Tbsp. balsamic vinegar mixture.
7. Arrange lettuce on individual serving plates. Top with tomato mixture and asparagus. Add avocado just before serving. Drizzle with remaining balsamic vinegar mixture.
Note: To make ahead, toss together tomatoes, bell pepper, and onion without dressing. Store these ready-to-use ingredients in an airtight container in the refrigerator up to 5 hours. The dressing and asparagus can also be made up to 8 hours before serving.
Time-Saver: Use bottled dressing for Roasted Asparagus Salad.

PER SERVING: CALORIES 193; FAT 17.1G (SAT 2.3G, MONO 10.8G, POLY 1.4G); PROTEIN 3.2G; CARB 8.8G; FIBER 2.9G; CHOL 0MG; IRON 1.4MG; SODIUM 181MG; CALC 33MG

Orange-Berry Cream Parfait

MAKES 4 SERVINGS
HANDS-ON TIME: 20 MIN.
TOTAL TIME: 20 MIN.

This recipe doubles as a nutritious breakfast snack and a delicious dessert.

1. Peel and section 3 medium oranges. Stir together 1 (7-oz.) container 2% low-fat Greek yogurt, 2 Tbsp. honey, ½ tsp. orange zest, and ½ tsp. vanilla extract in a small bowl. Layer 3 orange sections, 2 Tbsp. fresh blueberries, 1 rounded tablespoonful yogurt mixture, and 2 Tbsp. granola in each of 4 parfait glasses; repeat layers once.

PER SERVING: CALORIES 133; FAT 1.2G (SAT 0.8G, MONO 0G, POLY 0G); PROTEIN 5.3G; CARB 29.6G; FIBER 5.6G; CHOL 2.5MG; IRON 0.4MG; SODIUM 24MG; CALC 92MG

The Power of Color

Our guide to the benefits of and best sources for the healthiest hues.

REDS

Major benefits: promote heart health; help to lower cancer risks; protect against memory loss

Eat lots of: beets, strawberries, red bell pepper, cranberries, tomatoes, radishes, raspberries, blood oranges, red grapefruit, watermelon, red potatoes, pomegranates, cherries

ORANGES & YELLOWS

Major benefits: support the immune system and vision health, reduce cancer risk, promote collagen formation and healthy joints

Eat lots of: carrots, cantaloupe, pumpkin, corn, oranges, sweet potatoes, mangoes, yellow squash, peaches, apricots, yellow peppers

GREENS

Major benefits: promote vision health, lower blood pressure, normalize digestion time, boost immune system, reduce cancer risk

Eat lots of: dark lettuce, kiwifruit, avocados, cucumbers, celery, honeydew, green beans, leeks, okra, broccoli, asparagus

BLUES & PURPLES

Major benefits: increase memory function, lower LDL cholesterol, improve urinary tract health, reduce cancer risk, encourage healthful aging

Eat lots of: blackberries, blueberries, purple grapes, figs, plums, eggplant, raisins, purple cabbage

Baby Carrot Soup

MAKES 5 CUPS **HANDS-ON TIME:** 10 MIN.
TOTAL TIME: 45 MIN.

Smoky adobo sauce gives this creamy soup a subtle touch of heat.

- 1 (7-oz.) can chipotle peppers in adobo sauce
- 1 small sweet onion, chopped
- 1 Tbsp. olive oil
- 1 (32-oz.) container low-sodium fat-free chicken broth
- 1 (16-oz.) package baby carrots
- ⅓ cup half-and-half
- 1 tsp. salt
  Toppings: chopped fresh chives, chopped dried chile peppers, reduced-fat sour cream

1. Remove 2 tsp. adobo sauce from can; reserve peppers and remaining sauce for another use.

2. Sauté onion in hot oil in a Dutch oven over medium heat 3 to 4 minutes or until tender. Stir in broth, carrots, and 2 tsp. adobo sauce; cover, increase heat to medium-high, and bring to a boil. Reduce heat to medium, and simmer, partially covered, 15 to 20 minutes or until carrots are tender. Remove from heat, and let cool 10 minutes.

3. Process carrot mixture in a blender or food processor 1 minute or until smooth, stopping to scrape down sides as needed. Return carrot mixture to Dutch oven. Stir in half-and-half and salt. Cook over low heat 2 to 4 minutes or until thoroughly heated. Serve with desired toppings.

INSPIRED BY TERRI MATHEWS
LEEDS, ALABAMA

PER CUP: **CALORIES** 105; **FAT** 4.9G (**SAT** 1.6G, **MONO** 2.2G, **POLY** 0.3G); **PROTEIN** 2.5G; **CARB** 13.4G; **FIBER** 3.4G; **CHOL** 6MG; **IRON** 1MG; **SODIUM** 967MG; **CALC** 59MG

Artful Garnish ⋯⋯⋯⋯⋯⋯⋯⋯⋯⋯⋯⋯⋯

Stir together about 1 Tbsp. reduced-fat sour cream and 2 tsp. water; drizzle over soup, and swirl with a wooden pick. Top with chives and chopped chile peppers if you wish. For extra crunch, top it with veggie chips, such as Terra Stix.

Ginger-Whole Wheat Waffles

MAKES 8 WAFFLES **HANDS-ON TIME:** 34 MIN.
TOTAL TIME: 50 MIN. (INCLUDING SYRUP)

Crystallized ginger and honey offer spicy-sweet flavor. Top these warm waffles with our syrup or your favorite bottled brand.

- 1¼ cups whole wheat pancake-and-waffle mix
- ⅓ cup chopped crystallized ginger
- 1 tsp. ground ginger
- 1 cup whole milk
- 4 Tbsp. honey
- 3 Tbsp. olive or canola oil
- 1 large egg
  Strawberry-Maple Syrup

1. Stir together first 3 ingredients in a medium bowl. Add milk and next 3 ingredients, stirring until smooth. Let stand 5 minutes.

2. Cook batter in a preheated, lightly greased waffle iron until crisp and brown. Serve immediately with Strawberry-Maple Syrup.

Note: We tested with Aunt Jemima Whole Wheat Blend Pancake & Waffle mix.

PER SERVING (INCLUDING ABOUT 2¾ TBSP. SYRUP): **CALORIES** 320; **FAT** 7.4G (**SAT** 1.6G, **MONO** 4.6G, **POLY** 0.9G); **PROTEIN** 4.6G; **CARB** 62.3G; **FIBER** 1.9G; **CHOL** 29.5MG; **IRON** 3MG; **SODIUM** 420MG; **CALC** 130MG

Strawberry-Maple Syrup:

MAKES 1⅓ CUPS **HANDS-ON TIME:** 11 MIN.
TOTAL TIME: 11 MIN.

1. Combine ¾ cup maple syrup and ¾ cup quartered fresh strawberries in a small saucepan. Cook syrup mixture over medium heat, stirring occasionally, 6 to 8 minutes or until thoroughly heated. Serve immediately.

PER TBSP.: **CALORIES** 30; **FAT** 0G (**SAT** 0G, **MONO** 0G, **POLY** 0G); **PROTEIN** 0G; **CARB** 7.8G; **FIBER** 0.1G; **CHOL** 0MG; **IRON** 0.2MG; **SODIUM** 1MG; **CALC** 8MG

Fresh, Main-Dish Salads

These chop-and-toss recipes have restaurant-quality flavor, but they're easy enough to make at home.

Tex-Mex Beef-and-Beans Chopped Salad

MAKES 6 SERVINGS
HANDS-ON TIME: 25 MIN.
TOTAL TIME: 25 MIN.

Find refrigerated salsa in your grocer's produce or deli area. We prefer it in this recipe for chunky texture and fresh flavor. This recipe is also great with pulled pork.

- ¾ cup bottled Ranch dressing
- ¾ cup refrigerated salsa
- 1 (22-oz.) package romaine lettuce hearts, chopped
- 1 (15-oz.) can black beans, drained and rinsed
- 3 cups crushed tortilla chips
- 6 oz. pepper Jack cheese, cut into small cubes
- 1 cup seeded and chopped cucumber
- 1 cup diced jicama
- 3 plum tomatoes, seeded and chopped
- 1 medium avocado, chopped
- ¾ lb. barbecued beef brisket (without sauce), chopped and warmed*

1. Stir together ¾ cup Ranch dressing and salsa.
2. Toss together romaine and next 7 ingredients. Drizzle with dressing mixture, and top with brisket. Serve immediately.
*Grilled flank steak, chopped, may be substituted.

Dressed-Up Chopped Caesar Salad

MAKES 4 SERVINGS
HANDS-ON TIME: 25 MIN.
TOTAL TIME: 30 MIN.

These flavorful croutons are made in the microwave.

- 2 Tbsp. butter
- 1 garlic clove, minced
- 4 pumpernickel bread slices, cut into 1-inch cubes
  Salt and pepper
- 2 romaine lettuce hearts, chopped
- 3 cups chopped cooked turkey breast
- 1 pt. cherry tomatoes, cut in half
- 4 oz. Asiago cheese, cut into small cubes
- 4 thick bacon slices, cooked and crumbled
- 2 green onions, thinly sliced
- ½ cup bottled creamy Caesar dressing

1. Microwave butter in a microwave-safe pie plate at HIGH 30 seconds or until melted. Stir in garlic, and microwave 45 seconds or until fragrant. Stir in bread cubes and desired amounts of salt and pepper. Microwave 4 minutes or until crisp, stirring at 1-minute intervals. Let cool 5 minutes.
2. Toss together romaine lettuce and next 5 ingredients. Drizzle with dressing; toss gently. Sprinkle with croutons.

Spicy Pork-and-Orange Chopped Salad

MAKES 4 SERVINGS
HANDS-ON TIME: 28 MIN.
TOTAL TIME: 33 MIN.

Combining romaine and coleslaw mix makes this dish crispy and crunchy. The soy sauce-flavored almonds are a new favorite in our Test Kitchen. Find them sold in cans alongside cocktail peanuts. (pictured on page 168)

- 1 lb. pork tenderloin, cut into ½-inch pieces
- 2½ tsp. Szechwan seasoning blend
- ½ tsp. salt
- 1 Tbsp. olive oil
- 2 oranges
- ½ cup bottled low-fat sesame-ginger dressing
- 1 cup seeded and chopped cucumber
- ¼ cup chopped fresh cilantro
- 1 romaine lettuce heart, chopped
- 3 cups shredded coleslaw mix
- ½ cup wasabi-and-soy sauce-flavored almonds
  Garnish: orange slices

1. Toss pork with Szechwan seasoning and salt to coat. Sauté pork in hot oil in a large nonstick skillet over medium-high heat 8 to 10 minutes or until done.
2. Peel oranges, and cut into ½-inch-thick slices. Cut slices into chunks.
3. Pour dressing into a salad bowl. Stir in oranges, cucumber, and cilantro. Let stand 5 minutes. Add romaine, coleslaw mix, and pork; toss gently. Sprinkle with almonds. Garnish, if desired. Serve immediately.
Note: We tested with McCormick Gourmet Collection Szechwan Seasoning and Blue Diamond Bold Wasabi & Soy Sauce Almonds.

Chicken-and-Melon Chopped Salad

MAKES 4 SERVINGS
HANDS-ON TIME: 20 MIN.
TOTAL TIME: 20 MIN.

¾ cup bottled red wine vinaigrette
1 Tbsp. lime juice
⅓ cup thinly sliced red onion
2 romaine lettuce hearts, chopped
2½ cups chopped grilled chicken breasts
1½ cups cubed cantaloupe
1½ cups seeded and cubed watermelon
⅔ cup crumbled feta cheese
¼ cup chopped fresh basil
½ cup dry-roasted, salted pistachios
Salt and pepper to taste

1. Stir together first 2 ingredients in a large bowl; let stand 10 minutes.
2. Meanwhile, soak onion slices in hot water to cover 10 minutes; drain and pat dry.
3. Add onion, romaine, and next 5 ingredients to dressing mixture; toss to combine. Sprinkle with pistachios. Season with salt and pepper to taste. Serve immediately.

Mediterranean Chopped Salad

MAKES 4 SERVINGS
HANDS-ON TIME: 20 MIN.
TOTAL TIME: 30 MIN.

A few chickpeas will pop while sautéing.

1 (15½-oz.) can chickpeas, drained, rinsed, and patted dry
½ tsp. salt
¼ tsp. coarsely ground pepper
1 Tbsp. olive oil
1 garlic clove, minced
2 romaine lettuce hearts, chopped
1 (12-oz.) jar roasted red bell peppers, drained and coarsely chopped
½ cup golden raisins
⅓ cup bottled balsamic vinaigrette
¼ cup chopped fresh basil
3 oz. goat cheese, crumbled

1. Sauté chickpeas, salt, and pepper in hot oil in a skillet over medium-high heat 8 minutes. Stir in garlic, and cook 30 seconds to 1 minute or until chickpeas are golden brown. Remove from heat, and let stand 10 minutes.
2. Toss together romaine lettuce, chickpea mixture, and remaining ingredients. Serve immediately.

Texas Float

THE SODA FOUNTAIN TREAT OF YOUR CHILDHOOD IS ALL GROWN UP NOW. Remember that ice-cream float you loved as a child? Well, this ain't it. This one's brimming with Texas flavor, and it's for the big kids. We started with some of the best vanilla ice cream this side of your granddaddy's hand-crank freezer. Scoop ice cream into tall glasses, and top with coffee porter beer. Sprinkle with fresh raspberries.

Note: We used Blue Bell Homemade Vanilla ice cream and Real Ale Shade Grown Coffee Porter, but you can substitute another Texas brew—Shiner Bohemian Black Lager.

Cool Party Punches

Stir up a colorful palette of eye-catching beverages for your next spring bash.

Mango Tango Tea

MAKES 4 QT.
HANDS-ON TIME: 10 MIN.
TOTAL TIME: 3 HR., 20 MIN.

Find bottled mango nectar with other shelf-stable juices.

- 5 family-size tea bags
- 2 cups hot water
- 1 (12-oz.) can frozen lemonade concentrate, thawed
- 1 (6-oz.) can frozen limeade concentrate, thawed
- 1 (33.8-oz.) bottle mango nectar
- 4 cups cold water

1. Combine tea bags and hot water in a 4-cup glass measuring cup, and steep 10 minutes. Remove and discard tea bags.
2. Stir together tea, lemonade and limeade concentrates, mango nectar, and 4 cups cold water. Cover and chill 3 hours. Serve over ice.

Berry Ice Cubes

MAKES 16 ICE CUBES **HANDS-ON TIME:** 10 MIN. **TOTAL TIME:** 4 HR., 10 MIN.

Turn ordinary ice cubes into an extraordinary garnish. Serve them in any of these beverages, or add them to soft drinks and juices for a pop of color.

Place 5 to 6 **blueberries** in each compartment of 1 ice-cube tray (about 1 cup blueberries). Stir together ½ cup **white cranberry juice** and ½ cup **water**; pour over berries. Freeze 4 hours or until firm. Store cubes in an airtight container in the freezer for up to 1 month.

Kentucky Mimosa

MAKES ABOUT 3 CUPS
HANDS-ON TIME: 13 MIN.
TOTAL TIME: 18 MIN.

- ½ cup sugar
- 6 large fresh sage leaves
- 1¼ cups club soda
- 1 cup orange juice
- ⅓ cup bourbon or orange juice

1. Stir together sugar and ½ cup water in a small saucepan over medium heat. Bring to a light boil, and cook, stirring occasionally, 3 minutes or until sugar is dissolved. Remove from heat; add sage leaves, and let stand 5 minutes. Remove and discard leaves.
2. Stir together syrup, club soda, orange juice, and bourbon in a large pitcher; add ice cubes to fill. Serve immediately.

RECIPE FROM ELIZABETH BENNETT
MILL CREEK, WASHINGTON

Berry Splash

MAKES ABOUT 2 QT.
HANDS-ON TIME: 10 MIN.
TOTAL TIME: 10 MIN.

If your family likes a sweeter drink, stir in more sugar, ¼ cup at a time.

- 1 (0.13-oz.) package unsweetened cherry drink mix
- 6 cups white cranberry juice
- ¼ cup sugar
- Garnish: fresh mint sprigs or strawberry leaves

1. Stir together first 3 ingredients and 2 cups water in a large pitcher until sugar is dissolved. Cover and chill. Garnish, if desired.
Note: We tested with Kool-Aid Cherry Unsweetened Soft Drink Mix.

Lemon Squares

Bake these classic bar cookies from scratch, or try our quick-prep version with weeknight appeal.

Recipes from

Trisha Stevens
Scottsdale, Arizona

and

Amanda Stevens
Hoover, Alabama

❧ **WHY WE LOVE**

Mama's Way

- Buttery shortbread crust
- Rich, fresh lemon filling
- Classic dusting of powdered sugar

Luscious Lemon Bars

make-ahead

MAKES ABOUT 2 DOZEN
HANDS-ON TIME: 20 MIN.
TOTAL TIME: 2 HR., 5 MIN.

2¼	cups all-purpose flour, divided
½	cup powdered sugar
1	cup cold butter, cut into pieces
4	large eggs
2	cups granulated sugar
1	tsp. lemon zest
⅓	cup fresh lemon juice
½	tsp. baking powder
	Powdered sugar

1. Preheat oven to 350°. Line bottom and sides of a 13- x 9-inch pan with heavy-duty aluminum foil or parchment paper, allowing 2 to 3 inches to extend over sides; lightly grease foil.
2. Stir together 2 cups flour and ½ cup powdered sugar. Cut in butter using a pastry blender or fork until crumbly. Press mixture onto bottom of prepared pan.
3. Bake at 350° for 20 to 25 minutes or until lightly browned.
4. Meanwhile, whisk eggs in a large bowl until smooth; whisk in granulated sugar, lemon zest, and lemon juice. Stir together baking powder and remaining ¼ cup flour; whisk into egg mixture. Pour mixture over hot baked crust.
5. Bake at 350° for 25 minutes or until filling is set. Let cool in pan on a wire rack 30 minutes. Lift from pan, using foil sides as handles. Cool completely on a wire rack (about 30 minutes). Remove foil, and cut into bars; sprinkle with powdered sugar.
Note: To make ahead, prepare as directed. Cover tightly, and freeze up to 1 month.

❧ **WHY WE LOVE**

Your Way

- Easy-to-mix crust
- No-measuring lemon filling
- Hint of brown sugar taste

Lemon Drop Squares

family favorite

MAKES ABOUT 2 DOZEN
HANDS-ON TIME: 10 MIN.
TOTAL TIME: 1 HR., 30 MIN.

2½	cups all-purpose flour
1	cup butter, cubed
⅔	cup granulated sugar
½	cup uncooked quick-cooking oats
⅓	cup firmly packed brown sugar
2	(10-oz.) jars lemon curd

1. Line bottom and sides of a 13- x 9-inch pan with heavy-duty aluminum foil or parchment paper, allowing 2 to 3 inches to extend over sides; lightly grease foil.
2. Preheat oven to 350°. Beat flour, butter, granulated sugar, oats, and brown sugar with an electric mixer until crumbly and mixture resembles wet sand. Reserve 1¼ cups mixture. Press remaining mixture onto bottom of prepared pan.
3. Bake at 350° for 20 to 22 minutes until light golden brown.
4. Meanwhile, microwave both jars of lemon curd at the same time at HIGH 1 minute or until pourable. Spread lemon curd over hot baked crust, and sprinkle with reserved crumb mixture.
5. Bake at 350° for 30 minutes or until bubbly and brown. Let cool in pan on a wire rack 30 minutes. Lift from pan, using foil sides as handles. Cool completely on a wire rack (about 30 minutes). Remove foil, and cut into squares.

April

The Season's Easiest Shower Menu

Hosting a party for the bride and groom doesn't get easier than this. You provide the toppings, and guests grill their own pizzas.

iTunes Party Playlist

Menu

SERVES 6
(double or triple the menu to suit your crowd)

Pizza with sauces and toppings
of your choice

Greek Caesar Salad

Simple Antipasto Platter

Raspberry Beer Cocktail

Easy Cheesecake Bars

If there's a season for weddings in the South, it's now. And chances are you know a soon-to-be-wed couple in need of a party. So shower them with gifts and plenty of good food with this delicious, easygoing menu anchored by personal pizzas from the grill. Guests will gather around the grill once they catch the irresistible scent of fire-baked flatbread and fresh toppings. The menu's supporting recipes are mostly make-ahead, leaving you plenty of time to mingle with guests and celebrate with the lucky couple.

Chicken Alfredo Pizza
make-ahead • party perfect

MAKES 6 SERVINGS
HANDS-ON TIME: 29 MIN.
TOTAL TIME: 29 MIN.

Use a deli-roasted rotisserie chicken to ease the prep.

    Vegetable cooking spray
1½ lb. bakery pizza dough
    All-purpose flour
    Plain yellow cornmeal
¾ cup Creamy Alfredo Sauce
    (facing page)
1 (6-oz.) package fresh baby spinach,
    thoroughly washed
2 cups chopped cooked chicken
1½ cups (6 oz.) shredded fontina
    cheese
2 tsp. lemon juice
¼ tsp. salt
¼ tsp. pepper

1. Coat cold cooking grate of grill with cooking spray, and place on grill. Preheat grill to 350° (medium) heat.
2. Divide dough into 6 equal portions. Lightly sprinkle flour on a large surface. Roll each portion into a 6-inch round (about ¼-inch thick). Carefully transfer pizza dough rounds to a cutting board or baking sheet sprinkled with cornmeal.
3. Slide pizza dough rounds onto cooking grate of grill; spread Creamy Alfredo Sauce over rounds, and top with spinach, chicken, and cheese. Sprinkle with lemon juice, salt, and pepper.
4. Grill, covered with grill lid, 4 minutes. Rotate pizzas one-quarter turn, and grill, covered with grill lid, 5 to 6 more minutes or until pizza crusts are cooked. Serve immediately.
Note: Individual pizza dough rounds may be made ahead. Roll out as directed, and place between pieces of wax paper sprinkled with flour and cornmeal; place in a gallon-size zip-top plastic bag. Seal bag, and chill 8 hours.

Three Easy Sauces

1 | Zesty Pizza Sauce

Sauté 1 large **onion**, chopped, and 4 **garlic** cloves, minced, in 2 Tbsp. hot **olive oil** in a 3-qt. saucepan over medium-high heat 10 minutes or until tender. Stir 1 (28-oz.) can diced **tomatoes**, 1 Tbsp. dried **Italian seasoning**, ¾ tsp. **salt**, ½ tsp. **pepper**, and ¼ tsp. **dried crushed red pepper** into onion mixture. Bring to a boil; reduce heat to low, and simmer, stirring occasionally, 1 hour. Let stand 15 minutes. Process tomato mixture in a blender or food processor, in batches, until smooth. Cover and chill up to 5 days. Reheat in a saucepan over medium-low heat. Makes 3 cups. Hands-on time: 20 min.; Total time: 1 hr., 45 min.

2 | Creamy Alfredo Sauce

Sauté 1 minced **garlic** clove in 1 tsp. hot **olive oil** in a large skillet over medium-high heat 1 minute. Reduce heat to medium-low; stir in 1 (10-oz.) container refrigerated **Alfredo sauce**, 1 Tbsp. chopped fresh **basil** and ½ tsp. freshly **ground pepper**. Cook, stirring constantly, 2 minutes or until thoroughly heated. Cover and chill up to 5 days. Reheat in a saucepan over medium-low heat. Makes 1 cup. Hands-on time: 8 min., Total time: 8 min. **Note:** We tested with Buitoni Alfredo Sauce.

3 | Garden Pesto Sauce

Preheat oven to 350°. Bake ¼ cup each of **pine nuts** and chopped **pecans** in a single layer in a shallow pan 8 minutes or until toasted and fragrant. Let cool 5 minutes. Process 2½ cups firmly packed fresh **basil leaves**, ½ cup chopped fresh **parsley**, 2 chopped **garlic** cloves, and ⅓ cup **olive oil** in a food processor until a coarse paste forms. Add nuts and ¾ cup (3 oz.) shredded **Parmesan cheese**, and process until blended. With processor running, pour ⅓ cup **olive oil** through food chute in a slow, steady stream; process until smooth. Cover and chill up to 5 days. Makes 1¼ cups. Hands-on time: 10 min.; Total time: 23 min.

Shrimp-Pesto Pizza

make-ahead • party perfect

MAKES 6 SERVINGS
HANDS-ON TIME: 37 MIN.
TOTAL TIME: 37 MIN.

We found fresh pizza dough available in the deli section at Publix. If you're expecting a larger crowd, you can buy pizza dough in bulk from your local wholesale club or even a favorite pizza restaurant. (pictured on page 171)

Vegetable cooking spray
1 lb. unpeeled, large raw shrimp (31/35 count)
1 large yellow onion, chopped
1 red bell pepper, chopped
¼ tsp. salt
¼ tsp. pepper
1½ tsp. olive oil
1½ lb. bakery pizza dough
All-purpose flour
Plain yellow cornmeal
½ cup Garden Pesto Sauce* (above)
¾ cup freshly grated Parmesan cheese

1. Coat cold cooking grate of grill with cooking spray, and place on grill. Preheat grill to 350° (medium) heat.
2. Peel shrimp, and slice in half lengthwise; devein, if desired.
3. Sauté onion, bell pepper, salt, and pepper in ½ tsp. hot oil in a large skillet over medium heat 5 minutes or until tender. Transfer onion mixture to a large bowl. Sauté shrimp in remaining 1 tsp. hot oil 3 minutes or just until shrimp turn pink. Add shrimp to onion mixture, and toss
4. Divide dough into 6 equal portions. Lightly sprinkle flour on a large surface. Roll each portion into a 6-inch round (about ¼-inch thick). Carefully transfer pizza dough rounds to a cutting board or baking sheet sprinkled with cornmeal.
5. Slide pizza dough rounds onto cooking grate of grill; spread Garden Pesto Sauce over rounds, and top with shrimp mixture. Sprinkle each with 2 Tbsp. Parmesan cheese.
6. Grill, covered with grill lid, 4 minutes. Rotate pizzas one-quarter turn, and grill, covered with grill lid, 5 to 6 more minutes or until pizza crusts are cooked. Serve immediately.
*Refrigerated store-bought pesto may be substituted.
Note: Individual pizza dough rounds may be made ahead. Roll out as directed, and place between pieces of wax paper sprinkled with flour and cornmeal; place in a gallon-size zip-top plastic bag. Seal bag, and chill 8 hours.

Let partygoers fill a memory jar, instead of a guest book. Look for card stock, ribbons, and pens at any crafts store.

Greek Caesar Salad

quick prep • make-ahead • party perfect

MAKES 6 SERVINGS

HANDS-ON TIME: 10 MIN.

TOTAL TIME: 10 MIN.

- ¾ cup olive oil
- ¼ cup lemon juice
- ¼ cup egg substitute
- 2 garlic cloves, pressed
- 1 tsp. dried oregano
- ¼ tsp. salt
- ⅛ tsp. pepper
- 1 head romaine lettuce, torn
- ¾ cup kalamata olives
- 1 small red onion, thinly sliced
- ½ cup crumbled feta cheese
  Croutons

1. Whisk together olive oil and next 6 ingredients in a small bowl. Cover and chill up to 2 days.

2. Combine lettuce and next 3 ingredients in a large bowl; gradually add enough olive oil mixture to coat leaves, tossing gently. Sprinkle with croutons, and serve with remaining olive oil mixture.

Simple Antipasto Platter

quick prep • party perfect

MAKES 8 SERVINGS

HANDS-ON TIME: 10 MIN.

TOTAL TIME: 10 MIN.

- 1 (5-oz.) goat cheese log
- 2 Tbsp. chopped fresh parsley
- 1 (16-oz.) jar pickled okra, drained
- 1 (8-oz.) jar kalamata olives, drained and rinsed
- 1 (7-oz.) jar roasted red bell peppers, drained and cut into pieces
- 4 oz. sliced salami
  Assorted crackers and breadsticks

1. Roll goat cheese log in parsley; place on a serving platter. Arrange okra and next 3 ingredients on platter around goat cheese. Serve with assorted crackers and breadsticks.

Add a personal touch to Easy Cheesecake Bars by piping on the couple's monogram. If you can fill a zip-top plastic bag with store-bought chocolate frosting, then you can pipe a letter. Simply snip a corner of the filled bag (not too big, not too small), and squeeze. Practice first on a piece of paper. Use lower-case letters for a modern look, or get fancy with cursive.

Raspberry Beer Cocktail

Editor's Favorite

quick prep • make-ahead • party perfect

MAKES 6 SERVINGS
HANDS-ON TIME: 5 MIN.
TOTAL TIME: 5 MIN.

You can use fresh raspberries, but frozen taste just as good. (pictured on page 170)

- ¾ cup frozen raspberries*
- 3½ (12-oz.) bottles beer, chilled
- 1 (12-oz.) container frozen raspberry lemonade concentrate, thawed
- ½ cup vodka
  Garnish: lemon and lime slices

1. Stir together first 4 ingredients. Serve over ice. Garnish, if desired.
*Fresh raspberries may be substituted.
Note: To make ahead, stir together lemonade concentrate and vodka in a large container. Chill up to 3 days. Stir in raspberries and beer just before serving. Garnish, if desired.

Easy Cheesecake Bars

quick prep • make-ahead • party perfect

MAKES 1 DOZEN
HANDS-ON TIME: 15 MIN.
TOTAL TIME: 5 HR., 53 MIN.

(pictured on page 170)

- 1 cup all-purpose flour
- ⅓ cup firmly packed light brown sugar
- ¼ cup butter, softened
- 3 (8-oz.) packages cream cheese, softened
- ¾ cup granulated sugar
- 3 large eggs
- ⅓ cup sour cream
- ½ tsp. vanilla extract
- 1 (15.5-oz.) container ready-to-spread chocolate frosting (optional)
  Garnish: fresh raspberries

1. Preheat oven to 350°. Beat first 3 ingredients at medium-low speed with an electric mixer until combined. Increase speed to medium, and beat until well blended and crumbly. Pat mixture into a lightly greased 13- x 9-inch pan. Bake 13 to 15 minutes or until lightly browned.
2. Beat cream cheese at medium speed with an electric mixer until creamy. Gradually add granulated sugar, beating until well blended. Add eggs, 1 at a time, beating at low speed just until blended after each addition. Add sour cream and vanilla, beating just until blended. Pour over baked crust.
3. Bake at 350° for 25 minutes or until set. Cool completely on a wire rack (about 1 hour). Cover and chill 4 to 24 hours; cut into bars.
4. If desired, spoon frosting into a zip-top plastic freezer bag. (Do not seal.) Snip 1 corner of bag to make a small hole. Pipe a frosting monogram on each bar. Garnish, if desired.

Sweet on Strawberries

The South's most prized spring fruit gets a delicious update in these impressive desserts.

Strawberry-Orange Shortcake Tart

MAKES 8 SERVINGS
HANDS-ON TIME: 20 MIN.
TOTAL TIME: 1 HR., 25 MIN.

Baking the shortcake in a tart pan produces a sweet-and-sturdy base for the berries and whipped cream. (pictured on page 8)

- 1¾ cups all-purpose flour
- ¼ cup plain yellow cornmeal
- 2 Tbsp. sugar
- ¾ tsp. baking powder
- ½ tsp. salt
- 6 Tbsp. cold butter, cut into pieces
- 1 large egg, lightly beaten
- ⅔ cup buttermilk
- 1 Tbsp. orange marmalade
- 1 (16-oz.) container fresh strawberries, cut in half
- ½ cup orange marmalade
- 2 cups heavy cream
- 2 Tbsp. sugar
  Garnishes: fresh mint sprigs, sweetened whipped cream

1. Preheat oven to 425°. Place first 6 ingredients (in order of ingredient list) in a food processor. Process 20 seconds or until mixture resembles coarse sand. Transfer to a large bowl.
2. Whisk together egg and buttermilk; add to flour mixture, stirring just until dry ingredients are moistened and a dough forms. Turn dough out onto a lightly floured surface, and knead 3 to 4 times. Press dough on bottom and up sides of a lightly greased 9-inch tart pan.

3. Bake at 425° for 20 to 22 minutes or until golden and firm to touch.
4. Microwave 1 Tbsp. marmalade at HIGH 10 seconds; brush over crust. Cool 45 minutes.
5. Stir together strawberries and ½ cup marmalade.
6. Beat heavy cream with 2 Tbsp. sugar at medium speed with an electric mixer until soft peaks form. Spoon onto cornmeal crust; top with strawberry mixture. Garnish, if desired.

Vanilla-Stuffed Strawberry Cupcakes

make-ahead • party perfect

MAKES 2 DOZEN
HANDS-ON TIME: 30 MIN.
TOTAL TIME: 4 HR. (INCLUDING CUSTARD)

Cupcakes will rise over baking cup edges. Use a paring knife to gently loosen from pan. (pictured on page 8)

  Vanilla Bean Custard (facing page)
- 24 paper baking cups
- 1 (16-oz.) package angel food cake mix
- 2 tsp. vanilla bean paste*
- 3 cups halved fresh strawberries
  Garnish: fresh mint sprigs

1. Prepare Vanilla Bean Custard.
2. Meanwhile, preheat oven to 325°. Place baking cups in 2 (12-cup) muffin pans. (Do not grease.) Prepare angel food cake batter according to package

Bountiful Berries

The plump, juicy strawberries filling farm stands across the South this month inspired our top-rated Southern desserts.

Wash fresh strawberries just before using.

directions using a paddle attachment. Stir in vanilla bean paste. Spoon batter into baking cups, filling completely full.

3. Bake at 325° on middle oven rack 20 to 25 minutes or until a wooden pick inserted in center comes out clean. Cool in pans on wire racks 10 minutes.

4. Gently run a knife around edges of cupcakes to loosen. Remove from pans to wire racks, and cool completely (about 20 minutes).

5. Scoop out centers of cupcakes, leaving a ½ inch border on bottom and sides. Spoon or pipe Vanilla Bean Custard into centers of cupcakes. Top with strawberries. Cover and chill until ready to serve. Garnish, if desired.

*2 tsp. vanilla extract may be substituted.

Note: We tested with a number of brands of cake mix and preferred Duncan Hines Angel Food Premium Cake Mix.

Vanilla Bean Custard:

make-ahead

MAKES 3 CUPS
HANDS-ON TIME: 20 MIN.
TOTAL TIME: 3 HR., 20 MIN.

Don't be tempted to substitute a pudding mix here. The delicate flavor is well worth a bit of effort.

2½ cups milk
¾ cup sugar
⅓ cup all-purpose flour
2 egg yolks
2 tsp. vanilla bean paste*

1. Whisk together first 4 ingredients in a heavy 3-qt. saucepan. Cook over medium heat, whisking constantly, 10 to 12 minutes or until thickened. Remove from heat; stir in vanilla bean paste. Cover and chill 3 hours.

*2 tsp. vanilla extract may be substituted.

Five Easy Shrimp Appetizers

Take your pick from budget-stretching nachos to a bold and sassy twist on the classic shrimp cocktail.

Tex-Mex Shrimp Cocktail

quick prep • make-ahead • party perfect

MAKES 4 TO 6 SERVINGS
HANDS-ON TIME: 15 MIN.
TOTAL TIME: 4 HR., 15 MIN.

Fiery jalapeño pepper jelly adds a sweet kick to this traditional dish. (pictured on page 7)

¼ cup hot red jalapeño pepper jelly
1 Tbsp. lime zest
¼ cup fresh lime juice
1 lb. peeled, large cooked shrimp (31/40count)
1 cup diced mango
½ cup diced red bell pepper
¼ cup chopped fresh cilantro
1 small avocado, diced
　Garnishes: lime slices, fresh cilantro sprigs

1. Whisk together first 3 ingredients. Pour into a large zip-top plastic freezer bag; add shrimp and next 3 ingredients, turning to coat. Seal and chill 4 hours, turning occasionally. Add avocado. Garnish, if desired.

 ## Shrimp Nachos

party perfect

MAKES 4 DOZEN
HANDS-ON TIME: 20 MIN.
TOTAL TIME: 28 MIN.

1½ cups (6 oz.) shredded pepper Jack cheese
1 cup chopped cooked shrimp
1 (4.5-oz.) can chopped green chiles, drained
½ cup reduced-fat mayonnaise
⅓ cup chopped green onions
¼ cup sliced black olives
¼ cup chopped fresh cilantro
48 tortilla chip scoops

1. Preheat oven to 350°. Stir together pepper Jack cheese and next 6 ingredients. Spoon into tortilla chip scoops; place on a baking sheet. Bake 8 minutes or until cheese is melted.

RECIPE FROM LEISA BAILEY
YANKTON, SOUTH DAKOTA

Shrimp-and-Bacon Deviled Eggs

party perfect

MAKES 12 SERVINGS
HANDS-ON TIME: 20 MIN.
TOTAL TIME: 4 HR., 20 MIN.

12 hard-cooked eggs, peeled
¾ cup reduced-fat mayonnaise
1 Tbsp. Dijon mustard
½ tsp. ground red pepper
⅛ tsp. salt
1 cup chopped cooked shrimp
⅓ cup cooked and crumbled bacon
¼ cup chopped fresh chives

1. Cut eggs in half lengthwise; remove yolks. Process yolks, mayonnaise, and next 3 ingredients in a food processor until smooth. Stir in shrimp, bacon, and chives; spoon into egg white halves. Cover and chill 4 hours.

Seaside Shrimp

quick prep • party perfect

MAKES 8 SERVINGS
HANDS-ON TIME: 10 MIN.
TOTAL TIME: 28 MIN.

Serve shrimp with crusty French bread.

2   lb. peeled, large raw shrimp (31/40 count)
1   cup bottled Caesar dressing
¼   cup chopped fresh parsley
¼   cup fresh lime juice
2   garlic cloves, pressed
1   tsp. freshly ground pepper

1. Preheat oven to 375°. Place all ingredients in a 13- x 9-inch baking dish, tossing to coat. Bake 18 minutes or just until shrimp turn pink, stirring after 9 minutes.

Curried Shrimp Tarts

quick prep • make-ahead • party perfect

MAKES 4 TO 6 SERVINGS
HANDS-ON TIME: 15 MIN.
TOTAL TIME: 15 MIN.

Speedy Curried Shrimp Tarts use ready-made pastry shells.

1   cup chopped cooked shrimp
½   (8-oz.) package cream cheese, softened
3   Tbsp. chopped green onions
1   Tbsp. fresh lime juice
¾   tsp. curry powder
¼   tsp. ground red pepper
15   mini-phyllo pastry shells
2½   Tbsp. jarred mango chutney
     Toppings: chopped fresh chives, toasted sweetened flaked coconut

1. Stir together first 6 ingredients. Spoon mixture into pastry shells. Spoon ½ tsp. mango chutney over each tart; sprinkle with desired toppings.

RECIPE INSPIRED BY APRIL COX
CHARLESTON, SOUTH CAROLINA

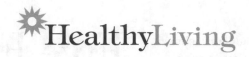

3 Delicious Super-foodsTo Try Now

These nutrient-packed ingredients deliver a bounty of healthful benefits (that's what makes them super).

Sweet Potato-and-Edamame Hash

good for you

MAKES 8 SERVINGS
HANDS-ON TIME: 42 MIN.
TOTAL TIME: 42 MIN.

Serve Sweet Potato-and-Edamame Hash over fresh arugula with a poached egg.

1   (8-oz.) package diced smoked lean ham
1   sweet onion, finely chopped
1   Tbsp. olive oil
2   sweet potatoes, peeled and cut into ¼-inch cubes
1   garlic clove, minced
1   (12-oz.) package uncooked frozen, shelled edamame (green soybeans)
1   (12-oz.) package frozen whole kernel corn
¼   cup chicken broth
1   Tbsp. chopped fresh thyme
½   tsp. kosher or table salt
½   tsp. freshly ground pepper

1. Sauté ham and onion in hot oil in a nonstick skillet over medium-high heat 6 to 8 minutes or until onion is tender and ham is lightly browned.

Edamame

This calcium-rich legume helps maintain bone density.

Stir in sweet potatoes, and sauté 5 minutes. Add garlic; sauté 1 minute. Stir in edamame and next 3 ingredients. Reduce heat to medium. Cover and cook, stirring occasionally, 10 to 12 minutes or until potatoes are tender. Stir in salt and pepper.

Note: We tested with Birds Eye Steamfresh Super Sweet Corn.

PER SERVING (NOT INCLUDING ARUGULA AND POACHED EGG): CALORIES 192; FAT 5.8G (SAT 0.8G, MONO 2.1G, POLY 0.5G); PROTEIN 13.9G; CARB 22.1G; FIBER 4.9G; CHOL 16MG; IRON 2.6MG; SODIUM 164MG; CALC 50MG

Green Tea

An excellent source of concentrated antioxidants that may help inhibit cancer growth

 READER RECIPE ## Honey-Ginger Tea
quick prep • good for you

MAKES 1 CUP

HANDS-ON TIME: 10 MIN.

TOTAL TIME: 13 MIN.

We like it with a touch of fresh lemon juice. This recipe also easily doubles or triples.

1. Grate 1 (1-inch) piece of fresh ginger, peeled, using the large holes of a box grater, to equal 1 Tbsp. Squeeze juice from ginger into a teacup; discard solids. Place 1 regular-size green tea bag, 1 Tbsp. fresh lemon juice, and 2 Tbsp. honey in teacup; add 1 cup boiling water. Cover and steep 3 minutes. Remove and discard tea bag, squeezing gently.

RECIPE FROM ROSE MARIE CROWE
TRUSSVILLE, ALABAMA

Note: We tested with Twinings Green Tea.

PER SERVING: CALORIES 134; FAT 0G (SAT 0G, MONO 0G, POLY 0G), PROTEIN 0.2G; CARB 36.6G; FIBER 0.2G; CHOL 0MG; IRON 0.2MG; SODIUM 12MG; CALC 11MG

Tex-Mex Fajitas
good for you

MAKES 8 FAJITAS

HANDS-ON TIME: 40 MIN.

TOTAL TIME: 40 MIN.

Crisp sautéed tofu adds texture and healthy benefits to your favorite fajitas.

- 1 (14-oz.) package extra-firm tofu, drained and cut crosswise into ½-inch-thick pieces*
- 1 tsp. ground cumin
- 1 tsp. chili powder
- 7 tsp. vegetable oil, divided
- ½ medium-size sweet onion, thinly sliced
- 1 red bell pepper, cut into thin strips
- ½ cup chunky salsa
- 2 tsp. cider vinegar
- 1 tsp. salt
- 8 (6-inch) fajita-size flour tortillas, warmed

1. Sprinkle tofu with cumin and chili powder; gently toss to coat all sides.
2. Cook half of tofu in 3 tsp. hot oil in a large nonstick skillet over medium heat 5 minutes on each side. Remove tofu, and keep warm. Repeat procedure with 3 tsp. oil and remaining tofu.
3. Sauté sliced onion and bell pepper in remaining 1 tsp. hot oil in skillet over medium-high heat 2 minutes or until tender. Stir in salsa, vinegar, and salt; cook 2 minutes. Pour mixture over tofu. Remove from heat. Serve with warm tortillas and your favorite toppings.

*1 lb. chopped cooked chicken breasts may be substituted for tofu. Cook 7 minutes, stirring often.

Note: We tested with Nasoya Extra Firm Tofu and Pace Chunky Salsa.

PER FAJITA (NOT INCLUDING TOPPINGS): CALORIES 169; FAT 8.9G (SAT 1.8G, MONO 0.6G, POLY 1.8G); PROTEIN 6.5G; CARB 15.8G; FIBER 1.4G; CHOL 0MG; IRON 1.4MG; SODIUM 563MG; CALC 72MG

Tofu

Contains omega-3 fats that prevent cholesterol from clogging arteries

Easter Flavors From TV's Cat Cora

This Mississippi native (and only female Iron Chef) shares a few of her favorite Easter dishes reflecting her Greek heritage.

She learned to hold her ground early working in her family's restaurant. Now, Cat Cora goes head-to-head with the macho superchefs on the Food Network. At home, though, it's all about family again, where she shares her culinary legacy with her children. Enjoy the flavors of a classic Greek Easter with her perfectly delicious holiday recipes.

Easter Dinner

SERVES 8

Roasted Lamb

Oregano Green Beans

Church-Style Lemon-Roasted Potatoes

Dinner rolls

Bakery Easter cookies

Cat Gives Back

In 2004, Cat established Chefs for Humanity, a nonprofit organization focused on reaching out to the culinary community to raise funds and lend support for important emergency, educational, and hunger-relief causes. Modeled after Doctors Without Boarders, Cat and her colleagues have touched lives internationally in Africa and Central America. Here in the U.S., Chefs for Humanity has established outreach programs such as Every Kid C.A.N. (Culinary Awareness Now) providing nutrition education to school-aged children. For more information, visit **www.chefsforhumanity.org.**

Roasted Lamb

party perfect

MAKES 8 SERVINGS
HANDS-ON TIME: 20 MIN.
TOTAL TIME: 2 HR., 30 MIN.
(pictured on page 174)

- 1 (5-lb.) boneless leg of lamb
- 2 lemons, halved and divided
- ¼ cup chopped fresh oregano
- 2½ tsp. salt
- 2 tsp. pepper
- Kitchen string
- 1 garlic bulb, unpeeled
- ¼ cup olive oil
- 1 cup low-sodium chicken broth
- Garnishes: roasted garlic cloves, baby carrots, radishes, lettuce leaves

1. Preheat oven to 350°. Unroll lamb, if necessary. Rub 1 lemon half on all sides of lamb, squeezing juice from lemon. Stir together oregano, salt, and pepper; rub on lamb. Roll up lamb, and tie with kitchen string.

2. Place lamb on a lightly greased rack in a roasting pan. Separate garlic cloves (do not peel), and place around roast. Drizzle olive oil over lamb and garlic cloves.

3. Squeeze juice from remaining 1½ lemons into a bowl. Stir together juice and chicken broth; pour into roasting pan.

4. Bake at 350° for 2 hours to 2 hours and 15 minutes or until a meat thermometer inserted into thickest portion registers 140° (medium) or to desired degree of doneness. Remove lamb from pan; cover with aluminum foil, and let stand 10 minutes before slicing. Garnish, if desired.

Feta Spread (Htipiti)

Not only does this deliciously sharp dip make a great starter for the Easter feast, but it also pairs beautifully with the roasted lamb.

Pulse 8 oz. crumbled **feta cheese**, 2 Tbsp. **olive oil**, 1 Tbsp. lemon juice, 1 tsp. finely chopped pepperoncini salad peppers, 1 tsp. minced garlic, 1 tsp. chopped fresh oregano, ¼ to ½ tsp. dried crushed red pepper, and ⅛ tsp. black pepper in a food processor 6 to 8 times or until combined, stopping to scrape down sides. Cover and chill 2 hours before serving. Store in refrigerator up to 3 days. Serve with crostini or pita chips. Garnish with dried crushed red pepper and olive oil, if desired. Makes 1 cup. Hands-on time: 10 min.; Total time: 2 hr., 10 min.

Note: To serve as a sauce, prepare as directed, processing mixture 3 to 4 minutes. Serve immediately.

TRY THIS TWIST!

Roasted Boston Butt: Substitute 1 (5-lb.) bone-in pork shoulder roast (Boston butt) for lamb. Rub lemon and oregano mixture over roast as directed. (Do not tie up roast.) Proceed as directed, increasing bake time to 3 to 3½ hours or until fork-tender. Shred pork into large pieces using two forks, if desired. Hands-on time: 20 min. Total time: 3 hr., 30 min.

Oregano Green Beans

MAKES 8 SERVINGS
HANDS-ON TIME: 27 MIN.
TOTAL TIME: 42 MIN.
(pictured on page 175)

- 2 cups chopped onion
- 2 Tbsp. olive oil
- 1 garlic clove, minced
- 1 lb. fresh green beans, trimmed
- 1 (14½-oz.) can diced tomatoes, drained
- ½ cup vegetable or low-sodium chicken broth
- 1 Tbsp. chopped fresh oregano
- 1 Tbsp. chopped fresh parsley
- ¾ tsp. salt
- ½ tsp. pepper
- 1 Tbsp. fresh lemon juice
- ½ cup crumbled feta cheese

1. Sauté onion in hot oil in a Dutch oven over medium heat 8 minutes or until tender. Add garlic; cook, stirring often, 4 minutes or until garlic is tender and golden brown. Add beans and next 6 ingredients; bring to a boil. Reduce heat to low; cover and simmer 10 minutes or until beans are tender. Stir in lemon juice. Transfer to a serving dish; sprinkle with feta. Serve with a slotted spoon.

Church-Style Lemon-Roasted Potatoes

MAKES 6 TO 8 SERVINGS
HANDS-ON TIME: 28 MIN.
TOTAL TIME: 1 HR., 8 MIN.

If you don't want to peel little potatoes, you can use larger peeled Yukons. Simply cut into large chunks, and bake as directed. Any leftover potatoes are great for potato salad the next day. (pictured on page 175)

- 3 Tbsp. olive oil
- 1½ Tbsp. butter
- 3 lb. small Yukon gold or red potatoes, peeled
- ¼ cup lemon juice
- 4 tsp. chopped fresh thyme
- ¾ tsp. salt
- ½ tsp. pepper

1. Preheat oven to 400°. Cook olive oil and butter in a skillet over medium heat, stirring constantly, 3 to 4 minutes or until butter begins to turn golden brown. Remove butter mixture from heat, and add peeled potatoes, tossing gently to coat.
2. Spread potatoes in a single layer in a 15- x 10-inch jelly-roll pan.
3. Bake at 400° for 40 to 45 minutes or until potatoes are golden brown and tender, stirring twice. Transfer potatoes to a large serving bowl, and toss with lemon juice, chopped fresh thyme, salt, and pepper until well coated. Serve potatoes immediately.

Mama's Way or Your Way?
Two Takes on Ham

One is a showstopping Southern classic; the other cooks in half the time. Both get rave reviews.

Recipes from

Gloria Nelson and **Nicole McLaughlin**
Hoover, Alabama

❀ WHY WE LOVE
Mama's Way

- Delicious hot or cold
- Bone-in delivers exceptional flavor
- Beautiful on a holiday buffet

Honey-Bourbon Glazed Ham

party perfect

MAKES 15 SERVINGS
HANDS-ON TIME: 20 MIN.
TOTAL TIME: 3 HR., 20 MIN.

- 1 (9¼-lb.) fully cooked, bone-in ham
- 40 whole cloves
- ½ cup firmly packed light brown sugar
- ½ cup honey
- ½ cup bourbon
- ⅓ cup Creole mustard
- ⅓ cup molasses

Ham 101

- Cooked ham can be served directly from the refrigerator. If you'd like to serve it hot, heat in a 350° oven to an internal temperature of 140°.
- Uncooked ham should be heated to an internal temperature of 160° in a 350° oven. Plan to cook it 18 to 20 minutes per pound.
- Dry-cured ham is rubbed with salt and seasonings, and then stored until the salt fully penetrates the meat.
- Wet-cured ham is seasoned with a brine solution, which keeps the meat moist and the texture tender.

---

1. Preheat oven to 350°. Remove skin from ham, and trim fat to ¼-inch thickness. Make shallow cuts in fat 1 inch apart in a diamond pattern; insert cloves in centers of diamonds. Place ham in an aluminum foil-lined 13- x 9-inch pan.

2. Stir together brown sugar and next 4 ingredients; spoon over ham.

3. Bake at 350° on lowest oven rack 2 hours and 30 minutes, basting with pan juices every 30 minutes. Shield ham with foil after 1 hour to prevent excessive browning. Remove ham from oven, and let stand 30 minutes.

TRY THIS TWIST!
Honey-Bourbon Boneless Glazed Ham: Substitute 1 (4-lb.) smoked, fully cooked boneless ham for bone-in. Reduce cloves to 3 (do not insert into ham). Stir together brown sugar mixture as directed in Step 2; stir in cloves. Place ham in a foil-lined 13- x 9-inch pan. Pour sauce over ham. Bake as

---

directed, reducing bake time to 1 hour and basting every 30 minutes. Makes 10 servings. Hands-on time: 10 min.; Total time: 1 hr., 10 min.

❀ WHY WE LOVE
Your Way

- Faster cook time
- Perfect size for small families
- Easy to carve

Orange Glazed Ham

quick prep

MAKES 10 SERVINGS
HANDS-ON TIME: 10 MIN.
TOTAL TIME: 1 HR., 50 MIN.

- 1 (4-lb.) smoked, fully cooked boneless ham
- 1 cup orange marmalade
- 1 cup orange juice
- ¼ cup firmly packed brown sugar
- 2 Tbsp. creamy Dijon mustard
- 1 tsp. ground ginger

1. Preheat oven to 350°.

2. Place ham in an aluminum foil-lined 13- x 9-inch pan.

3. Stir together marmalade and next 4 ingredients; spoon mixture over ham.

4. Bake at 350° on lowest oven rack 1 hour and 30 minutes, basting with pan juices every 30 minutes. Remove ham from oven, and let stand 10 minutes before slicing.

Add Flavor with Leeks and Shallots

These sweet, mild cousins of the onion star in everything from a savory main-dish tart to a versatile vinaigrette.

Bacon-and-Leek Tart

party perfect

MAKES 6 SERVINGS
HANDS-ON TIME: 33 MIN.
TOTAL TIME: 53 MIN.

This top-rated tart is so easy to make and great for company. (pictured on page 6)

- 4   medium leeks
- 3   thick hickory-smoked bacon slices
- 1   cup (4 oz.) shredded Gruyère cheese, divided*
- 2   tsp. chopped fresh thyme**
- ½   tsp. pepper
- ½   tsp. salt
- ½   (17.3-oz.) package frozen puff pastry sheets, thawed
- 1   egg white

1. Preheat oven to 400°. Remove and discard root ends and dark green tops of leeks. Thinly slice leeks, and rinse thoroughly under cold running water to remove grit and sand.
2. Cook bacon in a large skillet over medium-high heat 8 to 11 minutes or until crisp; remove bacon, and drain on paper towels, reserving 1 Tbsp. drippings in skillet. Crumble bacon.
3. Sauté leeks in hot drippings over medium heat 5 to 7 minutes or until tender. Stir in ½ cup cheese, thyme, pepper, and salt.
4. Unfold pastry sheet; fit into a 9-inch square tart pan. Whisk egg white until light and frothy. Brush egg white onto pastry sheet.
5. Bake at 400° for 15 to 20 minutes or until browned. Remove from oven. Press pastry with back of a spoon to flatten. Top with leek mixture; sprinkle with crumbled bacon and remaining ½ cup cheese. Bake 5 to 7 minutes or until cheese is melted.

RECIPE FROM LIZ HOLLEY
BIRMINGHAM, ALABAMA

* Swiss cheese may be substituted.
** 1 tsp. dried thyme may be substituted.

Stuffed Mushrooms with Pecans

party perfect

MAKES 8 APPETIZER SERVINGS
HANDS-ON TIME: 28 MIN.
TOTAL TIME: 53 MIN.

Use mushrooms of equal size for even cooking. (pictured on page 7)

- 2   medium leeks
- 1   (16-oz.) package fresh mushrooms (about 24 medium-size mushrooms)
- 1   tsp. salt, divided
- 2   shallots, minced
- 2   garlic cloves, minced
- 2   Tbsp. olive oil
- ½   cup grated Parmesan cheese
- ¼   cup fine, dry breadcrumbs
- ¼   cup pecans, chopped
- 2   Tbsp. chopped fresh basil
    Garnish: fresh basil sprigs

1. Preheat oven to 350°. Remove and discard root ends and dark green tops of leeks. Thinly slice leeks, and rinse thoroughly under cold running water to remove grit and sand.
2. Rinse mushrooms, and pat dry. Remove and discard stems. Place mushrooms, upside down, on a wire rack in an aluminum foil-lined jelly-roll pan. Sprinkle with ½ tsp. salt; invert mushrooms.
3. Bake at 350° for 15 minutes.
4. Sauté leeks, shallots, and garlic in hot oil in a large skillet over medium heat 3 to 5 minutes or until tender. Transfer mixture to a large bowl. Stir in ¼ cup Parmesan cheese, next 3 ingredients, and remaining ½ tsp. salt until well combined. Spoon 1 heaping teaspoonful leek mixture into each mushroom cap. Sprinkle with remaining ¼ cup Parmesan cheese. Bake at 350° for 10 minutes or until golden. Garnish, if desired.

Roasted Shallot Vinaigrette

quick prep • make-ahead

MAKES ABOUT ⅔ CUP
HANDS-ON TIME: 10 MIN.
TOTAL TIME: 45 MIN.

Serve over a mixed green salad with blue cheese, or toss with steamed green beans.

- 5 shallots
- 1 Tbsp. olive oil
- 2 Tbsp. white wine vinegar
- 2 Tbsp. balsamic vinegar
- ¾ tsp. salt
- ½ tsp. sugar
- ½ tsp. pepper
- ⅓ cup olive oil

1. Preheat oven to 400°. Peel shallots, and toss with 1 Tbsp. olive oil in a large bowl. Arrange shallots on an aluminum foil-lined baking sheet.

2. Bake at 400° for 25 minutes or until shallots are very tender, turning once after 15 minutes. Remove from oven, and let cool 10 minutes.

3. Pulse roasted shallots, white wine vinegar, and next 4 ingredients in a food processor 3 to 5 times or until thoroughly blended. With processor running, slowly pour ⅓ cup olive oil through food chute in a slow, steady stream, processing 15 to 20 seconds or until mixture is blended and smooth. Serve immediately. Store vinaigrette in an airtight container in refrigerator for up to 5 days. Let stand at room temperature for 10 minutes, and whisk just before serving.

10 Meals in 30 Minutes or Less

Our time-saving ingredients and handy tips help you create delicious meals for even your busiest days.

Spring Chicken Cobb Salad

good for you

MAKES 4 SERVINGS
HANDS-ON TIME: 23 MIN.
TOTAL TIME: 28 MIN. (INCLUDING VINAIGRETTE)

- 1 large sweet onion
- 2 tsp. olive oil
- ¼ tsp. salt
- ¼ tsp. pepper
- 1 (5-oz.) package arugula, thoroughly washed
- 2 cups chopped or shredded roasted chicken
- 2 avocados, sliced
- 1 cup drained and chopped jarred roasted red bell peppers
- 4 fully cooked bacon slices, chopped
- 4 oz. crumbled goat cheese
  Yogurt-Basil Vinaigrette

1. Cut onion into ¼-inch-thick slices. Brush with olive oil, and sprinkle with salt and pepper. Heat a grill pan over medium-high heat; cook onion slices 4 to 5 minutes on each side or until lightly charred and tender.

2. Arrange arugula on a serving platter; top with onions, chicken, and next 4 ingredients. Drizzle with Yogurt-Basil Vinaigrette.

Yogurt-Basil Vinaigrette:

good for you • make-ahead

MAKES 1 CUP
HANDS-ON TIME: 5 MIN.
TOTAL TIME: 5 MIN.

- ½ cup plain fat-free yogurt
- ¼ cup olive oil
- 2 Tbsp. chopped fresh basil
- 2 Tbsp. red wine vinegar
- 1 Tbsp. honey
- ½ tsp. salt
- ⅛ tsp. pepper

1. Whisk together all ingredients. Serve immediately, or cover and chill up to 8 hours. If chilled, let stand at room temperature 30 minutes before serving.

TRY THIS TWIST!

Salmon Cobb Salad: Omit chicken. Season 4 (4-oz.) salmon fillets with ¾ tsp. salt and ¼ tsp. pepper. Cook salmon, covered, in 1 Tbsp. hot olive oil in a large skillet over medium heat 8 to 10 minutes on each side or until done. Proceed with recipe as directed.

Grilled Chicken with Corn and Slaw

party perfect

MAKES 4 SERVINGS
HANDS-ON TIME: 30 MIN.
TOTAL TIME: 30 MIN.

Dice leftover grilled chicken, and then combine with leftover slaw for a tasty lunch. (pictured on page 172)

- 1 cup mayonnaise
- ¼ cup chopped fresh cilantro
- 6 Tbsp. white wine vinegar, divided
- ¾ tsp. salt, divided
- ⅛ tsp. pepper
- 4 skinned and boned chicken breasts (about 1 lb.)
- 4 ears fresh corn, husks removed
- ¼ cup melted butter
- 1 (10-oz.) package shredded coleslaw mix
- 3 Tbsp. olive oil
- ½ tsp. sugar
- ¼ tsp. pepper

1. Combine mayonnaise, cilantro, 3 Tbsp. vinegar, ¼ tsp. salt, and ⅛ tsp. pepper in a small bowl. Reserve ¾ cup mayonnaise mixture. Brush chicken with remaining ¼ cup mayonnaise mixture.

2. Preheat grill to 350° to 400° (medium-high) heat. Grill chicken and corn at the same time, covered with grill lid. Grill chicken 7 to 10 minutes on each side or until done; grill corn 14 to 20 minutes or until done, turning every 4 to 5 minutes and basting with melted butter.

3. Toss coleslaw mix with oil, sugar, ¼ tsp. pepper, and remaining 3 Tbsp. vinegar and ½ tsp. salt. Season chicken and corn with salt and pepper to taste. Serve with coleslaw and reserved mayonnaise mixture.

Test Kitchen Notebook

TIME-SAVING TIPS TO MAKE PREP EVEN FASTER:

- Turn on the oven before you start prepping.
- Read the recipe first before you begin.
- Gather all ingredients before you cook.
- Chop veggies ahead of time for even quicker prep times.

Steamed Mussels with Herbs

good for you

MAKES 4 SERVINGS
HANDS-ON TIME: 23 MIN.
TOTAL TIME: 23 MIN.

Serve with crusty bread to dip into the flavorful broth.

- 2 lb. fresh mussels
- 4 garlic cloves, minced
- 2 shallots, minced
- 2 Tbsp. olive oil
- 2 cups dry white wine
- 2 Tbsp. Dijon mustard
- 1 (14.5-oz.) can vegetable broth
- ¼ tsp. salt
- ¼ cup chopped fresh basil
- ¼ cup chopped fresh cilantro

1. Scrub mussels thoroughly with a scrub brush, removing beards. Discard any opened shells.

2. Sauté garlic and shallots in hot oil in a Dutch oven over medium heat 1 to 2 minutes. Stir in wine and mustard; cook 2 to 3 minutes. Add broth and salt, and bring to a boil. Add mussels. Cook, covered, stirring occasionally, 5 minutes or until all mussels have opened. Remove from heat. Stir in basil and cilantro.

Chicken with Couscous, Tomatoes, and Hummus

good for you

MAKES 4 SERVINGS
HANDS-ON TIME: 30 MIN.
TOTAL TIME: 30 MIN.

Orzo pasta (prepared according to package directions) will work in place of couscous.

- 1 (10-oz.) package plain couscous
- 4 (4- to 6-oz.) skinned and boned chicken breasts
- 2 Tbsp. olive oil, divided
- 1¼ tsp. salt, divided
- ½ tsp. pepper, divided
- 6 plum tomatoes, seeded and diced
- 1 garlic clove, minced
- 3 Tbsp. chopped fresh basil
- 2 Tbsp. minced red onion
- 1 Tbsp. lemon juice
- 1 (7-oz.) container hummus
- 4 pita bread rounds, cut into quarters

1. Prepare couscous according to package directions.

2. Brush chicken with 1 Tbsp. oil; sprinkle with ¾ tsp. salt and ¼ tsp. pepper.

3. Cook chicken, covered, in a large nonstick skillet or grill pan, over medium-high heat 8 to 10 minutes on each side or until done.

4. Meanwhile, combine tomatoes, next 4 ingredients, and remaining 1 Tbsp. oil, ½ tsp. salt, and ¼ tsp. pepper. Stir tomato mixture into prepared couscous.

5. Divide couscous mixture, hummus, and pita bread quarters among 4 serving plates; top each with 1 chicken breast.

Cheesy BBQ Sloppy Joes

quick prep

MAKES 4 SERVINGS
HANDS-ON TIME: 28 MIN.
TOTAL TIME: 28 MIN.

Thick-cut, store-bought frozen Texas toast gives you a head start. (pictured on page 173)

- 1½ lb. lean ground beef
- 1 (14.5-oz.) can diced tomatoes
- 1 cup ketchup
- ½ cup bottled barbecue sauce
- 1 Tbsp. Worcestershire sauce
- 2 Tbsp. chopped pickled jalapeño peppers (optional)
- 1 Tbsp. liquid from pickled jalapeño peppers (optional)
- 1 (11.25-oz.) package frozen garlic Texas toast
- ½ cup (2 oz.) shredded sharp Cheddar cheese

1. Brown ground beef in a large skillet over medium-high heat, stirring often, 8 to 10 minutes or until beef crumbles and is no longer pink; drain well. Return to skillet. Stir in tomatoes, next 3 ingredients, and, if desired, jalapeño peppers and liquid. Cover and cook 10 minutes.
2. Meanwhile, prepare Texas toast according to package directions. Serve beef mixture over Texas toast; sprinkle with cheese.

Pork Tenderloin Tacos with Radish-Avocado Salsa

good for you • party perfect

MAKES 4 SERVINGS
HANDS-ON TIME: 25 MIN.
TOTAL TIME: 25 MIN.

SALSA

- 1 (6-oz.) package radishes
- ½ small red onion, diced
- 1 avocado, diced
- 1 jalapeño pepper, seeded and minced
- ¼ cup chopped fresh cilantro
- 2 Tbsp. lime juice
- ¼ tsp. salt

TACOS

- 2 Tbsp. brown sugar
- 3 Tbsp. olive oil
- 2 tsp. salt
- 1 tsp. ground cumin
- ½ tsp. ground red pepper
- 1 lb. pork tenderloin, cut into 1-inch cubes
- 8 (6-inch) fajita-size corn or flour tortillas, warmed

1. Prepare Salsa: Process radishes in a food processor until finely chopped. Stir together radishes, onion, and next 5 ingredients; cover and chill salsa until ready to serve.
2. Prepare Tacos: Stir together brown sugar and next 4 ingredients. Toss pork with brown sugar mixture. Heat grill pan over medium-high heat; cook pork, in 2 batches, 2½ minutes on each side or until done. Serve pork in warm tortillas with salsa.

Oven-Fried Pork Chops with Roasted Green Beans and Pecans

MAKES 4 SERVINGS
HANDS-ON TIME: 30 MIN.
TOTAL TIME: 30 MIN.

Panko breadcrumbs give these hearty chops a crunchy crust. (pictured on page 173)

- 2 (12-oz.) packages fresh cut green beans
- 1 Tbsp. olive oil
- 1 tsp. salt, divided
- 4 (4- to 6-oz.) bone-in center-cut pork chops
- ¼ tsp. pepper
- ½ cup Japanese breadcrumbs (panko)
- ¼ cup freshly grated Parmesan cheese
- 1 Tbsp. lemon zest
- 1 tsp. chopped fresh thyme
- ¼ cup vegetable oil
- ¼ cup chopped pecans
- ½ Tbsp. butter

1. Preheat oven to 450°. Drain and rinse beans. Combine beans, 1 Tbsp. olive oil, and ¾ tsp. salt in a large bowl, tossing to coat. Spread beans in a single layer in a jelly-roll pan. Bake 18 to 20 minutes or until beans are tender and slightly browned.
2. Meanwhile, sprinkle pork chops with pepper and remaining ¼ tsp. salt.
3. Stir together breadcrumbs and next 3 ingredients in a large shallow dish. Dredge pork chops in breadcrumb mixture.
4. Cook chops in ¼ cup hot vegetable oil in a large skillet over medium heat 5 to 6 minutes on each side or until done.
5. Stir pecans and butter into beans; bake 5 to 6 more minutes or until pecans are golden. Serve pork chops with green beans.

Cilantro-Ginger Flank Steak with Edamame Rice

good for you

MAKES 4 SERVINGS
HANDS-ON TIME: 30 MIN.
TOTAL TIME: 30 MIN.

This recipe is also terrific made with chicken breasts or pork chops.

- 1 Tbsp. grated fresh ginger
- 1 Tbsp. olive oil
- 6 Tbsp. chopped fresh cilantro, divided
- 1 (1-lb.) flank steak
- 1 tsp. salt
- ½ tsp. pepper
- ½ lime
- 2 (8.5-oz.) pouches ready-to-serve basmati rice
- 2 cups fully cooked shelled frozen edamame, thawed

1. Preheat grill to 400° to 450° (high) heat. Stir together ginger, oil, and 2 Tbsp. cilantro in a small bowl. Rub cilantro mixture on steak. Sprinkle with salt and pepper.

2. Grill steak, covered with grill lid, 6 to 7 minutes on each side or to desired degree of doneness. Remove from grill; squeeze juice from lime over steak. Cover loosely with foil, and let stand 10 minutes.

3. Meanwhile, prepare rice according to package directions, and stir in edamame and remaining 4 Tbsp. cilantro. Cut steak across the grain into thin slices; serve over rice.

Fettuccine with Green Peas and Fresh Mint

quick prep

MAKES 3 TO 4 SERVINGS
HANDS-ON TIME: 15 MIN.
TOTAL TIME: 30 MIN.

- 1 (9-oz.) package refrigerated fettuccine
- 1 Tbsp. butter
- ¾ cup frozen baby sweet peas
- ⅔ cup half-and-half
- ½ cup ricotta cheese
- ¼ cup chopped fresh mint
- ¼ cup freshly grated Parmesan cheese
- 2 garlic cloves, minced
- 1 tsp. lemon zest
- ¼ tsp. salt
- ¼ tsp. pepper
  Garnish: fresh shaved Parmesan cheese

1. Prepare pasta according to package directions.

2. Melt butter in a large skillet over medium heat. Add peas and next 8 ingredients. Reduce heat to low, and cook, stirring constantly, 5 minutes or until cheese is melted. Stir in hot cooked pasta, and serve immediately. Garnish, if desired.

Speedy Black Beans and Mexican Rice

quick prep • good for you

MAKES 4 SERVINGS
HANDS-ON TIME: 12 MIN.
TOTAL TIME: 12 MIN.

This hearty dish is the perfect answer for a meatless main-dish choice.

- 2 (8.8-oz.) pouches ready-to-serve Spanish-style rice
- 2 (15-oz.) cans black beans, drained and rinsed
- 2 (4-oz.) cans chopped green chiles
- ¼ cup chopped fresh cilantro
  Toppings: sour cream, salsa, diced tomato, shredded Cheddar cheese

1. Prepare rice according to package directions.

2. Combine black beans and green chiles in a microwave-safe bowl. Microwave at HIGH 2 minutes or until thoroughly heated. Stir in rice and cilantro. Serve immediately with desired toppings.

Note: We tested with Uncle Ben's Spanish Style Ready Rice.

Cooking Class
Omelets Made Easy

Whip up the perfect omelet for breakfast or supper. Grab your blender and nonstick skillet, and we'll show you how.

Spinach-and-Cheese Omelet

quick prep

MAKES 1 SERVING
HANDS-ON TIME: 14 MIN.
TOTAL TIME: 14 MIN.

- 2 large eggs
- 1 Tbsp. butter
- 1 cup coarsely chopped spinach
- ⅓ cup chopped tomatoes
- ⅛ tsp. salt
- ⅓ cup (1½ oz.) shredded Swiss cheese
- ⅛ tsp. pepper

Test Kitchen Notebook

- Refrigerate eggs in their original carton at a temperature below 40°.

- Use raw eggs within four weeks and leftover yolks and whites within four days.

- Never leave eggs at room temperature for more than an hour.

- ¼ cup egg substitute = 1 large egg

Three Easy Steps

1 | Blend and Pour

Process eggs and 2 Tbsp. water in a blender until blended. Melt butter in an 8-inch nonstick skillet over medium heat; add spinach and tomatoes, and sauté 1 minute or until spinach is wilted. Add salt and egg mixture to skillet.

2 | Lift and Tilt

As egg mixture starts to cook, gently lift edges of omelet with a spatula, and tilt pan so uncooked egg mixture flows underneath, cooking until almost set (about 1 minute). Cover skillet, and cook 1 minute.

3 | Fold and Serve

Sprinkle omelet with cheese and pepper. Fold omelet in half, allowing cheese to melt. Slide cooked omelet onto a serving plate, and season with salt to taste. Serve with buttered toast and fresh fruit.

May

Fresh off the Grill

It's open season in the South for carefree entertaining, and these easy-to-make favorites are guaranteed to fire up some delicious backyard fun.

Spicy Grilled Pork Tenderloin with Blackberry Sauce

quick prep • party perfect

MAKES 6 TO 8 SERVINGS
HANDS-ON TIME: 15 MIN.
TOTAL TIME: 40 MIN.

- 2 (¾-lb.) pork tenderloins
- 1 Tbsp. olive oil
- 1½ Tbsp. Caribbean jerk seasoning
- 1 tsp. salt
- ⅔ cup seedless blackberry preserves
- ¼ cup Dijon mustard
- 2 Tbsp. rum or orange juice
- 1 Tbsp. orange zest
- 1 Tbsp. grated fresh ginger

1. Preheat grill to 350° to 400° (medium-high) heat. Remove silver skin from tenderloins, leaving a thin layer of fat. Brush tenderloins with oil, and rub with seasoning and salt.
2. Grill tenderloins, covered with grill lid, 10 minutes on each side or until a meat thermometer inserted into thickest portion registers 155°. Remove from grill, and let stand 10 minutes.
3. Meanwhile, whisk together blackberry preserves and next 4 ingredients in a small saucepan, and cook over low heat, whisking constantly, 5 minutes or until thoroughly heated.
4. Cut pork diagonally into thin slices, and arrange on a serving platter; drizzle with warm sauce.

Lexington-Style Grilled Chicken

quick prep • party perfect

MAKES 8 TO 10 SERVINGS
HANDS-ON TIME: 15 MIN.
TOTAL TIME: 2 HR., 50 MIN.

- 2 cups cider vinegar
- ¼ cup firmly packed dark brown sugar
- ¼ cup vegetable oil
- 3 Tbsp. dried crushed red pepper
- 4 tsp. salt
- 2 tsp. pepper
- 2 (2½- to 3-lb.) cut-up whole chickens

1. Stir together first 6 ingredients until blended.
2. Divide vinegar mixture and chicken between 2 large zip-top plastic freezer bags, and seal bags. Chill 2 to 8 hours, turning bags occasionally.
3. Preheat grill to 350° to 400° (medium-high) heat. Remove chicken from marinade, discarding marinade.
4. Grill chicken, covered with grill lid, 35 to 40 minutes or until done, turning occasionally.

Grilled Chicken Thighs with White Barbecue Sauce

party perfect

MAKES 5 SERVINGS
HANDS-ON TIME: 31 MIN.
TOTAL TIME: 6 HR., 41 MIN., INCLUDING SAUCE
(pictured on page 176)

- 1 Tbsp. dried thyme
- 1 Tbsp. dried oregano
- 1 Tbsp. ground cumin
- 1 Tbsp. paprika
- 1 tsp. onion powder
- ½ tsp. salt
- ½ tsp. pepper
- 10 skin-on, bone-in chicken thighs (about 3 lb.)
  White Barbecue Sauce

1. Combine first 7 ingredients until blended. Rinse chicken, and pat dry; rub seasoning mixture over chicken. Place chicken in a zip-top plastic freezer bag. Seal and chill 4 hours.
2. Preheat grill to 350° to 400° (medium-high) heat. Remove chicken from bag, discarding bag.
3. Grill chicken, covered with grill lid, 8 to 10 minutes on each side or until a meat thermometer inserted into thickest portion registers 180°. Serve with White Barbecue Sauce.

White Barbecue Sauce:

MAKES 1¾ CUPS
HANDS-ON TIME: 10 MIN.
TOTAL TIME: 2 HR., 10 MIN.

1. Stir together 1½ cups mayonnaise; ¼ cup white wine vinegar; 1 garlic clove, minced; 1 Tbsp. coarse ground pepper; 1 Tbsp. spicy brown mustard; 1 tsp. sugar; 1 tsp. salt; and 2 tsp. horseradish until blended. Cover and chill 2 to 4 hours. Store in an airtight container up to 1 week.

Our Favorite Grilled Corn

Preheat grill to 350° to 400° (medium-high) heat. Remove husks from 6 ears of fresh **corn**. Coat corn lightly with vegetable **cooking spray**. Sprinkle with desired amount of **salt** and freshly ground **pepper**. Grill, covered with grill lid, 15 minutes or until golden brown, turning occasionally; remove from grill. Stir together 2 Tbsp. each **reduced-fat mayonnaise** and **fat-free sour cream**. Spread corn with mayonnaise mixture; sprinkle with 3 Tbsp. finely grated **Parmesan cheese** and 1 to 2 Tbsp. **chili powder**. Cut 2 **limes** into wedges, and squeeze over corn. Makes 6 servings. Hands-on time: 25 min.; Total time: 25 min.

Grilled Shrimp-and-Green Bean Salad

party perfect

MAKES 4 TO 6 SERVINGS
HANDS-ON TIME: 38 MIN. **TOTAL TIME:** 1 HR., 18 MIN., INCLUDING VINAIGRETTE
(pictured on page 177)

- 8 (12-inch) wooden skewers
- 2 lb. peeled, medium-size raw shrimp (21/25 count)
  Basil Vinaigrette, divided
- 1½ lb. fresh green beans, trimmed
- 6 cooked bacon slices, crumbled
- 1⅓ cups (5½ oz.) shredded Parmesan cheese
- ¾ cup chopped roasted, salted almonds
  Cornbread (optional)

1. Soak wooden skewers in water to cover 30 minutes.
2. Meanwhile, combine shrimp and ¾ cup Basil Vinaigrette in a large zip-top plastic bag; seal and chill 15 minutes, turning occasionally.
3. Preheat grill to 350° to 400° (medium-high) heat.
4. Cook green beans in boiling salted water to cover 4 minutes or until crisp-tender; drain. Plunge into ice water to stop the cooking process; drain, pat dry, and place in a large bowl.
5. Remove shrimp from marinade, discarding marinade. Thread shrimp onto skewers.

6. Grill shrimp, covered with grill lid, 2 minutes on each side or just until shrimp turn pink. Remove shrimp from skewers, and toss with green beans, crumbled bacon, Parmesan cheese, roasted almonds, and remaining ¾ cup Basil Vinaigrette. Serve over hot cooked cornbread, if desired.

Basil Vinaigrette:

MAKES ABOUT 1½ CUPS
HANDS-ON TIME: 10 MIN.
TOTAL TIME: 10 MIN.

1. Whisk together ½ cup chopped fresh basil; ½ cup balsamic vinegar; 4 large shallots, minced; 3 garlic cloves, minced; 1 Tbsp. brown sugar; 1 tsp. seasoned pepper; and ½ tsp. salt until blended. Gradually add 1 cup olive oil, whisking constantly until blended.

Jalapeño-Lime Grilled Grouper

quick prep • party perfect

MAKES 4 SERVINGS
HANDS-ON TIME: 22 MIN.
TOTAL TIME: 32 MIN., INCLUDING RELISH

Vegetable cooking spray
- 3 Tbsp. chopped fresh cilantro
- 2 Tbsp. fresh lime juice
- 1½ to 2 Tbsp. chopped pickled jalapeño pepper
- 1 Tbsp. grated fresh ginger
- 1½ tsp. minced fresh garlic
- 4 grouper fillets (about 1½ lb.)*
- 1 tsp. salt
- ½ tsp. pepper
  Mango Relish

1. Preheat grill to 350° to 400° (medium-high) heat. Coat a grill tray or basket with cooking spray, and place on grill. Heat, covered with grill lid, 10 minutes.
2. Meanwhile, combine cilantro and next 4 ingredients.
3. Sprinkle fish with salt and pepper.
4. Place fish on hot grill tray. Grill fish, covered with grill lid, 6 to 8 minutes on each side or until fish flakes with a fork, spreading fish with cilantro mixture during the last 2 minutes of grilling.
5. Serve fish with Mango Relish.
*Amberjack, tilapia, or mahi-mahi may be substituted.

Mango Relish:

MAKES ABOUT 2 CUPS
HANDS-ON TIME: 10 MIN.
TOTAL TIME: 10 MIN.

1. Stir together 1½ cups diced fresh mango or nectarines, ½ cup diced red bell pepper, ¼ cup diced red onion, ¼ cup chopped fresh basil, 1 Tbsp. honey, 1 Tbsp. fresh lime juice, and ¼ tsp. salt.

Beef and Chicken Fajitas

party perfect

MAKES 8 SERVINGS
HANDS-ON TIME: 30 MIN.
TOTAL TIME: 2 HR., 40 MIN.

Serve with warm flour tortillas and your favorite toppings, such as shredded cheese and lettuce, diced tomato and avocado, and sour cream.

½ cup bottled Italian dressing
1 Tbsp. chili powder
1 tsp. ground cumin
½ tsp. brown sugar
½ tsp. pepper
¼ tsp. salt
⅛ tsp. garlic powder
⅛ tsp. chipotle seasoning
3 skinned and boned chicken breasts (about 2 lb.)
1 (2-lb.) flank steak

1. Whisk together first 8 ingredients. Pour half of marinade into a large zip-top plastic freezer bag, and add chicken breasts; seal bag. Repeat procedure with remaining marinade and flank steak. Chill 2 hours.
2. Preheat grill to 350° to 400° (medium-high) heat. Remove beef and chicken from marinade, discarding marinade.
3. Grill chicken and steak at the same time. Grill steak, covered with grill lid, 10 minutes on each side or to desired degree of doneness; grill chicken, covered with grill lid, 5 to 6 minutes on each side or until done.
4. Remove from grill, and let stand 10 minutes. Cut steak and chicken diagonally into ¼-inch-thick strips.

Skewered Flank Steak with Horseradish-Lemon Dipping Sauce

party perfect

MAKES 8 APPETIZER SERVINGS
HANDS-ON TIME: 41 MIN.
TOTAL TIME: 9 HR., 21 MIN., INCLUDING DIPPING SAUCE

⅓ cup olive oil
2 tsp. lemon zest
¼ cup fresh lemon juice
1 tsp. salt
¼ tsp. dried crushed red pepper
2 (2-lb.) flank steaks, cut diagonally into 32 (¼-inch-thick) slices
Horseradish-Lemon Dipping Sauce
32 (12-inch) wooden skewers

1. Combine first 5 ingredients in a large shallow dish or zip-top plastic freezer bag; add steak. Cover and chill 8 hours, turning occasionally.
2. Meanwhile, prepare Horseradish-Lemon Dipping Sauce.
3. Soak skewers in water to cover 30 minutes.
4. Preheat grill to 350° to 400° (medium-high) heat. Remove steak from marinade, discarding marinade. Thread 1 steak slice onto each skewer.
5. Grill steak, in batches, covered with grill lid, 4 to 5 minutes on each side or to desired degree of doneness. Serve with Horseradish-Lemon Dipping Sauce.

Horseradish-Lemon Dipping Sauce:

MAKES 2¼ CUPS
HANDS-ON TIME: 10 MIN.
TOTAL TIME: 8 HR., 10 MIN.

1. Stir together 1 (16-oz.) container light sour cream, 1 Tbsp. horseradish, 1 tsp. lemon zest, 3 Tbsp. fresh lemon juice, and ½ tsp. salt. Cover and chill 8 hours.

Molasses-Balsamic Steak Kabobs with Peaches and Green Tomatoes

good for you • party perfect

MAKES 4 TO 6 SERVINGS
HANDS-ON TIME: 38 MIN.
TOTAL TIME: 1 HR., 8 MIN.

We also loved these kabobs with pork tenderloin and plums in place of steak and peaches.

8 (12-inch) wooden or metal skewers
1 (1½-lb.) boneless sirloin steak, trimmed and cut into 1½-inch pieces
4 small, firm peaches, quartered
2 medium-size green tomatoes, cut into eighths
2 medium-size red onions, cut into eighths
2 tsp. seasoned salt
2 tsp. pepper
½ cup molasses
¼ cup balsamic vinegar

1. Soak wooden skewers in water to cover 30 minutes.
2. Preheat grill to 350° to 400° (medium-high) heat. Thread steak and next 3 ingredients alternately onto skewers, leaving a ¼-inch space between pieces. Sprinkle kabobs with seasoned salt and pepper. Stir together molasses and vinegar.
3. Grill kabobs, covered with grill lid, 4 minutes on each side. Baste with half of molasses mixture, and grill 2 minutes. Turn, baste with remaining half of molasses mixture, and grill 2 more minutes or until done.

Try Pickled Okra: We've been pickling okra in the South since Granny was a girl. And no wonder: It's a versatile gem loaded with flavor. Serve it all by itself or bobbing in an ice-cold Bloody Mary. Or get really uptown by stuffing pickled pods with cream cheese and wrapping them with prosciutto. If you didn't inherit the family pickling recipe, you have lots of store-bought options to choose from. Here are our favorites: Wickles Wicked Okra (for a sweet flavor), *wickles.com*; Talk O' Texas Crisp Okra Pickles (for a tangy version), *talkotexas.com*; and Old South Okra Pickles (which is right down the sweet-tangy middle), *boiledpeanuts.com*.

Grilled Maple Chipotle Pork Chops

party perfect

MAKES 6 SERVINGS
HANDS-ON TIME: 28 MIN.
TOTAL TIME: 43 MIN., INCLUDING GRITS

½ cup barbecue sauce
½ cup maple syrup
2 Tbsp. minced canned chipotle peppers in adobo sauce
6 (1¼-inch-thick) bone-in pork loin chops (about 4½ lb.)
1 tsp. salt
1 tsp. pepper
Smoked Gouda Grits

1. Preheat grill to 350° to 400° (medium-high) heat. Whisk together first 3 ingredients; reserve half.
2. Sprinkle pork chops with salt and pepper.
3. Grill pork, covered with grill lid, 9 minutes on each side or until a meat thermometer inserted into thickest portion registers 155°, basting with remaining half of barbecue sauce mixture during last 5 minutes of grilling. Remove from grill, and drizzle with reserved barbecue sauce mixture. Serve over Smoked Gouda Grits.

Smoked Gouda Grits:

MAKES 6 SERVINGS
HANDS-ON TIME: 10 MIN.
TOTAL TIME: 15 MIN.

1. Bring 4 cups water, 4 cups milk, 1 tsp. salt, and ½ tsp. ground white pepper to a boil in a large saucepan; gradually whisk in 2 cups uncooked quick-cooking grits. Cook, whisking often, 5 minutes or until thickened. Remove from heat. Whisk in 1⅔ cups (6½ oz.) shredded smoked Gouda cheese and 3 Tbsp. butter, whisking until blended.

All-Time Favorite Potato Salads

Every good cook south of the Mason-Dixon Line has a special recipe for this classic side. We reveal the secrets, from adding colorful sweet potatoes to amping up the flavor with the salty snap of bacon and blue cheese.

Picnic Potato Salad

quick prep • make-ahead • party perfect

MAKES 8 SERVINGS
HANDS-ON TIME: 20 MIN.
TOTAL TIME: 1 HR., 15 MIN.

You'll find a version of this hearty salad everywhere from backyard cookouts to bereavement platters. Add a sprinkling of cooked and crumbled bacon just before serving to put it over the top.

- 4 lb. Yukon gold potatoes
- 3 hard-cooked eggs, peeled and grated
- 1 cup mayonnaise
- ½ cup diced celery
- ½ cup sour cream
- ⅓ cup finely chopped sweet onion
- ¼ cup sweet pickle relish
- 1 Tbsp. spicy brown mustard
- 1 tsp. salt
- ¾ tsp. freshly ground pepper

1. Cook potatoes in boiling water to cover 40 minutes or until tender; drain and cool 15 minutes. Peel potatoes, and cut into 1-inch cubes.
2. Combine potatoes and eggs.
3. Stir together mayonnaise and next 7 ingredients; gently stir into potato mixture. Serve immediately, or cover and chill 12 hours.

Lemon-Garlic Potato Salad

make-ahead • party perfect

MAKES 8 SERVINGS
HANDS-ON TIME: 25 MIN.
TOTAL TIME: 1 HR., 15 MIN.

Choose small to medium-size potatoes of similar diameter for this colorful recipe. (pictured on page 10)

- 1½ lb. Yukon gold potatoes
- 1½ lb. sweet potatoes
- ⅔ cup olive oil
- 2 tsp. lemon zest
- ¼ cup fresh lemon juice
- 3 garlic cloves, minced
- 1 Tbsp. Dijon mustard
- 1 tsp. salt
- ¾ tsp. freshly ground pepper
- ½ cup chopped lightly salted, roasted pecans
- ¼ cup chopped fresh basil

1. Cook potatoes in boiling water to cover 30 minutes or until tender; drain and cool 20 minutes.
2. Meanwhile, whisk together olive oil and next 6 ingredients; let stand 30 minutes.
3. Peel potatoes, and cut into ¼-inch-thick slices. Arrange potatoes in rows in a shallow 2-qt. baking dish, alternating Yukon gold and sweet potatoes. Pour olive oil mixture over potatoes; sprinkle with pecans and basil.

Big Daddy's Grilled Blue Cheese-and-Bacon Potato Salad

READER RECIPE

make-ahead • party perfect

MAKES 6 SERVINGS
HANDS-ON TIME: 30 MIN.
TOTAL TIME: 1 HR, 5 MIN.

Grilling the potatoes in an easy-to-fold aluminum foil packet adds a subtle note of smoky flavor—plus it makes cleanup a breeze. (pictured on page 11)

- 3 lb. baby red potatoes, cut in half
- 2 Tbsp. olive oil
- 1 tsp. salt
- 1 tsp. freshly ground pepper
- 1 cup mayonnaise
- ¼ cup chopped fresh parsley
- ¼ cup white balsamic vinegar*
- 2 tsp. sugar
- 2 tsp. Dijon mustard
- 1 cup thinly sliced red onion
- 4 oz. crumbled blue cheese
- 6 bacon slices, cooked and crumbled

Test Kitchen Notebook

- Baby red-skinned potatoes and Yukon golds are our top choice for salads. Low in starch, they absorb less water and hold their shape better than Idahos or russets.

- Choose same-sized potatoes for even cooking. They're done when easily pierced with a fork.

- Stir in the dressing when the potatoes are still warm. After cooling, surface starch prevents the seasoning from penetrating.

- Hellmann's mayonnaise was our closest-to-homemade favorite in taste testing.

1. Preheat grill to 350° to 400° (medium-high) heat. Place potatoes in a single layer in center of a large piece of heavy-duty aluminum foil. Drizzle with olive oil; sprinkle with salt and pepper. Bring up foil sides over potatoes; double fold top and side edges to seal, making 1 large packet.

2. Grill potatoes, in foil packet, covered with grill lid, 15 minutes on each side. Remove packet from grill. Carefully open packet, using tongs, and let potatoes cool 5 minutes.

3. Whisk together mayonnaise and next 4 ingredients in a large bowl; add potatoes, tossing gently to coat. Stir in onion, blue cheese, and bacon.

*Balsamic vinegar may be substituted but it will darken the color of the dressing.

RECIPE FROM DAVID MCALEESE
NORCROSS, GEORGIA

Six Fast Fixes

Stir together 3 lb. cooked and quartered baby red potatoes with any of the following combinations of ingredients. Season with salt and freshly ground pepper to taste just before serving.

- 1 cup Greek yogurt; 1 cup peeled, seeded, and finely chopped cucumber; 2 garlic cloves, pressed; 2 Tbsp. chopped fresh dill; and 2 tsp. lemon juice. (Serve this version immediately.)

- ½ cup mayonnaise; ½ cup sour cream; ½ cup thinly sliced green onions; ⅓ cup chopped fresh cilantro; 2 Tbsp. sauce from canned chipotle peppers in adobo sauce; ¾ tsp. lime zest; and 2 Tbsp. lime juice

- 1 cup mayonnaise; 1 Tbsp. chopped fresh rosemary; 1 garlic clove, pressed; and ¾ tsp. lemon zest

- 1 cup (4 oz.) shredded Asiago cheese; ½ cup coarsely chopped fresh basil; ½ cup toasted pine nuts; ½ cup olive oil; and 2 garlic cloves, pressed

- ¾ cup sour cream; ⅓ cup diced red onion; ⅓ cup chopped fresh chives; ¼ cup mayonnaise; and 2 Tbsp. horseradish

- 1 cup crumbled feta cheese with sun-dried tomatoes; ⅔ cup pitted and coarsely chopped kalamata olives; ½ cup bottled Italian or Greek dressing; and 3 Tbsp. chopped fresh oregano

READER RECIPE
Creole Potato Salad

make-ahead • party perfect

MAKES 10 TO 12 SERVINGS
HANDS-ON TIME: 35 MIN.
TOTAL TIME: 1 HR., 43 MIN.

- 5 lb. baby red potatoes
- ¼ cup dry shrimp-and-crab boil seasoning
- 12 hard-cooked eggs, peeled and chopped
- 1½ cups finely chopped celery
- 1 cup finely chopped green onions
- 1½ Tbsp. Creole seasoning
- 2 cups mayonnaise
- ⅓ cup Creole mustard

1. Bring potatoes, shrimp-and-crab boil, and 4 qt. water to a boil in a large stockpot over high heat. Boil 20 minutes or until tender; drain and cool 20 minutes.

2. Peel potatoes; cut into ¾-inch pieces. Toss together potatoes, eggs, and next 3 ingredients; stir in mayonnaise and mustard.

RECIPE FROM SHARON CHEADLE
SLIDELL, LOUISIANA

Note: We tested with Zatarain's Pro Boil and Tony Chachere's Creole Seasoning.

TRY THIS TWIST!
Cajun Shrimp Potato Salad: Stir in 1 lb. peeled, medium-size cooked shrimp (51/60 count).

A Little Southern Know-How

Our Favorite Pimiento Cheese

Make this crowd-pleaser in minutes—but every step counts, so no fudging!

1 Make the Mayo Mixture

In a large bowl, stir together 1½ cups of high-quality mayonnaise, such as Hellmann's or Duke's; 1 (4-oz.) jar diced pimiento, drained; 1 tsp. Worcestershire sauce; 1 tsp. finely grated onion; and ¼ tsp. ground red pepper until blended.

2 Toast the Pecans

Toasting brings out the rich flavor of the nuts. Preheat your oven to 350°. Bake 1 cup chopped pecans in a single layer in a shallow pan 8 to 10 minutes or until toasted and fragrant, stirring halfway through. (Stirring helps to ensure even browning.)

3 Shred the Cheese

Trust us—texture matters. Using the small side of a box grater, finely shred 1 (8-oz.) block extra-sharp Cheddar cheese. Then use the large side of the grater to coarsely shred 1 (8-oz.) block sharp Cheddar cheese. Fresh cheese makes a difference.

4 Stir and Enjoy

Add pecans and shredded cheeses to mayo mixture, stirring until blended. You can store it in the refrigerator up to 1 week. Serve with celery sticks and assorted crackers, or make a grilled pimiento cheese sandwich in a skillet or panini press.

Beverage Bar

Easy Party Idea: Let guests help themselves to their beverage of choice. Simply display small carafes—filled with iced tea, water, lemonade, or juice—nestled in ice in a large serving bowl.

Look for carafes at kitchen shops or restaurant supply stores.

Lighten Up
Fried Shrimp

Oven "frying" gets the crunch we love in oil-cooked shrimp with less fat.

This oven-fried favorite gets its tropical flavor from jerk seasoning and coconut and its crispy coating from Japanese breadcrumbs. It's as tasty as the fried version without all the mess and fat grams. Serve with creamy Honey-Mustard Sauce, made with nonfat yogurt, coarse-grained mustard, honey, and a kick of horseradish.

Coconut Shrimp

quick prep • good for you • party perfect

MAKES 4 SERVINGS **HANDS-ON TIME:** 20 MIN.
TOTAL TIME: 35 MIN., INCLUDING SAUCE

- 1½ lb. unpeeled, large raw shrimp (21/25 count)
  Vegetable cooking spray
- 2 egg whites
- ¼ cup cornstarch
- 1 Tbsp. Caribbean jerk seasoning
- 1 cup sweetened flaked coconut
- 1 cup Japanese breadcrumbs (panko)
- 1 tsp. paprika
  Honey-Mustard Sauce

1. Preheat oven to 425°. Peel shrimp, leaving tails on; devein shrimp, if desired.
2. Place a wire rack coated with cooking spray in a 15- x 10-inch jelly-roll pan.

3. Whisk egg whites in a bowl just until foamy.
4. Stir together cornstarch and Caribbean jerk seasoning in a shallow dish.
5. Stir together coconut, breadcrumbs, and paprika in another shallow dish.
6. Dredge shrimp, 1 at a time, in cornstarch mixture; dip in egg whites, and dredge in coconut mixture, pressing gently with fingers. Lightly coat shrimp with cooking spray; arrange shrimp on wire rack.
7. Bake at 425° for 10 to 12 .minutes or just until shrimp turn pink, turning after 8 minutes. Serve with Honey-Mustard Sauce.

PER SERVING: CALORIES 446; **FAT** 10G (**SAT** 6G, **MONO** 1G, **POLY** 1.3G); **PROTEIN** 40.5G; **CARB** 47.9G; **FIBER** 1.9G; **CHOL** 259MG; **IRON** 4.7MG; **SODIUM** 774MG; **CALC** 137MG

TRY THIS TWIST!
Coconut Chicken: Substitute 1½ lb. chicken breast tenders for shrimp. Proceed with recipe as directed, beginning with Step 2 and increasing bake time to 18 to 20 minutes or until chicken is done, turning once after 12 minutes. Sprinkle with salt to taste, if desired.

PER SERVING (NOT INCLUDING SALT TO TASTE): CALORIES 448; **FAT** 11G (**SAT** 6.6G, **MONO** 1.9G, **POLY** 1G); **PROTEIN** 40.3G; **CARB** 46.4G; **FIBER** 1.9G; **CHOL** 94MG; **IRON** 1.7MG; **SODIUM** 604MG; **CALC** 65MG

Coatings help seal in moisture.

Honey-Mustard Sauce:

quick prep • good for you • party perfect

MAKES ABOUT 1¼ CUPS **HANDS-ON TIME:** 5 MIN.
TOTAL TIME: 5 MIN.

- ½ cup plain nonfat yogurt
- ¼ cup coarse-grained mustard
- ¼ cup honey
- 2 Tbsp. horseradish

1. Stir together all ingredients. Serve immediately, or cover and chill up to 3 days.

PER TBSP.: CALORIES 16; **FAT** 0G (**SAT** 0G, **MONO** 0G, **POLY** 0G); **PROTEIN** 0.3G; **CARB** 4.1G; **FIBER** 0.1G; **CHOL** 0.1MG; **IRON** 0MG; **SODIUM** 47MG; **CALC** 9MG

In Her Mother's Footsteps

Working in the *Southern Living* Test Kitchen has brought Marian Cairns full circle to a career inspired by her mom, Jane. She shares her story and recipes with us.

When Marian Cairns, Test Kitchen Specialst/ Food Stylist, was in the third grade, her mother, Jane, took a job in the *Southern Living* Test Kitchen. Marian would watch her get out of the car every night around 5 with a brown paper bag. The question was always: What's inside?

Marian and her sister knew it was leftovers from that day's tasting, always on a white oval Chinet plate in a zip-top plastic bag. It could be a casserole that had gone horribly wrong, poached fish, or—if they were really lucky—a dish that had gotten a high rating. The mystery of that paper bag is just one of the things she remembers when she thinks of her mother.

Marian works for *Southern Living* now herself, as a Test Kitchen Professional, the same job her mother held for 10 years. But if you told her 10 years ago she'd be working here, she'd have said you were crazy. Marian's mother was always against her having a food career. In high school, Marian just mentioned the *possibility* of attending culinary school, and her mother said, "Absolutely not!" She wanted Marian to find her own path, which she definitely did. Marian was the girl with pink hair who dropped out of college and worked in retail.

But Marian always loved food and entertaining. As a kid, she would sit on the beat-up kitchen stool and talk to her mom as she cooked. She'd offer little tips like, "Marian, you never want to have more than one crunchy thing in your menu." Marian learned so much from her. They always discussed the contents of that day's brown bag during the meal. And when they went out to eat, they'd rate the food just like they were at taste testing! Marian just thought that was normal.

Marian's mom was great at entertaining. Her food was always beautifully presented, though she sometimes went over the top. Once, as a house guest was leaving after a weekend of huge meals, she ran down the driveway after him, waving a package of her sausage biscuits for the road. She was very Southern and proper—she always, always wrote thank-you notes—but she knew how to loosen up and have fun too.

When Jane died in 2002, they were all devastated. Marian was a total mess. Her dad had recently told her to find a career that mattered to her, so Marian knew she had to do that. Marian met her husband, Lee, six weeks before her mom died. He was the one who really encouraged her to go to culinary school. He made Marian believe she could do it and that it was *worth* doing.

When Marian was invited to interview for a position in the Test Kitchen, she had a real feeling of coming home. Here she was at the same dining table where her mother had taste-tested recipes for so many years, with editors who had known her. One of them said, "Marian's a legacy," just as if she were joining a sorority. Marian thought, "I want to be a part of that sorority." Now she is, and she absolutely loves it.

Marian honestly thinks her mom would be glad she ended up where she is. Her mom loved working with *Southern Living* and appreciated the caring that her co-workers showed. During her illness, one of them, Judy Feagin, would often call to say, "I'm dropping supper by." Her offering was all too familiar: an oval Chinet plate in a brown paper bag with leftovers from the Test Kitchen. Marian has no doubt her mom was silently rating those recipes right up until the end. Enjoy Marian's fresh takes on some of her mom's signature recipes.

Black Beans and Coconut-Lime Rice

good for you

MAKES 6 SERVINGS
HANDS-ON TIME: 35 MIN.
TOTAL TIME: 48 MIN.

Marian says she was probably the only child sent off to college with packets of yellow rice mix and canned black beans tucked into her dorm room necessities. This is her latest tropical version.

- 1 cup sweetened flaked coconut
- 1½ cups chicken broth
- ¼ tsp. salt
- ¼ tsp. pepper
- 3 Tbsp. butter, divided
- 1¼ cups uncooked basmati rice
- 1 small onion, chopped
- 1 poblano pepper, diced
- 2 (15-oz.) cans black beans, drained and rinsed
- 2 tsp. chili powder
- 1 tsp. ground cumin
- 1 lime
- 2 green onions, thinly sliced
- ½ cup chopped fresh cilantro
  Toppings: lime wedges, diced mango, sliced radishes, sliced fresh jalapeño peppers, sour cream

1. Preheat oven to 350°. Bake coconut in a single layer on a baking sheet 8 to 10 minutes or until toasted.

2. Bring broth, next 2 ingredients, 2 Tbsp. butter, and 1 cup water to a boil in a 2-qt. saucepan. Stir in rice. Cover, reduce heat to low, and cook 15 to 20 minutes or until rice is tender and water is absorbed.

3. Meanwhile, melt remaining 1 Tbsp. butter in a medium saucepan over medium-high heat; add onion and poblano pepper, and sauté 5 minutes or until tender. Stir in black beans, chili powder, cumin, and ¾ cup water. Cook over medium-low heat, stirring occasionally, 15 minutes.

4. Grate zest from lime, avoiding pale bitter pith, into a bowl; squeeze juice from lime into bowl.

5. Fluff rice with a fork. Fold lime zest and juice, coconut, green onions, and cilantro into hot cooked rice. Serve bean mixture over rice with desired toppings.

Simple Beet Salad

quick prep • good for you • make-ahead

MAKES 6 TO 8 SERVINGS
HANDS-ON TIME: 20 MIN.
TOTAL TIME: 2 HR., 5 MIN.

Pickled beets were a point of contention between Marian and her mother, but she thinks they would have agreed on this fresher version. (pictured on page 169)

2 lb. assorted medium beets
⅓ cup bottled balsamic vinaigrette
   Salt and pepper
½ cup chopped walnuts
   Garnish: fresh parsley leaves

1. Preheat oven to 400°. Divide beets between 2 large pieces of heavy-duty aluminum foil, drizzle with balsamic vinaigrette, and sprinkle with desired amount of salt and pepper. Seal foil, making 2 loose packets.

2. Bake at 400° for 45 to 55 minutes until fork-tender.

3. Let cool 1 hour in packets, reserving accumulated liquid.

4. Bake walnuts at 400° in a single layer in a shallow pan 8 to 10 minutes or until toasted and fragrant.

5. Peel beets, and cut into slices or wedges. Arrange beets on a serving platter or in a bowl. Drizzle with reserved liquid, and sprinkle with walnuts. Garnish, if desired.

Cava Sangria

quick prep • party perfect

MAKES 4¼ CUPS
HANDS-ON TIME: 5 MIN.
TOTAL TIME: 5 MIN.

Marian's mom always served a big punch bowl cocktail for parties. Make this fast version for parties of 4 or 24.

8 large mint leaves
1 (750-milliliter) bottle Cava sparkling wine, chilled*
¾ cup white grape juice, chilled
½ cup sliced fresh strawberries
¼ cup orange liqueur
   Garnish: fresh sugar cane sticks

1. Press mint leaves against sides of a large pitcher with back of a wooden spoon to release flavors. Stir in sparkling wine and next 3 ingredients. Serve immediately over ice. Garnish, if desired.

*Other sparkling wine or Champagne may be substituted.

Note: We tested with Cointreau and Grand Marnier orange liqueurs.

Pavlova with Lemon Cream and Berries

MAKES 8 SERVINGS
HANDS-ON TIME: 30 MIN.
TOTAL TIME: 14 HR.

Marian's mother's signature dessert. Assemble it just before serving, but you can make the meringue up to two days ahead; store in an airtight container. (pictured on page 9)

1 cup sugar
1 Tbsp. cornstarch
4 egg whites, at room temperature
¼ tsp. cream of tartar
   Pinch of salt
¼ tsp. vanilla extract
   Parchment paper
1 (10-oz.) jar lemon curd
⅓ cup sour cream
   Assorted fresh berries
   Garnish: fresh lemon zest

1. Preheat oven to 225°. Whisk together sugar and cornstarch. Beat egg whites at medium-high speed with a heavy-duty electric stand mixer 1 minute; add cream of tartar and salt, beating until blended. Gradually add sugar mixture, 1 Tbsp. at a time, beating at medium-high speed until mixture is glossy, stiff peaks form, and sugar dissolves. (Do not overbeat.) Beat in vanilla. Gently spread mixture into a 7-inch round on a parchment paper-lined baking sheet, making an indentation in center of meringue to hold filling.

2. Bake at 225° for 1 hour and 30 minutes or until pale golden and outside has formed a crust. Turn oven off; let meringue stand in oven, with door closed and light on, 12 hours.

3. Meanwhile, whisk together lemon curd and sour cream until smooth. Cover and chill.

4. Spoon lemon mixture into center of meringue, and top with berries. (Center of meringue may fall once the lemon mixture and berries have been added.) Garnish, if desired.

Chocolate Chip Bundt Cake

make-ahead • party perfect

MAKES 12 SERVINGS **HANDS-ON TIME:** 25 MIN.
TOTAL TIME: 2 HR., 25 MIN.

This is Marian's sister Jennifer's favorite birthday cake. She has been known to ask for two on her special day (one for her and one for everyone else).

- ⅔ cup chopped pecans
- ¼ cup butter, softened
- 2 Tbsp. granulated sugar
- 2¾ cups all-purpose flour
- 1 tsp. baking soda
- 1 tsp. salt
- 1 cup butter, softened
- 1 cup firmly packed dark brown sugar
- ½ cup granulated sugar
- 1 Tbsp. vanilla extract
- 4 large eggs
- 1 cup buttermilk
- 1 (12-oz.) package semisweet chocolate mini-morsels
  Garnishes: whipped cream, cherries

1. Preheat oven to 350°. Stir together first 3 ingredients in a small bowl, using a fork. Sprinkle in a greased and floured 12-cup Bundt pan.
2. Whisk together flour, baking soda, and salt.
3. Beat butter, brown sugar, granulated sugar, and vanilla at medium speed with a heavy-duty electric stand mixer 3 to 5 minutes or until fluffy. Add eggs, 1 at a time, beating just until blended. Add flour mixture alternately with buttermilk, beginning and ending with flour mixture. Beat at low speed just until blended after each addition, stopping to scrape bowl as needed. Beat in chocolate mini-morsels. (Mixture will be thick.) Spoon batter into prepared pan.
4. Bake at 350° for 50 to 55 minutes or until a long wooden pick inserted in center comes out clean. Cool in pan on a wire rack 10 minutes; remove from pan to wire rack, and cool completely (about 1 hour). Garnish, if desired.

Cooking Class
Classic Pound Cake

It takes only six ingredients and two easy steps to create this buttery, from-scratch Southern staple.

Two-Step Pound Cake

quick prep • make-ahead • party perfect

MAKES 10 TO 12 SERVINGS
HANDS-ON TIME: 15 MIN.
TOTAL TIME: 2 HR., 55 MIN.

You'll need a heavy-duty stand mixer with a 4-qt. bowl and paddle attachment for this recipe.

- 4 cups all-purpose flour
- 3 cups sugar
- 2 cups butter, softened
- ¾ cup milk
- 6 large eggs
- 2 tsp. vanilla extract

Test Kitchen Notebook

"It's simple to soften butter to that just-right stage," says Angela Sellers, Test Kitchen Professional. "Remove butter from the refrigerator 2 hours before using, and let it stand in a cool, shaded spot. Test softness by gently pressing the top of the stick with your index finger. If an indentation remains and the stick of butter still holds its shape, it's ready to use."

Two Easy Steps

1 Layer Ingredients & Mix

Preheat oven to 325°. Place flour, sugar, butter, milk, eggs, and vanilla (in that order) in 4-qt. bowl of a heavy-duty electric stand mixer. Beat at low speed 1 minute, stopping to scrape down sides. Beat at medium speed 2 minutes.

2 Pour & Bake

Pour into a greased and floured 10-inch (16-cup) tube pan, and smooth. Bake at 325° for 1 hour and 30 minutes or until a long wooden pick inserted in center comes out clean. Cool in pan on a wire rack 10 minutes. Remove from pan to wire rack, and cool completely (about 1 hour).

Mama's Way or Your Way?
Squash Casserole

One bakes in the oven. The other cooks in the microwave. Both are luscious and loaded with flavor.

Recipes from

Becky Saarela and Tiffany Andrews

Alpharetta, Georgia

Two-Cheese Squash Casserole

MAKES 10 TO 12 SERVINGS
HANDS-ON TIME: 25 MIN.
TOTAL TIME: 1 HR., 8 MIN.

For a tasty and colorful twist, substitute sliced zucchini for half of the yellow squash.

- 4   lb. yellow squash, sliced
- 1   large sweet onion, finely chopped
- 1   cup (4 oz.) shredded Cheddar cheese
- ½   cup chopped fresh chives
- 1   (8-oz.) container sour cream
- 1   tsp. garlic salt
- 1   tsp. freshly ground pepper
- 2   large eggs, lightly beaten
- 2½ cups soft, fresh breadcrumbs, divided
- 1¼ cups (5 oz.) freshly shredded Parmesan cheese, divided
- 2   Tbsp. butter, melted

1. Preheat oven to 350°. Cook yellow squash and onion in boiling water to cover in a Dutch oven 8 minutes or just until tender; drain squash mixture well.

2. Combine squash mixture, Cheddar cheese, next 5 ingredients, 1 cup breadcrumbs, and ¾ cup Parmesan cheese. Spoon into a lightly greased 13- x 9-inch baking dish.

3. Stir together melted butter and remaining 1½ cups breadcrumbs and ½ cup Parmesan cheese. Sprinkle breadcrumb mixture over top of casserole.

4. Bake at 350° for 35 to 40 minutes or until set.

Summer Squash Casserole

quick prep

MAKES 6 TO 8 SERVINGS
HANDS-ON TIME: 10 MIN.
TOTAL TIME: 40 MIN.

- 2½ lb. yellow squash, sliced
- ¾   cup chopped green onions
- 1   cup reduced-fat mayonnaise
- 2   large eggs, lightly beaten
- 1   Tbsp. all-purpose flour
- ½   tsp. salt
- 1   (10-oz.) block sharp Cheddar cheese, shredded
- 1   cup soft, fresh breadcrumbs
- 2   Tbsp. butter, melted

1. Combine squash and green onions in a large microwave-safe bowl. Cover tightly with plastic wrap, folding back a small edge to allow steam to escape. Microwave at HIGH 8 minutes or until squash is tender. (Do not drain.)

2. Whisk together mayonnaise and next 3 ingredients in a large bowl; stir in squash mixture and cheese. Spoon mixture into a lightly greased 11- x 7-inch baking dish; cover tightly with plastic wrap, folding back a small edge to allow steam to escape. Microwave at HIGH 10 minutes or until casserole is set; remove from microwave, and let stand 10 minutes.

3. Stir together breadcrumbs and melted butter; microwave 2 minutes. Sprinkle over casserole.

Squash Tip: When selecting yellow squash, be sure to look at the stem; it can indicate the quality of the squash. If the stem is hard, dry, shriveled, or dark, the squash is not fresh.

Half-Hour Hostess

Kick off your KENTUCKY DERBY PARTY in just 30 minutes with delicious biscuits, a festive cheese nibble, and a classic cocktail.

Blackberry Mustard and Lemon-Herb Butter can both be made while mint syrup stands.

1 | Country Ham and Biscuits

For a Derby Day classic, bake **frozen tea biscuits** (Mary B's is one of our favorite brands), and fill with thin slices of **country ham** that have been browned in a hot skillet 1 to 2 minutes on each side. Have guests dress biscuits with **flavored butter** and **mustard blends**.

2 | Blackberry Mustard

Stir together ½ cup **blackberry preserves** and 2 Tbsp. **Dijon mustard**. Makes about ⅔ cup. Hands-on time: 5 min.; Total time: 5 min.

Recipe Note

Microwave a cold stick of butter for five seconds to quickly soften for Lemon-Herb Butter. Order authentic Kentucky beaten biscuits and sliced country ham from Browning's Country Hams and Gifts (*paulwbrowning.com/countryhams* or 859/987-2702).

---

3 | Lemon-Herb Butter

Stir together ½ cup softened **butter**, 2 Tbsp. chopped fresh **parsley**, 2 tsp. chopped fresh **chives**, and 2 tsp. **lemon zest**. Makes about ½ cup. Hands-on time: 5 min.; Total time: 5 min.

Serve with assorted crackers and precut veggies.

4 | Derby Cheese Hat

Place 1 (13.2-oz., 5¼-inch) **Brie round** on a serving platter. Top with 1 (5.2-oz., 2¾-inch) round buttery **garlic-and-herb spreadable cheese**. Garnish with ribbon and an herb bouquet of fresh **lavender**, fresh **thyme** sprigs, and fresh **mint** sprigs. **Note:** We used Boursin cheese for spreadable cheese.

The mint syrup is also terrific stirred into iced tea.

5 | Mint Julep

Bring 2 cups **sugar** and 2 cups water to a boil in a small saucepan, and stir until sugar dissolves. Remove from heat. Add 1 (1-oz.) package fresh **mint**, torn. Let stand 10 minutes. Pour through a wire-mesh strainer into a bowl. Pour 2 Tbsp. mint syrup over ice into a 12-oz. julep cup. Fill with **bourbon** and, if desired, a splash of **club soda**. Reserve remaining mint syrup for another use. Garnish with fresh **mint**, if desired. Makes 1 serving. Hands-on time: 5 min.; Total time: 20 min.

June

The Lazy Days of Summerland

In Georgia's pastoral hills, renowned chef Anne Quatrano escapes the Atlanta heat to chill out with friends at Summerland Farm.

When you see her spoons, you understand something essential about Anne Quatrano. Dozens of antique-looking spoons sit under a glass box in her home kitchen in Cartersville, Georgia. Teaspoons, salt spoons, silver dessert spoons, common table stirrers. All bear silver etchings and lettering, family initials, and heirloom patterns, and the collection lies together in prominent view. The James Beard award-winning chef sits at a long heart-pine table inside her spacious farmhouse kitchen about an hour northwest of her foodie utopia on Atlanta's west side, where restaurants Bacchanalia and Abbatoir and gourmet general store Star Provisions anchor a surging neighborhood. It is the middle of summer here, in Bartow County, and the reddish Etowah River softly eddies and floats along the edge of Summerland, Anne's sixth-generation family farm, the river's rush long lessened since its beginning near Amicalola Falls.

It is the chef's day off, and Anne (her friends call her Annie) is cooking a meal. She pulls dragon tongue and yellow wax pole beans from her home garden to dry fry in a hot pan, while friends from the restaurants scurry about fixing what in a few hours will be a summer feast. Andy Carson, a chef at Bacchanalia, layers pickled Georgia white shrimp with mustard seeds, peppercorns, coriander, sliced fennel bulbs, and torpedo onions, in a glass jar the size of a hydrant. Melissa Khorry, former sous chef at Abbatoir, salts a bowl of plump red, yellow, and orange tomatoes, and Matt Adolphi, yet another chef from Bacchanalia, walks in with culinary supplies.

"Ohhh, you got good butter," Anne says with a gush. "Southern butter." The slow-churned sticks come from a plantation dairy in South Louisiana. "What kind of fat do you have for the trout?" she asks.

Outside the kitchen, others set a huge harvest table underneath a shade tree, steps from curious horses. Anne's vintage bottles and jars rest on the table and hold cuttings from the lush river valley: umbrella fern, feverfew, lily grass, and Queen Anne's lace. Clifford Harrison, Anne's partner and co-executive chef, carries freshly plucked thyme and rosemary under a scuppernong archway, a trio of wet dogs bouncing behind. The table will seat everyone, a dozen of her staff, whom Anne treats more like dear friends. You can tell, by her peaceful disposition and her precise attention to the day's details, that the summer meal on her farm matters greatly to the chef. She is known widely for her style and her menus; what stands out on Summerland on this day is her playful wonder at all things related to a gathering. The relaxed, airy sophistication of the table setting. The simple, homegrown menu of June harvest. The basket of candles hanging from the tree.

"On my fiftieth birthday, my best friends came together from all over—Nantucket, San Francisco, New York, Atlanta," Anne says. "And each one gave me a spoon. Heirlooms and antiques." Holding half a dozen in her hands, she looks down like they were pictures of kin. A light breeze picks up as the sun leans toward the western treeline. Her guests circle the table, making their plates, pouring fruit tea, laughing. Annie beams. It is not a meal. It is family supper.

Blackberry Cocktail
quick prep • party perfect

MAKES 5 CUPS

HANDS-ON TIME: 20 MIN.

TOTAL TIME: 20 MIN.

"This drink is a refreshing use of Southern mint and early-summer blackberries."

- 1 (0.75-oz.) package fresh mint sprigs
- 12 (¼-inch-thick) cucumber slices
- 2 (6-oz.) packages fresh blackberries
- ¾ cup fresh lime juice (about 3 limes)
- 8 to 12 tsp. turbinado sugar*
- 1 cup plus 2 Tbsp. gin
- 1 cup cold club soda
   Crushed ice
   Garnishes: cucumber slices, fresh blackberries, lime wedges, lemon mint sprigs

1. Place first 5 ingredients in a large pitcher. Gently press mint leaves, cucumbers, and blackberries against side of pitcher with a wooden spoon to release flavors. Stir in gin and club soda. Serve over ice. Garnish, if desired.
*Superfine or powdered sugar may be substituted.
Note: We tested with Hendrick's Gin.

Pickled Beets
quick prep • make-ahead

MAKES 4 SERVINGS
HANDS-ON TIME: 20 MIN.
TOTAL TIME: 10 HR., 10 MIN.

"Pickled beets are something you can put in the refrigerator and have all the time."

- 4 medium beets (1 lb.)
- 1 Tbsp. white vinegar
- 1 tsp. honey
- ⅛ tsp. salt
- ⅛ tsp. pepper
- ½ cup red wine vinegar
- 2½ Tbsp. honey
- 1 Tbsp. minced crystallized ginger
- 1 shallot, minced
- ½ tsp. salt
- ⅛ tsp. pepper
- ¼ cup olive oil

1. Preheat oven to 300°. Trim beet stems to 1 inch; gently wash beets. Place on an aluminum foil-lined 15- x 10-inch jelly-roll pan.
2. Stir together 1 Tbsp. white vinegar, 1 tsp. honey, and 1 cup water; pour mixture over beets. Season with ⅛ tsp. each salt and pepper. Cover pan tightly with foil.
3. Bake at 300° for 1½ hours or until tender. Uncover; let cool 20 minutes.
4. Meanwhile, whisk together ½ cup red wine vinegar and next 5 ingredients in a bowl. Add oil in a slow, steady stream, whisking constantly until smooth.
5. Peel beets, and remove stem ends. Cut beets into 1-inch wedges. Place beets in 1 (16-oz.) jar. Pour vinegar mixture over beets. Cover and chill 8 hours before serving. Store in refrigerator up to 4 days.

Anne's Favorite Southern Cheeses

For your summer gathering, try these regional cheesemakers.

- **"Kelle's Blue"**; Sweet Grass Dairy, Thomasville, Georgia; *sweetgrassdairy.com*

- **"Awe Brie"**; Kenny's Farmhouse Cheese, Austin, Kentucky; *kennyscountrycheese.com*

- **"Red Hill Cheddar"**; Yellow Moon Cheese Co., Alexandria, Alabama; *yellowmooncheese.com*

- **"Singing Brook"**; Blackberry Farm, Walland, Tennessee; *blackberryfarmshop.com*

Goat Cheese Cheesecakes with Summer Berries
quick prep • make-ahead • party perfect

MAKES 10 SERVINGS
HANDS-ON TIME: 30 MIN.
TOTAL TIME: 8 HR., 27 MIN., INCLUDING BERRIES

"You can make the cake ahead of time, cook it in the jars, and then add berries just before serving."

- 1 cup graham cracker crumbs
- 4 Tbsp. melted butter
- 1 Tbsp. sugar
  Pinch of salt
- 1 (0.25-oz.) envelope unflavored gelatin
- ⅓ cup milk
- ½ (8-oz.) package cream cheese, softened
- 1 (4-oz.) goat cheese log
- ⅓ cup sugar
- 2 tsp. lemon zest
  Pinch of salt
- 1¼ cups heavy cream
  Summer Berries

1. Stir together graham cracker crumbs, butter, sugar, and salt. Divide mixture among 10 (8-oz.) glasses (about 1 heaping tablespoonful each); press mixture onto bottoms of glasses. Chill 30 minutes.
2. Sprinkle gelatin over milk in a small saucepan, and let stand 1 minute. Cook milk mixture over medium-low heat, whisking constantly, 3 to 5 minutes or until gelatin is dissolved. Remove from heat.
3. Beat cream cheese and goat cheese at medium speed with a heavy-duty electric stand mixer, using whisk attachment, until smooth. Beat in ⅓ cup sugar, lemon zest, and salt. Slowly add milk mixture, beating until combined.
4. Beat heavy cream at high speed, using whisk attachment, until soft peaks form. Gently fold into cheese mixture. Divide mixture among glasses (about ⅓ cup each). Cover and chill 6 to 48 hours. Let stand at room temperature 30 minutes. Top with Summer Berries just before serving.

Summer Berries:

MAKES ABOUT 3 CUPS
HANDS-ON TIME: 5 MIN.
TOTAL TIME: 1 HR., 5 MIN.

- 1 cup fresh blackberries
- 1 cup fresh blueberries
- 1 cup fresh raspberries
- ½ cup sugar
- 2 Tbsp. fresh lemon juice

1. Stir together all ingredients; cover and chill 1 hour.

A Laid-back Party

Simplify your entertaining with this quick
and easy menu.

If Willson Powell and Karen Brosius invite you to supper, by all means, go. Karen, executive director of the Columbia (South Carolina) Museum of Art, is a terrific cook and often hosts the museum's young professionals group at casual gatherings. The vibe is relaxed, fun, and definitely delicious.

Lemon Chicken

quick prep • good for you

MAKES 8 SERVINGS
HANDS-ON TIME: 30 MIN.
TOTAL TIME: 30 MIN.
(pictured on page 179)

- 4 skinned and boned chicken breasts (about 1½ lb.)
- 1 tsp. salt
- ½ tsp. pepper
- ⅓ cup all-purpose flour
- 4 Tbsp. butter, divided
- 2 Tbsp. olive oil, divided
- ¼ cup chicken broth
- ¼ cup lemon juice
- 8 lemon slices
- ¼ cup chopped fresh flat-leaf parsley
  Garnish: lemon slices

1. Cut each chicken breast in half lengthwise. Place chicken between 2 sheets of heavy-duty plastic wrap; flatten to ¼-inch thickness, using a rolling pin or flat side of a meat mallet. Sprinkle chicken with salt and pepper. Lightly dredge chicken in flour, shaking off excess.
2. Melt 1 Tbsp. butter with 1 Tbsp. olive oil in a large nonstick skillet over medium-high heat. Cook half of chicken in skillet 2 to 3 minutes on each side or until golden brown and done. Transfer chicken to a serving platter, and keep warm. Repeat procedure with 1 Tbsp. butter and remaining olive oil and chicken.
3. Add broth and lemon juice to skillet, and cook 1 to 2 minutes or until sauce is slightly thickened, stirring to loosen particles from bottom of skillet. Add 8 lemon slices.
4. Remove skillet from heat; add parsley and remaining 2 Tbsp. butter, and stir until butter melts. Pour sauce over chicken. Serve immediately. Garnish, if desired.

Green Beans with Goat Cheese, Tomatoes, and Almonds

quick prep • good for you

MAKES 6 TO 8 SERVINGS
HANDS-ON TIME: 21 MIN.
TOTAL TIME: 27 MIN.
(pictured on page 179)

- ½ cup sliced almonds
- 2 lb. haricots verts (tiny green beans), trimmed
- 3 Tbsp. sherry vinegar*
- 2 Tbsp. fresh lemon juice
- ¾ tsp. salt
- ½ tsp. pepper
- ⅓ cup olive oil
- 1 pt. cherry tomatoes, halved
- 2 shallots, thinly sliced
- 2 garlic cloves, minced
- ½ (4-oz.) goat cheese log, crumbled

1. Preheat oven to 350°. Bake almonds in a single layer in a shallow pan 6 to 8 minutes or until lightly toasted and fragrant, stirring halfway through.
2. Cook green beans in boiling salted water to cover 6 to 8 minutes or until crisp-tender; drain. Plunge beans into ice water to stop the cooking process; drain.
3. Whisk together vinegar and next 3 ingredients in a large bowl; add olive oil in a slow, steady stream, whisking constantly, until blended and smooth. Add cherry tomatoes, shallots, garlic, and green beans; toss to coat.
4. Top green bean mixture with crumbled goat cheese and toasted almonds.
*White wine vinegar may be substituted.

Carrot Orzo

good for you

MAKES 6 TO 8 SERVINGS
HANDS-ON TIME: 41 MIN.
TOTAL TIME: 41 MIN.

Though made with orzo rather than rice, this colorful dish is similar to risotto. (pictured on page 179)

 8 oz. carrots, cut into 1-inch pieces (about 2 cups)
2½ cups chicken broth
 3 Tbsp. butter
 1 medium onion, chopped
 2 cups uncooked orzo pasta
 2 garlic cloves, minced
 1 tsp. salt
 ½ tsp. pepper
 1 cup freshly grated Parmesan cheese
 3 Tbsp. chopped fresh chives
 1 tsp. chopped fresh thyme
     Garnish: carrot curls

1. Process carrots in a food processor 15 seconds or until finely chopped.
2. Combine 2½ cups water and broth in a microwave-safe measuring cup. Microwave at HIGH 5 minutes or until very hot.
3. Meanwhile, melt butter in a large saucepan over medium heat. Add carrots and onion, and cook, stirring occasionally, 5 minutes or until tender. Add orzo and garlic, and cook 1 minute.
4. Slowly stir hot broth mixture, salt, and pepper into orzo mixture. Cook, stirring often, 15 to 18 minutes or until liquid is absorbed.
5. Stir in Parmesan cheese, chives, and thyme until blended. Serve orzo immediately. Garnish, if desired.

Profiteroles with Coffee Whipped Cream

Profiteroles with Coffee Whipped Cream

MAKES ABOUT 2 DOZEN
HANDS-ON TIME: 20 MIN.
TOTAL TIME: 1 HR., 10 MIN., INCLUDING COFFEE WHIPPED CREAM

These small cream puffs are surprisingly easy to make. Use a 1-inch scoop coated with cooking spray to drop dough onto baking sheet. Store cooled, unfilled puffs in an airtight container up to 2 days. (pictured on page 13)

 ¾ cup all-purpose flour
1½ tsp. sugar
 ⅓ cup butter
 3 large eggs, beaten
     Parchment paper
     Coffee Whipped Cream
     Hot fudge topping

1. Preheat oven to 400°. Stir together flour and sugar.
2. Bring butter and ¾ cup water to a boil in a 3-qt. saucepan over medium-high heat, stirring occasionally. Immediately remove from heat, and quickly stir in flour mixture all at once. Beat with a wooden spoon until mixture is smooth and leaves sides of pan, forming a ball of dough. Gradually add eggs, beating until mixture is smooth and glossy.
3. Drop dough by rounded tablespoonfuls onto a parchment paper–lined baking sheet.

4. Bake at 400° for 20 minutes or until puffy and golden brown. Remove from oven to a wire rack. Pierce 1 side of each cream puff with a knife to allow steam to escape. Cool completely on baking sheet (about 20 minutes).
5. Cut each cream puff in half horizontally. Dollop Coffee Whipped Cream onto bottom halves; top with remaining halves. Cover and chill until ready to serve. Drizzle with hot fudge topping just before serving.

TRY THIS TWIST!
Profiteroles with Coffee Ice Cream: Substitute 1½ cups coffee ice cream for Coffee Whipped Cream.

Coffee Whipped Cream:

MAKES ABOUT 2 CUPS
HANDS-ON TIME: 5 MIN.
TOTAL TIME: 5 MIN.

Stir together 2 Tbsp. coffee liqueur and 1 tsp. instant espresso until blended. Beat 1 cup heavy cream at medium-high speed with an electric mixer until foamy. Add liqueur mixture and 2 Tbsp. powdered sugar, and beat until soft peaks form.
Note: We tested with Kahlúa coffee liqueur.

Carolina Peach Sangria

quick prep • make-ahead • party perfect

MAKES ABOUT 9 CUPS
HANDS-ON TIME: 10 MIN.
TOTAL TIME: 8 HR., 10 MIN.

Be sure to use rosé, not white Zinfandel, in this cool drink. It is best to make this refreshing beverage the day before the party so that flavors will have a chance to blend. (pictured on page 178)

- 1 (750-milliliter) bottle rosé wine
- ¾ cup vodka*
- ½ cup peach nectar
- 6 Tbsp. thawed frozen lemonade concentrate
- 2 Tbsp. sugar
- 1 lb. ripe peaches, peeled and sliced
- 1 (6-oz.) package fresh raspberries**
- 2 cups club soda, chilled

1. Combine first 5 ingredients in a pitcher; stir until sugar is dissolved. Stir in peaches and raspberries. Cover and chill 8 hours.

2. Stir in chilled club soda just before serving.

*Peach-flavored vodka may be substituted. Omit peach nectar.

**1 cup frozen raspberries may be substituted.

In Season
Peaches

Golden and fragrant, with that beautiful rosy blush, the South's sweetest, juiciest peaches are just beginning to ripen. Break out your garden basket!

GRILLED PEACHES WITH BLACKBERRY–BASIL BUTTER : Stir together ½ cup softened butter, ¼ cup seedless blackberry preserves, and 2 Tbsp. finely chopped fresh basil until blended. Garnish with fresh basil leaves. Serve with warm grilled peaches, or spread inside hot biscuits filled with thinly sliced pork tenderloin. Makes ¾ cup butter.

Mama's Way or Your Way?
Peach Cobbler

One dessert is a rich summer classic. The other equally delectable version takes a much lighter approach.

Pecan-Peach Cobbler
party perfect

MAKES 10 TO 12 SERVINGS
HANDS-ON TIME: 45 MIN.
TOTAL TIME: 1 HR., 41 MIN.
(pictured on page 181)

- 12 to 15 fresh peaches, peeled and sliced (about 16 cups)
- ½ cup all-purpose flour
- ½ tsp. ground nutmeg
- 3 cups sugar
- ⅔ cup butter
- 1¼ tsp. vanilla extract
- 2 (14.1-oz.) packages refrigerated piecrusts
- ½ cup chopped pecans, toasted
- 5 Tbsp. sugar, divided
- Sweetened whipped cream

1. Preheat oven to 475°. Stir together peaches, flour, nutmeg, and 3 cups sugar in a Dutch oven. Bring to a boil over medium heat; reduce heat to low, and simmer 10 minutes. Remove from heat; stir in butter and vanilla. Spoon half of mixture into a lightly greased 13- x 9-inch baking dish.

2. Unroll 2 piecrusts. Sprinkle ¼ cup pecans and 2 Tbsp. sugar over 1 piecrust; top with other piecrust. Roll to a 14- x 10-inch rectangle. Trim sides to fit baking dish. Place pastry over peach mixture in dish.

3. Bake at 475° for 20 to 25 minutes or until lightly browned. Unroll remaining 2 piecrusts. Sprinkle 2 Tbsp. sugar and remaining ¼ cup pecans over 1 piecrust; top with remaining piecrust. Roll into a 12-inch circle. Cut into 1-inch strips, using a fluted pastry wheel. Spoon remaining peach mixture over baked pastry. Arrange pastry strips over peach mixture; sprinkle with remaining 1 Tbsp. sugar. Bake 15 to 18 minutes or until lightly browned. Serve warm or cold with whipped cream.

So-Easy Peach Cobbler
party perfect

MAKES 6 SERVINGS
HANDS-ON TIME: 30 MIN.
TOTAL TIME: 30 MIN.

- ¼ cup butter
- 7 fresh peaches, peeled and sliced (about 7 cups, 3 lb.)
- 1 cup sugar
- 2 Tbsp. all-purpose flour
- 2 Tbsp. fresh lemon juice
- ¼ tsp. ground cinnamon
- ½ (14.1-oz.) package refrigerated piecrusts
  Parchment paper
- 1 egg white, lightly beaten
- 1 Tbsp. sugar

1. Preheat oven to 450°. Melt butter in a Dutch oven over medium heat. Add peaches, 1 cup sugar, and next 3 ingredients; bring to a boil over medium heat, stirring occasionally. Reduce heat to medium-low; simmer 7 to 8 minutes or until tender.

2. Meanwhile, unroll piecrust on a flat surface. Cut into 12 circles, using a 3½-inch round cutter with fluted edges. Make 4 small holes in center of each circle, using a plastic straw. Place circles on a parchment paper-lined baking sheet. Whisk together egg white and 1 Tbsp. water. Brush circles with egg mixture; sprinkle with 1 Tbsp. sugar.

3. Bake at 450° for 8 to 10 minutes or until lightly browned.

4. Place 1 pastry circle in each of 6 (7-oz.) ramekins. Spoon peach mixture over pastry circles; top with remaining pastry circles.

Shrimp Sauces with a Twist

Stir up these easy, flavorful recipes to dip, dunk, or drench the South's favorite seafood.

Summer Shrimp Party

SERVES 4 TO 6

2 to 3 lbs boiled shrimp

Green Goddess Dipping Sauce

Carolina-Style Mignonette

Smoky Pecan Relish

Spicy Glazed Shrimp and Vegetable Kabobs

Hot cooked rice

Crusty French bread

Green Goddess Dipping Sauce

quick prep • make-ahead • party perfect

MAKES 1½ CUPS

HANDS-ON TIME: 10 MIN.

TOTAL TIME: 1 HR., 10 MIN.

No need for lots of chopping; let the food processor do all the work in this delicious herb-packed sauce.

- ¾ cup sour cream
- ½ cup firmly packed fresh parsley leaves
- ½ cup mayonnaise
- 1 green onion, chopped
- 1 Tbsp. firmly packed fresh dill leaves
- 1 Tbsp. firmly packed fresh tarragon leaves
- 2 tsp. lemon zest
- 1 Tbsp. lemon juice
- 1 garlic clove
- ½ tsp. salt
- ¼ tsp. pepper

Garnish: fresh dill sprig

1. Process first 11 ingredients in a food processor or blender 30 seconds or until smooth, stopping to scrape sides as needed. Cover and chill 1 hour before serving. Garnish, if desired. Store in refrigerator up to 1 week.

Carolina-Style Mignonette

quick prep • make-ahead • party perfect

MAKES 1 CUP

HANDS-ON TIME: 20 MIN.

TOTAL TIME: 2 HR., 50 MIN.

Sweet 'n' spicy!

Mignonette is a classic French vinegar-based sauce traditionally served with oysters. We gave it a Southern spin by adding a barbecue base with a touch of horseradish.

- 1 cup cider vinegar
- ¼ cup ketchup
- 3 Tbsp. brown sugar
- 1 Tbsp. coarse-grained Dijon mustard
- 2 shallots, minced
- 2 tsp. horseradish
- ½ tsp. salt
- ¼ to ½ tsp. dried crushed red pepper

1. Bring all ingredients to a boil in a medium-size nonaluminum saucepan over medium heat; reduce heat to low, and simmer, stirring occasionally, 5 minutes. Remove from heat, and let stand 30 minutes. Cover and chill 2 hours before serving. Store in refrigerator up to 2 weeks.

Smoky Pecan Relish

quick prep • good for you • make-ahead • party perfect

MAKES ABOUT 1½ CUPS

HANDS-ON TIME: 15 MIN.

TOTAL TIME: 3 HR., 8 MIN.

This Southern version of romesco sauce uses pecans instead of almonds. We also love this tasty relish served over grilled chicken.

- ½ cup pecan halves
- 1 (12-oz.) jar roasted red bell peppers, drained and rinsed
- 3 Tbsp. extra virgin olive oil
- 1 Tbsp. red wine vinegar
- 1 garlic clove, minced
- 1½ tsp. smoked paprika*
- ½ tsp. salt
- ¼ tsp. ground red pepper

1. Preheat oven to 350°. Bake pecans in a single layer in a shallow pan 8 to 10 minutes or until toasted and fragrant. Let cool 15 minutes.
2. Pat peppers dry with paper towels. Combine peppers, pecans, oil, and remaining ingredients in a food processor. Pulse 8 to 10 times or until finely chopped (but not smooth). Cover and chill 2 hours before serving. Store in refrigerator up to 1 week. Let stand at room temperature 30 minutes before serving.

*1 tsp. regular paprika with ½ tsp. ground cumin may be substituted.

Shrimp 1-2-3

Bring a large pot of heavily salted water to a boil, add shrimp (peeled or unpeeled), wait about 3 minutes or just until shrimp turn pink, and drain. Serve warm, or shock in ice water, drain, and chill.

Spicy Glazed Shrimp and Vegetable Kabobs

good for you • party perfect

MAKES 4 TO 6 SERVINGS
HANDS-ON TIME: 45 MIN.
TOTAL TIME: 1 HR., 15 MIN.

Serve these party-ready grilled kabobs with any of our three flavorful sauces on facing page.

Soak 16 (7- to 8-inch) **wooden skewers** in water 30 minutes. Stir together 2 Tbsp. each **honey** and **spicy brown mustard.** Toss 1½ lb. peeled, jumbo-size raw **shrimp** with tails (16/20 count) with 1 Tbsp. **Caribbean jerk seasoning,** 2 Tbsp. **olive oil,** and ¼ tsp. **salt.** Thread onto 8 skewers. Thread 3 **yellow squash,** cut into ¼- to ½-inch slices; 2 **zucchini,** cut into ¼- to ½-inch slices; and 1 **red bell pepper,** cut into 1½-inch pieces, onto remaining skewers. Brush vegetable kabobs with 1 Tbsp. olive oil; sprinkle with **salt and pepper** to taste. Grill kabobs, covered with grill lid, over 350° to 400° (medium-high) heat. Grill vegetables 15 minutes or until tender, turning occasionally. Grill shrimp 2 minutes on each side or just until shrimp turn pink. Baste shrimp with honey mixture. Serve immediately.

Test Kitchen Notebook

SHRIMP SECRETS

- When purchasing shrimp, the flesh should feel firm and slippery and have a mild, almost sweet odor. Avoid purchasing shrimp with an odor of ammonia, which indicates deterioration.

- Store shrimp in the refrigerator for up to two days. Shrimp can be frozen raw in the shell or cooked, peeled, and frozen for longer storage.

- To peel shrimp, run your finger along the underside of the shrimp between the legs and remove the shell. The tail can be left on the shrimp for show, if desired.

Season with Fresh Herbs

A handful of fragrant basil or a scattering of rosemary and thyme is all it takes to turn up the flavor in these easy-to-make summer dishes.

Blueberry-Gorgonzola Salad

quick prep • good for you • party perfect

MAKES 4 SERVINGS

HANDS-ON TIME: 15 MIN.

TOTAL TIME: 15 MIN.

This salad features a tasty mix of tender-leafed herbs and salad greens.

- 1 (5-oz.) package mixed salad greens
- 2 cups fresh blueberries
- 1 cup loosely packed fresh flat-leaf parsley leaves
- 1 cup loosely packed basil leaves
- 1 cup roasted, salted almonds*
- ¾ cup sliced fresh chives (about 1-inch pieces)
- ¾ cup crumbled Gorgonzola cheese
- ¾ cup bottled raspberry-walnut vinaigrette
- ½ cup loosely packed fresh tarragon leaves

1. Toss together all ingredients in a large serving bowl.

*Glazed walnuts may be substituted.

Olive Oil Dipping Sauce

quick prep • good for you • make-ahead • party perfect

MAKES 1¼ CUPS

HANDS-ON TIME: 10 MIN.

TOTAL TIME: 10 MIN.

Serve in small shallow bowls with warm, crusty bread.

- 1 cup olive oil
- 2 garlic cloves, minced
- 2 Tbsp. chopped fresh parsley
- 2 Tbsp. chopped fresh basil
- 2 tsp. chopped fresh oregano
- 2 tsp. chopped fresh rosemary
- 2 tsp. freshly ground pepper
- ½ tsp. dried crushed red pepper
- ½ tsp. salt

1. Stir together all ingredients. Serve immediately, or cover and chill up to 3 days.

Grilled Onions

quick prep • good for you

MAKES 6 SERVINGS

HANDS-ON TIME: 10 MIN.

TOTAL TIME: 30 MIN.

- ¼ cup olive oil
- ¼ cup balsamic vinegar
- 1 Tbsp. chopped fresh parsley
- 1 Tbsp. chopped fresh basil
- 1 Tbsp. chopped fresh thyme
- ½ tsp. salt
- ¼ tsp. pepper
- 4 large sweet onions

1. Preheat grill to 350° to 400° (medium-high) heat. Whisk together first 7 ingredients. Cut onions into ½-inch-thick slices; brush with herb mixture. Grill onions, covered with grill lid, 10 minutes on each side or until golden brown. Remove from grill. Pour remaining herb mixture over onions, and serve immediately.

Parmesan-Herb Hash Browns

quick prep

MAKES 4 SERVINGS

HANDS-ON TIME: 25 MIN.

TOTAL TIME: 25 MIN.

- 1 (30-oz.) package frozen shredded hash browns
- 1 cup (4 oz.) shredded Parmesan cheese
- ¼ cup chopped fresh parsley
- ¼ cup chopped fresh chives
- 1 Tbsp. chopped fresh rosemary
- 2 tsp. freshly ground pepper
- ½ tsp. salt

1. Toss together all ingredients. Prepare hash brown mixture according to package directions.

Marinated Mozzarella

quick prep • make-ahead • party perfect

MAKES 6 SERVINGS
HANDS-ON TIME: 10 MIN.
TOTAL TIME: 2 HR., 10 MIN.

- 1 lb. fresh baby mozzarella cheese balls
- ¼ cup olive oil
- ¼ cup chopped fresh basil
- ¼ cup chopped fresh chives
- 2 Tbsp. chopped fresh oregano
- 2 Tbsp. fresh lemon juice
- ½ tsp. salt
- ½ tsp. freshly ground pepper

1. Toss together all ingredients. Cover and chill 2 to 3 hours.

Fresh Herb Spoon Rolls

quick prep • good for you

MAKES 2 DOZEN
HANDS-ON TIME: 20 MIN.
TOTAL TIME: 45 MIN.

These rolls start with a quick stir-and-bake batter.

- 1 (1¼-oz.) envelope active dry yeast
- 2 cups warm water (110°)
- 4 cups self-rising flour
- ¾ cup melted butter
- ¾ cup chopped fresh chives
- ½ cup chopped fresh parsley
- ¼ cup sugar
- 1 large egg, lightly beaten

1. Preheat oven to 400°. Combine yeast and 2 cups warm water in a large bowl; let stand 5 minutes. Stir in flour and remaining ingredients. Spoon batter into 2 lightly greased 12-cup muffin pans, filling three-fourths full.
2. Bake at 400° for 20 to 22 minutes or until golden brown.

Fresh Herb Mayonnaise

quick prep • make-ahead

MAKES ABOUT 2¼ CUPS
HANDS-ON TIME: 10 MIN.
TOTAL TIME: 10 MIN.

- 2 cups mayonnaise
- 2 Tbsp. chopped fresh parsley
- 2 Tbsp. chopped fresh chives
- 1 Tbsp. chopped fresh basil
- 1 Tbsp. chopped fresh dill
- 1 Tbsp. chopped fresh oregano

1. Stir together all ingredients.

Summer Alfredo Sauce

quick prep

MAKES 1½ CUPS
HANDS-ON TIME: 10 MIN.
TOTAL TIME: 15 MIN.

Serve over hot cooked pasta and grilled vegetables, or toss with hot cooked cheese-filled ravioli.

- 1 (1.6-oz.) envelope Alfredo sauce mix
- 1 Tbsp. chopped fresh parsley
- 1 Tbsp. chopped fresh chives
- 1 Tbsp. chopped fresh basil
- 1 Tbsp. chopped fresh oregano

1. Prepare Alfredo sauce mix according to package directions. Whisk in parsley and remaining ingredients. Serve immediately.

Gremolata

quick prep • good for you • party perfect

MAKES ½ CUP
HANDS-ON TIME: 10 MIN.
TOTAL TIME: 10 MIN.

Sprinkle over grilled meats, poultry, or seafood just before serving.

- ½ cup finely chopped fresh flat-leaf parsley
- 1 Tbsp. lemon zest
- 2 garlic cloves, minced
- ¼ tsp. salt

Stir together all ingredients.

Toasted Pecan Pesto

quick prep • make-ahead

MAKES ABOUT 1 CUP
HANDS-ON TIME: 10 MIN.
TOTAL TIME: 38 MIN.

- ½ cup chopped pecans
- 2 cups loosely packed fresh basil leaves
- ½ cup (2 oz.) shredded Parmesan cheese
- ½ cup olive oil
- 3 large garlic cloves
- ⅛ tsp. salt

1. Preheat oven to 350°. Bake pecans in a single layer in a shallow pan 8 to 10 minutes or until toasted and fragrant. Let cool 20 minutes.
2. Process pecans and remaining ingredients in a food processor until smooth.

Our Favorite Mini Desserts

Here are four little ways to tame your sweet tooth. We matched luscious fillings with simple crusts to create irresistible treats.

Lemon-Almond Tarts

make-ahead • party perfect

MAKES 6 SERVINGS
HANDS-ON TIME: 30 MIN.
TOTAL TIME: 3 HR.

Find almond paste in the baking aisle, either in a tube-shaped plastic wrapper (which we call for in this recipe) or a can. If you find it only in a can, use ¾ cup. (pictured on page 180)

VANILLA WAFER CRUSTS
- 75 vanilla wafers
- ¼ cup powdered sugar
- ½ cup butter, melted

LEMON-ALMOND FILLING
- 1 (7-oz.) package almond paste
- 2 large eggs
- ¼ cup granulated sugar
- 2 Tbsp. melted butter
- ⅔ cup lemon curd
- 2 (6-oz.) packages fresh raspberries
  Garnish: fresh mint sprigs

1. Prepare crusts: Preheat oven to 350°. Pulse vanilla wafers in a food processor 8 to 10 times or until finely crushed. Stir together crushed wafers, powdered sugar, and butter in a medium bowl. Press crumb mixture on bottom and up sides of 6 lightly greased 4-inch tart pans with removable bottoms. Place on a baking sheet.
2. Bake at 350° for 10 to 12 minutes or until lightly browned. Transfer to a wire rack. Let cool completely (about 30 minutes).
3. Meanwhile, prepare filling: Reduce oven temperature to 325°. Beat almond paste and next 3 ingredients at medium speed with an electric mixer until well blended. Pour mixture into crusts.
4. Bake at 325° for 18 to 20 minutes or until set and just beginning to brown around edges. Let cool on a wire rack 30 minutes. Spread 1½ Tbsp. lemon curd onto each tart. Cover and chill 1 to 24 hours. Remove tarts from pans, and top with raspberries just before serving. Garnish, if desired.
Note: We tested with Odense Pure Almond Paste.

Cream Cheese Tarts with Fresh Fruit

make-ahead • party perfect

MAKES 6 SERVINGS
HANDS-ON TIME: 20 MIN.
TOTAL TIME: 2 HR.

Top this simple dessert with colorful fruit combinations such as blueberries and sliced kiwifruit; blackberries and sliced peaches; or chopped mango, raspberries, and pineapple.

SHORTBREAD CRUSTS
- 1 (10-oz.) package shortbread cookies
- 6 Tbsp. unsalted butter, melted

FILLING
- ⅔ cup cream cheese, softened
- ¼ cup sugar
- ½ tsp. vanilla extract
  Assorted fresh fruit

1. Prepare crusts: Preheat oven to 325°. Pulse cookies in a food processor 8 to 10 times or until finely crushed. Stir together crumbs and melted butter. Press crumb mixture on bottom and up sides of 6 (4-inch) tart pans with removable bottoms. Place on a baking sheet.
2. Bake at 325° for 9 to 10 minutes until lightly browned. Transfer to a wire rack. Let cool completely (about 30 minutes).
3. Meanwhile, prepare filling: Beat cream cheese, sugar, and vanilla at medium speed with an electric mixer until smooth. Spoon mixture into crusts. Cover and chill 1 to 24 hours. Remove tarts from pans, and top with assorted fresh fruit just before serving.
Note: We tested with Nabisco Lorna Doone Shortbread Cookies.

Raspberry Tiramisù Bites

test kitchen favorite

MAKES 8 SERVINGS
HANDS-ON TIME: 30 MIN.
TOTAL TIME: 2 HR., 30 MIN.

- 3 Tbsp. seedless raspberry preserves
- 1 Tbsp. orange liqueur
- 1 (3-oz.) package cream cheese, softened
- ¼ cup sugar
- ½ cup heavy cream
- 8 ladyfingers, halved crosswise
- 8 fresh raspberries

1. Microwave raspberry preserves in a small microwave-safe bowl at HIGH 20 seconds. Stir in liqueur.
2. Beat cream cheese and sugar at medium speed with an electric mixer until creamy (about 1 minute).
3. Beat heavy cream with an electric mixer until soft peaks form. Fold into cream cheese mixture. Spoon into a zip-top plastic bag. (Do not seal.) Snip 1 corner of bag with scissors to make a hole (about ½ inch in diameter).
4. Press 1 ladyfinger half onto bottom of 1 (1½-oz.) shot glass. Repeat procedure with 7 more shot glasses. Drizzle about ½ tsp. raspberry mixture into each glass.

Chocolate Truffle Bites

party perfect

MAKES 45 POPPERS
HANDS-ON TIME: 20 MIN.
TOTAL TIME: 2 HR., 50 MIN.

- 3 (2.1-oz.) packages frozen mini-phyllo pastry shells, thawed
- 1 (8-oz.) package cream cheese, softened
- ½ cup powdered sugar
- 1 tsp. vanilla extract
- ½ (8-oz.) container frozen whipped topping, thawed
- 1 cup pecans, finely chopped
- ½ cup sweetened flaked coconut
- 3 Tbsp. butter, melted
- ½ cup jarred caramel topping (optional)

1. Preheat oven to 350°. Bake pastry shells on a baking sheet 3 to 5 minutes. Cool completely (about 30 minutes).
2. Beat cream cheese, sugar, and vanilla at medium speed with an electric mixer until blended. Fold in whipped topping. Spoon or pipe cream cheese mixture into pastry shells. Cover and chill 2 to 8 hours.
3. Meanwhile, stir together pecans, coconut, and butter in a small bowl. Spread mixture in a 9-inch square pan. Bake at 350° for 10 to 15 minutes or until toasted, stirring occasionally. Let cool 30 minutes. Sprinkle each tart with about 1 tsp. pecan mixture. Drizzle with caramel topping, if desired. Serve immediately.

RECIPE INSPIRED BY SHAREE PARKER
YADKINVILLE, NORTH CAROLINA

Pipe a small amount of cream cheese mixture evenly into each glass. Repeat procedure with remaining ladyfingers, raspberry mixture, and cream cheese mixture. Top each glass with 1 raspberry. Cover and chill 2 hours.

Chocolate Truffle Bites

MAKES 30 SERVINGS
HANDS-ON TIME: 20 MIN
TOTAL TIME: 1 HR., 57 MIN.

Making chocolate shavings for a garnish is easy. Pick up an extra chocolate bar, and use a vegetable peeler to shave bits of chocolate off the side.

- 1½ (14.1-oz.) packages refrigerated piecrusts
- 2 (4-oz.) semisweet chocolate baking bars, chopped
- 1 cup whipping cream
- 1½ tsp. vanilla extract
  Pinch of salt
  Sweetened whipped cream
  Garnish: chocolate shavings

1. Preheat oven to 425°. Unroll 3 piecrusts, and stack on top of one another. Cut piecrust stack 10 times using a 4-inch round cutter, making 30 rounds. Press rounds into bottoms of ungreased muffin cups. (Dough will come halfway up sides, forming a cup.) Flute edges with a fork, if desired.
2. Bake rounds at 425° for 8 to 10 minutes or until golden. Let cool on a wire rack 10 minutes. Remove from pans to wire racks, and let cool completely (about 20 minutes).
3. Meanwhile, stir together chocolate and cream in a 3½-qt. heavy saucepan over low heat, and cook, stirring constantly, 4 to 5 minutes or until chocolate is melted and mixture is smooth. Remove from heat; stir in vanilla and salt. Let cool 30 minutes.
4. Pour 1 Tbsp. chocolate mixture into each piecrust. Cover and chill 1 to 24 hours. Top each with a dollop of sweetened whipped cream. Garnish, if desired.

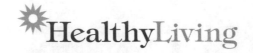
Lighten Up!

Banana Pudding

The delicious skinny on this all-time favorite.

When it comes to banana pudding, Food Editor Shannon Sliter Satterwhite's sweet tooth requires three things—a velvety rich custard, ripe banana flavor, and vanilla wafers so soft they melt in your mouth. Add an irresistible golden-baked meringue topping and she's in heaven. This recipe has all of the above, and it's lower in fat and calories than traditional versions. Taste it. You truly won't believe it's lightened.

Banana Pudding

good for you • quick prep

MAKES 8 SERVINGS
HANDS-ON TIME: 30 MIN.
TOTAL TIME: 1 HR., 20 MIN.

These make great individual party desserts. We love it with extra wafers.

⅓	cup all-purpose flour
	Dash of salt
2½	cups 1% low-fat milk
1	(14-oz.) can fat-free sweetened condensed milk
2	egg yolks, lightly beaten
2	tsp. vanilla extract
3	cups sliced ripe bananas
48	reduced-fat vanilla wafers
4	egg whites
¼	cup sugar

1. Preheat oven to 325°. Combine flour and salt in a medium saucepan. Gradually stir in 1% milk, sweetened condensed milk, and yolks, and cook over medium heat, stirring constantly, 8 to 10 minutes or until thickened. Remove from heat; stir in vanilla.

2. Layer 3 banana slices, 3½ Tbsp. pudding, and 3 vanilla wafers in each of 8 (1-cup) ramekins or ovenproof glass dishes. Top each with 6 banana slices, 3½ Tbsp. pudding, and 3 vanilla wafers.

3. Beat egg whites at high speed with an electric mixer until foamy. Add sugar, 1 Tbsp. at a time, beating until stiff peaks form and sugar dissolves (2 to 4 minutes). Spread about ½ cup meringue over each pudding.

4. Bake at 325° for 15 to 20 minutes or until golden. Let cool 30 minutes.

Note: An 8-inch square baking dish may be substituted for glass dishes. Arrange 1 cup bananas on bottom of dish. Top with one-third pudding mixture and 16 vanilla wafers. Repeat layers twice, ending with pudding. Arrange remaining 16 wafers around inside edge of dish, gently pressing wafers into pudding. Spread meringue over pudding, sealing edges; bake 20 to 25 minutes; cool as directed.

PER SERVING: CALORIES 359; **FAT** 3.6G **(SAT** 1G, **MONO** 0.7G, **POLY** 0.3G**); PROTEIN** 11G; **CARB** 70.7G; **FIBER** 1.3G; **CHOL** 58MG; **IRON** 1.1MG; **SODIUM** 234MG; **CALC** 242MG

TEST KITCHEN *Secret*

Fat-free sweetened condensed milk is the secret to this rich-and-creamy custard. It can be used as a base for puddings, pie fillings, and many other desserts. Plus, this shelf-stable gem is already sweetened, so no additional sugar is needed in most recipes.

July

Summer's Glorious Trinity

Perfectly ripe tomatoes, okra, and sweet corn inspire a bounty of irresistible new Southern favorites—from a colorful gumbo salad to garden-fresh griddle cakes.

You won't find the usual offerings in this collection of simple-to-fix recipes. Peppery grilled okra and shrimp team up with a fresh corn vinaigrette for an elegant but easy one-dish meal. Diced peaches sweeten an heirloom tomato salad—a fabulous go-to side. And barbecue-topped griddle cakes head south of the border with a speedy homemade salsa. These are the seasonal delights our winter dreams are made of. Enjoy!

Test Kitchen Tip

1 medium-size ear of fresh corn yields about ½ cup kernels.

Grilled Shrimp Gumbo Salad

good for you • party perfect

MAKES 6 TO 8 SERVINGS
HANDS-ON TIME: 1 HR.
TOTAL TIME: 1 HR., 40 MIN., INCLUDING VINAIGRETTE

Terrific flavors from the garden and grill come together in this summery twist on a New Orleans favorite. Served in smaller portions, it also makes a great first course. (pictured on page 182)

- 6 (12-inch) wooden skewers
- 1 lb. unpeeled, large raw shrimp (36/40 count)
- 2 Tbsp. olive oil, divided
- 2½ tsp. Cajun seasoning, divided
- 1 lb. fresh okra
- 6 (½-inch-thick) sweet onion slices
- 1 green bell pepper, quartered
- 2 (16-oz.) packages baby heirloom tomatoes, cut in half
  Fresh Corn Vinaigrette

1. Soak wooden skewers in water 30 minutes.
2. Preheat grill to 350° to 400° (medium-high) heat. Peel shrimp; devein, if desired. Drizzle shrimp with 1 Tbsp. olive oil, and sprinkle with ½ tsp. Cajun seasoning. Thread shrimp onto skewers.
3. Drizzle okra, onion, and bell pepper with remaining 1 Tbsp. olive oil; sprinkle with remaining 2 tsp. Cajun seasoning.

4. Grill okra, covered with grill lid, 4 minutes on each side or until tender. Grill onion slices and bell pepper, covered with grill lid, 6 minutes on each side or until tender. Grill shrimp, covered with grill lid, 2 minutes on each side or just until shrimp turn pink.
5. Cut okra in half lengthwise. Coarsely chop bell pepper. Toss together okra, bell pepper, and onion in a large bowl.
6. Remove shrimp from skewers, and toss with okra mixture, tomatoes, and Fresh Corn Vinaigrette.

Fresh Corn Vinaigrette:

MAKES 1½ CUPS
HANDS-ON TIME: 10 MIN.
TOTAL TIME: 10 MIN.

1. Whisk together 1 cup fresh corn kernels; ⅔ cup olive oil; ¼ cup fresh lemon juice; 1 garlic clove, minced; 2 Tbsp. balsamic vinegar; 1 Tbsp. Creole mustard; and 1 tsp. chopped fresh thyme. Season with salt and freshly ground pepper to taste.

Okra Chowchow

quick prep • make-ahead

MAKES ABOUT 2 CUPS
HANDS-ON TIME: 8 MIN.
TOTAL TIME: 8 MIN.

1. Spoon this spicy-sweet mix of tomatoes, onion, and peppers over fresh peas.
2. Sauté ½ lb. chopped fresh okra in 1 Tbsp. hot olive oil in a large skillet over medium-high heat 3 to 4 minutes or until crisp-tender. Remove skillet from heat, and stir in 1 (16-oz.) jar tomato relish.
Note: We tested with Mrs. Renfro's Mild Tomato Relish.

Tomato-and-Corn Pizza

quick prep • good for you

MAKES 4 SERVINGS
HANDS-ON TIME: 10 MIN.
TOTAL TIME: 44 MIN.
(pictured on page 184)

- 3 small plum tomatoes, sliced
- ¼ tsp. salt
- ⅛ tsp. freshly ground pepper
- 1 (14-oz.) package prebaked Italian pizza crust
  Parchment paper
- ⅓ cup refrigerated pesto
- ½ cup fresh corn kernels
- ¼ cup grated Parmesan cheese
- 1 tsp. sugar
- 8 oz. fresh mozzarella, sliced
- 3 Tbsp. fresh whole or torn basil leaves

1. Preheat oven to 450°. Place tomato slices on paper towels. Sprinkle with salt and pepper; let stand 20 minutes.
2. Place pizza crust on a parchment paper-lined baking sheet; spread with pesto. Stir together corn, Parmesan, and sugar. Top pizza with corn mixture, tomatoes, and mozzarella slices.
3. Bake at 450° for 14 minutes or until cheese is melted and golden. Remove from oven, and top with basil leaves.
Note: We tested with Boboli Original Pizza Crust.

3 Ways with Buttermilk Fried Okra

1 | **Fried Okra Tacos** (Pictured on page 185) Fill warm tortillas with shredded lettuce, hot Buttermilk Fried Okra (recipe below), and Fresh Tomato Salsa (page 117). Serve with shredded pepper Jack cheese, guacamole, and sour cream.

2 | **Okra Panzanella** Toss together Buttermilk Fried Okra, coarsely chopped fresh tomatoes, diced red onion, chopped fresh basil, and red wine vinaigrette. Serve immediately.

3 | **Fried Okra Croutons** Sprinkle Buttermilk Fried Okra over a crisp green salad with Ranch dressing or a Greek salad with tomatoes, black olives, and feta cheese. Or top off a favorite soup just before serving—we love the fresh crunch fried okra adds to tomato soup.

Buttermilk Fried Okra

MAKES 8 CUPS
HANDS-ON TIME: 30 MIN.
TOTAL TIME: 30 MIN.

A sprinkling of sugar in the cornmeal coating caramelizes as the okra cooks, creating a crisp, golden crust.

- 1 lb. fresh okra, cut into ½-inch-thick slices
- ¾ cup buttermilk
- 1½ cups self-rising white cornmeal mix
- 1 tsp. salt
- 1 tsp. sugar
- ¼ tsp. ground red pepper
  Vegetable oil

1. Stir together okra and buttermilk in a large bowl. Stir together cornmeal mix and next 3 ingredients in a separate large bowl. Remove okra from buttermilk, in batches, using a slotted spoon. Dredge in cornmeal mixture, and place in a wire-mesh strainer. Shake off excess.
2. Pour oil to depth of 1 inch into a large, deep cast-iron skillet or Dutch oven; heat to 375°. Fry okra, in batches, 4 minutes or until golden, turning once. Drain on paper towels.

Okra-and-Corn Maque Choux

party perfect

MAKES 8 SERVINGS
HANDS-ON TIME: 28 MIN.
TOTAL TIME: 28 MIN.

(pictured on page 11)

- ¼ lb. spicy smoked sausage, diced
- ½ cup chopped sweet onion
- ½ cup chopped green bell pepper
- 2 garlic cloves, minced
- 3 cups fresh corn kernels
- 1 cup sliced fresh okra
- 1 cup peeled, seeded, and diced tomato (½ lb.)
  Salt and freshly ground pepper to taste

1. Sauté sausage in a large skillet over medium-high heat 3 minutes or until browned. Add onion, bell pepper, and garlic, and sauté 5 minutes or until tender. Add corn, okra, and tomato; cook, stirring often, 10 minutes.
2. Season with salt and pepper to taste.
Note: We tested with Conecuh Original Spicy and Hot Smoked Sausage.

Griddle Cake Sandwiches

Reader Mary Ann Upchurch from Hominy, Oklahoma, inspired these sandwiches, named after her mother's home state. A favorite summer comfort food, the griddle cakes her mom made were sandwiched with sliced tomato and Vidalia onion.

Arkansas Tomato Sandwiches: (pictured on page 183) Process 1 cup mayonnaise, 1 cup loosely packed fresh cilantro leaves, 1 tsp. lime zest, 1 Tbsp. fresh lime juice, and 1 garlic clove in a blender until smooth. Spread mayonnaise mixture over warm Summer Griddle Cakes. Sprinkle tomato slices with salt and freshly ground pepper to taste, and sandwich tomato slices with salad greens and thinly sliced red onion between griddle cakes.

Barbecue-Topped Griddle Cakes: Top hot Summer Griddle Cakes with shredded or chopped barbecued pork or chicken (without sauce) and Fresh Tomato Salsa (facing page). Serve with barbecue sauce.

Summer Griddle Cakes

MAKES 17 (3½-INCH) CAKES
HANDS-ON TIME: 35 MIN.
TOTAL TIME: 35 MIN.

Stir finely chopped fresh cilantro into softened butter, and serve alongside a bread basket of these treats.

- 4 bacon slices
- 1 cup finely chopped okra
- 1½ cups self-rising white cornmeal mix
- ½ cup all-purpose flour
- 1 Tbsp. sugar
- 1⅔ cups buttermilk
- 3 Tbsp. butter, melted
- 2 large eggs, lightly beaten

1. Cook bacon in a large skillet over medium-high heat 8 to 10 minutes or until crisp; remove bacon, and drain on paper towels, reserving drippings in skillet. Finely chop bacon.

2. Sauté okra in hot drippings 3 minutes or until crisp-tender.
3. Whisk together cornmeal mix and next 5 ingredients just until moistened; stir in okra and bacon.
4. Pour about ¼ cup batter for each griddle cake onto a hot, lightly greased griddle or large nonstick skillet. Cook cakes 2 to 3 minutes or until tops are covered with bubbles and edges look dry and cooked; turn and cook other side 1 to 2 minutes or until done.

Fried Corn

MAKES 4 SERVINGS
HANDS-ON TIME: 23 MIN.
TOTAL TIME: 23 MIN.

After cutting the kernels from fresh corn, scrape the knife blade down each cob to get all the milky liquid.

1. Melt 3 Tbsp. butter in a large cast-iron skillet over medium-high heat. Add 4 cups fresh corn kernels, and sauté 8 to 10 minutes or until mixture is thickened. Stir in 1 tsp. sugar and ½ tsp. each of salt and freshly ground pepper.

Fresh Corn-and-Asiago Cheese Bread Pudding

party perfect
MAKES 12 SERVINGS
HANDS-ON TIME: 20 MIN.
TOTAL TIME: 1 HR., 35 MIN.

- 1½ cups milk
- 1 cup whipping cream
- 3 large eggs
- ½ tsp. salt
- ½ tsp. freshly ground pepper
- 1 (12-oz.) French bread loaf, cut into 1-inch cubes (8 cups)
- 4 cups fresh corn kernels
- 1½ cups (6 oz.) shredded Asiago cheese

1. Whisk together first 5 ingredients in a large bowl; add bread, tossing to coat. Let stand 30 minutes.
2. Preheat oven to 375°. Stir corn and cheese into bread mixture; spoon into a well-buttered 13- x 9-inch baking dish. Bake at 375° for 45 minutes or until set and golden brown.

Heirloom Tomatoes with Fresh Peaches, Goat Cheese, and Pecans

party perfect
MAKES 6 SERVINGS
HANDS-ON TIME: 20 MIN.
TOTAL TIME: 20 MIN.

1. Whisk together ⅓ cup white balsamic vinegar; 1 garlic clove, minced; 2 Tbsp. brown sugar; 2 Tbsp. olive oil; and ⅛ tsp. salt. Stir in 1 large peeled and diced fresh peach and 2 Tbsp. chopped fresh basil. Spoon over sliced heirloom tomatoes (about 2 lb.); top with 3 oz. crumbled goat cheese and ½ cup coarsely chopped toasted pecans. Sprinkle with freshly ground pepper to taste.

Fresh Tomato Salsa

quick prep • good for you • make-ahead

MAKES ABOUT 5 CUPS
HANDS-ON TIME: 15 MIN.
TOTAL TIME: 15 MIN.

Serve this salsa with Fried Okra Tacos (page 115). We also loved it with our Barbecue-Topped Griddle Cakes (facing page).

- 3 cups seeded and diced tomatoes (about 1½ lb.)
- 1 large avocado, diced
- 1 small green bell pepper, diced
- 1 (2.25-oz.) can sliced black olives, drained
- ½ cup chopped green onions
- ⅓ cup chopped fresh cilantro
- 1½ tsp. balsamic vinegar
- ½ tsp. seasoned salt
  Table salt to taste

1. Stir together diced tomatoes and next 7 ingredients. Season with table salt to taste.

RECIPE INSPIRED BY SHERLYNE HUTCHINSON
CORNELIUS, OREGON

TRY THIS TWIST!

Fresh Tomato-Peach Salsa: Omit black olives. Prepare recipe as directed, stirring in 2 peeled and diced fresh peaches (about 2 cups).

Cream of the Crop

Think most ice creams are just a bit … vanilla? Get the scoop on Grown-up Banana Pudding Ice Cream—or any of our other top-rated flavors. You're sure to love one of the delectable tastes that we churned up.

Grown-up Banana Pudding Ice Cream

quick prep • make-ahead

MAKES ABOUT 1 QT.
HANDS-ON TIME: 20 MIN.
TOTAL TIME: 10 HR., 10 MIN., NOT INCLUDING FREEZING TIME

- ¾ cup sugar
- 2 Tbsp. cornstarch
- ⅛ tsp. salt
- 2 cups milk
- 1 cup heavy whipping cream
- 1 egg yolk
- 1½ tsp. vanilla bean paste*
- 3 medium-size ripe bananas, cut into ½-inch slices
- ⅓ cup firmly packed light brown sugar
- 1 Tbsp. butter
- 2 Tbsp. banana liqueur, divided (optional)
- 1 cup coarsely crumbled vanilla wafers

1. Whisk together first 3 ingredients in a large heavy saucepan. Gradually whisk in milk and cream. Cook over medium heat, stirring constantly, 10 to 12 minutes or until mixture thickens slightly. Remove from heat.
2. Whisk egg yolk until slightly thickened. Gradually whisk about 1 cup hot cream mixture into yolk. Add yolk mixture to remaining cream mixture, whisking constantly. Whisk in vanilla bean paste. Cool 1 hour, stirring occasionally.

3. Meanwhile, preheat oven to 400°. Combine bananas, brown sugar, butter, and, if desired, 1 Tbsp. banana liqueur in a 2-qt. baking dish. Bake 20 minutes or until browned and softened, stirring after 10 minutes. Let cool 30 minutes.
4. Coarsely mash banana mixture; stir into cooled cream mixture. Place plastic wrap directly on cream mixture, and chill 8 to 24 hours.
5. Pour mixture into freezer container of a 1½-qt. electric ice-cream maker, and freeze according to manufacturer's instructions. (Instructions and time may vary.) Before transferring ice cream to an airtight container for further freezing, stir in vanilla wafers, and, if desired, remaining 1 Tbsp. banana liqueur.
*Vanilla extract may be substituted.

Test Kitchen Notebook

TABLETOP ICE-CREAM MAKER
We like the Cuisinart Ice Cream Maker (about $50) for these recipes. It's clean and easy (no rock salt or ice needed), fits on a kitchen counter, and makes excellent ice cream.

Peach-and-Toasted Pecan Ice Cream

make-ahead

MAKES ABOUT 1 QT.
HANDS-ON TIME: 32 MIN.
TOTAL TIME: 10 HR., 32 MIN., NOT INCLUDING FREEZING TIME

- ¾ cup sugar
- 2 Tbsp. cornstarch
- ⅛ tsp. table salt
- 2 cups milk
- 1 cup heavy whipping cream
- 1 egg yolk
- 1½ tsp. vanilla bean paste*
- 1 cup peeled and coarsely chopped peaches
- 2 Tbsp. light corn syrup
- 1½ Tbsp. butter
- 1 cup coarsely chopped pecans
- ¼ tsp. kosher salt

1. Whisk together first 3 ingredients in a large heavy saucepan. Gradually whisk in milk and whipping cream. Cook over medium heat, stirring constantly, 10 to 12 minutes or until mixture thickens slightly. Remove from heat.

2. Whisk egg yolk until slightly thickened. Gradually whisk about 1 cup hot cream mixture into yolk. Add yolk mixture to remaining cream mixture, whisking constantly. Whisk in vanilla bean paste. Cool 1 hour, stirring occasionally.

3. Meanwhile, cook peaches and corn syrup in a small saucepan over medium heat, stirring often, 4 to 5 minutes. Coarsely mash, and let cool 30 minutes. Stir peach mixture into cooled cream mixture.

4. Place plastic wrap directly on cream mixture, and chill 8 to 24 hours.

5. Meanwhile, melt butter in a small skillet over medium heat; add pecans, and cook, stirring constantly, 8 to 9 minutes or until toasted and fragrant. Remove from heat, and sprinkle with ¼ tsp. kosher salt. Cool completely (about 30 minutes).

6. Pour chilled cream mixture into freezer container of a 1½-qt. electric ice-cream maker, and freeze according to manufacturer's instructions. (Instructions and time may vary.) Before transferring ice cream to an airtight container for further freezing, stir in pecan mixture.

*Vanilla extract may be substituted.

❖

Peach-and-Toasted Pecan Ice Cream is sublimely Southern.

Vanilla Bean Ice Cream

quick prep • make-ahead

MAKES ABOUT 1 QT.
HANDS-ON TIME: 20 MIN.
TOTAL TIME: 9 HR., 20 MIN., NOT INCLUDING
FREEZING TIME

- ¾ cup sugar
- 2 Tbsp. cornstarch
- ⅛ tsp. salt
- 2 cups milk
- 1 cup heavy whipping cream
- 1 egg yolk
- 1½ tsp. vanilla bean paste*

1. Whisk together first 3 ingredients in a large heavy saucepan. Gradually whisk in milk and cream. Cook over medium heat, stirring constantly, 10 to 12 minutes or until mixture thickens slightly. Remove from heat.
2. Whisk egg yolk until slightly thickened. Gradually whisk about 1 cup hot cream mixture into yolk. Add yolk mixture to remaining cream mixture, whisking constantly. Whisk in vanilla bean paste. Cool 1 hour, stirring occasionally.
3. Place plastic wrap directly on cream mixture, and chill 8 to 24 hours.
4. Pour mixture into freezer container of a 1½-qt. electric ice-cream maker, and freeze according to manufacturer's instructions. (Instructions and time may vary.)
*Vanilla extract may be substituted.

TRY THESE TWISTS!
Chocolate-Raspberry Ice Cream:
Before transferring ice cream to a container for further freezing, stir in 4 oz. finely chopped semisweet chocolate, and gently fold in ¼ cup melted seedless raspberry preserves.

Coconut Cream Pie Ice Cream: Reduce milk to 1 cup. Stir 1 cup coconut milk into sugar mixture with milk. Before transferring ice cream to a container for further freezing, stir in ¾ cup toasted, sweetened flaked coconut.

Mocha Latte Ice Cream

MAKES ABOUT 1 QT.
HANDS-ON TIME: 20 MIN.
TOTAL TIME: 9 HR., 20 MIN., NOT INCLUDING
FREEZING TIME
(pictured on page 12)

- ¾ cup sugar
- 2 Tbsp. cornstarch
- 1 Tbsp. instant espresso
- ⅛ tsp. salt
- 2 cups milk
- 1 cup heavy whipping cream
- 1 egg yolk
- 1½ tsp. vanilla bean paste*
- 1 cup chopped pecans
- 2 oz. finely chopped semisweet chocolate
  Garnish: dark-chocolate sticks

1. Whisk together first 4 ingredients in a large heavy saucepan. Gradually whisk in milk and whipping cream. Cook over medium heat, stirring constantly, 10 to 12 minutes or until mixture thickens slightly. Remove from heat.
2. Whisk egg yolk until slightly thickened. Gradually whisk about 1 cup hot cream mixture into yolk. Add yolk mixture to remaining cream mixture, whisking constantly. Whisk in vanilla bean paste. Cool 1 hour, stirring occasionally.
3. Place plastic wrap directly on cream mixture, and chill 8 to 24 hours.
4. Meanwhile, preheat oven to 350°. Bake pecans in a single layer in a shallow pan 8 minutes or until toasted and fragrant, stirring once halfway through. Cool completely (about 30 minutes).
5. Pour chilled cream mixture into freezer container of a 1½-qt. electric ice-cream maker, and freeze according to manufacturer's instructions. (Instructions and time may vary.) Before transferring ice cream to an airtight container for further freezing, stir in pecans and chocolate. Garnish, if desired.
*Vanilla extract may be substituted.

Peach-Cinnamon Ice Cream

Test kitchen favorite

MAKES ABOUT 6 TO 8 SERVINGS
HANDS-ON TIME: 40 MIN.
TOTAL TIME: 4 HR., 40 MIN., NOT INCLUDING
FREEZING TIME

- 4 cups peeled, diced fresh peaches (about 3 lb.)
- 1 cup peach nectar
- ½ cup sugar
- 3 egg yolks
- 4 cups milk
- 1 cup half-and-half
- 1 tsp. lemon juice
- ½ tsp. ground cinnamon
Garnish: sliced fresh peaches

1. Combine first 3 ingredients in a medium bowl. Process peach mixture, in batches, in a food processor until smooth, stopping to scrape down sides. Set aside.
2. Whisk together yolks and milk in a heavy saucepan over medium heat; cook, stirring constantly, 20 minutes or until mixture thickens and coats a spoon. Do not boil.
3. Remove from heat; whisk in peach mixture, half-and-half, lemon juice, and ground cinnamon. Cover and chill 4 hours.
4. Pour mixture into freezer container of a 6-quart electric ice-cream maker. Freeze according to manufacturer's instructions. (Instructions and times may vary.) Garnish, if desired.

Top-Rated Burgers

We turned up the flavor and fun on these cookout-ready quarter-pounders.

Sweet-and-Savory Burgers

party perfect

MAKES 8 SERVINGS
HANDS-ON TIME: 25 MIN.
TOTAL TIME: 4 HR., 25 MIN.

Press your thumb into centers of patties before grilling for burgers that cook up flat, rather than domed, across the top.

- ¼ cup soy sauce
- 2 Tbsp. light corn syrup
- 1 Tbsp. fresh lemon juice
- ½ tsp. ground ginger
- ¼ tsp. garlic powder
- 2 green onions, thinly sliced
- 2 lb. ground beef
- ¼ cup chili sauce
- ¼ cup hot red pepper jelly
- 8 hamburger buns, toasted
  Toppings: grilled sweet onion, pineapple slices

1. Stir together first 6 ingredients. Reserve 3 Tbsp. mixture; cover and chill. Pour remaining soy sauce mixture into a shallow pan or baking dish.
2. Shape beef into 8 (½-inch-thick) patties; place in a single layer in soy sauce mixture in pan, turning to coat. Cover and chill 4 hours.
3. Preheat grill to 350° to 400° (medium-high) heat. Remove patties from marinade, discarding marinade. Grill patties, covered with grill lid, 5 minutes on each side or until beef is no longer pink in center, basting occasionally with reserved 3 Tbsp. soy sauce mixture.
4. Stir together chili sauce and jelly. Serve burgers on buns with chili sauce mixture and desired toppings.

RECIPE FROM HAZEL J. KING
NACOGDOCHES, TEXAS

Check Out Our New Book!

To make your Fourth of July barbecue truly unforgettable, pick up a copy of the *Southern Living Big Book of BBQ* (Oxmoor House, 2010).

Fig-Glazed Burgers with Red Onion Jam

Editor's Favorite

party perfect

MAKES 4 SERVINGS
HANDS-ON TIME: 42 MIN.
TOTAL TIME: 52 MIN.

Don't skip topping burgers with fig preserves before adding the cheese. It adds a wonderful sweet touch that's great with the tartness of the Red Onion Jam.

RED ONION JAM

- 4 cups thinly sliced red onions (about 2 medium)
- 1 tsp. olive oil
- ¼ cup sugar
- ¼ cup red wine vinegar
- ¾ tsp. chopped fresh thyme

CHEESEBURGERS

- Vegetable cooking spray
- 1½ lb. ground round
- 2 Tbsp. chopped fresh oregano
- 1 tsp. salt
- ¼ tsp. garlic powder
- 3 Tbsp. fig preserves
- 4 (½-oz.) Muenster cheese slices
- 4 hamburger buns, toasted

1. Prepare onion jam: Sauté onions in hot oil in a large nonstick skillet over medium-high heat 10 minutes. Reduce heat to low; stir in sugar, vinegar, and thyme. Cover and cook 10 minutes or until onion is very tender. Keep warm.
2. Prepare burgers: Coat cold cooking grate of grill with vegetable cooking spray, and place on grill. Preheat grill to 350° to 400° (medium-high) heat. Gently stir together ground round and next 3 ingredients. Shape mixture into 4 (½-inch-thick) patties.
3. Grill patties, covered with grill lid, 5 minutes on each side. Top with preserves and cheese; grill 2 minutes or until beef is no longer pink in center and cheese is melted. Serve burgers on buns with desired amount of Red Onion Jam.

10-Minute Burger Sauces

Make basic ground beef burgers better with these revved-up spreads.

Horseradish Mayonnaise: Stir together ½ cup mayonnaise, 1 Tbsp. horseradish, 2 tsp. chopped fresh chives, 2 tsp. lemon juice, and ¼ tsp. pepper. Store in an airtight container in refrigerator up to 1 week. Makes ½ cup.

Tex-Mex Secret Sauce: Stir together ½ cup sour cream, ⅓ cup ketchup, 1 (4.5-oz.) can chopped green chiles, and 1 Tbsp. minced fresh cilantro. Makes 1 cup.

Cajun Mustard: Stir together ½ (8-oz.) jar spicy brown mustard, 1 Tbsp. finely chopped green onion, 1 tsp. minced garlic, 1 tsp. hot sauce, and 1 tsp. honey. Store in an airtight container in refrigerator up to 3 days. Makes ½ cup.

Spicy Cheddar-Stuffed Burgers

party perfect

MAKES 6 SERVINGS
HANDS-ON TIME: 27 MIN.
TOTAL TIME: 57 MIN.

Remaining chipotle pepper puree may be frozen in a zip-top plastic freezer bag to use at another time. Shape patties like a pro: Cut the unwrapped ground meat into the number of patties called for in the recipe; then gently roll portions into balls, and flatten by pressing each one once with the palm of your hand.

- 1 (7-oz.) can chipotle peppers in adobo sauce
- 2 lb. ground chuck
- 2 tsp. Montreal steak seasoning
- ½ (10-oz.) block sharp Cheddar cheese, cut into 6 thick slices
- 6 sesame seed hamburger buns
  Toppings: tomato slices, red onion slices, romaine lettuce leaves, yellow mustard, mayonnaise

1. Process chipotle peppers in a blender until smooth. Combine ground beef, steak seasoning, and 3 to 4 tsp. chipotle pepper puree in a large bowl until blended. (Do not overwork meat mixture.) Reserve remaining puree for another use.

2. Shape beef mixture into 12 (4-inch) patties; place 1 cheese slice on each of 6 patties. Top with remaining 6 patties, pressing edges to seal. Cover and chill 30 minutes to 8 hours.

3. Preheat grill to 350° to 400° (medium-high) heat. Grill patties, covered with grill lid, 6 to 7 minutes on each side or until beef is no longer pink in center. Serve burgers on buns with desired toppings.

Note: We tested with McCormick Grill Mates Montreal Steak Seasoning.

Greek Turkey Burgers

party perfect

MAKES 4 SERVINGS
HANDS-ON TIME: 25 MIN.
TOTAL TIME: 25 MIN.

To create a fancier burger, make cucumber ribbons. Use Y-shaped vegetable peeler to cut thin slices of cucumber lengthwise. If you're in a hurry, cut the cucumber into thin, round slices.

- 1⅓ lb. ground turkey breast
- 1 (4-oz.) package crumbled feta cheese
- ¼ cup finely chopped red onion
- 1 tsp. dried oregano
- 1 tsp. lemon zest
- ½ tsp. salt
  Vegetable cooking spray
- ½ cup grated English cucumber
- 1 (6-oz.) container fat-free Greek yogurt
- 1 Tbsp. chopped fresh mint
- ½ tsp. salt
- 4 French hamburger buns, split and toasted
  Toppings: lettuce leaves, tomato slices, thinly sliced cucumber
  Garnish: pepperoncini salad peppers

1. Stir together first 6 ingredients. Shape mixture into 4 (½-inch-thick) patties.

2. Heat a grill pan over medium-high heat. Coat grill pan with cooking spray. Add patties; cook 5 minutes on each side or until done.

3. Stir together cucumber, yogurt, mint, and ½ tsp. salt in a small bowl. Serve burgers on buns with cucumber sauce and desired toppings. Garnish, if desired.

Lighten Up!
Key Lime Pie

This slice of tropical heaven offers the best of both worlds—rich, creamy texture with fewer fat grams.

Key Lime Pie

quick prep • good for you • make-ahead • party perfect

MAKES 8 SERVINGS
HANDS-ON TIME: 10 MIN.
TOTAL TIME: 4 HR., 27 MIN.

Don't be tempted to substitute bottled lime juice—it doesn't compare to fresh. Prepare Key Lime Pie up to one day ahead.

- 1 (14-oz.) can fat-free sweetened condensed milk
- ¾ cup egg substitute
- ½ cup fresh Key lime juice*
- 2 tsp. Key lime zest*
- 1 (6-oz.) reduced-fat ready-made graham cracker crust
- 1 (8-oz.) container fat-free frozen whipped topping, thawed
- Garnish: lime peel strips

1. Preheat oven to 350°. Whisk together first 4 ingredients until well blended. Pour mixture into piecrust; place pie on a baking sheet.
2. Bake at 350° for 17 minutes or until pie is set. Remove pie from baking sheet to a wire rack, and let pie cool completely (about 1 hour).
3. Chill 3 to 24 hours. Top with whipped topping just before serving. Garnish, if desired.
*Regular fresh lime juice and zest may be substituted.

PER SERVING: CALORIES 301; FAT 4.3G (SAT 0.7G, MONO 0.2G, POLY 0.4G); PROTEIN 7.7G; CARB 55.4G; FIBER 0.1G; CHOL 7MG; IRON 0.9MG; SODIUM 194MG; CALC 142MG

Try it with Lemon! Substitute fresh lemon juice for lime juice and lemon zest for lime zest.

Mama's Way or Your Way?

One is a deep-fried Delta favorite, while a baked crust gives the other delicious crunch.

❖ WHY WE LOVE
Mama's Way

- Deep-fried goodness
- Peppery cornmeal coating
- Moist, tender interior

Classic Fried Catfish
quick prep

MAKES 6 TO 8 SERVINGS
HANDS-ON TIME: 20 MIN.
TOTAL TIME: 8 HR., 20 MIN.

For an extra-crispy crust, use stone-ground yellow cornmeal, if available. Serve with lemon slices and your favorite tartar sauce. The secret to this recipe is maintaining an oil temperature of 360° to ensure a crispy, golden crust.

- 1½ cups buttermilk
- ¼ tsp. hot sauce
- 6 (4- to 6-oz.) catfish fillets
- ⅓ cup plain yellow cornmeal
- ⅓ cup masa harina (corn flour)*
- ⅓ cup all-purpose flour
- 2 tsp. salt
- 1 tsp. ground black pepper
- 1 tsp. ground red pepper
- ¼ tsp. garlic powder
  Peanut oil

1. Whisk together buttermilk and hot sauce.
2. Place catfish in a single layer in a 13- x 9-inch baking dish; pour buttermilk mixture over fish. Cover and chill 8 hours, turning once.
3. Combine cornmeal and next 6 ingredients in a shallow dish.

4. Let fish stand at room temperature 10 minutes. Remove from buttermilk mixture, allowing excess to drip off. Dredge fish in cornmeal mixture, shaking off excess.
5. Pour oil to depth of 2 inches into a large, deep cast-iron or heavy-duty skillet; heat to 360°.
6. Fry fish, in batches, 2 minutes on each side or until golden brown. Transfer to a wire rack on a paper towel-lined jelly-roll pan. Keep warm in a 225° oven until ready to serve.
*All-purpose flour or plain yellow cornmeal may be substituted.

❖ WHY WE LOVE
Your Way

- Easy cleanup
- Crispy, low-fat crust
- Hands-free cooking

Crispy Oven-Fried Catfish
quick prep • good for you

MAKES 4 SERVINGS
HANDS-ON TIME: 15 MIN.
TOTAL TIME: 45 MIN.

Cornflakes are the secret to a crisp baked coating. Serve with sautéed mixed veggies, such as squash, zucchini, and carrots, and a green salad.

- 1 cup low-fat buttermilk
- 4 (6-oz.) catfish fillets
- 1½ to 2 tsp. Creole seasoning
- 3 cups cornflakes cereal, crushed
  Vegetable cooking spray
  Lemon wedges

1. Place buttermilk in a large zip-top plastic freezer bag; add catfish, turning to coat. Seal and chill 20 minutes, turning once.
2. Preheat oven to 425°.
3. Remove fish from buttermilk, discarding buttermilk. Sprinkle fish with Creole seasoning.
4. Place crushed cornflakes in a shallow dish.
5. Dredge fish in cornflakes, pressing cornflakes gently onto each fillet. Place fish on a wire rack coated with cooking spray in a roasting pan.
6. Bake at 425° for 30 to 35 minutes or until fish flakes with a fork. Serve immediately with lemon wedges.
Note: We tested with Tony Chachere's Original Creole Seasoning.

What's for Supper?

Streamline weeknight cooking with these delicious main-dish recipes paired with simple ideas for sides.

 ## Pork Fried Rice

quick prep

MAKES 6 SERVINGS

HANDS-ON TIME: 30 MIN.

TOTAL TIME: 30 MIN.

You need only one skillet to make this tasty favorite.

Easy side: Stir together 1 English cucumber, thinly sliced lengthwise; 3 Tbsp. sesame-ginger vinaigrette; 1 Tbsp. chopped fresh cilantro; and 1 tsp. toasted sesame seeds. Cover and chill until ready to serve.

- 1 lb. boneless pork chops, cut into strips
- ½ tsp. pepper
- 1 Tbsp. sesame oil, divided
- ¾ cup diced carrots
- ½ cup chopped onion
- 3 green onions, chopped
- 1 Tbsp. butter
- 2 large eggs, lightly beaten
- 2 cups cooked long-grain white or jasmine rice, chilled
- ½ cup frozen English peas, thawed (optional)
- ¼ cup soy sauce

1. Season pork with pepper. Cook pork in 1½ tsp. hot sesame oil in a large skillet over medium heat 7 to 8 minutes or until done. Remove pork from skillet.
2. Heat remaining 1½ tsp. sesame oil in skillet; sauté carrots and onion in hot oil 2 to 3 minutes or until tender. Stir in green onions, and sauté 1 minute.

Remove mixture from skillet. Wipe skillet clean.
3. Melt butter in skillet. Add eggs to skillet, and cook, without stirring, 1 minute or until eggs begin to set on bottom. Gently draw cooked edges away from sides of pan to form large pieces. Cook, stirring occasionally, 30 seconds to 1 minute or until thickened and moist. (Do not overstir.) Add pork, carrot mixture, rice, and, if desired, peas to skillet; cook over medium heat, stirring often, 2 to 3 minutes or until thoroughly heated. Stir in soy sauce. Serve immediately.

RECIPE INSPIRED BY BRIDGET ECKHARDT
RICHMOND, TEXAS

Note: Chilling rice will help keep it from clumping while stir-frying. Use leftover rice, or prepare 1 (8-oz.) pouch ready-to-serve jasmine rice according to package directions, and chill.

 ## Vegetable Melt

MAKES 4 SANDWICHES

HANDS-ON TIME: 32 MIN. **TOTAL TIME:** 32 MIN.

Easy side: Prepare frozen sweet potato fries as directed. Stir together 1 (14.5-oz.) can fire-roasted diced tomatoes with garlic, drained; ½ cup ketchup; 1 garlic clove, minced; and ½ tsp. dried rosemary. Serve with fries.

HERB MAYONNAISE

- ¼ cup mayonnaise
- 1 Tbsp. chopped fresh parsley
- ½ tsp. lemon zest
- 1 Tbsp. fresh lemon juice

SANDWICHES

- 8 multigrain bread slices
- 1 (6-oz.) package mozzarella cheese slices
- ¼ cup finely chopped roasted red bell peppers
- 1 (6-oz.) jar marinated artichoke hearts, drained and chopped
- 1 cup firmly packed arugula
- ¼ cup butter, softened

1. Prepare Herb Mayonnaise: Combine all ingredients. Chill until ready to use.
2. Prepare Sandwiches: Spread Herb Mayonnaise on 1 side of each bread slice. Layer 4 bread slices, mayonnaise sides up, each with 1 cheese slice, 1 Tbsp. red bell peppers, 1 rounded tablespoonful artichoke hearts, and ¼ cup arugula. Top with remaining cheese and bread slices, mayonnaise sides down. Spread butter on outside of each sandwich.
3. Cook sandwiches in a large nonstick skillet or griddle over medium-high heat 3 to 4 minutes on each side or until lightly browned and cheese is melted. Serve immediately.

RECIPE INSPIRED BY LINDA COOK
RIDGELAND, MISSISSIPPI

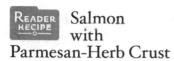

Salmon with Parmesan-Herb Crust

quick prep • good for you

MAKES 4 SERVINGS
HANDS-ON TIME: 15 MIN.
TOTAL TIME: 35 MIN.

Easy side: Boil 2 lb. peeled and chopped potatoes until tender; drain and mash. Stir in 1 cup warm milk, 3 oz. softened cream cheese, 1 Tbsp. chopped fresh chives, ½ tsp. salt, and ¼ tsp. pepper. Serve immediately.

- 4 (6-oz.) salmon fillets
- ¼ tsp. salt
- 1 Tbsp. fresh lime juice
- 1 tsp. olive oil
- ½ cup fine, dry breadcrumbs
- ½ cup (2 oz.) shredded Parmesan cheese
- 2 Tbsp. melted butter
- 1½ tsp. salt-free tomato-basil seasoning blend

1. Preheat oven to 375°. Sprinkle salmon with salt.
2. Place salmon on a lightly greased aluminum foil-lined 15- x 10-inch jelly-roll pan; pour lime juice and olive oil over salmon.
3. Stir together breadcrumbs and next 3 ingredients; spread over salmon.
4. Bake at 375° for 20 minutes or just to desired degree of doneness. Serve immediately.

RECIPE FROM CINDY MCGEORGE
LEXINGTON, KENTUCKY

Note: We tested with Mrs. Dash Tomato Basil Garlic Seasoning Blend.

Balsamic-Garlic Chicken Breasts

quick prep

MAKES 4 SERVINGS
HANDS-ON TIME: 22 MIN.
TOTAL TIME: 22 MIN.

Have this delicious dish on the table in less than 30 minutes.

Easy side: Stir together 1 cup uncooked orzo pasta, cooked according to package directions, and ¼ cup refrigerated pesto. Sprinkle with freshly grated Parmesan cheese, if desired.

- 4 (6-oz.) skinned and boned chicken breasts
- 1 tsp. salt
- 1 tsp. pepper
- 2 Tbsp. butter
- 1 Tbsp. vegetable oil
- ½ cup chicken broth
- ¼ cup balsamic vinegar
- 1 Tbsp. fresh lemon juice
- 3 garlic cloves, chopped
- 1½ tsp. honey

1. Sprinkle chicken breasts with salt and pepper.
2. Melt butter with oil in a large skillet over medium-high heat; add chicken, and cook 6 to 7 minutes on each side or until done. Remove chicken, and keep warm.
3. Add chicken broth and next 4 ingredients to skillet, and cook 5 minutes or until slightly thickened, stirring to loosen particles from bottom of skillet. Serve chicken with sauce.

Beef Brisket Tostados

quick prep

MAKES 4 SERVINGS
HANDS-ON TIME: 10 MIN.
TOTAL TIME: 18 MIN.

Easy side: Cut 2 ripe avocados in half. Scoop avocado pulp into bowl; mash just until chunky. Stir in 2 Tbsp. finely chopped red onion; 2 Tbsp. lime juice; ½ medium-size jalapeño pepper, seeded and chopped; 1 garlic clove, pressed; and ¾ tsp. salt. Serve immediately.

- ½ cup fresh salsa
- 1 Tbsp. chopped fresh cilantro
- 1 (16-oz.) can fat-free refried beans
- 6 corn tostada shells
- 1 lb. chopped barbecued beef brisket (without sauce), warmed*
- ¼ cup chopped red onion
  Toppings: shredded lettuce, chopped tomatoes, shredded pepper Jack cheese

1. Preheat oven to 400°. Stir together salsa and cilantro. Spread beans on tostada shells. Place shells on a jelly-roll pan; top with brisket, onion, and salsa mixture.
2. Bake at 400° for 8 to 10 minutes or until thoroughly heated. Serve immediately with desired toppings.
*Chopped grilled steak or pot roast may be substituted.

Party Chicken Salads

Start with a few cups of chopped cooked chicken and dress it up with fresh seasonal flavors. Simple!

Chicken-and-Broccoli Salad

quick prep • make-ahead • party perfect

MAKES 6 SERVINGS
HANDS-ON TIME: 15 MIN.
TOTAL TIME: 23 MIN.

- ½ cup chopped pecans
- 1 cup mayonnaise
- 3 Tbsp. sugar
- 2 Tbsp. cider vinegar
- 4 cups chopped cooked chicken
- 2 cups finely chopped fresh broccoli
- ½ cup diced red onion
- ½ cup sweetened dried cranberries
  Salt and pepper to taste
- ⅓ cup chopped cooked bacon

1. Preheat oven to 350°. Bake pecans in a single layer in a shallow pan 8 to 10 minutes or until toasted and fragrant, stirring halfway through.
2. Whisk together mayonnaise, sugar, and vinegar in a large bowl. Stir in chicken, next 3 ingredients, and pecans. Add salt and pepper to taste. Sprinkle with bacon just before serving.

Curried Chicken Salad

quick prep • make-ahead • party perfect

MAKES 6 SERVINGS
HANDS-ON TIME: 15 MIN.
TOTAL TIME: 20 MIN.

- ¾ cup sweetened flaked coconut
- ½ cup sour cream
- ½ cup mayonnaise
- 1 Tbsp. grated fresh ginger
- 2 tsp. curry powder
- 4 cups chopped cooked chicken
- ¾ cup golden raisins
- ½ cup minced green onions
  Salt and pepper to taste
- ⅓ cup coarsely chopped honey-roasted peanuts

1. Preheat oven to 350°. Bake coconut in a single layer in a shallow pan 5 to 7 minutes or until lightly toasted, stirring halfway through.
2. Whisk together sour cream and next 3 ingredients. Stir in chicken, raisins, green onions, and coconut. Add salt and pepper to taste. Sprinkle with peanuts.

Waldorf Chicken Salad

quick prep • make-ahead • party perfect

MAKES 6 SERVINGS
HANDS-ON TIME: 15 MIN.
TOTAL TIME: 21 MIN.

- ½ cup chopped walnuts
- 3 cups chopped cooked chicken
- 1 cup seedless red grapes, halved
- 1 large Gala apple, diced
- 1 cup diced celery
- ½ cup mayonnaise
- ½ cup honey mustard
  Salt and pepper to taste

1. Preheat oven to 350°. Bake walnuts in a single layer in a shallow pan 6 to 8 minutes or until toasted and fragrant, stirring halfway through.
2. Stir together chicken, next 5 ingredients, and walnuts. Add salt and pepper to taste.

Southwestern Chicken Salad

quick prep • make-ahead • party perfect

MAKES 6 SERVINGS
HANDS-ON TIME: 20 MIN.
TOTAL TIME: 20 MIN.

- ¾ cup mayonnaise
- ¼ cup chopped fresh cilantro
- 3 Tbsp. fresh lime juice
- 2 tsp. chili powder
- 1 tsp. minced garlic
- ½ tsp. ground cumin
- 4 cups chopped grilled chicken
- ¾ cup diced poblano pepper
  Salt to taste
  Soft taco-size flour tortillas, warmed
  Toppings: diced mango, diced avocado, diced tomatoes, shredded Monterey Jack cheese

1. Whisk together first 6 ingredients in a large bowl. Stir in chicken, poblano pepper, and salt. Serve in warm tortillas with desired toppings.

Strawberry-Spinach Chicken Salad

quick prep • make-ahead • party perfect

MAKES 6 SERVINGS
HANDS-ON TIME: 20 MIN.
TOTAL TIME: 20 MIN.

1 (6-oz.) package fresh baby spinach
2 cups sliced strawberries
1 cup diced nectarines
¾ cup diced English cucumber
½ cup sliced red onion
4 cups coarsely chopped grilled chicken breasts
1 (3.5-oz.) package roasted glazed pecan pieces
1 (8-oz.) bottle poppy seed dressing
½ cup sweetened dried cranberries
½ cup crumbled blue cheese

1. Toss together first 5 ingredients. Top with chopped chicken and pecan pieces. Stir together poppy seed dressing, cranberries, and crumbled blue cheese; serve with salad.

Confetti Chicken Salad

quick prep • make-ahead • party perfect

MAKES 6 SERVINGS
HANDS-ON TIME: 20 MIN.
TOTAL TIME: 20 MIN.

2 cups mayonnaise
¾ tsp. ground red pepper
6 cups chopped cooked chicken
1 cup diced celery
1 cup diced yellow bell pepper
½ cup diced water chestnuts
½ cup chopped fresh parsley
⅓ cup diced red onion
Salt and pepper to taste

1. Whisk together mayonnaise and ground red pepper in a large bowl. Stir in chicken and next 5 ingredients. Add salt and pepper to taste.

Chicken-and-Wild Rice Salad

Chicken-and-Wild Rice Salad

quick prep • make-ahead • party perfect

MAKES 6 SERVINGS
HANDS-ON TIME: 15 MIN.
TOTAL TIME: 25 MIN.

Serve this salad on a bed of watercress for a complete meal.

1 cup chopped pecans
3 Tbsp. soy sauce
3 Tbsp. rice wine vinegar
2 Tbsp. sesame oil
1 (8.5-oz.) pouch ready-to-serve whole grain brown and wild rice mix
3 cups shredded cooked chicken
1 cup diced red bell pepper
1 cup coarsely chopped watercress
¼ cup minced green onions
Pepper to taste

1. Preheat oven to 350°. Bake pecans in a single layer in a shallow pan 10 to 12 minutes or until toasted and fragrant, stirring halfway through.
2. Whisk together soy sauce, vinegar, and sesame oil in a large bowl.
3. Prepare brown and wild rice mix according to package directions. Stir chicken, next 3 ingredients, toasted pecans, and rice into soy sauce mixture. Add pepper to taste.

Chicken-and-Artichoke Salad

quick prep • make-ahead • party perfect

MAKES 6 SERVINGS
HANDS-ON TIME: 15 MIN.
TOTAL TIME: 22 MIN.

1 cup slivered almonds
4 cups chopped cooked chicken
1 (14-oz.) can artichoke hearts, drained and coarsely chopped
1 cup diced celery
1 cup mayonnaise
¼ cup chopped fresh chives
2 Tbsp. chopped fresh tarragon
2 tsp. lemon zest
Salt and freshly ground pepper to taste
Garnish: fresh chives

1. Preheat oven to 350°. Bake almonds in a single layer in a shallow pan 7 to 9 minutes or until toasted and fragrant, stirring halfway through.
2. Stir together chicken, next 7 ingredients, and almonds. Garnish, if desired.

Our Favorite Margaritas

Southern Living Test Kitchen pro and master mixologist Norman King offers five refreshing ways to shake it up.

Classic Margaritas on the Rocks

quick prep • party perfect

MAKES 1½ CUPS

HANDS-ON TIME: 10 MIN.

TOTAL TIME: 10 MIN.

These are potent, yet amazingly smooth-tasting when you use good-quality tequila and orange liqueur and thoroughly shake the mixture with ice before pouring over ice cubes to serve.

> Lime wedge
> Margarita salt
> ¾ cup tequila
> ½ cup powdered sugar
> ½ cup fresh lime juice (about 3 limes)
> ¼ cup orange liqueur
> Garnish: lime wedges

1. Rub rims of 4 chilled glasses with lime wedge; dip rims in salt to coat. Fill glasses with ice.
2. Stir together tequila and next 3 ingredients in a small pitcher, stirring until sugar is dissolved.
3. Fill a cocktail shaker half full with ice. Add desired amount of margarita mixture, cover with lid, and shake until thoroughly chilled. Strain into prepared glasses. Garnish, if desired. Serve immediately.
Note: We tested with Jose Cuervo Especial for tequila and Triple Sec for orange liqueur.

TRY THESE TWISTS!

Pomegranate Margaritas: Decrease lime juice to ¼ cup. Stir ½ cup pomegranate juice into tequila mixture in Step 2. Makes about 2 cups.

Strawberry Margaritas: Substitute red decorator sugar crystals for margarita salt. Reduce powdered sugar to ¼ to ⅓ cup and lime juice to ¼ cup. Process 1 (10-oz.) package frozen strawberries in light syrup, thawed, in blender 30 seconds or until smooth. Stir strawberry puree into tequila mixture in Step 2. Makes 2½ cups.

Frozen Blue Margaritas

quick prep • party perfect

MAKES ABOUT 5 CUPS

HANDS-ON TIME: 10 MIN.

TOTAL TIME: 10 MIN.

We found using limeade concentrate for frozen margaritas to be a great time-saver over squeezing fresh limes. Blue curaçao is an orange-flavored liqueur that's tinted blue.

> 1 (6-oz.) can frozen limeade concentrate, thawed
> ¾ cup tequila
> ¼ cup blue curaçao liqueur

1. Combine all ingredients in a blender. Fill with ice to 5-cup level, and process until mixture is smooth. Serve immediately.

Frozen Mango Margaritas

quick prep • party perfect

MAKES ABOUT 10 CUPS

HANDS-ON TIME: 15 MIN.

TOTAL TIME: 15 MIN.

> 1 (20-oz.) jar refrigerated sliced mangoes
> Colored decorator sugar crystals
> 1 (6-oz.) can frozen limeade concentrate, thawed
> 1 cup tequila
> ½ cup orange liqueur

1. Spoon 3 Tbsp. juice from mangoes into a shallow dish; pour mangoes and remaining juice into a blender.
2. Dip rims of glasses into 3 Tbsp. mango juice; dip in sugar crystals to coat.
3. Add limeade concentrate, tequila, and orange liqueur to blender; process until smooth, stopping to scrape down sides. Reserve half of mixture in a small pitcher.
4. Add ice to remaining mango mixture in blender to 5-cup level; process until slushy, stopping to scrape down sides. Pour into prepared glasses. Repeat procedure with reserved mango mixture and additional ice. Serve immediately.
Note: We tested with Triple Sec for orange liqueur.

August

Carolina Harvest Party

Join award-winning North Carolina winemaker Sean McRitchie and his family as they host a relaxed vineyard dinner to kick off the harvest season in the Blue Ridge foothills.

Casual Vineyard Menu

SERVES 8

Southwest Shrimp Tacos

Chunky Tomato-Fruit Gazpacho

Grilled Corn with Creamy Chipotle Sauce

Sweet-and-Sour Veggie Pickles

Blackberry Wine Sorbet

Things really get hoppin' around here when harvest kicks off in late August," says Sean McRitchie as he squeezes a wedge of lime over Southwest Shrimp Tacos. "So we take the first part of the month to gather with family and friends before working around the clock through October to bring in all the grapes."

Sean and his wife, Patricia, produce some of the South's top wines at McRitchie Winery & Ciderworks in Thurmond, North Carolina, nestled in the foothills of the Blue Ridge Mountains.

The couple's also known for their laid-back entertaining. "The keys for us are to relax, have fun, and enjoy the wonderful fresh foods grown and produced in our region. It's the perfect way to showcase our wines," Patricia says with a smile. Once you try these recipes, all graced with a touch of the McRitchies' festive spirit, you and your family will agree.

Southwest Shrimp Tacos

good for you • party perfect

MAKES 8 SERVINGS
HANDS-ON TIME: 34 MIN.
TOTAL TIME: 34 MIN.

Hot sauce and ancho chile powder give this dish a tasty kick. Serve with additional hot sauce, Mexican crema or regular sour cream, and chopped radishes.

- 10 to 12 (10-inch) wooden skewers
- 2 lb. unpeeled, large raw shrimp (21/25 count)
  Vegetable cooking spray
- 2 Tbsp. hot sauce
- 1 Tbsp. olive oil
- 1½ tsp. ancho chile powder
- 1½ tsp. ground cumin
- ¾ tsp. salt
- 16 to 20 (8-inch) soft taco-size corn or flour tortillas
- 3 cups shredded cabbage
- 1 cup grated carrots
  Lime wedges

1. Soak skewers in water 20 minutes.
2. Meanwhile, peel shrimp; devein, if desired. Coat cold cooking grate of grill with cooking spray, and place on grill. Preheat grill to 350° to 400° (medium-high) heat.
3. Toss shrimp with hot sauce and next 4 ingredients. Thread shrimp onto skewers. Grill shrimp, covered with grill lid, 1 to 2 minutes on each side or just until shrimp turn pink. Grill tortillas 1 minute on each side or until warmed.
4. Combine cabbage and carrots. Remove shrimp from skewers just before serving. Serve shrimp in warm tortillas with cabbage mixture and lime wedges.

Chunky Tomato-Fruit Gazpacho

good for you • make-ahead
• party perfect

MAKES ABOUT 9 CUPS
HANDS-ON TIME: 30 MIN.
TOTAL TIME: 2 HR., 30 MIN.

The mango, melon, and peaches, along with the cucumbers, give the gazpacho a sweet spin. Don't seed the jalapeño if you like a soup with more zip. If time permits, prepare the day before to allow the flavors to develop fully.

- 2 cups finely diced cantaloupe
- 2 cups finely diced honeydew melon
- 2 cups finely diced tomatoes
- 1 mango, finely diced
- 2 salad cucumbers, finely diced
- 1 jalapeño pepper, seeded and finely chopped
- 1 cup finely diced peaches
- 2 cups fresh orange juice
- ½ cup finely chopped sweet onion
- ¼ cup chopped fresh basil
- 3 Tbsp. chopped fresh mint
- 3 Tbsp. fresh lemon juice
- 1 tsp. sugar
- ½ tsp. salt
  Garnish: fresh basil sprigs

1. Combine first 14 ingredients in a large bowl. Cover and chill 2 to 24 hours. Garnish, if desired.

Wine Pairing Philosophy

"When it comes to wine, the only rule we have is to drink what you enjoy with the foods you enjoy," says Sean. Here are some picks from the McRitchie portfolio for this menu.

- Chunky Tomato-Fruit Gazpacho— Fallingwater White ($15)

- Southwest Shrimp Tacos—Pale Rider Rosé ($16), Chardonnay ($15)

- Blackberry Wine Sorbet—North Carolina Blackberry ($16), North Carolina Semi-Sweet Hard Cider ($14)

To learn more about McRitchie Winery & Ciderworks, visit mcritchiewine.com.

Grilled Corn with Creamy Chipotle Sauce

party perfect

MAKES 8 SERVINGS
HANDS-ON TIME: 25 MIN.
TOTAL TIME: 25 MIN.

To remove the silks from an ear of corn, rub with a damp paper towel or a damp, soft-bristled toothbrush. We doubled the sauce to serve with the tacos. Also try it with grilled steak or chicken.

- Vegetable cooking spray
- 2 garlic cloves
- 1 canned chipotle pepper in adobo sauce
- ½ tsp. salt
- 1 cup cottage cheese
- ¼ cup loosely packed fresh cilantro leaves
- ¼ cup mayonnaise
- ¼ cup plain yogurt
- 1 to 2 tsp. adobo sauce from can
- 8 ears fresh corn, husks removed

1. Coat cold cooking grate of grill with cooking spray, and place on grill. Preheat grill to 350° to 400° (medium-high) heat.
2. Place garlic, pepper, and salt in a food processor; process until minced. Add cottage cheese and next 3 ingredients; process until smooth, stopping to scrape down sides as needed. Stir in adobo sauce. Cover and chill until ready to serve (up to 24 hours).
3. Grill corn, covered with grill lid, 10 minutes or until tender, turning often. Serve corn with sauce.

Sweet-and-Sour Veggie Pickles

make-ahead

MAKES ABOUT 8 CUPS

HANDS-ON TIME: 20 MIN.

TOTAL TIME: 2 HR., 25 MIN., PLUS 1 DAY FOR CHILLING

Baby carrots, zucchini, and pattypan squash form a colorful trio in this recipe. Serve these pickles with cocktails or with grilled poultry or fish. This recipe makes four (1-pt.) jars—enough to keep and give away to friends and neighbors.

- 2 cups seasoned rice vinegar
- 2 cups white vinegar
- ⅔ cup sugar
- 2 tsp. salt
- 2 lb. assorted baby vegetables (carrots, zucchini, pattypan squash)
- 2 shallots, thinly sliced
- 4 garlic cloves, crushed
- 4 (¼-inch-thick) fresh ginger slices, peeled
- 12 fresh cilantro sprigs
- 12 black peppercorns
- 1 Tbsp. sesame seeds
- ½ tsp. dried crushed red pepper

1. Combine first 4 ingredients in a medium saucepan; bring to a boil.
2. Cut baby vegetables in half, if desired. Combine baby vegetables and next 7 ingredients in a large bowl. Pour hot vinegar mixture over vegetable mixture. Toss well. Let stand 2 hours. Cover and chill 24 hours before serving, stirring occasionally. Store in refrigerator up to 1 week.
Note: Vegetable mixture can be evenly divided among 4 (1-pt.) jars.

Blackberry Wine Sorbet

quick prep • make-ahead

MAKES ABOUT 5 CUPS

HANDS-ON TIME: 18 MIN.

TOTAL TIME: 12 HR., 18 MIN., NOT INCLUDING SOME FREEZING TIME, WHICH VARIES

You'll need 1 (750-milliliter) bottle of wine. The secrets to this dessert: Make sure all liquids are cold, and don't overfill the freezer container. For best results, freeze the sorbet for at least eight hours before serving. (pictured on page 15)

- 3 cups blackberry wine*
- 1 cup sugar
- ⅓ cup fresh lime juice
- 1 cup fresh blackberries
- 1 cup fresh blueberries
- ½ cup fresh raspberries
- 2 Tbsp. sugar
- 2 Tbsp. blackberry wine
- ½ tsp. lime zest

1. Cook first 3 ingredients and 1 cup water in a small saucepan over medium heat, stirring occasionally, 3 minutes or just until sugar dissolves. Fill a large bowl with ice; place saucepan in ice, and let stand, stirring wine mixture occasionally, until cold (about 1 hour).
2. Pour mixture into freezer container of a 1½-qt. electric ice-cream maker; freeze according to manufacturer's instructions. (Instructions and times will vary.) Spoon sorbet into an airtight container; cover and freeze at least 8 hours.
3. Combine blackberries and next 5 ingredients; toss gently. Cover and chill up to 2 hours. Serve sorbet topped with berries.
*Riesling or a dry rosé may be substituted.

In Season: Figs

The warm honeyed taste of just gathered figs is the sum of summer's goodness. Savor their sweetness.

The names alone are a seductive roll call of Southern sweetness and earthy delight: 'Alma,' 'Celeste,' 'Magnolia,' and 'Texas Everbearing'—each promises subtle nuances of flavor and texture that are not to be missed.

Baked Fig Crostini

make-ahead • party perfect

1. Preheat oven to 350°. Stir together 4 oz. chopped cooked bacon or country ham; 4 oz. crumbled goat cheese, softened; 1 Tbsp. finely chopped toasted pecans; and 1 tsp. chopped fresh thyme. Cut 12 fresh figs in half. Press back of a small spoon into centers of fig halves, making a small indentation in each. Spoon bacon mixture into indentations. Bake on a baking sheet 7 minutes. Drizzle with 1 Tbsp. honey. Serve immediately with toasted baguette slices

Baked Fig Crostini

Fig Facts

Everything you need to know from market to table.

TO BUY: Choose plump, fragrant, locally grown figs that feel heavy for their size. A supple bend in the stem and slightly puckered skin indicate perfect.

TO STORE: Enjoy them right away. Once picked, figs are highly perishable and won't continue to sweeten. Leave at room temperature or refrigerate up to 2 days.

TO COOK: Pan-sear halved figs with pork chops, broil with a sprinkling of brown sugar and balsamic vinegar, or brush with oil and grill until golden.

TO SERVE: Pair with salty aged cheese, country ham, or peppery salad greens. For dessert, poach them in spiced syrup, drizzle with cream, or dollop with mascarpone.

Get Figgy With It

FEEL THE GLOW: Essenza Hour Glass Candle Fig Tea, *amazon.com*; $19.50

SET A BEAUTIFUL TABLE: Acorn and Fig Ceramics Collection Serving Bowl, *surlatable.com*; $39.95

EMBRACE THE SCENT: Pacifica Mediterranean Fig Soap, *pacificaperfume.com*; $5

SPOON INTO SOMETHING WONDERFUL: Braswell's Select Fig Preserves, *braswells.com*; $5 and $6.25

Six-Ingredient Suppers

You'll be amazed at how much flavor we coaxed from so few ingredients.

Hearty main dishes from only six ingredients? Yep. It was a challenge, but our Test Kitchen Professionals aced the assignment. From Barbecued Pork Chops with Potato Salad to Grilled Chicken-and-Veggie Tortellini, all these recipes are surprisingly delicious and easy to prepare. Add a simple side and you've got supper.

Caribbean Crab Sandwich

quick prep • good for you

MAKES 6 SERVINGS
HANDS-ON: 15 MIN.
TOTAL TIME: 22 MIN.

- 2 limes
- 1 lb. fresh crabmeat, drained
- ¼ cup chopped fresh cilantro
- 6 hoagie rolls
- 1 mango, peeled and chopped
- 1 avocado, chopped

1. Preheat oven to 350°. Grate zest from 1 lime to equal ½ tsp. Squeeze juice from limes to equal 6 Tbsp. Gently combine zest, lime juice, crabmeat, and cilantro.
2. Bake buns at 350° for 7 minutes or until toasted.
3. Spoon crabmeat mixture into buns; sprinkle with mango and avocado. Serve immediately.

 ## Creamy Tomato Penne with Shrimp

quick prep

MAKES 4 SERVINGS
HANDS-ON TIME: 17 MIN.
TOTAL TIME: 22 MIN.

- ¾ lb. peeled, large raw shrimp (21/30 count)
- 1 (8-oz.) package penne pasta
- 1 (24-oz.) jar pasta sauce
- ½ cup freshly grated Parmesan cheese
- 1 cup heavy cream
- ½ cup firmly packed fresh basil leaves, shredded

1. Devein shrimp, if desired. Prepare pasta according to package directions.
2. Meanwhile, bring pasta sauce to a boil in a medium saucepan over medium heat. Gradually stir in cheese and cream; cook, stirring often, 3 minutes or until cheese melts and mixture begins to simmer. Stir in shrimp; cook 4 minutes or just until shrimp turn pink.
3. Combine sauce and pasta; toss to coat. Sprinkle with basil.

RECIPE INSPIRED BY KATHERINE SCULLY
SAINT JAMES, NEW YORK

Grilled Tomato-Peach Pizza

quick prep

MAKES 4 SERVINGS
HANDS-ON TIME: 26 MIN.
TOTAL TIME: 26 MIN.
(pictured on page 187)

- Vegetable cooking spray
- 2 tomatoes, sliced
- ½ tsp. salt
- 1 large peach, peeled and sliced
- 1 lb. bakery pizza dough
- ½ (16-oz.) package fresh mozzarella, sliced
- 4 to 6 fresh basil leaves
- Garnishes: coarsely ground pepper, olive oil

1. Coat cold cooking grate of grill with cooking spray, and place on grill. Preheat grill to 350° (medium) heat.
2. Sprinkle tomatoes with salt; let stand 15 minutes. Pat tomatoes dry with paper towels.
3. Grill peach slices, covered with grill lid, 2 to 3 minutes on each side or until grill marks appear.
4. Place dough on a large baking sheet coated with cooking spray; lightly coat dough with cooking spray. Roll dough to ¼-inch thickness (about 14 inches in diameter). Slide pizza dough from baking sheet onto cooking grate.
5. Grill, covered with grill lid, 2 to 3 minutes or until lightly browned. Turn dough over, and reduce temperature to 250° to 300° (low) heat; top with tomatoes, grilled peaches, and mozzarella. Grill, covered with grill lid, 5 minutes or until cheese melts. Arrange basil leaves over pizza. Serve immediately. Garnish, if desired.

Mediterranean Tuna Couscous

quick prep • good for you

MAKES 6 SERVINGS
HANDS-ON TIME: 10 MIN.
TOTAL TIME: 15 MIN.

- 1 (5.6-oz.) package toasted pine nut couscous mix
- 1 (8-oz.) container marinated Greek salad mix
- 2 (5-oz.) aluminum foil pouches solid white tuna chunks in water
- ¼ cup chopped fresh parsley
- 2 Tbsp. fresh lemon juice
  Lemon wedges (optional)

1. Prepare couscous according to package directions.
2. Drain Greek salad mix, reserving 3 Tbsp. liquid. Combine Greek salad mix, reserved liquid, tuna, parsley, and lemon juice in a large bowl. Add couscous, and toss to coat. Serve with lemon wedges, if desired.
Note: We tested with Bumble Bee Premium Albacore Tuna in Water pouches and Gia Russa Greek Salad.

Barbecued Pork Chops with Potato Salad

quick prep

MAKES 6 SERVINGS
HANDS-ON TIME: 25 MIN.
TOTAL TIME: 6 HR., 25 MIN.

Make the potato salad the night before; then pop the chops in the slow cooker before leaving in the morning to have dinner ready when you get home. Serve with purchased coleslaw or a salad.

- 6 (1-inch-thick) bone-in pork loin chops
- 1 (18-oz.) bottle barbecue sauce
- 2 lb. baking potatoes, peeled and cut into ½-inch cubes
- 2 tsp. salt
- ½ cup mayonnaise
- ¼ cup sweet salad cube pickles

1. Place pork chops and barbecue sauce in a 6-qt. slow cooker; cover and cook on LOW 6 to 8 hours or to desired degree of tenderness.
2. Bring potatoes, salt, and water to cover to a boil in a Dutch oven over medium-high heat. Reduce heat to low; cook 10 minutes or until tender. Drain.
3. Combine mayonnaise and pickles in a medium bowl; add potatoes, and gently stir to coat. Cover and chill, if desired. Serve with pork chops.
Note: We tested with Stubb's Mild Bar-B-Q Sauce.

Grilled Chicken-and-Veggie Tortellini

quick prep

MAKES 4 SERVINGS
HANDS-ON TIME: 22 MIN.
TOTAL TIME: 32 MIN.

- 4 small zucchini, cut in half lengthwise (about 1¼ lb.)
- 2 skinned and boned chicken breasts (13 oz.)
- 1 Tbsp. freshly ground Italian herb seasoning
- 1 (19-oz.) package frozen cheese-filled tortellini
- 1 (7-oz.) container refrigerated reduced-fat pesto
- 2 large tomatoes, seeded and chopped
  Garnish: grated Parmesan cheese

1. Preheat grill to 300° to 350° (medium) heat. Sprinkle zucchini and chicken with seasoning.
2. Grill zucchini and chicken at the same time, covered with grill lid. Grill zucchini 6 to 8 minutes on each side or until tender. Grill chicken 5 to 6 minutes on each side or until done. Remove from grill; let stand 10 minutes.
3. Meanwhile, prepare tortellini according to package directions.
4. Coarsely chop chicken and zucchini. Toss tortellini with pesto, tomatoes, chicken, and zucchini. Serve immediately. Garnish, if desired.
Note: We tested with McCormick Italian Herb Seasoning Grinder.

Cooking Class
Grilled Baby Back Ribs

Our unique stacking method from Test Kitchen Director Lyda Jones Burnette gives you fall-off-the-bone tender results every time you grill.

Grilled Baby Back Ribs

party perfect

MAKES 6 SERVINGS
HANDS-ON TIME: 30 MIN.
TOTAL TIME: 11 HR., 40 MIN.

- 1 Tbsp. kosher salt
- 1 Tbsp. ground black pepper
- ½ tsp. dried crushed red pepper
- 3 slabs baby back pork ribs (about 5½ lb.)
- 2 limes, halved
  Bottled barbecue sauce

Secret to recipe!

Must-Have Tool

Good Grips Silicone Basting Brush is odor resistant, dishwasher-safe, and angled for easy basting. About $10 at oxo.com

Four Easy Steps

1 Make Meat Tender

Combine kosher salt and next 2 ingredients. Remove thin membrane from back of ribs by slicing into it with a knife and pulling it off.

2 Add Spicy Flavor

Rub ribs with cut sides of limes, squeezing as you rub. Massage salt mixture into meat, covering all sides. Wrap tightly with plastic wrap. Place in a 13- x 9-inch baking dish; cover and chill 8 hours.

3 Stack & Grill

Light 1 side of grill, heating to 350° to 400° (medium-high) heat; leave other side unlit. Let slabs stand at room temperature 30 minutes. Remove plastic wrap. Place slabs over unlit side of grill, stacking one on top of the other. Grill, covered with grill lid, 40 minutes. Rotate slabs, moving bottom slab to top; grill 40 minutes. Rotate again; grill 40 minutes.

4 Separate & Baste

Lower grill temperature to 300° to 350° (medium) heat; place slabs side by side over unlit side of grill. Baste with barbecue sauce. Grill 30 minutes, covered with grill lid, basting with sauce occasionally. Remove from grill; let stand 10 minutes.

Frittatas for Any Occasion

Liven up brunch or supper with our basic oven omelet recipe and updated variations.

 Tomato-Herb Frittata

MAKES 6 TO 8 SERVINGS
HANDS-ON TIME: 27 MIN.
TOTAL TIME: 44 MIN.

The secret to this recipe is an ovenproof nonstick pan, which allows the eggs to cook properly, keeps them from sticking, and simplifies cleanup.

- 2 Tbsp. olive oil
- 1 garlic clove, minced
- ½ (6-oz.) package fresh baby spinach
- 1 (10-oz.) can mild diced tomatoes and green chiles, drained
- ¼ tsp. salt
- ¼ tsp. pepper
- 12 large eggs, beaten*
- ½ cup crumbled garlic-and-herb feta cheese**

TEST KITCHEN Secret

Sauté spinach or mushrooms first to prevent them from adding too much liquid to the finished product.

1. Preheat oven to 350°. Heat oil in a 10-inch (2-inch-deep) ovenproof nonstick skillet over medium-high heat.
2. Add garlic, and sauté 1 minute. Stir in spinach, and cook, stirring constantly, 1 minute or just until spinach begins to wilt.
3. Add tomatoes and green chiles, salt, and pepper, and cook, stirring frequently, 2 to 3 minutes or until spinach is wilted. Add eggs, and sprinkle with cheese. Cook 3 to 5 minutes, gently lifting edges of frittata with a spatula and tilting pan so uncooked portion flows underneath.
4. Bake at 350° for 12 to 15 minutes or until set and lightly browned. Remove from oven, and let stand 5 minutes. Slide frittata onto a large platter, and cut into 8 wedges.

RECIPE FROM DEVON GEARHART
SPRING BRANCH, TEXAS

*1 (32-oz.) carton egg substitute may be substituted. Increase bake time to 16 to 18 minutes or until set.
**Plain feta cheese may be substituted.
Note: We tested with Ro-Tel Mild Diced Tomatoes and Green Chilies.

TRY THESE TWISTS!
Tomato-Sausage Frittata: Brown ½ lb. ground pork sausage in a 10-inch (2-inch-deep) ovenproof nonstick skillet over medium-high heat, stirring often, 7 to 8 minutes or until meat crumbles and is no longer pink; remove from skillet, and drain. Wipe skillet clean. Proceed with recipe as directed, adding sausage with tomatoes and green chiles in Step 3. Hands-on time: 34 min.; Total time: 51 min.

Bacon-Mushroom Frittata: Prepare recipe as directed in Step 1, sautéing ½ cup sliced fresh mushrooms in hot oil 2 to 3 minutes or until browned. Proceed with recipe as directed, stirring 3 cooked and chopped bacon slices in with tomatoes. Hands-on time: 24 min.; Total time: 46 min.

Test Kitchen Notebook

ADD IN GOODNESS
Jazz up any frittata recipe with your favorite diced veggies.

Eggplant-and-Olive Frittata: Prepare recipe as directed in Step 1, sautéing 1 cup peeled and chopped eggplant 5 minutes or until tender. Proceed with recipe as directed, stirring in ½ cup sliced black olives with tomatoes. Hands-on time: 32 min.; Total time: 49 min.

Summer Squash Frittata
test kitchen favorite

MAKES 6 TO 8 SERVINGS
HANDS-ON TIME: 32 MIN.
TOTAL TIME: 1 HR., 5 MIN.

- 3 Tbsp. butter
- 2 small zucchini, chopped into ½ inch cubes (about 2 cups)
- 2 small summer squash, chopped into ½-inch cubes (about 2 cups)
- 1 small onion, coarsely chopped (½ cup)
- 12 large eggs, lightly beaten
- ½ cup sour cream
- 1 tsp. kosher salt
- ¾ tsp. freshly ground pepper
- ⅓ cup chopped fresh basil leaves

1. Preheat oven to 350°. Melt 3 Tbsp. butter in a 10-inch ovenproof skillet over medium-high heat; add chopped zucchini, squash, and onion, and sauté 12 to 14 minutes or until onion is tender. Remove skillet from heat.
2. Whisk together eggs and next 3 ingredients until well blended. Pour over vegetable mixture in skillet.
3. Bake at 350° for 33 to 35 minutes or until edges are lightly browned and center is set. Sprinkle evenly with chopped fresh basil.

"I have a bumper crop of cucumbers.

How can I use them in new ways?"

Cucumber-Melon Salad

good for you • make-ahead
• party perfect

MAKES 4 SERVINGS
HANDS-ON TIME: 10 MIN.
TOTAL TIME: 40 MIN.

Stir together 2 Tbsp. olive oil, 1 tsp. lime zest, 3 Tbsp. fresh lime juice, and 1 tsp. chili-lime seasoning. Gently toss with 1 English cucumber, cut into half moons; 2 cups chopped cantaloupe; and 6 radishes, thinly sliced. Cover and chill 30 minutes to 2 hours. Serve over 1 (5-oz.) package arugula.
Note: We tested with Cholula Chili Lime Seasoning.

Test Kitchen Notebook

TIMESAVING TIP:
It's not necessary to remove the seeds from a cucumber, but if you prefer them seedless, cut the cucumber in half lengthwise, and scrape out the seeds with a spoon or melon baller.

Creamy Cucumber Soup

quick prep • good for you • make-ahead
• party perfect

MAKES ABOUT 2 QT.
HANDS-ON TIME: 20 MIN.
TOTAL TIME: 4 HR., 20 MIN.

English, or hothouse, cucumbers have thin skins, few seeds, and mild flavor. English cucumbers are sold wrapped in plastic, rather than coated in wax.

- ¾ cup chicken broth
- 3 green onions
- 2 Tbsp. white vinegar
- ½ tsp. salt
- ¼ tsp. pepper
- 3 large English cucumbers (about 2½ lb.), peeled, seeded, and chopped
- 3 cups fat-free Greek yogurt*
  Garnishes: toasted slivered almonds, freshly ground pepper, chopped red bell pepper

1. Process chicken broth, green onions, vinegar, salt, pepper, and half of chopped cucumbers in a food processor until smooth, stopping to scrape down sides.
2. Add yogurt, and pulse until blended. Pour into a large bowl; stir in remaining chopped cucumbers. Cover and chill 4 to 24 hours. Season with salt to taste just before serving. Garnish, if desired.
*Plain low-fat yogurt may be substituted. Decrease chicken broth to ½ cup.

Fried Cucumbers

quick prep

MAKES ABOUT 5½ TO 6 DOZEN
HANDS-ON TIME: 37 MIN.
TOTAL TIME: 57 MIN.

Kirby cucumbers are short (about 6 inches long) and very crisp, which makes them ideal for pickling and frying.

- 4 small Kirby cucumbers (about 1 lb.), cut into ⅛- to ¼-inch-thick slices
- 1 tsp. kosher salt, divided
- ¾ cup cornstarch
- ½ cup self-rising white cornmeal mix
- ¼ tsp. ground black pepper
- ¼ tsp. ground red pepper
- ¾ cup lemon-lime soft drink
- 1 large egg, lightly beaten
  Vegetable oil
  Ranch dressing or desired sauce

1. Arrange cucumber slices between layers of paper towels. Sprinkle with ½ tsp. kosher salt, and let stand 20 minutes.
2. Combine cornstarch and next 3 ingredients. Stir in soft drink and egg. Dip cucumber slices into batter.
3. Pour oil to depth of ½ inch into a large cast-iron or heavy skillet; heat to 375°. Fry cucumbers, 6 to 8 at a time, about 1½ minutes on each side or until golden. Drain on paper towels. Sprinkle with remaining ½ tsp. kosher salt, and serve immediately with dressing or sauce.
Note: We tested with White Lily Self-Rising White Cornmeal Mix.

Lighten Up!
Potato Salad

This Southern picnic favorite gets a healthy makeover with light, summer-fresh flavor.

Move over, mayonnaise. Here's a lighter spin on Southern potato salad that's just as good as traditional creamy versions.

Olive oil, lemon juice, seasonings, and fresh herbs create a not-so-heavy dressing that offers a heart-healthy dose of monounsaturated fat. Plus, it's perfectly portable—you can serve it at room temperature or chilled.

Lemony Potato Salad
good for you • make-ahead •party perfect

MAKES 6 SERVINGS
HANDS-ON TIME: 25 MIN.
TOTAL TIME: 50 MIN.

- 2 lb. red potatoes, cut into eighths
- ¼ cup olive oil
- 3 Tbsp. lemon juice
- ¾ tsp. salt
- ½ tsp. dry mustard
- ¼ tsp. freshly ground pepper
- 3 green onions, thinly sliced
- 2 Tbsp. chopped fresh parsley

1. Bring potatoes and salted cold water to cover to a boil in a large Dutch oven; boil 15 to 17 minutes or just until tender. Drain and let cool 5 minutes.
2. Whisk together olive oil and next 4 ingredients in a large bowl. Add warm potatoes, green onions, and parsley; toss to coat. Serve at room temperature or chilled.

PER SERVING: CALORIES 196; **FAT** 9.7G (**SAT** 1.4G, **MONO** 7.2G, **POLY** 0.9G); **PROTEIN** 3.1G; **CARB** 25.4G; **FIBER** 2.9G; **CHOL** 0MG; **IRON** 1.3MG; **SODIUM** 302MG; **CALC** 24MG

TEST KITCHEN *Secret*

Leaving the skins on potatoes not only makes a prettier presentation but also adds more antioxidants and fiber to your dish. The red skins are chock-full of healthful flavonoids, which help protect against cardiovascular disease and certain cancers.

Quick and Delicious Summer Salads

Layer, toss, and serve—all in a cool 30 minutes.

Chicken, Apple, and Smoked Gouda Salad

quick prep • make-ahead • party perfect

MAKES 4 TO 6 SERVINGS
HANDS-ON TIME: 20 MIN.
TOTAL TIME: 30 MIN., INCLUDING DRESSING

One deli-style rotisserie chicken yields the perfect amount for this recipe.

- 2 large Gala apples, thinly sliced (about 1 lb.)
- 2 Tbsp. fresh lemon juice
- 1 (6-oz.) package baby spinach and spring greens mix
- 3 cups shredded cooked chicken
- 1 small red onion, halved and sliced
- 1½ cups (6 oz.) shredded smoked Gouda cheese
- 1½ cups thinly sliced celery
- 1 cup sweetened dried cranberries
- 1 cup salted roasted pecans
  Honey-Mustard Dressing

1. Toss apple slices with lemon juice.
2. Layer salad greens, apples, chicken, and next 5 ingredients in a large glass bowl. Serve immediately, or cover and chill up to 8 hours. Toss salad with ¼ cup Honey-Mustard Dressing just before serving. Serve with remaining dressing.
Note: We tested with Fresh Express 50/50 Spring Mix and Baby Spinach.

TEST KITCHEN *Secret*

Need a fabulous party dish? Each of these versatile salads can be layered and chilled up to eight hours ahead.

Honey-Mustard Dressing:

MAKES 1¾ CUPS
HANDS-ON TIME: 10 MIN.
TOTAL TIME: 10 MIN.

1. Whisk together 1 cup mayonnaise; ¼ cup chopped fresh basil; ¼ cup each yellow mustard, Dijon mustard, and honey; and ½ tsp. ground red pepper.

Cobb Salad with Barbecue-Ranch Dressing

quick prep • make-ahead • party perfect

MAKES 6 TO 8 SERVINGS
HANDS-ON TIME: 20 MIN.
TOTAL TIME: 25 MIN., INCLUDING DRESSING

This dressing also makes a tasty dipping sauce for fried chicken tenders and wings.

- 1 large head romaine lettuce, shredded
- 1 lb. chopped smoked chicken
- 1 cup (4 oz.) shredded sharp Cheddar cheese
- 3 large tomatoes, seeded and diced
- 2 large avocados
- 1 Tbsp. fresh lemon juice
- 1 bunch green onions, sliced
- 1 (4-oz.) package crumbled blue cheese
- 6 bacon slices, cooked and crumbled
  Barbecue-Ranch Dressing

1. Layer first 4 ingredients on a large serving platter.
2. Peel and chop avocados; toss with lemon juice.
3. Layer avocado, green onions, crumbled blue cheese, and crumbled bacon over salad. Serve immediately, or cover and chill up to 8 hours. Serve with Barbecue-Ranch Dressing.

Barbecue-Ranch Dressing:

MAKES 2⅓ CUPS
HANDS-ON TIME: 5 MIN.
TOTAL TIME: 5 MIN.

1. Prepare 1 (1-oz.) envelope buttermilk Ranch dressing mix according to package directions; stir in ½ cup barbecue sauce.

Melon-and-Mozzarella Salad

quick prep • make-ahead • party perfect

MAKES 8 TO 10 SERVINGS
HANDS-ON TIME: 20 MIN.
TOTAL TIME: 30 MIN., INCLUDING DRESSING

The real beauty of this salad is how easy It is to assemble. (pictured on page 186)

- 3 cups peeled, coarsely chopped fresh peaches (about 1½ lb.)
- 1 (8-oz.) tub fresh small mozzarella cheese balls, cut in half
- 3 Tbsp. chopped fresh basil
- ¾ cup Lemon-Poppy Seed Dressing
- 4 cups seeded and cubed watermelon
- 4 cups cubed honeydew melon
- 3 cups sliced fresh strawberries
- 2 cups seedless green grapes, cut in half
  Garnishes: fresh raspberries, mint leaves

1. Toss first 3 ingredients with ¼ cup Lemon-Poppy Seed Dressing.
2. Layer watermelon, peach mixture, honeydew, berries, and grapes in a large glass trifle dish or tall glass bowl. Serve immediately, or cover and chill up to 8 hours. Toss with remaining ½ cup dressing just before serving. Garnish, if desired.

Lemon-Poppy Seed Dressing:

MAKES 1⅓ CUPS
HANDS-ON TIME: 10 MIN.
TOTAL TIME: 10 MIN.

1. Process ⅔ cup vegetable oil, ½ cup sugar, ⅓ cup fresh lemon juice, 1½ Tbsp. poppy seeds, 2 tsp. finely chopped onion, 1 tsp. Dijon mustard, and ½ tsp. salt in a blender until smooth. Store in refrigerator up to 1 week; serve at room temperature.

Strawberry Fields Salad

quick prep • make-ahead • party perfect

MAKES 6 TO 8 SERVINGS
HANDS-ON TIME: 20 MIN.
TOTAL TIME: 30 MIN., INCLUDING DRESSING

Ripe nectarines add a colorful layer of flavor to Strawberry Fields Salad.

- 4 large nectarines, cut into ¼-inch-thick wedges
- ¾ cup Lemon-Poppy Seed Dressing
- 1 (10-oz.) package gourmet mixed salad greens
- 2 cups sliced fresh strawberries
- 1 (4-oz.) package crumbled feta cheese
- 1 large green tomato, diced*
- ½ cup chopped fresh basil
- 1 (3.5-oz.) package roasted glazed pecan pieces

1. Toss nectarines with ¼ cup Lemon-Poppy Seed Dressing.
2. Layer gourmet mixed salad greens, nectarines, strawberries, and next 4 ingredients in a large glass bowl. Serve immediately, or cover and chill up to 8 hours. Toss salad with remaining ½ cup dressing just before serving.
*1½ cups halved miniature heirloom green tomatoes may be substituted.

Berry Delicious Summer Salad

test kitchen favorite

MAKES 6 TO 8 SERVINGS
HANDS-ON TIME: 5 MIN.
TOTAL TIME: 5 MIN.

This quick-to-make and refreshing salad is perfect for a weeknight dinner or for a summer night gathering

- 8 cups mixed salad greens
- 2 cups fresh blueberries
- ½ cup Gorgonzola or blue cheese
- ¼ cup chopped and toasted walnuts or pecans
  Bottled vinaigrette

1. Toss together first 4 ingredients; drizzle with desired amount of vinaigrette, tossing gently to coat.
Note: For testing purposes only, we used Newman's Own Light Raspberry & Walnut Dressing.

Cookies Anytime

Why buy slice-and-bake cookies when you can quickly mix our doughs, keep 'em on hand, and bake fresh cookies in minutes.

 Spicy Oatmeal Cookies

quick prep • make-ahead

MAKES ABOUT 5 DOZEN
HANDS-ON TIME: 20 MIN.
TOTAL TIME: 2 HR., 18 MIN.

You get both crispy and chewy in each bite of these cookies.

- ¾ cup chopped pecans
- ½ cup butter
- 1½ cups sugar
- ½ cup molasses
- 2 large eggs
- 1 tsp. vanilla extract
- 1¾ cups all-purpose flour
- 1 tsp. salt
- 1 tsp. baking soda
- 1 tsp. ground cinnamon
- ¼ tsp. ground nutmeg
- 2 cups uncooked regular oatmeal
- 1 cup raisins
  Parchment paper

1. Preheat oven to 375°. Bake pecans in a single layer in a shallow pan 8 to 9 minutes or until toasted and fragrant, stirring halfway through. Let cool completely (about 30 minutes).
2. Beat butter at medium speed with an electric mixer until creamy; gradually add sugar and molasses, beating well. Add eggs and vanilla; beat well.
3. Stir together flour and next 4 ingredients. Add to butter mixture; beat at low speed until well blended. Stir in oatmeal, raisins, and pecans. (If desired, store dough in an airtight container in refrigerator up to 1 week.)
4. Drop cookie dough by heaping tablespoonfuls 2 inches apart onto parchment paper-lined or lightly greased baking sheets.
5. Bake at 375° for 9 to 10 minutes or until lightly browned. (Bake chilled dough 10 to 11 minutes.) Cool on baking sheets on a wire rack 5 minutes; transfer to wire racks, and cool completely (about 30 minutes).

RECIPE FROM CHRIS BRYANT
JOHNSON CITY, TENNESSEE

 Cappuccino Blossoms

quick prep • make-ahead

MAKES ABOUT 3½ DOZEN
HANDS-ON TIME: 20 MIN.
TOTAL TIME: 1 HR., 53 MIN.

This is our coffee-and-almond redo of the classic kiss-topped cookies. Our amounts of granulated and light brown sugar are correct—the liqueur also adds sweetness. And, surprisingly, the recipe does not call for eggs. (pictured on page 188)

- 1 cup butter, softened
- 6 Tbsp. granulated sugar
- ¼ cup firmly packed light brown sugar
- ½ cup coffee liqueur
- 2⅔ cups all-purpose flour
- 2 tsp. instant espresso
- 1 tsp. baking soda
- ½ tsp. ground cinnamon
- ¼ tsp. salt
- 1 cup chopped salted, roasted almonds*
  Parchment paper
- 42 dark chocolate kisses

1. Preheat oven to 375°. Beat butter at medium speed with an electric mixer until creamy; gradually add sugars; beating well. Add coffee liqueur; beat well.
2. Stir together flour and next 4 ingredients. Add to butter mixture; beat at low speed until well blended. Stir in almonds. (If desired, store dough in an airtight container in refrigerator up to 1 week.)
3. Drop cookie dough by heaping tablespoonfuls 2 inches apart onto parchment paper-lined or lightly greased baking sheets.
4. Bake at 375° for 10 to 12 minutes or until edges are golden. (Bake chilled dough 11 to 12 minutes.) Remove from oven, and immediately press 1 dark chocolate kiss into center of each cookie. Cool on baking sheets on a wire rack 3 minutes; transfer to wire racks, and cool completely (about 1 hour).

RECIPE FROM MARIE RIZZIO
INTERLOCHEN, MICHIGAN

Note: Be sure to unwrap candies while cookies bake. You'll be ready to quickly pop them onto hot cookies.
*Toasted, slivered almonds or dry-roasted salted peanuts may be substituted.

Easiest-Ever Chocolate Chip Cookies

quick prep • make-ahead

Kid Approved

MAKES ABOUT 4½ DOZEN
HANDS-ON TIME: 20 MIN.
TOTAL TIME: 1 HR.

- ½ cup butter, softened
- 1⅔ cups firmly packed light brown sugar
- 2 large eggs
- 1 tsp. vanilla extract
- 2 cups self-rising flour
- 1 (12-oz.) package semisweet chocolate morsels
  Parchment paper

1. Preheat oven to 350°. Beat butter at medium speed with an electric mixer until creamy; gradually add sugar, beating well. Add eggs and vanilla; beat well. Add flour; beat at low speed until well blended. Stir in chocolate morsels. (If desired, store dough in an airtight container in refrigerator up to 1 week.)

2. Drop cookie dough by heaping tablespoonfuls 2 inches apart onto parchment paper-lined or lightly greased baking sheets.

3. Bake at 350° for 11 to 12 minutes or until lightly browned. (Bake chilled dough 12 to 13 minutes.) Cool on baking sheets on a wire rack 5 minutes; transfer to wire racks, and cool completely (about 30 minutes).

RECIPE FROM CLAIRE TOWNSEND
LAKE CITY, FLORIDA

Peanut Buttery-Chocolate Chunk Cookies

quick prep • make-ahead

MAKES ABOUT 5½ DOZEN
HANDS-ON TIME: 20 MIN.
TOTAL TIME: 1 HR., 48 MIN.

- 1 cup butter, softened
- 1 cup creamy or chunky peanut butter
- 1 cup granulated sugar
- 1 cup firmly packed light brown sugar
- 1 large egg
- 1½ tsp. vanilla extract
- 2½ cups all-purpose flour
- 1½ tsp. baking powder
- 1 tsp. salt
- 1 (11.5-oz.) package semisweet chocolate chunks
  Parchment paper

1. Preheat oven to 350°. Beat butter and peanut butter at medium speed with an electric mixer until creamy; gradually add sugars beating well. Add egg and vanilla; beat well.

2. Stir together flour, baking powder, and salt. Add to butter mixture; beat at low speed until well blended. Stir in chocolate chunks. (If desired, store dough in an airtight container in refrigerator up to 1 week.)

3. Drop cookie dough by heaping tablespoonfuls 2 inches apart onto parchment paper-lined or lightly greased baking sheets.

4. Bake at 350° for 11 to 12 minutes or until edges of cookies are brown. (Bake chilled dough 13 to 14 minutes.) Cool on baking sheets on a wire rack 3 minutes; transfer to wire racks, and cool completely (about 30 minutes).

RECIPE FROM RENEE BISCHOFF
CINCINNATI, OHIO

Chunky Chocolate Gobs

test kitchen favorite

MAKES ABOUT 2½ DOZEN
HANDS-ON TIME: 18 MIN.
TOTAL TIME: 1 HR., 12 MIN.

- ¾ cup unsalted butter, softened
- ⅓ cup butter-flavored shortening
- 1 cup granulated sugar
- ⅔ cup firmly packed dark brown sugar
- 2 large eggs
- 2 tsp. vanilla extract
- 2 cups all-purpose flour
- ⅔ cup unsweetened cocoa
- 1 tsp. baking soda
- ¼ tsp. salt
- 2 cups cream-filled chocolate sandwich cookies, coarsely chopped (16 cookies)
- 3 (1.75-oz.) Mounds bars, chilled and chopped
- 1 to 2 cups semisweet chocolate morsels

1. Beat butter and shortening at medium speed with an electric mixer until creamy; gradually add sugars, beating until light and fluffy. Add eggs and vanilla, beating until blended..

2. Preheat oven to 350°. Combine flour and next 3 ingredients; gradually add to butter mixture, beating until blended. Stir in cookies, candy bars, and desired amount of chocolate morsels. Chill dough 30 minutes.

3. Drop dough by ¼ cupfuls 2 inches apart onto baking sheets lined with parchment paper. Bake at 350° for 10 to 12 minutes or until barely set. Cool on baking sheets 10 minutes. Transfer to wire racks to cool completely.

Mama's Way or Your Way?
Cool Lemon Pie

One has a from-scratch crust and lemony-rich baked filling; the other is a delicious no-cook favorite. Both are ready to impress.

Zesty Lemon Pie

quick prep • make-ahead • party perfect

MAKES 8 SERVINGS

HANDS-ON TIME: 25 MIN.

TOTAL TIME: 6 HR., 20 MIN.

If you don't have a 9-inch deep dish, you can use a regular 10-inch pie plate instead. Prepare recipe, without whipped cream, up to 2 days ahead. (pictured on page 189)

1 cup graham cracker crumbs
3 Tbsp. powdered sugar
3 Tbsp. butter, melted
6 egg yolks
2 (14-oz.) cans sweetened condensed milk
1 cup fresh lemon juice
1 cup whipping cream
2 Tbsp. powdered sugar
Garnishes: lemon slices, fresh mint leaves

1. Preheat oven to 350°. Stir together first 2 ingredients; add butter, stirring until blended. Press mixture on bottom and up sides of a 9-inch deep-dish pie plate. Bake 10 minutes. Let cool completely on a wire rack (about 30 minutes).

2. Whisk together egg yolks, sweetened condensed milk, and lemon juice. Pour into prepared crust.

3. Bake at 350° for 15 minutes. Let cool completely on a wire rack (about 1 hour). Cover and chill 4 hours.

4. Beat whipping cream at high speed with an electric mixer until foamy; gradually add powdered sugar, beating until soft peaks form; dollop over chilled pie. Garnish, if desired.

Lemonade Pie

quick prep • make-ahead • party perfect

MAKES 8 SERVINGS

HANDS-ON TIME: 15 MIN.

TOTAL TIME: 8 HR., 15 MIN.

For a homemade look, freeze crust for five minutes, and then slip it into your favorite pie plate before adding filling.

1 (12-oz.) can evaporated milk
2 (3.4-oz.) packages lemon instant pudding mix
1 Tbsp. lemon zest
2 (8-oz.) packages cream cheese, softened
½ tsp. vanilla extract
1 (12-oz.) can frozen lemonade concentrate, thawed
1 (9-inch) ready-made graham cracker piecrust
Thawed frozen whipped topping
Garnish: crushed lemon drop candies

1. Whisk together evaporated milk and next 2 ingredients in a bowl 2 minutes or until mixture is thickened.

2. Beat cream cheese and vanilla at medium speed with an electric mixer until fluffy. Add lemonade concentrate, beating until smooth; add milk mixture, and beat until blended. Pour into crust. Cover and chill 8 hours or until firm. Dollop each slice with whipped topping. Garnish, if desired.

September

Secrets from our Test Kitchen

Meet our Test Kitchen experts up close as they share their never-before-revealed entertaining tips, easy cooking techniques, and a few of their favorite dishes.

Angela's Spicy Buffalo Wings

party perfect

MAKES 4 SERVINGS
HANDS-ON TIME: 30 MIN.
TOTAL TIME: 55 MIN., INCLUDING SAUCES

Serve with plenty of cool beverages. (pictured on page 14)

- 2½ lb. chicken wing pieces (wings already cut)
- 2 tsp. salt
- ¾ tsp. ground black pepper
- ¼ tsp. ground red pepper
- ¼ tsp. onion powder
- 1 cup all-purpose flour
  Vegetable oil
  Spicy Buffalo Sauce
  Cool Ranch Sauce
  Celery sticks

1. Sprinkle wings with salt and next 3 ingredients. Dredge in flour, shaking to remove excess.

2. Pour oil to depth of 2 inches into a large deep skillet; heat to 350°. Fry wings, in batches, 3 to 4 minutes on each side or until done. Drain on a wire rack over paper towels. Toss wings in Spicy Buffalo Sauce; serve immediately with Cool Ranch Sauce and celery sticks.

Spicy Buffalo Sauce:

MAKES 1¼ CUPS
HANDS-ON TIME: 15 MIN.
TOTAL TIME: 15 MIN.

Cook 1 (8-oz.) can tomato sauce, 1 (5-oz.) bottle hot sauce, 1 tsp. Worcestershire sauce, ½ tsp. each salt and sugar, and ¼ tsp. pepper in a saucepan over medium heat 8 to 10 minutes or until slightly thickened.

Note: We tested with Cholula Original Hot Sauce.

Cool Ranch Sauce:

MAKES 1¼ CUPS
HANDS-ON TIME: 10 MIN.
TOTAL TIME: 10 MIN.

1. Whisk together ½ cup mayonnaise; ½ cup sour cream; ¼ cup buttermilk; 1 Tbsp. chopped fresh chives; ¼ tsp. lemon zest; 2 tsp. lemon juice; 1 garlic clove, minced; and salt and pepper to taste until smooth.

"A cast-iron skillet helps keep the oil at the perfect temperature while you fry—it maintains heat better than other skillets. Clip a candy thermometer to the inside of the skillet to monitor the oil temperature while you are frying."

ANGELA SELLERS

Get to know
NORMAN KING

1. How long have you been cooking? Since I was 12 years old.

2. Name a kitchen tool you can't live without. Spring-loaded tongs—they're essential for turning whatever's cooking in a pan. And it's the one tool my friends are guaranteed not to have when we cook together, so I always travel with an extra pair.

3. What's in your fridge right now? Pancetta, fresh sage, romaine lettuce, carrots, tortillas, eggs, Parmesan cheese, buttermilk, bottled lemon and lime juice, and Miller High Life.

4. What's a fast meal you like to make at home? Pan-roasted chicken breasts or thighs with yellow rice and black beans. It takes about 30 minutes to make—40 if I add a chopped salad.

5. Name three pantry items you always keep on hand. Dried beans, rice, and canned crushed tomatoes.

Norman's Stove-Top Popcorn

quick prep

MAKES ABOUT 4 CUPS
HANDS-ON TIME: 10 MIN.
TOTAL TIME: 10 MIN.

With so little oil, this is lighter than store-bought. Use a glass lid to watch the fun!

- ⅓ cup popcorn kernels
- 1 tsp. canola oil
- 1 Tbsp. melted butter
- ½ tsp. kosher salt
- ¼ tsp. freshly ground pepper

1. Combine kernels and oil in a heavy 3-qt. saucepan. Cover with lid, and cook over medium heat 2 to 3 minutes or until kernels begin to pop. Cook, shaking pan often, 2 more minutes or until popping slows. Transfer popcorn to a serving bowl. Drizzle with butter, and sprinkle warm popcorn with kosher salt and pepper; toss to coat.

Get to know
LYDA JONES BURNETTE

1. How long have you been cooking? Since age 14. I grew up watching and helping Mawtea, our family cook, who taught me everything I know.

2. Name a kitchen tool you can't live without. My chef's knife—I take it on vacation with me.

3. What's in your fridge right now? Milk, sippie cups for my kids, homemade white barbecue sauce, four kinds of mustard, three types of pepper jelly.

Lyda's Cream of Carrot Soup

good for you • make-ahead

MAKES 8 CUPS
HANDS-ON TIME: 1 HR., 5 MIN.
TOTAL TIME: 1 HR., 10 MIN.

Here's a delicious, low-fat way to get the kids to eat their veggies. (pictured on page 191)

- 2 Tbsp. butter
- 1 (1-lb.) package baby carrots, chopped
- 1 (1-lb.) package parsnips, peeled and chopped
- 1 medium-size yellow onion, chopped
- ½ tsp. salt
- ¼ tsp. freshly ground pepper
- 2 (32-oz.) containers chicken broth
- ⅓ cup uncooked long-grain rice
- ⅓ cup half-and-half (optional)
  Toppings: sour cream, chopped fresh chives, freshly ground pepper

1. Melt butter in a large Dutch oven over medium heat; add carrots and next 4 ingredients; sauté 8 minutes or until onion is tender. Stir in chicken broth. Bring to a boil over medium-high heat. Reduce heat to medium, and simmer, stirring often, 20 minutes. Stir in rice, and cook, stirring often, 18 minutes or until rice is tender.

2. Remove from heat. Process mixture with a handheld blender until smooth. Stir in half-and-half, if desired. Serve with desired toppings.

"We call this Peter Rabbit Soup at my house—the recipe is inspired by Julia Child's The Way To Cook. *I use a handheld immersion blender for ease."*

LYDA JONES BURNETTE

Marian's Apple-Fennel Salad

good for you • make-ahead

MAKES 6 TO 8 SERVINGS
HANDS-ON TIME: 20 MIN.
TOTAL TIME: 20 MIN.

Raw fennel is crisp and tasty, a perfect complement to apples and arugula. (pictured on page 191)

- ½ cup coarsely chopped walnuts
- ½ cup extra virgin olive oil
- ¼ cup lemon juice
- 1 shallot, minced
- 1 Tbsp. brown sugar
- 1 tsp. Dijon mustard
- Salt and pepper to taste
- 1 Gala apple, cut into quarters
- 1 medium-size fennel bulb
- 1 celery rib
- 1 (5-oz.) package fresh arugula
- 1 cup loosely packed fresh parsley leaves

1. Preheat oven to 350°. Bake walnuts in a single layer in a shallow pan 7 to 9 minutes or until toasted and fragrant, stirring halfway through.

2. Meanwhile, whisk together olive oil and next 4 ingredients; season with salt and pepper to taste.

3. Cut apple, fennel, and celery into thin slices, using a mandoline or sharp knife. Toss arugula with a small amount of vinaigrette. Arrange arugula on a serving platter. Toss apple, fennel, celery, and parsley with desired amount of vinaigrette. Top arugula with apple mixture; sprinkle with walnuts and salt and pepper to taste. Serve immediately with any remaining vinaigrette.

TRY THIS TWIST!
Crunchy Carrot-Beet Salad: Substitute 2 medium-size peeled beets and 2 large carrots for apples, fennel, and celery. To prevent hands from being stained, hold beets with a paper towel or wear rubber gloves while slicing.

"For ultrathin slices, I like to use a handheld mandoline slicer. It has a super-sharp blade for precision cutting, and it's faster than using a knife."

MARIAN COOPER CAIRNS

Rebecca's Black Bottom Icebox Pie

make-ahead • party perfect

MAKES 8 TO 10 SERVINGS
HANDS-ON TIME: 35 MIN.
TOTAL TIME: 9 HR., 35 MIN.

With a rich, creamy filling and melt-in-your-mouth crust, this is quite possibly the best chocolate pie ever.

- 1 (9-oz.) package chocolate wafers
- ½ cup butter, melted
- ⅔ cup sugar
- 3 Tbsp. cornstarch
- 4 egg yolks
- 2 cups milk
- 2 (4-oz.) bittersweet chocolate baking bars, chopped
- 1 Tbsp. dark rum
- 1½ tsp. vanilla extract
- 2 cups heavy whipping cream
- ¼ cup sugar
- Garnish: bittersweet chocolate shavings

1. Pulse chocolate wafers in a food processor 8 to 10 times or until finely crushed. Stir together wafer crumbs and butter, and firmly press mixture on bottom, up sides, and onto lip of a lightly greased 9-inch pie plate. Freeze crust 30 minutes.

2. Whisk together ⅔ cup sugar and 3 Tbsp. cornstarch in a 3-qt. heavy saucepan.

3. Whisk together egg yolks and milk in a small bowl; whisk yolk mixture into sugar mixture in pan, and cook over medium heat, whisking constantly, 10 to 12 minutes or until mixture thickens. Cook 1 more minute. Remove from heat.

4. Microwave chocolate in a microwave-safe glass bowl at HIGH 1½ minutes or until melted, stirring at 30-second intervals. Whisk melted chocolate, rum, and vanilla into thickened filling. Spoon filling into prepared crust. Place plastic wrap directly onto filling (to prevent a film from forming), and chill 8 to 24 hours.

5. Beat whipping cream and ¼ cup sugar at medium-high speed with an electric mixer until soft peaks form. Top pie with whipped cream, and garnish, if desired.

Note: We tested with Nabisco FAMOUS Chocolate Wafers and Ghirardelli 60% Cacao Bittersweet Chocolate Baking Bars.

Vanessa's Make-Ahead Beefy Lasagna

make-ahead • party perfect

MAKES 8 SERVINGS
HANDS-ON TIME: 25 MIN.
TOTAL TIME: 1 HR., 35 MIN.

- 12 uncooked lasagna noodles
- 1 (24-oz.) container 4% small-curd smooth-and-creamy cottage cheese
- 1 (16-oz.) container ricotta cheese
- 2 large eggs, lightly beaten
- ½ cup refrigerated pesto
- 1 tsp. salt
- 2½ cups (10 oz.) shredded mozzarella cheese, divided
- 1 lb. lean ground beef
- ½ cup finely chopped onion
- 2 (24-oz.) jars tomato-and-basil pasta sauce

1. Preheat oven to 375°. Prepare noodles according to package directions.

2. Meanwhile, stir together cottage cheese and next 4 ingredients. Stir in 1 cup mozzarella cheese.

3. Cook ground beef and onion in a large skillet over medium-high heat, stirring often, 6 to 7 minutes or until meat crumbles and is no longer pink; drain. Stir in pasta sauce.

4. Layer 1 cup beef mixture, 3 noodles, and 2½ cups cottage cheese mixture in a lightly greased 13- x 9-inch baking dish. Top with 3 noodles, 2 cups beef mixture, and 3 more noodles. Top with remaining cottage cheese mixture, 3 noodles, and beef mixture. Sprinkle with remaining 1½ cups mozzarella cheese.

5. Bake, covered, at 375° for 40 to 45 minutes. Uncover and bake 20 minutes or until cheese is browned. Let stand 10 to 15 minutes before serving.

Note: Freeze unbaked lasagna up to 3 months. To bake, thaw in refrigerator 24 hours. Let stand 30 minutes; bake as directed. We tested with Classico Di Napoli Tomato & Basil Pasta Sauce and both LeGrand Garden Pesto and Buitoni Reduced Fat Pesto with Basil.

"Line the dish with foil for easy freezing. Assemble and freeze in dish; then remove it from dish, wrap completely in foil, and freeze. Unwrap and return to dish to bake."

VANESSA MCNEIL ROCCHIO

Pam's Country Crust Bread

make-ahead

MAKES 2 LOAVES
HANDS-ON TIME: 25 MIN.
TOTAL TIME: 3 HR., 50 MIN.

This top-rated bread has a tender crumb and soft crust. (pictured on page 14)

2 (¼-oz.) envelopes active dry yeast
2 cups warm water (105° to 115°)
½ cup sugar
2 large eggs
¼ cup vegetable oil
1 Tbsp. salt
1 Tbsp. lemon juice
6 to 6½ cups bread flour
1 Tbsp. vegetable oil
1½ Tbsp. butter, melted

Pam's Country
Crust Bread

1. Combine yeast, warm water, and 2 tsp. sugar in bowl of a heavy-duty electric stand mixer; let stand 5 minutes. Stir in eggs, next 3 ingredients, 3 cups flour, and remaining sugar. Beat dough at medium speed, using paddle attachment, until smooth. Gradually beat in remaining 3 to 3½ cups flour until a soft dough forms.
2. Turn dough out onto a well-floured surface, and knead until smooth and elastic (about 8 to 10 minutes),

sprinkling surface with flour as needed. Place dough in a lightly greased large bowl, turning to grease top. Cover and let rise in a warm place (85°), free from drafts, about 1 hour or until doubled in bulk.
3. Punch dough down; turn out onto a lightly floured surface. Divide dough in half.
4. Roll each dough half into an 18- x 9-inch rectangle. Starting at 1 short end, tightly roll up each rectangle,

jelly-roll fashion, pressing to seal edges as you roll. Pinch ends of dough to seal, and tuck ends under dough. Place each dough roll, seam side down, in a lightly greased 9- x 5-inch loaf pan. Brush tops with oil. Cover and let rise in a warm place (85°), free from drafts, 1 hour or until doubled in bulk.
5. Preheat oven to 375°. Bake 25 to 30 minutes or until loaves are deep golden brown and sound hollow when tapped. Remove from pans to a wire rack, and brush loaves with melted butter. Let cool completely (about 1 hour).

TRY THESE TWISTS!
Country Crust Wheat Bread: Substitute 3 cups wheat flour for 3 cups bread flour.
Country Crust Cheese Bread: Sprinkle 1 cup (4 oz.) freshly shredded sharp Cheddar cheese onto each dough rectangle before rolling up.

"I love the Pampered Chef Pastry Mat— the nonskid silicone is perfect for sizing and rolling out dough."

PAM LOLLEY

Get to know ....
PAM LOLLEY

1. How long have you been baking? I baked my first batch of cookies when I was 8 years old. From there, I played with cake mixes and eventually experimented with real "from-scratch" recipes.
2. What is your secret weapon for easy entertaining? Keep it simple—quick and easy finger foods and make-ahead main dishes.
3. Name a kitchen tool you can't live without. My heavy-duty stand mixer.
4. What's in your fridge right now? Real butter, eggs, milk, and buttermilk.
5. What's a fast meal you like to make at home? A quick sauté of onion, garlic, olive oil, and whatever fresh veggies I have around stirred into pasta with some refrigerated pesto.
6. Name three pantry items you always keep on hand. Canned tomatoes, olive oil, and assorted pastas.

Three Easy Upside-Down Cakes

Tender layers of rich, moist cake and perfectly caramelized fruit bake together in one pan. As incredibly simple as it is deliciously seasonal.

Blackberry-Apple Upside-Down Cake

quick prep • make-ahead • party perfect

MAKES 8 SERVINGS
HANDS-ON TIME: 20 MIN.
TOTAL TIME: 1 HR., 15 MIN.

A handful of berries adds a sweet Southern twist to this dessert. If using frozen berries, add them straight from the freezer so they hold their shape. (pictured on page 188)

- ¾ cup butter, softened and divided
- ½ cup firmly packed light brown sugar
- ¼ cup honey
- 2 large Gala apples, peeled and cut into ¼-inch-thick slices
- 1 cup fresh or frozen blackberries*
- 1 cup granulated sugar
- 2 large eggs
- 1½ cups all-purpose flour
- 1 tsp. baking powder
- ½ cup milk
- 1 tsp. vanilla extract

1. Preheat oven to 350°. Melt ¼ cup butter in a lightly greased 9-inch round cake pan (with sides that are at least 2 inches high) over low heat. Remove from heat. Sprinkle with brown sugar; drizzle honey over brown sugar. Arrange apple slices in concentric circles over brown sugar mixture, overlapping as needed; sprinkle with blackberries.

TEST KITCHEN Secret

Flip an upside-down cake out of the pan when it's still hot, before the sugar syrup has set. After about 10 minutes (cake will still be hot), place a serving plate on top of the skillet or pan, and invert the cake directly onto the plate.

2. Beat granulated sugar and remaining ½ cup butter at medium speed with an electric mixer until blended. Add eggs, 1 at a time, beating until blended after each addition.
3. Stir together flour and baking powder. Add flour mixture to sugar mixture alternately with milk, beginning and ending with flour mixture. Beat at low speed just until blended after each addition. Stir in vanilla. Spoon batter over blackberries in pan.
4. Bake at 350° for 45 to 50 minutes or until a wooden pick inserted in center comes out clean. Cool in pan on a wire rack 10 minutes. Carefully run a knife around edge of cake to loosen. Invert cake onto a serving plate, spooning any topping in pan over cake.
*1 cup fresh or frozen cranberries may be substituted.

Pineapple Upside-Down Carrot Cake

quick prep • make-ahead • party perfect

MAKES 8 SERVINGS
HANDS-ON TIME: 20 MIN.
TOTAL TIME: 1 HR., 15 MIN.

One quick flip and this cake slips from a skillet.

- ¼ cup butter
- ⅔ cup firmly packed brown sugar
- 1 (20-oz.) can pineapple slices in juice, drained
- 7 maraschino cherries (without stems)
- 1 cup granulated sugar
- ½ cup vegetable oil
- 2 large eggs
- 1 cup all-purpose flour
- 1 tsp. baking powder
- 1 tsp. ground cinnamon
- ¾ tsp. baking soda
- ½ tsp. salt
- 1½ cups grated carrots
- ½ cup finely chopped pecans

1. Preheat oven to 350°. Melt butter in a lightly greased 10-inch cast-iron skillet or a 9-inch round cake pan (with sides that are at least 2 inches high) over low heat. Remove from heat. Sprinkle with brown sugar. Arrange 7 pineapple slices in a single layer over brown sugar, reserving remaining pineapple slices for another use. Place 1 cherry in center of each pineapple slice.
2. Beat granulated sugar, oil, and eggs at medium speed with an electric mixer until blended. Combine flour and next 4 ingredients; gradually add to sugar mixture, beating at low speed just until blended. Stir in carrots and pecans. Spoon batter over pineapple slices.
3. Bake at 350° for 45 to 50 minutes or until a wooden pick inserted in center comes out clean. Cool in skillet on a wire rack 10 minutes. Carefully run a knife around edge of cake to loosen. Invert cake onto a serving plate, spooning any topping in skillet over cake.

In Season: Sorghum Syrup

In the mountain South, it's known as "long sweetnin'" for its lingering rich-as-honey finish. Steeped in backcountry tradition, sorghum syrup making is an art—a magical, end-of-summer alchemy bottled in a Mason jar.

SORGHUM SAVVY: All about this natural sweetener, from sources to syrup fests

TO BUY: Look for 100% pure sorghum syrup at farm stands or specialty markets, or order online. Unlike molasses, sorghum has a buttery complexity.

TO STORE: Tuck it into a dark kitchen cupboard, ready to drizzle over baked apples, hot cornbread, or a down-home version of caramel macchiato.

TO COOK: Substitute it in equal amounts for corn syrup, maple syrup, honey, or molasses in recipes. Try it in Sweet Potato-Pecan Upside-Down Cake (below).

TO PARTY: Syrup-making festivals with hand-harvested sorghum cane and mule-drawn presses are held across the South from late August to mid-October.

Sweet Potato-Pecan Upside-Down Cake

make-ahead • party perfect

MAKES 8 SERVINGS
HANDS-ON TIME: 25 MIN.
TOTAL TIME: 1 HR., 15 MIN.

Brown sugar, butter, and sorghum syrup create a golden sticky bun topping for this delicately spiced cake.

1½ cups coarsely chopped pecans
½ cup firmly packed light brown sugar
⅓ cup butter, melted
¼ cup sorghum syrup or corn syrup
1 cup granulated sugar
½ cup butter, softened
2 large eggs
1¼ cups all-purpose flour
1½ tsp. pumpkin pie spice
1 tsp. baking soda
½ tsp. salt
1 (15-oz.) can sweet potatoes, drained and mashed
⅓ cup buttermilk
1 tsp. vanilla extract

1. Preheat oven to 350°. Stir together first 4 ingredients and 2 Tbsp. water, and spread on bottom of a lightly greased 10-inch cast-iron skillet or a 9-inch round cake pan (with sides that are at least 2 inches high).

2. Beat granulated sugar and ½ cup softened butter at medium speed with an electric mixer until smooth. Add eggs, 1 at a time, beating until blended after each addition.

3. Combine flour, pumpkin pie spice, baking soda, and salt. Gradually add flour mixture to butter mixture, beating at low speed just until blended and stopping to scrape bowl as needed. Add sweet potatoes, buttermilk, and vanilla, beating at medium speed until smooth. Spoon batter over pecan mixture in skillet.

4. Bake on an aluminum foil-lined jelly-roll pan at 350° for 40 to 45 minutes or until a wooden pick inserted in center comes out clean. Cool in skillet on a wire rack 10 minutes. Carefully run a knife around edge of cake to loosen. Invert cake onto a serving plate, spooning any topping in skillet over cake.

Mama's Way or Your Way?
Chicken Tetrazzini

One is a classic; the other, a contemporary twist tossed with Italian prosciutto and peas. Both are pure Southern comfort.

❀ WHY WE LOVE
Mama's Way

- Made-from-scratch Mornay sauce
- Toasted almond-and-Parmesan cheese topping
- Freezes beautifully

Classic Chicken Tetrazzini
quick prep • make-ahead • party perfect

MAKES 8 TO 10 SERVINGS
HANDS-ON TIME: 20 MIN.
TOTAL TIME: 55 MIN.

A speedy Italian classic, Chicken Tetrazzini can be made ahead for easy weeknight dinners. Freeze an unbaked casserole up to 1 month, if desired. Thaw overnight in refrigerator. Let stand 30 minutes at room temperature, and bake as directed.

- 1½ (8-oz.) packages vermicelli
- ½ cup butter
- ½ cup all-purpose flour
- 4 cups milk
- ½ cup dry white wine
- 2 Tbsp. chicken bouillon granules
- 1 tsp. seasoned pepper
- 2 cups freshly grated Parmesan cheese, divided
- 4 cups diced cooked chicken
- 1 (6-oz.) jar sliced mushrooms, drained
- ¾ cup slivered almonds

1. Preheat oven to 350°. Prepare pasta according to package directions.
2. Meanwhile, melt butter in a Dutch oven over low heat; whisk in flour until smooth. Cook 1 minute, whisking constantly. Gradually whisk in milk and wine; cook over medium heat, whisking constantly, 8 to 10 minutes or until mixture is thickened and bubbly. Whisk in bouillon granules, seasoned pepper, and 1 cup Parmesan cheese.
3. Remove from heat; stir in diced cooked chicken, sliced mushrooms, and hot cooked pasta.
4. Spoon mixture into a lightly greased 13- x 9-inch baking dish; sprinkle with slivered almonds and remaining 1 cup Parmesan cheese.
5. Bake at 350° for 35 minutes or until bubbly.

❀ WHY WE LOVE
Your Way

- Light and creamy Parmesan sauce
- Sautéed fresh mushrooms and Marsala
- Weeknight-easy shortcuts

Chicken Marsala Tetrazzini
quick prep • make-ahead • party perfect

MAKES 6 TO 8 SERVINGS
HANDS-ON TIME: 10 MIN.
TOTAL TIME: 45 MIN.

Served from a silver chafing dish on a sideboard or passed around the kitchen table for a casual supper, this updated version of a Southern classic will please everyone.

- 1 (8-oz.) package vermicelli
- 2 Tbsp. butter
- 1 (8-oz.) package sliced fresh mushrooms
- 3 oz. finely chopped prosciutto
- 3 cups chopped cooked chicken
- 1 cup frozen baby English peas, thawed
- 1 (10 ¾-oz.) can reduced-fat cream of mushroom soup
- 1 (10-oz.) container refrigerated light Alfredo sauce
- ½ cup chicken broth
- ¼ cup Marsala
- 1 cup (4 oz.) shredded Parmesan cheese

1. Preheat oven to 350°. Prepare pasta according to package directions. Meanwhile, melt butter in a large skillet over medium-high heat; add mushrooms and prosciutto, and sauté 5 minutes.
2. Stir together mushroom mixture, chicken, next 5 ingredients, and ½ cup cheese; stir in pasta. Spoon mixture into a lightly greased 11- x 7-inch baking dish; sprinkle with remaining ½ cup cheese.
3. Bake at 350° for 35 minutes or until bubbly.

What's for Supper?

Streamline weeknight cooking with these four delicious main dishes paired with simple sides.

Bow-Tie Pasta with Sausage

MAKES 6 SERVINGS
HANDS-ON TIME: 34 MIN.
TOTAL TIME: 34 MIN.

Easy side: Combine 2 Tbsp. chopped fresh parsley, ¼ cup softened butter, and 2 minced garlic cloves. Spread on French bread slices, and bake at 375° until golden brown.

- 1 (12-oz.) package farfalle (bow-tie) pasta
- ¾ lb. Italian sausage, casings removed
- 1 medium onion, chopped
- 4 garlic cloves, minced
- ¼ cup balsamic vinegar
- 1 (14½-oz.) can chicken broth
- 1 (9-oz.) package fresh spinach*
- 6 oz. crumbled feta cheese
- ¼ tsp. salt
- 4 fresh basil leaves, thinly sliced

1. Prepare pasta according to package directions.
2. Meanwhile, cook sausage in a Dutch oven over medium heat, stirring often, 8 to 10 minutes or until meat crumbles and is no longer pink. Add onion, and sauté 5 minutes. Add garlic, and sauté 1 minute. Stir in vinegar, and cook 3 minutes. Add chicken broth; cook 5 minutes. Stir in spinach and next 3 ingredients; cook 2 minutes or until thoroughly heated. Stir in hot cooked pasta, and serve immediately.
*Fresh baby spinach may be substituted for regular spinach.

Lemony Shrimp and Spinach

good for you

MAKES 4 SERVINGS
HANDS-ON TIME: 33 MIN.
TOTAL TIME: 33 MIN.

Easy side: Prepare 1 (10-oz.) package plain couscous according to package directions. Stir in ½ cup chopped roasted red bell peppers, ½ cup grated Parmesan cheese, and ¼ cup chopped fresh parsley.

- 1 lb. unpeeled, large raw shrimp (31/35 count)
- 3 garlic cloves, minced
- 2 Tbsp. olive oil
- ½ cup chicken broth
- 1 tsp. lemon zest
- 3 Tbsp. fresh lemon juice
- ¼ to ½ tsp. dried crushed red pepper
- 1 (6-oz.) package fresh baby spinach
  Salt and pepper to taste

1. Peel shrimp; devein, if desired.
2. Sauté shrimp and garlic in hot oil in a large skillet over medium-high heat 3 to 4 minutes or just until shrimp turn pink. Remove shrimp from skillet; keep warm.
3. Add chicken broth and next 3 ingredients to skillet, stirring to loosen particles from bottom of skillet. Cook 4 to 5 minutes or until liquid is reduced by half. Add spinach, and cook 2 minutes or just until spinach is wilted. Stir in shrimp. Season with salt and pepper to taste. Serve immediately.

RECIPE INSPIRED BY JOANN BELACK
BRADENTON, FLORIDA

Black Beans and Rice

quick prep • good for you

MAKES 6 SERVINGS
HANDS-ON TIME: 20 MIN.
TOTAL TIME: 55 MIN.

Easy side: Toss together 1 (5-oz.) package mixed salad greens, ½ cup (2 oz.) shredded mozzarella cheese, 8 quartered baby carrots, and 1 sliced green onion. Drizzle with your favorite bottled salad dressing. (pictured on page 190)

- 1½ cups uncooked long-grain rice
- 3 (15-oz.) cans black beans, divided
- 1 cup chopped onion
- 1 cup chopped green bell pepper
- 3 garlic cloves, minced
- 2 tsp. olive oil
- 1 (14-oz.) can chicken broth
- 1 (6-oz.) can tomato paste
- 1 tsp. ground cumin
- ¾ tsp. dried crushed red pepper
  Salt to taste
  Toppings: shredded Cheddar cheese, sliced radishes, chopped tomatoes, chopped fresh cilantro, sliced green onions, sliced jalapeño peppers

1. Prepare rice according to package directions.
2. Meanwhile, drain and rinse 2 cans black beans. (Do not drain remaining can of black beans.)
3. Sauté onion, bell pepper, and garlic in hot oil in a Dutch oven over medium-high heat 5 minutes or until tender. Stir in drained and undrained beans, chicken broth, tomato paste, cumin, and dried crushed red pepper. Bring to a boil; reduce heat, and simmer, stirring occasionally, 30 minutes. Add salt to taste. Serve with hot cooked rice and desired toppings.

Chicken Thigh Cacciatore

good for you

MAKES 4 SERVINGS

HANDS-ON TIME: 35 MIN.

TOTAL TIME: 35 MIN.

Easy side: Microwave 1 (12-oz.) package fresh broccoli florets, 1 minced garlic clove, 2 Tbsp. water, and ½ tsp. salt, covered with plastic wrap, at HIGH 3 to 4 minutes or until tender.

8   skinned and boned chicken thighs (about 2 lb.)

2   tsp. salt-free dried Italian seasoning

1   tsp. salt

2   Tbsp. vegetable oil

1   small onion, chopped

1   medium-size green bell pepper, chopped

1   garlic clove, minced

1   (24-oz.) jar tomato-and-basil pasta sauce

Hot cooked fettuccine

¼   cup finely grated Parmesan cheese

⅓   cup chopped fresh parsley (optional)

1. Sprinkle chicken with Italian seasoning and salt. Cook chicken in hot oil in a 12-inch skillet over medium-high heat 5 to 6 minutes on each side or until done. Remove chicken; reserve drippings in skillet.

2. Sauté onion and bell pepper in hot drippings 5 to 6 minutes. Add garlic, and sauté 1 minute. Return chicken to skillet; pour pasta sauce over chicken. Bring to a boil over medium heat. Reduce heat to medium-low, and simmer 3 to 5 minutes or until thoroughly heated.

3. Spoon chicken mixture over hot cooked fettuccine. Sprinkle with cheese and, if desired, parsley.

5 Reasons Avocados will make you healthier right now

1 | They protect your eyes from disease.

Avocados have a high content (more than any other fruit) of the carotenoid lutein, which protects against cataracts and macular degeneration—a leading cause of blindness.

2 | They will lower your cholesterol.

Avocados are high in beta-sitosterol, a natural substance that has been shown to lower blood pressure and cholesterol. In one study, 45 people saw an average drop in cholesterol of 17% after eating avocados for just one week.

3 | They help regulate and reduce blood pressure.

Avocados are a great source of potassium, containing even more than bananas. Studies confirm that eating foods high in potassium (and low in sodium) can lower blood pressure and reduce your risk of stroke.

4 | They are a great source of vitamin E.

Avocados are the greatest fruit source of vitamin E, an antioxidant that protects against many diseases and helps maintain overall health.

5 | They will moisturize your skin.

Avocado butter and oil, two deep-conditioning emollients, will soften skin, eliminate dry patches, and restore your skin's elasticity. Look for beauty products enriched with avocado butter.

A Favorite Way to Enjoy Avocados

MAKE GUACAMOLE

quick prep • good for you • make-ahead • party perfect

Mash pulp from **2 avocados.** Stir in ⅓ **cup drained chilled salsa** and **2 Tbsp. lime juice;** season with **salt and pepper** to taste. Makes 1¾ cups.

The Secret to Being Southern

Living in the South is the next best thing to being alive. Where else do people crown Strawberry Queens, know shrimpers by name, and trade pass-along daylilies? Celebrate the traditions and recipes that best reflect the sweetest life we know.

Welcome Friends with a Beautiful Table

Atlanta's preeminent hostess, tastemaker Danielle Rollins, shares her five cardinal rules for setting the perfect Southern table.

1 Use Heirloom Linens:

In the napkin arena, nothing's nicer than a generous 22-inch hemstitched piece of white linen, monogrammed and crisply ironed. And the more it's laundered, the better it becomes.

To buy: No. Four Eleven. Oversize linens with (or without) a monogram. Savannah, GA; numberfoureleven.com or 912/443-0065

2 Mix-andMatch China and Glassware:

Select the basics and add embellishments for a look that is "uniquely you." Use simple stemware to counter-balance more decorative china, or vice versa.

To buy: Replacements, Ltd. A veritable warehouse of patterns. Greensboro, NC; replacements.com or 800/737-5223

3 Use Vintage Silver:

Silver adds the sparkle to a table. Don't have all the pieces you need? Beg, borrow, or improvise! Mixing settings can give an updated look.

To buy: Scott Antique Markets. Open the second weekend of every month, a treasure hunt through 3,300 exhibit booths. Atlanta, GA; scottantiquemarket.com or 404/361-2000

4 Set Place Cards:

Place cards take the guesswork out of where to sit. Split up couples, and place people with something in common near each other. Writing names in your own handwriting makes it personal.

To buy: Gadabout Paper. Hand-drawn cards with monograms. Atlanta, GA; agadabout.com or 843/325-6488

5 Arrange Seasonal Flowers:

Stick to low, loosely arranged flowers. With rectangular tables, use multiple bouquets; for a round or square table, a single vase is perfect. Keep scents subtle.

To buy: Wakefield-Scearce Galleries. Mint julep cups, a Southern twist on bud vases. Shelbyville, KY; wakefieldscearce.com

Make a Perfect Apple Pie

Cornmeal Crust Dough

MAKES 2 DOUGH DISKS
HANDS-ON TIME: 15 MIN.
TOTAL TIME: 1 HR., 15 MIN.

2⅓ cups all-purpose flour
¼ cup plain yellow cornmeal
2 Tbsp. sugar
¾ tsp. salt
¾ cup cold butter, cut into ½-inch pieces
¼ cup cold shortening, cut into ½-inch pieces
8 to 10 Tbsp. chilled apple cider

1. Stir together first 4 ingredients in a large bowl. Cut in butter and shortening with a pastry blender until mixture resembles small peas.
2. Mound flour mixture on 1 side of bowl. Drizzle 1 Tbsp. apple cider along edge of mixture in bowl. Using a fork, gently toss a small amount of flour mixture into cider just until dry ingredients are moistened. Move mixture to other side of bowl, and repeat procedure with remaining cider, 1 Tbsp. at a time, until a dough forms.
3. Gently gather dough into 2 flat disks. Wrap in plastic wrap, and chill 1 to 24 hours.

Homemade Apple Pie

MAKES 8 SERVINGS
HANDS-ON TIME: 30 MIN.
TOTAL TIME: 4 HR., 45 MIN., INCLUDING CRUST

1. Preheat oven to 375°. Stir together 4½ lb. Granny Smith apples, peeled and cut into ½-inch-thick wedges; 1 cup sugar; ¼ cup all-purpose flour; ¾ tsp. ground cinnamon; and ¼ tsp. salt. Let stand 15 minutes, gently stirring occasionally.
2. Roll 1 Cornmeal Crust Dough disk to ⅛-inch thickness (about 11 inches wide) on a well-floured surface. Gently press dough into a 9-inch glass pie plate.

Spoon apple mixture into crust, packing tightly and mounding in center; dot with 1 Tbsp. butter cut into pieces.
3. Roll remaining dough disk to ⅛-inch thickness (about 13 inches wide). Gently place dough over filling; fold edges under, and crimp, sealing to bottom crust. Place pie on a jelly-roll pan. Cut 4 to 5 slits in top of pie for steam to escape.
4. Bake at 375° on an oven rack one-third up from bottom of oven 50 minutes. Cover loosely with aluminum foil, and bake 40 minutes. Transfer to a wire rack, and cool 1½ to 2 hours before serving.

Keep It Sweet

Southern Sweet Tea

MAKES 2½ QT.
HANDS-ON TIME: 5 MIN.
TOTAL TIME: 21 MIN.

If you like tea that's really sweet, add the full cup of sugar.

3 cups water
2 family-size tea bags
½ to 1 cup sugar
7 cups cold water

1. Bring 3 cups water to a boil in a saucepan; add tea bags. Boil 1 minute; remove from heat. Cover and steep 10 minutes.
2. Remove and discard tea bags. Add desired amount of sugar, stirring until dissolved. Pour into a 1-gal. container, and add 7 cups cold water. Serve over ice.

Peach Iced Tea

1. Prepare Southern Sweet Tea using ½ cup sugar. Stir together 1½ qt. tea, 1 (46-oz.) bottle peach nectar, and 2 Tbsp. lemon juice. Serve over ice. Makes 3 qt. Hands-on time: 5 min.; Total time: 26 min.

Tips for Celebrating the South

Smoke Like a Pitmaster

John A. Fullilove of Smitty's Market in Lockhart, Texas, shares his secrets.

Four Easy Steps

1 Choose Your Wood

Texas pitmasters preach post oak, but fruitwoods give a sweet finish. Soak the wood chunks in water for a slow burn.

2 Build the Fire

The key is indirect heat: Meat never goes directly above the coals. The smoker temperature should hang around 225°.

3 Smoke Slowly

Don't lift the lid like it's show-and-tell. Brisket might take up to six hours in your chamber. Aim for a meat temp of 195°.

4 Dig In

Let the finished meat rest for 10 minutes to allow the juices to redistribute. When your knife cuts in like butter, it's go time.

Cooking Class
Put up Pickled Okra

Pickled Okra

MAKES 7 (1-PT.) JARS
HANDS-ON TIME: 30 MIN.
TOTAL TIME: 12 HR., 40 MIN.

- 1 (9-piece) canning kit, including canner, jar lifter, and canning rack
- 7 (1-pt.) canning jars
- 2½ lb. small fresh okra
- 7 small fresh green chile peppers
- 7 garlic cloves
- 2 Tbsp. plus 1 tsp. dill seeds
- 4 cups white vinegar (5% acidity)
- ½ cup salt
- ¼ cup sugar

Four Easy Steps

1 Bring canner half-full with water to a boil; simmer. Meanwhile, place jars in a large stockpot with water to cover; bring to a boil, and simmer. Place bands and lids in a large saucepan with water to cover; bring to a boil, and simmer. Remove hot jars 1 at a time using jar lifter.

2 Pack okra into hot jars, filling to ½ inch from top. Place 1 pepper, 1 garlic clove, and 1 tsp. dill seeds in each jar. Bring vinegar, salt, sugar, and 4 cups water to a boil over medium-high heat. Pour over okra, filling to ½ inch from top.

3 Wipe jar rims; cover at once with metal lids, and screw on bands (snug but not too tight). Place jars in canning rack, and place in simmering water in canner. Add additional boiling water as needed to cover by 1 to 2 inches.

4 Bring water to a rolling boil; boil 10 minutes. Remove from heat. Cool jars in canner 5 minutes. Transfer jars to a cutting board; cool 12 to 24 hours. Test seals of jars by pressing center of each lid. If lids do not pop, jars are properly sealed. Store in a cool, dry place at room temperature up to 1 year.

Lighten Up!

French Fries

These four recipes for oven-baked, better-than-drive-through fries deliver fast-food ease without the oil and mess.

From-Scratch Oven Fries

quick prep • good for you

MAKES 4 SERVINGS

HANDS-ON TIME: 20 MIN.

TOTAL TIME: 1 HR.

1½ lb. medium-size baking potatoes, peeled and cut into ½-inch-thick strips

1 Tbsp. vegetable oil

½ tsp. kosher or table salt
    Ketchup (optional)

1. Preheat oven to 450°. Rinse potatoes in cold water. Drain and pat dry. Toss together potatoes, oil, and salt in a large bowl.

2. Place a lightly greased wire rack in a jelly-roll pan. Arrange potatoes in a single layer on wire rack.

3. Bake at 450° for 40 to 45 minutes or until browned. Serve immediately with ketchup, if desired.

PER SERVING (NOT INCLUDING KETCHUP): CALORIES 152; **FAT** 3.6G (**SAT** 0.5G, **MONO** 0.8G, **POLY** 2.3G); **PROTEIN** 2.6G; **CARB** 28.2G; **FIBER** 2G; **CHOL** 0MG; **IRON** 0.5MG; **SODIUM** 247MG; **CALC** 7MG

Try These Twists!

Three more ways to enjoy our From-Scratch Oven Fries

1 **Buffalo Oven Fries** Omit salt. Toss 2 tsp. mesquite seasoning, 1 tsp. hot sauce, ½ tsp. celery salt, and ½ tsp. garlic powder with potatoes and vegetable oil; bake as directed. Serve with Blue Cheese Dip and bottled hot wing sauce, if desired.

PER SERVING (INCLUDING 2 TBSP. BLUE CHEESE DIP; NOT INCLUDING WING SAUCE): CALORIES 211; **FAT** 8.8G (**SAT** 1.8G, **MONO** 1.3G, **POLY** 4G); **PROTEIN** 4.2G; **CARB** 32.4G; **FIBER** 2.1G; **CHOL** 5MG; **IRON** 0.5MG; **SODIUM** 537MG; **CALC** 44MG

2 **Italian-Parmesan Oven** Fries Toss 2 tsp. freshly ground Italian seasoning with potato mixture, and bake as directed. Sprinkle warm fries with 2 Tbsp. grated Parmesan cheese. Serve with warm Easy Marinara Sauce (below), if desired.

Note: We tested with McCormick Italian Herb Seasoning Grinder.

PER SERVING (INCLUDING ¼ CUP MARINARA SAUCE): CALORIES 258; **FAT** 11.7G (**SAT** 2G, **MONO** 5.8G, **POLY** 3.3G); **PROTEIN** 5.4G; **CARB** 35.6G; **FIBER** 4.3G; **CHOL** 3MG; **IRON** 1.3MG; **SODIUM** 489MG; **CALC** 95MG

3 **Spicy Cheese Oven Fries** Toss a pinch of ground red pepper with potato mixture, and bake as directed. Sprinkle with ⅓ cup (1½ oz.) shredded reduced-fat pepper Jack cheese. Bake 1 more minute or until cheese is melted. Serve with ketchup, if desired.

PER SERVING (NOT INCLUDING KETCHUP): CALORIES 184; **FAT** 5.9G (**SAT** 1.9G, **MONO** 0.8G, **POLY** 2.3G); **PROTEIN** 5.3G; **CARB** 28.9G; **FIBER** 2G; **CHOL** 8MG; **IRON** 0.5MG; **SODIUM** 230MG; **CALC** 83MG

Quick Dips

Our oven fries are delicious as is, or serve them with one of these quick-and-tasty dipping sauces.

Blue Cheese Dip: Stir together ½ cup light mayonnaise, ¼ cup crumbled blue cheese, 1 Tbsp. lemon juice, 1 minced garlic clove, and ¼ tsp. each salt and freshly ground pepper. Cover and chill 30 minutes to 1 hour. Makes ⅔ cup. Hands-on time: 5 min.; Total time: 35 min.

PER TBSP.: CALORIES 29; **FAT** 2.6G (**SAT** 0.6G, **MONO** 0.3G, **POLY** 0.8G); **PROTEIN** 0.8G; **CARB** 1.9G; **FIBER** 0G; **CHOL** 3MG; **IRON** 0MG; **SODIUM** 199MG; **CALC** 19MG

Easy Marinara Sauce: Sauté 2 minced garlic cloves in 2 Tbsp. hot olive oil in a saucepan over medium heat 1 minute. Add 1½ Tbsp. tomato paste; cook, stirring constantly, 1 minute. Stir in 1 (14½-oz.) can petite diced tomatoes and 1 Tbsp. lemon juice; reduce heat to low, and cook 10 minutes. Remove from heat. Mash tomatoes with a potato masher until tomatoes are crushed. Stir in 2 Tbsp. chopped fresh basil. Season with salt and pepper to taste. Makes 1 cup. Hands-on time: 20 min.; Total time: 20 min.

PER ¼ CUP (NOT INCLUDING SALT AND PEPPER TO TASTE): CALORIES 89; **FAT** 7G (**SAT** 1G, **MONO** 5G, **POLY** 1G); **PROTEIN** 1.2G; **CARB** 6.9G; **FIBER** 2G; **CHOL** 0MG; **IRON** 0.6MG; **SODIUM** 179MG; **CALC** 24MG

Salted Caramel-Chocolate
Cupcakes, Cappuccino Cupcakes,
and Mocha Latte Cupcakes *(page 39)*

Easy Chicken and Dumplings *(page 36)*

Parmesan-Pecan Fried
Catfish with Pickled Okra
Salsa *(page 29)*

Chocolate Fudge Pie *(page 48)*

Lemon-Cheesecake Bars *(page 48)*

Spicy Pickled Shrimp *(page 52)*

Sizzling Flounder, Bacon-Fried Okra, and Hot Slaw à la Greyhound Grill *(pages 53-54)*

Benne Brittle *(page 54)*

Spicy Pork-and-Orange
Chopped Salad *(page 63)*

Roasted Asparagus Salad *(page 60)*

Simple Beet Salad *(page 95)*

Raspberry Beer Cocktail *(page 71)*

Easy Cheesecake Bars *(page 71)*

Shrimp-Pesto Pizza *(page 69)*

Grilled Chicken with Corn
and Slaw *(page 81)*

Cheesy BBQ Sloppy
Joes *(page 82)*

Oven-Fried Pork Chops with
Roasted Green Beans and
Pecans *(page 82)*

Roasted Lamb *(page 76)*

Oregano Green Beans *(page 77)*

Church-Style Lemon-Roasted Potatoes *(page 77)*

Grilled Chicken Thighs with White Barbecue Sauce *(page 86)*

Grilled Shrimp-and-Green
Bean Salad *(page 87)*

Carolina Peach
Sangria *(page 104)*

Lemon Chicken; Carrot Orzo; and Green Beans with Goat Cheese Tomatoes, and Almonds
(pages 102-103)

Berry-topped Lemon-Almond Tarts *(page 110)*

Pecan-Peach Cobbler
(pages 105)

**Grilled Shrimp
Gumbo Salad** (*page 114*)

Chicken Parmesan
Pizza *(page 44)*

Arkansas Tomato
Sandwiches *(page 116)*

Tomato-and-Corn Pizza *(page 115)*

Fried Okra Tacos (*page 115*)

Melon-and-Mozzarella Salad *(page 141)*

Grilled Tomato-Peach Pizza *(page 134)*

**Cappuccino
Blossoms** (*page 142*)

**Blackberry-Apple
Upside-Down Cake** (*page 151*)

Zesty Lemon Pie *(page 144)*

Black Beans and Rice (*page 154*)

Lyda's Cream of Carrot
Soup *(page 147)*

Marian's Apple-Fennel Salad *(page 148)*

**Fresh Apple Cake
with Browned-Butter
Frosting** *(page 210)*

Southern Living
Food for Today

Duncan Hines

Satisfy your sweet tooth with one of these delicious desserts.

Mint Brownie Ice-Cream Pie

MAKES 10 TO 12 SERVINGS
HANDS-ON TIME: 15 MIN.
TOTAL TIME: 4 HR., 50 MIN.

- 1 (4.67-oz.) package thin crème de menthe chocolate mints
- 1 (17.6-oz.) package DUNCAN HINES Chocolate Lover's Walnut Brownie Mix
- 4 cups vanilla ice cream

1. Preheat oven to 350°. Chop chocolate mints; reserve 3 Tbsp. chopped mints. Prepare brownie batter according to package directions for cake-like brownies, stirring remaining chopped mints into batter. Pour batter into a lightly greased 10-inch springform pan.

2. Bake at 350° for 25 minutes or until a wooden pick inserted in center comes out with a few moist crumbs. Cool completely in pan on a wire rack (about 1 hour).

3. Meanwhile, let ice cream stand at room temperature 20 minutes or until slightly softened. Spread over cooled crust in pan. Freeze 3 hours or until firm.

4. Remove sides of pan. Let pie stand at room temperature 10 minutes before serving. Top with reserved chocolate mints.

Mint Brownie Ice-Cream Pie

Southern Living Food for Today

Black Cherry Brownies with Cherry Frosting

MAKES 12 SERVINGS
HANDS-ON TIME: 15 MIN.
TOTAL TIME: 1 HR., 27 MIN.

Stir the preserves in a small bowl after measuring to smooth the consistency.

- 1 (19.95-oz.) package DUNCAN HINES Family-Style Chewy Fudge Brownie Mix
- 2 cups frozen dark, sweet pitted cherries
- 1 (16.2-oz.) container DUNCAN HINES Fluffy Whipped White Frosting
- ⅓ cup black cherry preserves

1. Preheat oven to 350°. Prepare brownie batter according to package directions for cake-like brownies. Pour into a lightly greased 13- x 9-inch pan. Sprinkle batter with frozen cherries.
2. Bake at 350° for 27 to 30 minutes or until a wooden pick inserted in center comes out with a few moist crumbs. Cool completely in pan on a wire rack (about 45 minutes). Spread frosting over cooled brownies. Spoon preserves over frosting; gently swirl with a long wooden skewer or knife. Cut into squares.

Peanut Brittle Brownie Bites

MAKES ABOUT 4 DOZEN
HANDS-ON TIME: 35 MIN.
TOTAL TIME: 1 HR., 35 MIN.

It helps to run a sharp knife around edges of brownies when removing from pans.

- 1 (19.95-oz.) package DUNCAN HINES Family-Style Chewy Fudge Brownie Mix
- ½ cup chopped salted peanuts
- ¾ cup semisweet chocolate morsels
- 3 Tbsp. whipping cream
- ¾ cup chopped peanut brittle

1. Preheat oven to 350°. Prepare brownie batter according to package directions for fudgy brownies, stirring peanuts into batter. Pour into 2 (24-cup) lightly greased miniature muffin pans.
2. Bake at 350° for 15 to 17 minutes or until a wooden pick inserted in center comes out with a few moist crumbs. Cool in pans on wire racks 5 minutes. Remove from pans to wire racks, and completely cool (about 45 minutes).
3. Microwave chocolate morsels and cream in a microwave-safe bowl at HIGH 30 to 45 seconds or until melted and smooth, stirring at 15-second intervals. Spread chocolate mixture over brownies, and sprinkle with peanut brittle.

Grilled Peach Trifle

MAKES 8 TO 10 SERVINGS
HANDS-ON TIME: 30 MIN.
TOTAL TIME: 2 HR., 40 MIN.

Parchment paper
- 1 (16-oz.) package DUNCAN HINES Angel Food Cake Mix

Vegetable cooking spray
- 8 firm, ripe peaches, peeled and halved

½ cup peach preserves
- 1 (16-oz.) package fresh blueberries, divided

2 to 3 Tbsp. granulated sugar
- 1 Tbsp. chopped fresh mint
- 1 Tbsp. lemon juice
- 1 cup whipping cream
- ½ tsp. lemon juice
- ¼ cup powdered sugar

1. Preheat oven to 350°. Line a 13- x 9-inch pan with parchment paper. Prepare angel food cake batter according to package directions. Pour batter into prepared pan.
2. Bake at 350° for 30 to 33 minutes or until a wooden pick inserted in center comes out clean. Cool in pan on a wire rack 10 minutes. Remove from pan to wire rack, and cool completely (about 30 minutes).
3. Meanwhile, coat cold cooking grate of grill with cooking spray, and place on grill. Preheat grill to 350° to 400° (medium-high) heat. Coat peaches with cooking spray, and grill, without grill lid, 2 to 4 minutes on each side until tender and slightly charred. Remove from grill, and let cool 5 minutes; cut into large pieces.
4. Microwave preserves in a large microwave-safe bowl at HIGH 30 to 45 seconds or until melted. Toss peaches and 1½ cups blueberries with warm preserves. Stir in granulated sugar and next 2 ingredients.
5. Invert cake onto a cutting board. Carefully remove parchment paper, and discard. Trim and discard edges of cake. Cut cake into 32 equal pieces.
6. Beat whipping cream and lemon juice at medium speed with an electric mixer until foamy; gradually add powdered sugar, beating until soft peaks form.
7. Arrange about one-third of cake pieces in a 3-qt. trifle dish. Top with one-third of peach mixture. Repeat layers twice. Top with whipped cream. Cover and chill 1 hour. Top with remaining ½ cup blueberries just before serving.

Angel Coffee Sundaes

MAKES 15 SERVINGS
HANDS-ON TIME: 35 MIN.
TOTAL TIME: 1 HR., 50 MIN.

    2   cups chopped pecans
Parchment paper
    1   (16-oz.) package DUNCAN HINES
        Angel Food Cake Mix
    4   tsp. instant coffee granules
    4   tsp. hot water
    1   cup butter, softened
    4   cups sifted powdered sugar
    1   qt. vanilla ice cream
    ¾   cup jarred chocolate sauce
    ¾   cup jarred caramel sauce

1. Preheat oven to 350°. Bake pecans in a single layer in a shallow pan 5 to 6 minutes or until lightly toasted and fragrant, stirring halfway through.

2. Line a 13- x 9-inch pan with parchment paper. Prepare angel food cake batter according to package directions. Pour batter into prepared pan.

3. Bake at 350° for 30 to 33 minutes or until a wooden pick inserted in center comes out clean. Cool in pan on a wire rack 10 minutes. Remove from pan to wire rack, and cool completely (about 30 minutes).

4. Meanwhile, dissolve coffee granules in 4 tsp. hot water. Beat butter at medium speed with an electric mixer until creamy; gradually add sugar, beating until light and fluffy. Add coffee, and beat until spreading consistency.

5. Trim and discard edges from cake. Cut cake into 15 equal pieces. Spread frosting on top and sides of each piece of cake; roll in pecans. Serve with ice cream, chocolate sauce, and caramel sauce.

Lemon-Raspberry Angel Food Cupcakes

MAKES 24 CUPCAKES
HANDS-ON TIME: 30 MIN.
TOTAL TIME: 1 HR., 32 MIN.

CUPCAKES
    1   (16-oz.) package DUNCAN HINES
        Angel Food Cake Mix
    24 paper baking cups
    ¾ cup seedless raspberry jam

CREAM CHEESE FROSTING
    1½ (8-oz.) packages cream cheese,
        softened
    ¼   cup butter, softened
    ¼   cup fresh lemon juice
    1   (16-oz.) package powdered sugar,
        sifted
    2   tsp. lemon zest

GARNISH
Fresh raspberries

1. Prepare Cupcakes: Preheat oven to 325°. Prepare angel food cake batter according to package directions. Place paper baking cups into 2 (12-cup) muffin pans. Spoon batter into cups.

2. Bake at 325° for 22 to 25 minutes or until a wooden pick inserted in center comes out clean. Cool in pans on wire racks 10 minutes. Remove from pans to wire racks, and cool completely (about 30 minutes).

3. Make a small hole in tops of cupcakes with a knife or end of a wooden spoon. Pipe or spoon about 1 tsp. raspberry jam into centers of cupcakes.

4. Prepare Frosting: Beat cream cheese and butter at medium speed with an electric mixer until creamy; add lemon juice, beating just until blended. Gradually add powdered sugar, beating at low speed until blended; stir in lemon zest.

5. Spread Cream Cheese Frosting on tops of cupcakes. Garnish, if desired.

Angel Coffee Sundaes

Green Onion-Bacon Dip with Mozzarella Bites and Vegetables

Farm Rich

Use flavorful snacks to whip up a variety of scrumptious favorites.

Green Onion-Bacon Dip with Mozzarella Bites and Vegetables

MAKES ABOUT 1½ CUPS
HANDS-ON TIME: 15 MIN.
TOTAL TIME: 23 MIN.

This dip can be made up to 1 hour ahead and chilled until you're ready to serve it.

DIP:

- 4 bacon slices
- 2 green onions, finely chopped
- ¾ cup sour cream
- ½ cup buttermilk
- 1 (3-oz.) package cream cheese, softened
- 1 Tbsp. Ranch dressing mix

SERVE WITH:

1 (22-oz.) package frozen FARM RICH Mozzarella Bites, prepared according to package directions

Cucumber and carrot slices, red bell pepper strips, and celery sticks

Garnishes: Chopped cooked bacon, chopped green onions

1. Prepare Dip: Cook bacon in a large skillet over medium-high heat 6 to 8 minutes or until crisp; remove bacon, and drain on paper towels. Discard drippings. Chop bacon.

2. Stir together bacon, green onions, and next 4 ingredients in a small bowl. Serve with mozzarella bites, cucumber and carrot slices, red bell pepper strips, and celery sticks. Garnish, if desired.

Oven-Roasted Cheese Sticks Caprese

MAKES 6 TO 8 APPETIZER SERVINGS
HANDS-ON TIME: 10 MIN.
TOTAL TIME: 25 MIN.

The tomatoes and cheese sticks are placed on two different pans, but bake them at the same time to make this appetizer quick and easy.

- 1 Tbsp. olive oil
- 1 Tbsp. balsamic vinegar
- 1 garlic clove, pressed
- ¼ tsp. kosher salt
- ⅛ tsp. pepper
- 1 (10-oz.) package grape tomatoes
- ½ (28-oz.) package frozen FARM RICH Cheese Sticks, thawed and cut in half lengthwise
- 2 Tbsp. thin fresh basil strips

1. Preheat oven to 400°. Whisk together first 5 ingredients in a large bowl. Toss tomatoes in olive oil mixture, and place on a broiler pan.
2. Arrange cheese sticks, cut sides up, on a lightly greased 15- x 10-inch jelly-roll pan.
3. Bake cheese sticks and tomatoes, at the same time in separate pans, at 400° for 15 minutes or until cheese sticks are lightly golden and tomatoes begin to burst, stirring tomatoes occasionally.
4. Place cheese sticks on a platter. Spoon tomatoes and any accumulated liquid over cheese. Sprinkle with basil. Serve immediately.

Holiday Meatballs

MAKES 10 TO 12 APPETIZER SERVINGS
HANDS-ON TIME: 30 MIN.
TOTAL TIME: 30 MIN.

For a main-dish meal, serve meatballs over rice with cooked vegetables. You may also prepare meatballs in a 6-qt. slow cooker at HIGH for 2 hours.

- 1 (16-oz.) can whole-berry cranberry sauce
- 1 (12-oz.) bottle chili sauce
- ¼ cup orange marmalade
- 2 Tbsp. soy sauce
- 2 Tbsp. red wine vinegar
- 1 tsp. dried crushed red pepper
- 1 (32-oz.) package frozen FARM RICH Original Meatballs

Garnish: chopped fresh parsley

1. Stir together first 6 ingredients in a large Dutch oven over medium heat. Cook, stirring occasionally, 5 minutes or until smooth.
2. Add meatballs, and cook, stirring occasionally, 20 to 25 minutes or until thoroughly heated. Garnish, if desired.

Häagen-Dazs

Add a personal touch to rich and flavorful ice cream using one of these delicious recipes.

Fresh Cherry Cobbler with Vanilla Ice Cream

MAKES 12 SERVINGS
HANDS-ON TIME: 25 MIN.
TOTAL TIME: 1 HR., 20 MIN.

- 6 cups pitted fresh cherries (about 1½ lb.)
- 3 Tbsp. cornstarch
- 1½ cups sugar, divided
- 3 Tbsp. butter
- 1 tsp. lemon zest
- 1 cup all-purpose flour
- 1 tsp. baking powder
- ½ tsp. salt
- ½ cup milk
- 1 tsp. vanilla extract
- ¼ cup butter, softened
- 1 large egg
- 2 (14-oz.) containers HÄAGEN-DAZS FIVE® Vanilla Bean All Natural Ice Cream

Garnish: fresh mint leaves

1. Preheat oven to 350°. Bring cherries, cornstarch, ¾ cup sugar, and ½ cup water to a boil in a medium saucepan over medium-high heat, stirring constantly. Boil, stirring constantly, 1 minute. Remove from heat; stir in 3 Tbsp. butter and lemon zest. Pour into a lightly greased 11- x 7-inch baking dish.

Lemon Ice-Cream-Strawberry Shortcake

2. Combine flour, baking powder, salt, and remaining ¾ cup sugar in a large bowl. Add milk, vanilla, and ¼ cup butter, and beat at medium speed with an electric mixer 2 minutes. Add egg, and beat 2 more minutes. Spoon batter over cherry mixture.

3. Bake at 350° for 40 to 45 minutes or until golden, shielding with aluminum foil during last 10 minutes of baking to prevent excessive browning, if necessary. Cool on a wire rack 15 to 20 minutes. Serve warm with ice cream. Garnish, if desired.

Lemon Ice-Cream-Strawberry Shortcake

MAKES 10 TO 12 SERVINGS

HANDS-ON TIME: 20 MIN.

TOTAL TIME: 1 HR.

- 1 (16-oz.) container fresh strawberries, quartered
- 1 Tbsp. chopped fresh mint
- 1 Tbsp. honey
- 1¾ cups all-purpose flour
- ¼ cup plain yellow cornmeal
- 6 Tbsp. cold butter, cut into pieces
- 2 Tbsp. sugar
- 1½ tsp. baking powder
- ½ tsp. salt
- ¼ tsp. lemon zest
- 1 large egg, lightly beaten
- ⅔ cup whipping cream
- 1 Tbsp. butter, melted
- ½ tsp. sugar
- 2 (14-oz.) containers HÄAGEN-DAZS FIVE® Lemon All Natural Ice Cream

1. Preheat oven to 425°. Toss together first 3 ingredients in a large bowl, and let stand at room temperature 20 minutes.

2. Meanwhile, process flour and next 6 ingredients in a food processor 20 seconds or until mixture resembles coarse sand. Transfer mixture to a large bowl.

3. Whisk together egg and cream; add to flour mixture, stirring just until dry ingredients are moistened and a dough forms.

4. Turn dough out onto a lightly floured surface, and knead 3 to 4 times. Pat dough to ½-inch thickness using floured hands; cut with a 2-inch round cutter, and place, side by side, on a lightly greased or parchment paper-lined jelly-roll pan. (Dough rounds should touch.)

5. Bake at 425° for 18 to 23 minutes or until golden and firm to touch. Brush tops with melted butter, and sprinkle with ½ tsp. sugar.

6. Serve shortcakes with ice cream and strawberry mixture.

Lemon-and-Ginger Ice-Cream Tart

MAKES 8 SERVINGS
HANDS-ON TIME: 15 MIN.
TOTAL TIME: 4 HR., 5 MIN.

- ½ (16-oz.) package crisp gingersnap cookies
- 3 Tbsp. melted butter
- 3 Tbsp. sugar, divided
- 1 (14-oz.) container HÄAGEN-DAZS FIVE® Lemon All Natural Ice Cream
- 1 cup fresh blackberries
- 1 cup fresh raspberries
- 2 Tbsp. chopped crystallized ginger
- ½ tsp. lemon juice

1. Preheat oven to 325°. Place cookies in a large zip-top plastic bag; seal bag, and finely crush cookies using a rolling pin (about 2 cups crushed); pour into a large bowl. Stir in melted butter and 2 Tbsp. sugar. Press on bottom and up sides of a 9-inch square tart pan with removable bottom. Place on a baking sheet.
2. Bake crust at 325° for 10 to 12 minutes or until lightly browned. Let cool 10 minutes; freeze 20 minutes or until cold.
3. Meanwhile, let ice cream stand at room temperature 20 minutes or until slightly softened. Spread over cooled crust in pan. Freeze 3 hours or until firm.
4. Toss together blackberries, next 3 ingredients, and remaining 1 Tbsp. sugar in a medium bowl. Let berry mixture and tart stand at room temperature 10 minutes. Remove tart from pan, and place on a serving stand or plate. Top with berry mixture.

Mahatma Rice

Weeknight cooking just got a lot easier using this favorite ingredient.

Saffron-Ginger Rice with Thai Red Curry Soup

MAKES 4 SERVINGS
HANDS-ON TIME: 15 MIN.
TOTAL TIME: 40 MIN.

SAFFRON-GINGER RICE

- 2 cups vegetable broth
- 1 cup MAHATMA Jasmine Enriched Thai Fragrant Long Grain Rice
- 1 tsp. grated fresh ginger
- ½ tsp. kosher salt
- ⅛ tsp. ground saffron

THAI RED CURRY SOUP

- 1 lb. unpeeled, medium-size raw shrimp (31/40 count)
- 2 (14-oz.) cans light coconut milk
- ½ cup vegetable broth
- 1½ Tbsp. red curry paste
- ½ tsp. kosher salt
- 1⅓ cups halved sugar snap peas
- 1 (4-oz.) package sliced fresh gourmet mushroom blend
- 1 cup loosely packed fresh cilantro leaves

1. Prepare Rice: Bring 2 cups vegetable broth and next 4 ingredients to a boil in a medium saucepan over medium-high heat. Cover, reduce heat to low, and simmer 15 to 18 minutes or until liquid is absorbed and rice is tender. Remove from heat, and keep warm.
2. Prepare Soup: Peel shrimp; devein, if desired.

3. Bring coconut milk and next 3 ingredients to a boil in a large saucepan over medium heat. Add shrimp, peas, and mushrooms. Reduce heat to low, and simmer, stirring occasionally, 5 to 6 minutes or just until shrimp turn pink and vegetables are tender.
4. Spoon rice into bowls. Top with soup, and sprinkle with cilantro. Season with salt to taste.

Baby Spinach and Red Pepper Rice

MAKES 4 TO 6 SERVINGS
HANDS-ON TIME: 10 MIN.
TOTAL TIME: 33 MIN.

This is a delicious take on risotto, made completely in the microwave.

- ½ cup finely chopped sweet onion
- 2 Tbsp. butter
- 1 Tbsp. olive oil
- 1 garlic clove, minced
- 1 cup MAHATMA Extra Long Grain White Rice
- 2¾ cups low-sodium chicken broth
- ¼ cup dry white wine
- ½ cup (2 oz.) shredded Italian six-cheese blend
- ¼ to ½ cup low-sodium chicken broth
- Salt and pepper to taste
- ½ cup jarred chopped roasted red bell peppers
- 3 cups firmly packed fresh baby spinach

1. Stir together first 4 ingredients in a medium-size microwave-safe bowl. Microwave at HIGH 3 minutes. Stir in rice, and microwave at HIGH 2 minutes.
2. Stir in 2 ¾ cups broth and ¼ cup wine. Cover tightly with plastic wrap. (Do not vent.) Microwave at HIGH 9 minutes. Carefully swirl bowl without uncovering (to incorporate the mixture), and microwave at HIGH 8

Baby Spinach and
Red Pepper Rice

minutes. Carefully remove and discard plastic wrap. Stir in cheese and ¼ cup chicken broth, stirring 30 seconds to 1 minute or until creamy. Add up to ¼ cup additional broth, 1 Tbsp. at a time, for desired consistency. Season with salt and pepper to taste.

3. Stir in red peppers and spinach, and microwave at HIGH 1 minute or until spinach is wilted.

Note: We tested with a 1,100-watt microwave oven and a 1½-liter glass bowl. We found that press-and-seal plastic wrap will not work in this application.

Almond-and-Pistachio Brown Rice Pilaf

MAKES 4 TO 6 SERVINGS
HANDS-ON TIME: 17 MIN.
TOTAL TIME: 1 HR., 5 MIN.

- 1 small onion, finely chopped
- 2 tsp. olive oil
- 1 cup MAHATMA Natural Whole Grain Brown Rice
- 1 tsp. garam masala
- 2 garlic cloves, minced
- 2½ cups vegetable broth
- ½ tsp. salt
- ⅓ cup slivered almonds
- ⅓ cup roasted, salted pistachios
- ⅓ cup dried currants
- 2 Tbsp. chopped fresh parsley

1. Sauté onion in hot oil in a large skillet over medium-high heat 3 to 4 minutes or until tender. Stir in rice and garam masala, and cook, stirring often, 3 minutes or until fragrant and rice is lightly browned; add garlic, and cook 1 minute.

2. Add broth and salt, and bring to a boil. Cover, reduce heat to low, and cook 45 minutes or until rice is tender.

3. Meanwhile, preheat oven to 350°. Bake almonds in a single layer in a shallow pan 6 to 8 minutes or until lightly toasted and fragrant.

4. Fluff rice mixture with a fork. Stir in almonds and remaining ingredients.

Sauza Tequila

Enjoy the fresh flavor of a refreshing margarita any night of the week.

Drink Responsibly Sauza® Tequila, 40% alc./vol.
©2010 Sauza Tequila Import Company, Deerfield, IL

Grapefruit Margaritas

MAKES 4 SERVINGS (ABOUT 7 CUPS)
HANDS-ON TIME: 5 MIN.
TOTAL TIME: 5 MIN.

 2 **cups no-sugar-added ruby red grapefruit juice***
 ⅔ **cup SAUZA® Silver Tequila**
 ¼ **cup sweetened lime juice**
 2 **cups ginger ale**
 2 **cups crushed ice**
Garnish: sliced grapefruit

1. Stir together first 3 ingredients in a large pitcher. Stir in ginger ale and crushed ice. Serve immediately. Garnish, if desired.

*Not-from-concentrate grapefruit juice may be substituted.

Grapefruit Margaritas

Raspberry Beer 'Garitas

MAKES 9 SERVINGS (ABOUT 6½ CUPS)
HANDS-ON TIME: 5 MIN.
TOTAL TIME: 5 MIN.

- 1½ cups SAUZA® Silver Tequila
- 1 (12-oz.) can frozen limeade concentrate, thawed
- 1 (12-oz.) bottle raspberry-flavored beer
- 1 cup frozen raspberries

Crushed ice

Garnish: sliced limes

1. Stir together first 3 ingredients and 1½ cups water in a large pitcher until blended. Stir in raspberries. Serve immediately over crushed ice. Garnish, if desired.

Note: For fast measuring, you can use the empty can of limeade concentrate to measure the tequila. One 12-oz. can is equivalent to 1 ½ cups.

Blackberry Margaritas

MAKES 4 SERVINGS (ABOUT 8 CUPS)
HANDS-ON TIME: 10 MIN.
TOTAL TIME: 10 MIN.

- 1 cup fresh blackberries
- 1 Tbsp. sugar
- ¾ cup SAUZA® Silver Tequila
- 1 (12-oz.) can frozen lemonade concentrate, thawed
- 3 cups club soda
- 3 cups ice cubes

Garnish: fresh blackberries

1. Mash together blackberries and sugar in a medium bowl with a potato masher. Press mixture through a fine wire-mesh strainer into a small bowl, using back of a spoon to squeeze out juice. Discard pulp and seeds.

2. Pour blackberry mixture into a large pitcher. Stir in tequila and lemonade

concentrate until blended. Stir in club soda and ice cubes. Serve immediately. Garnish, if desired.

Note: For fast measuring, you can use the empty can of limeade concentrate to measure the tequila. Half of a 12-oz. can is equivalent to ¾ cup.

National Peanut Board

Discover scrumptious ways to satisfy your cravings for both sweet and savory with this favorite nut.

Cream Cheese-Banana Bread with Peanut Butter Streusel

MAKES 2 LOAVES
HANDS-ON TIME: 20 MIN.
TOTAL TIME: 2 HR., 15 MIN.

- ¾ cup butter, softened
- 1 (8-oz.) package cream cheese, softened
- 2 cups sugar
- 2 large eggs
- 1½ cups unsifted all-purpose flour
- 1½ cups sifted light roast peanut flour made with USA-GROWN PEANUTS
- ½ tsp. baking powder
- ½ tsp. baking soda
- ½ tsp. salt
- 1½ cups mashed ripe bananas (about 4 medium)
- 1 cup chopped salted USA-GROWN PEANUTS
- ½ tsp. vanilla extract

Peanut Butter Streusel

1. Preheat oven to 350°. Beat butter and cream cheese at medium speed with an electric mixer until creamy. Gradually add sugar, beating until light and fluffy. Add eggs, 1 at a time, beating just until blended after each addition.

2. Combine all-purpose flour and next 4 ingredients; gradually add to butter mixture, beating at low speed just until blended. Stir in bananas, peanuts, and vanilla. Spoon batter into 2 greased and floured 8- x 4-inch loaf pans. Sprinkle Peanut Butter Streusel over batter in pans.

3. Bake at 350° for 1 hour and 10 minutes or until a long wooden pick inserted in center comes out clean and sides pull away from pan, shielding with aluminum foil after 55 minutes to prevent excessive browning, if necessary. Cool bread in pans on wire racks 10 minutes. Remove from pans to wire racks, and cool 30 minutes before slicing.

Peanut Butter Streusel: Combine ½ cup plus 1 Tbsp. all-purpose flour and ½ cup firmly packed brown sugar in a small bowl. Cut in ¼ cup cold butter and 3 Tbsp. creamy peanut butter made with USA-GROWN PEA-NUTS with a pastry blender or fork until mixture resembles small peas. Makes 1 ½ cups. Hands-on Time: 5 min., Total Time: 5 min.

PER ½-INCH-THICK SLICE: CALORIES 226; FAT 12G (SAT 6G, MONO 4G, POLY 1G); PROTEIN 4G; CARB 27G; FIBER 1G; CHOL 34MG; IRON 1MG; SODIUM 152MG; CALC 25MG

Peanut Hummus

MAKES 1 CUP

HANDS-ON TIME: 20 MIN.

TOTAL TIME: 20 MIN.

Boiled peanuts can be found canned or in the refrigerated produce section of your local market. We tested with canned boiled peanuts; it takes about 1½ cans to make this recipe.

- 1 cup shelled boiled USA-GROWN PEANUTS
- 1 Tbsp. chopped fresh parsley
- 2 Tbsp. creamy peanut butter made with USA-GROWN PEANUTS
- 2 Tbsp. fresh lemon juice
- 1 tsp. minced fresh garlic
- ¼ tsp. ground cumin
- Pinch of ground red pepper
- 2 Tbsp. olive oil
- SERVE WITH: pita chips, sliced carrots and cucumbers, bell pepper strips, quartered radishes

1. Process first 7 ingredients in a food processor until coarsely chopped, stopping to scrape down sides as needed. With processor running, pour olive oil through food chute in a slow, steady stream, processing until mixture is smooth. Stir in up to 5 Tbsp. water, 1 Tbsp. at a time, for desired consistency. Serve with pita chips, sliced carrots and cucumbers, bell pepper strips, and quartered radishes.

PER TBSP.: CALORIES 64; **FAT** 5G (**SAT** 1G, **MONO** 3G, **POLY** 1G); **PROTEIN** 2G; **CARB** 3G; **FIBER** 1G; **CHOL** 0MG; **IRON** 0.2MG; **SODIUM** 94MG; **CALC** 8MG

Peanut Butter Pancakes

Peanut Butter Pancakes

MAKES ABOUT 20 (4-INCH) PANCAKES

HANDS-ON TIME: 30 MIN.

TOTAL TIME: 30 MIN.

These pancakes don't cook exactly the same as traditional pancakes. Turn them as soon as the edges look cooked so that the pancakes do not overcook.

- 1 cup sifted light roast peanut flour made with USA-GROWN PEANUTS
- 1 cup unsifted all-purpose flour
- 3 Tbsp. baking powder
- ¼ tsp. salt
- ¾ cup creamy peanut butter made with USA-GROWN PEANUTS
- ¼ cup honey
- 2 Tbsp. vegetable oil
- 2 large eggs
- 2 cups milk
- 1 cup strawberry preserves
- Toppings: banana slices, strawberry slices, chopped USA-GROWN PEANUTS

1. Process first 9 ingredients in a food processor until smooth, stopping once to scrape down sides.

2. Pour ¼ cup batter for each pancake onto a hot, lightly greased griddle or large nonstick skillet. Cook pancakes 3 to 4 minutes or until edges look cooked. Turn and cook 3 to 4 minutes or until done.

3. Microwave strawberry preserves in a microwave-safe bowl at HIGH 45 seconds to 1 minute, stirring after 30 seconds. Serve pancakes with preserves and desired toppings.

PER PANCAKE (WITHOUT PRESERVES AND TOPPINGS): **CALORIES** 141; **FAT** 8G (**SAT** 2G, **MONO** 4G, **POLY** 2G); **PROTEIN** 6G; **CARB** 13G; **FIBER** 1G; **CHOL** 20MG; **IRON** 1MG; **SODIUM** 311MG; **CALC** 161MG

October

Christy's Recipes for Success

Southern charm and recipes like these Sunday dinner favorites have made blogger Christy Jordan an Internet sensation.

Read Christy Jordan's blog SouthernPlate.com and you'll know how much she appreciates tradition—including gathering around the table after church. "I like to cook a big meal to share with our friends and their kids," the energetic Huntsville, Alabama, native says. "I make anything I'm in the mood to cook: ham, Jordan Rolls, a couple gallons of tea, maybe some casseroles. My favorite meals are like family reunions—real casual."

This relaxed, confident attitude toward cooking and her love of family have earned Christy legions of faithful followers. Her upbeat personality and absolute sincerity endear her to viewers, who can't get enough of Christy's homespun stories, playful comments, and step-by-step recipes with photos.

"I try to talk in plain terms and show the food the way it would look if you did it at your house," she says. It's unpretentious, budget-conscious family fare. "We're making food to eat here, not to build a shrine to!" she quips.

Christy has always loved the way Southerners see food as a way to bring friends and family together—and the way it connects one generation to the next. Most of her recipes have come from her mother and grandmothers, which is why she encourages people to get in the kitchen with their kids and pass it along. "Cooking is a way of handing down the history of your family," she says.

Christy's First Book!

Enjoy more of Christy's wisdom and recipes in her new cookbook, *Southern Plate*, sold in bookstores and on amazon.com.

Her success has brought fresh opportunities, including a *Southern Plate* cookbook to be published October, 2010. She's putting family first, though, with a book tour that allows her to be home with her children on weekends. And she's still keeping her food simple because Christy would be the first to tell you that it's not how long you stayed in the kitchen—it's how much fun you had around the table.

Lela's Baked Ham

make-ahead • party perfect

MAKES 8 TO 10 SERVINGS

HANDS-ON TIME: 20 MIN.

TOTAL TIME: 3 HR., 40 MIN.

Choose the size ham that best suits your family. Bake it 20 minutes per pound and 20 minutes more once you add the second layer of glaze. Sop up the drippings with warm rolls.

1 (8-lb.) smoked, ready-to-cook, bone-in ham
1 cup firmly packed light brown sugar
2 Tbsp. cola soft drink
1 Tbsp. yellow mustard
   Garnish: fresh sage sprigs

1. Preheat oven to 350°. If necessary, trim skin or excess fat from ham. Stir together brown sugar and next 2 ingredients in a small bowl. Brush half of glaze over ham. Wrap ham tightly with heavy-duty aluminum foil. Place in a foil-lined 13- x 9-inch pan.
2. Bake ham at 350° for 2 hours and 40 minutes or until a meat thermometer inserted into ham registers 148°. Uncover ham and brush with remaining glaze. Bake, uncovered, 20 to 30 minutes or until lightly browned. Transfer to a serving dish; let stand 20 minutes. Skim fat from pan drippings, and serve with ham. Garnish, if desired.

Apple Julep

Stir together 1 qt. **apple juice**, 1 cup **pineapple juice**, 1 cup **orange juice**, and ¼ cup **lemon juice**. Serve over ice. Garnish with apple slices, lemon slices, and fresh mint sprigs, if desired. Makes 6 cups. This recipe may be made ahead and chilled. Double or triple it for larger groups or to keep in the refrigerator for sippin'.

Sweet-and-Sour Green Beans

make-ahead

MAKES 8 TO 10 SERVINGS
HANDS-ON TIME: 27 MIN.
TOTAL TIME: 27 MIN.

Christy says, "I make a triple batch of these and freeze leftovers in quart-size freezer bags to use at another meal on a busy day."

- 6 bacon slices, cut into 1-inch pieces
- ½ medium onion, chopped
- 2 (16-oz.) packages frozen whole or cut green beans
- 2 Tbsp. cider vinegar
- 2 Tbsp. sugar
  Salt and pepper to taste

1. Cook bacon and onion in a Dutch oven over medium heat, stirring often, 6 to 8 minutes or until browned. Transfer bacon mixture to a plate, reserving drippings in Dutch oven.
2. Cook beans in hot drippings, stirring often, 8 to 10 minutes or to desired degree of tenderness. Stir in vinegar, sugar, and bacon mixture. Cook, stirring often, 3 minutes or until thoroughly heated. Season with salt and pepper to taste.

Vidalia-Honey Vinaigrette

make-ahead

MAKES ABOUT 1⅓ CUPS
HANDS-ON TIME: 23 MIN.
TOTAL TIME: 3 HR., 28 MIN.

Christy serves this over a salad of mixed greens, chopped apple, toasted pecans, and dried cranberries.

- ½ cup chopped Vidalia onion
- ¾ cup vegetable oil, divided
- ¼ cup cider vinegar, divided
- ¼ cup honey
- 1 Tbsp. Dijon mustard
- ½ tsp. salt
- ½ tsp. pepper

1. Sauté onion in 1 Tbsp. hot oil in a medium skillet over medium heat, stirring often, 8 minutes or until caramel colored. Add 2 Tbsp. vinegar, stirring to loosen particles from bottom of skillet. Remove from heat; cool 5 minutes.
2. Process onion mixture, honey, next 3 ingredients, and remaining oil and vinegar in a blender 30 seconds or until blended. Cover and chill 3 to 24 hours.

Jordan Rolls
make-ahead

MAKES 1½ DOZEN
HANDS-ON TIME: 25 MIN.
TOTAL TIME: 1 HR., 35 MIN.

This is Christy's family's recipe. "We love them served alongside our meals," she says. "But they are especially good when you have ham, because they make the best little sandwiches for leftovers!"

½ cup sugar
2 (¼-oz.) envelopes rapid-rise yeast
1½ tsp. salt
5 cups all-purpose flour
½ cup shortening
2 large eggs, lightly beaten
1½ cups warm water (110° to 120°)
¾ cup butter, melted and divided

1. Combine first 3 ingredients and 2 cups flour in a large bowl. Cut in shortening with a fork or pastry blender until crumbly. Stir in eggs. (Mixture will be lumpy and dry.) Stir in warm water, ½ cup melted butter, and remaining 3 cups flour until well blended. (Mixture will remain lumpy.) Cover with a kitchen towel, and let rise in a warm place (85°), free from drafts, 20 minutes. (Rolls will rise only slightly.)
2. Turn dough out onto a floured surface. Sprinkle lightly with flour; knead 3 to 4 times. Pat or roll into a 13- x 9-inch rectangle (about ¾ inch thick). Cut dough into 18 rectangles using a pizza cutter. Place in a lightly greased 13- x 9-inch pan, and cover with towel. Let rise in a warm place (85°), free from drafts, 20 minutes.
3. Preheat oven to 350°. Bake rolls 25 minutes. Brush with remaining ¼ cup melted butter, and bake 5 more minutes or until golden.

The Recipe that Launched a Career

Christy's first post was the recipe for her favorite made-from-scratch banana pudding. This vanilla wafer-filled dessert is even better the next day. Find Christy on the Web at *southernplate.com*.

Banana Pudding

Banana Pudding
make-ahead • party perfect

MAKES 8 SERVINGS
HANDS-ON TIME: 30 MIN.
TOTAL TIME: 2 HRS., 15 MIN.

This is definitely a cookie lover's version. Serve right away if you like crispy cookies, or chill overnight for a softer texture. Delicious served warm, at room temperature, or chilled. If you omit the meringue, you won't need to bake the pudding.

PUDDING
1 (12-oz.) package vanilla wafers
5 ripe bananas, sliced
2 cups milk
½ cup sugar*
⅓ cup all-purpose flour
3 egg yolks
⅛ tsp. salt
½ tsp. vanilla extract

MERINGUE
3 egg whites
¼ cup sugar

1. Prepare Pudding: Preheat oven to 325°. Arrange one-third of vanilla wafers in a medium-size ovenproof bowl (about 2 qt.); cover with one-third of banana slices. Repeat layers twice with remaining vanilla wafers and bananas.
2. Whisk together milk and next 4 ingredients in a heavy saucepan. Cook over medium-low heat, whisking constantly, 15 minutes or until pudding-like thickness. Remove from heat, and stir in vanilla. Pour over vanilla wafers and bananas in bowl.
3. Prepare Meringue: Beat egg whites at medium speed with an electric mixer until foamy. Gradually add sugar, beating until sugar dissolves and stiff peaks form. Spread meringue over pudding, sealing to edge of bowl.
4. Bake at 325° for 15 minutes or until golden. Serve immediately, or let cool completely (about 30 minutes), and cover and chill 1 hour before serving.
*½ cup no-calorie sweetener may be substituted. We tested with Splenda No-calorie Granulated Sweetener. (Do not substitute sweetener in meringue.)

Mama's Way or Your Way?

Fresh-Baked Cinnamon Rolls

One is a classic baked in a cast-iron skillet; the other, a miniature twist on pecan sticky buns. Both deliver big homemade flavor.

Cinnamon-Pecan Rolls

make-ahead

MAKES 12 ROLLS
HANDS-ON TIME: 20 MIN.
TOTAL TIME: 1 HR., 20 MIN.

Simple enough for a beginning baker, this easy yeast-roll dough rises in just 30 minutes.

- 1   cup chopped pecans
- 1   (16-oz.) package hot roll mix
- ½   cup butter, softened
- 1   cup firmly packed light brown sugar
- 2   tsp. ground cinnamon
- 1   cup powdered sugar
- 2   Tbsp. milk
- 1   tsp. vanilla extract

1. Preheat oven to 350°. Bake pecans in a single layer in a shallow pan 5 to 7 minutes or until toasted and fragrant, stirring halfway through.
2. Prepare hot roll dough as directed on back of package; let dough stand 5 minutes. Roll dough into a 15- x 10-inch rectangle; spread with softened butter. Stir together brown sugar and cinnamon; sprinkle over butter. Sprinkle pecans over brown sugar mixture. Roll up tightly, starting at one long end; cut into 12 slices. Place rolls, cut sides down, in a lightly greased 12-inch cast-iron skillet or 13- x 9-inch pan. Cover loosely with plastic wrap and a cloth towel; let rise in a warm place (85°), free from drafts, 30 minutes or until doubled in bulk.
3. Preheat oven to 375°. Uncover rolls, and bake for 20 to 25 minutes or until center rolls are golden brown and done. Let cool in pan on a wire rack 10 minutes. Stir together powdered sugar, milk, and vanilla; drizzle over rolls.
Note: We tested with Pillsbury Specialty Mix Hot Roll Mix.

Bite-Size Cinnamon-Pecan Twirls

quick prep • make-ahead

MAKES 20 MINIATURE ROLLS
HANDS-ON TIME: 15 MIN.
TOTAL TIME: 33 MIN.

- ½   cup chopped pecans
- ¼   cup butter
- ¼   cup firmly packed light brown sugar
- 2   Tbsp. corn syrup
- 1   tsp. ground cinnamon, divided
- 1   (8-oz.) can refrigerated crescent rolls
- 1½ tsp. granulated sugar

1. Preheat oven to 375°. Bake pecans and butter in a lightly greased 8-inch round cake pan 2 minutes. Swirl pan to combine, and bake 2 more minutes. Remove from oven, and stir in brown sugar, corn syrup, and ½ tsp. cinnamon; spread mixture evenly over bottom of pan.
2. Unroll crescent roll dough, and separate into 4 rectangles, pressing perforations to seal. Stir together granulated sugar and remaining ½ tsp. cinnamon; sprinkle over rectangles. Roll up each rectangle tightly, starting at 1 long side; press edges to seal. Cut each log into 5 slices; place slices, cut sides down, in prepared pan. (Space slices equally in pan; slices will not touch.)
3. Bake at 375° for 14 to 16 minutes or until center rolls are golden brown and done. Remove from oven, and immediately invert pan onto a serving plate. Spoon any topping in pan over rolls.

Our Best-Ever Apple Cake

Frost it. Glaze it. Sprinkle on a streusel topping. One irresistible cake, 5 easy twists—each delicious variation of this test kitchen favorite tempts you to try another.

Fresh Apple Cake

MAKES 12 TO 15 SERVINGS
HANDS-ON TIME: 25 MIN.
TOTAL TIME: 2 HR., NOT INCLUDING FROSTING

Thinly sliced apples create rich, moist layers of fruit within the cake. (pictured on page 192)

- 1½ cups chopped pecans
- ½ cup butter, melted
- 2 cups sugar
- 2 large eggs
- 1 tsp. vanilla extract
- 2 cups all-purpose flour
- 2 tsp. ground cinnamon
- 1 tsp. baking soda
- 1 tsp. salt
- 2½ lb. Granny Smith apples (about 4 large), peeled and cut into ¼-inch-thick wedges
  Browned-Butter Frosting, Dark Chocolate Frosting, or Cream Cheese Frosting (right and facing page)

1. Preheat oven to 350°. Bake pecans in a single layer in a shallow pan 5 to 7 minutes or until lightly toasted and fragrant, stirring halfway through.
2. Stir together butter and next 3 ingredients in a large bowl until blended.
3. Combine flour and next 3 ingredients; add to butter mixture, stirring until blended. Stir in apples and 1 cup pecans. (Batter will be very thick, similar to a cookie dough.) Spread batter into a lightly greased 13- x 9-inch pan.
4. Bake at 350° for 45 minutes or until a wooden pick inserted in center comes out clean. Cool completely in pan on a wire rack (about 45 minutes). Spread your choice of frosting over top of cake; sprinkle with remaining ½ cup pecans.

Choose Your Frosting

Creating a special signature look for our Fresh Apple Cake is as easy as spreading on a different frosting. Here's a trio of simple-to-fix favorites.

Dark Chocolate Frosting

MAKES ABOUT 2 CUPS
HANDS-ON TIME: 10 MIN.
TOTAL TIME: 30 MIN.

Indulge your cravings. If you're a fan of chocolate-dipped caramel apples, this is the frosting for you.

- 1 (12-oz.) package semisweet chocolate morsels
- ½ cup whipping cream
- 3 Tbsp. butter

1. Microwave semisweet chocolate morsels and whipping cream in a 2-qt. microwave-safe bowl at MEDIUM (50% power) 2½ to 3 minutes or until chocolate begins to melt.
2. Whisk until chocolate melts and mixture is smooth. Whisk in butter; let stand 20 minutes. Beat at medium speed with an electric mixer 3 to 4 minutes or until mixture forms soft peaks. Use immediately.

Try these Twists!

1 Caramel-Apple Cobbler Cake

Prepare Fresh Apple Cake batter, and bake as directed. Cool on a wire rack 10 minutes. Omit frosting. Spread Caramel Glaze over cake, and cool 30 minutes. Sprinkle with remaining ½ cup pecans. Spoon this super-moist cake out of the pan, cobbler-style, and serve with ice cream. Hands-on time: 25 min.; Total time: 2 hr., 5 min., including glaze

Caramel Glaze: Bring 1 cup firmly packed **light brown sugar**, ½ cup **butter**, and ¼ cup **milk** to a boil in a small saucepan over medium heat, stirring constantly; boil, stirring constantly, 1 minute. Remove from heat, and stir in 1 tsp. **vanilla extract.** Stir 2 minutes; use immediately.

2 Apple Streusel Coffee Cake

Prepare Fresh Apple Cake batter as directed; sprinkle with Streusel Topping. Bake and cool cake as directed. Omit frosting and ½ cup pecans from top of cake. Hands-on time: 25 min.; Total time: 2 hr., 10 min., including topping

Streusel Topping: Pour 2 Tbsp. melted **butter** in a small bowl, and stir in ½ cup firmly packed **brown sugar**, 2 Tbsp. **all-purpose flour**, and 1 tsp. **ground cinnamon.** Add 1 cup chopped **pecans,** stirring until mixture is crumbly.

Browned-Butter Frosting

MAKES ABOUT 3½ CUPS
HANDS-ON TIME: 10 MIN.
TOTAL TIME: 1 HR., 16 MIN.

Taste the difference. Browning and chilling the butter adds a rich nutty flavor and subtle hint of caramel.

- 1 cup butter
- 1 (16-oz.) package powdered sugar
- ¼ cup milk
- 1 tsp. vanilla extract

1. Cook butter in a small heavy saucepan over medium heat, stirring constantly, 6 to 8 minutes or until butter begins to turn golden brown. Remove pan from heat immediately, and pour butter into a small bowl. Cover and chill 1 hour or until butter is cool and begins to solidify.
2. Beat butter at medium speed with an electric mixer until fluffy; gradually add powdered sugar alternately with milk, beginning and ending with powdered sugar. Beat mixture at low speed until well blended after each addition. Stir in vanilla.

Cream Cheese Frosting

MAKES ABOUT 1⅔ CUPS
HANDS-ON TIME: 10 MIN.
TOTAL TIME: 10 MIN.

Go for a classic. This perfectly complements the warm spices in a fruit-filled apple cake.

- 1 (8-oz.) package cream cheese, softened
- 3 Tbsp. butter, softened
- 1½ cups powdered sugar
- ⅛ tsp. salt
- 1 tsp. vanilla extract

1. Beat cream cheese and butter at medium speed with an electric mixer until creamy. Gradually add sugar and salt, beating until blended. Stir in vanilla.

In Season *Caramel Apples*

Branch out and get creative with some of our favorite toppings.

SOUTHERN-STYLE CARAMEL APPLES: Remove the stems from 6 apples, and insert food-safe branches (see below). Microwave 1 (14-oz.) package caramels, 1 Tbsp. vanilla extract, and 1 Tbsp. water until melted, stirring every 30 seconds. Quickly dip or drizzle apples with caramel mixture; roll or sprinkle with crushed peanut brittle or toasted pecans, if desired. Stand apples on lightly greased wax paper, and chill 15 minutes before serving. Makes 6 servings. Hands-on time: 15 min., Total time: 30 min.

Please note: We used Southern magnolia twigs; other branches may render the apples inedible. When in doubt, use craft sticks or large pretzel sticks.

Our Most Comforting Soups

Make a big batch of hearty soup tonight, and freeze the leftovers up to a month for a delicious meal ready when you are.

White Bean-and-Collard Soup

make-ahead • party perfect

MAKES 12 CUPS
HANDS-ON TIME: 30 MIN.
TOTAL TIME: 1 HR., 45 MIN.

- 2 thick hickory-smoked bacon slices
- 2 cups chopped smoked ham
- 1 medium onion, finely chopped
- 5 (16-oz.) cans navy beans
- 1 cup barbecue sauce
- 1 (6-oz.) can tomato paste
- 1 Tbsp. chicken bouillon granules
- 1 tsp. ground chipotle chile pepper
- ½ tsp. dried thyme
- ½ tsp. freshly ground pepper
- 3 cups shredded collard greens
  Hot sauce

1. Cook bacon in a large Dutch oven over medium-high heat 4 to 5 minutes or until crisp; remove bacon, and drain on paper towels, reserving 2 Tbsp. drippings in Dutch oven. Crumble bacon.
2. Sauté ham and onion in hot drippings 10 minutes or until tender.
3. Add beans, next 6 ingredients, and 8 cups water. Bring to a boil over medium-high heat. Cover, reduce heat to medium-low, and simmer, stirring occasionally, 1 hour. Stir in collards; cook 10 minutes or until tender. Serve with crumbled bacon and hot sauce.

Basil Tomato Soup

good for you • make-ahead • party perfect

MAKES 15 CUPS
HANDS-ON TIME: 45 MIN.
TOTAL TIME: 1 HR., 10 MIN.

- 2 medium onions, chopped
- 4 Tbsp. olive oil, divided
- 3 (35-oz.) cans Italian-style whole peeled tomatoes with basil
- 1 (32-oz.) can chicken broth
- 1 cup loosely packed fresh basil leaves
- 3 garlic cloves
- 1 tsp. lemon zest
- 1 Tbsp. lemon juice
- 1 tsp. salt
- 1 tsp. sugar
- ½ tsp. pepper
- 1 (16-oz.) package frozen breaded cut okra

1. Sauté onions in 2 Tbsp. hot oil in a large Dutch oven over medium-high heat 9 to 10 minutes or until tender. Add tomatoes and chicken broth. Bring to a boil, reduce heat to medium-low, and simmer, stirring occasionally, 20 minutes. Process mixture with a handheld blender until smooth.
2. Process basil, next 4 ingredients, ¼ cup water, and remaining 2 Tbsp. oil in a food processor until smooth, stopping to scrape down sides. Stir basil mixture, sugar, and pepper into soup. Cook 10 minutes or until thoroughly heated.
3. Meanwhile, cook okra according to package directions. Serve with soup.

Creamy Chicken Divan Soup

party perfect

MAKES 12 CUPS
HANDS-ON TIME: 32 MIN.
TOTAL TIME: 47 MIN.

Pick up a rotisserie chicken from the supermarket deli for quick prep and lots of flavor.

- 2 Tbsp. butter
- 1 medium-size sweet onion, chopped
- 1 garlic clove, chopped
- ¼ tsp. dried crushed red pepper
- 1 (48-oz.) container chicken broth
- 2 (12-oz.) packages fresh broccoli florets (about 12 cups)
- 1 (8-oz.) package cream cheese, cut into cubes
- 4 cups chopped cooked chicken
- 1 (8-oz.) block sharp Cheddar cheese, shredded
  Salt and pepper to taste
  Toasted slivered almonds (optional)

1. Melt butter in a Dutch oven over medium-high heat; add onion, and sauté 5 to 6 minutes or until tender. Add garlic and red pepper, and cook 2 minutes. Stir in chicken broth and broccoli. Cover and bring to a boil; reduce heat to medium, and cook 10 to 15 minutes or until broccoli is tender. Stir in cream cheese.
2. Process mixture with a handheld blender until smooth. Add chicken and shredded cheese. Cook, stirring occasionally, 5 minutes or until cheese is melted. Season with salt and pepper to taste. Serve immediately with almonds, if desired.
Note: If you don't have a handheld immersion blender, let mixture cool slightly; process mixture, in batches, in a regular blender until smooth, stopping to scrape down sides as needed. Return mixture to Dutch oven, and proceed as directed.

Grilled Pimiento Cheese Sandwiches

MAKE A SOUP AND SANDWICH

Stir together 1 cup **mayonnaise;** 1 (4-oz.) jar **diced pimiento,** drained; 1 tsp. **Worcestershire sauce;** and 1 tsp. finely grated onion. Stir in 2 (8-oz.) blocks **sharp Cheddar cheese,** shredded. (Store in an airtight container in refrigerator up to 1 week, if desired.) Spread ¼ cup pimiento cheese mixture on 1 side of a **white bread** slice; top with another bread slice. Lightly spread both sides of sandwich with mayonnaise. Repeat with remaining pimiento cheese mixture for desired number of sandwiches. Cook, in batches, on a hot griddle or large nonstick skillet over medium heat 4 to 5 minutes on each side or until golden brown and cheese melts. Makes 11 sandwiches.

Fried okra-topped Basil Tomato Soup and Grilled Pimiento Cheese Sandwiches

Cream of Potato-and-Onion Soup

party perfect

MAKES 12 CUPS

HANDS-ON TIME: 1 HR.

TOTAL TIME: 1 HR., 40 MIN.

- 2 Tbsp. butter
- 1 Tbsp. olive oil
- 4 large sweet onions, chopped (about 5 cups)
- 1 tsp. sugar
- 3 Tbsp. all-purpose flour
- 1 (32-oz.) container chicken broth
- 1 (32-oz.) package frozen Southern-style cubed hash browns
- ½ tsp. dried thyme
- 1 bay leaf
- 1 tsp. salt
- ½ tsp. pepper
- 1 cup grated Gruyère or Swiss cheese
- 1 cup half-and-half
  Garnishes: chopped fresh chives, freshly ground pepper

1. Melt butter with oil in a large Dutch oven over medium heat. Add onions and sugar. Cook, stirring often, 45 to 50 minutes or until onions are caramel colored.

2. Sprinkle onions with flour, and stir to coat. Add chicken broth. Bring to a boil over medium heat, and cook 20 minutes. Add hash browns and 2 cups water. Reduce heat to low, add thyme and next 3 ingredients, and simmer 30 minutes.

3. Stir in cheese and half-and-half; cook, stirring constantly, over medium heat 5 minutes or until cheese is melted. Remove bay leaf before serving. Garnish, if desired.

Lighten Up!
Skillet Cornbread

Low-fat kitchen staples keep this cornbread moist and delicious. Enjoy it as a side to any meal, or use this recipe as an ingredient in our fabulous breakfast or brunch variation.

Sour Cream Cornbread

quick prep • good for you • make-ahead

MAKES 8 SERVINGS
HANDS-ON TIME: 10 MIN.
TOTAL TIME: 37 MIN.

- 1½   cups self-rising white cornmeal mix
- ½   cup all-purpose flour
- 1   (14.75-oz.) can low-sodium cream-style corn
- 1   (8-oz.) container light sour cream
- 3   large eggs, lightly beaten
- 2   Tbsp. chopped fresh cilantro
- ½   cup (2 oz.) 2% reduced-fat shredded Cheddar cheese (optional)

1. Preheat oven to 450°. Heat a 10-inch cast-iron skillet in oven 5 minutes.
2. Stir together cornmeal mix and flour in a large bowl; add corn and next 3 ingredients, stirring just until blended. Pour batter into hot lightly greased skillet. Top with cheese, if desired.

3. Bake at 450° for 22 to 24 minutes or until golden brown and cornbread pulls away from sides of skillet.

PER SERVING (NOT INCLUDING CHEESE TOPPING): CALORIES 224; **FAT** 4.8G (**SAT** 2.4G, **MONO** 0.8G, **POLY** 0.5G); **PROTEIN** 8.1G; **CARB** 36.1G; **FIBER** 2.9G; **CHOL** 68MG; **IRON** 2.1MG; **SODIUM** 403MG; **CALC** 102MG

Mix It Up!

You can also use Sour Cream Cornbread in the recipe below—just omit the cheese topping.

Farmhouse Eggs Benedict:
Prepare 1 (0.9-oz.) envelope hollandaise sauce mix according to package directions, using 1 cup 2% reduced-fat milk and 2 Tbsp. lemon juice and omitting butter. Cut 4 cornbread wedges in half lengthwise, and toast under the broiler. Top 2 toasted cornbread halves with 1 low-sodium ham slice, 1 poached egg, and 1 Tbsp. hollandaise sauce. Repeat with remaining cornbread. Makes 4 servings.

PER SERVING: CALORIES 334; **FAT** 12.9G (**SAT** 5.1G, **MONO** 3.7G, **POLY** 1.2G); **PROTEIN** 19.9G; **CARB** 34.9G; **FIBER** 2.6G; **CHOL** 297MG; **IRON** 3.1MG; **SODIUM** 896MG; **CALC** 78MG

Cheddar-topped
Sour Cream Cornbread

5 Reasons Honey Will Make You Healthier Right Now

1 It's a natural way to enhance energy.

Need a morning pick-me-up or extra lift before a workout? Don't turn to addictive energy drinks. Instead, try a spoonful of honey. Its natural sugars, both glucose and fructose, are absorbed by the body quickly—giving you an instant boost.

2 It can soothe a sore throat.

This is no old wives' tale. Add honey, lemon juice, and a pinch of salt to warm water and either gargle or sip to ease the inflammation associated with a cold or flu. In addition to relief, honey can also kill certain bacteria that's at the root of the infection.

3 It will help skin stay supple.

Due to its thick texture and ability to absorb moisture from the air, honey is a useful moisturizer. Over time, mature skin becomes thin and dry. Using beauty products enriched with honey helps hydrate and restore skin's elasticity.

4 It can heal wounds, burns, and cuts.

Honey has long been used as a natural first-aid treatment, thanks to its anti-bacterial properties. Among its many benefits: It helps keep wounds clean and infection-free, reduces swelling and scarring, and acts as an anti-inflammatory.

5 It's the healthiest sweetener.

While it contains more calories than table sugar, honey (in moderation) has its benefits. Because it's sweeter than regular sugar, you don't need as much. And, in studies involving both healthy subjects and those with high cholesterol, natural honey reduced both total cholesterol and blood sugar by 6%-8%.

Drizzle It Over Breakfast

Layer ¼ cup 2% reduced-fat Greek yogurt, 2 Tbsp. granola, and ¼ cup fresh raspberries in a small 6-oz. glass cup. Top with ¼ cup 2% reduced-fat Greek yogurt, and drizzle with 1 Tbsp. honey.

7 Slow-Cooker Favorites

We've got dinnertime covered every night of the week with flavor-packed entrées plus fast, fresh sides to match.

Slow Cooker Barbecue Pork

Slow Cooker Barbecue Pork

quick prep • make-ahead

MAKES 6 SERVINGS

HANDS-ON TIME: 5 MIN.

TOTAL TIME: 8 HR., 5 MIN.

Serve this simple-to-fix recipe with buns and slaw, fill a quesadilla, or spoon over hot cooked cheese grits or toasted cornbread.

- 1 (3- to 4-lb.) boneless pork shoulder roast (Boston butt), trimmed
- 1 (18-oz.) bottle barbecue sauce
- 1 (12-oz.) can cola soft drink

1. Place roast in a lightly greased 6-qt. slow cooker; pour barbecue sauce and cola over roast. Cover and cook on LOW 8 to 10 hours or until meat shreds easily with a fork.

2. Transfer pork to a cutting board; shred with two forks, removing any large pieces of fat. Skim fat from sauce, and stir in shredded pork.

Note: We tested with Cattlemen's Kansas City Classic barbecue sauce.

Italian Pot Roast

quick prep • make-ahead

MAKES 6 SERVINGS
HANDS-ON TIME: 18 MIN.
TOTAL TIME: 8 HR., 58 MIN.

Easy Side: Sauté 2 cups diced zucchini, 1 cup frozen sweet peas, and ½ cup diced onion in 3 Tbsp. olive oil until tender. Toss with 20 oz. hot cooked cheese and spinach tortellini, and ½ cup each shredded Parmesan cheese and chopped fresh basil. Season with salt and pepper to taste.

- 1 (8-oz.) package sliced fresh mushrooms
- 1 large sweet onion, cut in half and sliced
- 1 (3- to 4-lb.) boneless chuck roast, trimmed
- 1 tsp. pepper
- 2 Tbsp. olive oil
- 1 (1-oz.) envelope dry onion soup mix
- 1 (14-oz.) can beef broth
- 1 (8-oz.) can tomato sauce
- 3 Tbsp. tomato paste
- 1 tsp. dried Italian seasoning
- 2 Tbsp. cornstarch

1. Place mushrooms and onion in a lightly greased 5- to 6-qt. slow cooker.
2. Sprinkle roast with pepper. Cook roast in hot oil in a large skillet over medium-high heat 2 to 3 minutes on each side or until browned.
3. Place roast on top of mushrooms and onion in slow cooker. Sprinkle onion soup mix over roast; pour beef broth and tomato sauce over roast. Cover and cook on LOW 8 to 10 hours or until meat shreds easily with a fork.
4. Transfer roast to a cutting board; cut into large chunks, removing any large pieces of fat. Keep roast warm.
5. Skim fat from juices in slow cooker; stir in tomato paste and Italian seasoning. Stir together cornstarch and 2 Tbsp. water in a small bowl until smooth; add to juices in slow cooker, stirring until blended. Increase slow cooker heat to HIGH. Cover and cook 40 minutes or until mixture is thickened. Stir in roast.

Spicy Steak and Black Bean Chili

quick prep • make-ahead

MAKES 8 SERVINGS
HANDS-ON TIME: 19 MIN.
TOTAL TIME: 8 HR., 19 MIN.

Easy Side: Prepare batter from 2 (6-oz.) packages buttermilk cornbread mix according to package directions. Cook batter, in batches, in a preheated, oiled waffle iron until done.

- 2 lb. boneless top sirloin steak, cubed*
- 2 Tbsp. vegetable oil
- 3 (15.5-oz.) cans black beans
- 2 (14.5-oz.) cans diced tomatoes
- 2 (4.5-oz.) cans chopped green chiles
- 1 large sweet onion, diced
- 1 green bell pepper, diced
- 4 garlic cloves, minced
- 1 (12-oz.) can beer
- 1 (3.625-oz.) package chili seasoning kit
  Toppings: shredded Cheddar cheese, diced tomatoes, avocado, sour cream, sliced green onions, chopped fresh cilantro

1. Sauté steak in hot oil in a large skillet over medium-high heat 4 to 5 minutes or until browned.
2. Place steak in a lightly greased 6-qt. slow cooker; stir in black beans and next 6 ingredients. Stir in packets from chili kit, omitting masa and red pepper packets. Cover and cook on LOW 8 hours. Serve with desired toppings.
*2 lb. ground round may be substituted. Omit oil. Brown ground round in a large skillet over medium-high heat, stirring often, 8 minutes or until meat crumbles and is no longer pink; drain. Proceed with recipe as directed. Hands-on time: 23 min.; Total time: 8 hr., 23 min.

Note: We tested with Wick Fowler's 2 Alarm Chili Kit at one tasting and with 1 (4-oz.) package Carroll Shelby's Original Texas Brand Chili Kit at another. Both worked fine.

Creole Chicken with Field Pea Succotash

quick prep • make-ahead

MAKES 6 SERVINGS
HANDS-ON TIME: 10 MIN.
TOTAL TIME: 5 HR., 10 MIN.

Easy Side: Drizzle sliced fresh tomatoes with oil-and-vinegar dressing; season with salt and pepper to taste.

- 1 (16-oz.) package frozen field peas with snaps, thawed
- 1 (10-oz.) package frozen vegetable gumbo mix, thawed
- 1 (16-oz.) package baby gold and white corn, thawed
- 2 tsp. chicken bouillon granules
- 4 tsp. Creole seasoning, divided
- 1½ tsp. paprika
- 6 skinned, bone-in chicken thighs (about 2½ lb.)

1. Stir together first 4 ingredients and 2 tsp. Creole seasoning in a lightly greased 6-qt. oval shaped slow cooker.
2. Combine paprika and remaining 2 tsp. Creole seasoning; rub over chicken. Arrange chicken on top of vegetable mixture. Cover and cook on LOW 5 to 6 hours or until chicken is done.

Meatloaf

quick prep • make-ahead

MAKES 6 SERVINGS
HANDS-ON TIME: 15 MIN.
TOTAL TIME: 5 HR., 25 MIN.

Easy Side: Prepare 1 (30-oz.) package frozen country-style shredded hash browns according to package directions. Stir in ¼ cup each chopped fresh parsley, sour cream, and bottled Ranch dressing, 1 tsp. freshly ground pepper, and ½ tsp. salt.

- 2 lb. ground round
- 1 (1-oz.) envelope dry onion soup mix
- 1 cup (4 oz.) shredded sharp Cheddar cheese
- ¾ cup fine, dry breadcrumbs
- 1 large egg
- 1 Tbsp. Worcestershire sauce
- 1 cup ketchup, divided
- 1 Tbsp. light brown sugar
- 1 tsp. yellow mustard

1. Combine first 6 ingredients, ½ cup ketchup, and ¼ cup water; shape mixture into an 8- x 4-inch loaf. Line bottom and sides of a 4-qt. oval-shaped slow cooker with aluminum foil, allowing 2 inches to extend over sides. Lightly grease foil. Place loaf in slow cooker.
2. Stir together brown sugar, mustard, and remaining ½ cup ketchup; spread over top of loaf. Cover and cook on LOW 5 to 6 hours or until a meat thermometer registers 160°. Lift loaf from slow cooker, using foil sides as handles. Let stand 10 minutes before serving.
Note: You may also prepare in a 5-qt. slow cooker. Cover and cook on LOW 3½ hours or until a meat thermometer registers 160°.

Test Kitchen Tip

Removing the slow cooker's lid during the last 30 minutes of cooking gives casseroles like King Ranch Chicken and Chicken-and-Spinach Lasagna oven-baked flavor and texture.

King Ranch Chicken

quick prep • make-ahead

MAKES 6 SERVINGS
HANDS-ON TIME: 10 MIN.
TOTAL TIME: 4 HR., 10 MIN.

Easy Side: Whisk together ⅓ cup white balsamic vinegar and ¼ cup pepper jelly. Toss with 1 quartered and thinly sliced English cucumber, 1 quartered and thinly sliced small red onion, 4 cups fresh arugula, 2 cups halved grape tomatoes, and 1 cup diced yellow bell pepper.

- 4 cups chopped cooked chicken
- 1 large onion, chopped
- 1 large green bell pepper, chopped
- 1 (10¾-oz.) can cream of chicken soup
- 1 (10¾-oz.) can cream of mushroom soup
- 1 (10-oz.) can diced tomatoes and green chiles
- 1 garlic clove, minced
- 1 tsp. chili powder
- 12 (6-inch) fajita-size corn tortillas
- 2 cups (8 oz.) shredded sharp Cheddar cheese

1. Stir together first 8 ingredients. Tear tortillas into 1-inch pieces; layer one-third of tortilla pieces in a lightly greased 6-qt. slow cooker. Top with one-third of chicken mixture and ⅔ cup cheese. Repeat layers twice.
2. Cover and cook on LOW 3½ hours or until bubbly and edges are golden brown. Uncover and cook on LOW 30 minutes.

Chicken-and-Spinach Lasagna

quick prep • make-ahead

MAKES 6 SERVINGS
HANDS-ON TIME: 20 MIN.
TOTAL TIME: 4 HR., 30 MIN.

Easy Side: Toss 1 (5-oz.) package mixed salad greens with 2 cups each refrigerated unsweetened pink grapefruit sections and diced avocado, ½ cup sweetened dried cranberries, and ⅓ cup bottled poppy seed dressing.

- 1 (10-oz.) package frozen chopped spinach, thawed
- 3 cups chopped cooked chicken
- 2 cups matchstick carrots
- 2 (10-oz.) packages refrigerated Alfredo sauce*
- 1 (10¾-oz.) can cream of mushroom soup**
- 1 cup chicken broth
- ½ tsp. pepper
- 4 cups (16 oz.) shredded Italian cheese blend, divided
- 9 uncooked lasagna noodles
- ¼ cup chopped fresh basil

1. Drain spinach well, pressing between paper towels. Stir together spinach, chicken, next 5 ingredients, and 3 cups Italian cheese blend in a large bowl.
2. Spoon one-fourth of chicken mixture into a lightly greased 6-qt. slow cooker. Arrange 3 noodles over chicken mixture, breaking to fit. Repeat layers twice. Top with remaining chicken mixture and 1 cup cheese. Cover and cook on LOW 3½ hours or until noodles are done, mixture is bubbly, and edges are golden brown. Uncover and cook on LOW 30 minutes. Sprinkle with basil. Let stand 10 minutes before serving.
*Reduced-fat Alfredo sauce may be substituted.
**Reduced-fat cream of mushroom soup may be substituted.

November

Celebrate the *Season*

Mix-and-match recipes from these four no-fail menus, perfected in our Test Kitchen for your holiday gatherings.

Choose Your Menu

Traditional Family Dinner (BELOW)

Fun Girls' Lunch (PAGE 223)

Casual Texas Thanksgiving (PAGE 226)

Easy Holiday Brunch (PAGE 230)

Traditional Family Dinner

Each December, Victoria Amory rings in the season with a special family dinner. Enjoy some of her favorite dishes—then top them off with Upside-Down Apple Tart on page 229.

Meet the Hostess

VICTORIA AMORY

An elegant family dinner might seem to be a waste in a house full of boys, but quintessential hostess Victoria Amory says her brood is all the more reason to gussy up, polish the heirloom silver, and gather 'round the table. During the holidays, she welcomes the family's oldest son home from school with a festive dinner. It sets the tone for the season and creates memories for her children who will one day do the same for their families. "It is very important to learn about food, tradition, and togetherness," she says, "and the table is the perfect place to do that."

Victoria's Menu

SERVES 8

Roasted Pork
with Dried Fruit
and Port Sauce

Brussels Sprouts
with Pancetta

Mashed Potatoes
en Croûte

Celebrate *the* Season

Plan Ahead

Decorating the table can be as important to the success of a dinner party as the menu itself. Here are some of Victoria's tips.

- Set the table and pick out the serving dishes early in the day. "I take out the platters and label them—it helps me mentally prepare for the last-minute rush."

- Limit your table setting to no more than three colors. When in doubt use simple white linens. "I love white with accents of blue and red because it's elegant and holidayish without being over-the-top."

- Keep centerpiece arrangements low. "Otherwise, guests won't be able to see each other."

- Use heirloom china and silver to add a personal touch to the table.

Roasted Pork with Dried Fruit and Port Sauce

party perfect

MAKES 8 SERVINGS
HANDS-ON TIME: 21 MIN.
TOTAL TIME: 49 MIN.

"Prepare the meat and sauce separately," Victoria says, "and then warm them together just before the guests arrive."

- 3 lb. pork tenderloin
- 1 tsp. salt
- ½ tsp. pepper
- 7 tsp. olive oil, divided
- 1 cup dried apricots
- 1 cup dried pitted plums
- 1 cup dried peaches
- ½ cup dried tart cherries
- ¼ cup pine nuts
- 1 cup port wine
- 1 cup pomegranate juice
- 2 (2½-inch) cinnamon sticks
- ½ cup chicken broth

1. Preheat oven to 425°. Remove silver skin from tenderloin, leaving a thin layer of fat. Sprinkle pork with salt and pepper. Cook pork in 6 tsp. hot oil in a large skillet over medium-high heat 3 minutes on each side or until golden brown. Transfer pork to a lightly greased jelly-roll or roasting pan, reserving drippings in skillet.

2. Bake pork at 425° for 18 to 20 minutes or until a meat thermometer inserted into thickest portion registers 150°. Remove from oven; cover and let stand 10 minutes or until thermometer registers 155°.

3. Meanwhile, add remaining 1 tsp. oil to hot drippings in skillet. Add apricots and next 4 ingredients, and sauté over medium-high heat 3 minutes or until pine nuts are toasted and fragrant. Add port wine and next 2 ingredients. Bring to a boil; reduce heat to low, and simmer 5 minutes or until mixture slightly thickens. Stir in broth, and simmer 15 minutes or until fruit is tender. Serve with pork.

Brussels Sprouts with Pancetta

quick prep

MAKES 8 SERVINGS
HANDS-ON TIME: 10 MIN.
TOTAL TIME: 27 MIN.

- 2 lb. fresh Brussels sprouts, trimmed and halved
- 2 Tbsp. olive oil
- ¼ tsp. salt
- ¼ tsp. pepper
- 6 (⅛-inch-thick) pancetta slices
- 1 Tbsp. freshly grated Parmesan cheese

1. Preheat oven to 425°. Toss together Brussels sprouts and next 3 ingredients in a 15- x 10-inch jelly-roll pan. Bake 17 to 20 minutes or until sprouts are tender and edges are lightly browned, stirring occasionally.

2. Meanwhile, cook pancetta in a large skillet over medium heat 8 to 10 minutes or until crisp. Remove pancetta, and drain on paper towels. Crumble pancetta.

3. Remove sprouts from oven, and place in a large serving dish. Top with cheese and crumbled pancetta.

Fast Flourish

Add a decorative fall touch to Mashed Potatoes en Croûte by topping it with pretty pastry leaves. Simply cut out leaves from another puff pastry sheet, using a small leaf-shaped cutter, and arrange on top of the crust before baking.

Mashed Potatoes en Croûte

party perfect

MAKES 10 TO 12 SERVINGS
HANDS-ON TIME: 30 MIN.
TOTAL TIME: 1 HR., 24 MIN.

Victoria recommends mashing Yukon gold potatoes by hand. "Don't even think about using a blender or food processor. Giving in to such temptation will result in a dense, inedible paste."

- 4 lb. Yukon gold potatoes, peeled and cut into 1-inch cubes
- ½ cup milk
- 2 bay leaves
- ½ cup butter
- ½ cup heavy cream
- 1 tsp. salt
- ½ tsp. freshly ground pepper
- ¼ tsp. ground nutmeg
- 2 egg yolks
- ¼ cup freshly grated Parmesan cheese
- 1 (17.3-oz.) package frozen puff pastry sheets, thawed
- 1 large egg
- 1 Tbsp. half-and-half

1. Preheat oven to 425°. Bring 2 qt. salted water to a boil in a large Dutch oven over medium-high heat. Add potatoes and next 2 ingredients, and cook 25 minutes or until potatoes are tender. Drain potatoes, and discard bay leaves. Mash potatoes with a potato masher until soft and fluffy.

2. Microwave butter and cream in a small microwave-safe bowl at HIGH 1 minute. Stir until smooth; add salt, pepper, and nutmeg. Stir butter mixture into mashed potatoes. Stir in egg yolks and cheese until smooth.

3. Press 1 pastry sheet into a 9-inch deep-dish pie plate, allowing edges to hang over sides. Spoon mashed potatoes into pie plate, and top with remaining pastry sheet. Crimp and fold edges inward. Cut several slits in top of pastry for steam to escape. Whisk together egg and half-and-half; brush over pastry.

4. Bake at 425° for 24 minutes or until pastry is golden and has risen slightly.

Fun Girls' Lunch

To kick off the holiday season, two work-at-home moms invited their Atlanta-area neighbors for a home-based version of an office party. Eight years later, the Jingle Mingle is still going strong.

Meet the Hostesses

KRISTI GORINAS, back row, third from left, began a baby-gear business, kristig.com, from home. Her neighbor, **BETH MARTIN,** front row on right, has now gone back to work full-time, but the friends are committed to their long-running holiday luncheon. Kristi says, "It's the epitome of Southern hospitality."

The Girls' Menu

SERVES 8

Latina Lasagna

Green Beans with Garlic

Leafy Green Salad with Pears

Warm Lemon-Rosemary Olives

Mexican Chocolate Pound Cake

Latina Lasagna

make-ahead • party perfect

MAKES 8 SERVINGS
HANDS-ON TIME: 28 MIN.
TOTAL TIME: 1 HR., 48 MIN.

You can assemble and chill this up to two days ahead to bake before serving. Simply add 20 to 30 minutes to the baking time.

- 1½ lb. fresh chorizo sausage, casings removed
- 2 (24-oz.) jars tomato-and-basil pasta sauce
- 1 cup chopped fresh cilantro
- 1 (4.5-oz.) can chopped green chiles
- 1 (15-oz.) container ricotta cheese
- 1 cup whipping cream
- 2 large eggs, lightly beaten
- 12 no-boil lasagna noodles
- 1 (16-oz.) package shredded Mexican four-cheese blend

1. Preheat oven to 375°. Cook sausage in a Dutch oven over medium heat 8 to 10 minutes or until meat is no longer pink, breaking sausage into pieces while cooking. Drain; return sausage to Dutch oven. Reduce heat to medium-low. Stir in pasta sauce, cilantro, and chiles; cook, stirring often, 5 minutes.

2. Stir together ricotta cheese, whipping cream, and eggs until smooth.

3. Spoon 1 cup sauce mixture into a lightly greased 13- x 9-inch pan. Top with 4 lasagna noodles. Top with half of ricotta cheese mixture, one-third of shredded Mexican cheese blend, and one-third of remaining sauce mixture. Repeat layers once, beginning with noodles. Top with remaining 4 noodles, sauce mixture, and shredded cheese blend. Cover with aluminum foil.

4. Bake at 375° for 45 minutes. Uncover and bake 15 minutes or until golden and bubbly. Let stand 20 minutes before serving.

Green Beans with Garlic

make-ahead

MAKES 12 TO 16 SERVINGS

HANDS-ON TIME: 23 MIN.

TOTAL TIME: 23 MIN.

- 3 lb. green beans, trimmed
- 3 large garlic cloves, thinly sliced
- 2 Tbsp. olive oil
- 1 tsp. salt
- ½ tsp. freshly ground pepper

1. Cook beans in boiling salted water to cover 5 minutes or just until tender. Drain well.

2. Cook half of garlic in 1 Tbsp. hot oil in a Dutch oven over medium heat 1 minute or until golden. Add half of beans, and sprinkle with ½ tsp. salt and ¼ tsp. pepper. Cook, stirring constantly, 3 minutes. Transfer to a serving dish. Repeat procedure with remaining garlic, oil, beans, salt, and pepper.

Leafy Green Salad with Pears

quick prep • good for you • make-ahead • party perfect

MAKES 16 SERVINGS

HANDS-ON TIME: 10 MIN.

TOTAL TIME: 10 MIN.

1. Stir 1 Tbsp. honey into ½ cup bottled olive oil-and-vinegar dressing. Place 8 cups torn butter lettuce and 2 Anjou pears, sliced, in a bowl. Drizzle with dressing, and sprinkle with 1 (3.5-oz.) package roasted glazed pecan pieces.

Note: We tested with Naturally Fresh Salad Toppings Roasted & Glazed Pecan Pieces.

Warm Lemon-Rosemary Olives

Warm Lemon-Rosemary Olives

quick prep • good for you • party perfect

MAKES 3 CUPS

HANDS-ON TIME: 10 MIN.

TOTAL TIME: 40 MIN.

Mixed olives are available at most groceries.

- 3 cups mixed olives
- 2 fresh rosemary sprigs
- 1 tsp. dried crushed red pepper
- 1 tsp. lemon zest
- 1 tsp. olive oil
  Garnishes: rosemary sprig, lemon zest strips

1. Preheat oven to 400°. Place first 4 ingredients on a large piece of aluminum foil; drizzle with oil. Fold foil over olive mixture, and pinch edges to seal.

2. Bake at 400° for 30 minutes. Serve warm. Garnish, if desired.

Celebrate the *Season*

Mexican Chocolate Pound Cake

quick prep • make-ahead • party perfect

MAKES 16 SERVINGS
HANDS-ON TIME: 16 MIN.
TOTAL TIME: 3 HR., 14 MIN., INCLUDING SAUCE

We replicated the flavor profile of Mexican chocolate using semisweet chocolate and cinnamon. If you prefer to use Mexican chocolate, look for it with the hot drink mixes or on the Hispanic food aisle. This moist cake is equally delicious without the sauce.

- 1 (8-oz.) package semisweet chocolate baking squares, chopped*
- 1 cup butter, softened
- 1½ cups granulated sugar
- 4 large eggs
- ½ cup chocolate syrup
- 2 tsp. vanilla extract
- 2½ cups all-purpose flour
- 1 tsp. ground cinnamon
- ¼ tsp. baking soda
- ⅛ tsp. salt
- 1 cup buttermilk
  Powdered sugar (optional)
  Mexican Chocolate Sauce
  Garnish: toasted sliced almonds

1. Preheat oven to 325°. Microwave chocolate baking squares in a microwave-safe bowl at HIGH 1 minute and 15 seconds or until chocolate is melted and smooth, stirring at 15-second intervals.
2. Beat butter at medium speed with a heavy-duty electric stand mixer 2 minutes or until creamy. Gradually add granulated sugar, beating 5 to 7 minutes or until light and fluffy. Add eggs, 1 at a time, beating just until yellow disappears after each addition. Stir in melted chocolate, chocolate syrup, and vanilla until smooth.

3. Combine flour and next 3 ingredients; add to butter mixture alternately with buttermilk, beginning and ending with flour mixture. Beat at low speed just until blended after each addition. Pour batter into a greased and floured 10-inch (14-cup) tube pan.
4. Bake at 325° for 1 hour and 10 minutes or until a long wooden pick inserted in center of cake comes out clean. Cool in pan on a wire rack 10 to 15 minutes; remove from pan to wire rack, and let cool completely (about 1 hour and 30 minutes). Sprinkle with powdered sugar, if desired. Serve with Mexican Chocolate Sauce. Garnish, if desired.
*2 (4.4-oz.) packages Mexican chocolate, chopped, may be substituted. Omit ground cinnamon.
Note: We tested with Nestlé Abuelita Marqueta Mexican chocolate.

Mexican Chocolate Sauce:

MAKES ABOUT 1½ CUPS
HANDS-ON TIME: 8 MIN.
TOTAL TIME: 8 MIN.

- 1 (8-oz.) package semisweet chocolate baking squares, chopped
- ¾ cup whipping cream
- 2 tsp. light brown sugar
- ¼ tsp. ground cinnamon
- ¼ tsp. almond extract
  Pinch of salt
- 1 Tbsp. butter

1. Cook first 6 ingredients in a small saucepan over low heat, whisking occasionally, 3 to 4 minutes or until mixture is smooth and chocolate is melted. Remove from heat. Whisk in butter until melted. Serve immediately.

Mexican Chocolate Pound Cake with Mexican Chocolate Sauce

Casual Texas Thanksgiving

Chef Maiya Keck of Marfa shares her relaxed feast with family and friends.

Meet the Hostess

MAIYA KECK

"I spent many college breaks here," says artist and self-taught chef Maiya Keck, who settled in this quaint-but-quirky desert oasis after graduating from Rhode Island School of Design. Now she's a busy mother of two and runs a popular downtown restaurant called Maiya's.

About 200 miles southeast of El Paso, little Marfa, Texas, defines the word "unusual." It's where the Wild West meets the international food and art community. Surrounded by three mountain ranges and iffy cell phone reception, Marfa and its unlikely population of fourth-generation ranchers, renowned artists, and tourists who never left enjoy some of the best food this side of the border.

Maiya's Thanksgiving Menu is no exception. "I like to start with simple ingredients and create recipes from there," she says. From chipotle sweet potatoes to turkey and hazelnut dressing, this menu delivers tremendous flavor.

Maiya's Menu

SERVES 8

White Bean-and-Black Olive Crostini

Roasted Turkey Stuffed
with Hazelnut Dressing

Citrus-Walnut Salad

Roasted Green Beans
with Sun-dried Tomatoes

Chipotle Smashed Sweet Potatoes

Upside-Down Apple Tart

Sparkling Sipper

White Bean-and-Black Olive Crostini

MAKES ABOUT 3 DOZEN
HANDS-ON TIME: 20 MIN.
TOTAL TIME: 28 MIN.

- 1 (8.5-oz.) French bread baguette, cut diagonally into ¼-inch slices
  Olive oil cooking spray
  Salt and pepper to taste
- 1 (15.5-oz.) can cannellini beans, drained and rinsed
- ¼ cup olive oil
- ¼ tsp. salt
- ¼ tsp. pepper
- ½ cup pitted kalamata olives, coarsely chopped
- ½ cup diced jarred roasted red bell peppers
- 1 Tbsp. olive oil
  Garnish: torn basil leaves

1. Preheat oven to 425°. Arrange bread slices on a baking sheet, and coat with cooking spray. Sprinkle with desired amount of salt and pepper. Bake 8 minutes or until toasted.

Celebrate the Season

2. Process beans and next 3 ingredients in a food processor until smooth, stopping to scrape down sides as needed. Toss together olives and next 2 ingredients. Spread bean mixture on toasted bread slices, and dollop with olive mixture. Garnish, if desired.

Roasted Turkey Stuffed with Hazelnut Dressing

party perfect

MAKES 10 TO 12 SERVINGS
HANDS-ON TIME: 55 MIN.
TOTAL TIME: 6 HR., 53 MIN., PLUS 2 DAYS FOR CHILLING

"I always use kosher salt," says Maiya. "It allows me to control the saltiness better than regular table salt. The pepper and herbs in the brine solution also help infuse a lot of flavor."

TURKEY

- 1 (18- to 20-lb.) whole fresh turkey*
- 3 cups firmly packed dark brown sugar
- 1 cup kosher salt
- 1 (18- to 20-qt.) food-safe plastic container
- 4 cups hot water
- 4 cups ice cubes
- ¼ cup black peppercorns
- 1 (1-oz.) package fresh thyme
- 6 qt. cold water

HAZELNUT DRESSING

- 1½ cups coarsely chopped hazelnuts or pecans
- 1½ cups butter
- 2 medium-size yellow onions, chopped
- 8 celery ribs, chopped
- 16 cups assorted day-old bread cubes (such as pumpernickel, sourdough, rustic white, and wheat; about 3 loaves)
- Salt and pepper to taste

REMAINING INGREDIENTS

- Wooden picks
- Kitchen string
- 3 Tbsp. olive oil
- 1 Tbsp. kosher salt
- 2 tsp. pepper
- 2 cups water

1. Prepare turkey: Remove giblets and neck. Combine dark brown sugar and kosher salt in plastic container. Add 4 cups hot water to container; stir until sugar and salt dissolve. Add ice cubes, peppercorns, and thyme; place turkey in brine. Add cold water to cover (about 6 qt.). Weight turkey down using a cast-iron lid, if necessary. Cover and chill 48 hours.

2. Prepare dressing: Preheat oven to 350°. Bake hazelnuts in a single layer in a shallow pan 8 to 10 minutes or until toasted and fragrant, stirring halfway through.

3. Melt butter in a large Dutch oven over medium-high heat. Add onions and celery, and sauté 10 to 12 minutes or until tender. Add bread cubes and hazelnuts; stir to coat. Season with salt and pepper to taste. Let cool completely (about 1 hour).

4. Remove turkey from brine; discard brine. Place turkey, breast side down, on a work surface, and spoon 4 to 5 cups dressing into neck cavity, pressing firmly. Replace skin over neck cavity, and secure using wooden picks. Turn turkey over, and spoon remaining dressing into body cavity. Tie ends of legs together with string; tuck wingtips under. Pat turkey dry with paper towels. Brush turkey with 3 Tbsp. olive oil; sprinkle with 1 Tbsp. salt and 2 tsp. pepper. Place turkey, breast side down, on a rack in a large roasting pan. Pour 2 cups water into pan.

5. Bake at 350° for 2 to 2½ hours. Turn turkey over, breast side up. Bake 2 to 2½ hours or until a meat thermometer inserted into thigh registers 180° and center of dressing registers 165°, shielding with aluminum foil during last hour of baking. Let turkey stand 20 minutes before carving.

*Frozen whole turkey, thawed, may be substituted.

Note: Depending on the size of your turkey cavity, you may have leftover dressing. Stir ½ to 1 cup chicken broth into remaining dressing, and place in a lightly greased 11- x 7-inch baking dish. Bake at 350° for 25 to 30 minutes or until thoroughly heated.

Citrus-Walnut Salad

quick prep • good for you • party perfect

MAKES 8 SERVINGS
HANDS-ON TIME: 15 MIN.
TOTAL TIME: 30 MIN., INCLUDING VINAIGRETTE

½ **cup walnut pieces**
8 **heads Belgian endive (about 2¼ lb.)**
½ **cup firmly packed fresh parsley leaves**
   Cumin-Dijon Vinaigrette
2 **red grapefruits, peeled and sectioned**

1. Preheat oven to 350°. Bake walnuts in a single layer in a shallow pan 6 to 8 minutes or until toasted and fragrant, stirring halfway through.
2. Remove and discard outer leaves of endive. Rinse endive with cold water, and pat dry. Cut each endive head diagonally into ¼-inch-thick slices, and place in a serving bowl. Add walnuts, parsley leaves, and desired amount of dressing; gently toss to coat. Top with grapefruit. Serve with any remaining dressing.

Cumin-Dijon Vinaigrette

MAKES ¾ CUP
HANDS-ON TIME: 10 MIN.
TOTAL TIME: 10 MIN.

½ **cup extra virgin olive oil**
3 **Tbsp. white wine vinegar**
2 **Tbsp. Dijon mustard**
¼ **tsp. ground cumin**
¼ **tsp. salt**
¼ **tsp. sugar**

1. Whisk together all ingredients.

Fast Simple Syrup

Bring equal parts sugar and water to a boil in a medium saucepan. Boil, stirring often, 1 minute or until sugar is dissolved. Remove from heat; cool completely. You can also find bottled simple syrup, such as Stirrings, in larger supermarkets.

Sparkling Sipper

MAKES 1 SERVING
HANDS-ON TIME: 10 MIN.
TOTAL TIME: 10 MIN.

One bottle of Prosecco yields about 6 servings for this recipe, so buy at least two bottles for a larger crowd.

Sparkling Sipper

1. Fill a 10-oz. glass with ice. Add Prosecco, filling three-fourths full. Top with 1 Tbsp. Campari and 2 Tbsp. simple syrup . Garnish with kumquats and lime slices, if desired. Serve immediately.

Roasted Green Beans with Sun-dried Tomatoes

quick prep • party perfect

MAKES 8 TO 10 SERVINGS
HANDS-ON TIME: 15 MIN.
TOTAL TIME: 27 MIN.

1½ **lb. fresh green beans, trimmed**
½   **cup sun-dried tomatoes in oil, chopped**
⅓   **cup pine nuts**
3   **Tbsp. butter, melted**
3   **Tbsp. olive oil**
1   **tsp. salt**
½   **tsp. pepper**

1. Preheat oven to 425°. Toss together all ingredients. Place mixture on an 18- x 12-inch jelly-roll pan. Bake 12 to 15 minutes or to desired degree of doneness, stirring twice.

TRY THIS TWIST!
Roasted Brussels Sprouts with Sun-dried Tomatoes: Substitute 2 lb. fresh Brussels sprouts for 1½ lb. green beans. Remove discolored leaves from Brussels sprouts, cut off stem ends, and halve. Toss together all ingredients except sun-dried tomatoes. Bake at 425° for 25 to 30 minutes or until golden and tender, stirring once halfway through and adding sun-dried tomatoes during the last 5 minutes of baking time.

Celebrate *the Season*

Chipotle Smashed Sweet Potatoes

party perfect

MAKES 8 SERVINGS
HANDS-ON TIME: 25 MIN.
TOTAL TIME: 30 MIN.

Chipotle peppers are smoked jalapeños that come canned in adobo sauce and can be found in most grocery stores. Maiya warns, "They have tremendous flavor and a lot of heat—a little goes a long way."

- 3 lb. fresh sweet potatoes, peeled and chopped
- ½ cup butter, cut into pieces
- 1 to 2 Tbsp. minced canned chipotle peppers in adobo sauce
- ¼ cup heavy cream
  Salt to taste

1. Bring sweet potatoes and salted water to cover to a boil in a Dutch oven over high heat. Reduce heat to medium, and simmer 10 to 15 minutes or until tender. Drain, reserving ½ cup water.
2. Return potatoes to Dutch oven. Add butter, minced peppers, and cream; mash with a potato masher, adding reserved water, a little at a time, for desired consistency. Season with salt to taste. Transfer to a serving bowl.

Add Spiked Ice Cream

The combination of vanilla ice cream, coffee, and bourbon pairs deliciously with Maiya's buttery apple tart—a yummy treat for grown-ups.

Coffee-Bourbon Ice Cream: Drizzle premium bourbon, such as Basil Hayden's Kentucky Straight Bourbon Whiskey, over a scoop of vanilla-bean ice cream. Sprinkle with fresh finely ground coffee.

Upside-Down Apple Tart

make-ahead • party perfect

MAKES 8 TO 10 SERVINGS
HANDS-ON TIME: 30 MIN.
TOTAL TIME: 4 HR., 35 MIN.

Be sure to use the larger cooking eye on your stovetop when making the apple mixture. Resist the temptation to overstir the apples—stir just once every 15 minutes for even cooking.

- 1 cup cold butter, cut up
- 2 cups all-purpose flour
  Pinch of salt
- 1¾ cups sugar, divided
- ½ cup ice-cold water
- 1 (3-lb.) package small Granny Smith apples, peeled and quartered
- ½ cup butter, cut up

1. Freeze 1 cup cut-up butter 30 minutes. Pulse cold butter, flour, salt, and ¼ cup sugar in a food processor 7 to 8 times or until mixture resembles coarse meal. Add ½ cup ice-cold water, 1 Tbsp. at a time, and pulse just until mixture comes together and a dough forms. Turn dough out onto a piece of plastic wrap, and shape into a disk. Wrap in plastic wrap, and chill 2 to 24 hours.
2. Gently stir together apples, ½ cup butter, and remaining 1½ cups sugar in a large bowl. Place apple mixture in a 10-inch cast-iron skillet. (Skillet will be very full.) Cook over medium-low heat 1 hour to 1 hour and 15 minutes or until liquid is reduced, thickened, and turns golden, stirring only once every 15 minutes. (Depending on your stovetop, you might need to lower the temperature if mixture begins to scorch on the bottom.)
3. Preheat oven to 425°. Unwrap dough, and turn out onto a lightly floured surface. Roll dough to a 12-inch circle; place over warm apple mixture, tucking edges into sides of skillet.
4. Bake at 425° for 25 minutes or until crust is golden brown and flaky. Let cool 10 minutes. Run a knife around edge of skillet; invert tart onto a cutting board or serving plate.

Easy Holiday Brunch

Follow our step-by-step tips and you'll pull off these recipes with ease and time to spare.

Streusel Coffee Cake

quick prep • good for you • party perfect

MAKES 8 TO 10 SERVINGS

HANDS-ON TIME: 20 MIN.

TOTAL TIME: 1 HR., 25 MIN., INCLUDING TOPPING

To make one day ahead, just bake, cool completely, and wrap in aluminum foil.

- ½ cup butter, softened
- 1 (8-oz.) package cream cheese, softened
- 1¼ cups sugar
- 2 large eggs
- 2 cups all-purpose flour
- 2 tsp. baking powder
- ½ tsp. baking soda
- ½ tsp. salt
- ½ cup milk
- 1 tsp. vanilla extract
- ½ tsp. almond extract
  Crumb Topping

1. Preheat oven to 350°. Beat butter and cream cheese at medium speed with an electric mixer until creamy. Gradually add sugar, beating at medium speed until light and fluffy. Add eggs, 1 at a time, beating just until yellow disappears.

2. Sift together flour and next 3 ingredients; add to butter mixture alternately with milk, beginning and ending with flour mixture. Beat at low speed just until blended after each addition. Stir in vanilla and almond extracts. Pour batter into a greased 13-x 9-inch pan; sprinkle with Crumb Topping.

3. Bake at 350° for 35 to 40 minutes or until a wooden pick inserted in center comes out clean. Let cool 20 minutes before serving.

Crumb Topping

MAKES ABOUT 1½ CUPS

HANDS-ON TIME: 10 MIN.

TOTAL TIME: 10 MIN.

1. Stir together ½ cup all-purpose flour, ½ cup sugar, and ½ cup coarsely chopped pecans in a bowl. Cut in ¼ cup butter with a pastry blender or fork until mixture resembles small peas.

Serve buttery Streusel Coffee Cake for breakfast or as a dessert anytime.

Celebrate *the Season*

Three Easy Steps

GRITS-AND-GREENS BREAKFAST BAKE

1 Slowly whisk grits into boiling water to prevent lumps from forming.

2 Make 8 indentations in casserole using the back of a spoon.

3 Break eggs and pour each egg, one at a time, into each indentation.

Grits-and-Greens Breakfast Bake

party perfect

MAKES 8 SERVINGS
HANDS-ON TIME: 25 MIN.
TOTAL TIME: 2 HR., 7 MIN.

Give yourself a head start: Make Simple Collard Greens up to three days ahead.

- 1 tsp. salt
- 1½ cups uncooked quick-cooking grits
- 1 cup (4 oz.) shredded white Cheddar cheese
- 3 Tbsp. butter
- ½ cup half-and-half
- ¼ tsp. freshly ground black pepper
- ¼ tsp. ground red pepper
- 10 large eggs, divided (not separated)
- 3 cups Simple Collard Greens, drained
  Hot sauce (optional)

1. Preheat oven to 375°. Bring salt and 4 cups water to a boil in a large saucepan over medium-high heat; gradually whisk in grits. Reduce heat to medium, and cook, whisking often, 5 to 7 minutes or until thickened. Remove from heat, and stir in cheese and butter.
2. Whisk together half-and-half, next 2 ingredients, and 2 eggs in a medium bowl. Stir half-and-half mixture into grits mixture. Stir in Simple Collard Greens. Pour mixture into a lightly greased 13- x 9-inch baking dish.
3. Bake at 375° for 25 to 30 minutes or until set. Remove from oven.
4. Make 8 indentations in grits mixture with back of a large spoon. Break remaining 8 eggs, 1 at a time, and slip 1 egg into each indentation. Bake 12 to 14 minutes or until eggs are cooked to desired degree of doneness. Cover loosely with aluminum foil, and let stand 10 minutes. Serve with hot sauce, if desired.

Simple Collard Greens

quick prep • good for you • make-ahead party perfect

MAKES 3 CUPS
HANDS-ON TIME: 10 MIN.
TOTAL TIME: 50 MIN.

- ½ medium-size sweet onion, chopped
- 2 Tbsp. olive oil
- 1 (16-oz.) package fresh collard greens, washed, trimmed, and chopped
- 1½ tsp. salt

1. Cook onion in hot oil in a large Dutch oven over medium heat, stirring occasionally, 10 minutes or until tender. Add collard greens, salt, and 3 cups water. Bring to a boil; reduce heat, and simmer 30 minutes or until tender.

Cornmeal-and-Brown Sugar Crusted Bacon

quick prep • party perfect

MAKES 8 SERVINGS
HANDS-ON TIME: 15 MIN.
TOTAL TIME: 1 HR.

- ¼ cup plain yellow cornmeal
- 3 Tbsp. brown sugar
- 1½ tsp. freshly ground pepper
- 16 thick bacon slices

1. Preheat oven to 400°. Combine first 3 ingredients in a shallow dish. Dredge bacon slices in cornmeal mixture, shaking off excess.
2. Place half of bacon in a single layer on a lightly greased wire rack in a jelly-roll pan. Repeat procedure with remaining bacon, placing on another lightly greased wire rack in a second jelly-roll pan.
3. Bake at 400° for 40 to 45 minutes or until browned and crisp. Let stand 5 minutes.

Coffee Milk Punch

Two Easy Steps

CORNMEAL-AND-BROWN SUGAR-CRUSTED BACON

1 Dredge each bacon slice in cornmeal mixture, shaking off excess.

2 Place bacon on a wire rack in a jelly-roll pan. For easy cleanup, line jelly-roll pans with aluminum foil.

Coffee Milk Punch

quick prep • make-ahead • party perfect

MAKES 9 CUPS
HANDS-ON TIME: 15 MIN.
TOTAL TIME: 15 MIN.

- 6 cups strong brewed hot coffee
- ½ cup hot fudge topping
- ¼ cup sugar
- 2 cups half-and-half
- 1 cup coffee liqueur
- 1 Tbsp. vanilla extract

1. Whisk together hot coffee, fudge topping, and sugar in a large Dutch oven until smooth. Add half-and-half and remaining ingredients, stirring until blended. Bring mixture to a simmer over medium-high heat. Serve immediately, or let cool, cover, and chill 1 to 24 hours, and serve over ice.

In Season
Mulling Spices

Infuse holiday recipes with seasonal flavors and aromas using homemade spice bags. Here are five ways to spread the joy.

2 | **Drizzle it:** Simmer 12 oz. maple syrup and a Spice Bag over low heat 5 minutes. Cover and chill 24 hours. Discard Spice Bag. Store in refrigerator up to 2 weeks. Serve warm with pancakes or waffles.

3 | **Sip it:** Combine 1 gal. apple cider, 2 qt. cranberry juice cocktail, and a Spice Bag in a large Dutch oven. Bring to a boil; partially cover, reduce heat, and simmer 30 minutes. Discard Spice Bag before serving. Serve hot or cold.

1 | **Gift it:** Wrap up a Spice Bag by placing 8 black peppercorns, 6 whole allspice, 6 whole cloves, 2 (3-inch) cinnamon sticks, and 3 (3- x 1-inch) orange zest strips on a 5-inch square of cheesecloth. Gather the edges, and tie securely with kitchen string. Give it as a gift, and see the delicious ways to use it on this page.

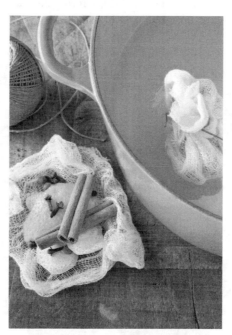

4 | **Simmer it:** Bring 2 Spice Bags and 8 cups water to a boil over medium heat; reduce heat to low, and simmer 3 to 4 hours. Before parties, this will create a festive home fragrance.

5 | **Toss it:** Simmer 16 oz. apple cider vinegar and a Spice Bag 1 minute. Remove from heat; let stand 3 hours. Discard bag. Store up to 2 weeks as a vinaigrette to toss with salads.

Makeovers for Leftovers

Wondering what to do with Thanksgiving leftovers? Do we have answers for you! Test Kitchen pro Marian Cooper Cairns created six fresh-tasting recipes—from Southwest-inspired Turkey Tostadas to rich Loaded Potato Soup—that give the actual turkey day feast a run for its money.

Loaded Potato Soup

quick prep

Made with leftover ham, mashed potatoes, sweet peas, dinner rolls

1. Preheat broiler. Melt 2 Tbsp. butter in a 3-qt. saucepan; add 1 cup diced smoked ham, 4 sliced green onions, and 1 minced garlic clove. Sauté until golden. Stir in 2 cups mashed potatoes, 1 (14-oz.) can low-sodium chicken broth, 1 cup milk, ⅓ cup sweet peas, and 2 tsp. chopped fresh thyme. Bring to a boil; reduce heat. Simmer 8 minutes or until thickened. Season with salt and pepper. Spoon into 4 broiler-safe bowls. Top with 2 cups torn dinner rolls; sprinkle with 1 cup (4 oz.) shredded Cheddar cheese. Place bowls on a baking sheet. Broil 3 minutes or until golden brown.

Cranberry Old-Fashioned Cocktail

quick prep • party perfect

Made with leftover cranberry sauce

1. Mash 1 orange wedge, 1 sugar cube, and a dash of bitters against bottom and sides of a 10-oz. old fashioned glass using a muddler or wooden spoon. Fill glass with crushed ice. Stir in ¼ cup bourbon, 2 Tbsp. whole-berry cranberry sauce, and a splash of club soda. Garnish with orange twist and fresh cranberries, if desired. Serve immediately.

Cranberry Old-Fashioned Cocktail

Savory Hand Pies

make-ahead • party perfect

Made with leftover turkey, mashed potatoes, green beans, gravy

MAKES 18 PIES
HANDS-ON TIME: 30 MIN.
TOTAL TIME: 48 MIN.

Add leftover chopped herbs for extra flavor.

- 1 cup finely chopped roasted turkey
- ¾ cup mashed potatoes
- ½ (8-oz.) package cream cheese, softened
- ½ cup cut green beans, cooked
- 1 carrot, grated
- 2 Tbsp. chopped fresh parsley
  Salt and pepper
- 1½ (14.1-oz.) packages refrigerated piecrusts
- 1 large egg, beaten
  Poppy seeds (optional)
  Turkey gravy, warmed

1. Stir together first 6 ingredients. Season with desired amount of salt and pepper.
2. Preheat oven to 400°. Unroll each piecrust. Lightly roll each into a 12-inch circle. Cut each piecrust into 6 circles using a 4-inch round cutter. Place about 3 Tbsp. turkey mixture just below center of each dough circle. Fold dough over filling, pressing and folding edges to seal.
3. Arrange pies on a lightly greased baking sheet. Brush with egg, and, if desired, sprinkle with poppy seeds.
4. Bake at 400° for 18 to 20 minutes or until golden brown. Serve with warm gravy.
Note: Unbaked pies can be frozen up to 1 month. Bake frozen pies 30 to 32 minutes or until golden brown.

Harvest Pizza

quick prep • party perfect

Made with leftover sweet potatoes, turkey

1. Preheat oven to 450°. Roll 1 lb. pizza crust dough into a 12-inch circle. Transfer to a baking sheet sprinkled with cornmeal. Spread 1 cup mashed sweet potatoes or leftover sweet potato casserole (without toppings) over dough. Top with 1 cup each shredded roasted turkey and spinach, ½ cup each sliced shiitake mushrooms and red onion, 1½ cups (6 oz.) shredded Havarti cheese, and 1 tsp. freshly ground Italian seasoning. Bake directly on oven rack 18 minutes or until edges are browned.

Turkey Tostadas with Spicy Cranberry-Chipotle Sauce

quick prep

Made with leftover turkey

MAKES 8 SERVINGS

HANDS-ON TIME: 18 MIN.

TOTAL TIME: 38 MIN., INCLUDING SAUCE

Find tostada shells near tortillas or other Mexican foods. To make your own, fry corn tortillas, one at a time, in ¼-inch hot vegetable oil in a skillet over medium-high heat until golden and crisp. Drain on paper towels.

- 1 large onion, sliced
- 1 poblano pepper, seeded and sliced
- 1 large red bell pepper, sliced
- 2 Tbsp. olive oil
- 3 cups shredded roasted turkey
- 2 garlic cloves, minced
  Salt to taste
- 8 tostada shells
- 1 cup refried black beans
  Spicy Cranberry-Chipotle Sauce
- 1 cup crumbled queso fresco (fresh Mexican cheese)
- ½ cup loosely packed fresh cilantro leaves
- 8 lime wedges

Turkey Tostadas with Spicy Cranberry-Chipotle Sauce

1. Preheat oven to 400°. Sauté first 3 ingredients in hot oil in a large non-stick skillet over medium-high heat 6 to 8 minutes or until onion is golden. Stir in turkey and garlic; cook 2 to 3 minutes or until thoroughly heated. Season with salt to taste.

2. Bake tostada shells on a baking sheet at 400° for 3 minutes. Spread shells with refried beans; top with turkey mixture. Drizzle with a small amount of Spicy Cranberry-Chipotle Sauce. Sprinkle with queso fresco.

3. Bake at 400° for 10 to 12 minutes or until thoroughly heated. Serve with fresh cilantro, lime wedges, and remaining sauce.

Spicy Cranberry-Chipotle Sauce

Made with leftover cranberry sauce

MAKES ABOUT 1⅓ CUPS

HANDS-ON TIME: 5 MIN.

TOTAL TIME: 7 MIN.

1. Microwave 1 cup whole-berry cranberry sauce; ⅓ cup taco sauce; 1 canned chipotle pepper in adobo sauce, minced; 1 tsp. chili powder; and ½ tsp. ground cumin at HIGH 2 to 3 minutes or until thickened, stirring halfway through. Season with salt to taste.

Festive Slow-Cooker Sides

Forget about juggling bake times and wedging casseroles around a 20-pound turkey in a tiny oven. Countertop cooking is the secret to this delicious sideshow.

Sweet Onion Pudding

make-ahead • party perfect

MAKES 10 SERVINGS
HANDS-ON TIME: 55 MIN.
TOTAL TIME: 4 HR., 55 MIN.

- ½ cup butter
- 6 medium-size sweet onions, thinly sliced
- 6 large eggs, lightly beaten
- 2 cups whipping cream
- 1 cup (4 oz.) shredded Parmesan cheese
- 3 Tbsp. all-purpose flour
- 2 Tbsp. sugar
- 2 tsp. baking powder
- 1 tsp. salt
- 2 cups soft, fresh breadcrumbs

1. Melt butter in a large skillet over medium heat; add onions. Cook, stirring often, 30 to 40 minutes or until caramel colored; remove from heat.
2. Whisk together eggs, cream, and Parmesan cheese in a large bowl. Combine flour and next 3 ingredients in a separate bowl; gradually whisk into egg mixture until blended. Stir onions and breadcrumbs into egg mixture; spoon into a lightly greased 6-qt. slow cooker.
3. Cover and cook on LOW 4 to 5 hours or until center is set and edges are golden brown.
Note: Onions can be cooked up to 2 days ahead. Cover and chill until ready to assemble pudding.

Squash Casserole

make-ahead

MAKES 10 TO 12 SERVINGS
HANDS-ON TIME: 30 MIN.
TOTAL TIME: 3 HR., 40 MIN.

Soft, white breadcrumbs are the secret to this classic casserole's tender, soufflé-like texture. To make fresh breadcrumbs, tear day-old slices of sandwich bread into pieces, and pulse several times in the food processor until coarse crumbs form.

- 2 lb. yellow squash, sliced
- 2 lb. zucchini, sliced
- 1 large sweet onion, finely chopped
- 2 cups (8 oz.) shredded sharp Cheddar cheese
- 2 cups soft, fresh breadcrumbs
- 1 (8-oz.) container sour cream
- 2 large eggs, lightly beaten
- 1½ tsp. garlic salt
- ½ tsp. freshly ground pepper
- ¾ cup (3 oz.) freshly shredded Parmesan cheese

1. Cook first 3 ingredients in boiling water to cover in a Dutch oven 10 to 12 minutes or just until tender; drain well in a colander, gently pressing squash mixture against sides with a wooden spoon.
2. Stir together squash mixture, Cheddar cheese, and next 5 ingredients. Spoon into a lightly greased 6-qt. oval-shaped slow cooker. Sprinkle Parmesan cheese over top.
3. Cover and cook on LOW 2½ to 3 hours or until center is set and edges are golden brown; uncover and cook 30 minutes. Let stand 10 minutes.
Note: Yellow squash, zucchini, and onions may be cooked and drained as directed up to 2 days ahead. Cover and chill until ready to assemble casserole.

Over the River and Through the Woods

If you're taking a slow-cooker dish to grandmother's house, you may want to invest in a model that features a lock top and insulated carrying case. Or you can attach heavy-duty rubber bands around the handles and lid and then wrap the slow cooker in towels or newspaper.

Balsamic Root
Vegetables

Cornbread Dressing
quick prep • make-ahead • party perfect
MAKES 12 TO 16 SERVINGS
HANDS-ON TIME: 20 MIN.
TOTAL TIME: 4 HR., 20 MIN.

- 5 cups crumbled cornbread
- 1 (14-oz.) package herb stuffing
- 2 (10¾-oz.) cans cream of chicken soup
- 2 (14-oz.) cans chicken broth
- 1 large sweet onion, diced
- 1 cup diced celery
- 4 large eggs, lightly beaten
- 1 Tbsp. rubbed sage
- ½ tsp. pepper
- 2 Tbsp. butter, cut up

1. Combine first 9 ingredients in a large bowl.
2. Pour cornbread mixture into a lightly greased 6-qt. slow cooker. Dot with butter. Cover and cook on LOW 4 to 6 hours or until set and thoroughly cooked.
Note: We tested with Pepperidge Farm Herb Seasoned Stuffing. Two (6-oz.) packages of Martha White Buttermilk Cornbread & Muffin Mix, prepared according to package directions, yields 5 cups crumbs.

TRY THIS TWIST!
Sausage-Apple Cornbread Dressing:
Cook 1 (16-oz.) package ground pork sausage in a large skillet over medium-high heat, stirring often, 8 to 10 minutes or until meat crumbles and is no longer pink; drain. Stir sausage and 2 Granny Smith apples, peeled and diced, into cornbread mixture in Step 1.

Balsamic Root Vegetables
quick prep • good for you • make-ahead
party perfect
MAKES 6 TO 8 SERVINGS
HANDS-ON TIME: 25 MIN.
TOTAL TIME: 4 HR., 25 MIN.

For a delicious twist, top with a sprinkling of cooked and crumbled bacon just before serving.

- 1½ lb. sweet potatoes
- 1 lb. parsnips
- 1 lb. carrots
- 2 large red onions, coarsely chopped
- ¾ cup sweetened dried cranberries
- 1 Tbsp. light brown sugar
- 3 Tbsp. olive oil
- 2 Tbsp. balsamic vinegar
- 1 tsp. salt
- ½ tsp. freshly ground pepper
- ⅓ cup chopped fresh flat-leaf parsley

1. Peel first 3 ingredients, and cut into 1½-inch pieces. Combine parsnips, carrots, onions, and cranberries in a lightly greased 6-qt. slow cooker; layer sweet potatoes over top.
2. Whisk together sugar and next 4 ingredients in a small bowl; pour over vegetable mixture. (Do not stir.)
3. Cover and cook on HIGH 4 to 5 hours or until vegetables are tender. Toss with parsley just before serving.

Green Bean Casserole

quick prep • make-ahead • party perfect

MAKES 10 SERVINGS
HANDS-ON TIME: 15 MIN.
TOTAL TIME: 4 HR., 45 MIN.

- 2 (16-oz.) packages frozen French-cut green beans, thawed
- 1 (10-oz.) container refrigerated Alfredo sauce
- 1 (8-oz.) can diced water chestnuts, drained
- 1 (6-oz.) jar sliced mushrooms, drained
- 1 cup (4 oz.) shredded Parmesan cheese
- ½ tsp. freshly ground pepper
- 1 (6-oz.) can French fried onions, divided
- ½ cup chopped pecans

1. Stir together first 6 ingredients and half of French fried onions; spoon mixture into a lightly greased 4-qt. slow cooker.
2. Cover and cook on LOW 4½ hours or until bubbly.
3. Heat pecans and remaining half of French fried onions in a small nonstick skillet over medium-low heat, stirring often, 1 to 2 minutes or until toasted and fragrant; sprinkle over casserole just before serving.

Wild Rice Pilaf

quick prep • good for you • make-ahead party perfect

MAKES 8 TO 10 SERVINGS
HANDS-ON TIME: 15 MIN.
TOTAL TIME: 4 HR.

Lightly coating rice with butter or oil before adding the broth prevents the grains from sticking together. Less liquid is used during slow cooking because it doesn't evaporate as quickly as when cooking rice on the stovetop.

- 1 cup uncooked brown rice
- 1 cup uncooked wild rice
- 2 Tbsp. butter, melted
- 1 (32-oz.) container chicken broth
- 1 cup diced sweet onion
- ¾ tsp. freshly ground pepper
- 1 (5.5-oz.) package dried cherries, coarsely chopped (about 1 cup)
- 1 cup coarsely chopped pecans

1. Stir together first 3 ingredients in a lightly greased 3-qt. slow cooker, stirring until rice is coated. Stir in chicken broth, onion, and pepper.
2. Cover and cook on HIGH 3½ to 4 hours or until rice is tender. Stir in cherries with a fork; turn off heat, cover, and let stand 15 minutes.
3. Meanwhile, heat pecans in a small nonstick skillet over medium-low heat, stirring often, 3 to 4 minutes or until toasted and fragrant. Stir into rice with a fork just before serving.

Cranberry Sauce

quick prep • make-ahead • party perfect

MAKES ABOUT 5½ CUPS
HANDS-ON TIME: 20 MIN.
TOTAL TIME: 12 HR., 50 MIN.

Quickly grate fresh ginger and citrus zest using a Microplane zester.

- 2 (12-oz.) packages fresh cranberries
- 1 cup granulated sugar
- 1 cup firmly packed light brown sugar
- 1 cup fresh orange juice
- 2 Tbsp. grated fresh ginger
- 1 cup sweetened dried cranberries
- 1 Tbsp. orange zest

1. Stir together first 5 ingredients and ½ cup water in a lightly greased 3½- to 4-qt. slow cooker.
2. Cover and cook on HIGH 3 to 3½ hours or until cranberries begin to pop.
3. Uncover and cook 30 minutes. Stir in dried cranberries and orange zest. Cool completely, stirring often (about 1 hour; mixture will thicken as it cools). Cover and chill 8 hours. Store in refrigerator up to 2 weeks.

Easy As Pie

This impressive dessert showcases one of fall's sweetest gems. With simple prep and make-ahead ease, it only looks like you spent hours in the kitchen.

Sweet Potato Pie with Marshmallow Meringue

quick prep • make-ahead • party perfect

MAKES 8 TO 10 SERVINGS
HANDS-ON TIME: 20 MIN.
TOTAL TIME: 2 HR., 30 MIN.

Be sure to lightly pack the mashed sweet potatoes in your measuring cup for a fluffy filling. (pictured on page 1)

CRUST

- ½ (14.1-oz.) package refrigerated piecrusts
- Parchment paper
- 1 egg yolk, lightly beaten
- 1 Tbsp. whipping cream

FILLING

- ¼ cup butter, melted
- 1 cup sugar
- ¼ tsp. salt
- 3 large eggs
- 3 cups lightly packed, cooked, mashed sweet potatoes (about 2½ lb. sweet potatoes)
- 1 cup half-and-half
- 1 Tbsp. lemon zest
- 3 Tbsp. lemon juice
- ¼ tsp. ground nutmeg

MARSHMALLOW MERINGUE

- 3 egg whites
- ½ tsp. vanilla extract
- ⅛ tsp. salt
- ¼ cup sugar
- 1 (7-oz.) jar marshmallow crème

Two Easy Steps

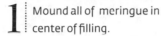
1 | Mound all of meringue in center of filling.

2 | Swirl and spread with offset spatula or back of a spoon.

1. Prepare crust: Preheat oven to 425°. Roll piecrust into a 13-inch circle on a lightly floured surface. Fit into a 9-inch pie plate; fold edges under, and crimp. Prick bottom and sides with a fork. Line piecrust with parchment paper; fill with pie weights or dried beans. Bake 9 minutes. Remove weights and parchment paper.

2. Whisk together egg yolk and cream; brush bottom and sides of crust with yolk mixture. Bake 6 to 8 more minutes or until crust is golden. Transfer to a wire rack, and cool. Reduce oven temperature to 350°.

3. Prepare filling: Stir together melted butter, 1 cup sugar, and next 2 ingredients in a large bowl until mixture is well blended. Add sweet potatoes and next 4 ingredients; stir until mixture is well blended. Pour sweet potato mixture into prepared piecrust. (Pie will be very full.)

4. Bake at 350° for 50 to 55 minutes or until a knife inserted in center comes out clean, shielding with aluminum foil to prevent excessive browning. Transfer pie to wire rack, and cool completely (about 1 hour).

5. Prepare meringue: Beat egg whites and next 2 ingredients at high speed with a heavy duty electric stand mixer until foamy. Gradually add sugar, 1 Tbsp. at a time, beating until stiff peaks form.

6. Beat one-fourth of marshmallow crème into egg white mixture; repeat 3 times with remaining marshmallow crème, beating until smooth (about 1 minute). Spread over pie.

7. Bake at 400° for 6 to 7 minutes or until meringue is lightly browned.

Note: Pie can be made up to a day ahead. Prepare recipe as directed through Step 4; cover and chill up to 24 hours. Proceed as directed in Steps 5 through 7.

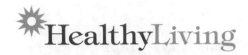
Lighten Up!
Sweet Potato Casserole

We cut more than half the fat and sugar in our favorite Thanksgiving side, and we like it better than the original!

Cornflake, Pecan, and Marshmallow-Topped Sweet Potato Casserole

quick prep • good for you • party perfect

MAKES 8 SERVINGS
HANDS-ON TIME: 20 MIN.
TOTAL TIME: 2 HR., 30 MIN.

SWEET POTATO FILLING

2½ lb. sweet potatoes (about 5 medium)
 2 Tbsp. butter, softened
 ½ cup firmly packed brown sugar
 ½ cup 2% reduced-fat milk
 1 large egg
 ½ tsp. salt
 ½ tsp. vanilla extract
    Vegetable cooking spray

CORNFLAKE, PECAN, AND MARSHMALLOW TOPPING

1¼ cups cornflakes cereal, crushed
 ¼ cup chopped pecans
 1 Tbsp. brown sugar
 1 Tbsp. melted butter
1¼ cups miniature marshmallows

1. Prepare filling: Preheat oven to 400°. Bake sweet potatoes on a baking sheet 1 hour or until tender. Reduce oven temperature to 350°. Let potatoes stand until cool to touch (about 20 minutes); peel and mash with a potato masher.
2. Beat mashed sweet potatoes, 2 Tbsp. softened butter, and next 5 ingredients at medium speed with an electric mixer until smooth. Spoon mixture into an 11- x 7-inch baking dish coated with cooking spray.

3. Prepare topping: Stir together crushed cornflakes cereal and next 3 ingredients. Sprinkle over sweet potato mixture in diagonal rows 2 inches apart.
4. Bake at 350° for 30 minutes. Remove from oven; let stand 10 minutes. Sprinkle miniature marshmallows in alternate rows between cornflake mixture, and bake 10 more minutes.

PER SERVING: CALORIES 267; FAT 7.9G (SAT 3.3G, MONO 3G, POLY 1.1G); PROTEIN 3.7G; CARB 46.7G; FIBER 3.6G; CHOL 35MG; IRON 2MG; SODIUM 302MG; CALC 69MG

More Irresistible Options

Golden Meringue-Topped Sweet Potato Casserole: Omit Corn-flake, Pecan, and Marshmallow Topping. Bake Sweet Potato Filling at 350° for 30 minutes. Remove from oven; let stand 10 minutes. Beat 4 egg whites at high speed with an electric mixer until foamy. Gradually add ¼ cup granulated sugar, 1 Tbsp. at a time, beating until stiff peaks form and sugar is dissolved. Spread meringue over sweet potato mixture; bake 10 more minutes or until golden. hands-on time: 30 min.; total time: 2 hr., 40 min.

PER SERVING: CALORIES 216; FAT 3.8G (SAT 2.1G, MONO 1.1G, POLY 0.2G); PROTEIN 4.8G; CARB 41.3G; FIBER 3.1G; CHOL 31MG; IRON 1MG; SODIUM 271MG; CALC 66MG

Pecan-Topped Sweet Potato Casserole: Omit Cornflake, Pecan, and Marshmallow Topping. Pulse 3 Tbsp. all-purpose flour and ¼ cup firmly packed brown sugar in a food processor until combined. Add 1 Tbsp. cold butter, cut into small pieces, and process 45 seconds or until mixture resembles coarse meal; stir in ⅓ cup finely chopped pecans. Sprinkle mixture over Sweet Potato Filling in baking dish. Bake at 350° for 40 to 45 minutes or until topping is golden brown. Hands-on time: 20 min.; Total time: 2 hr., 20 min.

PER SERVING: CALORIES 267; FAT 8.8G (SAT 3.4G, MONO 3.5G, POLY 1.4G); PROTEIN 3.7G; CARB 44.5G; FIBER 3.6G; CHOL 35MG; IRON 1.4MG; SODIUM 256MG; CALC 75MG

5 Reasons Almonds Will Make You Healthier

1 They help you lose weight. Studies show people who eat a serving of almonds at least twice a week are less likely to gain weight. Almonds are high in calories, though; stick to no more than ⅓ cup—a small handful—each day. Pick whole, roasted almonds. (Sugar-coated almonds are not a super food.)

Italian-Roasted Almonds

Preheat oven to 325°. Combine 1 (11-oz.) bag whole natural almonds, 1 Tbsp. freshly ground Italian seasoning, 1 Tbsp. olive oil, and ¾ tsp. kosher salt. Bake on a parchment-lined baking sheet 20 minutes or until toasted and fragrant.

Our Favorite Ways To Enjoy Almonds

Give this natural soap as a gift; the almond oil fights autumn's drier skin. Honeybee Mine soap, $6; *8thstreet soap.etsy.com*

Remove impurities and treat yourself to a mini-facial with this gentle cleanser that's paraben-free. Be fine Exfoliating Cleanser with Brown Sugar, Sweet Almond & Oats, $25; *befine.com*

Maintain shiny, healthy hair each morning with this hydrating shampoo, enriched with almond milk. Phyto Phytolactum + Intelligent Shampoo, $24; *sephora.com*

Pucker up with a peppermint-scented lip gloss that's ultra-moisturizing—thanks to vitamin E and almond oil. Philosophy Kiss Me lip balm in Red or Pink, $10-$12 each; *philosophy.com*

Smooth dry winter skin with body cream. c.Booth Honey & Almond Body Butter, $6.99; *shop .deliciousbrandsllc.com*

2 They provide a natural beauty boost. Almonds are high in vitamin E, an antioxidant that fights the effects of sun and environmental pollutants. Beauty products enriched with almond oil soften skin. To add luster to your hair, massage a few drops of almond oil into your scalp, let sit for 15 minutes, rinse, and voilà—shiny locks!

3 They lower your risk of heart disease. Almonds are high in monounsaturated ("good") fats, which help lower cholesterol. By adding almonds to a low-fat diet, you can reduce your chance of heart disease by 30% to 45%. Choose nuts with little or no salt, which can raise blood pressure.

4 They're a quick source of protein. No time to make eggs in the morning? Here's a fun fact: A ¼ cup of almonds (approximately 20-25) provides just as much protein as a single egg, strengthening everything from your eyes to your nails. So when you're reaching for an afternoon almond snack, you're not only satisfying cravings but also supporting your entire body.

5 They help strengthen bones. Just one serving of almonds contains 10% of your daily recommended calcium intake, making for strong, resilient bones. They're also high in magnesium, which supports calcium in keeping teeth healthy.

December

The Best Christmas Dinner Ever

Give your holiday meal a delicious (and memorable) makeover.

We've granted your wish for a beef tenderloin menu that inspires the creative cook in you, while pleasing guests who love a traditional meal. With a few easy-to-find ingredients you can add a crispy pancetta crust to the beef and perk up green beans with fresh lemon and basil. From the start to the grand finish—Chocolate Truffle Cheesecake—this Christmas celebration will be one for the memory book.

An Elegant Holiday Dinner

SERVES 8

Cherry-Pecan Brie

Pancetta-Wrapped Beef Tenderloin with Whipped Horseradish Cream

Crispy Potatoes with Fennel

Lemon-Garlic Green Beans

Tossed Greens-and-Grapes Salad

Easy Asiago-Olive Rolls

Chocolate Truffle Cheesecake

Cherry-Pecan Brie

1. Stir together ⅓ cup cherry preserves, 1 Tbsp. balsamic vinegar, ⅛ tsp. freshly ground pepper, and ⅛ tsp. salt in a bowl. Drizzle over 1 (16-oz.) warm Brie round (rind removed from top). Top with chopped toasted pecans. Serve with assorted crackers.

Pancetta-Wrapped Beef Tenderloin with Whipped Horseradish Cream

MAKES 8 SERVINGS
HANDS-ON TIME: 20 MIN.
TOTAL TIME: 1 HR., 25 MIN., INCLUDING CREAM

Buy pancetta, or Italian bacon, freshly sliced from the deli department. For the best price on beef tenderloin, watch for it on sale at grocery stores or buy from a wholesale club. Tenderloins are usually sealed in airtight packaging. Refrigerate no longer than the use-by date, or freeze. Let thaw 2 days in fridge.

- 1 (5- to 6-lb.) beef tenderloin, trimmed
- 2 tsp. kosher salt
- 1 tsp. coarsely ground pepper
- 3 Tbsp. olive oil, divided
- 14 very thin pancetta slices
  Wax paper
- 3 garlic cloves, minced
- 2 Tbsp. chopped fresh rosemary
  Kitchen string
  Whipped Horseradish Cream
  Garnish: fresh herbs

1. Preheat oven to 425°. Sprinkle tenderloin with salt and pepper. Cook tenderloin in 2 Tbsp. hot oil in a large skillet over medium-high heat 5 minutes on each side or until browned. Let cool 5 minutes.

2. Meanwhile, arrange pancetta slices in 2 rows on a large piece of wax paper, overlapping to form a rectangle the same length and width of tenderloin.

3. Sprinkle garlic and rosemary over tenderloin. Place tenderloin on edge of 1 long side of pancetta. Tightly roll up tenderloin with pancetta, using wax paper as a guide. Discard wax paper. Tie tenderloin with kitchen string, securing at 1-inch intervals. Transfer to an aluminum foil-lined baking sheet, and brush with remaining 1 Tbsp. oil.

4. Bake at 425° for 30 minutes or until pancetta is crispy and a meat thermometer inserted into center of tenderloin registers 120° (rare). Let stand 10 minutes. Discard kitchen string before slicing. Serve with Whipped Horseradish Cream. Garnish, if desired.

Note: For medium-rare, cook tenderloin to 135°, or to 150° for medium. We tested with Boar's Head Pancetta.

Whipped Horseradish Cream:

MAKES 2¼ CUPS
HANDS-ON TIME: 10 MIN.
TOTAL TIME: 10 MIN.

- 1 cup whipping cream
- ¼ cup horseradish
- 2 Tbsp. chopped fresh parsley
- ¼ tsp. salt

1. Beat whipping cream at medium speed with a heavy-duty electric stand mixer 1 minute or until soft peaks form. Fold in remaining ingredients. Serve immediately, or cover and chill up to 8 hours.

Get-Ahead Prep Steps

Hosting the big Christmas dinner with ease is about snatching spare minutes to complete a few steps or prepare recipes ahead. Here's how.

- Stir together topping for the Brie the day before and chill. Toast pecans up to 2 weeks ahead and freeze in an airtight container.

- Allow 2 days for beef tenderloin to thaw in refrigerator if frozen.

- Prepare Whipped Horseradish Cream 8 hours before serving; cover and chill.

- Gather a pretty bouquet of fresh herbs for garnishing. Keep in a glass of water, in fridge, up to 2 days.

- Trim and slice fennel for potatoes. Wrap in a damp paper towel, seal in a zip-top bag, and chill up to 1 day.

- Make vinaigrette 2 days ahead. Cover and chill. Let stand at room temperature 30 minutes, whisk, and serve.

- Bake cheesecake 1 day ahead—the texture and flavor is better when well chilled. Cheesecake may also be frozen. Double wrap in heavy-duty aluminum foil; freeze up to 1 month.

Crispy Potatoes with Fennel

MAKES 8 SERVINGS
HANDS-ON TIME: 15 MIN.
TOTAL TIME: 1 HR., 5 MIN.

The best skillet for this recipe is cast-iron. It's made for high oven temperatures and browns food evenly. Do not use a traditional cookware skillet unless the skillet and handle are labeled oven-safe to at least 475°.

- 1 fennel bulb
- 3 Tbsp. olive oil
- 2 lb. red potatoes, thinly sliced
- 2 tsp. chopped fresh thyme
- 1½ tsp. salt
- ½ tsp. pepper
  Garnish: fresh thyme sprigs

1. Preheat oven to 475°. Rinse fennel thoroughly. Trim and discard root end of fennel bulb. Trim stalks from bulb, reserving fronds for another use. Thinly slice bulb.

2. Add oil to a 9-inch cast-iron skillet. Arrange half of potato slices in cast-iron skillet. Layer with fennel slices and remaining potatoes. Sprinkle with thyme, salt, and pepper. Cover with aluminum foil.
3. Bake at 475° for 35 minutes. Uncover and bake 15 more minutes or until vegetables are browned. Serve hot or at room temperature. If desired, transfer to serving bowl, and garnish, if desired.

Lemon-Garlic Green Beans

MAKES 8 SERVINGS
HANDS-ON TIME: 15 MIN.
TOTAL TIME: 21 MIN.

Haricot vert is a French term that describes young, tiny, slender green beans prized for their thinness. They're generally cooked whole.

- 1½ lb. fresh haricots verts (tiny green beans), trimmed
- 2 tsp. salt, divided
- 3 garlic cloves, minced
- 3 shallots, sliced
- 2 Tbsp. olive oil
- ¼ cup chopped fresh basil
- 3 Tbsp. fresh lemon juice
- ¼ tsp. pepper
  Garnishes: lemon zest, fresh basil leaves

1. Cook beans with 1 tsp. salt in boiling water to cover 4 to 5 minutes or until crisp-tender; drain. Plunge beans into ice water to stop the cooking process; drain.
2. Cook garlic and shallots in hot oil in a large nonstick skillet over medium heat 2 minutes or until just golden brown; remove from heat. Stir in basil, next 2 ingredients, and remaining 1 tsp. salt. Add green beans, and toss to coat. Garnish, if desired.

Relocate Your Tree

Who doesn't love gathering around the Christmas tree? Try a different twist, moving the tree to the dining room. Or use the tree as a room divider between the dining room and living areas. It's a perfect solution for homes with open floor plans.

This Season's Best Wines for $15 or Less

Food Executive Editor and resident wine expert ,Scott Jones, shares his top wine picks to pair with this delicious menu.

WHITE

- Justin, Paso Robles Chardonnay, California
- Cline, Viognier, California

RED

- Concannon, Conservancy Cabernet Sauvignon, California
- Liberty School, Syrah, California

DESSERT

- JDotson-Cervantes, Gotas de Oro, Muscat Canelli, Texas (Actually, this wine retails for around $30, but it's definitely worth the holiday splurge.)

Tossed Greens-and-Grapes Salad

MAKES 8 SERVINGS
HANDS-ON TIME: 15 MIN.
TOTAL TIME: 15 MIN.

Manchego cheese has a firm texture with a nutty, buttery, mildly sharp flavor that's easy to like. Use a vegetable peeler to shave cheese into big pieces.

- ¾ cup olive oil
- ¼ cup red wine vinegar
- 1½ Tbsp. Dijon mustard
- 1½ tsp. honey
- ⅛ tsp. salt
- ⅛ tsp. pepper
- 1 (5-oz.) package spring greens mix or sweet baby greens
- 2 cups seedless red grapes, halved
- 1 cup salted, roasted cashews
- 2 oz. Manchego cheese, shaved

1. Stir together first 6 ingredients in a large serving bowl. Add spring greens and next 3 ingredients, and toss. Serve immediately.

Easy Asiago-Olive Rolls

MAKES 8 TO 10 SERVINGS
HANDS-ON TIME: 10 MIN.
TOTAL TIME: 25 MIN.

Asiago [ah-SAYH-goh] has a sweeter flavor than Parmesan and Romano and works well with the saltiness of the olive tapenade.

- 1 (13.8-oz.) can refrigerated classic pizza crust dough
- ¼ cup refrigerated olive tapenade
- ½ cup grated Asiago cheese
- 1 tsp. chopped fresh rosemary
- 1 Tbsp. butter, melted

1. Preheat oven to 450°. Unroll pizza crust dough. Spread olive tapenade over dough, leaving a ¼-inch border. Sprinkle with cheese and rosemary. Gently roll up dough, starting at 1 long side. Cut into 10 (1¼-inch-thick) slices. Place slices in a lightly greased 9-inch round cake pan. Brush top of dough with melted butter. Bake 15 to 20 minutes or until golden. Serve immediately.
Note: We tested with Pillsbury Classic Pizza Crust.

Chocolate Truffle Cheesecake

MAKES 10 SERVINGS
HANDS-ON TIME: 20 MIN.
TOTAL TIME: 12 HR., 25 MIN., INCLUDING GANACHE

- 1½ cups crushed dark chocolate-and-almond shortbread cookies (about 18 cookies)
- 2 Tbsp. melted butter
- 2 (4-oz.) semisweet chocolate baking bars, chopped
- 1 cup whipping cream
- 4 (8-oz.) packages cream cheese, softened
- 1 (14-oz.) can sweetened condensed milk
- 2 tsp. vanilla extract
- 4 large eggs
  Ganache Topping
  Garnish: fresh raspberries or White Chocolate Snowflake

1. Preheat oven to 300°. Combine crushed cookies and butter. Press mixture on bottom of a 9-inch springform pan.
2. Microwave chocolate and cream in a microwave-safe bowl at HIGH 1½ minutes or until melted, stirring at 30-second intervals.
3. Beat cream cheese at medium speed with a heavy-duty electric stand mixer 2 minutes or until smooth. Add sweetened condensed milk and vanilla, beating just until combined. Add eggs, 1 at a time, beating at low speed just until blended after each addition. Add chocolate mixture, beating just until blended. Pour batter into prepared crust.
4. Bake at 300° for 1 hour and 5 minutes or just until center is set. Turn oven off. Let cheesecake stand in oven with door closed 30 minutes. Remove cheesecake from oven; gently run a knife around outer edge of cheesecake to loosen from sides of pan. Cool completely in pan on a wire rack (about 1 hour). Cover and chill 8 to 24 hours.

5. Remove sides of pan, and place cheesecake on a serving plate. Slowly pour warm Ganache Topping over cheesecake, spreading to edges. Chill 1 hour before serving. Garnish, if desired.
Note: We tested with Keebler Dark Chocolate Almond Shortbread Sandies.

Ganache Topping:

MAKES 1¼ CUPS
HANDS-ON TIME: 10 MIN.
TOTAL TIME: 30 MIN.

- 1 cup whipping cream
- 1 (4-oz.) semisweet chocolate baking bar
- 1 (4-oz.) dark chocolate baking bar

1. Bring cream to a light boil in a saucepan over medium heat.
2. Process chocolate bars in a food processor until coarsely chopped. With processor running, pour cream through food chute in a slow, steady stream, processing until smooth. Let mixture cool until slightly warm (about 20 minutes).

Create a Snowflake Garnish

Play up winter by topping the Chocolate Truffle Cheesecake with our White Chocolate Snowflake. You'll find the stencil on page 336.

Place a sheet of parchment paper over snowflake stencil on a jelly-roll pan. Microwave 1 (4-oz.) white chocolate baking bar, chopped, in a 2-qt. microwave-safe glass bowl at HIGH 1 minute or until chocolate is glossy. Let stand 5 minutes; stir just until melted and smooth. (Be careful not to overstir or chocolate will lose its gloss and firm up.) Spoon chocolate into a zip-top plastic freezer bag. Snip 1 corner of bag to make a small hole. Pipe chocolate onto parchment paper, using stencil as a guide. Freeze 10 minutes or until chocolate hardens. Carefully lift snowflake from parchment paper using a spatula, and place on cheesecake.

Luscious Golden Caramel

The magic starts with just a spoonful of sugar.

 Tiny Caramel Tarts

MAKES 6 DOZEN
HANDS-ON TIME: 30 MIN.
TOTAL TIME: 4 HR., 30 MIN., INCLUDING PASTRY SHELLS

Add a festive touch! Just before serving, sprinkle tarts with finely chopped chocolate, crystallized ginger, toffee, or Buttered Pecans (recipe on page 250).

     2 cups sugar, divided
     ½ cup cold butter, sliced
     6 Tbsp. all-purpose flour
     4 egg yolks
     2 cups milk
        Cream Cheese Pastry Shells
        Sweetened whipped cream

1. Cook 1 cup sugar in a medium-size heavy skillet over medium heat, stirring constantly, 6 to 8 minutes or until sugar melts and turns golden brown. Stir in butter until melted.
2. Whisk together flour, egg yolks, milk, and remaining 1 cup sugar in a 3-qt. heavy saucepan; bring just to a simmer over low heat, whisking constantly. Add sugar mixture to flour mixture, and cook, whisking constantly, 1 to 2 minutes or until thickened. Cover and chill 4 hours.
3. Meanwhile, prepare Cream Cheese Pastry Shells. Spoon caramel mixture into pastry shells, and top with whipped cream.

RECIPE FROM TELIA JOHNSON
BIRMINGHAM, ALABAMA

Cream Cheese Pastry Shells:

MAKES 6 DOZEN
HANDS-ON TIME: 35 MIN.
TOTAL TIME: 2 HR., 20 MIN.

     1 cup butter, softened
     1 (8-oz.) package cream cheese, softened
    3½ cups all-purpose flour

1. Preheat oven to 400°. Beat butter and cream cheese at medium speed with a heavy-duty electric stand mixer until creamy. Gradually add flour to butter mixture, beating at low speed just until blended. Shape dough into 72 (¾-inch) balls, and place on a baking sheet; cover and chill 1 hour.
2. Place dough balls in cups of lightly greased miniature muffin pans; press dough to top of cups, forming shells.
3. Bake at 400° for 10 to 12 minutes. Remove from pans to wire racks, and cool completely (about 15 minutes).
Test Kitchen Tip: Baked pastry shells may be made up to 1 month ahead and frozen in an airtight container. Thaw at room temperature before filling.

RECIPE FROM TELIA JOHNSON
BIRMINGHAM, ALABAMA

Caramel Pecan Bars

MAKES ABOUT 2 DOZEN
HANDS-ON TIME: 25 MIN.
TOTAL TIME: 2 HR., 15 MIN.

    3½ cups coarsely chopped pecans
     2 cups all-purpose flour
     ⅔ cup powdered sugar
     ¾ cup butter, cubed
     ½ cup firmly packed brown sugar
     ½ cup honey
     ⅔ cup butter
     3 Tbsp. whipping cream

1. Preheat oven to 350°. Line bottom and sides of a 13- x 9-inch pan with heavy-duty aluminum foil, allowing 2 to 3 inches to extend over sides. Lightly grease foil.
2. Bake pecans in a single layer in a shallow pan 8 to 10 minutes or until lightly toasted and fragrant, stirring halfway through.
3. Pulse flour, powdered sugar, and ¾ cup butter in a food processor 5 or 6 times or until mixture resembles coarse meal. Press mixture on bottom and ¾ inch up sides of prepared pan. Bake at 350° for 20 minutes or until edges are lightly browned. Cool bars completely on a wire rack (about 15 minutes).
4. Bring brown sugar and next 3 ingredients to a boil in a 3-qt. saucepan over medium-high heat. Stir in toasted pecans, and spoon hot filling into prepared crust.
5. Bake at 350° for 25 to 30 minutes or until golden and bubbly. Cool completely on a wire rack (about 30 minutes). Lift baked bars from pan, using foil sides as handles. Transfer to a cutting board; cut into bars.

Caramel Italian Cream Cake

MAKES 12 SERVINGS
HANDS-ON TIME: 25 MIN.
TOTAL TIME: 2 HR., 25 MIN., INCLUDING FROSTINGS

Brown sugar is the shortcut to quick caramel flavor in both the cake layers and the frosting.

- 3 cups shaved coconut
- 1 cup finely chopped pecans
- ½ cup butter, softened
- ½ cup shortening
- 1½ cups granulated sugar
- ½ cup firmly packed dark brown sugar
- 5 large eggs, separated
- 1 Tbsp. vanilla extract
- 2 cups all-purpose flour
- 1 tsp. baking soda
- 1 cup buttermilk
- 1 cup sweetened flaked coconut
  Quick Caramel Frosting
  Cream Cheese Frosting

1. Preheat oven to 350°. Place shaved coconut in a single layer in a shallow pan. Place pecans in a second shallow pan. Bake coconut and pecans at the same time 5 to 7 minutes or until coconut is toasted and pecans are lightly toasted and fragrant, stirring halfway through.

2. Beat butter and shortening at medium speed with an electric mixer until fluffy; gradually add granulated and brown sugars, beating well. Add egg yolks, 1 at a time, beating until blended after each addition. Add vanilla, beating until blended.

3. Combine flour and baking soda; add to butter mixture alternately with buttermilk, beginning and ending with flour mixture. Beat at low speed just until blended after each addition. Stir in pecans and 1 cup sweetened flaked coconut.

4. Beat egg whites at high speed until stiff peaks form, and fold into batter. Pour batter into 3 greased and floured 9-inch round cake pans.

5. Bake at 350° for 23 to 25 minutes or until a wooden pick inserted in center comes out clean. Cool in pans on wire racks 10 minutes; remove from pans to wire racks, and cool completely (about 1 hour). Prepare Quick Caramel Frosting. Immediately spread caramel frosting between layers and on top of cake. Spread Cream Cheese Frosting over sides of cake; press 3 cups toasted shaved coconut onto sides of cake.

Quick Caramel Frosting:

MAKES 5 CUPS
HANDS-ON TIME: 20 MIN.
TOTAL TIME: 20 MIN.

Like the classic caramel frosting, this one hardens quickly—so cool the cake layers before you start to make it.

- 1 cup butter
- 1 cup firmly packed light brown sugar
- 1 cup firmly packed dark brown sugar
- ½ cup heavy cream
- 4 cups powdered sugar, sifted
- 2 tsp. vanilla extract

1. Bring first 3 ingredients to a rolling boil in a 3½-qt. saucepan over medium heat, whisking constantly (about 7 minutes). Stir in cream, and bring to a boil; remove from heat. Pour into bowl of a heavy-duty electric stand mixer. Gradually beat in powdered sugar and vanilla at medium speed, using whisk attachment; beat 8 to 12 minutes or until thickened. Use immediately.
Test Kitchen Tip: Don't panic if you overbeat the frosting—thin to a spreadable consistency by adding 1 to 2 tsp. hot water.

Cream Cheese Frosting:

MAKES ABOUT 1¾ CUPS
HANDS-ON TIME: 10 MIN.
TOTAL TIME: 10 MIN.

1. Beat ¼ cup butter, softened, and ½ (8-oz.) package cream cheese, softened, at medium speed with an electric mixer until creamy. Gradually add 2 cups powdered sugar, beating at low speed until blended; stir in 1 tsp. vanilla extract.

The Midas Touch ·············

Caramelizing sugar may seem like tricky business, but the secret is all in the timing. As the color deepens, caramel loses sweetness and develops a rich mellow flavor—too dark, and it becomes bitter.

STOP SHORT: Once sugar begins to caramelize, the color changes rapidly—from pale yellow, to gold, to amber, to dark brown, to black. Remove from heat just before it reaches the desired color.

CHILL OUT: Residual heat continues to darken the caramel after the pan is removed from the stove. To stop the cooking process, place the bottom half of the saucepan in ice water.

BE FEARLESS: Adding cold butter or cream causes hot caramel to bubble up and spatter, and sometimes creates lumps. Just step back and keep stirring.

All That Glitters ...

Tissue-thin flakes of edible gold leaf add instant glamour to a flurry of holiday garnish—from fresh cranberries to shards of coarsely chopped white chocolate. It's super-easy to apply—just press it on. Order online from *surlatable.com, goldleaf. com,* or *fancyflour.com* ($28-$41). It's a splurge, but stored in a dry place it will last for years of celebrations yet to come.

Caramel Crunch Ice-Cream Pie

MAKES 8 SERVINGS

HANDS-ON TIME: 22 MIN.

TOTAL TIME: 1 HR., 54 MIN., INCLUDING PECANS, PLUS 1 DAY FOR FREEZING

- 1 cup Buttered Pecans
- 1½ cups sugar
- 2 (14-oz.) containers coffee ice cream
- 1 (6-oz.) ready-made chocolate crumb piecrust
- 1 cup heavy cream
- ¼ cup coffee liqueur
- ½ cup finely chopped semisweet chocolate

1. Prepare Buttered Pecans as directed. Meanwhile, combine sugar and 1 cup water in a 2-qt. heavy saucepan; cook over medium heat 12 to 15 minutes or until sugar caramelizes and turns light golden brown, tipping pan to incorporate mixture. (Once the sugar begins to caramelize, the color will deepen from light to dark very quickly.) Stir in pecans, and immediately pour onto a lightly greased jelly-roll pan. Cool completely (about 1 hour). Break pecan mixture into pieces, and finely chop.

2. Transfer ice cream to bowl of a heavy-duty electric stand mixer. Let stand at room temperature 10 minutes. Beat ice cream at low speed, using paddle attachment, 5 to 10 seconds. Add pecan pieces, and beat just until combined. Immediately spread ice cream mixture into piecrust; cover and freeze 24 hours.

3. Beat whipping cream and liqueur at medium speed until stiff peaks form. Spread whipped cream mixture over ice-cream filling; sprinkle with chopped chocolate. Serve immediately.

Buttered Pecans

MAKES 2 CUPS

HANDS-ON TIME: 10 MIN.

TOTAL TIME: 22 MIN.

Delicious paired with caramel, these salty nuts can also be used to garnish a cake, sprinkle over a salad, or stir into a cheese spread.

1. Preheat oven to 350°. Stir together 2 cups coarsely chopped pecans and ¼ cup melted butter. Spread in a single layer in a 13- x 9-inch pan. Bake 12 to 15 minutes or until toasted and fragrant, stirring halfway through. Remove from oven, and let cool in pan.

White Chocolate-Cranberry Crème Brûlée

MAKES 6 SERVINGS

HANDS-ON TIME: 30 MIN.

TOTAL TIME: 9 HR., 20 MIN.

- 2 cups whipping cream
- 4 oz. white chocolate
- 1 tsp. vanilla extract
- 5 egg yolks
- ½ cup sugar, divided
- ½ (14-oz.) can whole-berry cranberry sauce
  Ice cubes
  Garnish: gold-leafed fresh cranberries

1. Preheat oven to 300°. Combine ½ cup cream and chocolate in a heavy saucepan; cook over low heat, stirring constantly, 2 to 3 minutes or until chocolate is melted. Remove from heat. Stir in vanilla and remaining 1½ cups cream.

2. Whisk together egg yolks and ¼ cup sugar until sugar is dissolved and mixture is thick and pale yellow. Add cream mixture, whisking until well blended. Pour mixture through a fine wire-mesh strainer into a large bowl.

3. Spoon 1½ Tbsp. cranberry sauce into each of 6 (4-oz.) ramekins. Pour cream mixture into ramekins; place ramekins in a large roasting pan. Add water to pan to depth of ½ inch.

4. Bake at 300° for 45 to 55 minutes or until edges are set. Cool custards in pan on a wire rack 25 minutes. Remove ramekins from water; cover and chill 8 hours.

5. Preheat broiler with oven rack 5 inches from heat. Sprinkle remaining sugar over ramekins. Fill a large roasting pan or 15- x 10-inch jelly-roll pan with ice; arrange ramekins in pan.

6. Broil 3 to 5 minutes or until sugar is melted and caramelized. Let stand 5 minutes. Garnish, if desired.

Test Kitchen Tip: Filling the roasting pan with ice before broiling keeps the custards cool while caramelizing the tops.

Caramel-Cream Cheese Flan

MAKES 8 SERVINGS
HANDS-ON TIME: 15 MIN.
TOTAL TIME: 7 HR., 10 MIN.

- 1½ cups sugar, divided
- 7 egg yolks
- 1 (14-oz.) can sweetened condensed milk
- 1 (12-oz.) can evaporated milk
- ¾ cup milk
- 1½ tsp. vanilla extract
- ⅛ tsp. salt
- 4 egg whites
- 1 (8-oz.) package cream cheese, softened

1. Preheat oven to 350°. Cook 1 cup sugar in a 9-inch round cake pan over medium heat, stirring occasionally, 5 minutes or until sugar melts and turns golden brown. Remove pan from heat, and let stand 5 minutes. (Sugar will harden.)

2. Meanwhile, whisk together egg yolks and next 5 ingredients in a large bowl. Process egg whites, cream cheese, and remaining ½ cup sugar in a blender until smooth. Add 2 cups egg yolk mixture, and process until smooth. Stir egg white mixture into remaining egg yolk mixture until blended. Pour custard over caramelized sugar in pan. Place cake pan in a large shallow pan. Add hot water to large pan to depth of one-third up sides of cake pan.

3. Bake at 350° for 50 to 60 minutes or until a knife inserted into center of flan comes out clean. Remove pan from water; cool completely on a wire rack (about 2 hours). Cover and chill 4 hours to 2 days.

4. Run a knife around edge of flan to loosen; invert onto a serving plate. (Once inverted, the flan will take about 30 seconds to slip from the pan. Be sure to use a serving plate with a lip to catch the extra caramel sauce.)

In Season
A Snowy Drift of Coconut

The coming of winter always brings sweet dreams of a white Christmas.

COCONUT CREAM TARTS: Whisk together ¾ cup sugar, ⅓ cup all-purpose flour, 4 large eggs, and 2 cups milk in a heavy saucepan. Cook over medium heat, whisking constantly, 10 minutes or until a chilled pudding-like thickness. Remove from heat; stir in 1 cup sweetened flaked coconut and 1 Tbsp. vanilla extract. Cover and chill 6 to 24 hours. Bake 1 (8-oz.) package frozen tart shells according to package directions; cool completely. Spoon custard into tart shells. Dollop with sweetened whipped cream; sprinkle with additional coconut. Makes 8 tarts. Hands-on time: 20 min.; Total time: 7 hr., 18 min.

Caramel Sauce

MAKES 3 CUPS
HANDS-ON TIME: 10 MIN.
TOTAL TIME: 40 MIN.

A small amount of lemon juice doesn't affect the flavor, but it does prevent the sugar from crystallizing.

- 1 cup butter
- 2 cups sugar
- 2 tsp. lemon juice
- 1 cup whipping cream

1. Melt butter in a 3-qt. heavy saucepan over medium heat; add sugar and lemon juice, and cook, stirring constantly with a long-handled wooden spoon, 8 to 10 minutes or until mixture turns light golden brown. Gradually add cream, and cook, stirring constantly, 1 to 2 minutes or until smooth. (Mixture will bubble and spatter when adding cream.) Remove from heat, and cool 30 minutes.

Lighten Up!
Bread Pudding

Go ahead and indulge in this delicious, individually baked treat. You'll get all the satisfaction of the classic dessert without the extra calories.

Berry Bread Pudding

MAKES 6 SERVINGS

HANDS-ON TIME: 20 MIN.

TOTAL TIME: 3 HR., 55 MIN., INCLUDING CHILL TIME AND SAUCE

- ½ (16-oz.) Italian bread loaf, cut into 1-inch pieces (about 6 cups)
  Vegetable cooking spray
- 3 large eggs
- 1¼ cups 2% reduced-fat milk
- 1 (12-oz.) can fat-free evaporated milk
- ¼ cup sugar
- ½ tsp. almond extract
- 6 Tbsp. seedless raspberry preserves
  Raspberry Sauce

1. Place bread in 6 (8-oz.) oval-shaped cast-iron baking dishes coated with cooking spray.

2. Whisk together eggs and next 4 ingredients; pour over bread in baking dishes (about ⅔ cup egg mixture each). Dot top of each with 1 Tbsp. preserves. Cover and chill 2 to 3 hours.

3. Preheat oven to 350°. Remove baking dishes from refrigerator, and let stand 15 minutes. Bake 38 to 40 minutes or until tops are crisp and golden brown. Let stand 10 minutes. Serve with Raspberry Sauce.

PER SERVING (INCLUDING 1 TBSP. RASPBERRY SAUCE): **CALORIES** 319; **FAT** 4.6G (**SAT** 1.6G, **MONO** 1.6G, **POLY** 0.9G); **PROTEIN** 12.69G; **CARB** 56.1G; **FIBER** 1.2G; **CHOL** 96.1MG; **IRON** 1.8MG; **SODIUM** 346MG; **CALC** 270MG

Note: For a one-dish dessert, place bread in a lightly greased 11- x 7-inch baking dish. Proceed with recipe as directed in Step 2, dotting top of bread mixture with all 6 Tbsp. raspberry preserves. Bake at 350° for 45 to 50 minutes or until top is crisp and golden brown. Let stand 10 minutes. Serve with sauce. Makes 6 servings. Hands-on time: 15 min.; Total time: 3 hr., 25 min.

Raspberry Sauce:

MAKES ABOUT 1⅔ CUPS

HANDS-ON TIME: 5 MIN.

TOTAL TIME: 35 MIN.

This tangy-sweet sauce is delicious over pancakes and waffles too.

- 1 (12-oz.) package frozen unsweetened raspberries, thawed
- ⅔ cup sugar
- ¼ cup orange juice

1. Reserve 1 cup raspberries. Process remaining berries, sugar, and orange juice in a food processor until smooth. Pour raspberry mixture through a fine wire-mesh strainer into a bowl; discard pulp and seeds. Stir in 1 cup reserved raspberries. Cover and chill 30 minutes.

PER TBSP.: CALORIES 25; **FAT** 0G (**SAT** 0G, **MONO** 0G, **POLY** 0G); **PROTEIN** 0.1G; **CARB** 6.3G; **FIBER** 0.2G; **CHOL** 0MG; **IRON** 0.1MG; **SODIUM** 0.1MG; **CALC** 0.9MG

TRY THIS TWIST!

Whey Low sweeteners offer a great-tasting reduced-sugar option. Find them at Whole Foods Market, or order online at wheylow. com.

Reduced-Sugar Bread Pudding and Reduced-Sugar Raspberry Sauce: Prepare Berry Bread Pudding and Raspberry Sauce as directed, substituting Whey Low Granular for sugar in each.

PER SERVING (INCLUDING 1 TBSP. SAUCE): **CALORIES** 267; **FAT** 4.6G (**SAT** 1.6G, **MONO** 1.6G, **POLY** 0.9G); **PROTEIN** 12.6G; **CARB** 55.6G; **FIBER** 1.2G; **CHOL** 96.1MG; **IRON** 1.8MG; **SODIUM** 346MG; **CALC** 270MG

Two More Easy Sauces

Serve these with Berry Bread Pudding, or drizzle over low-fat ice cream for a quick and delicious dessert.

WHISKEY SAUCE: Combine ¼ cup firmly packed brown sugar, 2 Tbsp. half-and-half, and 2 Tbsp. butter in a small saucepan over medium heat. Bring to a light boil, and cook, stirring occasionally, 1 minute. Remove from heat; stir in 2 Tbsp. whiskey. Serve warm. Makes about ⅓ cup. Hands-on time: 10 min., Total time: 10 min.

PER TBSP.: CALORIES 85; **FAT** 4.4G **(SAT** 2.8G, **MONO** 1G, **POLY** 0.1G**); PROTEIN** 0.2G; **CARB** 9.2G; **FIBER** 0G; **CHOL** 11.9MG; **IRON** 0.2MG; **SODIUM** 33MG; **CALC** 14MG

TOASTED PECAN-CARAMEL SAUCE: Sprinkle ¾ cup sugar in a small 2-qt. saucepan. Stir together ⅓ cup water and 1 tsp. light corn syrup, and pour over sugar in saucepan. Cook, without stirring, over medium-high heat 12 to 14 minutes or until sugar is dissolved and mixture is golden. Remove from heat. Gradually whisk in ½ cup evaporated milk. (Mixture will bubble.) Stir in ¼ cup chopped toasted pecans and 1½ tsp. butter. Makes about 1 cup. Hands-on time: 20 min., Total time: 20 min.

PER TBSP.: CALORIES 64; **FAT** 2.3G **(SAT** 0.7G, **MONO** 1G, **POLY** 0.4G**); PROTEIN** 0.7G; **CARB** 10.8G; **FIBER** 0.2G; **CHOL** 3.2MG; **IRON** 0.1MG; **SODIUM** 11MG; **CALC** 22MG

Look Good Feel Great!
5 Reasons Pomegranates Will Make You Healthier

1 **They keep your teeth clean.** Rich in polyphenolic flavonoids—compounds with antibacterial properties—pomegranate juice has been found to be just as effective as prescription mouthwash at ridding the mouth of plaque, the bacteria that causes cavities and gingivitis.

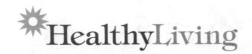
Sip A Healthy Cocktail

Pour 2 Tbsp. refrigerated 100% pomegranate juice and ½ cup chilled Prosecco or sparkling wine into a Champagne flute. Serve immediately. Makes 1 serving. Hands-on time: 5 MIN., Total time: 5 MIN.

DID YOU KNOW? When selecting a pomegranate, consider that the heavier the fruit is, the juicier it will be.

Our Favorite Ways To Enjoy Pomegranates

Reduce Wrinkles: Use this serum, which contains pomegranate, nightly to smooth skin with doctor's office results. Repairwear Laser Focus by Clinique, $44.50; *clinique.com*

Refresh Skin: Great for travel, these gentle wipes remove makeup, tone, and cleanse skin. Pomegranate extract helps reduce the size of pores. Pomegranate Cleansing and Make Up Removing Wipes by Korres, $12 for 25; *korresusa.com*

Try It in the Shower: This fragrant body wash uses pomegranate and rice to soften and hydrate skin. Active Naturals Body Wash in Smoothing by Aveeno, $7; *aveeno.com*

Carry-on a Candle: We love this cute tin package and how it transforms an office cubicle or hotel room with its sweet scent. Makes a great stocking stuffer! Bon Chic Soy Travel Candle in Raspberry Pomegranate by Seda France, $13.50; *sedafrance.com*

Wear a Signature Scent: This intense, almost woodsy perfume will perk up the winter doldrums. Pomegranate Noir cologne by Jo Malone, $100 for 100 ml; *jomalone.com*

2 They regulate cholesterol. Pomegranates contain paraoxonase—a naturally occurring enzyme in the body that helps keep LDL (bad cholesterol) from accumulating in arteries. In one study, subjects who drank pomegranate juice for two weeks had an 18 percent increase in production of the enzyme.

3 They can help prevent arthritis. Studies have shown that both pomegranate seed oil and pomegranate fruit extract have anti-inflammatory effects that stop the destruction to joints caused by osteoarthritis.

4 They are a great source of fiber. "A single pomegranate contains nearly one-quarter of the USDA's daily recommended amount of dietary fiber, which helps you feel full and, in turn, maintain a healthy weight," says Jennifer Franklin, a registered dietitian at the Vanderbilt Nutrition Clinic in Nashville, Tennessee.

5 They protect your skin. Packed with potent antioxidants (including the powerful ellagic acid), pomegrantes help limit the damage of UV rays. Additionally, they defend against harmful free radicals by increasing collagen production.

Easy Appetizer Party

For a holiday gathering with flair, serve these standout appetizers and beverages. They're mostly make-ahead, giving you an additional reason to celebrate.

Spiced Butternut-Pumpkin Soup

MAKES 15 CUPS
HANDS-ON TIME: 30 MIN.
TOTAL TIME: 1 HR., 35 MIN.

This yields more than enough for appetizer-size servings. Divide up the leftovers and freeze for a last-minute meal in busy December.

- 2 Tbsp. butter
- 1 large sweet onion, diced
- 1 large red bell pepper, chopped
- 3 garlic cloves, minced
- 2 Tbsp. finely grated fresh ginger
- 1 medium-size butternut squash, peeled and cubed (about 1¾ lb.)
- 1 small pumpkin, peeled and cubed (about 1¾ lb.)
- 1 large sweet potato, peeled and cubed
- 1 large Granny Smith apple, peeled and cubed
- 1 (32-oz.) container low-sodium chicken broth
- 2 bay leaves
- 1½ tsp. red curry paste*
- ½ tsp. ground pepper
- ¾ cup whipping cream
- 1 Tbsp. fresh lime juice
  Salt and pepper to taste

1. Melt butter in a large Dutch oven over medium-high heat; add onion and bell pepper, and sauté 8 minutes or until golden. Stir in garlic and ginger, and cook 1 minute. Add squash, next 7 ingredients, and 4 cups water. Bring to a boil, reduce heat to medium-low, and simmer 20 minutes or until vegetables are tender. Remove from heat, and let stand 30 minutes, stirring occasionally. Remove and discard bay leaves.

2. Process soup, in batches, in a blender until smooth. Return to Dutch oven, and stir in cream. Bring to a simmer over medium heat; stir in lime juice, and season with salt and pepper to taste.

*1 tsp. curry powder may be substituted for red curry paste.

Note: 1 (3-lb.) butternut squash may be substituted for 1¾ lb. butternut squash and 1¾ lb. pumpkin.

Caesar Salad Bites

MAKES 8 SERVINGS
HANDS-ON TIME: 20 MIN.
TOTAL TIME: 20 MIN.

Turn these appetizers into a pretty salad by layering veggies and croutons in a clear ice bucket or trifle dish and topping with dressing and parsley.

- 2 romaine lettuce hearts
- ⅔ cup bottled refrigerated creamy Caesar dressing
- ½ English cucumber, chopped
- 1¼ cups small seasoned croutons
- 1 cup halved grape tomatoes
- ¼ cup coarsely chopped fresh parsley
  Freshly ground pepper to taste

1. Separate romaine hearts into 24 medium leaves, and arrange on a large platter. Spoon dressing lightly down center of each leaf. Top with cucumbers and next 3 ingredients. Sprinkle with pepper to taste.

Note: We tested with Marie's Creamy Caesar Dressing.

Bacon-Grits Fritters

MAKES ABOUT 32
HANDS-ON TIME: 35 MIN.
TOTAL TIME: 4 HR., 40 MIN.

- 1 cup uncooked quick-cooking grits
- 4 cups milk
- 1 tsp. salt
- 1½ cups (6 oz.) shredded extra-sharp white Cheddar cheese
- ½ cup cooked and finely crumbled bacon (about 8 slices)
- 2 green onions, minced
- ½ tsp. freshly ground pepper
- 2 large eggs
- 3 cups Japanese breadcrumbs (panko)
  Vegetable oil

1. Prepare grits according to package directions, using 4 cups milk and 1 tsp. salt. Remove from heat, and let stand 5 minutes. Stir in cheese and next 3 ingredients, stirring until cheese is melted. Spoon mixture into a lightly greased 8-inch square baking dish or pan, and chill 4 to 24 hours.

2. Preheat oven to 225°. Roll grits into 1½-inch balls. Whisk together eggs and ¼ cup water. Dip balls in egg wash, and roll in breadcrumbs.

3. Pour oil to depth of 3 inches in a large heavy skillet; heat over medium-high heat to 350°. Fry fritters, in batches, 3 to 4 minutes or until golden brown.

4. Drain on paper towels. Keep fritters warm on a wire rack in a pan in a 225° oven up to 30 minutes. Serve warm.

Note: To make ahead, prepare recipe as directed through Step 2. Cover and chill in a single layer up to 4 hours. Fry as directed. You may also prepare through Step 2 and freeze on a baking sheet for 30 minutes or until firm. Transfer to a zip-top plastic bag, and freeze. Cook frozen fritters as directed in Step 3, increasing cooking time to 5 to 6 minutes or until golden and centers are thoroughly heated.

Baked Goat Cheese Dip

MAKES 12 SERVINGS
HANDS-ON TIME: 20MIN.
TOTAL TIME: 45 MIN.

- 1 small onion, diced
- 1 Tbsp. olive oil
- 2 garlic cloves, minced
- 2 Tbsp. tomato paste
- ¼ tsp. dried crushed red pepper
  Pinch of sugar
- 1 (14.5-oz.) can petite diced tomatoes
- ¼ cup chopped sun-dried tomatoes in oil
- ¼ cup torn basil leaves
  Salt and pepper to taste
- 2 (4-oz.) goat cheese logs, softened
- 1 (8-oz.) package cream cheese, softened
  Assorted cut vegetables and bread cubes

1. Preheat oven to 350°. Sauté onion in hot oil in a 3-qt. saucepan over medium-high heat 5 minutes or until tender. Stir in garlic and next 3 ingredients, and cook, stirring constantly, 1 minute. Stir in diced and sun-dried tomatoes.
2. Reduce heat to medium-low, and simmer, stirring occasionally, 10 minutes or until very thick. Remove from heat, and stir in basil and salt and pepper to taste. Stir together goat cheese and cream cheese until well blended. Spread into a lightly greased 9-inch shallow ovenproof dish. Top with tomato mixture.
3. Bake at 350° for 15 to 18 minutes or until thoroughly heated. Serve with assorted vegetables and bread cubes.
Note: To make ahead, prepare recipe as directed through Step 2. Cover and freeze up to 1 month. Thaw in refrigerator overnight. Let stand at room temperature 30 minutes. Bake as directed.

Sparkling Pear
Brandy Cider

Creamy Sorghum Eggnog: Whisk together 1 cup bourbon and ½ cup sorghum in a punch bowl or large pitcher. Stir in 2 qt. refrigerated eggnog and 3 cups milk. Chill until ready to serve. Sprinkle individual servings with crushed gingersnaps. Makes about 12½ cups. Hands-on time: 5 min., Total time: 5 min.

Sparkling Pear Brandy Cider: Stir together 2 cups chilled pear nectar, ¼ cup honey, and, if desired, 1 cup brandy in a punch bowl or large pitcher. Stir in 2 (750-milliliter) bottles chilled sparkling apple cider, and 1 (1-liter) bottle chilled club soda. Garnish with star anise pods and sliced pears. Makes about 14 cups. Hands-on time: 5 min.; Total time: 5 min.

Southern Pineapple Punch: Stir together 1 (2-liter) bottle chilled ginger ale; 1 (12-oz.) container frozen pineapple-orange juice concentrate, thawed; 1 cup mango nectar; 1 Tbsp. finely grated fresh ginger, and, if desired, 1½ cups Southern Comfort in a punch bowl. Garnish with sliced kiwifruit and fresh pineapple rings. Serve over crushed ice. Makes about 11 cups. Hands-on time: 10 min.; Total time: 10 min.
Note: We tested with Old Orchard Pineapple-Orange Frozen Juice Concentrate.

Bourbon Margarita Slushies: Stir together 1 (1-liter) bottle club soda, 1 (12-oz.) can frozen limeade concentrate, thawed; 1½ cups water; 1 cup tequila; 1 cup bourbon; and ¾ cup orange liqueur. Divide mixture between 2 large zip-top plastic freezer bags; seal bags. Freeze 24 hours or up to 1 week. Serve in salt-rimmed glasses with lime slices. Makes about 9 cups. Hands-on time: 10 min.; Total time: 24 hr., 10 min.

Note: We tested with Triple Sec orange liqueur.

RECIPE FROM JAN GUATRO
BIRMINGHAM, ALABAMA

Apple-Spiced Iced Tea: Stir together 2 qt. hot unsweetened tea; 1 (12-oz.) can apple juice concentrate; 3 (3-inch) cinnamon sticks; 1 vanilla bean, split; 1 (3-inch) piece fresh ginger, sliced; and 1 lemon, sliced. Chill 24 hours, stirring occasionally. Remove cinnamon, vanilla bean, and ginger. Serve over ice with lemon slices and fresh rosemary sprigs. Makes about 9½ cups. Hands-on time: 10 min.; Total time: 24 hr., 10 min.

Apple-Spiced Iced Tea

Poinsettia Gimlet: Stir together 1 (12-oz.) bottle sweetened lime juice, 1 cup gin, ½ cup pomegranate juice, and ¼ cup fresh lime juice in a large pitcher. Chill 2 hours. Stir in 4 (12-oz.) cans lemon-lime soft drink, chilled. Serve over ice in chilled glasses. Garnish with lime slices. Makes about 9 cups. Hands-on time: 10 min.; Total time: 2 hr., 10 min.

Note: We tested with Rose's Lime Juice.

Warm Spiced Sangría: Place 8 black peppercorns, 6 whole allspice, 6 whole cloves, 2 (3-inch) cinnamon sticks, and 3 (3- x 1-inch) orange rind strips on a 5-inch square of cheesecloth. Gather edges of cheesecloth, and tie securely with kitchen string. Combine 3 cups orange juice, 1½ cups apple cider, ¾ cup sugar, and spice bag in a 6-qt. slow cooker. Cover and cook on HIGH 2 hours. Stir in 2 (750-milliliter) bottles dry red wine; ½ cup brandy; 1 orange, sliced; and 2 small Granny Smith apples, sliced. Cover and cook on LOW 30 minutes or until thoroughly heated. Makes 1½ cups. Hands-on time: 10 min.; Total time: 2 hr., 40 min.

Cranberry-Key Lime Punch: Combine 2 cups fresh cranberries, 1 cup sugar, and 1 cup water in a saucepan. Cook mixture over medium heat, stirring occasionally, 8 minutes or until cranberries begin to pop. Pour mixture through a wire-mesh strainer into a large pitcher, discarding solids; cool completely (about 1 hour). Stir in 5 to 6 cups chilled club soda, ½ cup fresh Key lime juice, and, if desired, 1 cup vodka. Serve over ice. Garnish with Key lime slices and fresh cranberries. Makes about 7½ cups. Hands-on time: 15 min.; Total time: 1 hr., 15 min.

Honey-Green Tea Fizz: Steep 8 regular-size ginger-flavored green tea bags in 4 cups boiling water according to package directions. Stir in ½ cup honey and ¼ cup sugar until dissolved; cool completely (about 2 hours). Combine tea, 1 (2-liter) bottle chilled ginger ale, and ¼ cup fresh lemon juice. Serve over ice. Makes about 13 cups. Hands-on time: 10 min., Total time: 2 hr. 10 min.

Note: We tested with Tazo Tea.

RECIPE INSPIRED BY MONNIE SULLIVAN
LILLINGTON, NORTH CAROLINA

Raspberry Wine Zinger: Stir together 1 (750-milliliter) bottle dry white wine, 2 (12-oz.) bottles raspberry lambic beer, 1 (1-liter) bottle chilled club soda, and ¾ cup simple syrup in a large punch bowl. Scoop 1 pt. raspberry sorbet into wine mixture. Add 1 cup frozen raspberries. Garnish with rosemary sprigs. Makes about 13 cups. Hands-on time: 10 min., Total time: 10 min.

Note: We tested with Stirrings Simple Syrup and Lindeman's Framboise Raspberry Lambic Beer.

Blackberry Mojito Punch: Stir together 3 cups blueberry-blackberry juice blend, 2 (12-oz.) cans frozen mojito mix, 2 (1-liter) bottles chilled club soda, 1½ cups white rum, 3 sliced limes, and 1 (12-oz.) package frozen blackberries in a large punch bowl. Serve over ice. Garnish with fresh mint sprigs. Makes about 16 cups. Hands-on time: 5 min., Total time: 5 min.

Iced Hello Dolly: Stir together 6 cups milk, 3 cups chilled strong brewed hazelnut-flavored coffee, 1½ cups chocolate syrup, and ¾ tsp. coconut extract. Chill until ready to serve (up to 8 hours). Top each serving with refrigerated instant whipped cream and chocolate syrup. Makes about 10 cups. Hands-on time: 5 min.; Total time: 5 min.

Seven Southern Classics

Sample a few quintessential Southern dishes from *Southern Living*'s latest cookbook, *1001 Ways to Cook Southern*.

Uptown Collards

MAKES 8 TO 10 SERVINGS
HANDS-ON TIME: 20 MIN.
TOTAL TIME: 1 HR., 10 MIN.

7 lb. fresh collard greens*
1 medium onion, quartered
1 cup dry white wine
1 Tbsp. sugar
1 Tbsp. bacon drippings
1 red bell pepper, diced

1. Remove and discard stems from greens. Wash leaves thoroughly, and cut into 1-inch-wide strips.
2. Pulse onion in a food processor 3 to 4 times or until minced.
3. Bring onion, next 3 ingredients, and 1 cup water to a boil in a Dutch oven.
4. Add greens and bell pepper; cook, covered, over medium heat 45 minutes to 1 hour or until greens are tender.
* 2 (1-lb.) packages fresh collard greens may be substituted.

Super-Moist Cornbread

MAKES 8 SERVINGS
HANDS-ON TIME: 10 MIN.
TOTAL TIME: 40 MIN.

You can bake this cornbread one day in advance. Allow it to cool completely; then wrap tightly in aluminum foil or plastic wrap.

⅓ cup butter
1 (8-oz.) container sour cream
2 large eggs, lightly beaten
1 (8-oz.) can cream-style corn
1 cup self-rising white cornmeal mix

1. Preheat oven to 400°. Heat butter in a 9-inch cast-iron skillet in oven 5 minutes or until butter melts.
2. Combine sour cream, eggs, and corn in a medium bowl. Whisk in cornmeal mix just until combined. Whisk in melted butter. Pour batter into hot skillet.
3. Bake at 400° for 30 minutes or until golden brown.

Baked Ham with Bourbon Glaze

MAKES 12 TO 14 SERVINGS
HANDS-ON TIME: 15 MIN.
TOTAL TIME: 1 HR., 50 MIN.

1 cup honey
½ cup molasses
½ cup bourbon
¼ cup orange juice
2 Tbsp. Dijon mustard
1 (6- to 8-lb.) smoked fully cooked, semi-boneless ham

1. Preheat oven to 325°. Microwave honey and molasses in a 1-qt. microwave-safe dish at HIGH 1 minute; whisk until blended. Whisk in bourbon, orange juice, and mustard.
2. Remove skin and excess fat from ham, and place ham in a roasting pan.
3. Bake at 325° on lower oven rack 1½ to 2 hours or until a meat thermometer inserted into thickest portion registers 140°, basting occasionally with honey mixture.
4. Transfer ham to a serving platter, reserving drippings. Bring drippings and remaining honey mixture to a boil in a small saucepan. Boil 1 to 2 minutes. Remove from heat, and serve with sliced ham.

Cheddar Cheese Grits Casserole

MAKES 6 SERVINGS
HANDS-ON TIME: 15 MIN.
TOTAL TIME: 55 MIN.

Serve this with thick strips of bacon for a wonderful winter breakfast.

4 cups milk
¼ cup butter
1 cup uncooked quick-cooking grits
1 large egg, lightly beaten
2 cups (8 oz.) shredded sharp Cheddar cheese
1 tsp. salt
½ tsp. pepper
¼ cup grated Parmesan cheese

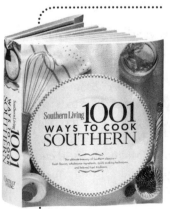

1001 Delicious Recipes!

A SOUTHERN FOOD BIBLE
1001 Ways to Cook Southern is a must-have for anyone who loves the food of this region. It's packed with classic recipes such as Smoked Baby Back Ribs, Red Velvet Cake, and Southern Turnip Greens and Ham Hocks. The book also features our staff's favorite ingredients and offers fast, fresh twists perfect for today's busy cooks. Give it as a gift, but be sure to get a copy for yourself, too. Available for $34.95 at *www.oxmoorhouse.com* and wherever books are sold.

1. Preheat oven to 350°. Bring milk just to a boil in a large saucepan over medium-high heat; gradually whisk in butter and grits. Reduce heat, and simmer, whisking constantly, 5 to 7 minutes or until grits are done.

2. Remove from heat. Stir in egg and next 3 ingredients. Pour into a lightly greased 11- x 7-inch baking dish. Sprinkle with grated Parmesan cheese.

3. Bake, covered, at 350° for 35 to 40 minutes or until mixture is set. Serve immediately.

Chicken and Dumplings

MAKES 4 TO 6 SERVINGS
HANDS-ON TIME: 25 MIN.
TOTAL TIME: 40 MIN.

We used a deli-roasted chicken for this recipe. One chicken yields about 3 cups.

- 1 (32-oz.) container low-sodium chicken broth
- 1 (14-oz.) can low-sodium chicken broth
- 3 cups shredded cooked chicken (about 1½ lb.)
- 1 (10¾-oz.) can reduced-fat cream of celery soup
- ¼ tsp. poultry seasoning
- 1 (10.2-oz.) can refrigerated jumbo buttermilk biscuits

1. Stir together first 5 ingredients in a Dutch oven over medium-high heat, and bring to a boil. Reduce heat to low; simmer, stirring occasionally, 15 minutes.

2. Meanwhile, place biscuits on a lightly floured surface. Roll or pat each biscuit to ⅛-inch thickness; cut into ½-inch-wide strips.

3. Return broth mixture to a low boil over medium-high heat. Drop strips, 1 at a time, into boiling broth. Reduce heat to low; simmer 10 minutes, stirring occasionally to prevent dumplings from sticking.

Muffuletta Calzones

MAKES 4 SERVINGS
HANDS-ON TIME: 20 MIN.
TOTAL TIME: 40 MIN.

- 1 cup jarred mixed pickled vegetables, rinsed and finely chopped
- 1 (7-oz.) package shredded provolone-Italian cheese blend
- 8 thin slices Genoa salami, chopped (about ⅛ lb.)
- ½ cup diced cooked ham
- ¼ cup sliced pimiento-stuffed Spanish olives
- 2 Tbsp. olive oil, divided
- 1 lb. bakery pizza dough
- 2 Tbsp. grated Parmesan cheese

1. Preheat oven to 425°. Stir together pickled vegetables, next 4 ingredients, and 1 Tbsp. olive oil.

2. Place dough on a lightly floured surface. Cut dough into 4 equal pieces. Roll each piece into a 7-inch circle.

3. Place 2 dough circles on a lightly greased baking sheet. Spoon vegetable mixture on top of circles, mounding mixture on dough and leaving a 1-inch border. Moisten edges of dough with water, and top with remaining 2 dough circles. Press and crimp edges to seal.

4. Cut small slits in tops of dough to allow steam to escape. Brush with remaining 1 Tbsp. olive oil, and sprinkle with Parmesan cheese.

5. Bake at 425° for 20 to 24 minutes or until golden brown.

Chicken-and-Sausage Creole

MAKES 6 SERVINGS
HANDS-ON TIME: 20 MIN.
TOTAL TIME: 45 MIN.

- 1 cup uncooked long-grain rice
- 2 (14-oz.) cans low-sodium fat-free chicken broth, divided
- ½ lb. smoked sausage, cut into ½-inch rounds
- 1 medium-size yellow onion, chopped (about 2 cups)
- 1 cup chopped celery
- 1 green bell pepper, chopped
- 2 garlic cloves, minced
- 3 cups chopped cooked chicken
- 1 (14½-oz.) can diced tomatoes
- 2 tsp. chopped fresh parsley
- 1 tsp. salt
- ⅛ tsp. ground red pepper
- 2 bay leaves

1. Prepare rice according to package directions, substituting 2 cups broth for water.

2. Sauté sausage and next 4 ingredients in a lightly greased Dutch oven over medium-high heat 5 minutes or until vegetables are tender.

3. Stir in chicken, next 5 ingredients, and remaining broth. Bring to a boil over medium-high heat. Reduce heat to low; simmer, stirring occasionally, 20 minutes. Remove and discard bay leaves, and serve over hot cooked rice.

Our Favorite Sweets to Swap

Impress your friends with these scrumptious treats plucked straight from the baking sheets of our annual Test Kitchen holiday sweet swap. From cinnamon-scented Snickerdoodles to buttery Pecan Sandies, these easy-to-make recipes are perfect for giving and nibbling.

Meet our Hosts

Left to right: Rebecca Kracke Gordon, *Assistant Test Kitchen Director*; Angela Sellers, *Test Kitchen Professional*; Lyda Jones Burnette, *Test Kitchen Director*; Vanessa McNeil Rocchio, *Test Kitchen Specialist/Food Styling*; Pam Lolley and Norman King, *Test Kitchen Professionals*; Not pictured: Marian Cooper Cairns, *Test Kitchen Specialist/Food Styling*

SNICKERDOODLES: "I like to use the bottom of a glass to flatten dough balls slightly before baking for a crackled appearance or bake dough balls without flattening for more of a 'snowball.'" **Lyda Jones Burnette**

ALMOND SNOWBALLS: "Don't be alarmed—the dough will be crumbly. The additional flour in this variation allows the cookies to bake up nice and round." **Norman King**

BLACKBERRY THUMBPRINTS: "Be sure the zip-top plastic bag you use to pipe preserves into cookies is a freezer bag and not a regular storage bag or you may experience a blowout...ask me how I know." **Norman King**

CANDY BAR-PEANUT BUTTER COOKIES: "This is my family's all-time favorite cookie. Don't feel like you have to bake all of the cookies at once. You can keep the dough covered in the refrigerator up to 1 week and bake small batches whenever you want to for that fresh-from-the-oven taste." **Pam Lolley**

SNOWFLAKE SHORTBREAD: "When I make sugar cookie cutouts, I omit the leavening or look for recipes without it so that cookies keep their shape during baking." **Rebecca Kracke Gordon**

PECAN SANDIES: "Feel free to omit the pecans and substitute with almonds or your favorite nut. You can also freeze the dough for up to 2 months." **Vanessa McNeil Rocchio**

SALTED CARAMEL-PECAN BARS: "If you like the look of cleaner edges, use a chef's knife to cut bars into irregular pieces." **Marian Cooper Cairns**

FLOURLESS PEANUT BUTTER-CHOCOLATE CHIP COOKIES: "When portioning dough, spray your tablespoon measure with cooking spray for easy release onto baking sheets." **Angela Sellers**

Snickerdoodles

MAKES 4½ DOZEN
HANDS-ON TIME: 20 MIN.
TOTAL TIME: 1 HR., 28 MIN.

Lyda Jones Burnette, our Test Kitchens Director, borrows this recipe from one of her favorite spice stores.

- 1 cup butter, softened
- 2 cups sugar
- 2 large eggs
- ¼ cup milk
- 1 tsp. vanilla extract
- 3¾ cups all-purpose flour
- 1 tsp. baking powder
- 2 tsp. ground cinnamon
- 3 Tbsp. sugar
- 1½ Tbsp. ground cinnamon

1. Preheat oven to 375°. Beat butter at medium speed with an electric mixer until creamy. Gradually add 2 cups sugar, beating well. Add eggs, milk, and vanilla, beating well.
2. Combine flour, baking powder, and 2 tsp. cinnamon; gradually add to butter mixture, beating at low speed just until blended. (If desired, store dough in an airtight container in refrigerator up to 1 week.)
3. Combine 3 Tbsp. sugar and 1½ Tbsp. cinnamon in a small bowl. Roll dough into 1¼-inch balls, and roll in sugar mixture.
4. Place on ungreased baking sheets, and flatten slightly.
5. Bake at 375° for 11 to 13 minutes or until lightly browned. Cool on baking sheets 5 minutes. Transfer to wire racks, and cool completely (about 30 minutes).

RECIPE FROM LYDA JONES BURNETTE

Flourless Peanut Butter–Chocolate Chip Cookies

MAKES 2 DOZEN
HANDS-ON TIME: 30 MIN.
TOTAL TIME: 1 HR., 14 MIN.

- 1 cup creamy peanut butter
- ¾ cup sugar
- 1 large egg
- ½ tsp. baking soda
- ¼ tsp. salt
- 1 cup semisweet chocolate morsels
  Parchment paper

1. Preheat oven to 350°. Stir together first 5 ingredients in a medium bowl until well blended. Stir in chocolate morsels.
2. Drop dough by rounded tablespoonfuls 2 inches apart onto parchment paper-lined baking sheets.
3. Bake at 350° for 12 to 14 minutes or until puffed and lightly browned. Cool on baking sheets on a wire rack 5 minutes. Transfer to wire rack, and let cool 15 minutes.

RECIPE FROM ANGELA SELLERS

Plan to wrap similar treats together so spice cookies don't pick up notes of peanut butter and chocolate. Use tissue paper, string, ribbon, and tags for an extra splash of holiday flair. Assorted containers for packaging can be found at your local grocery store, supercenter, or crafts store: Mason or jelly jars, brown paper lunch sacks, small white or brown bakery boxes, small silver or white aluminum tins, cellophane bags, and clear plastic containers with lids.

Blackberry Thumbprints

MAKES ABOUT 5 DOZEN
HANDS-ON TIME: 30 MIN.
TOTAL TIME: 2 HR., 5 MIN.

- ½ cup slivered almonds
- 1 cup butter, softened
- 1 cup powdered sugar
- 2 cups all-purpose flour
- ¼ tsp. salt
- ¼ tsp. ground cloves
- ¼ tsp. ground cinnamon
  Parchment paper
- ½ cup seedless blackberry preserves

1. Preheat oven to 350°. Bake almonds in a single layer in a shallow pan 6 minutes or until toasted and fragrant, stirring halfway through. Cool completely (about 20 minutes). Reduce oven temperature to 325°.
2. Process almonds in a food processor 30 seconds or until finely ground. Beat butter at medium speed with a heavy-duty electric stand mixer until creamy. Gradually add 1 cup powdered sugar, beating well.
3. Combine flour, next 3 ingredients, and almonds; gradually add to butter mixture, beating until blended.

4. Shape dough into ¾-inch balls, and place 2 inches apart on parchment paper-lined baking sheets. Press thumb into each ball, forming an indentation.
5. Bake at 325° for 12 to 15 minutes or until edges are lightly browned. Cool on baking sheets 2 minutes. Transfer to wire racks, and cool 30 minutes.
6. Place preserves in a zip-top plastic freezer bag; snip 1 corner of bag to make a small hole. Pipe preserves into indentations. Store in an airtight container up to 5 days.

TRY THIS TWIST!
Almond Snowballs: Omit cloves, cinnamon, and preserves. Increase flour to 2½ cups. Prepare recipe as directed through Step 4, beating in 1 tsp. vanilla extract with butter and sugar. (Dough will be crumbly.) Shape and bake dough as directed, without making indentations. Cool on baking sheets 2 minutes. Transfer to wire racks, and cool 10 minutes. Roll cookies in ½ cup powdered sugar. Makes about 5 dozen. Hands-on time: 25 min.; Total time: 1 hr., 37 min.

RECIPE FROM NORMAN KING

Snowflake Shortbread

MAKES ABOUT 7½ DOZEN
HANDS-ON TIME: 25 MIN.
TOTAL TIME: 1 HR., 42 MIN., INCLUDING GLAZE

- 1 cup butter, softened
- 1 cup powdered sugar
- 2 cups all-purpose flour
- ¼ tsp. salt
  Parchment paper
  Royal Icing
  Sparkling sugar

1. Preheat oven to 325°. Beat butter at medium speed with a heavy-duty electric stand mixer until creamy. Gradually add powdered sugar, beating well.
2. Combine flour and salt; gradually add to butter mixture, beating until blended.
3. Roll dough to ⅛-inch thickness on a lightly floured surface. Cut with a 2-inch snowflake-shaped cutter, and place 1 inch apart on parchment paper-lined baking sheets.
4. Bake at 325° for 11 to 13 minutes or until edges are lightly browned. Cool on baking sheets 5 minutes. Transfer to wire racks, and cool completely (about 40 minutes). Decorate with Royal Icing, and sprinkle with sparkling sugar.

Royal Icing:

MAKES ABOUT 1¾ CUPS
HANDS-ON TIME: 5 MIN.
TOTAL TIME: 5 MIN.

- 3 cups powdered sugar
- 2 Tbsp. meringue powder
- ¼ cup cold water

1. Beat all ingredients at high speed with a heavy-duty electric stand mixer, using a whisk attachment, until glossy, stiff peaks form. Place a damp cloth directly on surface of icing (to prevent a crust from forming) while icing cookies.

RECIPE FROM REBECCA KRACKE GORDON

Pecan Sandies

MAKES ABOUT 7 DOZEN
HANDS-ON TIME: 20 MIN.
TOTAL TIME: 3 HR.

My grandfather was a great cook who inspired me. These cookies, made with fresh Texas pecans, were always in his cookie jar. You can't stop with just one cookie.

- ⅓ cup finely chopped pecans
- 1 cup butter, softened
- ½ cup sugar
- 2½ cups all-purpose flour
- 1 tsp. vanilla extract
  Parchment paper

1. Preheat oven to 350°. Bake pecans in a single layer in a shallow pan 6 to 8 minutes or until toasted and fragrant, stirring halfway through.
2. Beat butter and sugar at medium speed with an electric mixer until fluffy. Gradually add flour, beating just until blended. Stir in pecans and vanilla.
3. Divide dough in half, and shape each portion into 2 (1¼-inch-thick) logs (about 12 inches long). Wrap in parchment paper, and cover and chill 1 hour or until firm.
4. Preheat oven to 325°. Cut logs into ¼-inch-thick rounds, and place ½ inch apart on parchment paper-lined baking sheets.
5. Bake at 325° for 18 to 20 minutes or until lightly golden. Let cool on baking sheets 5 minutes. Transfer to wire racks, and let cool completely (about 20 minutes). Store in an airtight container up to 1 week.

RECIPE FROM VANESSA MCNEIL ROCCHIO

Salted Caramel-Pecan Bars

MAKES 4 DOZEN
HANDS-ON TIME: 15 MIN.
TOTAL TIME: 1 HR., 5 MIN.

This is an old recipe Marian "updated" with a sprinkle of kosher salt and by adding a dark chocolate variation.

- 1 cup chopped pecans
- 12 whole graham crackers
- 1 cup firmly packed brown sugar
- ¾ cup butter
- 2 Tbsp. whipping cream
- 1 tsp. vanilla extract
- ¼ tsp. kosher salt

1. Preheat oven to 350°. Bake pecans in a single layer in a shallow pan 10 to 12 minutes or until toasted and fragrant, stirring halfway through.
2. Line a 15- x 10-inch jelly-roll pan with aluminum foil; lightly grease foil.
3. Arrange graham crackers in a single layer in prepared pan, slightly overlapping edges.
4. Combine sugar and next 2 ingredients in a medium-size heavy saucepan; bring to a boil over medium heat, stirring occasionally. Remove from heat, and stir in vanilla and pecans. Pour butter mixture over crackers, spreading to coat.
5. Bake at 350° for 10 to 11 minutes or until lightly browned and bubbly. Immediately sprinkle with salt, and carefully slide foil from pan onto a wire rack. Cool completely (about 30 minutes). Break into bars.

TRY THIS TWIST!

Chocolate-Pecan Caramel Bars: Prepare recipe as directed through Step 4. Top warm bars with 1 cup dark chocolate morsels. Let stand 3 minutes, and spread chocolate over bars. Proceed as directed. Chill 20 minutes before serving.

RECIPE FROM MARIAN COOPER CAIRNS

Candy Bar-Peanut Butter Cookies

MAKES 3 DOZEN
HANDS-ON TIME: 20 MIN.
TOTAL TIME: 1 HR., 50 MIN.

- 1 cup butter, softened
- 1 cup granulated sugar
- 1 cup firmly packed brown sugar
- 1 cup creamy peanut butter
- 2 large eggs
- 1 tsp. vanilla extract
- 2 cups all-purpose flour
- 1 tsp. baking soda
- ½ tsp. salt
- 36 bite-size chocolate-covered caramel-peanut nougat bars

1. Beat first 4 ingredients at medium speed with an electric mixer until smooth. Add eggs and vanilla, and beat until blended. Stir together flour and next 2 ingredients in a small bowl. Add to butter mixture, beating until blended. Cover and chill 30 minutes.
2. Preheat oven to 350°. Shape about 2 Tbsp. dough around each nougat bar, using lightly floured hands, and roll into balls. Place 3 inches apart on ungreased or parchment paper-lined baking sheets.
3. Bake at 350° for 13 to 14 minutes or until lightly browned. Cool on baking sheets 5 minutes. Transfer to wire racks, and cool completely (about 20 minutes).
Note: We tested with Snickers.

RECIPE FROM PAM LOLLEY

Sweet Holidays

Share the magic of the season with this decadent cake.

Spice Cake with Citrus Filling

MAKES 12 SERVINGS
HANDS-ON TIME: 25 MIN.
TOTAL TIME: 2 HR., 40 MIN., INCLUDING FILLING AND ICING
(Pictured on the cover)

  1 cup chopped pecans
  1 cup butter, softened
  2 cups sugar
  3 large eggs
  3¼ cups all-purpose flour
  1 tsp. baking soda
  ½ tsp. salt
  1½ cups buttermilk
  1 tsp. vanilla extract
  ½ tsp. ground cinnamon
  ½ tsp. ground allspice
  ¼ tsp. ground cloves
     Citrus Filling
     White Icing

1. Preheat oven to 350°. Bake pecans in a single layer in a shallow pan 5 to 7 minutes or until lightly toasted and fragrant, stirring halfway through. Let cool.
2. Meanwhile, beat butter at medium speed with a heavy-duty electric stand mixer until creamy. Gradually add sugar, beating until light and fluffy. Add eggs, 1 at a time, beating just until blended after each addition.
3. Stir together flour, baking soda, and salt; add to butter mixture alternately with buttermilk, beating at low speed just until blended, beginning and ending with flour mixture. Stir in vanilla.

4. Divide batter into 2 equal portions (about 3½ cups each); stir cinnamon, allspice, cloves, and pecans into 1 portion. Pour plain batter into 2 greased and floured 9-inch round cake pans (about 1¾ cups batter per pan). Pour spiced batter into 2 greased and floured 9-inch round cake pans (about 1¾ cups batter per pan).
5. Bake at 350° for 18 to 20 minutes or until a wooden pick inserted in center comes out clean. Cool in pans on wire racks 10 minutes; remove from pans to wire racks; cool completely (about 1 hour).
6. Place 1 plain cake layer on a serving plate or cake stand; spread top with ⅔ cup Citrus Filling, leaving a ¼-inch border around edges.
7. Top with a spice cake layer, and spread top with Citrus Filling as directed above. Repeat procedure with remaining plain cake layer and Citrus Filling. Top with remaining spice cake layer. Spread top and sides of cake with White Icing.
Note: For a pretty presentation, we used a kitchen torch to lightly brown the White Icing after frosting the cake.

Citrus Filling:

MAKES ABOUT 2 CUPS
HANDS-ON TIME: 5 MIN.
TOTAL TIME: 5 MIN.

  2 (10-oz.) jars lemon curd
  1½ cups sweetened flaked coconut
  1 Tbsp. orange zest
  1 Tbsp. fresh orange juice

1. Stir together all ingredients in a medium bowl until blended.

White Icing:

MAKES ABOUT 4 CUPS
HANDS-ON TIME: 15 MIN.
TOTAL TIME: 15 MIN.

  2 egg whites
  1¼ cups sugar
  1 Tbsp. corn syrup
  1 tsp. vanilla extract

1. Pour water to depth of 1½ inches into a 3½-qt. saucepan; bring to a boil over medium-high heat. Reduce heat to medium, and simmer. Combine egg whites, next 3 ingredients, and ¼ cup water in a 2½-qt. glass bowl; beat at high speed with an electric mixer until blended. Place bowl over simmering water, and beat at high speed 5 to 7 minutes or until soft peaks form; remove from heat. Beat to spreading consistency (about 2 to 3 minutes). Use immediately.

Turkey for a Small Crowd

Four simple-to-fix recipes (plus a trendy little spin on cornbread dressing) set the table with big holiday flavor.

Molasses Grilled Turkey Tenderloin

MAKES 8 TO 10 SERVINGS
HANDS-ON TIME: 30 MIN.
TOTAL TIME: 4 HR., 45 MIN.

  1 cup molasses
  ½ cup olive oil
  ½ cup soy sauce
  ¼ cup Worcestershire sauce
  2 Tbsp. grated fresh ginger
  2 garlic cloves, minced
  3 lb. turkey tenderloins
     Vegetable cooking spray
     Salt to taste

1. Combine first 6 ingredients in a large zip-top plastic freezer bag; add turkey. Seal and chill 4 hours, turning occasionally.

2. Coat cold cooking grate of grill with vegetable cooking spray, and place on grill. Preheat grill to 350° to 400° (medium-high) heat. Remove turkey from marinade, discarding marinade.

3. Grill turkey, covered with grill lid, 20 to 25 minutes or until a meat thermometer inserted into thickest portion registers 170°, turning turkey occasionally. Let stand 15 minutes. Cut turkey diagonally into thin slices, and arrange on a serving platter. Season with salt to taste.

Roasted Turkey Breast with Pan-fried Polenta and Hollandaise Sauce

MAKES 8 TO 10 SERVINGS
HANDS-ON TIME: 20 MIN.
TOTAL TIME: 4 HR., 45 MIN., INCLUDING POLENTA AND SAUCE

Prep and chill the polenta up to a day ahead, then cook while the turkey stands after roasting.

- 1 (5-lb.) skinned and boned turkey breast
- 3 garlic cloves, minced
- ½ tsp. salt
- 6 bacon slices
  Pan-fried Polenta
  Hollandaise Sauce

1. Preheat oven to 425°. Place turkey between 2 sheets of heavy-duty plastic wrap, and flatten to ¾-inch thickness, using a rolling pin or flat side of a meat mallet. Rub with garlic and salt; place on a rack in a broiler pan, and top with bacon slices.

2. Bake at 425° for 25 to 30 minutes or until done. Let stand 10 minutes before slicing. Serve with Pan-fried Polenta and Hollandaise Sauce.

Pan-fried Polenta:

MAKES 8 TO 10 SERVINGS
HANDS-ON TIME: 40 MIN.
TOTAL TIME: 3 HR., 40 MIN.

- ½ cup butter, divided
- ¾ cup finely chopped sweet onion
- ½ cup finely chopped celery
- 2 garlic cloves, minced
- 4 (14½-oz.) cans chicken broth
- 2 cups plain yellow cornmeal
- 3 Tbsp. finely chopped fresh sage
- ½ tsp. salt
- ½ tsp. pepper
- ½ cup freshly grated Parmesan cheese

1. Melt ¼ cup butter in a Dutch oven over medium heat; add onion, celery, and garlic, and sauté 3 to 5 minutes or until tender. Add broth, and bring to a boil; gradually stir in cornmeal and next 3 ingredients. Reduce heat to low, and cook, stirring often, 10 minutes.

2. Remove from heat, and stir in cheese. Pour mixture into a lightly greased 13- x 9-inch baking dish; cover and chill 3 to 12 hours or until firm. Cut polenta into 12 triangles.

3. Melt 1 Tbsp. butter in a large non-stick skillet over medium-high heat. Add 3 polenta triangles, and cook 2 to 3 minutes on each side or until golden brown. Transfer to a serving dish, and keep warm. Repeat procedure with remaining polenta triangles and 3 Tbsp. butter.

HOLLANDAISE SAUCE: Prepare 1 (0.9-oz.) envelope hollandaise sauce mix according to package directions, stirring in 1 Tbsp. fresh lemon juice. Serve immediately. Makes 2¼ cups. Hands-on time: 5 min.; Total time: 15 min.
Note: We tested with Knorr Hollandaise Sauce Mix.

Sugar-and-Spice Cured Turkey Breast

MAKES 6 TO 8 SERVINGS
HANDS-ON TIME: 10 MIN.
TOTAL TIME: 10 HR., 40 MIN.

To prevent a top-heavy turkey breast from tilting over onto its side, use kitchen shears to trim an inch or two from the bony, lower portion of the rib cage—just enough to level the underside of the breast so that it rests securely in the pan or on the grill.

- ¼ cup firmly packed light brown sugar
- 1 Tbsp. salt
- 1 tsp. onion powder
- ½ tsp. garlic powder
- ½ tsp. ground allspice
- ½ tsp. ground cloves
- 1 (5- to 6-lb.) bone-in, skin-on turkey
- 2½ to 3 cups chicken broth

1. Combine brown sugar and next 5 ingredients. Rub mixture over turkey breast; cover and chill 8 hours.

2. Preheat oven to 350°. Let turkey breast stand at room temperature 30 minutes. Place turkey breast on a rack in a roasting pan, breast side up. Pour broth in bottom of pan. Cover turkey loosely with aluminum foil.

3. Bake at 350° for 1 hour and 45 minutes or until a meat thermometer inserted into thickest portion registers 170°. Transfer turkey to a serving platter, and let stand 15 minutes before slicing.

Turkey Cutlets With Lemon Caper Sauce

MAKES 4 SERVINGS
HANDS-ON TIME: 25 MIN.
TOTAL TIME: 25 MIN.

⅓ cup all-purpose flour
½ tsp. salt
½ tsp. pepper
1 lb. turkey cutlets
3 Tbsp. butter, divided
1 Tbsp. olive oil
½ cup dry white wine
3 Tbsp. fresh lemon juice
2 garlic cloves, minced
2 Tbsp. chopped fresh flat-leaf parsley
2 Tbsp. capers
    Garnishes: lemon wedges, chopped fresh flat-leaf parsley

1. Combine flour, salt, and pepper; dredge turkey in mixture.
2. Melt 2 Tbsp. butter with oil in a large skillet over medium-high heat; add turkey, and cook, in batches, 1½ minutes on each side or until golden. Transfer to a serving dish, and keep warm.
3. Add wine, lemon juice, and remaining 1 Tbsp. butter to skillet, stirring to loosen particles from bottom of skillet. Cook mixture 2 minutes or just until thoroughly heated.
4. Stir in garlic, parsley, and capers; spoon over turkey. Garnish, if desired. Serve immediately.

Try Our Cherries Jubilee Ham

All it takes is a jar of preserves and slow baking to give this showstopping entrée a shimmery glaze and super-juicy results.

Cherries Jubilee-Black Pepper Glazed Ham

MAKES 10 SERVINGS
HANDS-ON TIME: 30 MIN.
TOTAL TIME: 4 HR., 45 MIN.

We baked this ham at a low temperature—275°—which made it juicier and more tender than at a higher temperature. For an open house or next day breakfast, serve ham in split biscuits with mustard and the chilled cherry sauce.

1 (10- to 12-lb.) smoked, ready-to-cook bone-in ham
1 (14-oz.) can low-sodium chicken broth
2¼ cups cherry preserves (about 2 [12-oz.] jars)
¾ cup brandy
¼ cup cider vinegar
1 Tbsp. freshly ground pepper
3 Tbsp. whole grain Dijon mustard
3 Tbsp. cane syrup
    Whole grain Dijon mustard
    Garnishes: fresh cherries, fresh sage sprigs

1. Remove skin from ham, and trim fat to ¼-inch thickness. Make shallow cuts in fat 1 inch apart in a diamond pattern. Place ham in an aluminum foil-lined roasting pan; add broth to pan.
2. Stir together preserves and next 5 ingredients in a saucepan; bring to a boil over mediumhigh heat, stirring constantly. Reduce heat to medium-low; simmer, stirring constantly, 5 minutes or until mixture is slightly reduced. Reserve 1½ cups of mixture. Cover and chill half of cherry mixture until ready to serve. Brush ham with remaining half of cherry mixture.
3. Bake ham at 275° on lower oven rack 4 hours to 4 hours and 30 minutes or until a meat thermometer inserted into thickest portion registers 148°, basting with remaining cherry mixture every 30 minutes. Let ham stand 15 minutes before slicing.
4. If desired, reheat reserved chilled cherry mixture. Serve ham with reserved cherry mixture and mustard. Garnish, if desired.
Note: We tested with Smucker's Cherry Preserves and Smithfield Hardwood Smoked, Ready-to-Cook Ham.

Test Kitchen Tip

Long-lasting carving knives that can be sharpened are usually from cutlery makers such as Wüsthof. If considering a fancy-looking set, check to be sure blades can be sharpened.

Lemon-Parsley Ham Spread

MAKES ABOUT 3 CUPS
HANDS-ON TIME: 15 MIN.
TOTAL TIME: 8 HR., 15 MIN.

- 2 cups firmly packed chopped cooked ham
- 6 oz. cream cheese, softened
- 2 tsp. lemon zest
- 1 Tbsp. fresh lemon juice
- 1 Tbsp. whole grain Dijon mustard
- ¼ tsp. coarsely ground pepper
- ¼ tsp. ground red pepper
- ¼ cup chopped fresh parsley
  Crackers
  Pickled okra

1. Pulse ham, in batches, in a food processor 6 times or until shredded. (Do not overprocess.)

2. Beat cream cheese and next 5 ingredients at medium speed with an electric mixer 1 to 2 minutes or until fluffy, stopping to scrape down sides as needed. Stir in ham and parsley. Cover and chill 8 hours. Let stand at room temperature 30 minutes before serving. Store in an airtight container in refrigerator up to 3 days. Serve with crackers and pickled okra.

Carving Made Simple

Be traditional, have Dad show off your beautifully garnished ham while you and your guests enjoy a festive salad. He can whisk it away to the kitchen and carve using this easy method.

1 Follow the lines

Start by cutting away the largest section. Cut into ham following the curve of the natural fat lines, using a thin-bladed knife about 10 inches long. Continue, cutting deeper, until this piece separates from the bone.

2 Remove the smaller sections

Cut an S shape around the bone to release the second largest section of ham. Repeat to remove the smallest. Trim away excess fat, if necessary.

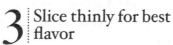

3 Slice thinly for best flavor

Cut sections into about ½-inch-thick slices to retain juicy tenderness. Steady the ham slices with the fork.

4 Final touches

Slide knife under slices, steady with the fork, and slide onto platter. Garnish and serve. For a big crowd, put a platter of ham at each end of the table.

Make It Special

Our Christmas gift to you is a terrific collection of our best recipes featuring your favorite holiday flavors. We've taken out the guess work and added lots of tips to make everything easy. Try it all or pick and choose. Either way, we promise you a Christmas the whole family will remember. Enjoy!

Magical Peppermint & Chocolate Treats

With only a few ingredients you can turn mint candies and chocolate into two playful desserts—Loaded Milk Chocolate-Peppermint Bark and Peppermint Patty Frappés. P.S. The bark makes great party favors and teacher gifts!

Loaded Milk Chocolate-Peppermint Bark

MAKES 2¾ LB.
HANDS-ON TIME: 25 MIN.
TOTAL TIME: 6 HR., 25 MIN.

Do not freeze. Frozen chocolate will get a powdery, chalky look called bloom.

 Parchment paper
1 tsp. butter
3 (11.5-oz.) packages milk chocolate morsels
12 cream-and-mint filled chocolate sandwich cookies, broken into pieces
1 cup small pretzel sticks
1¼ cups coarsely chopped soft peppermint candies

1. Line 1 (15- x 10-inch) jelly-roll pan with parchment paper; grease with 1 tsp. butter.

2. Microwave chocolate in a large microwave-safe bowl at HIGH 1 to 2 minutes or until smooth, stirring at 45-second intervals.
3. Gently stir cookies, pretzels, and ¾ cup peppermint candies into chocolate mixture. Spread mixture in prepared pan. Sprinkle with remaining ½ cup peppermint candy.
4. Let stand until firm (about 6 hours). Break or cut bark into pieces. Store in an airtight container in a cool place up to 3 days.
Note: We tested with Ghirardelli Milk Chocolate Chips, Oreo Double-Delight Chocolate Mint' N Creme Cookies, and Publix brand soft peppermint candies. You may also find King Leo Soft Peppermint Puffs in your local grocery stores.

Peppermint Patty Frappés

MAKES 3 CUPS
HANDS-ON TIME: 10 MIN.
TOTAL TIME: 10 MIN.

Make 'em minis! Small portions of this rich drinkable dessert are just right for the indulgent holidays.

2 cups vanilla ice cream
1 cup milk
9 miniature chocolate-covered peppermint patties, chopped*

1. Process all ingredients in a blender until smooth. Pour into glasses, and serve immediately.
*3 (1.4-oz.) chocolate-covered peppermint patties, chopped, may be substituted.
Note: We tested with York Peppermint Patties.

Grown-up Peppermint Patty Frappés: Decrease milk to ⅔ cup. Prepare recipe as directed, adding ⅓ cup crème de cacao.

Make It Special

Fancy Looks for Glasses

BLACK-BOTTOMED: Freeze serving glasses 2 hours. Pour about 1½ Tbsp. bottled chocolate fudge shell topping into bottom of each glass; swirl to coat. Freeze 30 minutes before serving.

SPARKLES & FUDGE RIMS: Microwave ½ (4-oz.) dark chocolate baking bar, finely chopped, in a small, shallow microwave-safe bowl at HIGH 45 seconds or until melted. Dip rims of 6 to 8 glasses into melted chocolate; sprinkle with finely chopped hard peppermint candy. Let stand at room temperature 20 minutes to 8 hours.

SPIKED WHIPPED CREAM: Beat ¾ cup whipping cream at medium-high speed with an electric mixer until foamy; gradually add 1 Tbsp. crème de cacao, beating until soft peaks form. Serve immediately, or cover and chill up to 6 hours.

Create a Festive Party Tray

Set the stage for fun holiday parties with our Dixie, Blue Ridge, or Creole appetizer trays. Each is an enticing collection of local artisan cheeses, grocery store pickups, and a recipe or two that offers marvelous regional flavor.

Dixie Party Tray

MAKES 12 TO 16 SERVINGS
HANDS-ON TIME: 10 MIN.
TOTAL TIME: 1 HR., 36 MIN., INCLUDING PECANS AND TOAST

Georgia cash crops peaches and pecans are on this tray. Try the Toast Points, an oldie but goodie, perfect for nostalgic holidays.

1 **(1- to 1½-lb.) tomme cheese wedge***
8 **oz. thinly sliced country ham**
1 **cup peach preserves**
   Brined Pecans (recipe at right)
   Toast Points (recipe at right) or table water crackers

1. Arrange all ingredients on a serving platter or cutting board.
*Manchego or Brie may be substituted.
Note: We tested with Sweet Grass Dairy Thomasville Tomme Cheese (sweetgrassdairy.com).

Our Cheese Pick

Georgia's Thomasville Tomme Cheese from Sweet Grass Dairy (*sweetgrassdairy.com*). Their tomme (a cheese originally produced in Switzerland) is mellow, buttery, and easy to love, making it a delicious balance with the stout flavors of country ham and Brined Pecans.

WINE PAIRING: Beachaven, Brut, Tennessee (*beachavenwinery.com*) or Domaine Chandon, Brut Classic, California

Brined Pecans

MAKES 2½ CUPS
HANDS-ON TIME: 10 MIN.
TOTAL TIME: 35 MIN.

Soaking pecans in sugar and water, then salting, guarantees the pecans will be dry, flavorful, and crisp.

1. Preheat oven to 350°. Stir together 2 cups warm water and ½ cup sugar, stirring until sugar is dissolved. Soak 2½ cups pecan halves in water mixture 10 minutes; drain well. Sprinkle 2 Tbsp. kosher salt in a 15- x 10-inch jelly-roll pan. Arrange pecans in a single layer in pan; sprinkle with 1 Tbsp. kosher salt. Bake 15 to 18 minutes or until toasted and fragrant. Toss pecans in a strainer to remove excess salt, if desired.
2. Store in an airtight container at room temperature 1 week, or freeze up to 2 months.

Buying Tips for Artisan Cheeses

- Label cheese with type and production city for a great conversion starter. (Note on the label the type milk used for any guests who might be allergic.)

- Order as early as possible for holiday parties. If this cheese is sold out, ask the cheesemaker for an alternative.

- Coordinate ship time with your party date. Cheese is perishable, only shipped on certain days, and is often sold in a minimum quantity.

Toast Points

MAKES 40
HANDS-ON TIME: 15 MIN.
TOTAL TIME: 51 MIN., INCLUDING COOL TIME

1. Preheat oven to 400°. Remove and discard crusts from 10 white bread slices; cut each slice into 4 triangles. Stir together 3 Tbsp. melted butter, ¼ tsp. onion powder, and ¼ tsp. salt. Lightly brush 1 side of bread triangles with butter mixture; place, buttered sides up, on a baking sheet. Bake 6 to 8 minutes or until toasted; cool on a wire rack 30 minutes.
Note: Toast points can be made up to 4 hours ahead.

Make It Special

Our Cheese Pick

Kentucky's Barron Co. Bleu Cheese (*kennysfarmhousecheese.com*) Kenny's Farmhouse Cheese, located in Austin, Kentucky, makes and sells this tangy and tart tasting yet subtle blue cheese. It's named after Barron County where it is made, and is an ideal flavor match to the apples and nuts on this tray.

WINE PAIRING: RayLen Vineyards, Cabernet Franc, North Carolina (*raylenvineyards.com*) or J. Lohr, Los Osos Merlot, California

Blue Ridge Party Tray

MAKES 12 TO 16 SERVINGS
HANDS-ON TIME: 10 MIN.
TOTAL TIME: 50 MIN., INCLUDING POTATO CHIPS

Golden Delicious apples are the state fruit of West Virginia, and North Carolina is known for sweet potatoes. Dollop chips with preserves and sprinkle with crumbled blue cheese for a fun flavor combo.

1 (1- to 1½-lb.) blue cheese wedge*
 Sweet Potato Chips (recipe at right)
2 Golden Delicious apples, sliced
1 (7-oz.) package glazed walnuts
 Apple preserves

1. Arrange all ingredients on a serving platter or cutting board.
* Stilton or Gorgonzola cheese may be substituted.
Note: We tested with Kenny's Farmhouse Barren Co. Bleu cheese (kennysfarmhousecheese. com) and Emerald Original Glazed Walnuts.

Sweet Potato Chips

MAKES 6 TO 8 SERVINGS
HANDS-ON TIME: 40 MIN.
TOTAL TIME: 40 MIN.

The secret to crisp sweet potato chips is to fry them in small batches, in peanut oil, at a low temperature. This makes 6 servings when served as a side, but will be plenty for 10 with the others foods on the tray.

1. Cut 2 peeled sweet potatoes (about 2 lb.) into ¹⁄₁₆-inch-thick slices, using a mandoline.
2. Pour peanut oil to depth of 3 inches into a Dutch oven; heat over medium-high heat to 300°. Fry potato slices, in small batches, stirring often, 4 to 4½ minutes or until crisp.
3. Drain on a wire rack over paper towels. Immediately sprinkle with desired amount of kosher salt.
Note: Cool completely, and store in an airtight container at room temperature up to 2 days.

Creole Party Tray

MAKES ABOUT 12 TO 16 SERVINGS
HANDS-ON TIME: 10 MIN.
TOTAL TIME: 1 HR., 10 MIN., INCLUDING ANDOUILLE AND FLATS

1 (1- to 1½-lb.) block Kashkaval Bulgarian-style yellow cheese*
1 (9.5-oz.) package sweet Cajun trail mix
 Smoked Paprika-Glazed Andouille (recipe on following page)
 Frenchie Flats (recipe on following page)
 Pickled okra

1. Arrange all ingredients on a serving platter or cutting board.
*White Cheddar, goat, or Gouda cheese may be substituted.
Note: We tested with Bittersweet Plantation Dairy Kashkaval-Bulgarian-style Yellow Cheese (jfolse.com/bittersweet_dairy/), Archer Farms Sweet Cajun Trail Mix (available at Target), and Wickles Pickled Okra.

Our Cheese Pick

Bittersweet Plantation Dairy Kashkaval-Bulgarian-style Yellow Cheese (*jfolse.com/bittersweet_dairy/*). Chef John Folse produces this cheese at his dairy in Gonzalez, Louisiana. It has a texture similar to Cheddar, and a friendly, tangy flavor that can stand up to our spicy andouille appetizer.

WINE PAIRING: Pontchartrain Vineyards, Louis D'Or, Louisiana (*pontchartrainvineyards.com*) or Milbrandt Vineyards, Traditions Chardonnay, Washington

Make It Special

Smoked Paprika-Glazed Andouille

MAKES 10 TO 12 SERVINGS
HANDS-ON TIME: 20 MIN.
TOTAL TIME: 20 MIN.

1. Cook 1 lb. andouille sausage, cut into ½-inch rounds, in 1 Tbsp. hot olive oil in a large skillet over medium-high heat 3 minutes on each side or until browned. Stir in 2 small garlic cloves, minced, and ½ tsp. smoked paprika, and cook 1 minute or until fragrant.
2. Add 2 Tbsp. sherry wine vinegar and 1 tsp. chopped fresh thyme, and cook, stirring often, 2 minutes or until sausage is glazed. Transfer to a shallow bowl. Serve with wooden picks.

Frenchie Flats

MAKES 10 TO 12 SERVINGS
HANDS-ON TIME: 15 MIN.
TOTAL TIME: 40 MIN.

1. Preheat oven to 350°. Cut 1 (14-oz.) package soft flatbreads into 1-inch strips. Place on a baking sheet. Brush with 3 Tbsp. olive oil, and sprinkle with desired amount of Creole seasoning. Bake 15 minutes or until toasted; cool 10 minutes. Store in an airtight container at room temperature up to 1 day.

Sweet-and-Spicy Finale

Fresh pears, a trio of spices, and bourbon-soaked fruits are cuddled in piecrust and baked, releasing the most intoxicating scents of the season.

Tipsy Spiced Fruit Tart with Buttermilk Whipped Cream

MAKES 8 SERVINGS
HANDS-ON TIME: 35 MIN.
TOTAL TIME: 2 HR., INCLUDING BUTTERMILK WHIPPED CREAM, PLUS 24 HR. FOR CHILLING

The bourbon-soaked fruits and bold flavors in this rustic pie make it an adults-only dessert. Splurge for premium brandy or bourbon—it's worth it.

- ⅔ **cup bourbon or brandy**
- ¾ **tsp. ground cinnamon**
- ¼ **tsp. ground allspice**
- ¾ **cup granulated sugar, divided**
- 1 **cup halved dried Mission figlets**
- 1 **(7-oz.) package dried apricots, coarsely chopped**
- 1 **cup jumbo raisins**
- 3 **ripe Bartlett pears, peeled and chopped**
- 2 **Tbsp. all-purpose flour**
- 2 **tsp. finely grated fresh ginger**
- 1 **(14.1-oz.) package refrigerated piecrusts**
  Parchment paper
- 1 **large egg, beaten**
- 2 **tsp. sugar**
  Buttermilk Whipped Cream Cook bourbon, next 2 ingredients, and

½ cup granulated sugar in a medium saucepan over medium-low heat, stirring often, 3 minutes or until sugar has dissolved and mixture is hot. Remove from heat, and stir in figlets, apricots, and raisins. Pour mixture into a large zip-top plastic freezer bag. Seal bag, removing as much air as possible; chill 24 hours.

1. Preheat oven to 350°. Transfer fruit mixture to a large bowl; stir in pears, flour, ginger, and remaining ¼ cup sugar.
2. Unroll and stack piecrusts on parchment paper. Roll into a 12-inch circle. Mound fruit mixture in center of piecrust (mixture will be slightly runny), leaving a 2- to 2½-inch border. Fold piecrust border up and over fruit, pleating as you go, leaving an opening about 5 inches wide in center. Brush piecrust with egg, and sprinkle with 2 tsp. sugar. Slide parchment paper onto a baking sheet.
3. Bake at 350° for 50 minutes or until filling is bubbly and crust is golden brown. Cool on baking sheet on a wire rack 30 minutes. Serve warm or at room temperature with Buttermilk Whipped Cream.
Note: We tested with Sun-Maid Mediterranean Apricots.

Make It Special

Test Kitchen Secrets

FOLLOW THESE TIPS FOR AN EASY, PERFECT TART.

1 | JUICES ARE GOOD
Once piecrusts are stacked and rolled out, mound fruit mixture with juices in the center, leaving about a 2½-inch border of crust. Tempted to not use the juices? Don't. We tried it and the fruit was very dry.

2 | PLEATING IS EASY
Lift parchment edges straight up, releasing crust onto fruit. Crust will naturally form folds or pleats. Adjust pleats to your liking—they can be uniform or free form.

3 | CASUAL DESSERTS NEED SPARKLE, TOO
Sprinkle crust with demerera sugar, instead of granulated, if desired. Demerera has bigger crystals and a golden-yellow color. Brushing egg on crust—before sprinkling with sugar—gives it a shiny, deep golden brown pastry once baked.

Buttermilk Whipped Cream

MAKES 3 CUPS
HANDS-ON TIME: 5 MIN.
TOTAL TIME: 5 MIN.

Freeze the bowl and beaters, and use cream and buttermilk right out of the fridge for perfect results.

1 cup heavy cream
½ cup buttermilk
2 Tbsp. sugar

1. Beat first 2 ingredients at high speed with an electric mixer until foamy; gradually add sugar, beating until soft peaks form. Serve immediately, or cover and chill up to 2 hours.

Spiced Rustic Apple Tart

MAKES 8 SERVINGS
HANDS-ON TIME: 35 MIN.
TOTAL TIME: 2 HR., 30 MIN., INCLUDING WHIPPED CREAM

We tested with Honeycrisp apples, but Braeburn or Granny Smith would also work well.

1½ lb. Honeycrisp apples, peeled and sliced
½ cup sugar
⅓ cup pear preserves
1 tsp. vanilla extract
¼ tsp. ground allspice
1 Tbsp. all-purpose flour
1 (14.1-oz.) package refrigerated piecrusts
Parchment paper
1 large egg, lightly beaten
1 Tbsp. sugar
Buttermilk Whipped Cream

1. Preheat oven to 350°. Stir together first 5 ingredients in a large bowl. Let stand 30 minutes, stirring occasionally. Stir in flour.

Unroll and stack piecrusts on parchment paper. Roll into a 12-inch circle. Mound apple mixture in center of piecrust using a slotted spoon (mixture will be slightly runny), leaving a 2- to 2½- inch border. Fold piecrust border up and over fruit, pleating as you go, leaving an opening about 5 inches wide in center. Drizzle apples with any remaining juice in bowl. Brush piecrust with egg, and sprinkle with 1 Tbsp. sugar. Slide parchment paper onto a baking sheet.

2. Bake at 350° for 50 to 55 minutes or until filling is bubbly and crust is golden brown. Cool on a baking sheet on a wire rack 30 minutes. Serve warm with Buttermilk Whipped Cream.

Update a Southern Classic

Spicy Cheddar cheese straws take shape in a delicious flight of holiday fancy.

Make It Special

Spicy Cheddar Cheese Straw Dough

MAKES 1 DOUGH BALL
HANDS-ON TIME: 15 MIN.
TOTAL TIME: 15 MIN.

- 1 (10-oz.) block sharp Cheddar cheese, shredded
- 1½ cups all-purpose flour
- ½ cup unsalted butter, cut into 4 pieces and softened
- 1 tsp. kosher salt
- ½ tsp. dried crushed red pepper
- 2 Tbsp. half-and-half

1. Pulse first 5 ingredients in a food processor at 5-second intervals until mixture resembles coarse crumbs. Add half-and-half, and process 10 seconds or until dough forms a ball.
Note: Dough may be wrapped in plastic wrap, sealed in a zip-top plastic bag, and chilled up to 3 days.

1 | Fancy Dinner Party Pickups

CHEDDAR CROSTINI WITH TOPPINGS:
Prepare dough, and divide in half. Roll each half into an 8-inch-long log. Wrap in parchment paper, and chill 2 hours. Preheat oven to 350°. Cut logs into ¼-inch-thick rounds. Place 1 inch apart on parchment paper-lined baking sheets, and bake 16 to 18 minutes; cool on baking sheets on wire racks 30 minutes. Top with desired toppings, such as whipped cream cheese spread, smoked salmon, caviar, chopped fresh chives, chopped cooked bacon, and chopped toasted pecans. Makes about 6½ dozen. Hands-on time: 20 min., Total time: 1 hr., 38 min., including dough.

2 | Fun for Casual Get-togethers

FOUR-SEED CHEDDAR TRIANGLES:
Preheat oven to 350°. Prepare dough, and divide in half. Roll each half into a 9- to 10-inch round. Transfer rounds to parchment paper-lined baking sheets. Whisk together 1 egg white and 1 tsp. water just until foamy. Stir together ¼ cup roasted, salted pumpkin seeds; ¼ cup roasted sunflower kernels; 2 Tbsp. toasted sesame seeds; and 2 Tbsp. black sesame seeds. Brush rounds with egg white mixture, and sprinkle with seed mixture. Cut each round into wedges of random sizes, using a fluted pastry wheel. Separate wedges about 1 inch apart. Bake 16 to 18 minutes; cool on baking sheets on wire racks 30 minutes. Makes 24 to 32 triangles. Hands-on time: 20 min., Total time: 1 hr., 22 min., including dough.
Note: You may substitute 1 cup chopped, lightly toasted pecans for seed mixture.

3 | Open House Buffet Nibbles

PECAN-CHEDDAR BUTTONS: Preheat oven to 300°. Prepare dough, and shape into 1-inch balls. Whisk together 2 egg whites and 2 tsp. water. Dip balls in egg white mixture, and roll in 2 cups finely chopped pecans. Place 1 inch apart on parchment paper-lined baking sheets. Bake 1 hour; cool on baking sheets on wire racks 30 minutes. Makes about 4½ dozen. Hands-on time: 30 min., Total time: 3 hr., including dough.

4 | Christmas Eve Munchies

SPICY CHEDDAR "LONG" STRAWS:
Preheat oven to 350°. Prepare dough, and turn out onto a well-floured surface; divide in half. Roll each half into a 12- x 8-inch rectangle (about ⅛ inch thick). Cut dough into ¾-inch-wide strips using a sharp knife or fluted pastry wheel, dipping knife or pastry wheel in flour after each cut to ensure clean cuts. Place on parchment paper-lined baking sheets. Bake 18 to 20 minutes or until edges are well browned; cool on baking sheets on wire racks 30 minutes. Makes about 3 dozen. Hands-on time: 15 min., Total time: 1 hr., 26 min., including dough.

5 | Cocktail Party Cool

SPICY CHEDDAR APPETIZER COOKIES:
Preheat oven to 350°. Prepare dough, and turn out onto a well-floured surface; divide in half. Roll each half to ⅛-inch thickness. Cut with assorted 2½- to 3½-inch cutters; place 2 inches apart on parchment paper-lined baking sheets. Bake 16 to 18 minutes; cool on baking sheets on wire racks 30 minutes. Makes 28 (3½-inch) cookies or 72 (2½-inch) cookies. Hands-on time: 20 min.;, Total time: 1 hr., 38 min., including dough.
Note: Position cookie cutters closely together to cut out shapes; dough will be tough if rerolled.

Sweet and Tart Cranberries

Sugar and citrus take fresh cranberries from too tart to just right in our Cranberry-Jalapeño Salsa and moonshine cocktails.

Cranberry-Moonshine Cocktail

MAKES 1 SERVING
HANDS-ON TIME: 5 MIN.
TOTAL TIME: 5 MIN., NOT INCLUDING MOONSHINE

If you like very dry martinis, you'll enjoy this cocktail.

- 2 cups ice cubes
- 3 Tbsp. Cranberry-Infused Moonshine*
- 1 Tbsp. orange liqueur
  Blood-orange Italian soda, chilled
  Garnish: lemon twist

1. Combine first 3 ingredients in a cocktail shaker. Cover with lid, and shake until thoroughly chilled. Remove lid, and strain into a chilled martini glass; top with Italian soda. Garnish, if desired. Serve immediately.
*Cranberry-Infused Vodka may be substituted.
Note: We tested with Grand Marnier for orange liqueur.

Frozen Cranberry-Moonshine Lemonade

MAKES 5 CUPS
HANDS-ON TIME: 10 MIN.
TOTAL TIME: 10 MIN.

For a sweet-tart drink, with a scent like Christmas, use "spiced" moonshine. To make it more tart than sweet, substitute Cranberry-Infused Moonshine. Sip this slushy drink slowly —it doesn't have a strong alcohol flavor, but it definitely packs a punch.

- 1 (12-oz.) can frozen lemonade concentrate
- ¾ cup sweet-and-spicy moonshine*
- ⅓ cup whole-berry cranberry sauce
- 2 Tbsp. orange liqueur
- 2 Tbsp. fresh lime juice
  Garnish: fresh cranberries, rosemary sprigs

1. Combine first 5 ingredients in a blender. Fill blender with ice to 5-cup level, and process until smooth. Garnish, if desired. Serve immediately.
*Cranberry-Infused Moonshine may be substituted.
Note: We tested with Catdaddy Carolina Moonshine and Triple Sec for orange liqueur.

Cranberry-Infused Moonshine

MAKES ABOUT 3¼ CUPS
HANDS-ON TIME: 10 MIN.
TOTAL TIME: 15 MIN., PLUS 3 DAYS FOR STAND TIME

This concoction is best used for our drink recipes, not straight up or on the rocks.

- 1 cup fresh cranberries
- ¼ cup sugar
- 1 (750-milliliter) bottle moonshine
- 2 (2- x 1-inch) orange zest strips

1. Cook cranberries, sugar, and 3 Tbsp. water in a small saucepan over medium heat 5 minutes or until sugar dissolves, liquid begins to turn a light pink color, and cranberries just begin to pop. Let cool slightly (about 10 minutes).
2. Pour cranberry mixture into a large glass jar; stir in moonshine and orange strips. Cover and let stand at room temperature 3 days. Pour mixture through a fine wire-mesh strainer into a bowl; discard solids. Return moonshine to jar. Store in refrigerator up to 2 months.
Note: We tested with Junior Johnson Midnight Moon Carolina Moonshine.

TRY THIS TWIST!
Cranberry-Infused Vodka: Substitute vodka for moonshine.

Make It Special

So Southern: Moonshine

Our moonshine cocktails will get party guests talking! Winning Nascar driver Junior Johnson led the comeback of this once illegal liquor. His distillery in the foothills of the Blue Ridge Mountains produces moonshine in small-batch, copper stills just as in the days of running bootleg. (Check availability at *piedmontdistillers.com*.)

Cranberry-Infused Moonshine (carafe); Frozen Cranberry-Moonshine Lemonade (short glasses); Cranberry-Moonshine Cocktail (martini glasses); Cranberry-Infused Moonshine (decanter); Cranberry-Jalapeño Salsa

Cranberry-Jalapeño Salsa

MAKES 2 CUPS
HANDS-ON TIME: 10 MIN.
TOTAL TIME: 2 HR., 10 MIN

Amazingly, this salsa can be frozen, then thawed, and still look and taste great. Try it spooned over cream cheese or goat cheese with crackers, served at room temperature with grilled or roasted pork tenderloin, or spread on a turkey sandwich.

1 (12-oz.) package fresh cranberries
⅓ to ½ cup sugar
2 to 3 green onions, chopped
1 jalapeño pepper, seeded and chopped
1 Tbsp. grated or finely chopped fresh ginger
1 Tbsp. fresh lime juice
½ tsp. salt
¼ cup chopped fresh cilantro
 Tortilla chips
 Garnish: lime wedges

1. Pulse cranberries and sugar in a food processor 3 or 4 times or until coarsely chopped, stopping to scrape down sides. Add green onions and next 4 ingredients; pulse 3 to 4 times or until chopped.

2. Transfer to a bowl, and stir in cilantro. Cover and chill 2 to 24 hours. Serve with chips. Garnish, if desired.
Note: To make ahead, prepare recipe as directed, omitting fresh cilantro. Freeze in an airtight container up to 1 month. Thaw in refrigerator 12 hours. Stir in cilantro just before serving.

RECIPE FROM JANE HOKE
BIRMINGHAM, ALABAMA

Fresh Holiday Salads

Lend holiday meals a lighter touch and bright flavor with these easy, enticing sides.

Cauliflower Salad

MAKES 4 SERVINGS
HANDS-ON TIME: 15 MIN.
TOTAL TIME: 20 MIN.

- 2 Tbsp. pine nuts
- 2 (10-oz.) packages cauliflower florets
- ¼ cup golden raisins
- ¼ cup chopped fresh parsley
- 2 Tbsp. olive oil
- 1 shallot, minced
- 1 garlic clove, minced
- 2 Tbsp. drained capers
- 2 Tbsp. fresh lemon juice
- ½ tsp. salt
- ¼ tsp. pepper
- ½ cup crumbled feta cheese

1. Heat pine nuts in a small nonstick skillet over medium heat, stirring occasionally, 2 to 3 minutes or until lightly toasted and fragrant.
2. Break apart larger cauliflower florets. Cook cauliflower in boiling salted water to cover 4 to 5 minutes or until tender; drain. Plunge into ice water to stop the cooking process; drain.
3. Stir together raisins and next 8 ingredients in a large bowl. Gently fold in cauliflower and feta until combined. Sprinkle with pine nuts just before serving.

Green Salad with White Wine Vinaigrette

MAKES 6 TO 8 SERVINGS
HANDS-ON TIME: 15 MIN.
TOTAL TIME: 20 MIN.

- 1 (8-oz.) package haricots verts (tiny green beans)
- ½ cup olive oil
- ¼ cup white wine vinegar
- 1 Tbsp. country-style Dijon mustard
- ½ tsp. salt
- ¼ tsp. pepper
- ½ (5-oz.) package fresh baby spinach
- ½ (5-oz.) package fresh arugula
- 2 cups torn Bibb lettuce
- 1 avocado, peeled and chopped
- ½ cup chopped fresh parsley
- ¼ cup chopped fresh tarragon
  Garnishes: shaved Parmesan cheese, croutons

1. Cook green beans in boiling salted water to cover 4 to 5 minutes or until crisp-tender; drain. Plunge into ice water to stop the cooking process; drain.
2. Whisk together olive oil and next 4 ingredients.
3. Toss together spinach, next 5 ingredients, and green beans in a large bowl. Drizzle with olive oil mixture; toss gently to coat. Garnish, if desired. Serve immediately.

Avocado, Citrus, and Jicama Salad

MAKES 6 SERVINGS
HANDS-ON TIME: 20 MIN.
TOTAL TIME: 30 MIN., INCLUDING VINAIGRETTE

- 1 lb. jicama
- 2 pink or red grapefruit
- 2 large navel oranges
- ⅓ cup thinly sliced red onion
  Citrus Vinaigrette
- 1 head red leaf lettuce, torn
- 2 avocados, peeled and sliced

1. Peel jicama, and cut into 2- x ⅛-inch sticks.
2. Cut a ¼-inch-thick slice from each end of grapefruit using a sharp, thin-bladed knife. Place grapefruit, flat ends down, on a cutting board, and remove peel in strips, cutting from top to bottom, following the curvature of fruit.
3. Remove any remaining bitter white pith. Holding peeled grapefruit in the palm of your hand and working over a bowl to catch juices, slice between membranes, and gently remove whole segments. Repeat procedure with oranges. Reserve juices for another use.
4. Combine jicama, grapefruit segments, orange segments, and onion in a medium bowl. Toss with Citrus Vinaigrette. Line a platter or salad plates with lettuce. Top with jicama mixture and avocado.

Citrus Vinaigrette:

MAKES ½ CUP
HANDS-ON TIME: 10 MIN.
TOTAL TIME: 10 MIN.

1. Whisk together ¼ cup olive oil, 2 Tbsp. chopped fresh cilantro, 2 Tbsp. fresh lime juice, 2 Tbsp. fresh orange juice, 1 tsp. sugar, and ¾ tsp. salt.

Make It Special

Roasted Root Vegetable Salad

MAKES 6 SERVINGS
HANDS-ON TIME: 30 MIN.
TOTAL TIME: 1 HR., 20 MIN.

- 2 large sweet potatoes (about 1½ lb.)
- 4 large parsnips (about 1 lb.)
- 6 medium beets (about 1½ lb.)
- 3 Tbsp. olive oil, divided
- 1¾ tsp. salt, divided
- 1 tsp. pepper, divided
- ½ cup bottled olive oil-and-vinegar dressing
- 1 Tbsp. chopped fresh parsley
- 1 Tbsp. horseradish
- 1 tsp. Dijon mustard
  Fresh arugula

1. Preheat oven to 400°. Peel sweet potatoes, and cut into ¾-inch cubes. Peel parsnips, and cut into ½-inch slices. Peel beets, and cut into ½-inch-thick wedges.
2. Toss sweet potatoes and parsnips with 2 Tbsp. olive oil in a large bowl; place in a single layer in a lightly greased 15- x 10-inch jelly-roll pan. Sprinkle with 1¼ tsp. salt and ½ tsp. pepper.
3. Toss beets with remaining 1 Tbsp. olive oil; arrange beets in a single layer on a separate aluminum foil-lined 15- x 10-inch jelly-roll pan. Sprinkle with remaining ½ tsp. salt and ½ tsp. pepper.
4. Bake at 400° for 40 to 45 minutes or just until tender. Let cool completely (about 20 minutes).
5. Meanwhile, whisk together dressing and next 3 ingredients. Place vegetables in a large bowl, and drizzle with desired amount of dressing; toss gently to coat. Serve at room temperature or chilled over arugula with any remaining dressing.

Chubba Bubba's Salad

MAKES 6 TO 8 SERVINGS
HANDS-ON TIME: 25 MIN.
TOTAL TIME: 1 HR., 25 MIN.

- ½ (16-oz.) package bacon
- 1 (12-oz.) package broccoli florets, chopped
- 1 (10-oz.) package cauliflower florets, chopped
- 1 cup (4 oz.) shredded Cheddar cheese
- ½ cup finely chopped carrot
- ¼ cup finely chopped red onion
- ½ cup mayonnaise
- 1 Tbsp. sugar
- 2 Tbsp. red wine vinegar

1. Cook bacon in a large skillet over medium-high heat 10 to 12 minutes or until crisp; remove bacon, and drain on paper towels. Crumble bacon.
2. Cook broccoli and cauliflower in boiling salted water to cover 2 minutes or until crisp-tender; drain. Plunge into ice water to stop the cooking process; drain well. Place cauliflower and broccoli in a large bowl. Add cheese, carrot, and onion.
3. Stir together mayonnaise, sugar, and vinegar. Pour over cauliflower mixture; toss to coat. Top with bacon. Cover and chill 1 to 8 hours.

RECIPE INSPIRED BY MARILYN J. SPRINGER
PIGEON FORGE, TENNESSEE

Chipotle Caesar Salad

MAKES 4 TO 6 SERVINGS
HANDS-ON TIME: 20 MIN.
TOTAL TIME: 20 MIN.

Star-shaped slices of jicama give this salad festive flair. But if you prefer, peel the jicama and cut it into strips.

- 1 large jicama
- 2 romaine lettuce hearts, torn
- 1 large red bell pepper, thinly sliced
  Chipotle Caesar Dressing

1. Cut jicama into thin slices. Cut each slice into a star using a 1½-inch star-shaped cutter.
2. Toss together lettuce, bell pepper, and desired amount of dressing in a large bowl. Top with jicama stars, and serve with remaining dressing.

Chipotle Caesar Dressing:

MAKES 1⅓ CUPS
HANDS-ON TIME: 10 MIN.
TOTAL TIME: 10 MIN.

- 1 to 2 canned chipotle peppers in adobo sauce
- 1 tsp. chopped garlic
- ½ tsp. salt
- ⅓ cup fresh lemon juice
- ⅓ cup egg substitute
- ¼ cup (1 oz.) shredded Parmesan cheese
- ½ cup olive oil

1. Pulse first 3 ingredients in a food processor 3 to 4 times or until garlic is minced. Add lemon juice, egg substitute, and Parmesan cheese. With processor running, pour oil though food chute in a slow, steady stream, processing until smooth. Cover and chill until ready to serve.

Season with Fresh Rosemary

Fragrant and captivating, rosemary adds rustic richness to our stunning potato side dish, biscuit croutons, and olive-and-okra appetizer.

Test Kitchen Secrets

Potent rosemary is a bossy herb that can take over a dish, so use it sparingly. We call for only 1 Tbsp. to season the entire Potato Gratin with Rosemary Crust. At one testing we tried a tiny amount in the potato layers. It overwhelmed the dish. Check out these other prep tips for success.

1 Sandwich in Flavor
One package refrigerated piecrusts contains 2 crusts. Sprinkle finely chopped rosemary, pepper, and shredded cheese over one crust. Top with second crust. Roll into a 13-inch circle.

2 No Perfection Needed
Don't stress when fitting crust in pan. Fold the double-stacked crust in half to move to springform pan. Unfold, lift, and drape crust until it settles into bottom of pan, pleating as needed. Take your time, being careful not to stretch or tear. Tuck excess crust under to finish edges.

3 Add Yummy Goodness
Layer the potatoes with salt and cheese. Don't pour warm cream directly into the center—instead pour in circles to evenly cover potatoes. Bake right away.

Make It Special

Potato Gratin with Rosemary Crust

MAKES 10 SERVINGS
HANDS-ON TIME: 45 MIN.
TOTAL TIME: 2 HR., 20 MIN.

Accurate baking means knowing your oven. Some bake hot, others slow, so times can easily vary 10 minutes. The crust will be richly browned.

- 1 (14.1-oz.) package refrigerated piecrusts
- 1 Tbsp. chopped fresh rosemary
- ¼ tsp. freshly ground pepper
- 2 cups (8 oz.) shredded Gruyère cheese, divided
- 1½ lb. Yukon gold potatoes
- 1½ lb. sweet potatoes
- 1 tsp. kosher salt
- ⅔ cup heavy cream
- 1 garlic clove, minced
  Garnish: fresh rosemary sprigs

1. Preheat oven to 450°. Unroll piecrusts on a lightly floured surface. Sprinkle rosemary, pepper, and ½ cup cheese over 1 piecrust; top with remaining piecrust. Roll into a 13-inch circle. Press on bottom and up sides of a 9-inch springform pan; fold edges under. Chill.
2. Meanwhile, peel and thinly slice Yukon gold and sweet potatoes. Layer one-third each of Yukon gold potatoes, sweet potatoes, and salt in prepared crust. Sprinkle with ¼ cup cheese. Repeat layers twice, pressing layers down slightly to fit.
3. Microwave cream and garlic in a 1-cup microwave-safe measuring cup at HIGH 45 seconds; pour over potato layers in pan. Sprinkle with remaining ¾ cup cheese. Cover with heavy-duty aluminum foil. Place on a baking sheet.
4. Bake at 450° for 1 hour. Uncover and bake 25 minutes or until golden, bubbly, and potatoes are done. Let stand 10 to 15 minutes.
5. Carefully transfer to a serving plate, and remove sides of pan. If desired, carefully slide gratin off bottom of pan using a long, thin knife or narrow spatula. Garnish, if desired.

Rosemary Biscuit Croutons

MAKES ABOUT 4 CUPS
HANDS-ON TIME: 10 MIN.
TOTAL TIME: 2 HR., 45 MIN.

Use leftover homemade biscuits in place of baking frozen. Let croutons be the star on a simple salad with pear slices, crumbled blue cheese, and vinaigrette.

- 6 frozen biscuits
- 2 tsp. chopped fresh rosemary
- ½ tsp. coarsely ground pepper
- 3 Tbsp. olive oil
- 2 Tbsp. freshly grated Parmesan cheese

1. Preheat oven to 400°. Place biscuits on a baking sheet. Bake 18 to 20 minutes or until golden brown. Let cool completely (about 30 minutes). Reduce oven temperature to 250°.
2. Cut biscuits into ½-inch cubes. Sauté rosemary and pepper in hot oil over medium heat 30 seconds to 1 minute or until fragrant. Toss biscuits with oil mixture, and place in a single layer on a lightly greased aluminum foil-lined jelly-roll pan.
3. Bake at 250° for 1 hour and 20 minutes or until golden brown and crisp, stirring every 20 to 30 minutes. Sprinkle with cheese; bake 10 more minutes. Let cool completely (about 15 minutes). Store in an airtight container up to 3 days.
Note: We tested with Mary B's Buttermilk Biscuits.

Spicy Olive-and-Okra-Topped Hummus

MAKES 8 SERVINGS
HANDS-ON TIME: 15 MIN.
TOTAL TIME: 20 MIN.

Find mixed pitted olives in your grocer's deli department.

- 1 tsp. lemon zest
- 1 small garlic clove, minced
- ¼ tsp. dried crushed red pepper
- 2 Tbsp. extra virgin olive oil
- 1 cup mixed pitted olives, coarsely chopped*
- 4 pickled okra, sliced
- 1 tsp. chopped fresh rosemary
- 1 (17-oz.) container hummus
  Pita bread or chips

1. Sauté first 3 ingredients in hot oil in a large skillet over medium heat 1 minute. Add olives; sauté 3 to 5 minutes.
2. Remove from heat, and stir in okra and rosemary. Let stand 5 minutes. Transfer hummus to a serving dish; top with warm olive mixture. Serve with pita bread or chips.
*1 (11-oz.) jar whole pitted kalamata olives, drained and chopped, or 1 (6-oz.) jar sliced kalamata olives, drained and chopped, may be substituted.

Irresistible Red Velvet Sweets

Kissed with chocolate, our Red Velvet Soufflés and Brownies are the dreamiest desserts of the season.

Red Velvet Soufflés with Whipped Sour Cream

MAKES 6 SERVINGS

HANDS-ON TIME: 20 MIN.

TOTAL TIME: 47 MIN., INCLUDING WHIPPED SOUR CREAM

To serve, "crack" or break centers of each soufflé with a spoon and pour Whipped Sour Cream into the opening. Just a note: Frozen soufflés do bake within the same time range as those baked immediately after mixing.

- 1 Tbsp. butter
- 3 Tbsp. granulated sugar
- 1 (4-oz.) bittersweet chocolate baking bar, chopped
- 5 large eggs, separated
- ⅓ cup granulated sugar
- 3 Tbsp. milk
- 1 Tbsp. red liquid food coloring
- 1 tsp. vanilla extract
    Pinch of salt
- 2 Tbsp. granulated sugar
    Powdered sugar
    Whipped Sour Cream

Test Kitchen Secrets for Perfect Soufflés

HELP SOUFFLÉS RISE
Buttering and sugaring ramekins provides a coarse texture the soufflé mixture clings to while baking, helping it rise and form a delicate crust that complements the soft inside.

CREATE A PRETTY TOP
Give your soufflés a "crown" by running a groove (or rim) about ½ inch deep around the edge of the ramekins using your thumb.

1. Preheat oven to 350°. Grease bottom and sides of 6 (8-oz.) ramekins with butter. Lightly coat with 3 Tbsp. sugar, shaking out excess. Place ramekins on a baking sheet.

2. Microwave chocolate in a large microwave-safe bowl at HIGH 1 minute to 1 minute and 15 seconds or until melted, stirring at 30-second intervals. Stir in 4 egg yolks, ⅓ cup sugar, and next 3 ingredients. (Discard remaining egg yolk.)

3. Beat 5 egg whites and salt at high speed with an electric mixer until foamy. Gradually add 2 Tbsp. sugar, beating until stiff peaks form. Fold egg white mixture into chocolate mixture, one-third at a time. Spoon into prepared ramekins. Run tip of thumb around edges of each ramekin, wiping clean and creating a shallow indentation around outside edge of egg mixture.

4. Bake at 350° for 20 to 24 minutes or until soufflés rise and are set. (A long

wooden pick inserted into centers will have a few moist crumbs.) Dust with powdered sugar; serve immediately with Whipped Sour Cream.

Note: We tested with Ghirardelli 60% Cacao Bittersweet Chocolate Baking Bar. To make ahead, soufflés can be assembled through Step 3, and frozen up to 1 week. Bake frozen soufflés as directed.

Whipped Sour Cream:

MAKES ABOUT 2 CUPS

HANDS-ON TIME: 5 MIN.

TOTAL TIME: 5 MIN.

1. Beat ¾ cup whipping cream, ½ cup sour cream, and 2 Tbsp. sugar with a heavy-duty electric stand mixer at medium-high speed 45 seconds or just until lightly whipped and pourable. Serve immediately.

Make It Special

Test Kitchen Tips

KEEP IN MIND

- Egg whites beaten to stiff peaks will have a glossy—not dry—appearance. Overbeaten whites lose the ability to stretch and trap air during baking, resulting in flat soufflés.

- Keep oven door closed until minimum bake time is up. (Keep kitchen activity calm, too.)

- Gather everyone 5 minutes before the timer rings. The old saying holds true— soufflés don't wait on guests. (Allow 2 to 5 minutes from oven to table for the biggest wow factor. If they fall, be cool about it—they'll be fudgy and delicious.

Cook's Stocking Stuffer

The new Oxo Good Grips Brownie Spatula has a sharp front edge to cut pieces cleanly, and is narrow and flexible enough to get under brownies, bar cookies, or coffee-cakes that are served from the pan. (About $5 at oxo.com).

How to Make Chocolate Curls

Pull a vegetable peeler along the side of about a 4-oz. white chocolate bar, allowing curls to fall onto wax paper. If the chocolate is too firm, microwave chocolate bar on a microwave-safe plate at MEDIUM at 5-second intervals until you are able to make curls.

Red Velvet Brownies with Cream Cheese Frosting

MAKES 16 SERVINGS
HANDS-ON TIME: 15 MIN.
TOTAL TIME: 3 HR., 9 MIN., INCLUDING FROSTING

Line pan with foil without tears or crinkles by trimming two long foil pieces to a 9-inch width. Fit strips, crossing each other, in the pan. Once baked, foil will easily peel away from brownies. We made the brownies tall and special-looking for the holidays by baking a generous recipe of batter in a 9-inch pan.

1 (4-oz.) bittersweet chocolate baking bar, chopped
¾ cup butter
2 cups sugar
4 large eggs
1½ cups all-purpose flour
1 (1-oz.) bottle red liquid food coloring
1½ tsp. baking powder
1 tsp. vanilla extract
⅛ tsp. salt
Cream Cheese Frosting
Garnish: white chocolate curls

1. Preheat oven to 350°. Line bottom and sides of a 9-inch square pan with aluminum foil, allowing 2 to 3 inches to extend over sides; lightly grease foil.
2. Microwave chocolate and butter in a large microwave-safe bowl at HIGH 1½ to 2 minutes or until melted and smooth, stirring at 30-second intervals. Whisk in sugar. Add eggs, 1 at a time, whisking just until blended after each addition. Gently stir in flour and next 4 ingredients. Pour mixture into prepared pan.
3. Bake at 350° for 44 to 48 minutes or until a wooden pick inserted in center comes out with a few moist crumbs. Cool completely on a wire rack (about 2 hours).
4. Lift brownies from pan, using foil sides as handles; gently remove foil. Spread Cream Cheese Frosting on top of brownies, and cut into 16 squares. Garnish, if desired.

Cream Cheese Frosting:

MAKES ABOUT 1⅓ CUPS
HANDS-ON TIME: 10 MIN.
TOTAL TIME: 10 MIN.

This is a small-batch recipe for our 9-inch pan of brownies and not enough to cover a cake.

1 (8-oz.) package cream cheese, softened
3 Tbsp. butter, softened
1½ cups powdered sugar
⅛ tsp. salt
1 tsp. vanilla extract

1. Beat cream cheese and butter at medium speed with an electric mixer until creamy. Gradually add sugar and salt, beating until blended. Stir in vanilla.

Great Holiday Appetizers

Sugared Nuts

MAKES 5 CUPS

HANDS-ON TIME: 5 MIN.

TOTAL TIME: 27 MIN.

Sprinkle these nuts over a salad, use them to garnish a dessert, or enjoy them as snacks.

- 1 large egg white
- 4 cups pecan halves, walnut halves, or whole almonds (blanched)
- 1 cup sugar

1. Preheat oven to 350°. Whisk egg white in a large bowl until foamy; stir in pecans, coating well. Stir in sugar, coating well. Spread pecan mixture in a single layer on a lightly greased 15- x 10-inch aluminum foil-lined jelly-roll pan.
2. Bake at 350° for 10 minutes. Stir gently with a wooden spoon; bake 10 to 12 more minutes or until sugar is light golden brown. Remove from oven, and cool completely on pan. Store in an airtight container up to 5 days.

Pecan-Havarti Quesadilla With Pear Preserves

MAKES 2 SERVINGS

HANDS-ON TIME: 5 MIN.

TOTAL TIME: 9 MIN.

Try this tasty quesadilla with your favorite Cabernet Sauvignon for a fresh twist on wine and cheese. Our resident wine expert, Scott Jones, suggests Columbia Crest Cabernet Sauvignon.

1. Sprinkle 1 side of an 8-inch flour tortilla with ⅓ cup shredded Havarti cheese; top with 2 Tbsp. chopped, toasted pecans. Fold tortilla over filling. Coat a nonstick skillet with vegetable cooking spray, and cook quesadilla over medium-high heat for 2 minutes on each side or until cheese melts. Remove from heat, slice into wedges, and serve with pear preserves. Pair it with a glass of Cabernet Sauvignon.
Note: This recipe can be easily doubled or tripled to serve more.

Tennessee Caviar

MAKES 4 CUPS

HANDS-ON TIME: 10 MIN.

TOTAL TIME: 2 HR., 10 MIN.

This Southern dip features down-home veggies. Make it a day ahead for the best flavor.

- 1 (15.8-oz.) can black-eyed peas
- 1 (11-oz.) can yellow corn with red and green bell peppers
- 3 plum tomatoes, seeded and chopped
- 1 small sweet onion, chopped
- 1 cup hot picante sauce
- ¼ cup chopped fresh cilantro
- 2 garlic cloves, minced
- 2 Tbsp. fresh lime juice
  Tortilla chips

1. Rinse and drain peas and corn. Stir together peas, corn, tomatoes, and next 5 ingredients in a serving bowl; cover and chill at least 2 hours. Serve with tortilla chips.

Marinated Mozzarella

MAKES ABOUT 4 CUPS

HANDS-ON TIME: 20 MIN.

TOTAL TIME: 8 HR., 20 MIN.

For a big crowd, double all the ingredients in this recipe except the black pepper and garlic powder. For those strong flavors, use one-and-a-half times the amount called for.

- 3 (8-oz.) blocks mozzarella cheese
- 1 (8.5-oz.) jar sun-dried tomatoes, drained and halved
- ½ cup olive oil
- 3 Tbsp. finely chopped fresh flat-leaf parsley
- 1 tsp. garlic powder
- 1 tsp. onion powder
- ½ tsp. dried oregano
- ½ tsp. dried Italian seasoning
- ¼ tsp. salt
- ¼ tsp. freshly ground pepper
  Garnish: flat-leaf parsley sprigs or fresh rosemary stems

1. Cut cheese into 1-inch cubes. Arrange cheese cubes and tomato halves in an 8-inch square dish.
2. Whisk together ½ cup olive oil, chopped parsley, and next 6 ingredients; pour evenly over cheese cubes. Cover and chill at least 8 hours or up to 24 hours. Transfer mixture to a serving plate. Garnish with fresh flat-leaf parsley sprigs, or spear tomato halves and cheese cubes with short rosemary stems, if desired. Drizzle with marinade, if desired.

Make It Special

Warm Turnip Green Dip

MAKES 4 CUPS
HANDS-ON TIME: 30 MIN.
TOTAL TIME: 34 MIN.

Transfer the dip to a 1- or 2-qt. slow cooker set on WARM so guests can enjoy this creamy dip throughout your party. To make it spicier, serve your favorite brand of hot sauce on the side.

- 5 bacon slices, chopped
- ½ sweet onion, chopped
- 2 garlic cloves, chopped
- ¼ cup dry white wine
- 1 (16-oz.) package frozen chopped turnip greens, thawed
- 12 oz. cream cheese, cut into pieces
- 1 (8-oz.) container sour cream
- ½ tsp. dried crushed red pepper
- ¼ tsp. salt
- ¾ cup freshly grated Parmesan cheese, divided

1. Preheat oven to broil. Cook bacon in a Dutch oven over medium-high heat 5 to 6 minutes or until crisp; remove bacon, and drain on paper towels, reserving 1 Tbsp. bacon drippings in Dutch oven. Cook onion and garlic in hot drippings 3 to 4 minutes. Add wine, and cook 1 to 2 minutes, stirring to loosen particles from bottom of Dutch oven. Stir in turnip greens, next 4 ingredients, and ½ cup Parmesan cheese. Cook, stirring often, 6 to 8 minutes or until cream cheese is melted and mixture is thoroughly heated.
2. Transfer to a lightly greased 1½-qt. baking dish. Sprinkle evenly with remaining ¼ cup Parmesan cheese. Broil 6 inches from heat 4 to 5 minutes or until cheese is lightly browned. Sprinkle evenly with bacon.

Chicken Fingers with Honey-Horseradish Dip

MAKES 8 SERVINGS
HANDS-ON TIME: 25 MIN.
TOTAL TIME: 43 MIN.

This recipe won our highest flavor rating. We think little and big kids will love it.

- 16 saltine crackers, finely crushed
- ¼ cup pecans, toasted and ground
- ½ tsp. salt
- ½ tsp. pepper
- 2 tsp. paprika
- 4 (6-oz.) skinned and boned chicken breast halves
- 1 egg white
  Vegetable cooking spray
  Honey-Horseradish Dip

1. Preheat oven to 425°. Stir together first 5 ingredients. Cut each breast half into 4 strips. Whisk egg white until frothy; dip chicken strips into egg white, and dredge in saltine mixture. Place a rack coated with cooking spray in a broiler pan. Coat chicken strips on each side with cooking spray; arrange on pan. Bake at 425° for 18 to 20 minutes or until golden brown. Serve with Honey-Horseradish Dip.

Honey-Horseradish Dip:

MAKES 1 CUP
HANDS-ON TIME: 5 MIN.
TOTAL TIME: 5 MIN.

- ½ cup plain nonfat yogurt
- ¼ cup coarse-grained mustard
- ¼ cup honey
- 2 Tbsp. horseradish

1. Stir together all ingredients.

Mini Cajun Burgers with Easy Rémoulade

MAKES 12 APPETIZER SERVINGS
HANDS-ON TIME: 30 MIN.
TOTAL TIME: 1 HR., 5 MIN., INCLUDING RÉMOULADE

- 1¼ lb. ground beef
- ½ lb. spicy Cajun sausage, finely chopped
- 2 tsp. Cajun seasoning
- 1 (14-oz.) package dinner rolls, split
  Green leaf lettuce
  Easy Rémoulade

1. Preheat grill to 350° to 400° (medium-high) heat. Combine ground beef and sausage in a large bowl. Shape mixture into 12 (2½-inch) patties, and place on a large baking sheet. Sprinkle patties evenly with Cajun seasoning. Cover and chill up to 1 day, if desired.
2. Grill, covered with grill lid, 5 minutes on each side or until burgers are no longer pink in center. Serve on split rolls with green leaf lettuce and Easy Rémoulade.

Easy Rémoulade:

MAKES 1 CUP
HANDS-ON TIME: 5 MIN.
TOTAL TIME: 35 MIN.

- ¾ cup light mayonnaise
- 2 Tbsp. Creole mustard
- 2 Tbsp. chopped fresh parsley

1. Combine all ingredients, stirring well. Cover and chill 30 minutes or up to 3 days.

Easy, Irresistible Scones

Buttery-rich scones are nothing more than glorified biscuits, but oh what delicious biscuits they are!

Test Kitchen Tips

- Make sure the dry ingredients are stirred together well to distribute the baking powder and salt.

- Quickly cut ice-cold butter into the flour mixture, leaving crumbly pieces the size of small peas. If the butter is softened or cut in too finely, the texture will be dense and coarse.

- Handle the dough as little as possible—the less you work it, the more tender the scones will be.

Best-Ever Scones

MAKES 8 SERVINGS
HANDS-ON TIME: 15 MIN.
TOTAL TIME: 33 MIN.

When reader Betty Joyce Mills from Birmingham shared her recipe for scones (she adds a half cup of sweetened dried cranberries), we thought they were the best we had ever tasted. Never fearing too much of a good thing, we created eight sweet and savory variations.

- 2 cups all-purpose flour
- ⅓ cup sugar
- 1 Tbsp. baking powder
- ½ tsp. salt
- ½ cup cold butter, cut into ½-inch cubes
- 1 cup whipping cream, divided
  Wax paper

1. Preheat oven to 450°. Stir together first 4 ingredients in a large bowl. Cut butter into flour mixture with a pastry blender until crumbly and mixture resembles small peas. Freeze 5 minutes. Add ¾ cup plus 2 Tbsp. cream, stirring just until dry ingredients are moistened.

2. Turn dough out onto wax paper; gently press or pat dough into a 7-inch round (mixture will be crumbly). Cut round into 8 wedges. Place wedges 2 inches apart on a lightly greased baking sheet. Brush tops of wedges with remaining 2 Tbsp. cream just until moistened.

3. Bake at 450° for 13 to 15 minutes or until golden.

Chocolate-Cherry Scones:
Stir in ¼ cup dried cherries, coarsely chopped, and 2 oz. coarsely chopped semisweet chocolate with cream.

Apricot-Ginger Scones:
Stir in ½ cup finely chopped dried apricots and 2 Tbsp. finely chopped crystallized ginger with cream.

Cranberry-Pistachio Scones:
Stir in ¼ cup sweetened dried cranberries and ¼ cup coarsely chopped roasted salted pistachios with cream.

Brown Sugar-Pecan Scones:
Substitute brown sugar for granulated sugar. Stir in ½ cup chopped toasted pecans with cream.

Bacon, Cheddar, and Chive Scones:
Omit sugar. Stir in ¾ cup (3 oz.) shredded sharp Cheddar cheese, ¼ cup finely chopped cooked bacon, 2 Tbsp. chopped fresh chives, and ½ tsp. freshly ground pepper with cream.

Ham-and-Swiss Scones:
Omit sugar. Stir in ¾ cup (3 oz.) shredded Swiss cheese and ¾ cup finely chopped baked ham with cream. (We love these served warm with mustard butter. Stir together ½ cup softened butter, 1 Tbsp. spicy brown mustard, and 1 Tbsp. minced sweet onion.)

Pimiento Cheese Scones:
Omit sugar. Stir in ¾ cup (3 oz.) shredded sharp Cheddar cheese and 3 Tbsp. finely chopped pimiento with cream.

Rosemary, Pear, and Asiago Scones:
Omit sugar. Stir in ¾ cup finely chopped fresh pear, ½ cup grated Asiago cheese, and 1 tsp. chopped fresh rosemary with cream.

What's for Supper?

Streamline weeknight cooking with these five delicious main-dish ideas paired with simple sides.

Cumin-Crusted Pork Cutlets

MAKES 4 TO 6 SERVINGS
HANDS-ON TIME: 27 MIN.
TOTAL TIME: 27 MIN.

Easy side: Sauté 4 cups shredded red cabbage, 1 cup thinly sliced sweet onion, and 1 thinly sliced Granny Smith apple in 2 Tbsp. hot olive oil until tender. Add 2 Tbsp. each red wine vinegar and brown sugar, and cook until sugar is dissolved. Sprinkle with salt and pepper to taste.

- 3 whole wheat bread slices
- 2 Tbsp. self-rising yellow cornmeal mix
- ½ tsp. ground cumin
- 8 thinly sliced boneless pork loin chops (about 1¼ lb.)
- ½ tsp. salt
- ¼ tsp. pepper
- 1 large egg
- 2 Tbsp. whole grain mustard
- ¼ cup olive oil

1. Process bread in a food processor until finely crumbled. Combine breadcrumbs, cornmeal mix, and cumin in a shallow bowl. Preheat oven to 200°. Sprinkle pork chops with salt and pepper. Whisk together egg, mustard, and 2 Tbsp. water until blended. Dip pork in egg mixture; dredge in breadcrumb mixture, pressing to adhere.
2. Cook half of pork in 2 Tbsp. hot oil in a large nonstick skillet over medium heat 3 to 4 minutes on each side or until golden brown. Keep warm in a 200° oven. Repeat procedure with remaining pork and oil. Serve warm.

Roasted Tomato and Feta Shrimp

MAKES 6 SERVINGS
HANDS-ON TIME: 10 MIN.
TOTAL TIME: 35 MIN.

Test Kitchen Favorite

Easy side: Serve with 1 (5-oz.) package mixed salad greens and your favorite Greek dressing.

- 2 pt. grape tomatoes
- 3 garlic cloves, sliced
- 3 Tbsp. olive oil
- 1 tsp. kosher salt
- ½ tsp. pepper
- 1½ lb. peeled and deveined, medium-size raw shrimp (31/40 count)
- ½ cup chopped jarred roasted red bell peppers
- ½ cup chopped fresh parsley
- 1 (4-oz.) package crumbled feta cheese
- 2 Tbsp. fresh lemon juice
  Crusty French bread, sliced

1. Preheat oven to 450°. Place tomatoes and next 4 ingredients in a 13- x 9-inch baking dish, tossing gently to coat. Bake 15 minutes. Stir in shrimp and peppers. Bake 10 to 15 minutes or just until shrimp turn pink. Toss with parsley, feta cheese, and lemon juice. Serve immediately with crusty French bread.

Chile Buttermilk Baked Chicken

MAKES 4 SERVINGS
HANDS-ON TIME: 15 MIN.
TOTAL TIME: 47 MIN.

Easy side: Cook 1 (12-oz.) package frozen steam-in-bag whole green beans according to package directions. Toss with 1 Tbsp. each butter, lemon zest, and lemon juice. Sprinkle with 3 Tbsp. roasted pecans-and-almond pieces and salt and pepper to taste.

- ¼ cup butter, cut into ½-inch pieces
- 4 skinned and boned chicken breasts
- ½ tsp. salt
- ½ tsp. ground cumin
- 1½ cups buttermilk, divided
- ½ cup all-purpose flour
- 1 (10¾-oz.) can reduced-fat cream of mushroom soup
- 1 (4.5-oz.) can chopped green chiles
- 1 cup (4 oz.) shredded Monterey Jack cheese
  Hot cooked rice
- ¼ cup chopped fresh cilantro

1. Preheat oven to 425°. Melt butter in a lightly greased 11- x 7-inch baking dish in oven 2 to 3 minutes.
2. Sprinkle chicken with salt and cumin. Dip chicken in ½ cup buttermilk, and dredge in flour. Arrange chicken in baking dish. Bake at 425° for 15 minutes.
3. Stir together cream of mushroom soup, chiles, and remaining 1 cup buttermilk. Pour over chicken, and bake 10 to 15 minutes or until chicken is done. Sprinkle with cheese, and bake 5 minutes or until cheese is melted. Serve chicken and sauce over hot cooked rice. Sprinkle with cilantro.

Beef and Pepper Hash with Eggs

MAKES 6 SERVINGS
HANDS-ON TIME: 46 MIN.
TOTAL TIME: 46 MIN.

This is a one-dish meal that doesn't need sides.

- 4 Tbsp. butter, divided
- 1 (28-oz.) package frozen shredded hash browns with onions and peppers, thawed
- 1 medium-size red bell pepper, cut into 1-inch pieces
- 1 large onion, cut into 1-inch pieces
- 2 garlic cloves, minced
- 1 (8-oz.) package sliced fresh mushrooms
- ½ tsp. dried thyme
- 1½ tsp. salt
- ¾ lb. barbecued brisket without sauce, coarsely chopped
- 6 large eggs
  Salt and pepper

1. Melt 3 Tbsp. butter in a heavy 12-inch skillet over medium-high heat. Add potatoes, next 3 ingredients, and 3 Tbsp. water. Cook mixture, stirring occasionally, 10 to 12 minutes or until potatoes begin to lightly brown.
2. Add mushrooms, thyme, and salt; cook, stirring occasionally, 6 to 8 minutes or until mushrooms are browned and tender. Add brisket, and cook, stirring occasionally, 6 to 8 minutes. Keep warm.
3. Melt remaining 1 Tbsp. butter in a large nonstick skillet over medium heat. Gently break eggs into hot skillet, and sprinkle with desired amount of salt and pepper. Cook 2 to 3 minutes on each side or to desired degree of doneness. Serve over hash.

Pinto Beans Enchilada Stack

MAKES 6 SERVINGS
HANDS-ON TIME: 22 MIN.
TOTAL TIME: 40 MIN.

- 1 lb. lean ground beef
- 1 (1.25-oz.) envelope taco seasoning mix
- 1 (16-oz.) can refried beans
- 1 (15-oz.) can pinto beans, drained and rinsed
- 5 (10-inch) burrito-size flour tortillas
- 2½ cups (10 oz.) shredded Mexican four-cheese blend
- 1 (10-oz.) can enchilada sauce
  Toppings: chopped plum tomatoes, chopped green onions, sour cream, chopped fresh cilantro, chopped avocado

1. Preheat oven to 425°. Cook ground beef in a large skillet over medium-high heat, stirring often, 6 to 7 minutes or until meat crumbles and is no longer pink. Add taco seasoning and ⅓ cup water, and cook 1 to 2 minutes or until thickened.
2. Stir together refried beans and pinto beans.
3. Place 1 tortilla on a lightly greased aluminum foil-lined jelly-roll pan. Top tortilla with half of meat mixture and ½ cup cheese; top with another tortilla, half of refried bean mixture, half of enchilada sauce, and ½ cup cheese. Top with another tortilla, and repeat layers once. Top with remaining tortilla.
4. Bake at 425° for 16 to 18 minutes or until thoroughly heated and browned. Top tortilla with remaining ½ cup cheese, and bake 2 to 3 minutes or until cheese is melted. Cut into wedges, and serve with desired toppings.

Mama's Way or Your Way?
Corn Pudding

One is a rich, from-scratch classic. The other takes a quicker approach with a cheesy Parmesan twist.

Parmesan Corn Pudding

MAKES 8 SERVINGS
HANDS-ON TIME: 15 MIN.
TOTAL TIME: 55 MIN.

- 2 (12-oz.) packages frozen white shoepeg corn, thawed and divided
- ⅓ cup sugar
- ¼ cup all-purpose flour
- 2 Tbsp. plain yellow cornmeal
- ½ tsp. salt
- 6 Tbsp. butter, melted
- 1½ cups milk
- 4 large eggs
- 2 Tbsp. chopped fresh chives
- ½ cup (2 oz.) shredded Parmesan cheese
  Garnish: chopped fresh chives

1. Preheat oven to 350°. Place 1 package of corn and next 7 ingredients (in order listed) in a large food processor. Process until smooth, stopping to scrape down sides.
2. Transfer to a large bowl; stir in chives and remaining corn. Pour mixture into a lightly greased 2-qt. baking dish. Sprinkle with cheese.
3. Bake at 350° for 40 to 45 minutes or until set. Garnish, if desired.

Tee's Corn Pudding

MAKES 8 SERVINGS
HANDS-ON TIME: 25 MIN.
TOTAL TIME: 1 HR., 10 MIN.

- 12 to 13 ears fresh corn, husks removed
- ¼ cup sugar
- 3 Tbsp. all-purpose flour
- 2 tsp. baking powder
- 1½ tsp. salt
- 6 large eggs
- 2 cups whipping cream
- ½ cup butter, melted

1. Preheat oven to 350°. Cut kernels from cobs into a large bowl (about 6 cups). Scrape milk and remaining pulp from cobs; discard cobs.
2. Combine sugar and next 3 ingredients. Whisk together eggs, whipping cream, and butter in a large bowl. Gradually add sugar mixture to egg mixture, whisking until smooth; stir in corn. Pour mixture into a lightly greased 13- x 9-inch baking dish.
3. Bake at 350° for 40 to 45 minutes or until set. Let stand 5 minutes.

Ask the Test Kitchen

"I usually serve pepper jelly with cream cheese and crackers.

Are there any fun new ways to use it in a recipe?"

Pepper Jelly-Cheddar Thumbprints

MAKES 4½ DOZEN
HANDS-ON TIME: 20 MIN.
TOTAL TIME: 1 HR., 8 MIN.

Preheat oven to 350°. Combine 2¼ cups all-purpose flour; 2 cups (8 oz.) shredded white Cheddar cheese; and 1 cup butter, softened and cut into 1-inch pieces, in a food processor. Pulse mixture in 5-second intervals until it forms a ball. Roll dough into ¾-inch balls, and place on lightly greased baking sheets. Press thumb in center of each ball to make an indentation. Cover and chill 30 minutes. Bake 18 minutes or until lightly golden. Transfer to wire racks, and spoon ¼ tsp. red or green pepper jelly into each indentation.

Test Kitchen Notebook

Y'ALL ASK US:
Whether you need fresh ideas for your favorite ingredient or have a cooking problem, we're happy to share our Test Kitchen expertise. Ask questions and see answers: southernliving.com/ask-the-tk.

Grilled Steak Kabobs with Pepper Jelly-Jezebel Sauce

MAKES 5 APPETIZER SERVINGS
HANDS-ON TIME: 34 MIN.
TOTAL TIME: 34 MIN.

- 10 (6-inch) wooden skewers
- ½ cup red pepper jelly
- ½ cup pineapple preserves
- 2 Tbsp. creamy horseradish
- 2 Tbsp. country-style Dijon mustard
- 1½ lb. beef strip steaks (1 inch thick)
- 1 large red bell pepper, cut into 1-inch squares
- 1½ tsp. Creole seasoning
   Garnish: fresh cilantro leaves

1. Soak skewers in water to cover 30 minutes.
2. Meanwhile, preheat grill to 350° to 400° (medium-high) heat. Whisk together pepper jelly and next 3 ingredients.
3. Trim steaks, and cut into 1-inch cubes. Thread beef and peppers alternately onto skewers, leaving a ¼-inch space between pieces. Sprinkle kabobs with Creole seasoning.
4. Grill kabobs, covered with grill lid, 2 to 3 minutes on each side or until beef reaches desired degree of doneness. Garnish, if desired. Serve with pepper jelly sauce.

Mango Salsa

MAKES 4 CUPS
HANDS-ON TIME: 15 MIN.
TOTAL TIME: 1 HR., 15 MIN.

We love it served over crisp pan-fried catfish, but it's also wonderful with grilled pork or chicken. For a quick and colorful appetizer, serve over cream cheese rolled in chopped fresh cilantro and toasted pecans.

- ½ cup diced red onion
- ⅓ cup hot jalapeño pepper jelly
- ¼ cup chopped fresh cilantro
- 1 Tbsp. lime zest
- 3 Tbsp. fresh lime juice
- ¼ tsp. salt
- 2 cups diced fresh mango
- 1 cup diced fresh strawberries
- 1 cup diced avocado
- 1 cup peeled, seeded, and diced cucumber

1. Whisk together first 6 ingredients in a large bowl; stir in mango and remaining ingredients. Cover and chill 1 to 8 hours.

Fried Catfish

MAKES 8 SERVINGS
HANDS-ON TIME: 20 MIN.
TOTAL TIME: 20 MIN.

1. . Pour vegetable oil to depth of 2 inches into a Dutch oven; preheat to 350°. Stir together 1 cup plain yellow cornmeal, ⅓ cup all-purpose flour, and 1 Tbsp. Creole seasoning. Dredge 8 medium-size catfish fillets in cornmeal mixture. Fry fillets, in batches, 5 to 6 minutes or until golden; drain on paper towels.

Make-Ahead Favorites

Appealing Appetizers

Deviled Eggs with Smoked Salmon and Cream Cheese

MAKES 12 SERVINGS
HANDS ON TIME: 18 MIN.
TOTAL TIME: 41 MIN.

Hard-cooked eggs get dolled up with the classic combination of smoked salmon and cream cheese. If you're buying smoked salmon for a special occasion, set aside some for this hors d'oeuvre.

- 6 large eggs
- 3 Tbsp. minced smoked salmon (about 1 oz.)
- 3 Tbsp. minced green onions
- 3 Tbsp. softened cream cheese
- 1 Tbsp. sour cream
- 1 tsp. Dijon mustard
- 2 tsp. lemon juice
- ¼ tsp. salt
- ⅛ tsp. ground red pepper
    Garnishes: fresh dill, smoked salmon slivers, sweet paprika

1. Place eggs and enough water to cover in a saucepan over medium heat; bring to a boil. Cover, remove from heat, and let stand 15 minutes. Drain; return eggs to saucepan, and add enough cold water and ice to cover. Let cool. Remove shells from eggs, halve each egg lengthwise, and scrape yolks into a bowl. Reserve egg whites.
2. Combine yolks, salmon, and next 7 ingredients, mashing with a fork until well blended. Spoon filling into reserved whites, cover loosely with plastic wrap, and refrigerate up to 2 days. Garnish, if desired.

Babaghanouj

MAKES 1⅔ CUPS
HANDS-ON TIME: 29 MIN.
TOTAL TIME: 1 HR., 9 MIN.

This dip (pronounced bah-bah-gah-NOOSH) gets wonderful smoky flavor from two sources—grilled eggplant and smoked paprika. Look for smoked paprika at specialty food stores or spice stores. It's one of those secret ingredients that turns an ordinary dish into an extraordinary one. Of course, you can make it with regular paprika, but you won't have the same smoky essence. This dip is best made ahead, as the flavors tend to mellow.

    Olive oil-flavored cooking spray
- 1 medium eggplant, cut in half lengthwise (about 1 lb.)
- 2 Tbsp. extra virgin olive oil
- 2 large garlic cloves, chopped
- 2 Tbsp. tahini*
- 2 Tbsp. fresh lemon juice
- 1 Tbsp. sour cream
- ½ tsp. salt
- ⅛ tsp. ground red pepper
    Extra virgin olive oil
    Smoked paprika
    Pitted kalamata olives, halved
    Pita chips

1. Preheat grill to medium-high (350° to 400°) heat. Spray cut sides of eggplant with cooking spray. Grill eggplant, skin side down, covered with grill lid 10 minutes. Turn eggplant halves over, and grill 4 minutes or until flesh is browned and tender. Remove from grill, and let stand 20 minutes or until cool to the touch.
2. Scoop pulp from eggplant halves into a large wire-mesh strainer; let drain 20 minutes. Combine drained pulp, 2 Tbsp. olive oil, and next 6 ingredients in a food processor. Process until smooth. Transfer to a bowl; cover and refrigerate up to 1 week. To serve, transfer dip to a serving bowl; drizzle with a small amount of olive oil, and sprinkle with smoked paprika and olives. Serve with pita chips.
*Tahini is a popular ingredient used in Middle Eastern cooking. It's a thick paste made from ground sesame seeds. Tahini can be found with the peanut butter or with organic foods at your grocer.

Hummus

MAKES 2 CUPS
HANDS-ON TIME: 7 MIN.
TOTAL TIME: 7 MIN.

This version of hummus was such a hit that we gave it our highest rating.

- 1 (19-oz.) can chickpeas
- 2 garlic cloves, chopped
- ⅓ cup extra-virgin olive oil
- ⅓ cup water
- ⅓ cup fresh lemon juice
- ⅓ cup tahini
- ½ tsp. salt
- 1 Tbsp. extra virgin olive oil
- 2 Tbsp. minced fresh flat-leaf parsley
- 2 Tbsp. pine nuts, toasted
    Pita bread, cut into wedges

1. Combine first 7 ingredients in a food processor; process until smooth. Transfer hummus to a serving bowl; cover and refrigerate up to 5 days before serving.
2. To serve, drizzle hummus with 1 Tbsp. olive oil, and sprinkle with parsley and toasted pine nuts. Serve with pita wedges.

Make-Ahead Favorites

Southwestern Spinach Dip

MAKES 1½ CUPS
HANDS-ON TIME: 10 MIN.
TOTAL TIME: 10 MIN.

- ⅔ cup mayonnaise
- ½ (8-oz.) package cream cheese, softened
- ½ cup fresh cilantro leaves
- 2 Tbsp. sliced green onions
- 1 tsp. lime zest
- 2 Tbsp. fresh lime juice
- ½ tsp. ground cumin
- ½ tsp. salt
- 1 jalapeño pepper, seeded and chopped
- 1 (10-oz.) package frozen chopped spinach, thawed and squeezed dry

1. Combine first 9 ingredients in a food processor; process until smooth. Add spinach, and pulse 3 times or until blended. Transfer dip to a bowl; cover and refrigerate up to 1 day. Serve with fresh cut vegetables, multigrain tortilla chips, or crackers.

Quick Creamy Vegetable Dip

MAKES ABOUT 1½ CUPS
HANDS-ON TIME: 10 MIN.
TOTAL TIME: 2 HR., 10 MIN.

Serve with raw vegetables or as a topping for chili or baked potatoes.

- ½ cup mayonnaise
- ½ cup sour cream
- 1 (2-oz.) jar diced pimiento, drained
- ¼ cup chopped onion
- ¼ cup diced green bell pepper
- ½ tsp. garlic salt
- ⅛ tsp. pepper
- ⅛ tsp. hot sauce

1. Stir together all ingredients. Cover and chill 2 hours.

Bean Dip

MAKES 1 CUP
HANDS-ON TIME: 10 MIN.
TOTAL TIME: 10 MIN.

- ½ cup sour cream
- ½ cup prepared black bean dip
- 1 tsp. minced chipotle peppers in adobo sauce
- 1 tsp. adobo sauce from can
- ¼ tsp. salt
  Garnishes: chopped tomato, chopped avocado

1. Combine first 5 ingredients; stir well. Cover and chill up to 3 days. Garnish, if desired. Serve with tortilla chips.

Black-eyed Pea-and-Ham Dip

MAKES 6 CUPS
HANDS-ON TIME: 23 MIN.
TOTAL TIME: 23 MIN.

You can prepare dip 24 hours in advance, then reheat before serving

- ½ cup diced country ham
- 2 (15.8-oz.) cans black-eyed peas, rinsed and drained
- 1 large tomato, finely chopped
- 2 green onions, sliced
- 1 celery rib, finely chopped
- ¼ cup chopped fresh parsley
- 2 Tbsp. olive oil
- 1 to 2 Tbsp. apple cider vinegar
  Cornbread crackers

1. Sauté ham in a lightly greased large nonstick skillet over medium-high heat 3 to 5 minutes or until lightly brown; stir in black-eyed peas and ¾ cup water. Reduce heat to medium, and simmer 8 minutes or until liquid is reduced by three-fourths. Partially mash beans with back of spoon to desired consistency

2. Stir together tomato and next 5 ingredients. Spoon warm bean mixture into a serving dish, and top with tomato mixture. Serve with crackers.
Note: Prepare dip 24 hours in advance, if desired; then reheat before serving.

Tzatziki

MAKES 2¾ CUPS
HANDS-ON TIME: 16 MIN.
TOTAL TIME: 16 MIN.

This refreshing cucumber yogurt dip can be served as part of the traditional Mezze, but it's also perfect as a sauce for poached salmon or other cold seafood. Be sure to look for Greek yogurt. It's thick, rich, and predrained. Plain yogurt can be substituted.

- 2 large cucumbers, peeled, seeded, and grated (about 1¼ pounds unpeeled)
- 2 cups Greek yogurt or 4 cups plain yogurt, drained (see note)
- 2 garlic cloves, minced
- 3 Tbsp. fresh lemon juice
- 1½ Tbsp. chopped fresh dill
- 1½ Tbsp. chopped fresh mint
- ½ tsp. salt

1. Press grated cucumber between layers of paper towels to remove excess moisture. Stir together cucumber, yogurt, and remaining ingredients. Cover and refrigerate up to 5 days.
Note: To drain plain yogurt, line a sieve with a double thickness of cheesecloth; set sieve over a bowl. Spoon yogurt into sieve, and let drain in refrigerator at least 3 hours.

Make-Ahead Favorites

Herbed Feta Spread

MAKES 2½ CUPS
HANDS-ON TIME: 10 MIN.
TOTAL TIME: 10 MIN.

- 1 (8-oz.) package feta cheese, softened
- 1 (8-oz.) package cream cheese, softened
- 3 Tbsp. chopped fresh basil
- 3 Tbsp. chopped fresh chives
- 2 Tbsp. olive oil
- 2 Tbsp. balsamic vinegar
- ⅓ cup pine nuts, toasted
  Garnish: fresh basil sprigs
  Toasted pita chips or baguette slices

1. Stir together first 6 ingredients until smooth. Cover and chill up to 1 week. Stir in pine nuts just before serving. Garnish, if desired. Serve with toasted pita chips or baguette slices.

Mexican Cheese Spread

MAKES 2 CUPS
HANDS-ON TIME: 13 MIN.
TOTAL TIME: 13 MIN.

Serve this creamy spread with stone-ground wheat crackers or bagel chips.

- 2 cups (8 oz.) shredded sharp Cheddar cheese
- ½ cup sour cream
- ¼ cup butter, softened
- 2 green onions, chopped
- 1 (2-oz.) jar diced pimiento, drained
- 2 Tbsp. chopped green chiles

1. Combine first 3 ingredients in a mixing bowl; beat at medium speed with an electric mixer until blended.
2. Stir in green onions, pimiento, and chiles. Cover and chill cheese spread, if desired.

Garlic-and-Dill Feta Cheese Spread

MAKES ABOUT 1 CUP
HANDS-ON TIME: 8 MIN.
TOTAL TIME: 8 HR., 8 MIN.

- 1 (8-oz.) package cream cheese, softened
- 1 (4-oz.) package crumbled feta cheese
- ¼ cup mayonnaise
- 1 garlic clove, minced
- 1 Tbsp. chopped fresh dill or ½ tsp. dried dillweed
- ¼ tsp. seasoned pepper
- ¼ tsp. salt
  Cucumber slices (optional)

1. Process first 7 ingredients in a food processor until smooth, stopping to scrape down sides. Cover and chill 8 hours. Serve with cucumber slices, if desired.
Note: Spread may be frozen in an airtight container up to 1 month. Thaw in refrigerator at least 24 hours. Stir before serving.

Honey-Peppered Goat Cheese with Fig Balsamic Drizzle

MAKES 6 TO 8 APPETIZER SERVINGS
HANDS-ON TIME: 8 MIN.
TOTAL TIME: 8 MIN.

- 1 (11-oz.) package or 4 (3-oz.) logs fresh goat cheese
- ⅓ cup olive oil
- ¼ cup honey
- ½ tsp. freshly ground black pepper
- 1 tsp. fresh thyme leaves
  Fig balsamic vinegar or balsamic vinegar
  Garnish: fresh thyme
  Lahvosh or other cracker bread

1. Using a sharp knife, carefully slice goat cheese in ½-inch-thick slices. Place cheese in an 11- x 7-inch dish or other serving platter. Drizzle with oil. Combine honey and pepper; drizzle over cheese. Sprinkle with 1 tsp. thyme leaves. Cover and chill up to 2 days.
2. Remove cheese from refrigerator 1 hour before serving. Just before serving, drizzle a little vinegar over cheese. Garnish, if desired. Serve with lahvosh or other specialty cracker bread.

Sweet 'n' Savory Snack Mix

MAKES 8 CUPS
HANDS-ON TIME: 5 MIN.
TOTAL TIME: 17 MIN.

This is the perfect after-school or in-the-car traveling snack mix.

- 3 cups crispy corn or rice cereal squares
- 1 cup small pretzels
- 1 (6-oz.) can roasted almonds
- 8 oz. salted peanuts
- ⅓ cup firmly packed light brown sugar
- 1½ Tbsp. Worcestershire sauce
  Butter-flavored cooking spray
- 1 cup bear-shaped graham crackers
- ½ cup raisins

1. Preheat oven to 325°. Combine first 4 ingredients in a large bowl. Stir together brown sugar and Worcestershire sauce until blended; pour over cereal mixture. Coat a 15- x 10-inch jelly-roll pan with butter-flavored cooking spray; spread cereal mixture in a single layer in pan, stirring to coat.
2. Bake at 325° for 12 minutes, stirring every 5 minutes. Stir in graham crackers and raisins. Cool completely. Store snack mix in an airtight container at room temperature.

Make-Ahead Favorites

Bourbon BBQ Baby Back Ribs

MAKES 5 SERVINGS

HANDS-ON TIME: 10 MIN.

TOTAL TIME: 10 HR., 49 MIN.

Prebaking these ribs gives them a rich browned exterior. The subsequent long, slow stint in the slow cooker produces fall-off-the-bone, fork-tender ribs.

- 5 lb. pork baby back ribs, racks cut in half
- 1½ tsp. salt
- 1 tsp. pepper
- 1 cup ketchup
- 1 cup firmly packed light brown sugar
- ½ cup bourbon
- ¼ cup prepared horseradish
- ½ tsp. hot sauce

1. Preheat oven to 475°. Place ribs, meaty-side up, in a large roasting pan. Sprinkle ribs with salt and pepper.
2. Bake at 475° for 30 minutes. Meanwhile, combine ketchup and next 4 ingredients in a small bowl.
3. Arrange ribs in a 6-qt. slow cooker, adding sauce on each layer of ribs. (Depending on the shape of your slow cooker—oval or round—you may have to cut each rib rack into thirds instead of in half.) Cover and cook ribs on LOW 9 hours. Remove ribs from slow cooker; cover to keep warm.
4. Pour drippings and sauce from slow cooker into a saucepan. (Skim a few ice cubes across the surface of sauce to remove fat, if desired, and discard.) Bring sauce to a boil; reduce heat, and simmer over medium heat 20 minutes or until sauce thickens. (Sauce will reduce by about half.) Brush sauce over ribs before serving.

Make Ahead: These ribs can hold for several hours after finishing in the slow cooker. Place sauced ribs on a rimmed baking sheet; cover tightly with foil. Place in a preheated 190° oven to keep warm.

Marinated Cheese, Olives, and Peppers

MAKES 6 TO 8 APPETIZER SERVINGS
HANDS-ON TIME: 15 MIN.
TOTAL TIME: 1 HR., 15 MIN.

- 1½ lb. cubed firm cheeses (such as Cheddar, Gouda, Havarti, or Monterey Jack)
- 2 cups olives
- 1 (7-oz.) jar roasted red bell peppers
  Cheese Marinade

1. Combine cheeses, olives, and peppers in a large zip-top plastic freezer bag or decorative airtight-container. Pour Cheese Marinade over mixture, and chill at least 1 hour or up to 2 days.

Cheese Marinade:

MAKES ABOUT 3 CUPS
HANDS-ON TIME: 10 MIN.
TOTAL TIME: 10 MIN.

- 1½ cups olive oil
- 1 cup white balsamic vinegar
- ¼ cup fresh thyme leaves
- 2 Tbsp. chopped fresh rosemary
- 1 tsp. salt
- ½ tsp. pepper

1. Whisk together all ingredients. Pour into an airtight jar or decorative container. Store in refrigerator up to 1 week.

Peach and Pecan Tapenade with Goat Cheese

MAKES 3¾ CUPS

HANDS-ON TIME: 17 MIN.

TOTAL TIME: 47 MIN.

We gave this traditional French condiment a Southern twist with pecans and dried peaches. The result is a beautiful spread that's sure to impress.

- 1 cup orange juice
- 2 cups dried peaches, chopped (we tested with Sunmaid)
- 1 cup pitted kalamata olives, chopped
- 2 Tbsp. olive oil
- 2 Tbsp. honey
- 1 Tbsp. capers, drained
- ½ tsp. dried thyme
- ¼ tsp. freshly ground pepper
- 1 cup chopped pecans, toasted
- 12 oz. goat cheese
  Specialty crackers

1. Bring orange juice to a boil in a small saucepan over medium heat. Remove from heat, and add chopped dried peaches. Cover and let stand 30 minutes. Drain, if necessary.
2. Combine olives and next 5 ingredients in a serving bowl. Stir in peaches and pecans. Place tapenade on a serving platter with goat cheese and crackers. Spread cheese on crackers, and smear with tapenade.
Note: Prepare tapenade, omitting nuts. Cover and store in refrigerator up to 2 days. Stir in pecans just before serving.

Main-Dish Marvels

Family and friends will rave over these enticing entrées.

Beef Lombardi

MAKES 6 SERVINGS
HANDS-ON TIME: 20 MIN.
TOTAL TIME: 1 HR., 31 MIN.

- 1 lb. lean ground beef
- 1 (14½-oz.) can diced tomatoes
- 1 (10-oz.) can diced tomatoes and green chiles
- 2 tsp. sugar
- 2 tsp. salt
- ¼ tsp. pepper
- 1 (6-oz.) can tomato paste
- 1 bay leaf
- 1 (6-oz.) package medium egg noodles
- 6 green onions, chopped (about ½ cup)
- 1 cup sour cream
- 1 cup (4 oz.) shredded sharp Cheddar cheese
- 1 cup shredded Parmesan cheese
- 1 cup (4 oz.) shredded mozzarella cheese
- Garnish: fresh parsley sprigs

1. Preheat oven to 350°. Cook ground beef in a large skillet over medium heat 5 to 6 minutes, stirring until it crumbles and is no longer pink. Drain. Stir in both cans of tomatoes and next 3 ingredients; cook 5 minutes. Stir in

tomato paste, and add bay leaf; cook 30 minutes. Discard bay leaf.
2. Meanwhile, cook egg noodles according to package directions, and drain. Stir together cooked egg noodles, chopped green onions, and 1 cup sour cream until blended.
3. Place noodle mixture in a lightly greased 13- x 9-inch baking dish. Top with beef mixture; sprinkle evenly with cheeses.
4. Bake, covered, at 350° for 35 minutes. Uncover and bake 5 more minutes. Garnish, if desired.
Note: Freeze casserole up to 1 month, if desired. Thaw in refrigerator overnight. Bake as directed.

Light Beef Lombardi: Substitute low-fat or fat-free sour cream and 2% reduced-fat Cheddar cheese. Reduce amount of cheeses on top to ½ cup each.

Garlic-Herb Steaks

MAKES 4 SERVINGS
HANDS-ON TIME: 30 MIN.
TOTAL TIME: 1 HR., 30 MIN.

Minced garlic in a jar can be found in the produce area of your grocery store.

- 4 (4-oz.) beef tenderloin fillets
- ¼ tsp. salt
- ¼ tsp. freshly ground pepper
- ¼ cup jarred minced garlic
- 1 Tbsp. minced fresh rosemary

1. Sprinkle fillets with salt and pepper; coat with garlic and rosemary. Chill 1 to 24 hours.
2. Light 1 side of grill, heating to 400° to 500° (high) heat; leave other side unlit. Place rack on grill. Arrange fillets over unlit side, and grill, covered with grill lid, 10 minutes on each side or until desired degree of doneness.

Chunky Italian Soup

MAKES 10 CUPS
HANDS-ON TIME: 20 MIN.
TOTAL TIME: 1 HR., 5 MIN.

- 1 lb. lean ground beef or beef tips
- 1 medium onion, chopped
- 2 (14½-oz.) cans Italian-style tomatoes
- 1 (10¾-oz.) can tomato soup
- 4 cups water
- 2 garlic cloves, minced
- 2 tsp. dried basil
- 2 tsp. dried oregano
- 1 tsp. salt
- ½ tsp. pepper
- 1 Tbsp. chili powder (optional)
- 1 (16-oz.) can kidney beans, drained
- 1 (16-oz.) can Italian green beans, drained
- 1 carrot, chopped
- 1 zucchini, chopped
- 8 oz. rotini pasta, cooked
- Freshly grated Parmesan cheese (optional)

1. Cook beef and onion in a Dutch oven over medium heat, stirring until beef crumbles and is no longer pink; drain. Return mixture to pan.
2. Stir in tomatoes, next 7 ingredients, and, if desired, chili powder; bring to a boil. Reduce heat; simmer, stirring occasionally, 30 minutes. Stir in kidney beans and next 3 ingredients; simmer, stirring occasionally, 15 minutes. Stir in pasta. (To freeze, let soup cool slightly, and spoon into freezer-proof containers or zip-top plastic freezer bags. Cover or seal, and freeze up to 1 month. Thaw overnight in the refrigerator, and reheat.) Sprinkle soup with cheese, if desired.

Make-Ahead Favorites

Meat Lover's Chili

MAKES 16 CUPS
HANDS-ON TIME: 17 MIN.
TOTAL TIME: 1 HR., 38 MIN.

This chili is better the second and even third day, but feel free to enjoy it freshly made with minced red onion, shredded Monterey Jack cheese, chopped fresh cilantro, sour cream, and a basket of warm flour tortillas.

- 3 lb. ground chuck
- 3 medium onions, chopped
- 1 large green bell pepper, chopped
- 3 Tbsp. minced garlic
- ½ cup chili powder
- 1 Tbsp. ground cumin
- 1 (14-oz.) can beef broth
- 1 Tbsp. dried oregano
- 1½ tsp. salt
- 2 (28-oz.) cans diced tomatoes, undrained
- 3 (15-oz.) cans pinto beans, rinsed and drained

1. Brown beef in a large Dutch oven over medium heat. Drain beef, reserving ¼ cup drippings in pan.
2. Add onion, bell pepper, and garlic to drippings; sauté over medium-high heat 6 to 8 minutes or until vegetables are tender. Return beef to Dutch oven.
3. Stir in chili powder and cumin; cook over medium heat 3 minutes, stirring occasionally. Stir in beef broth and next 3 ingredients. Reduce heat, and simmer, covered, 50 minutes, stirring occasionally. Add pinto beans, and cook 20 more minutes.

Company Beef Stew

MAKES 6 CUPS
HANDS-ON TIME: 30 MIN.
TOTAL TIME: 3 HR., 20 MIN.

- 1 (3-lb.) boneless chuck roast, cut into 1-inch cubes
- 1 large onion, sliced
- 1 garlic clove, minced
- 1 tablespoon dried parsley flakes
- 1 bay leaf
- ½ tsp. salt
- ½ tsp. pepper
- ½ tsp. dried thyme
- 1 cup dry red wine
- 2 Tbsp. olive oil
- 4 bacon slices, cut crosswise into ¼-inch pieces
- 3 Tbsp. all-purpose flour
- 1½ cups beef broth
- ½ lb. baby carrots
- 1 (16-oz.) package frozen pearl onions, thawed
- 2 Tbsp. butter
- 1 (8-oz.) package fresh mushrooms

1. Combine first 8 ingredients in a shallow dish or zip-top plastic freezer bag. Combine wine and oil; pour over meat mixture. Cover or seal; chill 1 hour. Drain well, reserving marinade.
2. Cook bacon in an ovenproof Dutch oven until crisp; remove bacon, reserving drippings in Dutch oven. Drain bacon on paper towels. (If desired, place bacon in a zip-top plastic freezer bag; seal and freeze up to 1 month. Thaw in refrigerator overnight.)
3. Brown meat mixture in reserved bacon drippings. Drain and return to Dutch oven. Sprinkle evenly with flour; cook, stirring constantly, 1 to 2 minutes. Add reserved marinade and beef broth; bring to a boil.
4. Bake, covered, at 300° for 1 hour and 30 minutes or until tender. Add carrots and onions; bake 30 more minutes.

5. Melt butter in a large skillet. Add mushrooms; sauté over medium-high heat until tender, and add to meat mixture. (To freeze, let soup cool slightly, and spoon into freezer-proof containers or zip-top plastic freezer bags. Cover or seal, and freeze up to 1 month. Thaw overnight in the refrigerator, and reheat.)
6. Cook over medium heat in a Dutch oven, stirring occasionally, until thoroughly heated. Discard bay leaf. Sprinkle with bacon.

French Club Sandwiches

MAKES 3 SERVINGS
HANDS-ON TIME: 13 MIN.
TOTAL TIME: 13 MIN.

Tailgating takes a tasty turn when this winning cream cheese club sandwich is served. This sandwich wraps and travels nicely chilled in a cooler.

- ½ (8-oz.) container chive-and-onion cream cheese, softened
- 1 Tbsp. mayonnaise
- ½ celery rib, chopped
- ¼ cup (1 oz.) shredded Cheddar cheese
- 1 (8-oz.) French baguette
- ½ lb. thinly sliced cooked ham
- 3 dill pickle stackers*

1. Combine first 4 ingredients, stirring until blended.
2. Slice baguette in half horizontally, and spread cream cheese mixture evenly over cut sides of bread. Place ham on bottom half of baguette, and top with pickles. Cover with top half of baguette. Cut baguette into 3 portions.
*We tested with Vlasic Dill Pickle Stackers.

Make-Ahead Favorites

Beef-and-Lime Rice Salad

MAKES 4 SERVINGS
HANDS-ON TIME: 15 MIN.
TOTAL TIME: 35 MIN.

Serve this salad right away, or chill and serve cold.

1   lb. lean ground beef
1   tsp. salt, divided
½   tsp. cumin
1½ cups uncooked long-grain rice
1   tsp. lime zest
1   Tbsp. fresh lime juice
     Toppings: salsa, shredded Cheddar cheese, sour cream, chopped tomatoes, chopped green onions, avocado slices

1. Cook beef and ½ tsp. salt in a 3-qt. saucepan over medium-high heat, stirring until beef crumbles and is no longer pink. Drain and pat dry with paper towels. Wipe pan clean.
2. Add 3 cups water, ½ tsp. cumin, and remaining ½ tsp. salt to saucepan. Bring to a boil, and add rice; cover, reduce heat, and cook 20 to 25 minutes or until water is absorbed and rice is tender. Stir in cooked beef, 1 tsp. lime zest, and 1 Tbsp. lime juice. Serve salad with desired toppings.

Make-Ahead Pork Dumplings

MAKES 116 DUMPLINGS
HANDS-ON TIME: 2 HR.
TOTAL TIME: 2 HR., 20 MIN.

This recipe makes a bunch, so ask a friend to help you assemble the dumplings; then freeze some for later.

1½ lb. lean boneless pork loin chops, cut into chunks
1   (12-oz.) package 50%-less-fat ground pork sausage
1½ tsp. salt
15   water chestnuts, finely chopped
1   to 2 Tbsp. minced fresh ginger
½   cup cornstarch
2   tsp. lite soy sauce
½   cup low-sodium fat-free chicken broth
4   Tbsp. sugar
1   tsp. teriyaki sauce
1   tsp. sesame oil
¼   cup chopped fresh parsley
4   green onions, diced
2   (16-oz.) packages wonton skins
     Ginger Dipping Sauce (optional)

1. Process pork loin in a food processor until finely chopped.
2. Combine pork loin, pork sausage, and next 11 ingredients.
3. Cut corners from wonton skins to form circles. Drop 1 tsp. mixture onto middle of each skin. Gather up skin sides, letting dough pleat naturally. Lightly squeeze the middle while tapping the bottom on a flat surface so it will stand upright.
4. Arrange dumplings in a bamboo steam basket over boiling water. Cover and steam 20 to 25 minutes. Serve with Ginger Dipping Sauce, if desired.

Note: To freeze, arrange dumplings on a baking sheet; freeze for 2 hours. Place in zip-top plastic freezer bags; label and freeze for up to 3 months. To cook dumplings from frozen state, steam for 22 to 25 minutes.

Ginger Dipping Sauce

MAKES ⅓ CUP (ABOUT 5 SERVINGS)
HANDS-ON TIME: 11 MIN.
TOTAL TIME: 11 MIN.

1   garlic clove, minced
1   Tbsp. minced fresh ginger
1   tsp. dark sesame oil
2   Tbsp. lite soy sauce
1   Tbsp. rice wine vinegar
2   tsp. teriyaki sauce
1   green onion, minced

1. Sauté garlic and ginger in hot oil 1 minute; remove from heat. Whisk in remaining ingredients.

Make-Ahead Favorites

Chunky Ham Pot Pie

MAKES 6 TO 8 SERVINGS
HANDS-ON TIME: 20 MIN.
TOTAL TIME: 1 HR., 25 MIN.

- 2 Tbsp. butter
- 1 cup chopped onion
- 1 (10-oz.) package frozen cut broccoli or florets
- 1 lb. new potatoes, coarsely chopped
- 1 (10¾-oz.) can cream of potato soup
- 1 (8-oz.) container sour cream
- 1 cup (4 oz.) shredded sharp Cheddar cheese
- ¾ cup milk
- ½ tsp. garlic powder
- ½ tsp. salt
- ¼ tsp. pepper
- 2½ cups chopped cooked ham
- ½ (14.1-oz.) package refrigerated piecrusts

1. Melt 2 Tbsp. butter in a large skillet over medium heat; add chopped onion. Cook, stirring often, 10 minutes or until onion is tender and begins to brown. Set aside.
2. Cook broccoli according to package directions; drain well, and set aside.
3. Cook chopped new potatoes in boiling water to cover 10 minutes or until barely tender; drain.
4. Combine cream of potato soup and next 6 ingredients in a large bowl, stirring well. Stir in onion, broccoli, new potatoes, and chopped ham. Spoon ham mixture into a lightly greased 3½-qt. casserole dish. (Cover and chill 8 hours, if desired. Let stand at room temperature 30 minutes before baking.)
5. Preheat oven to 400°. Unroll piecrust onto a lightly floured surface. Roll pastry to extend ¾ inch beyond edges of casserole. Place pastry over ham mixture. Seal edges, and crimp. Cut slits in pastry to allow steam to escape.

6. Bake, uncovered, at 400° for 45 minutes or until crust is golden. Let stand 10 minutes before serving.
Note: You can divide this pot pie into 2 (2 qt.) dishes. Bake one now, and freeze one for later. You will need the whole package of piecrusts for two casseroles. Top the casserole to be frozen with crust before freezing, but do not cut slits in top until ready to bake. Let frozen casserole stand at room temperature 30 minutes before baking.

Mushroom Chicken Bake

MAKES 8 SERVINGS
HANDS-ON TIME: 5 MIN.
TOTAL TIME: 40 MIN.

Mushroom soup and wine combine to create a savory sauce that's spooned over cheese-topped chicken breasts.

- 8 skinned and boned chicken breasts
- 8 (1-oz.) Swiss cheese slices
- 1¼ cups sliced fresh mushrooms
- 1 (10¾-oz.) can cream of mushroom or cream of chicken soup
- ¼ cup dry white wine
- 2 cups seasoned stuffing mix°
- ¼ cup butter, melted

1. Preheat oven to 350°. Place chicken in a single layer in a lightly greased 13-x 9-inch baking dish. Top each breast with a cheese slice; sprinkle with mushrooms. Combine soup and wine in a bowl; pour over chicken. Sprinkle with stuffing; drizzle with butter. Bake, uncovered, at 350° for 35 minutes or until chicken is done.
*We tested with Pepperidge Farm stuffing mix.

Chicken-and-Rice Casserole

MAKES 8 SERVINGS
HANDS-ON TIME: 20 MIN.
TOTAL TIME: 45 MIN.

Use a rotisserie chicken for this family-friendly casserole. The potato chip topping promises to be a hit.

- 2 Tbsp. butter
- 1 medium onion, chopped
- 1 (8.8-oz.) package microwaveable rice of choice
- 3 cups chopped cooked chicken
- 1½ cups frozen petite peas
- 1½ cups (6 oz.) shredded sharp Cheddar cheese
- 1 cup mayonnaise
- 1 (10¾-oz.) can cream of chicken soup
- 1 (8-oz.) can sliced water chestnuts, drained
- 1 (4-oz.) jar sliced pimientos, drained
- 3 cups coarsely crushed ridge potato chips

1. Preheat oven to 350°. Melt butter in a skillet over medium heat. Add onion, and sauté 5 minutes or until tender.
2. Cook rice in microwave according to package directions. Combine sautéed onion, rice, chicken, and next 6 ingredients in a large bowl; toss gently. Spoon mixture into a lightly greased 13- x 9-inch baking dish. Top with coarsely crushed potato chips.
3. Bake, uncovered, at 350° for 20 to 25 minutes or until bubbly.
Note: To make casserole ahead, prepare and spoon casserole into baking dish, leaving off crushed chips. Cover and refrigerate up to 24 ours. Uncover and add crushed chips before baking.

Make-Ahead Favorites

Tortilla Chicken Casserole

MAKES 8 SERVINGS
HANDS-ON TIME: 17 MIN.
TOTAL TIME: 1 HR., 17 MIN.

Get a jump-start on dinner with this southwestern comfort food casserole that can be made up to two days ahead. Serve with an array of toppings: diced avocado, sour cream, lime wedges, sliced pickled jalapeño, fresh cilantro, and salsa.

3 Tbsp. vegetable oil
1½ cups minced red bell pepper
1½ cups minced onion
2 Tbsp. minced garlic
½ tsp. salt
2½ tsp. ground cumin
¼ cup all-purpose flour
1½ cups chicken broth
1 cup sour cream
5 cups chopped cooked chicken or turkey
12 corn tortillas
3 cups (12 oz.) shredded Monterey Jack cheese

1. Heat oil in a large nonstick skillet over medium heat until hot. Add bell pepper and next 3 ingredients; cook 5 minutes or until vegetables are soft. Stir in cumin, and cook 1 minute. Stir in flour; cook 3 minutes. Add chicken broth and sour cream; simmer 5 minutes, stirring frequently. Add chicken, and stir to blend.
2. Soften tortillas by layering them between damp paper towels and heating in microwave, in several batches, at HIGH for 30 seconds.
3. Arrange 4 tortillas in a lightly greased 3-qt. baking dish. Top with one-third of chicken mixture (about 2 cups), sprinkle with 1 cup cheese, and cover with 4 more tortillas. Repeat layers with another one-third of chicken mixture, 1 cup cheese, 4 tortillas, and ending with remaining chicken and 1 cup cheese. Cover with aluminum foil, and refrigerate up to 2 days.
4. Bake, uncovered, at 350° for 35 to 45 minutes or until bubbling and browned.
Note: You can also freeze this casserole. Follow the make-ahead directions above but freeze after preparing. When ready to cook it, bake foil-covered frozen casserole at 350° for 1 hour and 15 minutes or until thoroughly heated.

Chicken à la King

MAKES 8 SERVINGS
HANDS-ON TIME: 25 MIN.
TOTAL TIME: 55 MIN.

A classic American dish evoking childhood memories for some of us, Chicken à la King is elegant enough for a party buffet, and yet comfort food at its best. Serve the creamy chicken over our Crisp Cheddar-Cornmeal Waffles, and it'll be a hit. The dish can be prepared 2 days ahead, stored, covered, and chilled.

4 cups chicken broth
2 lb. skinned and boned chicken breasts
6 Tbsp. butter, divided
4 red bell peppers, cut into ½-inch pieces
1 medium onion, cut into ½-inch pieces
1 (8-oz.) package fresh mushrooms, quartered
1 tsp. salt
⅛ tsp. ground red pepper
Crisp Cheddar-Cornmeal Waffles
6 Tbsp. all-purpose flour
2 cups whipping cream
3 Tbsp. dry sherry
2 Tbsp. lemon juice
Salt and pepper to taste
Garnishes: toasted sliced almonds, flat-leaf parsley

1. Pour broth in a Dutch oven or stockpot; bring to a boil. Add chicken; reduce heat to medium-low, and cook, uncovered, 10 minutes. Remove chicken from broth; coarsely chop, and set aside. Strain broth through a sieve into a saucepan; simmer, uncovered, over medium heat until reduced to 2½ cups (10 to 20 minutes).
2. Melt 3 Tbsp. butter in a large skillet over medium heat. Sauté red bell pepper and onion 4 minutes or until tender. Add mushrooms, salt, and ground red pepper; sauté 4 minutes. Remove from heat, and set aside.
3. While broth continues to simmer, preheat waffle iron, and cook waffles.
4. Melt remaining 3 Tbsp. butter in Dutch oven over low heat; whisk in flour until smooth. Cook 3 minutes, whisking constantly. Gradually whisk in reserved 2½ cups broth and cream; cook over medium heat, whisking constantly, until sauce is thickened and bubbly.
5. Add chicken and reserved vegetables to sauce. Stir in sherry and lemon juice; cook over medium heat, just until thoroughly heated. Add salt and pepper to taste. Serve over waffles. Garnish, if desired.

Make-Ahead Favorites

Crisp Cheddar-Cornmeal Waffles:

MAKES 16 (4-INCH) WAFFLES
HANDS-ON TIME: 12 MIN.
TOTAL TIME: 32 MIN.

These waffles are crisp and interesting on their own or with syrup, but crown them with some Chicken à la King (on facing page), and they become fancy brunch fare.

- 1 cup all-purpose flour
- 1 cup yellow cornmeal
- 2 tsp. baking powder
- 1 tsp. baking soda
- ½ tsp. salt
- 1½ cups (6 oz.) shredded sharp Cheddar cheese
- ½ cup chopped toasted pecans
- 3 large eggs
- 1 cup buttermilk
- 1 cup club soda
- ⅓ cup canola or vegetable oil

1. Preheat waffle iron. Sift together first 5 ingredients in a large bowl. Stir in cheese and pecans. Combine eggs and next 3 ingredients; gently stir into dry ingredients just until blended.
2. Preheat oven to 200°. Spoon a heaping 1 cup batter evenly onto a lightly greased waffle iron. Cook 5 to 10 minutes or until crisp and done. Repeat with remaining batter.
3. Transfer waffles to a baking sheet, and keep warm, uncovered, in the oven at 200° until ready to serve. Waffles can be frozen in zip-top plastic freezer bags and reheated in oven or toaster oven.
Note: To make Belgian waffles, spoon 2 cups batter into a preheated, greased Belgian waffle iron with 4 square grids. Cook until crisp and done.

Heavenly Chicken Lasagna

MAKES 8 TO 10 SERVINGS
HANDS-ON TIME: 30 MIN.
TOTAL TIME: 1 HR., 45 MIN.

- 1 Tbsp. butter
- ½ large onion
- 1 (10 ½-oz.) can reduced-fat cream of chicken soup
- 1 (10-oz.) container refrigerated reduced-fat Alfredo sauce*
- 1 (7-oz.) jar diced pimiento, undrained
- 1 (6-oz.) jar sliced mushrooms, drained
- ⅓ cup dry white wine
- ½ tsp. dried basil
- 1 (10-oz.) package frozen chopped spinach, thawed
- 1 cup cottage cheese
- 1 cup ricotta cheese
- ½ cup grated Parmesan cheese
- 1 large egg, lightly beaten
- 9 lasagna noodles, cooked
- 3 cups chopped cooked chicken
- 3 cups (12 oz.) shredded sharp Cheddar cheese, divided

1. Preheat oven to 350°. Melt butter in a skillet over medium-high heat. Add onion, and sauté 5 minutes or until tender. Stir in soup and next 5 ingredients. Reserve 1 cup sauce.
2. Drain spinach well, pressing between layers of paper towels.
3. Stir together spinach, cottage cheese, and next 3 ingredients.
4. Place 3 lasagna noodles in a lightly greased 13- x 9-inch baking dish. Layer with half each of sauce, spinach mixture, and chicken. Sprinkle with 1 cup Cheddar cheese. Repeat procedure. Top with remaining 3 noodles and reserved 1 cup sauce. Cover and chill up to 1 day ahead.

5. Bake at 350° for 45 minutes. Sprinkle with remaining 1 cup Cheddar cheese, and bake 5 more minutes or until cheese is melted. Let stand 10 minutes before serving.
*We tested with Cantadina Light Alfredo Sauce.

Marinated Shrimp Salad

MAKES 8 SERVINGS
HANDS-ON TIME: 12 MIN.
TOTAL TIME: 3 HR., 12 MIN.

- 1 cup bottled vinaigrette
- 1 bunch green onions, chopped
- 2 celery ribs, chopped
- 2 garlic cloves, minced
- 1¼ lb. cooked, peeled shrimp
- 8 cups mixed salad greens
  Garnishes: lemon wedges, paprika

1. Combine vinaigrette, green onions, celery, and garlic in a large bowl. Add shrimp, tossing to coat; cover and chill 3 hours.
2. Arrange shrimp mixture on salad greens, and, garnish, if desired.

Show-Stealing Sides

These tasty recipe will compete with the main dish for center stage on the dinner table.

Twice-Baked Smoky Sweet Potatoes

MAKES 6 SERVINGS
HANDS-ON TIME: 21 MIN.
TOTAL TIME: 1 HR., 33 MIN.

Like a twice-baked potato, this sweet potato version mashes yummy ingredients together and then gets a crusty cheese topping with a surprise ingredient. The results pair well with pork tenderloin, turkey, or ham.

- 6   medium sweet potatoes (3½ lb.)
- ⅓ cup butter
- ½ cup whipping cream, half-and-half, or milk
- ¼ tsp. salt
- ¼ tsp. smoked paprika
- ⅛ tsp. ground red pepper
- ½ cup crushed amaretti cookies (about 4 cookies)
- ¼ tsp. smoked paprika
- ¾ cup grated Parmigiano-Reggiano cheese

1. Preheat oven to 450°. Scrub potatoes, and prick each potato once. Place on a baking sheet. Bake at 450° for 1 hour or until tender.
2. When potatoes are cool enough to handle, cut a strip from top of each potato, carefully scoop out potato pulp, leaving ⅛-inch-thick shells. Set shells aside. Place pulp, butter, and next 4 ingredients in a medium bowl. Mash with a potato masher, or beat at medium speed with an electric mixer until smooth; spoon into potato shells. Cover and chill up to 2 days.
3. When ready to bake, place stuffed potatoes on a large, round microwave-safe, ovenproof platter, and cover with a paper towel. Microwave potatoes at HIGH 6 minutes or until thoroughly heated.
4. Combine crushed cookies, ¼ tsp. paprika, and cheese. Sprinkle over potatoes. Bake at 400° for 6 minutes or until browned.
Note: You can find smoked paprika at specialty grocery stores or spice stores.

Quick Double-Cheese Grits

MAKES 8 SERVINGS
HANDS-ON TIME: 15 MIN.
TOTAL TIME: 15 MIN.

- ½ tsp. salt
- 1½ cups quick-cooking grits
- 1   cup (4 oz.) shredded extra-sharp Cheddar cheese
- 1   cup (4 oz.) shredded Monterey Jack cheese
- 2   Tbsp. butter
- ½ tsp. pepper

1. Bring 6 cups water and salt to a boil in a large saucepan. Gradually stir in grits. Cook 4 to 5 minutes, stirring often, until thickened. Remove from heat. Add shredded cheeses, butter, and pepper, stirring until blended. Serve immediately.
Note: Grits may be chilled and reheated. Whisk ¼ cup warm water into grits over medium-heat, adding more water as necessary.

Carrot-Sweet Potato Puree

MAKES 6 SERVINGS
HANDS-ON TIME: 20 MIN.
TOTAL TIME: 37 MIN.

This recipe requires no stovetop cooking; it's all done in the microwave. We reduced calories, fat, and cholesterol by using light butter (and less of it) and light sour cream.

- 5   carrots, sliced
- ¼ cup light butter
- 1   (29-oz.) can sweet potatoes, drained
- 1   (16-oz.) can sweet potatoes, drained
- 1   (8-oz.) container light sour cream
- 1   Tbsp. sugar
- 1   tsp. lemon zest
- ½ tsp. ground nutmeg
- ¼ tsp. salt
- ¼ tsp. ground black pepper
- ⅛ tsp. ground red pepper

1. Microwave carrots and ¾ cup water in a glass bowl at HIGH 8 to 12 minutes or until tender. Drain.
2. Process carrots and butter in a food processor until mixture is smooth, stopping to scrape down sides. Add sweet potatoes; process until smooth.
3. Stir together sweet potato mixture, sour cream, and remaining ingredients in a bowl.
4. Spoon mixture into a 1½-qt. glass dish. Microwave at HIGH 4 to 5 minutes or until thoroughly heated.
Note: To make ahead, prepare and stir together ingredients as directed; cover and chill up to 2 days. Let stand at room temperature 30 minutes; microwave as directed.

Make-Ahead Favorites

Honey-Baked Tomatoes

MAKES 8 SERVINGS
HANDS-ON: 10 MIN.
TOTAL TIME: 45 MIN.

Prepare the crumb topping the day before you plan to serve these tasty tomatoes.

- 8 medium tomatoes, cut into 1-inch slices
- 4 tsp. honey
- 2 white bread slices
- 1 Tbsp. dried tarragon
- 1½ tsp. salt
- 2 tsp. freshly ground pepper
- 4 tsp. butter

1. Preheat oven to 350°. Place tomato slices in a single layer in a lightly greased aluminum foil-lined 15- x 10-inch jelly-roll pan. Drizzle with honey, spreading honey into hollows.
2. Process bread in a blender or food processor until finely chopped.
3. Stir together breadcrumbs and next 3 ingredients; sprinkle evenly over tomato slices. Dot with butter.
4. Bake at 350° for 30 minutes or until tomato skins begin to wrinkle. Increase oven temperature to broil.
5. Broil 5 inches from heat 5 minutes or until tops are golden. Serve warm.

Cherry Tomato-Caper Salad

MAKES 4 SERVINGS
HANDS-ON TIME: 10 MIN.
TOTAL TIME: 25 MIN.

Fresh basil leaves add a crisp herbal note to this colorful salad, and they're a snap to shred. Simply stack, roll, and slice. The sliced leaves will fall from the roll in perfect-size pieces.

- 2 Tbsp. balsamic vinegar
- 1 Tbsp. drained small capers
- 4 tsp. olive oil
- ½ tsp. freshly ground pepper
- 1 pint cherry or grape tomatoes, halved
- 6 fresh basil leaves, shredded
  Bibb lettuce leaves

1. Combine first 4 ingredients. Drizzle over tomato halves, tossing to coat. Let stand at least 15 minutes or up to 1 hour. Sprinkle with basil. Serve over Bibb lettuce.

Colorful Coleslaw

MAKES 6 SERVINGS
HANDS-ON TIME: 10 MIN.
TOTAL TIME: 10 MIN.

- 1 (10-oz.) package finely shredded cabbage
- 4 green onions, chopped
- 1 medium-size green bell pepper, chopped
- 1 medium tomato, seeded and chopped
- 3 Tbsp. mayonnaise
- ½ tsp. salt

1. Stir together all ingredients. Cover and chill, if desired.

Cantaloupe-Spinach Salad

MAKES 6 TO 8 SERVINGS
HANDS-ON TIME: 5 MIN.
TOTAL TIME: 8 MIN. (INCLUDING VINAIGRETTE)

Buy cubed cantaloupe from your supermarket's produce section to make this refreshing salad in a snap.

- 6 cups baby spinach leaves
- 1 large cantaloupe, cubed
- ½ cup pistachios, coarsely chopped
  Pistachio-Lime Vinaigrette or bottled vinaigrette

1. Place spinach on individual serving plates; arrange cantaloupe on top, and sprinkle with pistachios. Serve with Pistachio-Lime Vinaigrette.

Pistachio-Lime Vinaigrette:

MAKES ABOUT 2 CUPS
HANDS-ON TIME: 3 MIN.
TOTAL TIME: 3 MIN.

This vinaigrette is spicy-sweet.

- ⅓ cup fresh lime juice
- ⅓ cup honey
- ¼ cup coarsely chopped red onion
- 1 tsp. dried crushed red pepper
- ½ tsp. salt
- ¼ cup fresh cilantro leaves
- ¾ cup vegetable oil
- 1 cup pistachios

1. Process first 6 ingredients in a blender until smooth. With blender running, add oil in a slow, steady stream. Turn blender off; add pistachios, and pulse until pistachios are finely chopped. Cover and store in refrigerator.

Blackened Tomato Salad

MAKES 4 SERVINGS
HANDS-ON TIME: 28 MIN.
TOTAL TIME: 1 HR., 28 MIN.

The juice from the tomatoes creates the fantastic marinade for this salad.

- 4 large tomatoes
- 1 Tbsp. olive oil
- 3 Tbsp. sliced fresh basil
- ¼ cup olive oil
- 1½ Tbsp. red wine vinegar
- ½ tsp. salt
- 1 tsp. freshly ground pepper
  Garnish: sliced fresh basil leaves

1. Cut tomatoes into quarters; remove and discard seeds. Pat tomatoes dry, and brush sides evenly with 1 Tbsp. olive oil

2. Cook tomato quarters in a hot cast-iron skillet over high heat 1½ to 2 minutes on each side or until blackened. Remove from skillet, and, cool, reserving juice from skillet.

3. Toss tomato with reserved juice, 3 Tbsp. basil, and next 4 ingredients in a large bowl. Cover and let stand, stirring occasionally, 1 hour. Garnish, if desired.

Bountiful Breads

Bake up a batch of comforting feel-good breads.

Tiny Cream Cheese Biscuits

MAKES 1½ DOZEN
HANDS-ON TIME: 8 MIN.
TOTAL TIME: 23 MIN.

The three simple ingredients for this recipe are worth committing to memory so you can stir up these gems without even looking at the recipe.

- 1 (8-oz.) package cream cheese, softened
- ½ cup butter, softened
- 1 cup self-rising flour

1. Preheat oven to 400°. Beat cream cheese and butter in a small mixing bowl at medium speed with an electric mixer 2 minutes or until creamy.

2. Gradually add flour to cream cheese mixture, beating at low speed just until blended.

3. Spoon dough into ungreased miniature (1¾-inch) muffin pans, filling full. Bake at 400° for 15 to 17 minutes or until golden. Remove from pans immediately. Serve hot.

Biscuit Poppers

MAKES 2 DOZEN
HANDS-ON TIME: 10 MIN.
TOTAL TIME: 30 MIN.

These unbelievably easy biscuits have a buttery, flaky texture like the ones Grandma used to bake.

- 1 (8-oz.) container sour cream
- ½ cup butter, melted
- 2¼ cups all-purpose baking mix

1. Preheat oven to 350°. Whisk together sour cream and butter until smooth. Stir in baking mix just until moistened. With floured hands, roll into 1½-inch balls. Place in lightly greased miniature (1¾-inch) muffin pans.

2. Bake at 350° for 18 to 20 minutes or until biscuits are golden brown. Remove from pans immediately.

Cheese Garlic Biscuits

MAKES 10 TO 12 BISCUITS
HANDS-ON TIME: 10 MIN.
TOTAL TIME: 20 MIN.

The ¼ tsp. garlic powder in this recipe equals 2 minced garlic cloves or 1 tsp. jarred minced garlic. Take your pick.

- 2 cups all-purpose baking mix
- ⅔ cup milk
- ½ cup (2 ounces) shredded Cheddar cheese
- ¼ cup butter, melted
- ¼ tsp. garlic powder

1. Preheat oven to 450°. Stir together first 3 ingredients until soft dough forms. Stir vigorously 30 seconds. Drop by tablespoonfuls onto an ungreased baking sheet.

2. Bake at 450° for 8 to 10 minutes.

3. Stir together butter and garlic powder; brush over warm biscuits.

Make-Ahead Favorites

Raspberry-Streusel Muffins

MAKES 1 DOZEN
HANDS-ON TIME: 15 MIN.
TOTAL TIME: 35 MIN.

The streusel (German for "sprinkle") makes a delicious crown for these sweet muffins. It's a crumbly topping of flour, butter, sugar, and, in this recipe, chopped pecans.

- 1¾ cups all-purpose flour, divided
- 2 tsp. baking powder
- ½ cup granulated sugar
- 1 large egg, lightly beaten
- ½ cup milk
- ½ cup plus 2 Tbsp. butter, melted and divided
- 1 cup frozen unsweetened raspberries
- ¼ cup chopped pecans
- ¼ cup firmly packed brown sugar

1. Preheat oven to 375°. Combine 1½ cups flour, 2 tsp. baking powder, and sugar in a large bowl; make a well in center of mixture.
2. Combine egg, milk, and ½ cup butter; add to dry ingredients, stirring just until dry ingredients are moistened. Fold in raspberries. Spoon mixture into a lightly greased muffin pan, filling two-thirds full.
3. Combine remaining ¼ cup flour, remaining 2 Tbsp. butter, pecans, and brown sugar; sprinkle over muffins.
4. Bake at 375° for 20 to 25 minutes. Remove from pan immediately.

Broccoli Cornbread Muffins

MAKES 2 DOZEN
HANDS-ON TIME: 20 MIN.
TOTAL TIME: 38 MIN.

- 1 (8½-oz.) package corn muffin mix
- 1 (10-oz.) package frozen chopped broccoli, thawed
- 1 cup (4 oz.) shredded Cheddar cheese
- 1 small onion, chopped
- 2 large eggs
- ½ cup butter, melted and slightly cooled

1. Preheat oven to 325°. Combine first 4 ingredients in a large bowl; make a well in center of mixture.
2. Stir together eggs and butter, blending well; add to broccoli mixture, stirring just until dry ingredients are moistened.
3. Spoon into lightly greased miniature (1¾-inch) muffin pans, filling three-fourths full.
4. Bake at 325° for 15 to 20 minutes or until golden. Let stand 2 to 3 minutes before removing from pans.

Herb Bread

MAKES 12 SERVINGS
HANDS-ON TIME: 10 MIN.
TOTAL TIME: 35 MIN.

A medley of herbs creates a savory bread suitable for any entrée or soup.

- 1 (16-oz.) French bread loaf
- 1 cup butter, softened
- 1 (2¼-oz.) can chopped ripe olives
- ½ cup chopped fresh parsley
- ⅓ cup chopped green onions
- 1½ tsp. dried basil
- ½ tsp. garlic powder
- ½ tsp. dried tarragon
- ¼ tsp. celery seeds

1. Preheat oven to 350°. Slice bread in half horizontally.
2. Combine butter and remaining 7 ingredients; spread evenly over cut sides of bread. Place halves together; wrap in aluminum foil. Store in refrigerator until ready to bake, if desired.
3. Bake at 350° for 25 minutes or until thoroughly heated. Cut into slices to serve.

The Grand Finale

Complete your meal with one of these desserts that you can prepare in advance.

Chocolate-Pecan Cookies

MAKES 4½ DOZEN
HANDS-ON TIME: 5 MIN.
TOTAL TIME: 37 MIN. PER BATCH

If you love cookies but are short on time, try making these chocolaty treats that start with a cake mix.

- 1 (18.25-oz.) package chocolate or yellow cake mix
- ½ cup vegetable oil
- 2 large eggs
- 1 cup (6 oz.) semisweet chocolate morsels
- ½ cup chopped pecans

1. Preheat oven to 350°. Beat first 3 ingredients at medium speed with an electric mixer until batter is smooth. Stir in chocolate morsels and pecans. Drop by heaping teaspoonfuls onto ungreased baking sheets.
2. Bake at 350° for 8 to 10 minutes. Remove to wire racks to cool.

Gooey Turtle Bars

MAKES 2 DOZEN
HANDS-ON TIME: 10 MIN.
TOTAL TIME: 55 MIN.

- ½ cup butter, melted
- 1½ cups vanilla wafer crumbs
- 1 (12-oz.) package semisweet chocolate morsels
- 1 cup pecan pieces
- 1 (12-oz.) jar caramel topping

1. Preheat oven to 350°. Combine butter and wafer crumbs in a 13- x 9-inch pan; press into bottom of pan. Sprinkle with morsels and pecans.
2. Remove lid from caramel topping; microwave at HIGH 1 to 1½ minutes or until hot, stirring after 30 seconds. Drizzle evenly over pecans.
3. Bake at 350° for 12 to 15 minutes or until morsels melt; cool in pan on a wire rack. Cover and chill at least 30 minutes; cut into bars.

Texas Millionaires

MAKES 2 DOZEN
HANDS-ON TIME: 25 MIN.
TOTAL TIME: 1 HR., 30 MIN.

- 1 (14-oz.) package caramels
- 2 Tbsp. butter
- 3 cups pecan halves
- 1 cup semisweet chocolate morsels
- 8 (2-oz.) vanilla candy coating squares

1. Cook caramels, butter, and 2 Tbsp. water in a heavy saucepan over low heat, stirring constantly until smooth. Stir in pecans. Cool in pan 5 minutes.
2. Drop by tablespoonfuls onto lightly greased wax paper. Chill 1 hour, or freeze 20 minutes until firm.
3. Melt morsels and candy coating in a heavy saucepan over low heat, stirring until smooth. Dip caramel candies into chocolate mixture, allowing excess to drip; place on lightly greased wax paper. Let stand until firm.

Streusel Blueberry Shortcake

MAKES 1 (8-INCH) CAKE
HANDS-ON TIME: 15 MIN.,
TOTAL TIME: 43 MIN.

- 3 cups all-purpose baking mix
- ⅔ cup milk
- ¼ cup butter, melted
- ½ cup firmly packed brown sugar
- ½ cup chopped pecans
- ¼ cup butter
- 1 (8-oz.) container frozen whipped topping, thawed
- 2 pints fresh blueberries

1. Preheat oven to 400°. Combine first 3 ingredients in a large bowl; stir until a soft dough forms. Spread dough evenly into 2 lightly greased 8-inch square pans.
2. Combine brown sugar and pecans; cut in ¼ cup butter with a pastry blender until mixture is crumbly. Sprinkle nut mixture over dough.
3. Bake, uncovered, at 400° for 18 minutes or until a wooden pick inserted in center comes out clean. Cool in pans on wire racks 10 minutes; remove from pans, and cool completely on wire racks.
4. Place 1 cake layer on a serving plate. Spread half of whipped topping over layer, and arrange half of blueberries on top. Repeat procedure with remaining cake layer, whipped topping, and blueberries. Chill cake until ready to serve.

Make-Ahead Favorites

German Chocolate Cheesecake

MAKES 12 SERVINGS
HANDS-ON TIME: 37 MIN.
TOTAL TIME: 9 HR., 22 MIN.

- 1 cup chocolate wafer crumbs
- 2 Tbsp. sugar
- 3 Tbsp. butter, melted
- 3 (8-oz.) packages cream cheese, softened
- ¾ cup sugar
- ¼ cup unsweetened cocoa
- 2 tsp. vanilla extract
- 3 large eggs
- ⅓ cup evaporated milk
- ⅓ cup sugar
- ¼ cup butter
- 1 large egg, lightly beaten
- ½ tsp. vanilla extract
- ½ cup coarsely chopped pecans, toasted
- ½ cup organic coconut chips or sweetened flaked coconut

1. Preheat oven to 325°. Stir together first 3 ingredients; press into bottom of an ungreased 9-inch springform pan. Bake at 325° for 10 minutes. Cool crust.
2. Increase oven temperature to 350°. Beat cream cheese and next 3 ingredients at medium speed with an electric mixer until blended. Add eggs, 1 at a time, beating just until blended after each addition. Pour into prepared crust.
3. Bake at 350° for 35 minutes. Remove from oven; run a knife around edge of pan. Cool completely in pan on a wire rack. Cover and chill 8 hours.
4. Stir together evaporated milk and next 4 ingredients in a saucepan. Cook over medium heat, stirring constantly, 7 minutes. Stir in pecans and coconut. Remove sides of pan; spread topping over cheesecake.

Citrus Cheesecake

MAKES 12 SERVINGS
HANDS-ON TIME: 8 MIN.
TOTAL TIME: 9 HR., 3 MIN.

The beauty of pomegranate seeds nestled against sectioned oranges and candied orange peel gives this creamy cheesecake grande dame status. Baking it in a water bath makes it extra creamy.

- 4 navel oranges
- 1 cup sugar, divided
- 2 cups graham cracker crumbs
- ½ cup butter, melted
- ⅓ cup sugar
- ½ tsp. ground ginger
- 3 (8-oz.) packages cream cheese, softened
- 1¼ cups sugar
- 1 (8-oz.) container sour cream
- 4 large eggs
- 1 Tbsp. lemon zest
- 2 tsp. vanilla extract
- 1 tsp. orange extract
- 1 large pomegranate, seeds removed

1. Preheat oven to 350°. Using a zester and working from top of orange to bottom, remove peel from oranges in long strips. Combine ¾ cup sugar and ¾ cup water in a small saucepan over medium-low heat, stirring until sugar dissolves. Bring to a boil; reduce heat, and simmer 2 minutes. Add orange peel; simmer 15 minutes.
2. Meanwhile, peel and section zested oranges. Seal orange sections in a zip-top plastic bag, and refrigerate until ready to garnish cheesecake.
3. Drain orange peel well. Toss with ¼ cup sugar in a small bowl. Place candied peel in a thin layer on wax paper to dry. Store in an airtight container up to 2 days.

4. Combine graham cracker crumbs and next 3 ingredients; stir well. Press mixture firmly on bottom and 2 inches up sides of a lightly greased 9-inch springform pan.
5. Bake at 350° for 14 to 16 minutes; let cool. Wrap bottom and sides of pan in aluminum foil, and place in a large roasting pan; set aside. (Wrapping the pan is insurance against leaks in case your pan is older and not 100% airtight.)
6. Beat cream cheese at medium-high speed with an electric mixer until creamy. Gradually add 1¼ cups sugar, beating just until blended. Add sour cream, beating just until blended. Add eggs, 1 at a time, beating well after each addition. Stir in lemon zest and extracts.
7. Pour batter into baked crust. Add hot water to roasting pan to a depth of 2 inches. Bake at 350° for 55 minutes or until edges are set and center is almost set. Carefully remove pan from water bath, and immediately run a knife around edge of pan. Cool completely on a wire rack; cover and chill 8 hours.
8. To serve cheesecake, remove sides of springform pan. Place cheesecake on a serving platter. Arrange orange sections in concentric circles on top of cake. Pile pomegranate seeds in center of cheesecake. Decorate with candied orange peel.

Make-Ahead Favorites

Slow-Cooker Rocky Road Chocolate Cake

MAKES 8 TO 10 SERVINGS
HANDS-ON TIME: 15 MIN.
TOTAL TIME: 4 HR., 3 MIN.

1 (18.25-oz.) package German chocolate cake mix
1 (3.9-oz.) package chocolate instant pudding mix
3 large eggs, lightly beaten
1 cup sour cream
⅓ cup butter, melted
1 tsp. vanilla extract
3¼ cups milk, divided
1 (3.4-oz.) package chocolate cook-and-serve pudding mix
½ cup chopped pecans, toasted
1½ cups miniature marshmallows
1 cup semisweet chocolate morsels
Vanilla ice cream (optional)

1. Beat cake mix, next 5 ingredients, and 1¼ cups milk at medium speed with an electric mixer 2 minutes, stopping to scrape down sides as needed. Pour batter into a lightly greased 4-qt. slow cooker.
2. Cook remaining 2 cups milk in a heavy nonaluminum saucepan over medium heat, stirring often, 3 to 5 minutes or just until bubbles appear (do not boil); remove from heat.
3. Sprinkle cook-and-serve pudding mix over batter. Slowly pour hot milk over pudding. Cover and cook on LOW 3 hours and 30 minutes.
4. Turn off slow cooker. Sprinkle cake with pecans, marshmallows, and chocolate morsels. Let stand, partially covered, 15 minutes or until marshmallows are slightly melted. (The cake will look like it needs to cook just a little longer, but by the time the topping is set, it's ready to serve.) Spoon into dessert dishes, and serve with ice cream, if desired.

Easiest Peanut Butter Cookies

MAKES 2½ DOZEN
HANDS-ON TIME: 20 MIN.
TOTAL TIME: 50 MIN.

1 cup peanut butter
1 cup sugar
1 large egg
1 tsp. vanilla extract

1. Preheat oven to 325°. Combine all ingredients in a large bowl; stir until blended. Shape dough into 1-inch balls. Place balls 1 inch apart on ungreased baking sheets, and flatten gently with tines of a fork.
2. Bake at 325° for 15 minutes or until golden brown. Remove to wire racks to cool completely.

Triple Chocolate-Nut Clusters

MAKES 6 DOZEN
HANDS-ON TIME: 13 MIN.
TOTAL TIME: 4 HR., 13 MIN.

Candy making has never been so easy! The slow cooker is the perfect tool to keep this candy mixture warm while you're spooning it out.

1 (16-oz.) jar dry-roasted peanuts
1 (9.75-oz.) can salted whole cashews
2 cups pecan pieces
18 (2-oz.) chocolate candy coating squares, cut in half
1 (12-oz.) package semisweet chocolate morsels
4 (1-oz.) bittersweet chocolate baking squares, broken into pieces
1 Tbsp. shortening
1 tsp. vanilla extract

1. Combine first 7 ingredients in a 5-qt. slow cooker; cover and cook on LOW 2 hours or until chocolate is melted. Add vanilla, stirring to coat.
2. Drop candy by heaping teaspoonfuls onto wax paper. Let stand at least 2 hours or until firm. Store in an airtight container.

Bayou Brownies

MAKES 8 SERVINGS
HANDS-ON TIME: 10 MIN.
TOTAL TIME: 50 MIN.

Don't think chocolate when you try these brownies. Instead, think pecans and sweet cream cheese topping.

1 cup chopped pecans
½ cup butter, melted
3 large eggs, divided
1 (18.25-oz.) package yellow cake mix
1 (8-oz.) package cream cheese, softened
1 (16-oz.) package powdered sugar

1. Preheat oven to 325°. Combine pecans, butter, 1 egg, and cake mix, stirring until well blended; press into mixture into bottom of a lightly greased 13- x 9-inch pan.
2. Beat remaining 2 eggs, cream cheese, and powdered sugar at medium speed with an electric mixer until smooth. Pour over cake mix layer.
3. Bake at 325° for 40 minutes or until set. Cool in pan on a wire rack. Cut into squares. Store in refrigerator.

Holiday Favorites

Christmas Express

Check out this easy and fast holiday fare—each recipe is ready in 30 minutes or less and many can be made ahead.

Spicy Crawfish Spread

make-ahead • quick prep

MAKES 2¼ CUPS
HANDS-ON TIME: 4 MIN.
TOTAL TIME: 10 MIN.

Serve this sassy Cajun spread with corn chips, vegetable crudités, or crackers.

- 3 Tbsp. butter
- ¾ cup finely diced onion
- ¾ cup finely diced celery
- 4 garlic cloves, minced
- 2 Tbsp. all-purpose salt-free seasoning blend
- ½ tsp. ground red pepper
- 8 oz. peeled, cooked crawfish tails, finely chopped
- 1 (8-oz.) package cream cheese, softened
  Garnish: celery leaf

1. Melt butter in a small skillet over medium-high heat. Add onion, celery, and garlic; sauté 5 minutes or until onion and celery are tender. Add seasoning blend and pepper; sauté 30 seconds. Combine sautéed vegetables and crawfish tails in a bowl. Add softened cream cheese, and stir gently to combine. Garnish, if desired.
Note: We tested with Paul Prudhomme's Magic Seasoning.

Orecchiette with Broccoli in Garlic Oil

quick prep

MAKES 4 SERVINGS
HANDS-ON TIME: 4 MIN.
TOTAL TIME: 26 MIN.

This simple pasta dish offers a nice way to get kids to eat broccoli.

- 1 Tbsp. salt
- 1 (12-oz.) package orecchiette pasta (about 4 cups) or other small shaped pasta
- 1 (12-oz.) package fresh broccoli florets
- ½ cup olive oil
- 8 garlic cloves, thinly sliced
- ¾ tsp. salt
- ¼ tsp. dried crushed red pepper
- 3 Tbsp. minced fresh flat-leaf parsley

1. Stir 1 Tbsp. salt and pasta into 3 qt. boiling water in a Dutch oven. Cook 3 minutes less than package directions state. Stir in broccoli florets; cook 3 minutes or until pasta is al dente, and broccoli is crisp-tender. Drain and return pasta and broccoli to Dutch oven.
2. While pasta cooks, combine olive oil and next 3 ingredients in a small saucepan. Cook over medium-low heat 6 minutes or until garlic is golden, stirring often. Remove from heat. Add garlic oil and parsley to pasta, and toss well. Serve hot.

Stovetop Sweet Potatoes with Maple and Crème Fraîche

quick prep

MAKES 8 TO 10 SERVINGS
HANDS-ON TIME: 8 MIN.
TOTAL TIME: 23 MIN.

These sweet potatoes are beaten with a mixer and heated on the stove, keeping your oven free for other holiday baking. Crème fraîche is the surprise ingredient blended in along with maple syrup for an indulgent twist to traditional sweet potato casserole. And, instead of marshmallow topping, try these cinnamon-glazed pecans. You won't be able to stop nibbling on them.

- 2 cinnamon sticks, broken
- ¼ cup sugar
- 3 Tbsp. butter
- 1 cup pecan halves
- ¼ tsp. salt
- 3 (15-oz.) cans candied yams or sweet potatoes in syrup, drained
- ¼ cup butter, softened
- 2 Tbsp. finely chopped crystallized ginger
- 1 tsp. salt
- ¼ tsp. freshly grated nutmeg
- 1 cup crème fraîche*
- ¼ cup pure maple syrup
- 1 tsp. maple extract or vanilla extract
- 1 tsp. balsamic vinegar

1. Grind cinnamon sticks to a fine powder in a coffee grinder; set aside.
2. Cook sugar and 3 Tbsp. butter in a small saucepan over medium-high heat 3 minutes or until melted and golden. Add pecans, and cook 2 minutes until pecans are toasted and glazed, stirring frequently.
3. Stir in cinnamon and ¼ tsp. salt. Spread pecans on wax paper, and set aside to cool.

4. Combine sweet potatoes, ¼ cup butter, ginger, 1 tsp. salt, and nutmeg in a large bowl. Beat at low speed with a hand mixer 1 minute; beat at high speed 2 minutes.

5. Gently fold crème fraîche, maple syrup, extract, and balsamic vinegar into sweet potatoes. Transfer to a saucepan. Bring to a simmer over medium-low heat. Simmer, covered, 10 minutes, stirring occasionally. Spoon potatoes into a serving dish, and sprinkle with glazed pecans.

*Find crème fraîche with other specialty cheeses in the deli section of many upscale markets.

Raspberry-Glazed Beets with Chèvre

quick prep

MAKES 8 SERVINGS
HANDS-ON TIME: 2 MIN.
TOTAL TIME: 17 MIN.

Goat cheese makes a wonderful finishing touch for these slightly sweet, quick-to-heat beets.

- ¾ cup chicken broth
- ½ cup red raspberry preserves
- ¼ tsp. salt
- 3 (14½-oz.) cans sliced beets, drained
- ¼ cup butter
- ¼ cup crumbled chèvre

1. Bring first 3 ingredients to a boil in a large saucepan over high heat. Add beets, and boil 8 to 10 minutes or until liquid is reduced to a syrup, stirring often. Remove from heat. Stir in butter. Top each serving with crumbled chèvre. Serve immediately.
Note: We tested with Smucker's Simply Fruit.

Roasted Broccoli with Orange-Chipotle Butter

quick prep

MAKES 6 TO 8 SERVINGS
HANDS-ON TIME: 2 MIN.
TOTAL TIME: 17 MIN.

Here's a high-flavored side dish worthy of the finest dinner menu. Fresh orange flavor and smoky chipotle pepper hit hot roasted broccoli and sizzle with goodness. Chicken, beef, or pork make fine partners.

- 2 (12-oz.) packages fresh broccoli florets
- 2 Tbsp. olive oil
- ¼ cup butter, softened
- 2 tsp. orange zest
- 1 tsp. minced canned chipotle peppers in adobo sauce
- ½ tsp. salt

1. Preheat oven to 450°. Combine broccoli and oil in a large bowl; toss to coat. Place broccoli in a single layer on an ungreased jelly-roll pan. Roast at 450° for 15 to 17 minutes or until broccoli is crisp-tender.
2. While broccoli roasts, combine butter and next 3 ingredients in a large bowl. Add roasted broccoli to bowl, and toss to coat. Serve hot.

Crisp Chicken with Hearts of Palm Salad

quick prep

MAKES 4 SERVINGS
HANDS-ON TIME: 17 MIN.
TOTAL TIME: 26 MIN.

- 4 skinned and boned chicken breasts (about 1½ lb.)
- 1 cup Japanese breadcrumbs (panko)
- 1 large egg
- ½ tsp. salt
- ½ tsp. freshly ground black pepper, divided
- 5 Tbsp. olive oil, divided
- 1 (14-oz.) can hearts of palm, drained and sliced
- ½ cup diced red onion
- 1 small green bell pepper, diced
- 1 Tbsp. red wine vinegar
- 2 Tbsp. chopped fresh flat-leaf parsley or cilantro
  Garnish: flat-leaf parsley or cilantro

1. Place chicken between 2 sheets of heavy-duty plastic wrap; flatten to ¼-inch thickness using a meat mallet or rolling pin. Spread breadcrumbs in a shallow plate. Beat egg in a shallow bowl.
2. Sprinkle chicken with salt and ¼ tsp. pepper. Dip 1 chicken breast in beaten egg; coat with breadcrumbs. Repeat with remaining chicken. Cook chicken in ¼ cup hot oil in a large skillet over medium-high heat 4 minutes on each side or until done.
3. While chicken cooks, make salad. Gently toss together remaining 1 Tbsp. oil, remaining ¼ tsp. pepper, hearts of palm, and next 4 ingredients. Serve chicken topped with salad. Garnish, if desired.

HolidayFavorites

Turkey and Black Bean Chili

make-ahead • quick prep

MAKES 6 CUPS
HANDS-ON TIME: 5 MIN.
TOTAL TIME: 24 MIN.

Take advantage of packaged seasoning mixes, such as the chili mix called for below. Seasoning mixes are great because they include a number of spices in one package so they cut down on the time it takes to measure individual spices. We used canned black beans here but pinto or kidney beans are equally good.

- 2 Tbsp. olive oil
- 1¼ lb. ground turkey
- ½ tsp. salt
- 1 large onion, chopped
- 2 Tbsp. chopped garlic
- 1 (1.25-oz.) package chili seasoning mix
- 1 (15-oz.) can diced tomatoes in sauce or crushed tomatoes in puree
- 1 cup chicken broth
- 1 chipotle pepper in adobo sauce, chopped
- 1 Tbsp. adobo sauce
- 1 (15-oz.) can black beans, rinsed and drained
  Toppings: sour cream, shredded Monterey Jack cheese, fresh cilantro sprigs, diced avocado

1. Heat oil in a Dutch oven over medium-high heat. Add turkey and salt; cook, stirring until turkey crumbles and is no longer pink. Push meat to outer edges of pan, and add onion and garlic to center of pan. Sauté 3 minutes.
2. Add chili seasoning, and cook 1 minute. Add tomatoes, broth, chipotle pepper, and 1 Tbsp. adobo sauce. Bring to a boil. Cover, reduce heat, and simmer 5 minutes. Add beans; cook 5 minutes or until thoroughly heated. Serve with desired toppings.

Monterey Jack Omelets with Bacon, Avocado, and Salsa

quick prep

MAKES 2 SERVINGS
HANDS-ON TIME: 9 MIN.
TOTAL TIME: 16 MIN.

Omelets make wonderful quick suppers. This southwestern-flavored omelet makes two hefty servings or serves four.

- 6 fully cooked bacon slices
- 1 cup (4 oz.) shredded Monterey Jack cheese, divided
- 1 avocado, diced
- ¼ cup bottled salsa
- ¼ cup minced fresh cilantro
- 6 large eggs
- 2 Tbsp. water
- ½ tsp. salt
- ¼ tsp. freshly ground black pepper
- ¼ cup butter, divided

1. Reheat bacon according to package directions until crisp; coarsely crumble. Stir together bacon, ½ cup cheese, avocado, and salsa; set aside to use as filling. Combine remaining ½ cup cheese and cilantro in a bowl.
2. Whisk together eggs, water, salt, and pepper. Melt 2 Tbsp. butter in a 9-inch nonstick skillet over medium-high heat. Pour half of egg mixture into skillet, and sprinkle with half of cilantro-cheese mixture. As egg starts to cook, gently lift edges of omelet with a spatula, and tilt pan so uncooked portion flows underneath. Sprinkle 1 side of omelet with half of bacon filling. Fold in half. Cook over medium-low heat 45 seconds. Remove from pan, and keep warm. Repeat procedure with remaining butter, egg mixture, cilantro-cheese mixture, and bacon filling. Serve hot.

Sausage Italian Bread Pizza

MAKES 4 SERVINGS
HANDS-ON TIME: 12 MIN.
TOTAL TIME: 31 MIN.

Choose your favorite sauce for this quick pizza. Most supermarkets have a good selection of jarred pasta and pizza sauces ranging in flavor from simple marinara to roasted pepper.

- 1 lb. mild or hot Italian sausage
- 2 Tbsp. olive oil, divided
- 1 onion, halved and thinly sliced
- 2 garlic cloves, minced
- 1 cup pizza or pasta sauce
- 1½ tsp. dried oregano
- ¼ tsp. dried crushed red pepper
- ¼ tsp. salt
- 1 (1-lb.) loaf semolina bread (about 14 inches long)
- ⅔ cup ricotta cheese, divided
- 2 cups (8 oz.) shredded mozzarella cheese, divided
- ¼ cup grated Parmesan cheese, divided

1. Preheat oven to 425°. Remove and discard casings from sausage. Cook sausage in a large skillet over medium-high heat 8 minutes, stirring until meat crumbles and is no longer pink. Push meat to outer edges of pan; add 1 Tbsp. oil. Add onion and garlic; cook 5 minutes or until onion is softened. Remove from heat; stir in pizza sauce and next 3 ingredients.
2. Cut bread in half lengthwise using a serrated knife, and scoop out center of each bread half, leaving a ½-inch border; discard scooped-out bread or reserve for making breadcrumbs.
3. Spread ⅓ cup ricotta down center of each bread half. Top each evenly with sausage mixture, mozzarella, and

Parmesan cheese. Drizzle pizzas evenly with remaining 1 Tbsp. oil. Place pizzas on a lightly greased baking sheet.
4. Bake at 425° for 6 minutes or until cheese is melted and pizzas are thoroughly heated.

Pepper Steak with Roasted Red Pepper Pesto

quick prep

MAKES 4 TO 6 SERVINGS
HANDS-ON TIME: 4 MIN.
TOTAL TIME: 19 MIN.

Using a grill pan allows you to grill year-round. A cast-iron skillet works well as a grill pan substitute.

- 1½ lb. sirloin steak (1½ inch thick)
- ½ tsp. salt
- 1 Tbsp. coarsely ground black pepper
- 2 Tbsp. olive oil
- 1 (7-oz.) jar refrigerated pesto
- 1 (7-oz.) jar roasted red bell peppers, drained and chopped
- 1 Tbsp. lemon juice

1. Sprinkle both sides of steak with salt and 1 Tbsp. pepper; brush with olive oil. Place grill pan over medium-high heat until hot. Cook steak in hot grill pan 5 to 7 minutes on each side or until desired degree of doneness. Transfer steak to a carving board, and let stand 5 minutes.
2. Meanwhile, combine pesto, chopped roasted red pepper, and lemon juice in a small bowl.
3. Cut steak into thin slices, and transfer to a serving platter. Serve with red pepper pesto.

Broiled Sirloin with Smoky Bacon Mushrooms

quick prep

MAKES 4 TO 6 SERVINGS
HANDS-ON TIME: 8 MIN.
TOTAL TIME: 29 MIN.

Using precooked bacon and presliced mushrooms gets this gourmet fare to the table fast.

- 4 fully cooked hickory-smoked bacon slices
- 1 medium onion, cut vertically into thin slices
- 1 Tbsp. butter, melted
- 2 garlic cloves, minced
- 2 (8-oz.) packages sliced fresh mushrooms
- 1¾ tsp. salt, divided
- 3 Tbsp. chopped fresh flat-leaf parsley
- ⅛ tsp. freshly ground black pepper
- 2 (1-lb.) sirloin steaks (1¼ inch thick)
- ½ tsp. freshly ground black pepper

1. Preheat oven to broil. Reheat bacon according to package directions until crisp; coarsely crumble. Sauté onion in butter in a large skillet over medium heat 5 minutes until beginning to brown. Stir in garlic, mushrooms, and ¾ tsp. salt. Sauté 10 minutes or until mushrooms are tender and liquid evaporates. Stir in bacon, parsley, and ⅛ tsp. pepper.
2. While mushrooms cook, sprinkle both sides of steaks with remaining 1 tsp. salt and ½ tsp. pepper.
3. Broil 5½ inches from heat 7 minutes on each side or until desired degree of doneness. Let stand 5 minutes before slicing. Cut steaks into thin slices; arrange on a serving platter, and top with mushrooms.

Chicken with Cranberry Mojo

quick prep

MAKES 4 SERVINGS
HANDS-ON TIME: 9 MIN.
TOTAL TIME: 15 MIN.

- 1 tsp. salt
- 1 tsp. ground cumin
- ½ tsp. ground coriander
- ¼ tsp. freshly ground black pepper
- 6 skinned and boned chicken breasts
- 2 Tbsp. olive oil
  Cranberry Mojo

1. Combine first 4 ingredients in a small bowl; set aside.
2. Place chicken breasts between 2 sheets of heavy-duty plastic wrap, and flatten to ¼-inch thickness using a meat mallet or rolling pin.
3. Sprinkle chicken with spice mixture. Cook chicken in hot oil in a large nonstick skillet over medium heat 2 to 3 minutes on each side or until done. Serve with Cranberry Mojo.

Cranberry Mojo

MAKES 1½ CUPS
HANDS-ON TIME: 10 MIN.
TOTAL TIME: 10 MIN.

- 2 cups fresh cranberries
- ½ cup frozen cranberry juice concentrate, thawed
- ¼ cup fresh cilantro leaves
- 2 Tbsp. olive oil
- 1 Tbsp. fresh lime juice
- 1 Tbsp. honey
- 1 garlic clove, sliced
- ¼ tsp. ground cumin
- ¼ tsp. salt

1. Combine all ingredients in a food processor; pulse 3 times or until mixture is coarsely chopped. Serve over chicken.

Cranberry Chicken Salad Empanadas

quick prep

MAKES 8 EMPANADAS
HANDS-ON TIME: 10 MIN.
TOTAL TIME: 26 MIN.

Look for a premium, freshly made deli chicken salad, or use leftover holiday turkey. One empanada makes the perfect appetizer; two with a small salad fit the entrée bill.

- 1 (14.1-oz.) package refrigerated piecrusts
- 1 cup deli chicken salad
- ⅓ cup sweetened dried cranberries
- ⅓ cup pecan pieces, toasted
- 1 large egg, lightly beaten

1. Preheat oven to 400°. Working with 1 crust at a time, unroll piecrust according to package directions onto a lightly floured surface. Cut each piecrust into 4 (4½-inch) circles.
2. Combine chicken salad, cranberries, and pecans in a bowl. Spoon about 2 Tbsp. chicken salad mixture in center of each circle. Brush edges of circles with beaten egg. Fold dough over filling for each empanada, pressing edges with a fork to seal. Place empanadas onto a lightly greased baking sheet, and brush with beaten egg. Repeat procedure with remaining piecrust circles, chicken salad mixture, and beaten egg.
3. Bake at 400° for 16 minutes or until lightly browned. Serve warm or at room temperature.

Cranberry Parfaits

quick prep

MAKES 6 SERVINGS
HANDS-ON TIME: 22 MIN.
TOTAL TIME: 22 MIN.

You can also serve this tasty holiday dessert in wine glasses or other festive glasses for a pretty presentation.

- 1¼ cups fresh or frozen cranberries
- ½ cup light corn syrup
- 1 tsp. orange zest
- 1 cup whipping cream
- 1 cup sifted powdered sugar
- 1½ cups sour cream
- ½ tsp. vanilla extract
  Garnish: cranberries cut in half

1. Process 1¼ cups cranberries and corn syrup in a food processor until finely chopped. Transfer to a small bowl, and stir in orange zest.
2. Beat whipping cream until foamy; gradually add powdered sugar, beating until stiff peaks form.
3. Stir together sour cream and vanilla in a medium bowl. Fold in half of whipped cream. Fold in remaining whipped cream.
4. Spoon about 1 Tbsp. cranberry syrup into each of 6 parfait glasses; top with about ⅓ cup sour cream mixture. Repeat layers once. Garnish, if desired.

Ginger Streusel-Topped Cheesecake

editor's favorite • quick prep

MAKES 8 SERVINGS
HANDS-ON TIME: 5 MIN.
TOTAL TIME: 21 MIN.

This easy dressed-up cheesecake is topped with big chunks of crunchy ginger-snap streusel. Serve it warm from the oven, and scoop it into dessert bowls.

- 1 cup coarsely crushed gingersnaps
- 2½ cups butter, softened
- ½ cup sugar
- ½ cup all-purpose flour
- 1 Tbsp. finely chopped crystallized ginger
- 1 (30-oz.) frozen New York-style cheesecake

1. Preheat oven to 425°. Combine first 5 ingredients, mixing well with a spoon. Sprinkle streusel over top of frozen cheesecake. Bake at 425° for 16 to 19 minutes or until streusel is browned. Scoop warm cheesecake into serving bowls.
Note: We tested with Nabisco Ginger-snaps and Sara Lee Cheesecake.

Ginger Streusel-Topped Pumpkin Pie: Prepare topping as directed for cheesecake. Sprinkle topping over a small deli-baked pumpkin pie. Bake again at 425° for 18 to 20 minutes to brown the streusel. Let stand 15 minutes. Slice to serve.

Cheesecake-Stuffed Dark Chocolate Cake

editor's favorite • make-ahead

MAKES 12 SERVINGS
HANDS-ON TIME: 26 MIN.
TOTAL TIME: 2 HR., 8 MIN.

Though it isn't ready in 30 minutes, there's a lot that's express about this grand cake. It's even better once you've chilled it.

    Unsweetened cocoa
1   (18.25-oz.) package devil's food cake mix
1   (3.4-oz.) package chocolate instant pudding mix
3   large eggs
1¼ cups milk
1   cup canola oil
1   Tbsp. vanilla extract
1½ tsp. chocolate extract (optional)
1   tsp. almond extract
3   (1.55-oz.) milk chocolate bars, chopped
3   (16-oz.) cans homestyle cream cheese frosting
3   (7.75-oz.) boxes frozen cheesecake bites, coarsely chopped
1   (12-oz.) jar dulce de leche caramel sauce
    Double chocolate rolled wafer cookies, coarsely broken
    Chocolate fudge rolled wafer cookies, coarsely broken

1. Preheat oven to 350°. Grease 2 (9-inch) round cake pans, and dust with cocoa.
2. Beat cake mix and next 7 ingredients at low speed with an electric mixer 1 minute; then beat at medium speed 2 minutes. Fold in chopped milk chocolate bars. Pour batter into prepared pans.
3. Bake at 350° for 32 minutes or until cake springs back when lightly touched. Cool cake in pans on wire racks 10 minutes; remove from pans, and cool completely on wire racks. Wrap and chill cake layers at least 1 hour or up to 24 hours. (This step enables you to split cake layers with ease.)
4. Using a serrated knife, slice cake layers in half horizontally to make 4 layers. Place 1 layer, cut side up, on a cake plate. Spread with ½ cup cream cheese frosting; sprinkle with one-fourth of chopped cheesecake bites. Repeat procedure with remaining 3 layers, frosting, and cheesecake bites, omitting cheesecake bites on top of last layer. Frost top and sides of cake with remaining frosting. Drizzle desired amount of caramel sauce over cake, letting it drip down sides. Chill until ready to serve. Decorate cake with rolled wafer cookies and remaining chopped cheesecake bites. Store in refrigerator.
Note: We tested with Hershey's Chocolate Bars, Sara Lee Frozen Cheesecake Bites, Smucker's Dulce de Leche Caramel Sauce, Pirouline Chocolate Rolled Wafer Cookies, and Pepperidge Farm Fudge Rolled Wafer Cookies.

Snacks & Munchies Swap

Move over cookie swap; this get-together encourages savory or sweet pickup food of all kinds to sample and share with friends.

Christmas Gorp

quick prep

MAKES 18 CUPS
HANDS-ON TIME: 25 MIN.
TOTAL TIME: 25 MIN.

1½ cups white chocolate baking morsels
¾   cup creamy peanut butter
¼   cup plus 2 Tbsp. butter
1   Tbsp. honey
¼   tsp. ground cinnamon (optional)
8   cups crispy corn and rice cereal squares
1   (8-oz.) package pretzel-flavored fish-shaped crackers (3 cups)
1½ cups powdered sugar
2   cups salted, roasted almonds with skins
2   cups red and green candy-coated chocolate pieces
1½ cups sweetened dried cranberries or raisins

1. Combine first 4 ingredients and cinnamon, if desired, in a heavy saucepan. Cook over medium heat, stirring until morsels and butter melt. Place cereal and crackers in a large bowl; add melted white chocolate mixture. Stir until well coated. Let cool slightly.
2. Place powdered sugar in a large zip-top plastic bag. Add coated cereal mixture in batches; seal bag, and toss well to coat. Combine sugar-coated cereal mixture, almonds, and remaining ingredients in a large bowl. Stir gently to blend. Store in an airtight container.
Note: We tested with Crispix Cereal Squares.

Rocky Road Granola Clusters

gift idea • make-ahead • quick prep

MAKES 2 DOZEN

HANDS-ON TIME: 20 MIN.

TOTAL TIME: 25 MIN.

Look for sesame sticks in grocery markets that sell bulk nuts, candies, and snack mixes.

- 1 (16-oz.) package chocolate candy coating, chopped
- 2 Tbsp. shortening
- ¼ cup creamy peanut butter
- 2 to 3 cups coarsely chopped granola bars
- ¾ cup sesame sticks or thin pretzels
- 3 Tbsp. slivered almonds, toasted
- 1 cup miniature marshmallows
- 12 caramels, chopped

1. Combine chocolate coating and shortening in a large microwave-safe bowl; cover loosely with heavy-duty plastic wrap. Microwave at HIGH 1½ minutes or until melted, stirring once. Stir in peanut butter. Let stand 2 minutes. Stir in granola bars, sesame sticks, and almonds. Stir in marshmallows and caramels last so they don't melt. Drop by rounded tablespoonfuls onto parchment or wax paper. Let clusters stand until firm.

Note: We tested with Nature Valley Maple Brown Sugar Granola Bars.

Holiday Fortune Cookies

make-ahead

MAKES ABOUT 2 DOZEN

HANDS-ON TIME: 5 MIN.

TOTAL TIME: 15 MIN.

Wear gloves while shaping these fortune cookies fresh from the oven. They cool and crisp quickly, so bake and shape them two at a time. Bake more at one time if you have helpers. To make paper fortunes, type them, triple spaced, on a computer. Cut them out, fold in half, and place in middle of cookies before folding.

- ½ cup all-purpose flour
- 1 Tbsp. cornstarch
- ¼ cup sugar
- ¼ tsp. salt
- ¼ tsp. ground cinnamon
- ⅛ tsp. ground nutmeg
- ¼ cup canola oil
- 2 egg whites
- 1 tsp. vanilla extract
- 2 (2-oz.) vanilla candy coating squares
  Red decorator sugar
  Purple decorator sugar

1. Preheat oven to 300°. Whisk together first 6 ingredients in a medium bowl. Add oil and egg whites, whisking until smooth. Whisk in 1 Tbsp. water and vanilla.

2. Drop a rounded teaspoonful of batter onto a well-greased baking sheet. Using back of a spoon, spread batter into a 3-inch circle. Repeat procedure with another rounded teaspoonful of batter. Bake at 300° for 10 to 12 minutes or until light golden brown.

3. Working quickly, immediately remove each cookie from pan with a spatula, and flip over into gloved hand; place prepared fortune in center of each cookie, and fold each cookie in half. Grasp end of each cookie, and

place over the edge of a bowl, drawing the edges down to form a crease. Place cookies, ends down, in muffin pans to maintain shape; let cookies cool completely. Repeat procedure with remaining batter, baking 2 cookies at a time.

4. To decorate, microwave vanilla coating in a small bowl at MEDIUM (50% power) 2 minutes, stirring after 1 minute. Dip outer edge of each cookie in vanilla coating, and then into red or purple sugar; set aside to let coating harden.

Crispy Chocolate Popcorn

MAKES 29 CUPS

HANDS-ON TIME: 30 MIN.

TOTAL TIME: 1 HR., 30 MIN.

- 2 cups milk chocolate morsels, divided
- 1½ cups firmly packed light brown sugar
- ¾ cup butter
- ¾ cup light corn syrup
- ¾ tsp. salt
- 1½ tsp. vanilla extract
- ¾ tsp. baking soda
- 2 (3.5-oz.) bags natural-flavored microwave popcorn, popped
- 2 cups peanuts or cashews

1. Preheat oven to 250°. Combine 1 cup chocolate morsels, brown sugar, and next 3 ingredients in a heavy saucepan; cook over medium heat, stirring constantly, until mixture comes to a boil. Remove from heat, and stir in vanilla and baking soda.

2. Distribute popcorn and nuts evenly into 2 lightly greased roasting pans. Be sure to remove all unpopped kernels of popcorn before pouring chocolate mixture over popcorn. Pour chocolate

mixture evenly over popcorn and nuts, stirring well with a lightly greased spatula.

3. Bake at 250° for 1 hour, stirring every 15 minutes. Spread on wax paper to cool, breaking apart large clumps as mixture cools. Sprinkle remaining 1 cup chocolate morsels over hot popcorn; let cool. Store in airtight containers.

Famous Sausage Ball Muffins

make-ahead

MAKES 4 DOZEN
HANDS-ON TIME: 5 MIN.
TOTAL TIME: 18 MIN.

This recipe has been around for years, and every cook has definite opinions and memories related to it. We found the recipe fun to revisit as easy mini muffins and with some flavor variations.

- 2 cups all-purpose baking mix
- 1 lb. hot or regular pork sausage
- 2 cups (8 oz.) shredded sharp Cheddar cheese)

1. Preheat oven to 400°. Combine all ingredients in a large bowl, pressing together with hands. Spoon rounded tablespoonfuls into lightly greased miniature (1¾-inch) muffin pans. Bake at 400° for 13 to 15 minutes or until lightly browned. Remove from pans, and serve warm with desired sauce, such as Ranch dressing, honey mustard, or barbecue sauce.
Note: We tested with Jimmy Dean Pork Sausage and Cracker Barrel Cheddar cheese.

To make traditional Sausage Balls, shape mixture into ¾-inch balls, and place on ungreased baking sheets. Bake at 400° for 15 to 18 minutes or until lightly browned. Makes about 8 dozen. Freeze uncooked sausage balls, if desired. Bake frozen balls for 18 to 20 minutes.

Dressed-Up Sausage Ball Muffins: Add ⅓ cup finely chopped onion, 1 Tbsp. garlic powder, and ¼ tsp. hot sauce to sausage-cheese dough. Proceed with recipe. Makes 4 dozen.

Southwest Sausage Ball Muffins: Use Pepper Jack cheese instead of Cheddar, and add 1 (4.5-oz.) can chopped green chiles, drained and patted dry with paper towels, to sausage-cheese dough. Bake 20 minutes. Makes about 4½ dozen.

Mediterranean Sausage Ball Muffins: Add ⅔ cup chopped pimiento-stuffed green olives. Use 1 cup Cheddar cheese and 1 cup crumbled feta cheese. Proceed with recipe. Makes about 4½ dozen.

Sausage Ball Cocktail: Skewer 2 or 3 warm Sausage Balls onto a small wooden pick or skewer. Spoon a few tablespoons of Ranch dressing into a martini glass; add skewered sausage balls. Makes about 4 dozen.

Sea Salt and Cracked Pepper Pita Chips

make-ahead • quick prep

MAKES 4 DOZEN CHIPS
HANDS-ON TIME: 6 MIN.
TOTAL TIME: 21 MIN.

- 3 (6-inch) pita rounds
- ¼ cup olive oil
- ½ tsp. sea salt
- ½ tsp. freshly ground black pepper

1. Preheat oven to 350°. Split each pita round into 2 rounds. Cut each round into 8 wedges. Place wedges onto a lightly greased baking sheet. Brush rough side of each wedge with oil. Sprinkle with salt and pepper. Bake at 350° for 15 minutes or until crisp. Transfer to wire racks to cool.

Parmesan-Herb Pita Chips

make-ahead • quick prep

MAKES 4 DOZEN CHIPS
HANDS-ON TIME: 6 MIN.
TOTAL TIME: 21 MIN.

- ⅓ cup olive oil
- 4 tsp. dried Italian seasoning
- 1 tsp. garlic salt
- 3 (6-inch) pita rounds
- ½ cup freshly grated Parmesan cheese

1. Preheat oven to 350°. Combine olive oil, Italian seasoning, and garlic salt.
2. Split each pita round into 2 rounds. Cut each round into 8 wedges. Place wedges on a lightly greased baking sheet. Brush rough side of each wedge with oil mixture. Sprinkle wedges with cheese. Bake at 350° for 15 minutes or until crisp. Transfer to wire racks to cool.

Taco Pita Chips

make-ahead • quick prep

MAKES 4 DOZEN CHIPS
HANDS-ON TIME: 6 MIN.
TOTAL TIME: 21 MIN.

- ¼ cup olive oil
- 1½ Tbsp. taco seasoning
- 3 (6-inch) pita rounds
- 1 (8-oz.) package shredded Mexican four-cheese blend

1. Preheat oven to 350°. Combine olive oil and taco seasoning in a small bowl.
2. Split each pita round into 2 rounds. Cut each round into 8 wedges. Place wedges on a lightly greased baking sheet. Brush rough side of each wedge with oil mixture. Sprinkle wedges with cheese. Bake at 350° for 15 minutes or until crisp. Remove from oven; transfer to wire racks to cool.

Barbecue Pita Chips

make-ahead • quick prep

MAKES 4 DOZEN CHIPS
HANDS-ON TIME: 6 MIN.
TOTAL TIME: 21 MIN.

- ¼ cup butter, melted
- 1½ Tbsp. barbecue seasoning
- 1½ Tbsp. lemon juice
- 3 (6-inch) pita rounds

1. Preheat oven to 350°. Combine butter, barbecue seasoning, and lemon juice in a small bowl.
2. Split each pita round into 2 rounds. Cut each round into 8 wedges. Place wedges on a lightly greased baking sheet. Brush rough side of each wedge with butter mixture. Bake at 350° for 15 minutes or until crisp. Remove from oven; transfer to wire racks to cool.
Note: We tested with McCormick Grill Mates Barbecue Seasoning.

Bacon, Cheddar, and Ranch Pita Chips

make-ahead • quick prep

MAKES 4 DOZEN CHIPS
HANDS-ON TIME: 6 MIN.
TOTAL TIME: 21 MIN.

- ¼ cup olive oil
- 1½ Tbsp. Ranch dressing mix
- 3 (6-inch) pita rounds
- ⅓ cup real bacon bits
- ½ cup (2 oz.) shredded sharp Cheddar cheese

1. Preheat oven to 350°. Combine olive oil and dressing mix in a small bowl.
2. Split each pita round into 2 rounds. Cut each round into 8 wedges. Place wedges on a lightly greased baking sheet. Brush rough side of each wedge with oil mixture. Sprinkle wedges with bacon bits and then cheese. Bake at 350° for 15 minutes or until crisp. Remove from oven; transfer to wire racks to cool.
Note: We tested with Hormel Real Bacon Bits.

Simple Christmas

Keep things simple this holiday season. Start with these innovative and practically effortless recipes to stir you toward your goal.

Parmesan-Peppercorn Snowflakes

quick prep

MAKES 20 SNOWFLAKES
HANDS-ON TIME: 7 MIN.
TOTAL TIME: 14 MIN.

These delicate, cheesy gems are perfect for an appetizer buffet served alongside mixed nuts and olives.

- 2 cups freshly shredded Parmigiano-Reggiano cheese
- ½ tsp. crushed tricolor peppercorn blend

1. Preheat oven to 425°. Drop cheese by slightly heaping tablespoonfuls onto parchment paper-lined baking sheets, and spread into 3½-inch rounds. Sprinkle each portion of cheese lightly with crushed peppercorns. Bake at 425° for 5 to 6 minutes or until bubbly and browned. Cool for 2 to 3 minutes on baking sheets. Remove with a metal spatula to wire racks to cool completely (cheese crisps up as it cools).

Jalapeño-Cheese Sausage Cups

quick prep

MAKES 30 APPETIZERS
HANDS-ON TIME: 9 MIN.
TOTAL TIME: 23 MIN.

Serve these spicy sausage cups as pickup food for a ball game get-together.

- 1 lb. hot ground pork sausage
- ½ cup Ranch dressing
- 2 (2.1-oz.) packages frozen mini-phyllo pastry shells, thawed
- ½ cup pickled jalapeño slices, drained
- ½ cup shredded sharp Cheddar cheese

1. Preheat oven to 350°. Brown sausage in a large skillet over medium-high heat, stirring to crumble; drain. Return sausage to skillet; stir in Ranch dressing. Spoon sausage mixture evenly into phyllo shells. Place shells on a baking sheet. Top sausage cups evenly with pepper slices; sprinkle with cheese. Bake at 350° for 8 to 10 minutes or until pastry shells are browned.

Honey-Roasted Grape Tomato Crostini

editor's favorite • quick prep

MAKES 31 CROSTINI
HANDS-ON TIME: 2 MIN.
TOTAL TIME: 22 MIN.

1 pt. grape tomatoes
1 Tbsp. honey
1½ tsp. olive oil
¼ tsp. kosher salt
1 (4-oz.) log goat cheese
1 (6- to 8-oz.) container crostini*
Garnish: fresh rosemary

1. Preheat oven to 450°. Toss together first 3 ingredients on a lightly greased rimmed baking sheet. Bake at 450° for 20 minutes or until tomato skins burst and begin to wrinkle (do not stir). Transfer roasted tomatoes to a bowl, scraping accumulated juices into bowl. Stir salt into tomato mixture.
2. Microwave goat cheese at HIGH 8 to 10 seconds to soften. Smear goat cheese evenly over crostini; top with roasted tomatoes. Serve on a platter; garnish, if desired.
*We found numerous sizes of crostini packages available at large grocery chains. Look for a 6- to 8-oz. container so that you'll have plenty for this recipe. Enjoy any leftovers as croutons over salad greens.

Creole Fried Bow-Ties

make-ahead

MAKES 6 CUPS
HANDS-ON TIME: 7 MIN.
TOTAL TIME: 16 MIN.

This crispy snack is simply pasta that's cooked and then tossed in a spicy corn-meal coating and quickly fried. Serve these nibbles hot or at room temperature.

1 (8-oz.) package bow-tie pasta
⅓ cup yellow cornmeal
3 Tbsp. spicy Creole seasoning
Vegetable oil

1. Cook pasta according to package directions; drain well, and blot pasta dry with paper towels. Combine corn-meal and Creole seasoning in a large bowl. Toss pasta, a handful at a time, in cornmeal mixture to coat; shake off excess.
2. Pour oil to a depth of 2 inches in a Dutch oven; heat over medium-high heat to 375°. Fry pasta, in batches, 3 to 4 minutes or until golden brown. Drain on paper towels. Store pasta snacks up to a week in an airtight container.
Note: We tested with Tony Chachere's More Spice Creole Seasoning.

Balsamic-Splashed Bacon and Arugula Canapés

quick prep

MAKES 1 DOZEN
HANDS-ON TIME: 9 MIN.
TOTAL TIME: 14 MIN.

Ricotta salata is a dry salted ricotta cheese that can be found in specialty grocery stores.

6 fully cooked bacon slices
2 tsp. honey
⅛ tsp. ground red pepper
12 (½-inch-thick) French baguette slices, lightly toasted
24 arugula leaves
12 thinly shaved pieces ricotta salata or Parmesan cheese
2 Tbsp. balsamic glaze*

1. Preheat oven to 375°. Place bacon on a baking sheet lined with aluminum foil. Combine honey and pepper; brush onto bacon. Bake at 375° for 5 minutes or until hot. Cut bacon in half crosswise.
2. Place baguette slices on a serving platter; top with arugula leaves. Arrange bacon and cheese on arugula. Drizzle each canapé with ½ tsp. balsamic glaze. Serve immediately.
Note: We tested with Gia Russa Balsamic Glaze.
*Make your own balsamic glaze by reducing balsamic vinegar. Cook ½ cup balsamic vinegar in a small saucepan over medium heat 9 minutes or until syrupy and reduced to 3 Tbsp. Cool completely.

Pecan, Olive, and Parmesan Rugelach

quick prep

MAKES 16 PASTRIES
HANDS-ON TIME: 12 MIN.
TOTAL TIME: 27 MIN.

Rugelach, traditionally a Jewish pastry, is often filled with nuts and raisins or preserves. This easy savory takeoff is best served warm from the oven.

- ⅓ cup finely chopped pecans, toasted
- ⅓ cup finely chopped imported green olives
- ¼ cup freshly grated Parmesan cheese
- 2 tsp. minced fresh thyme
- 1 (8-oz.) can refrigerated crescent rolls
  Paprika

1. Preheat oven to 375°. Combine first 4 ingredients in a medium bowl.
2. Unroll crescent rolls onto a lightly floured cutting board. Sprinkle pecan mixture evenly over dough, pressing firmly into dough. Using a sharp knife, cut dough along perforations. Cut each triangle lengthwise into 2 equal triangles.
3. Roll up each triangle, starting at wide end. Place rugelach, point sides down, on an ungreased baking sheet, curving them into a crescent shape. Sprinkle with paprika. Bake at 375° for 15 minutes or until browned. Serve hot.
Note: We tested with Picholine Green Olives.

Rosemary-Lemon Olives

MAKES 2 CUPS
HANDS-ON TIME: 4 MIN.
TOTAL TIME: 44 MIN.

The infused oil resulting from this recipe is great for dipping crusty baguette slices. For gift giving, replace the baked rosemary and lemon peel with fresh sprigs of rosemary and fresh lemon peel.

- 6 (5-inch) strips lemon peel
- 2 (8-inch) fresh rosemary sprigs
- ⅛ tsp. crushed red pepper flakes
- 1 cup kalamata olives
- 1 cup Sicilian olives
- 1 cup extra virgin olive oil
  Garnish: fresh rosemary

1. Preheat oven to 300°. Place lemon peel, rosemary, and red pepper flakes in an 11- x 7-inch baking dish. Add olives, and drizzle with olive oil. Bake, uncovered, at 300° for 40 minutes. Cool to room temperature. Garnish, if desired, and serve immediately, or store in refrigerator up to 5 days. Bring refrigerated olives to room temperature before serving.

Bloody Mary Shrimp Cocktail

quick prep

Pile these spicy marinated shrimp in martini glasses for a fun way to present a classic appetizer.

MAKES 4 TO 6 APPETIZER SERVINGS
HANDS-ON TIME: 12 MIN.
TOTAL TIME: 8 HR., 15 MIN.

- 1 lb. unpeeled, large raw shrimp (about 30)
- 1 cup hot and spicy Bloody Mary cocktail mix
- ¼ cup chopped Spanish olives
- 1 to 2 Tbsp. capers, drained
  Garnishes: pimiento-stuffed Spanish olives, celery leaves

1. Bring 3 qt. water to a boil; add shrimp, and cook 3 to 5 minutes or just until shrimp turn pink. Drain and rinse with cold water. Peel shrimp.
2. Combine shrimp and cocktail mix in a large zip-top plastic freezer bag. Seal bag, and chill 8 hours.
3. Remove shrimp from marinade; discard marinade. For a fun presentation, divide shrimp among martini glasses. Sprinkle each serving with chopped olives and capers. Garnish, if desired.

Tuna Niçoise Canapés

quick prep

MAKES ABOUT 3 DOZEN
HANDS-ON TIME: 15 MIN.
TOTAL TIME: 15 MIN.

- 2 (5.5-oz.) cans solid light tuna in olive oil, well drained and flaked
- ¼ cup finely minced red onion
- 3 Tbsp. chopped kalamata or niçoise olives
- 2 Tbsp. capers, drained
- 2 tsp. extra virgin olive oil
- 2 tsp. Dijon mustard
- 2 tsp. balsamic vinegar
- ¼ to ½ tsp. freshly ground pepper
- ⅛ tsp. kosher salt
  Endive leaves or cucumber slices
  Garnishes: sliced kalamata olives, fresh flat-leaf parsley

1. Combine first 9 ingredients in a medium bowl. To serve, spoon tuna mixture onto endive leaves or cucumber slices. Garnish, if desired.
Note: We tested with Starkist Tuna.

Pimiento Cheese Fondue

MAKES 4 CUPS
HANDS-ON TIME: 9 MIN.
TOTAL TIME: 2 HR., 9 MIN.

- 4 cups (16 oz.) shredded extra-sharp Cheddar cheese
- 1 (8-oz.) package cream cheese, softened
- 1 cup heavy whipping cream
- 1 (7-oz.) jar diced pimiento, well drained
- ¼ cup thinly sliced green onions
- ¼ tsp. ground red pepper

1. Combine first 3 ingredients in a 3- or 4-qt. slow cooker. Cover and cook on LOW 1 hour. Stir to combine. Cover and cook on LOW 30 more minutes. Add pimiento, green onions, and red pepper. Stir to blend. Cover and cook on LOW 30 more minutes or until thoroughly heated. Serve fondue with raw vegetables, tortilla chips, or French bread chunks.

Pesto Chicken Quesadillas

editor's favorite • quick prep

MAKES 2 TO 4 SERVINGS
HANDS-ON TIME: 13 MIN.
TOTAL TIME: 21 MIN.

These skillet quesadillas are quick and delicious. Try a flavored rotisserie chicken or add some toasted pine nuts to kick up the flavor. Dollop with marinara or sour cream.

- 1 (3.5-oz.) jar pesto
- 4 (8-inch) flour tortillas
- 1½ cups shredded rotisserie chicken
- 1 (8-oz.) package shredded Italian cheese blend
  Softened butter or yogurt-based spread

1. Spread about 1½ Tbsp. pesto on each tortilla. Sprinkle a slightly heaping ⅓ cup chicken onto half of each tortilla; sprinkle cheese over chicken on each tortilla.
2. Fold each tortilla in half. Butter both sides of each folded tortilla.
3. Heat a large nonstick skillet over medium-high heat. Cook quesadillas, in 2 batches, 2 minutes on each side or until browned and crusty. Remove to a cutting board, and cut each quesadilla into 3 wedges.
Note: We tested with Alessi Pesto and Brummel & Brown yogurt-based spread.

Chicken Yakitori

MAKES 8 APPETIZER SERVINGS
HANDS-ON TIME: 11 MIN.
TOTAL TIME: 47 MIN.

Yakitori is a Japanese grilled chicken skewer that makes a great party appetizer-on-a-stick and goes well with Japanese beer.

- 6 green onions
- ½ cup teriyaki marinade and sauce
- 1½ Tbsp. grated fresh ginger
- 2 large garlic cloves, pressed
- 1 Tbsp. sugar
- 2 Tbsp. dark sesame oil
- 1 lb. boneless, skinless chicken breast, cut into 1-inch pieces

1. Preheat grill to 350° to 400° (medium-high) heat. Cut white and pale green parts of green onions into 1½-inch pieces. Thinly slice dark green onion tops. Set aside.
2. Combine marinade, ginger, garlic, sugar, and sesame oil in a zip-top plastic freezer bag; add chicken and 1½-inch green onion pieces, turning to coat. Seal and chill for at least 30 minutes or up to 2 hours.
3. Meanwhile, soak 8 (6-inch) wooden skewers in water to cover for 30 minutes. Drain.
4. Thread marinated chicken and green onion pieces onto skewers, discarding marinade. Grill chicken, covered with grill lid, 3 to 4 minutes on each side or until chicken is done.
5. Transfer skewers to an appetizer platter, and sprinkle with thinly sliced green onions.
Note: We tested with Kikkoman Teriyaki Marinade and Sauce.

Blue Chip Nachos

editor's favorite

MAKES 8 TO 10 SERVINGS
HANDS-ON TIME: 12 MIN.
TOTAL TIME: 17 MIN.

Your favorite blue cheese is essential for decadence here.

- 1 (4-oz.) wedge Maytag or other blue cheese
- 3 Tbsp. tub-style cream cheese, softened
- ⅓ cup whipping cream
- 1 (5-oz.) bag lightly salted crinkle-cut potato chips
- 1 cup chopped walnuts, toasted
- 2 tsp. chopped fresh thyme
- 2 tsp. chopped fresh rosemary
- 2 to 3 Tbsp. bottled balsamic glaze

1. Preheat oven to 400°. Combine cheeses and whipping cream in a small bowl, stirring well. Spread whole potato chips in a double layer on a parchment paper-lined baking sheet. Dollop cheese onto potato chips. Sprinkle with walnuts. Bake at 400° for 5 minutes or until heated. Remove from oven, and carefully slide chips and parchment paper onto a wooden board. Sprinkle with herbs; drizzle with desired amount of balsamic glaze. Serve immediately.

Note: We tested with Kettle Potato Chips and Gia Russa Balsamic Glaze.

Chocolate-Caramel-Pecan Potato Chips

MAKES ABOUT 9 DOZEN
HANDS-ON TIME: 34 MIN.
TOTAL TIME: 46 MIN.

These chips are best served the day they're made. Use the thickest ridged potato chips you can find.

- 1 (13-oz.) bag thick ruffled potato chips
- 1 (14-oz.) bag caramels
- ⅓ cup whipping cream
- 1 (11.5-oz.) bag milk chocolate morsels
- 2 Tbsp. shortening
- 1 cup finely chopped pecans, toasted

1. Spread whole potato chips in single layers on parchment paper-lined wire racks. Combine caramels and cream in a heavy saucepan over low heat, stirring constantly, until smooth; remove from heat. Drizzle caramel over chips.
2. Melt milk chocolate morsels and shortening in a small bowl in microwave at HIGH, 1½ to 2 minutes, stirring after 1 minute; cool slightly. Drizzle chocolate over caramel on potato chips; sprinkle with pecans. Cool until chocolate and caramel harden.

Note: We tested with Wavy Lays Potato Chips and Kraft Caramels.

Ranch Popcorn

quick prep

MAKES 9½ CUPS
HANDS-ON TIME: 1 MIN.
TOTAL TIME: 3 MIN.

This flavored popcorn is addictive.

- 1 (3-oz.) bag butter-flavored 94% fat-free popped microwave popcorn Butter-flavored cooking spray
- 1½ Tbsp. Ranch dressing mix

1. Pour popped corn into a large bowl; coat heavily with cooking spray. Sprinkle Ranch dressing mix over popcorn; toss well.

Note: We tested with Pop Secret Microwave Popcorn.

Spicy Nut Popcorn

quick prep

MAKES 8 SERVINGS
HANDS-ON TIME: 15 MIN.
TOTAL TIME: 15 MIN.

- 3 Tbsp. butter
- 1 cup pine nuts or pecans
- ¾ cup slivered almonds
- 1 tsp. chili powder
- ½ tsp. salt
- ½ tsp. lemon zest
- 1 Tbsp. fresh lime juice
- ¼ tsp. ground cloves
- ¼ tsp. pepper
- 1 (3-oz.) bag low-fat popcorn, popped

1. Melt butter in a large skillet over medium heat; add pine nuts and next 7 ingredients, and sauté 3 to 4 minutes. Pour warm mixture over popcorn, tossing to coat.

Note: We tested with Orville Redenbacher's Smart Pop Gourmet Popping Corn.

HolidayFavorites

Grilled Shrimp Caesar

quick prep

Smoked paprika is a delicious seasoning to have on hand. It's wonderful in marinades and as a seasoning for sauces and soups. It's made by smoke-drying red pepper pods before grinding and can range from sweet to spicy hot.

MAKES 4 SERVINGS
HANDS-ON TIME: 7 MIN.
TOTAL TIME: 13 MIN.

- 2 (8-oz.) packages complete Caesar salad mix
- 24 unpeeled, large raw shrimp
- 2 Tbsp. olive oil
- 2 Tbsp. fresh lemon juice
- 2 large garlic cloves, minced, or 2 tsp. jarred minced garlic
- 1 tsp. smoked paprika
- ½ tsp. salt
- ¼ tsp. freshly ground pepper

1. Preheat grill to 350° to 400° (medium-high) heat. Place lettuce and croutons from salad mix into a bowl; chill. Set aside salad dressing and Parmesan cheese packets.
2. Peel and, if desired, devein shrimp. Combine shrimp and next 6 ingredients in a bowl; toss to coat. Thread shrimp onto 4 (10-inch) metal skewers. Grill 3 minutes on each side or just until shrimp turn pink. Remove shrimp from skewers, if desired.
3. Lightly toss salad with desired amount of reserved dressing. Divide salad among individual serving plates. Top each salad with 6 shrimp, and sprinkle with reserved cheese.
Note: We tested with Fresh Express Caesar Salad Mix.

Apricot-Glazed Pork Tenderloin with Couscous

A two-ingredient glaze paints this pork with rich color and tangy-sweet flavor.

MAKES 4 SERVINGS
HANDS-ON TIME: 10 MIN.
TOTAL TIME: 33 MIN.

- 1 (1¼-lb.) pork tenderloin
- 1 Tbsp. olive oil
- ¼ tsp. salt
- ¼ tsp. pepper
- ⅓ cup apricot preserves
- 2 Tbsp. honey mustard
- 1 (10-oz.) box couscous
- ½ cup diced dried apricots
- ⅓ cup toasted sliced almonds

1. Preheat oven to broil. Brush pork with olive oil; season with salt and pepper. Place on an aluminum foil-lined broiler pan. Broil 5½ inches from heat 8 minutes or until browned, turning once.
2. Combine apricot preserves and honey mustard; spread over pork. Broil 10 more minutes, turning once, or until meat thermometer inserted in center of meat registers 155°. Cover pork with aluminum foil, and let stand 5 minutes.
3. Meanwhile, prepare couscous according to package directions. Fluff couscous; stir in apricots and almonds. Slice pork, and serve with couscous.
Note: We tested with Far East Couscous.

Baked Three-Cheese Ziti

MAKES 4 SERVINGS
HANDS-ON TIME: 11 MIN.
TOTAL TIME: 51 MIN.

- 1 (12-oz.) package uncooked ziti pasta
- 3 cups marinara sauce
- 1 (8-oz.) package shredded mozzarella cheese
- ½ cup freshly grated Parmesan cheese
- 1 cup ricotta cheese
- 3 Tbsp. jarred pesto sauce
- ¼ tsp. dried crushed red pepper
  Freshly grated Parmesan cheese

1. Preheat oven to 400°. Cook pasta according to package directions; drain and transfer to a large bowl. Add 2 cups marinara sauce, half of mozzarella cheese, half of Parmesan cheese, ricotta cheese, pesto, and red pepper, stirring gently to blend.
2. Spoon pasta mixture into a lightly greased 13- x 9-inch baking dish. Spoon remaining marinara sauce over pasta; sprinkle with remaining mozzarella and Parmesan cheese.
3. Bake, uncovered, at 400° for 30 minutes or until cheese is melted and bubbly. Serve extra Parmesan at the table.

Chicken Fajitas

quick prep

MAKES 4 SERVINGS
HANDS-ON TIME: 12 MIN.
TOTAL TIME: 22 MIN.

2 Tbsp. olive oil
1 red bell pepper, cut lengthwise into ½-inch strips
1 medium onion, sliced
½ tsp. ground cumin
½ tsp. salt
3 cups shredded cooked rotisserie chicken
3 Tbsp. minced fresh cilantro
1½ Tbsp. minced pickled jalapeño peppers
8 (8-inch) flour tortillas
 Toppings: salsa, guacamole, sour cream

1. Heat 2 Tbsp. olive oil in a large skillet over medium heat. Add bell pepper and next 3 ingredients. Cook 8 minutes or until pepper and onion are tender, stirring often. Add chicken, cilantro, and jalapeño peppers; cook 2 minutes or until thoroughly heated. Remove from heat, and keep warm.
2. Warm tortillas according to package directions.
3. Transfer chicken mixture to a serving platter. Serve with tortillas and desired toppings.

Chicken Pot Pie

This is easy comfort food with a puff pastry crust.

MAKES 6 SERVINGS
HANDS-ON TIME: 9 MIN.
TOTAL TIME: 55 MIN.

2 Tbsp. butter
1 small onion, minced
1 (8-oz.) pkg. sliced fresh mushrooms
½ tsp. salt
1 (10-oz.) package frozen mixed vegetables, thawed and drained
3 cups chopped rotisserie chicken
1 (10¾-oz.) can reduced-sodium cream of chicken soup
⅔ cup milk
1 to 2 Tbsp. dry sherry (optional)
1 Tbsp. fresh lemon juice
1 sheet frozen puff pastry, thawed

1. Preheat oven to 375°. Melt butter in a large skillet over medium heat. Add onion, and cook, stirring occasionally, 3 minutes or until tender. Add mushrooms and salt; sauté 8 minutes or until liquid evaporates and mushrooms are browned. Add vegetables and next 5 ingredients, stirring to blend.
2. Pour chicken mixture into a lightly greased 10-inch deep-dish pie plate, and cover with pastry; trim excess pastry. Bake at 375° for 30 to 35 minutes or until filling is bubbly and pastry is golden.

Chocolate Cream Martini

quick prep

This luxurious drink is both cocktail and dessert.

MAKES 2 SERVINGS
HANDS-ON TIME: 4 MIN.
TOTAL TIME: 4 MIN.

1 (1-oz.) square semisweet chocolate, melted
3 Tbsp. vanilla-flavored vodka
3 Tbsp. Irish cream liqueur
2 Tbsp. half-and-half
⅓ cup coffee-flavored liqueur
⅓ cup chocolate-flavored liqueur

1. Dip rims of 2 martini glasses in melted chocolate on a plate to form a thin layer. Place glasses in refrigerator until chocolate is firm.
2. Combine vodka and next 4 ingredients in a martini shaker filled with ice. Cover with lid; shake until thoroughly chilled. Remove lid; strain into chocolate-rimmed martini glasses. Serve immediately.
Note: We tested with Absolut Vanilla Vodka, Tia Maria coffee liqueur, and Godiva chocolate liqueur.

Chocolate Eggnog

quick prep

MAKES 9½ CUPS
HANDS-ON TIME: 15 MIN.
TOTAL TIME: 15 MIN.

1 qt. refrigerated eggnog
1 qt. milk
1 (16-oz.) can chocolate syrup
½ cup light rum (optional)
1 cup whipping cream
2 Tbsp. powdered sugar
 Unsweetened cocoa (optional)

1. Stir together first 3 ingredients and, if desired, rum in a punch bowl, stirring well.

2. Beat whipping cream at high speed with an electric mixer until foamy. Add powdered sugar, beating until medium peaks form. Dollop whipped cream over individual servings. Sift cocoa over whipped cream, if desired.

Brownie Buttons

Nestle miniature chocolate candies into freshly baked brownie bites for impressive little chocolate treats.

MAKES 20 BROWNIES
HANDS-ON TIME: 15 MIN.
TOTAL TIME: 47 MIN.

- 1 (16.5-oz.) refrigerated roll triple chocolate chunk brownie batter
- 1 bag assorted miniature peanut butter cup candies and chocolate-coated caramels

1. Preheat oven to 350°. Spray miniature (1¾-inch) muffin pans with cooking spray, or line pans with paper liners and spray liners with cooking spray. Spoon brownie batter evenly into each cup, filling almost full. Bake at 350° for 19 to 20 minutes. Cool in pans 3 to 4 minutes, and then gently press a miniature candy into each baked brownie until the top of candy is level with top of brownie. Cool 10 minutes in pans. Gently twist each brownie to remove from pan. Cool on a wire rack.
Note: We tested with Pillsbury refrigerated brownie batter and Rolo chocolate-coated caramels.

Hazelnut Mousse Crunch

quick prep

For a special effect, use a decorative tip to pipe the mousse into each glass. All you need is a large star tip and piping bag.

MAKES 6 SERVINGS
HANDS-ON TIME: 5 MIN.
TOTAL TIME: 6 MIN.

- 1 (13-oz.) jar hazelnut spread
- 1 (8-oz.) container frozen whipped topping, thawed
- 1 (6.88-oz) package bittersweet chocolate-dipped biscotti or other favorite biscotti

1. Remove and discard foil wrap from jar. Microwave hazelnut spread, uncovered, on HIGH for 25 seconds. Fold hazelnut spread and whipped topping together in a large bowl, leaving some chocolate streaks. Spoon mousse into a zip-top plastic freezer bag (do not seal). Snip 1 corner of bag to make a hole. Pipe mousse into parfait glasses. Serve with biscotti; or crush biscotti, and lightly sprinkle over each serving.
Note: We tested with Nutella Hazelnut Spread and Nonni's Chocolate-Dipped Biscotti.

Fudgy Toffee-Crunch Brownies

make-ahead

No one will detect that these decadent brownies start with a mix.

MAKES 2 DOZEN
HANDS-ON TIME: 16 MIN.
TOTAL TIME: 1 HR., 6 MIN.

- 2 (17.6-oz.) packages dark fudge brownie mix with chocolate chunks
- 2 large eggs
- ½ cup vegetable oil or canola oil
- ¼ cup water
- 1 Tbsp. instant espresso granules
- 1 (12-oz.) package miniature chocolate-covered toffee bars, coarsely crushed

1. Preheat oven to 325°. Beat first 4 ingredients at medium speed with an electric mixer for 3 minutes or until blended; stir in coffee granules and candy bars. Spoon batter into a lightly greased 13- x 9-inch pan, spreading evenly (batter will be very thick).
2. Bake at 325° for 50 to 52 minutes or until center is set. Cool in pan on a wire rack. Cut into bars.
Note: We tested with Duncan Hines Chocolate Lover's Dark Fudge Brownie Mix and Heath Miniatures chocolate-covered toffee bars.

Orange, Red Onion, and Mint Salad

make-ahead • quick prep

Prepare and chill this colorful salad up to three hours ahead. Lightly dress and toss greens right before serving. Use Valencia oranges; they're both sweet and tart with an intense citrus flavor.

MAKES 10 SERVINGS
HANDS-ON TIME: 16 MIN.
TOTAL TIME: 16 MIN.

- 2 heads romaine lettuce, chopped
- 5 Valencia or navel oranges, peeled and sectioned or sliced
- 1 small red onion, thinly sliced, separated into rings, and halved
- 2 avocados, sliced
- 2 Tbsp. lime juice
- 1 Tbsp. white or red wine vinegar
- ½ tsp. salt
- ½ tsp. ground cumin
- ¼ tsp. freshly ground black pepper
  Pinch of sugar
- ⅓ cup olive oil
- 3 Tbsp. minced fresh mint
- 8 fresh mint leaves

1. Combine first 4 ingredients in a salad bowl.
2. Combine lime juice and next 5 ingredients in a small bowl; slowly add oil in a thin stream, whisking constantly. Drizzle dressing over salad; sprinkle with minced mint, and toss. Top with mint leaves.

Mexican Rice and Cheese Casserole

editor's favorite • make-ahead

MAKES 10 SERVINGS
HANDS-ON TIME: 12 MIN.
TOTAL TIME: 57 MIN.

- 2 (8-oz.) packages Mexican rice
- 2 cups (8 oz.) shredded Monterey Jack cheese, divided
- 1 cup thinly sliced green onions
- 1 (8-oz.) container sour cream
- 1 tsp. salt
- ¼ tsp. ground red pepper
- ¼ tsp. smoked or sweet paprika

1. Preheat oven to 350°. Prepare rice according to package directions.
2. Combine hot cooked rice, 1½ cups shredded cheese, and next 4 ingredients in a large bowl; stir seasoned rice mixture until combined.
3. Transfer seasoned rice mixture to a greased 13- x 9-inch baking dish; sprinkle with remaining ½ cup cheese and paprika.
4. Bake, uncovered, at 350° for 25 to 30 minutes or until thoroughly heated.
Note: We tested with Vigo Mexican Rice.

Deep, Rich Mexican Hot Chocolate

quick prep

For a special touch, add a vanilla bean, split lengthwise, to each mug as a stirrer stick—vanilla "seeds" will permeate the hot chocolate as you stir.

MAKES 11 CUPS
HANDS-ON TIME: 6 MIN.
TOTAL TIME: 16 MIN.

- 9 cups milk
- ½ cup firmly packed dark brown sugar
- 2 (3.5-oz.) bars bittersweet chocolate, finely chopped
- ⅓ cup Dutch process or unsweetened cocoa
- 3 Tbsp. instant espresso powder
- 1½ tsp. ground cinnamon
- ⅔ cup coffee liqueur (optional)
  Garnishes: sweetened whipped cream*, ground cinnamon
  Vanilla beans, split lengthwise (optional)

1. Combine first 6 ingredients in a Dutch oven. Cook over medium heat 10 minutes or until chocolate melts and sugar dissolves, stirring occasionally. Remove from heat, and whisk vigorously until hot chocolate is frothy.
2. Immediately pour into mugs; stir a splash of coffee liqueur into each serving, if desired. Top with whipped cream, and sprinkle with cinnamon, if desired. Add a split vanilla bean to each mug as a stirrer stick, if desired.
Note: We tested with canned Reddi-wip topping. For party fun, it's quick and easy, and fun to squirt.

HolidayFavorites

Farmhouse Holiday Breakfast

A hearty country breakfast in front of a crackling fire is a dream come true on any winter morning. Farm-fresh eggs enhanced with herbs, sugar-smoked bacon, fluffy biscuits, and homestyle charm are the highlights of this meal.

Game Plan

2 WEEKS AHEAD:
- Make grocery list. Shop for non-perishables.
- Plan table centerpiece and/or decorations.

2 DAYS AHEAD:
- Do remaining shopping.
- Prepare Spiced Honey Butter; cover and refrigerate.

1 DAY AHEAD:
- Mix together coffee cake; cover and refrigerate unbaked.
- Prepare Cider-Glazed Christmas Fruit; cover and refrigerate.
- Measure out sugar and cocoa for Steaming Hot Mocha.

2 HOURS AHEAD:
- Prepare and bake bacon. Cool completely; cover loosely at room temperature.
- Bake coffee cake.
- Prepare and cut biscuit dough; place on baking sheet.

1 HOUR AHEAD:
- Prepare Steaming Hot Mocha; cover and keep hot until ready to serve.

40 MINUTES AHEAD:
- Prepare and bake cheese grits.
- Gather ingredients for scrambled eggs.

20 MINUTES AHEAD:
- Bake biscuits.
- Scramble eggs.
- Reheat Cider-Glazed Christmas Fruit.

Brunch for a Bunch

SERVES 12

Farmers Market Scramble

Smoky Brown Sugar Bacon

Puffy Cheese Grits

Jalapeño Biscuits   Spiced Honey Butter

Streusel-Spiced Coffee Cake

Cider-Glazed Christmas Fruit

Steaming Hot Mocha

Orange juice   Milk

Farmers Market Scramble

quick prep

Hearty scrambled eggs get a punch of flavor with fresh herbs and tomato.

MAKES 12 SERVINGS
HANDS-ON TIME: 10 MIN.
TOTAL TIME: 24 MIN.

- 24 large eggs
- ½ cup milk
- ¼ cup whipping cream
- 1½ tsp. salt
- ½ tsp. freshly ground pepper
- ½ tsp. hot sauce
- ¼ cup butter, divided
- 1 large tomato, chopped and drained on a paper towel
- ⅓ cup chopped fresh chives
- ¼ cup chopped fresh flat-leaf parsley

1. Whisk together first 6 ingredients in a large bowl.
2. Melt 2 Tbsp. butter in a large nonstick skillet over medium heat; add half of egg mixture, and cook, without stirring, until eggs begin to set on bottom. Draw a spatula across bottom of skillet to form large curds. Cook until eggs are thickened but still moist. (Do not stir constantly.) Stir in half of tomato. Remove from heat, and transfer to a warm platter. Repeat procedure with remaining butter, egg mixture, and tomato. Sprinkle whole platter of eggs with chives and parsley; serve hot.

Smoky Brown Sugar Bacon

editor's favorite

This bacon takes a little while to prepare, but it's more than worth it. The aroma alone gets our highest rating.

MAKES 24 SLICES
HANDS-ON TIME: 12 MIN.
TOTAL TIME: 30 MIN.

- 3 cups firmly packed light brown sugar
- 24 slices applewood smoked bacon

1. Preheat oven to 425°. Spread brown sugar onto a large plate; dredge half of bacon in sugar, pressing to be sure plenty of sugar sticks to both sides of bacon. Place bacon in a single layer on a large baking rack on an aluminum foil-lined rimmed baking sheet. Bake at 425° for 18 to 20 minutes or until crisp. Remove bacon from rack to a serving platter or parchment paper to cool. Repeat with remaining bacon and brown sugar.
Note: We tested with Nueske's Applewood Smoked Bacon.

Puffy Cheese Grits

This airy grits casserole stands tall as it finishes baking. Plan to bring it straight from the oven to the table.

MAKES 12 SERVINGS
HANDS-ON TIME: 21 MIN.
TOTAL TIME: 41 MIN.

- 1 cup milk
- 1 tsp. salt
- 1 cup uncooked quick-cooking grits
- ⅓ cup unsalted butter
- ¼ tsp. ground white pepper
- 4 large egg yolks
- 1½ cups (6 oz.) shredded Monterey Jack cheese
- 8 large egg whites
- ¼ tsp. cream of tartar

1. Preheat oven to 425°. Combine milk, 1 cup water, and salt in a large saucepan. Bring to a boil; stir in grits. Reduce heat, and simmer 3 minutes or until thickened, stirring often. Remove from heat; add butter and pepper, stirring until butter melts. Stir in egg yolks, 1 at a time, and cheese.
2. Beat egg whites and cream of tartar at high speed with an electric mixer until stiff peaks form. Fold one-third of beaten egg whites into grits, and carefully fold in remaining egg whites. Pour into a lightly greased 13- x 9-inch baking dish. Bake at 425° for 20 minutes or until puffed and browned. Serve immediately.

Jalapeño Biscuits

If you prefer less heat in these big yummy biscuits, seed the jalapeños before chopping them.

MAKES 20 BISCUITS
HANDS-ON TIME: 15 MIN.
TOTAL TIME: 31 MIN.

- 4 cups all-purpose flour
- 2 Tbsp. baking powder
- 1 tsp. salt
- ⅔ cup butter, chilled and cut into pieces
- 2 medium jalapeño peppers, minced (about ¼ cup)
- 1½ to 1¾ cups buttermilk
  Melted butter (optional)

1. Preheat oven to 425°. Combine first 3 ingredients; cut in ⅔ cup butter with a pastry blender or 2 knives until crumbly. Stir in jalapeño. Add buttermilk, stirring just until dry ingredients are moistened.
2. Turn out dough onto a lightly floured surface, and knead lightly 3 or 4 times. Pat or roll dough to ½-inch thickness; cut with a 2½-inch round cutter. Place on a lightly greased baking sheet. Bake at 425° for 16 to 18 minutes or until golden. Brush with melted butter, if desired, before serving.

Spiced Honey Butter

make-ahead • quick prep

Make this sweet and spicy butter in advance so that all the flavors have a chance to blend; it's wonderful spread over coffee cake or fresh-from-the-oven biscuits.

MAKES 1¼ CUPS
HANDS-ON TIME: 9 MIN.
TOTAL TIME: 9 MIN.

- 1 cup unsalted butter, softened
- ¼ cup raw honey or regular processed honey
- ¼ tsp. freshly grated nutmeg
- ¼ tsp. ground cinnamon
  Pinch of ground cloves

1. Combine all ingredients in a bowl; beat at medium speed with a handheld electric mixer until blended. Serve at room temperature. Store butter in refrigerator.

★ HolidayFavorites

Streusel-Spiced Coffee Cake

make-ahead

MAKES 12 SERVINGS
HANDS-ON TIME: 16 MIN.
TOTAL TIME: 8 HR., 51 MIN.

- ¾ cup unsalted butter, softened
- 1 cup granulated sugar
- 2 large eggs
- 1 cup sour cream
- 2 cups all-purpose flour
- 2 tsp. baking powder
- 1 tsp. baking soda
- ½ tsp. ground cinnamon
- ½ tsp. grated nutmeg
- ½ tsp. salt
- ¾ cup firmly packed light brown sugar
- 1 cup coarsely chopped pecans
- ½ tsp. ground cinnamon
- ¼ to ½ tsp. grated nutmeg

1. Preheat oven to 350°. Beat butter at medium speed with an electric mixer until fluffy; gradually add granulated sugar, beating well. Add eggs, 1 at a time, beating until blended after each addition. Add sour cream, mixing well.
2. Combine flour and next 5 ingredients; add to butter mixture, beating well. Spread batter into a greased and floured 13 x 9 inch pan.
3. Combine brown sugar, pecans, ½ tsp. cinnamon, and ¼ to ½ tsp. nutmeg in a small bowl. Sprinkle evenly over batter. Cover and refrigerate 8 hours.
4. Preheat oven to 350°. Uncover; bake at 350° for 35 minutes or until a wooden pick inserted in center comes out clean.

Cider-Glazed Christmas Fruit

An apple cider reduction and two kinds of apples create layers of flavor in this buttery glazed fruit that's equally good served over waffles, pancakes, or ice cream.

MAKES 6 CUPS
HANDS-ON TIME: 7 MIN.
TOTAL TIME: 32 MIN.

- 1 cup apple cider
- 6 Tbsp. unsalted butter, divided
- ¾ tsp. ground cinnamon
- 1 Tbsp. brown sugar
- 3 Granny Smith apples, peeled, cored, and sliced
- 3 Braeburn apples, unpeeled, if desired, cored, and sliced
- ½ cup granulated sugar
- 2 cups fresh cranberries

1. Pour apple cider into a medium skillet. Cook over medium-high heat 14 minutes or until syrupy. Remove from heat, and stir in 2 Tbsp. butter and cinnamon. Set aside.
2. Melt remaining ¼ cup butter in a large deep skillet over medium-high heat. Stir in brown sugar. Add apple slices, tossing to coat. Sprinkle apples with granulated sugar, and cook, stirring often, 8 minutes or until apples are mostly tender. Transfer apples to a serving bowl using a slotted spoon.
3. Add cranberries to buttery drippings in skillet. Cook, stirring constantly, 2 minutes or until cranberries begin to pop. Stir in apple cider reduction, and cook 1 minute. Pour cranberry mixture over apples in serving bowl, and fold in gently. Serve warm.
Make-Ahead Note: You can prepare Cider-Glazed Christmas Fruit up to 1 day ahead. Cover and refrigerate; reheat in microwave until warm.

Steaming Hot Mocha

quick prep

Coffee combines with hot chocolate for a bracing drink to be enjoyed on the coldest of mornings.

MAKES 15½ CUPS
HANDS-ON TIME: 4 MIN.
TOTAL TIME: 24 MIN.

- 2 cups sugar
- 1½ cups unsweetened cocoa
- ¼ tsp. salt
- 7 cups milk
- 7 cups strong brewed coffee
- 1 Tbsp. vanilla extract
  Marshmallow crème (optional)

1. Combine first 3 ingredients in a Dutch oven. Whisk in milk and coffee until smooth. Cook mixture over medium heat, stirring often, 20 minutes or just until bubbles appear (do not boil); remove from heat. Stir in vanilla. Top each serving with marshmallow crème, if desired.

Kids in the Kitchen

Little ones can help stir up these playful sweets for party fun or gift giving.

Wreath Cookies

make-ahead

With only a few ingredients, you can transform shredded wheat cereal into these whimsical holiday wreaths. Let the kids help shape and decorate them.

MAKES ABOUT 1½ DOZEN
HANDS-ON TIME: 25 MIN.
TOTAL TIME: 58 MIN.

- 1 (12-oz.) package vanilla candy coating, broken up
  Green paste food coloring
- 2½ cups coarsely crushed mini shredded whole wheat cereal biscuits
  Mini candy-coated chocolate pieces, red cinnamon candies, swirled holiday white morsels

1. Microwave vanilla candy coating in a medium bowl at MEDIUM (50% power) 3 minutes, stirring after every minute. Stir in desired amount of food coloring. Add cereal, stirring gently to coat. Drop cereal mixture by heaping tablespoonfuls onto wax paper; shape each spoonful into a wreath. Decorate with assorted candies. Let cookies stand about 30 minutes until firm.
Note: We tested with vanilla creme-flavored Frosted Mini Wheats.

Jelly Bean Thumbprint Cookies

make-ahead

Jelly beans make a fun middle for these classic vanilla cookies.

MAKES 1½ DOZEN
HANDS-ON TIME: 6 MIN.
TOTAL TIME: 8 HR., 19 MIN.

- 1 cup butter, softened
- ⅔ cup granulated sugar
- 2 egg yolks
- 1 tsp. vanilla extract
- 2¼ cups all-purpose flour
- ¼ tsp. salt
- ⅓ cup powdered sugar
- 2 Tbsp. heavy whipping cream
  Assorted jelly beans
  Additional powdered sugar

1. Beat butter at medium speed with an electric mixer until creamy; gradually add ⅔ cup sugar, beating well. Add egg yolks and vanilla, beating until blended.
2. Combine flour and salt; add to butter mixture, beating at low speed until blended. Cover and chill dough 8 hours.
3. Preheat oven to 350°. Shape dough into 1-inch balls, and place 2 inches apart on ungreased baking sheets. Press thumb into each cookie to make an indentation.
4. Bake at 350° for 12 to 13 minutes. Cool 1 minute on baking sheets; remove to wire racks. Make thumbprint indentations again while cookies are still warm; let cookies cool completely.
5. Meanwhile, combine ⅓ cup powdered sugar and heavy cream in a small bowl; stir with a fork until smooth.
6. Spoon icing into a zip-top plastic bag; cut a tiny hole in 1 corner of bag, and squirt a small amount of icing into indentation in each cookie. Press jelly beans into center of each cookie. Let set. Dust cookies with powdered sugar.

Fudge Ring

make-ahead

Spooning this cookie- and candy-filled fudge into a homemade ring mold makes a fun project that the kids will want to take part in.

MAKES 2 LB.
HANDS-ON TIME: 10 MIN.
TOTAL TIME: 37 MIN.

- 1 (12-oz.) package milk chocolate morsels
- 1 cup butterscotch morsels
- 1 (14-oz.) can sweetened condensed milk
- 1 tsp. vanilla extract
  Pinch of salt
  Butter
- 1¼ cups candy-coated chocolate pieces
- ½ cup coarsely crushed cream-filled chocolate sandwich cookies (about 5 cookies)

1. Combine first 3 ingredients in a saucepan, reserving condensed milk can. Cook over medium-low heat until all morsels melt, stirring often. Remove from heat; stir in vanilla and salt. Cool slightly (about 15 minutes).
2. Meanwhile, grease an 8-inch round cake pan or springform pan with butter. Line pan with 2 pieces of plastic wrap, overlapping edges and smoothing out any wrinkles. Wrap empty condensed milk can with aluminum foil, smoothing out wrinkles; place in center of cake pan.
3. Stir 1 cup candies and crushed cookies into fudge; spread fudge in cake pan, holding can firmly in center. (A second pair of hands is a big help here.) Sprinkle remaining ¼ cup chocolate candies over fudge, gently pressing candies into fudge. Cover and chill until firm (about 2 to 3 hours).

4. To unmold, carefully loosen edges with a sharp knife, and remove can from center of fudge. Carefully invert fudge onto a plate. Invert again on a serving plate or cardboard cake round for gift giving. Cut fudge into thin slices to serve.

Note: For an easy gift-giving "platter," we wrapped a cardboard cake round with wrapping paper.

Tutti Fruity Crispy Candy

make-ahead • quick prep

This simple candy recipe offers several opportunities for kids to help: Let them crush the pretzels in a zip-top plastic bag, stir the cereal into the melted vanilla coating, and, best of all, break the finished candy into pieces and sample it.

MAKES ABOUT 1¾ LB.
HANDS-ON TIME: 5 MIN.
TOTAL TIME: 1 HR., 7 MIN.

- 1 (24-oz.) package vanilla candy coating, broken up
- 2½ cups sweetened fruit-flavored multigrain cereal
- 1 cup thin pretzel sticks, coarsely broken

1. Line a lightly greased 15- x 10-inch jelly-roll pan with wax or parchment paper.
2. Melt candy coating in a large microwave-safe bowl according to package directions. Gently stir in cereal and pretzels. Spread candy onto wax paper. Let stand 1 hour or until firm. (Do not refrigerate.)
3. Break candy into pieces. Store in an airtight container.
Note: We tested with Froot Loops multigrain cereal.

Sugar Cookie Pops

make-ahead

You'll want to buy several containers of colored sugars and jimmies so you'll have plenty for coating these cookie balls.

MAKES 4½ DOZEN
HANDS-ON TIME: 24 MIN.
TOTAL TIME: 2 HR., 57 MIN.

- ½ cup butter, softened
- ½ cup shortening
- 1 cup granulated sugar
- 1 cup powdered sugar
- 2 large eggs
- ¾ cup canola or vegetable oil
- 2 tsp. vanilla extract
- 4 cups all-purpose flour
- 1 tsp. baking soda
- 1 tsp. salt
- 1 tsp. cream of tartar
  Colored sugars, sparkling sugars, and multicolored jimmies
  4-inch white craft sticks

1. Beat butter and shortening at medium speed with an electric mixer until fluffy; add sugars, beating well. Add eggs, oil, and vanilla, beating until blended.
2. Combine flour and next 3 ingredients; add to butter mixture, blending well. Cover and chill dough 2 hours or overnight.
3. Preheat oven to 350°. Shape dough into 1½-inch balls. Roll each ball in colored sugar or jimmies in individual bowls, pressing gently, if necessary, to coat balls. Place 2 inches apart on ungreased baking sheets. Insert craft sticks about 1 inch into each cookie to resemble a lollipop.
4. Bake at 350° for 10 to 11 minutes or until set. Let cool 2 minutes on baking sheets; remove cookie pops to wire racks to cool completely.

Peanut Butter 'n' Jelly Scones

MAKES 1 DOZEN
HANDS-ON TIME: 15 MIN.
TOTAL TIME: 33 MIN.

- 3¼ cups all-purpose flour
- ⅔ cup firmly packed light brown sugar
- 1 Tbsp. baking powder
- ¾ tsp. salt
- ½ cup cold unsalted butter, cut into pieces
- ½ cup chunky peanut butter, chilled
- ½ cup semisweet chocolate morsels (optional)
- ⅔ cup whipping cream, divided
- 2 tsp. vanilla extract
- 2 Tbsp. turbinado sugar
  About ¾ cup strawberry jelly

1. Preheat oven to 425°. Combine first 4 ingredients in a food processor. Pulse briefly until combined. Add butter, and pulse to make a coarse meal. Add peanut butter, and pulse briefly to disperse evenly. Be careful not to overmix.
2. Transfer dough to a large bowl. Add chocolate morsels, if desired. Make a well in center, and add ½ cup plus 1 Tbsp. whipping cream and vanilla. Stir with a fork just until dry ingredients are moistened. Knead dough in bowl 2 or 3 times to incorporate dry ingredients in bottom of bowl.
3. Drop mounds of dough using a ⅓-cup measure onto a baking sheet lined with parchment paper. Smooth tops, and brush scones with remaining cream. Sprinkle with turbinado sugar. Make a deep indentation in center of each scone using thumb or the back of a small spoon; fill each with a scant tablespoon jelly.
4. Bake at 425° for 18 to 20 minutes or until scones are lightly browned around edges. Cool completely.

Christmas Family Gathering

This bountiful menu delivers great flavor and evokes nostalgia for a simpler time. Pass these hearty dishes around the table family-style for some old-fashioned togetherness.

Game Plan

2 WEEKS AHEAD:
- Make grocery list. Shop for nonperishables.
- Plan table centerpiece and/or decorations.

3 OR 4 DAYS AHEAD:
- Finish remaining shopping.
- Place turkey in refrigerator to thaw, if frozen.

2 DAYS AHEAD:
- Make cake layers, wrap in plastic wrap, and refrigerate.
- Cook cauliflower, transfer to zip-top plastic bag; chill.
- Bake sweet potatoes; cool and chill.

1 DAY AHEAD:
- Make frosting, assemble cake, cover loosely with plastic wrap, and chill.
- Prepare dressing, and spoon into a baking dish; cover and chill, unbaked, overnight.
- Make sauce for cauliflower, assemble dish, cover, and chill.
- Make dressing for Brussels sprout salad.
- Prepare and chill Cranberry Chutney.

5 HOURS AHEAD:
- Assemble and bake Roasted Apples and Sweet Potatoes.

4 HOURS AHEAD:
- Prepare turkey; bake. Cover with aluminum foil.2 hours ahead:
- Cook giblets and neck for Bourbon Gravy.
- Roast Brussels sprouts.
- Let dressing come to room temperature.
- Let cauliflower casserole come to room temperature.
- Simmer green beans with bacon.

1½ HOURS AHEAD:
- Assemble Brussels sprout salad (don't add dressing).
- Bake cauliflower casserole.
- Bake Country Ham and Sage Dressing.

45 MINUTES AHEAD:
- Reheat Roasted Apples and Sweet Potatoes.
- Finish making Bourbon Gravy.
- Bake dinner rolls.
- Take cake out of refrigerator.

10 MINUTES AHEAD:
- Dress Brussels sprout salad.

Christmas Dinner

SERVES 12

Two-Herb Roasted Turkey with Bourbon Gravy

Country Ham and Sage Dressing

Cranberry Chutney

Roasted Brussels Sprout Salad

Roasted Apples and Sweet Potatoes in Honey-Bourbon Glaze

Old-Fashioned Green Beans

Creamed Cauliflower with Farmhouse Cheddar

Dinner rolls

Coconut Cake

Two-Herb Roasted Turkey with Bourbon Gravy

This tender and juicy bird is prepared with a traditional technique and has classic flavor. A bourbon-splashed gravy makes it extra-special. Be sure to set aside half of the gravy for the kids before adding bourbon.

MAKES 12 TO 14 SERVINGS
HANDS-ON TIME: 23 MIN.
TOTAL TIME: 3 HR., 38 MIN.

- 1 (12- to 14-lb.) fresh or frozen turkey, thawed
- 6 Tbsp. unsalted butter, softened
- 1½ Tbsp. minced fresh sage or 1½ tsp. rubbed sage
- 1½ Tbsp. fresh thyme leaves or 1½ tsp. dried thyme
- 2 tsp. salt
- 1 tsp. pepper
- 1 large onion, cut into wedges
- 2 celery ribs, coarsely chopped
- 3 garlic cloves, halved
  Bourbon Gravy
  Garnishes: fresh sage and fresh flat-leaf parsley

1. Preheat oven to 325°. Remove giblets and neck from turkey; place in refrigerator for use in gravy, if desired. Rinse turkey with cold water; pat dry with paper towels. Place turkey, breast side up, on a rack in a lightly greased roasting pan. Lift wing tips up and over back, and tuck under bird.

2. Combine butter and next 4 ingredients in a small bowl; rub 2 Tbsp. seasoned butter inside turkey cavity. Place onion, celery, and garlic inside turkey cavity. Rub remaining 4 Tbsp. seasoned butter all over outside of turkey, legs and all. Tie ends of legs together with heavy string, or tuck under flap of skin around tail.

3. Bake, uncovered, at 325° for 2½ to 3 hours or until a meat thermometer inserted into the meaty part of thigh registers 170°. Shield turkey with aluminum foil towards end of cooking, if necessary, to prevent overbrowning. Transfer turkey to a serving platter, reserving pan drippings for Bourbon Gravy. Let turkey stand, covered with foil, at least 15 minutes before carving. Garnish platter, if desired. Serve turkey with Bourbon Gravy.

Bourbon Gravy

editor's favorite

MAKES ABOUT 3 CUPS
HANDS-ON TIME: 5 MIN.
TOTAL TIME: 1 HR., 13 MIN.

    Giblets and neck reserved from
    turkey
    Pan drippings from turkey
½   cup all-purpose flour
½   tsp. garlic powder
2   Tbsp. bourbon

1. Combine giblets, neck, and 3 cups water in a saucepan. Bring to a boil; cover, reduce heat, and simmer 45 minutes to 1 hour or until giblets are tender.

Strain, reserving broth. Discard turkey neck. Coarsely chop giblets; set aside.

2. Add reserved broth (2 cups) to turkey pan drippings; stirring to loosen particles from bottom of roasting pan.

3. Transfer broth and drippings to a saucepan, if desired, or continue cooking in roasting pan placed over 2 burners on the stovetop. Stir in chopped giblets, if desired. Bring to a boil; reduce heat, and simmer, uncovered, 3 to 5 minutes.

4. Combine flour and ½ cup water, stirring until blended; gradually stir into gravy. Bring to a boil; boil 1 minute or until thickened. Set aside some plain gravy, if desired. Stir garlic powder and bourbon into remaining gravy. Serve hot.

Fix It Faster: Substitute canned chicken broth instead of making homemade broth, if desired.

Country Ham and Sage Dressing

make-ahead

This dressing is good any time of year. Serve it alongside roast chicken or pork.

MAKES 12 SERVINGS
HANDS-ON TIME: 25 MIN.
TOTAL TIME: 1 HR., 38 MIN.

1   (1½-lb.) loaf firm-textured white
    bread, cut into ¾-inch cubes
½   cup unsalted butter, divided
½   lb. country ham, cubed
2   medium onions, chopped (about 4
    cups)
4   celery ribs, chopped (about 2 cups)
6   garlic cloves, minced
2   cups chicken broth
1   large egg, beaten
1   tsp. pepper
⅔   cup chopped fresh flat-leaf parsley
3   Tbsp. minced fresh sage
1   Tbsp. minced fresh thyme

1. Preheat oven to 350°. Spread bread cubes in a single layer on 2 large baking sheets. Bake at 350° for 10 minutes or until toasted. Let cool, and transfer to a very large bowl. Increase oven temperature to 400°.

2. Melt 1 Tbsp. butter in a large deep skillet over medium-high heat; add country ham, and sauté 2 to 3 minutes. Add ham to bread in bowl.

3. Melt remaining butter in same skillet over medium heat; add onion and celery, and sauté 8 minutes. Add garlic, and sauté 2 minutes. Remove from heat; add to bread in bowl. Combine broth, egg, and pepper. Add broth mixture to bread, tossing well. Stir in fresh herbs. Spoon dressing into a lightly greased 13- x 9-inch baking dish.

4. Bake, covered, at 400° for 30 minutes. Uncover and bake 15 to 20 more minutes or until top is browned and crusty.

Make-Ahead Note: Prepare dressing a day ahead. Store dressing, unbaked, in refrigerator. The next day, let dressing stand at room temperature 30 minutes and bake as directed. Reheat briefly just before serving.

Cranberry Chutney

make-ahead

Prepare this dressed-up cranberry sauce up to 3 days ahead, and chill it.

MAKES 3½ CUPS
HANDS-ON TIME: 5 MIN.
TOTAL TIME: 5 MIN.

2   (16-oz.) cans whole-berry
    cranberry sauce
2   Tbsp. mango chutney
2   tsp. orange liqueur

1. Combine all ingredients in a bowl; stir well. Serve chilled or at room temperature.

HolidayFavorites

Roasted Brussels Sprout Salad

make-ahead

This vibrant holiday salad can be served warm or even made ahead and served at room temperature.

MAKES 12 SERVINGS
HANDS-ON TIME: 20 MIN.
TOTAL TIME: 45 MIN.

- 1 Tbsp. Dijon mustard
- 1 large garlic clove, finely minced
- 2 to 3 Tbsp. white wine vinegar
- ½ tsp. sugar
- ½ tsp. salt
- ¼ tsp. pepper
- ½ cup olive oil
- 3 lb. Brussels sprouts
- ⅓ cup olive oil
- 1 tsp. salt
- ½ tsp. pepper
- 2 cups grape or cherry tomatoes, halved
- ⅔ cup minced green onions
- ¼ cup minced fresh flat-leaf parsley

1. Preheat oven to 450°. Whisk together first 6 ingredients; gradually whisk in ½ cup oil until blended. Set aside.
2. Rinse Brussels sprouts thoroughly, and remove any discolored leaves. Trim stem ends; cut in half lengthwise. Combine Brussels sprouts and next 3 ingredients in a large bowl; toss to coat. Transfer Brussels sprouts to 1 or 2 large rimmed baking sheets, spreading into 1 layer.
3. Roast at 450° for 25 to 30 minutes or until tender and browned, stirring once. Transfer roasted Brussels sprouts to a serving bowl, and cool slightly. Add tomatoes, green onions, and parsley; toss to blend. Add desired amount of dressing, and toss to coat. Serve warm or at room temperature.

Roasted Apples and Sweet Potatoes in Honey-Bourbon Glaze

editor's favorite • make-ahead

MAKES 12 SERVINGS
HANDS-ON TIME: 32 MIN.
TOTAL TIME: 3 HR., 4 MIN.

- 5 large sweet potatoes, scrubbed (about 5 lb.)
- 3 Golden Delicious apples
- ¼ cup fresh lemon juice
- ⅔ cup firmly packed brown sugar
- ½ cup honey
- 6 Tbsp. unsalted butter
- ¼ cup bourbon
- 1 tsp. ground cinnamon
- ½ tsp. ground ginger
- ½ tsp. salt
- ⅔ cup coarsely chopped pecans

1. Preheat oven to 400°. Place sweet potatoes on a baking sheet; prick with a fork. Bake at 400° for 1 hour or until almost tender. Remove from oven. Let stand 45 minutes or until cooled.
2. Meanwhile, peel and core apples. Slice apples into ⅓-inch-thick wedges; toss with lemon juice in a bowl. Drain, reserving lemon juice.
3. Peel cooled potatoes, and slice ⅓ inch thick. Arrange potatoes and apples alternately in a greased 13- x 9-inch baking dish. Pour remaining lemon juice over potatoes and apples.
4. Combine brown sugar and next 6 ingredients in a saucepan, stirring well. Bring to a boil over medium heat, stirring occasionally; boil 2 minutes or until slightly thickened. Pour glaze over potatoes and apples. Bake, uncovered, at 400° for 30 minutes.
5. Remove from oven; baste with glaze in bottom of dish, and sprinkle nuts across top. Bake 14 to 15 more minutes or until apples look roasted. Baste with glaze just before serving.

Old Fashioned Green Beans

These beans are simmered long and slow with premium double-smoked bacon to develop that trademark "Southern-style" goodness. Red pepper flakes add a nice punch to the dish.

MAKES 12 SERVINGS
HANDS-ON TIME: 12 MIN.
TOTAL TIME: 1 HR., 7 MIN.

- ½ lb. double-smoked bacon, diced*
- 1 medium onion, chopped
- 3 lb. green beans, trimmed
- 1 tsp. dried crushed red pepper
- 1 tsp. salt
- 2 Tbsp. unsalted butter, softened
- 2 to 3 Tbsp. cider vinegar

1. Cook bacon in a Dutch oven over medium heat 10 minutes or until browned and crisp. Add onion, and sauté 5 minutes or until tender. Stir in green beans, red pepper, and salt. Add enough water to cover green beans. Bring to a boil; cover, reduce heat, and simmer 40 to 45 minutes or until beans are very tender. Drain beans, and transfer to a bowl. Add butter and vinegar; toss well. Serve hot.
*****We discovered 2 great online sources for the specialty bacon: Schaller and Weber from **www.germandeli.com** and **www.nodinesmokehouse.com.** Regular bacon is an option too but contributes a milder flavor.

☆ HolidayFavorites

Creamed Cauliflower with Farmhouse Cheddar

editor's favorite • make ahead

MAKES 12 TO 14 SERVINGS
HANDS-ON TIME: 12 MIN.
TOTAL TIME: 1 HR., 10 MIN.

- 2 large heads cauliflower (about 2½ lb. each), cut into florets
- 3 Tbsp. unsalted butter
- ½ cup minced green onions
- 2 large garlic cloves, minced
- 3 Tbsp. all-purpose flour
- 2 cups milk
- 2 cups heavy whipping cream
- ½ tsp. salt
- ½ tsp. freshly grated nutmeg
- ¼ tsp. black pepper
- ¼ tsp. ground red pepper
- 1 cup (4 oz.) shredded Farmhouse Cheddar cheese or sharp Cheddar cheese
- 1½ cups fresh breadcrumbs*
- ¼ cup freshly grated Parmesan cheese
- ½ tsp. salt
- ¼ tsp. pepper
- 3 Tbsp. unsalted butter, melted

1. Preheat oven to 400°. Bring 4 qt. salted water to a boil in a large Dutch oven over high heat. Add cauliflower; cook just until crisp-tender, stirring often. Drain; rinse under cold water. Let cool in colander.
2. Melt 3 Tbsp. butter in a large skillet over medium heat; add green onions and garlic, and sauté 3 minutes. Whisk in flour until smooth. Cook 1 minute, whisking constantly. Gradually whisk in milk and cream; cook over medium heat, whisking constantly, until mixture is thickened and bubbly. Stir in ½ tsp. each salt and nutmeg and ¼ tsp. each pepper. Add cheese, stirring until cheese melts. Remove from heat; add cauliflower, stirring to coat well.

Spoon cauliflower into a greased 13- x 9-inch baking dish.
3. Combine breadcrumbs and next 3 ingredients in a small bowl; sprinkle over cauliflower. Drizzle with melted butter. Bake, uncovered, at 400° for 35 minutes or until browned and bubbly.
*To make 1½ cups homemade breadcrumbs, place 3 slices bread, torn, in a mini chopper. Cover and pulse just until you have fine crumbs.
Note: Farmhouse Cheddar gets its distinction, in part, because it's made on a farmer's property, using only milk from his cows. We tested with Keen's.

Coconut Cake

MAKES 1 (2-LAYER) CAKE
HANDS-ON TIME: 10 MIN.
TOTAL TIME: 40 MIN.

- 1¼ cups unsalted butter, softened
- 1½ cups sugar
- 4 large eggs
- 3 cups all-purpose flour
- 2 tsp. baking powder
- ½ tsp. salt
- 1 cup coconut milk
- 1 tsp. vanilla extract
- 1 tsp. coconut extract
  Coconutty-Pecan Frosting

1. Preheat oven to 350°. Grease 2 (9-inch) round cake pans with shortening, line pans with wax paper, and grease paper. Dust with flour, shaking out excess.
2. Beat butter at low speed with an electric mixer 2 minutes or until creamy. Gradually add sugar, beating at medium speed 5 minutes or until light and fluffy. Add eggs, 1 at a time, beating just until yellow disappears.
3. Combine flour, baking powder, and salt in a medium bowl. With mixer at low speed, add dry ingredients

alternately with coconut milk, beginning and ending with dry ingredients. Add extracts. Pour batter into prepared pans.
4. Bake at 350° for 23 to 25 minutes or until a wooden pick inserted in center comes out clean. Cool layers in pans on wire racks 5 minutes; remove from pans, and cool completely on wire racks. Cake layers can be wrapped and chilled up to 2 days, if desired.
5. Spread Coconutty-Pecan Frosting between layers and on top of cake; let ooze down sides.

Coconutty-Pecan Frosting

MAKES 4¼ CUPS
HANDS-ON TIME: 5 MIN.
TOTAL TIME: 13 MIN.

- 1 (12-oz.) can evaporated milk
- 1½ cups sugar
- ¾ cup butter
- 4 egg yolks, lightly beaten
- 2½ cups unsweetened organic coconut flakes
- 1½ cups chopped pecans
- 2 tsp. vanilla extract

1. Combine milk, sugar, butter, and egg yolks in a 3-qt. heavy saucepan. Bring to a simmer over medium heat; cook 8 to 10 minutes or until frosting is thickened, stirring occasionally. Remove from heat. Stir in coconut, pecans, and vanilla. Let cool.

Appendices

Create a Snowflake Garnish

Place tissue or wax paper over the template
and trace. Follow the directions on page 247.

METRIC EQUIVILANTS

The recipes that appear in this cookbook use the standard United States method for measuring liquid and dry or solid ingredients (teaspoons, tablespoons, and cups). The information on this chart is provided to help cooks outside the U.S. successfully use these recipes. All equivalents are approximate.

METRIC EQUIVALENTS FOR DIFFERENT TYPES OF INGREDIENTS

A standard cup measure of a dry or solid ingredient will vary in weight depending on the type of ingredient. A standard cup of liquid is the same volume for any type of liquid. Use the following chart when converting standard cup measures to grams (weight) or milliliters (volume).

Standard Cup	Fine Powder	Grain	Granular	Liquid Solids	Liquid
	(ex. flour)	(ex. rice)	(ex. sugar)	(ex. butter)	(ex. milk)
1	140 g	150 g	190 g	200 g	240 ml
3/4	105 g	113 g	143 g	150 g	180 ml
2/3	93 g	100 g	125 g	133 g	160 ml
1/2	70 g	75 g	95 g	100 g	120 ml
1/3	47 g	50 g	63 g	67 g	80 ml
1/4	35 g	38 g	48 g	50 g	60 ml
1/8	18 g	19 g	24 g	25 g	30 ml

USEFUL EQUIVALENTS FOR DRY INGREDIENTS BY WEIGHT
(To convert ounces to grams, multiply the number of ounces by 30.)

1 oz	=	1/16 lb	=	30 g
4 oz	=	1/4 lb	=	120 g
8 oz	=	1/2 lb	=	240 g
12 oz	=	3/4 lb	=	360 g
16 oz	=	1 lb	=	480 g

USEFUL EQUIVALENTS FOR LENGTH
(To convert inches to centimeters, multiply the number of inches by 2.5.)

1 in				=		2.5 cm
6 in	=	1/2 ft	=	=		15 cm
12 in	=	1 ft		=		30 cm
36 in	=	3 ft	=	1 yd	=	90 cm
40 in				=		100 cm = 1 m

USEFUL EQUIVALENTS FOR LIQUID INGREDIENTS BY VOLUME

1/4 tsp	=					1 ml
1/2 tsp	=					2 ml
1 tsp	=					5 ml
3 tsp	=	1 tbls		=	1/2 fl oz =	15 ml
	=	2 tbls	= 1/8 cup	=	1 fl oz =	30 ml
	=	4 tbls	= 1/4 cup	=	2 fl oz =	60 ml
	=	5 1/3 tbls	= 1/3 cup	=	3 fl oz =	80 ml
	=	8 tbls	= 1/2 cup	=	4 fl oz =	120 ml
	= 10 2/3 tbls	= 2/3 cup	=	5 fl oz =	160 ml
	=	12 tbls	= 3/4 cup	=	6 fl oz =	180 ml
	=	16 tbls	= 1 cup	=	8 fl oz =	240 ml
	=	1 pt	= 2 cups	=	16 fl oz =	480 ml
	=	1 qt	= 4 cups	=	32 fl oz =	960 ml
					33 fl oz =	1000 ml = 1 l

USEFUL EQUIVALENTS FOR COOKING/OVEN TEMPERATURES

	Fahrenheit	Celsius	Gas Mark
Freeze Water	32° F	0° C	
Room Temperature	68° F	20° C	
Boil Water	212° F	100° C	
Bake	325° F	160° C	3
	350° F	180° C	4
	375° F	190° C	5
	400° F	200° C	6
	425° F	220° C	7
	450° F	230° C	8
Broil			Grill

Menu Index

This index lists every menu by suggested occasion. Recipes in bold type are provided with the menu and accompaniments are in regular type.

Menus for Company

Relaxed Summer Soirée

SERVES 6 TO 8

(page 102)

Lemon Chicken

Green Beans with Goat Cheese,
    Tomatoes, and Almonds

Carrot Orzo

Profiteroles with Coffee Whipped
    Cream

Carolina Peach Sangría

Summer Shrimp Party

SERVES 4 TO 6

(page 106)

2 to 3 lb. boiled shrimp

Green Goddess Dipping Sauce

Carolina-Style Mignonette

Smoky Pecan Relish

Spicy Glazed Shrimp and Vegetable
    Kabobs

Hot cooked rice

Crusty French bread

Casual Vineyard Menu

SERVES 8

(page 130)

Southwest Shrimp Tacos

Chunky Tomato-Fruit
    Gazpacho

Grilled Corn with
    Creamy Chipotle Sauce

Sweet-and-Sour
    Veggie Pickles

Blackberry Wine Sorbet

Game-Day Gathering

SERVES 4

Angela's Spicy Buffalo Wings
    (page 146)

Bean Dip *(page 293)*

Mexican Cheese Spread *(page 94)*

Lemon-Almond Tarts *(page 110)*

Christy's Sunday Dinner

SERVES 8

(page 206)

Lela's Baked Ham

Sweet-and-Sour Green Beans

Vidalia-Honey Vinaigrette,

Jordan Rolls

Apple Julep

Banana Pudding

Easy Appetizer Party

SERVES 8

Spiced Butternut-Pumpkin Soup
    (page 255)

Ceasar Salad Bites *(page 255)*

Bacon-Grits Fritters *(page 255)*

Baked Goat Cheese Dip *(page 256)*

Apple-Spiced Iced Tea *(page 257)*

Raspberry Wine Zinger *(page 257)*

Holiday Cocktail Party

SERVES 10 TO 15

Marinated Mozzarella *(page 284)*

Famous Sausage Ball Muffins
    (page 317)

Honey-Roasted Grape Tomato
    Crostini *(page 319)*

Balsamic-Splashed Bacon and
    Arugula Canapés *(page 319)*

Creamy Sorghum Eggnog *(page 256)*

Kids' Movie Night

SERVES 8

Chicken Fingers with Honey-
    Horseradish Dip *(page 285)*

From-Scratch Oven Fries
    (double recipe) *(page 160)*

Sliced apples

Crispy Chocolate Popcorn *(page 316)*

Make-Ahead Supper

SERVES 4

Garlic-Herb Steaks *(page 296)*

Twice-Baked Smoky Sweet Potatoes
    (page 302)

Mixed salad greens

Cheese Garlic Biscuits *(page 304)*

German Chocolate Cheesecake
    (page 307)

Fiesta Night

SERVES 6

Taco Pita Chips *(page 318)*

Pinto Beans Enchilada Stack *(page 288)*

Avocado and tomato salad

Warm Spiced Sangría *(page 257)*

Menus for Family

Down-Home Dinner

⋯⋯⋯⋯⋯⋯⋯⋯⋯⋯⋯⋯

SERVES 6

Parmesan-Pecan Fried Catfish with Pickled Okra Salsa *(page 29)*

Mashed potatoes

Upside-Down Caramelized Apple Cake *(page 29)*

Pancake Supper

SERVES 8

Pam-Cakes with Buttered Honey Syrup *(page 31)*

bacon and sausage

fresh fruit

Italian Supper

⋯⋯⋯⋯⋯⋯⋯⋯⋯⋯⋯⋯

SERVES 6 TO 8

Sausage-and-Ravioli Lasagna *(page 33)*

Cherry Tomato-Caper Salad (double recipe) *(page 303)*

Garlic bread

Gelato

Simple Supper

⋯⋯⋯⋯⋯⋯⋯⋯⋯⋯⋯⋯

SERVES 6

Chicken Dijon *(page 35)*

Rice Pilaf *(page 56)*

Blueberry-Gorgonzola Salad *(page 108)*

New Orleans Supper

⋯⋯⋯⋯⋯⋯⋯⋯⋯⋯⋯⋯

SERVES 6

Easy Chicken Gumbo *(page 42)*

Crusty French bread

Banana Bread Cobbler *(page 43)*

Southern Comfort Food

⋯⋯⋯⋯⋯⋯⋯⋯⋯⋯⋯⋯

SERVES 6

Slow-Cooker Pork Chops and Field Peas *(page 43)*

Hot cooked rice

Chowchow

Iced tea

Tex-Mex Dinner

⋯⋯⋯⋯⋯⋯⋯⋯⋯⋯⋯⋯

SERVES 4 TO 6

Mexican Beef 'n' Rice *(page 44)*

Chipotle Caesar Salad *(page 279)*

Cornbread with jalapeño

Lemonade

Pizza Night

⋯⋯⋯⋯⋯⋯⋯⋯⋯⋯⋯⋯

SERVES 4

Chicken Parmeasan Pizza *(page 44)*

Tossed salad

Oatmeal, Chocolate Chip, and Pecan Cookies *(page 49)*

Meat and Three

⋯⋯⋯⋯⋯⋯⋯⋯⋯⋯⋯⋯

SERVES 8

Bev's Famous Meatloaf *(page 47)*

Parmesan-Herb Hashbrowns (double recipe) *(page 108)*

Buttermilk Fried Okra *(page 115)*

Tee's Corn Pudding *(page 289)*

Taste of the Islands

⋯⋯⋯⋯⋯⋯⋯⋯⋯⋯⋯⋯

SERVES 4

Jamaican Chicken Burgers *(page 58)*

Sweet potato fries

Ice cream with bananas

Soup and Salad Supper

⋯⋯⋯⋯⋯⋯⋯⋯⋯⋯⋯⋯

SERVES 4

Baby Carrot Soup *(page 62)*

Spicy Pork-and-Orange Chopped Salad *(page 63)*

Assortment of crackers

Weekend Breakfast

⋯⋯⋯⋯⋯⋯⋯⋯⋯⋯⋯⋯

SERVES AS MANY AS NEEDED

Spinach-and-Cheese Omelet (make as many servings as needed) *(page 84)*

Tiny Cream Cheese Biscuits *(page 304)*

Fresh fruit

Summer Supper

....

SERVES 4

Tomato-and-Corn Pizza *(page 115)*

Peach-and-Toasted Pecan Ice Cream
  (page 118)

Burger Night

....

SERVES 4

**Fig-Glazed Burgers with Red Onion
  Jam** *(page 120)*

Colorful Coleslaw *(page 303)*

Potato chips

Catfish Supper

....

SERVES 6 TO 8

Classic Fried Catfish *(page 123)*

Coleslaw

Hushpuppies

Key Lime Pie *(page 122)*

Southwest Supper

....

SERVES 4

Beef Brisket Tostados *(page 125)*

Mashed avocados

Frozen Blue Margaritas *(page 128)*

Barbecue Night

....

SERVES 6

**Barbecued Pork Chops with Potato
  Salad** *(page 135)*

Coleslaw

Zesty Lemon Pie *(page 144)*

One-Dish Delish

....

SERVES 6 TO 8

Tomato-Herb Frittata *(page 137)*

Bakery biscuits

Vegetarian Night

....

SERVES 6

Black Beans and Rice *(page 154)*

Simple tossed salad

Banana Pudding *(page 112)*

Warm Winter Lunch

....

SERVES 11

Basil Tomato Soup *(page 212)*

Grilled Pimiento Cheese Sandwiches
  (page 213)

Slow-Cooker Supper

....

SERVES 6

King Ranch Chicken *(page 218)*

**Green Salad with White Wine
  Vinaigrette** *(page 278)*

Pork Chop Dinner

....

SERVES 4 TO 6

Cumin-Crusted Pork Cutlets *(page 287)*

Green beans

Broccoli Cornbread Muffins *(page 305)*

Simple Weeknight Dinner

....

SERVES 6 TO 8

Chunky Ham Pot Pie *(page 299)*

Cantaloupe-Spinach. Salad *(page 303)*

Bayou Brownies *(page 308)*

Menus for Special Occasions

Potluck Gathering

SERVES 4 TO 6

(page 34)

Hoppin' John Stew with White-Cheddar Cheese Grits
Good-for-You Collards
Bakery brownies

Shower Menu

SERVES 6

(page 68)

Pizza with sauces and toppings of your choice
Greek Caesar Salad
Simple Antipasto Platter
Raspberry Beer Cocktail
Easy Cheesecake Bars

Easter Dinner

SERVES 8

(page 76)

Roasted Lamb
Oregano Green Beans
Church-Style Lemon-Roasted Potatoes
Dinner rolls
Bakery Easter cookies

4th of July Cookout

SERVES 6

Spicy Cheddar-Stuffed Burgers
(page 121)
Big Daddy's Grilled Blue Cheese-and-Bacon Potato Salad *(page 90)*
Baked beans
So-Easy Peach Cobbler *(page 105)*
Beer

Victoria's Thanksgiving Menu

SERVES 8

(page 220)

Roasted Pork with Dried Fruit and Port Sauce
Brussels Sprouts with Pancetta
Mashed Potatoes en Croûte

The Girls' Menu

SERVES 8

(page 223)

Latina Lasagna
Green Beans with Garlic
Leafy Green Salad with Pears
Warm Lemon-Rosemary Olives
Mexican Chocolate Pound Cake

Maiya's Texas Thanksgiving Menu

SERVES 8

(page 226)

White Bean-and-Black Olive Crostini
Roasted Turkey Stuffed with Hazelnut Dressing
Citrus-Walnut Salad
Roasted Green Beans with Sun-dried Tomatoes
Chipotle Smashed Sweet Potatoes
Upside-Down Apple Tart
Sparkling Sipper

Cozy Morning Menu

SERVES 8

(page 230)

Streusel Coffee Cake
Grits-and-Greens Breakfast Bake
Cornmeal-and-Brown Sugar-Crusted Bacon
Coffee Milk Punch

Cookie Swap

SERVES A CROWD

Flourless Peanut Butter-Chocolate Chip Cookies *(page 261)*
Snickerdoodles *(page 261)*
Blackberry Thumbprints *(page 262)*
Snowflake Shortbread *(page 262)*
Pecan Sandies *(page 263)*
Salted Caramel-Pecan Bars *(page 263)*
Candy Bar-Peanut Butter Cookies *(page 263)*
Coffee and eggnog

Quick Christmas Eve Dinner

SERVES 4 TO 6

Pepper Steak with Roasted Red Pepper Pesto *(page 313)*
Stovetop Sweet Potatoes with Maple anc Créme Fraîche *(page 310)*
Roasted Broccoli with Orange-Chipotle Butter *(page 311)*
Bakery rolls
Cranberry Parfaits *(page 314)*

Christmas Dinner

SERVES 12

(page 332)

Two-Herb Roasted Turkey with Bourbon Gravy
Country Ham and Sage Dressing
Cranberry Chutney
Roasted Brussels Sprout Salad
Roasted Apples and Sweet Potatoes in Honey-Bourbon Glaze
Old-Fashioned Green Beans
Creamed Cauliflower with Farmhouse Cheddar
Dinner rolls
Coconut Cake

Recipe Title Index

This index alphabetically lists every recipe by exact title.

This index alphabetically lists every food article and accompanying recipes by month.

General Recipe Index

This index lists every recipe by food category and/or major ingredient.

Bacon (*continued*)

Mushrooms, Broiled Sirloin with Smoky
  Bacon, 313
Okra, Bacon-Fried, 53
Omelets with Bacon, Avocado, and Salsa,
  Monterey Jack, 312
Pancetta, Brussels Sprouts with, 222
Pancetta Crisps with Goat Cheese and Pear, 32
Pancetta-Wrapped Beef Tenderloin with
  Whipped Horseradish Cream, 244
Salad, Big Daddy's Grilled Blue Cheese-and-
  Bacon Potato, 90
Scones, Bacon, Cheddar, and Chive, 287
Smoky Brown Sugar Bacon, 328
Tart, Bacon-and-Leek, 79

BANANAS
Bread Cobbler, Banana, 43
Bread with Peanut Butter Streusel, Cream
  Cheese-Banana, 203
Ice Cream, Grown-up Banana Pudding, 117
Pudding, Banana, 112, 208

BARBECUE. SEE ALSO GRILLED.
Chips, Barbecue Pita, 318
Dressing, Barbecue-Ranch, 140
Griddle Cakes, Barbecue-Topped, 116
Pork
Baby Back Ribs, Bourbon BBQ, 295
Chops with Potato Salad, Barbecued Pork,
  135
Slow-Cooker Barbecue Pork, 216
Sauce, White Barbecue, 86
Sloppy Joes, Cheesy BBQ, 82

BEANS
Black
Chili, Spicy Steak and Black Bean, 217
Chili, Turkey and Black Bean, 312
Chili, Turkey-Black Bean, 32
Dip, Bean, 293
Rice, Black Beans and, 154
Rice, Black Beans and Coconut-Lime , 94
Speedy Black Beans and Mexican Rice, 83
Tostadas with Spicy Cranberry-Chipotle
  Sauce, Turkey, 235
Chili, Meat Lover's, 297
Chili, Super Quick, 50
Green
Casserole, Green Bean, 238
Garlic, Green Beans with, 224
Goat Cheese, Tomatoes, and Almonds,
  Green Beans with, 102
Lemon-Garlic Green Beans, 245
Old-Fashioned Green Beans, 334
Oregano Green Beans, 77
Roasted Green Beans and Cashews, 56
Roasted Green Beans and Pecans, Oven-
  Fried Pork Chops with, 82
Roasted Green Beans with Sun-dried
  Tomatoes, 228
Salad, Grilled Shrimp-and-Green Bean, 87
Salad with White Wine Vinaigrette, Green, 278
Sweet-and-Sour Green Beans, 207
Hummus, 292
Pinto Beans Enchilada Stack, 288
Salad, Mediterranean Chopped, 64
Salad, Tex-Mex Beef-and-Beans Chopped, 63
Soup, Chunky Italian, 296
Tostados, Beef Brisket, 125
White Bean-and-Black Olive Crostini, 226
White Bean-and-Collard Soup, 212

BEEF. SEE ALSO BEEF, GROUND.
Brisket
Salad, Tex-Mex Beef-and-Beans Chopped, 63

Tostados, Beef Brisket, 125
Hash with Eggs, Beef and Pepper, 288
Pot Roast, Italian, 217
Soup, Chunky Italian, 296
Steaks
Cajun Steaks with Louisiana Slaw, 59
Chili, Spicy Steak and Black Bean, 217
Fajitas, Beef and Chicken, 88
Flank Steak with Edamame Rice, Cilantro-
  Ginger, 83
Flank Steak with Horseradish-Lemon
  Dipping Sauce, Skewered, 88
Garlic-Herb Steaks, 296
Kabobs with Peaches and Green Tomatoes,
  Molasses-Balsamic Steak, 88
Kabobs with Pepper Jelly-Jezebel Sauce,
  Grilled Steak, 290
Pepper Steak with Roasted Red Pepper
  Pesto, 313
Sirloin with Smoky Bacon Mushrooms,
  Broiled, 313
Stew, Company Beef, 297
Tenderloin with Whipped Horseradish Cream,
  Pancetta-Wrapped Beef, 244

BEEF, GROUND
Burgers
Cheddar-Stuffed Burgers, Spicy, 121
Fig-Glazed Burgers with Red Onion Jam, 120
Mini Cajun Burgers with Easy Rémoulade,
  285
Sweet-and-Savory Burgers, 120
Casseroles
Lasagna, Vanessa's Make-Ahead Beefy, 149
Lombardi, Beef, 296
Lombardi, Light Beef, 296
Chili, Meat Lover's, 297
Chili, Super Quick, 50
Enchilada Stack, Pinto Beans, 288
Hamburger Steak with Sweet Onion-
  Mushroom Gravy, 59
Meatloaf, 218
Meatloaf, Bev's Famous, 47
Rice, Mexican Beef 'n', 44
Salad, Beef-and-Lime Rice, 298
Sloppy Joes, Cheesy BBQ, 82

BEETS
Pickled Beets, 101
Raspberry-Glazed Beets with Chèvre, 311
Salad, Crunchy Carrot-Beet, 148
Salad, Simple Beet, 95

BEVERAGES
Alcoholic
Cider, Sparkling Pear Brandy, 256
Cocktail, Blackberry, 100
Cocktail, Cranberry-Moonshine, 276
Cocktail, Cranberry Old-Fashioned, 234
Cocktail, Healthy, 254
Cocktail, Raspberry Beer, 71
Eggnog, Creamy Sorghum, 256
Frappés, Grown-up Peppermint Patty, 268
'Garitas, Raspberry Beer, 203
Gimlet, Poinsettia, 257
Hello Dolly, Iced, 257
Lemonade, Frozen Cranberry-
  Moonshine, 276
Margaritas, Blackberry, 203
Margaritas, Frozen Blue, 128
Margaritas, Frozen Mango, 128
Margaritas, Grapefruit, 202
Margaritas on the Rocks, Classic, 128
Margaritas, Pomegranate, 128

Margaritas, Strawberry, 128
Martini, Chocolate Cream, 324
Mint Julep, 98
Moonshine, Cranberry-Infused, 276
Sangría, Carolina Peach, 104
Sangría, Cava, 95
Sangría, Warm Spiced, 257
Sipper, Sparkling, 228
Slushies, Bourbon Margarita, 257
Vodka, Cranberry-Infused, 276
Zinger, Raspberry Wine, 257
Coffee, Maple, 31
Eggnog, Chocolate, 324
Fizz, Honey-Green Tea, 257
Frappés, Peppermint Patty, 268
Hot Chocolate, Deep, Rich
  Mexican, 326
Hot Mocha, Steaming, 329
Ice Cubes, Berry, 65
Julep, Apple, 207
Mimosa, Kentucky, 65
Punch
Blackberry Mojito Punch, 257
Coffee Milk Punch, 232
Cranberry-Key Lime Punch, 257
Lowcountry Punch, 52
Pineapple Punch, Southern, 256
Splash, Berry, 65
Syrup, Fast Simple, 228
Tea, Apple-Spiced Iced, 257
Tea, Honey-Ginger, 75
Tea, Mango Tango, 65
Tea, Peach Iced, 157
Tea, Southern Sweet, 157

BISCUITS
Cheese Garlic Biscuits, 304
Country Ham and Biscuits, 98
Cream Cheese Biscuits, Tiny, 304
Croutons, Rosemary Biscuit, 281
Jalapeño Biscuits, 328
Poppers, Biscuit, 304
Stir-and-Roll Biscuits, 43

BLACKBERRIES
Butter, Grilled Peaches with Blackberry-Basil,
  104
Cake, Blackberry-Apple Upside-Down, 151
Cocktail, Blackberry, 100
Margaritas, Blackberry, 203
Mustard, Blackberry, 98
Punch, Blackberry Mojito, 257
Sauce, Spicy Grilled Pork Tenderloin with
  Blackberry, 86
Sorbet, Blackberry Wine, 132
Thumbprints, Blackberry, 262
Vinaigrette, Blackberry-Basil, 32

BLUEBERRIES
Ice Cubes, Berry, 65
Parfait, Orange-Berry Cream, 60
Salad, Berry Delicious Summer, 141
Salad, Blueberry-Gorgonzola, 108
Shortcake, Streusel Blueberry, 306
Syrup, Blueberry-Lemon Maple, 30

BREADS. SEE ALSO BISCUITS; CORN-
BREADS; CROUTONS; MUFFINS;
PANCAKES; PIES, PUFFS, AND
PASTRIES; ROLLS; WAFFLES.
Bacon-Parmesan Crisps, 45
Banana Bread Cobbler, 43
Cream Cheese-Banana Bread with Peanut
  Butter Streusel, 203
Flats, Frenchie, 272

❖ *Favorite Recipes Journal*

Jot down your family's and your favorite recipes for quick and handy reference. And don't forget to include the dishes that drew rave reviews when company came for dinner.

Recipe	Source/Page	Remarks